Foundations of Macroeconomics

FOURTH EDITION
Study Guide Included

Saeid Mahdavi
The University of Texas at San Antonio

James F. Willis, Professor Emeritus
San Jose State University

M. Manfred Fabritius
Centre College

 CAT PUBLISHING

ISBN 978-1-56226-685-1

Table Of Contents

Preface

An educated person is one who has finally discovered that there are some questions to which nobody has the answers.
Anonymous

From our own observations as teachers and from recent developments in the field, two facts about the principles of economics course are apparent. First, enrollments are growing, and second, they are growing not just because students want to learn about economics, but also because they are *required* to take the course.

On the one hand, this boom gives those of us who teach economics a greater opportunity to expose students to our way of thinking, to economists' ideas on how to approach the understanding and solution of problems. On the other, it means that we have to provide students with some good reasons for learning about the subject, especially if we expect them to retain what they learn. It is our hope that this book will help students understand how economists think, and how applicable an economic perspective is to the problems of the real world. Furthermore, the basic questions facing our students, as political creatures in a democracy, are economic ones. This text should prepare them to understand policy debate in such areas as economic stabilization, the crisis of the cities; poverty, and agricultural policy. Obviously, an understanding of economics is also useful, if not necessary, for careers in such areas as business administration, sociology, psychology, history, and the administrative end of many types of engineering.

We have therefore tried to do two things. First, we have reduced the principles of economics in both volume and complexity to the point at which our students can grasp (and, we hope, *retain*) them. Second, we have applied the basic principles to problems that our students can recognize. We have tried to address particularly those students who are more concerned with a J.O.B. than a Ph.D. Many of the problems these students will face concern economics to some degree. And, although there are some questions in economics to which nobody knows the answers, there are even more for which there are *many* answers. Our students need to be able to analyze the alternatives, choose the most feasible one, and—perhaps most important—*know the basis on which the choice rests.*

Scope and Approach

In our experience, the greatest criticism of the principles of economics course is that we instructors try to do too much. Using the average textbook of 1,300-plus pages crammed with solid, valuable materials, the instructor naturally has to race in order to cover the ground. Furthermore, students tend to become swamped with the detail and diversity of the subject matter. They often become confused about what is most important. We have tried to avoid this situation.

Of necessity, we could not include in this text everything that our colleagues wanted us to—although we are grateful to them for their suggestions. We included those principles and problems that seemed most important *to us*, including what we did because both of us are teachers. In other words, we put in materials that work with our students. We have included the essential materials dealing with income determination, banking and money, government stabilization policy, supply and demand, the theory of the firm, and pricing of factors of production. In addition to this basic core, we have added materials on economic development, international trade, and other economic systems. We realize, however, that different instructors may wish to delve more deeply into an issue or expand on a problem in a particular chapter. Therefore, we have listed, at the end of chapters, a number of additional sources.

We feel that this principles of economics text has several distinct advantages over many others in the field:

1. It is not an encyclopedia of economics but, rather, contains enough theory to equip the student with a permanent level of economic literacy.

2. Most theoretical chapters contain extended applications that use the economic principles just covered to analyze practical economic problems. For example, an application deals with the financial crisis of 2008-2009 and how we have moved beyond the recession. That application illustrates how the principles of macroeconomic equilibrium may be used to understand the background, causes, and controversies surrounding efforts to combat a recession that began in December 2007.

3. The use of mathematics has been limited to the practical minimum by avoiding complex algebraic manipulations and difficult derivations of relationships, and by using, instead, simple two-dimensional diagrams to illustrate principles.

4. Every attempt has been made to communicate in the everyday language of the student rather than in the technical language of the economic journal.

5. Special attention has been given to chapter summaries, end-of-chapter materials, and the glossary in order to help the student review and to reinforce the concepts presented in each chapter.

The Study Guide

To help students obtain some drill in economic problem solving and find out how well they are grasping the material, we have prepared a study guide. Each unit of this guide starts with a review of key terms and essay questions and problems that are designed to make students rethink the material just learned. It ends with a self-test consisting of true/false, multiple-choice, and matching questions. After the self-test are all self-test answers and occasional problem answers.

We regard the study guide as an important supplement to *Foundations of Macroeconomics*. Since economics requires a lot of concentration and going over material again and again, we strongly advise that students arm themselves with this learning aid.

Acknowledgments

We have benefited from the advice and assistance of many people in preparing the two editions of *Foundations of Macroeconomics*. The management and staff of CAT Publishing have been exceptionally accommodating and helpful in the lengthy process of preparing and polishing the new manuscript. While that has been true of all at CAT, we want to express our particular gratitude to our publisher, Leslie Golden. As usual, we accept responsibility for any errors that remain.

M. Manfred Fabritius

Saeid Mahdavi

James F. Willis

SECTION I:
Introduction to a Market Economy

SECTION I

Introduction to a Market Economy

A Brief Background to Americas Market Economy

Over the more than two centuries of our existence as a nation and economic society, much as changed. From a small but prosperous nation of two and a half million citizens in the 1790s, we have grown to a nation of more than 300 million citizens in the early 21st century. From a rural, overwhelmingly agricultural society, we have experienced the tremendous structural changes that came to be known as the industrial revolution. By 1900, the U.S. was the world's largest industrial economy with its society ever more urban. This transformation has continued into the 21st century. Today, we are often described as a post-industrial society.

Change of this magnitude inevitably engenders resistance and controversy. Landowners for example resisted the transfer of resources to industrial uses. Property owners resisted government regulation. Throughout the process we continued to rely primarily on markets and market prices to allocate and reallocate resources.

During the 2008-2009 period, we were in the midst of a serious economic downturn (the "Great Recession"), one of many in our history. We will have much to say about the controversies arising from efforts to find solutions to the contemporary problems of the economy. These problems include the crisis of financial markets, high unemployment rates, and excessive risk taking by private financial firms. In addition, the very large federal deficits continued to add to the federal debt. These along with the declining strength of the U.S. dollar in global markets were sources of great concern. The U.S. economy has entered its recovery phase since 2009 with output growth resuming, the unemployment rate reaching half of its 10 percent peak value during the downturn, the federal deficits shrinking, the rise of public debt slowing down, and the dollar appreciating. These recent experiences illustrate instability as an important feature of a market based economy.

The dimensions of a market economy

Microeconomics study of a disaggregated market economy.

Macroeconomics: The study of an aggregated market economy.

The U.S., like the vast majority of today's economic societies is a market economy, one in which private buyers and sellers interact to make choices about what to produce, and to create the prices at which voluntary exchanges between the two groups will occur. The study of how this individual disaggregated (exchange) economy works is called *microeconomics*. It is based on assumptions about human behavior as well as on assumptions about the constraints humans face in seeking to solve economic problems. It is with that background to the "economic way of thinking" that we begin this text and the course in *macroeconomics* or aggregate economics in which you are enrolled.

Why, you may well ask, should we begin with some microeconomic fundamentals rather than plunging straight into macroeconomics or the "big picture" of a market economy in its aggregated form? Put simply, it is for two reasons: (1) We cannot understand the macroeconomy fully without first understanding its underlying microeconomic processes—inflation; ˙ or significant increases in overall prices, for example, cannot be understood or the problems of inflation dealt with unless we understand how the individual prices that add up to inflation are determined, and (2) the models of the macroeconomy that are developed in this book and course are only as valid as the microeconomics on which they are built.

This microeconomic introduction to the macroeconomy is developed in four chapters. In Chapter 1, you are introduced to the most fundamental of economic problems, scarcity, or the inability of societies to satisfy all material wants. In Chapter 2, you will see how attempts to solve the problem of scarcity have resulted in widely varying levels of economic development among nations. In Chapter 3, you will see how markets, the institutional arrangements through which buyers and sellers make exchanges, allocate a society's scarce resources through the guidance of prices. Finally, in Chapter 4 you will see who are the players in both the microeconomy and the macroeconomy. The economic roles of households, business firms, and governments are examined. The role of international trade, or that of exports and imports, is briefly introduced as well.

Chapter 1: Breaking the Ice

The Aims of the Economist

Economics has had a bad press ever since the nineteenth century Scottish essayist Thomas Carlyle referred to it as "the dismal science." Carlyle had in mind the gloomy predictions about the future welfare of the human race that many economists were making at the time. This was over a century ago, when economists were still being referred to as "political economists", an apt name for them, calling to mind Lenin's remark that "political institutions are a superstructure resting on an economic foundation."

Economics has changed in the years since Carlyle called it a dismal science. It has become more scientific and less dismal. The subjects that economists deal with, for example, prices, jobs, the distribution of income, the growth of output and real income, the prevention of inflation, have remained the same, but what has changed are the methods we use to investigate them, and the amounts and kinds of information we have. Our view of the future has also changed: most economists today are optimistic about the ability of people to solve economic problems.

Frequently, we hear it said that economists seem unable to agree on solutions to economic problems. Since economics is a way of thinking about such problems, and is designed to identify alternative solutions, the disagreement is understandable. For a long time, it was common to find economists divided on ideological grounds between those who favored systems of private enterprise and individual initiative and those who favored systems of collective activity and public control. A major convergence among those concerned with economic policy in the late twentieth century occurred on the question of which of these two systems should be given emphasis by societies seeking economic growth. Economists on the "left" now seem willing to grant the necessity for a society seeking growth to appeal to human acquisitiveness and self-interest. Generating incentives to work, to take risks, and to innovate seem to be an increasing priority in most parts of the world. We will say more about these developments in the application section in this chapter.

Solving Specific Economic Problems

Though most economists agree about the nature of economic behavior by individuals, there is room for disagreement about specific measures to solve particular economic problems. Should government intervene to prevent mergers and takeovers of firms? Will the United States fall into a recession next year and, if so, should interest rates be lowered now to fight this recession? Are foreign manufacturers increasing their share of key U.S. markets and, if so, should the American government intervene? These are but a few of the many economic policy questions that arise constantly and about which economists may have different opinions. In short, when you complete your course in economics you will not have a set of policy conclusions to carry with you but a way of examining the alternatives and formulating your own views about policy questions as they arise. Nonetheless, certain tools and methodology, such as quantitative methods and model building, are accepted by nearly all economists. Most economists accept a basic procedure for looking at aggregate economic problems, like unemployment, and at nonaggregate market problems as well.

At the end of this chapter, we have included several applications to illustrate the process by which economic principles are employed to identify a range of solutions to personal as well as national economic problems. The applications deal with problems such as the financial crisis of 2008, the future of the Social Security program, the problem of saving for retirement, that of improving public education, along with affordability of housing in the U.S. and the future of the nations health care system. We know it is early in your economic course to look at these problems analytically. Nonetheless, this introduction will give you an idea of the economists' approach. Embodied in that approach is the effort to identify alternative solutions, the costs along with the benefits of each.

The fact that today's economists, in the main, are optimistic about the future, should not seem strange. Though human history goes back many centuries, most of the increase in goods and services, the real income that improves the material well-being of people, has occurred in the last two centuries. While economic problems remain for all nations, we now know that improvement in economic organization and institutions combined with the enormous potential of further technological change make possible continued advance in standards of living. This is true not only for the relatively wealthy industrial nations but for the newly industrializing nations and for less developed nations as well. Can economic problems, then, be eliminated? Few economists would go so far as to say yes. However, the most famous economist of the twentieth century, John Maynard Keynes[1] (rhymes with *gains*), writing in 1930 and looking ahead to the next hundred years, put his view this way:

> *I draw the conclusion that, assuming no important wars and no important increase in population, the economic problem may be solved, or at least be within sight of solution, within a hundred years. This means that the economic problem is not, if we look into the future, the permanent problem of the human race.*

Keynes expressed this very optimistic view in the early years of the Great Depression of the 1930s. He was wrong, of course, in assuming that there

---

1. Keynes, J.M. "On the Economic Possibilities for our Grandchildren." *Nation and Atheneum*, London, 1930.

would be no major wars after 1930, but his assumption about no major increase in population may turn out to be correct, at least for the more developed industrial countries. Keynes's statement illustrates two things: (1) economists are no longer dismal about the future, and (2) economists develop economic principles not for the sake of abstract exercise, but to be able to analyze and propose solutions to problems constantly confronted by human beings. Economists are, in short, deeply concerned with *people* and their material well-being.

What Is Economics?

Now let's define economics in terms of the "economic problem" to which Keynes referred.

Economics
The social science that deals with the analysis of material problems and how societies allocate scarce resources to satisfy human wants.

        Economics is the social science that deals with the analysis of material problems. It identifies the various means by which people can satisfy their desires for goods and services by using the limited resources available to produce them. This is a very general definition, but a useful one, because it points out certain basic features of economics.

        1. *Economics is a social science.* It deals with the actions of groups of people in relation to society. Economics differs from physical science, which has laws established in the laboratory where conditions can be more readily controlled. The laboratory of economists is the world, in which nothing is certain and nothing can be controlled with surety. Economists base their principles on what they observe about people. For example, their willingness to spend money or to save it, or on their observation about the economic institutions that societies have created, such as private property rights, government planning, and economic institutions such as banks and stock and commodity markets that bring savers and investors together.

        2. *Experimental economics* provides data on economic behavior that arise from laboratory experiments. In 2002, the Nobel Prize in Economics was awarded to Vernon Smith who has for years espoused the use of such laboratory tests on humans to generate reliable data that can be used to test hypotheses about economic behavior. As The Wall Street Journal observed, "Economic experiments give us insights into how buyers and sellers interact to create a market." Thus, while it remains true that the rigorously controlled experiments of laboratory science are more difficult to replicate in economic experiments, the differences between the two have narrowed thanks to the work of Smith and others.

        3. *Economics is analytical.* Economists use the principles of economics to diagnose various problems, such as unemployment and poverty, and propose solutions to them. Instead of choosing one solution and saying, "Here's what to do," economists set forth the available alternative solutions to a given problem and point out the costs and benefits of each.

        4. *Economics is concerned with the material well being of people.* Economists measure current economic activity and project figures for the future. This does not mean that they feel it is only material well-being that counts, but they do insist that it takes the use of limited material resources (land, labor, capital, and entrepreneurship) to solve social problems. Solving economic problems, thus, is closely tied to efforts to solve other kinds of problems.

Macroeconomics and Microeconomics: Economic Principles From Two Perspectives

Macroeconomics
The study of aggregated economic activity such as the forces that determine the level of income and employment in a society.

Microeconomics
The study of disaggregated economic activities, or how a market economy allocates resources through prices.

Macroeconomics is the study of aggregated economic activity such as the forces that determine the level of income and employment in a society. Macroeconomics gives us the big picture of a society, or what economists call its aggregate performance. Macroeconomics builds models to better understand how important variables such as aggregate output/income, employment, and price levels are determined. These models help us to better understand the way economic activity in the private sector, policies of the government, and international trade interact to affect economic growth, unemployment, and inflation.

Microeconomics is the study of disaggregated economic activities. Microeconomics builds models of individual consumer and producer behavior assuming that they have limited resources and wish to maximize their satisfaction and profits, respectively. Microeconomics recognizes the importance of prices in a market economy and seeks to explain how prices for goods and services and factors of production are influenced by the degree of competition and other characteristics of the markets in which they are exchanged.

While macroeconomics and microeconomics differ in focus, each deals with the same basic subject matter of economic activity. It is not surprising, therefore, that some areas of study are taught in both micro and macro, though from a different perspective.

What Is The Economist's Method?

Even though economics is a social science, rather than a physical science, its method is scientific and based on facts and logic. An economist's starting point, like a chemist's or physicist's, is a hypothesis, or an assumption about a relationship between two things (or ten or twenty things). At this point, however, the economist steps outside the safety of the laboratory into the less predictable realm of the real world. We can best demonstrate the economist's job with an example using a three stage economic analysis.

Suppose that you are a young economist, a consultant to the President's Council of Economic Advisors, and are called to a meeting of the council. Everyone looks grave. The chairman explains that the country's economy is showing some alarming tendencies. Personal incomes in the last year have risen, but for some reason, consumer spending has fallen. People just aren't buying, and business is beginning to hurt. The President is deeply concerned, and so is Congress. You are to find out what has happened and tell the government what to do about it

Now you begin at stage 1 of the economist's three-stage process (see Figure 1-1). First you gather all the data you can that might explain what has happened. Exactly how much did incomes grow in the past year? Did spending on consumer goods change in any way, and if so, how? How do the figures for the past three-month period compare with the figures for the same quarter a year ago? Has there been a change in the relationship between income and spending?

What have people been doing with all the money they haven't been spending? Have they been saving it? Have they been using it to pay taxes?

After you have finished this fact-finding or *descriptive* stage, you embark on stage 2, the *theorizing* stage. You try to formulate a theory that will explain the way behavior changes as income changes. You want to express not only what is happening now, but also what is likely to happen a year from now, two years, or five years from now, given certain incomes, populations, and supplies and prices of goods. The theory you evolve may be a simple one (people have lost faith in material things and are giving all their money to churches), or more complex (people are more afraid of inflation and at the same time distrustful of anything modern, so they are putting all their money in gold, Renaissance paintings, and pre-1914 Rolls-Royces). In any event, you spend days writing up your version of the situation, using all the facts you have gathered, and expressing your opinion in the clearest manner possible..

Figure 1-1
The Three Basic Stages in Economic Analysis

Stage 1	Stage 2	Stage 3
Gathering the facts	*Formulating and testing theory*	*Making economic policy*
The economist gathers data that are relevant to the hypothesis or statement (this is called descriptive economics).	On the basis of the data, the economist sets forth a theory about economic behavior and tests the theory (this is the theorizing stage).	The policy maker, who is not necessarily the same person as the economist, formulates measures to deal with economic behavior and its consequences (this is the policy-making stage).

On the basis of the data you have collected, you form the hypothesis that short-term changes in consumer spending depend not only on changes in income but also on changes in other factors such as taxes and future expectations. You can use various statistical techniques to isolate the effect of one factor (short-term income changes) on another (consumer spending).

When you are setting up these theoretical interrelationships, you construct a *model*, a systematic analogy to real consumer behavior. This model enables you to interpret the statistical results.

Suppose you find that there is a weak (perhaps nearly zero) correlation, during any six-month period, between changes in people's incomes and changes in their spending habits. In other words, even if their incomes go up, their spending changes little, or perhaps not at all. Then you must explain the decline in consumer spending in terms of changes in other factors.

Your model may include the expectations people have about future changes in prices and in taxes (income taxes, excise taxes). Suppose your data show that taxes (and other important factors that might offer some explanation) have not changed in the past six months. Then you conclude that the decline in spending may be due to *expectations* about the future. People are putting off buying things until later in the year. They're waiting for inventory-reduction sales, or for the crops to come in, or for an expected drop in interest rates. For many reasons, they're just holding onto their money and waiting. You incorporate all these ideas in your report to the chairman of the President's Council of Economic Advisors.

The third stage is the *policy-making* stage. This stage is out of your hands, because the people who decide on the economic policy act on their own, although they may base their decisions on the economists' recommendations. The policy maker may be Congress, or the President, or the President and the Cabinet acting together. But bear in mind that a nation's economic policy is part of its overall social policy (including diplomatic, military, and political policies). Your role as an economist has been only to identify to the policy makers the nature of the problem, tell them how serious it is, and point out alternative solutions, with the costs and benefits of each.

(For a fascinating discussion of public policy decisions, (in several post-World War II presidencies), read *America's Hidden Success*, by John E. Schwartz, published by Norton. This book provides a reassessment of public policy from Kennedy to Reagan.

The Citizen and Economic Policy

The above example is fairly clear-cut. The policy maker here may decide on the basis of reports prepared by you and others that no change in economic policy is required. It appears in this case that consumer spending is going to rise in the long term, as prices fall and as people adjust to their higher incomes.

From this illustration, you might conclude that economic investigation and policy making are processes reserved for experts in politics and economics. This is not so. Whether the issue is local or federal taxes, or local or national economic policies, the United States needs an enlightened public. The *non*economist, *non*politician, just plain citizen can review, criticize, and in the long run even change economic policy. People can do this by discussion with others and by the way they vote.

This book is written with the conviction that (1) the economic principles a person needs to know to make intelligent decisions on economic issues are understandable, and that (2) such decisions should be founded in fact and logic.

Applications: Concrete Examples of Abstract Ideas

Much of economics consists of abstractions, theories, and discussions of curves and trends. But, as noted at the beginning of this chapter, it isn't all just theories; you already know a lot about economics. So the text tries to use the knowledge you already have to illustrate the theoretical part of economics. You will find a group of applications at the end of this chapter as well as at the end of chapters throughout the book. They show you one or more practical applications of the theory or principle that has just been explained. For example, in the chapter that introduces the theory of supply and demand, there is an application that discusses a concrete example of supply and demand: rent controls and the price of housing. These applications can serve as beacons to help you fix your position in unfamiliar surroundings as you explore the economic way of thinking. We begin that process in this introduction.

End-of-Chapter Summaries

At the end of each chapter, you'll find a section titled "Summing Up." These sections repeat, in condensed form, what the chapter or application is about. Even if you feel you understand the chapter as you read it, read "Summing Up" carefully. The repetition will help to imprint the material in your mind. Also, after the Summing Up sections to each chapter, there is a list of "Key Terms," concepts that are important to understand and remember.

These terms and their definitions can be checked by (1) rereading the margin notes in that chapter as well as by (2) checking the glossary at the end of the book.

Mathematics De-emphasized

One reason why economics has a reputation for being a tough subject is that many people are afraid of mathematics, and they associate math with economics. However, as you work your way through this book, you will realize that it contains very little mathematics. When economists write articles in professional journals, they may use advanced mathematics, but you do not need to know advanced mathematics to learn the basic principles of economics.

This book does contain a number of graphs and tables of data. The data serve to ensure that we are using facts as the basis for our discussions, and the graphs are simply devices to help you visualize abstract ideas. Figure 1-2 is an example of a graph.

All the graphs we use in this book are two-dimensional. That is, they measure the relationships between two factors. They have *height* (measured along the vertical axis) and *length* (measured along the horizontal axis).

The measure of the first factor to change (called the **independent variable**) comes from the vertical axis.

The measure of the factor whose value depends on that of the first factor (the **dependent variable**) comes from the horizontal axis.[2] As we go along, we will use graphs to chart the progress of a number of dependent and independent variables: prices of goods, quantities sold, demand for goods and services, jobs, wages, and so forth. In each case, the rule about reading graphs will remain the same.

Now look at Figure 1-2 and we'll discuss some of the kinds of relationships that may occur between dependent and independent variables. The lines drawn on this diagram are called *curves*, even though in this case they are straight lines.

- *Curve A* is a case in which the relationship between the independent and dependent variables is **inverse**. This means that as the independent variable increases (moves up the vertical axis), the dependent variable decreases (moves toward zero). As the independent variable decreases, the dependent variable increases. We say that curve A is *negatively sloped*, or that it *slopes downward*.

- *Curve B* is a case in which the independent variable doesn't change at all. All change occurs in the dependent variable. The dependent variable responds almost without limit at the given value of the independent variable; therefore curve B is horizontal.

- *Curve C* is a case in which the relationship between the independent and dependent variable is **direct**. As the independent variable increases, so does the dependent variable. As the independent variable decreases, so does the dependent variable. We say that curve C is *positively sloped*, or that it *slopes upward*.

Independent Variable
In a set of relationships, this is the variable that changes first.

Dependent Variable
In a set of relationships, the variable whose value depends on the value of the independent variable.

Inverse
The relationship between independent and dependent variables is inverse if the dependent variable changes in the opposite direction from the independent variable.

Direct
The relationship between the independent variable and the dependent variable is direct if the dependent variable changes in the same direction as the independent variable.

---

2. Note that this is a convention adopted in the United States in economics with supply and demand diagrams. In mathematics, though, the reverse is usually the case with the dependent variable on the vertical axis and the independent variable on the horizontal axis.

Figure 1-2

An Illustration of Graphing: From a basic Supply and Demand concept

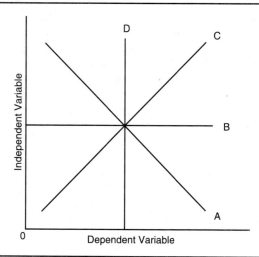

Note: the labeling of the axes reflects a convention in economics with supply and demand diagrams. Though in mathematics and in other economic diagrams (for example,. a consumption function) the reverse is usually the case with the dependent variable on the vertical axis and the independent variable on the horizontal axis.

• *Curve D* is a case in which the dependent variable doesn't change at all. All change in D takes place in the independent variable. The independent variable responds almost without limit at the given value of the dependent variable; therefore curve D is vertical.

If you keep these four cases in mind, you won't be confused by the graphs in this book. Indeed, the graphs will help you to visualize and understand relationships that might otherwise be hard to grasp.

Positive Versus Normative Economics

A person starting out in a first course in principles of physics or chemistry usually does so with no preconceived notions. Since we don't feel at home talking about subnuclear particles, we're willing to leave that subject to the physicists and take anything they say as the truth. However, most people approach economics with a considerable amount of built-in expertise. We have biases about economics, as we do about any social science. We cannot avoid having them, since from an early age we have all had considerable experience as members of the economic society. For example, we get jobs, spend income, pay taxes, and watch the government spend.

But we do not simply leave economic issues to the economists and the politicians. Citizens who are *not* economists, who are *not* politicians, still must in the long run make choices, through voting or in other ways. Citizens must choose among alternative solutions to economic problems, and they often have to approve or turn down choices that have already been made by some governing body. To be a good citizen, to make informed choices on voting day, one needs an understanding of economic principles, backed up by a knowledge of how those principles work out in actual application.

Normative Economics
Consists of making judgments about what should be.

Positive Economics
Consists of determining what is.

When you come to the point of choosing among alternative solutions, you enter the area of **normative economics**, or making judgments about what *should* be. **Positive economics**, on the other hand, consists of determining what is. It involves stating facts. We have pointed out that when you gather facts and apply economic principles in an attempt to find a solution to a problem, you do not always find just one answer, one unique "right" way; you find that there may be several alternative solutions. Normative economics involves looking at these various solutions and applying personal or collective value judgments, to decide what *should* be. (Generalizing about economic behavior naturally has some normative aspects. Therefore, in writing a book about economics, we cannot avoid a few judgments here and there. We have tried to keep them to a minimum. When they do appear, we try to point them out and you're free to agree or disagree.)

To be sure that you understand the difference between positive and normative statements, let's take an example. You go to a party and find an economist who is talking about food stamps and their economic impact. The following conversation takes place:

Economist: The United States spent $20 billion in 2008 on the food stamp program. (*Positive*)

You: But a lot of people were still going hungry because they had to present the food stamps at stores in person, and many elderly or disabled people were too feeble to go to the store. It wasn't fair. (*Normative*)

Economist: A family of four with an income of $16,000 a year or less can qualify for $150 a month in food stamps. (*Positive*)

You: A family of four can't live on $16,000 a year, not what I'd call living. (*Normative*)

See how hard it is to keep from being normative? (*Normative*)

A Word About Words

Economists sometimes speak what seems to be a language all their own. In fact, someone once defined an economist as a person who states the obvious in terms of the incomprehensible. When economists speak of contrived versus natural scarcities, implicit factor returns, and maximum-profit monopoly equilibrium, you may wonder if they're really speaking English. Throughout this book, we have tried to avoid speaking "economese," or what William F. Buckley called "econospeak." However, we could not weed out *all* the economese, because economics is a complex subject, full of precise language. When we introduce a term, we put it in italics and define it. Boldface type means that you can find the word defined and highlighted in the margin of the text page on which it appears as well as in the glossary at the back of the book. As you go along, whenever you are not certain of the meaning of something, don't look back through the book for the definition. Just turn to the glossary and look it up. Definitions are important in economics, because often a word means one thing in everyday usage and another in the language of economists. This book is designed to help you learn economics in the clearest and most painless way possible.

Application I: The Economic Crisis of 2008-2011: Background, Causes, and Effects

Background

Financial crises are not new to the American economy. Indeed, they have occurred throughout this nation's history. James Van Horne of Stanford University counts sixteen such events in our economic history. Beginning in 1819, these sharp downturns occurred in irregular cycles, some long, some sharp, and a few both sharp and long. The panics of 1897 and 1907 are among the sharpest. The crash of 1929 was not only sharp but so long lasting that its effects, together with its related events, have been characterized as the "Great Depression." In the late 2007, another major economic downturn, referred to as the "Great Recession," began. It was caused by crises in the financial and housing markets and turned out to be the most sever contraction since 1929. Can we isolate common threads in these major downturns? Van Horne concludes that the answer is yes and that commonalities include the following:

1. Almost all were preceded by speculative bubbles.
2. The bubbles had their origins in low interest rates or easy money.
3. Financial markets experienced deregulation and lax regulatory oversight prior to the crisis.
4. Most, but not all, lasted from five to seven years.

Will the current crisis follow this pattern? Let us begin by looking at its causes.

Causes

Reasons for the most recent financially induced economic downturn referred to as the "Great Recession" are varied and complex. The sharp downturn has been attributed to a number of factors including speculation, greed, outright fraud, and lax oversight of federal lending and mortgage agencies. Above all it seems to be the result of unconstrained risk taking by many financial institutions including banks, mortgage lending companies and insurance companies. It is, thus, not unlike some of the earlier downturns mentioned above. A key point in understanding the current downturn is that our capitalistic system depends on lenders extending credit to borrowers; when lenders are hesitant and unable to assess credit risk, transactions can decrease dramatically. As this happened globally in 2008, the Federal Reserve and other central banks injected hundreds of billions of dollars into global credit markets in an effort to combat the financial crisis.

It is commonly believed that the passing of the Gramm-Leach-Bliley (GLB) Act of 1999 was among the primary contributors toward the recent economic fall. The GLB Act was enacted to repeal the Glass-Steagall Act of 1933. Glass-Steagall was put into effect as a reaction to the collapse of a large portion of the American commercial banking system in the early 1930's. Too many commercial banks became involved in stock market investments and many scholars believe this to be the main reason for the 1929 stock market crash. The act was the first to separate bank types, by commercial and investment banks, and founded the FDIC. The FDIC was created by Congress to maintain stability and public confidence in insuring bank deposits.

In 1999, the GLB Act opened the market among banking, securities, and insurance companies that were banned by the Glass-Steagall Act. GLB allowed banks to become involved with other commercial banks, investment banks, security firms and insurance companies simultaneously. When the economy is good, people generally put more money into investments. Contrarily, when the economy is bad people tend to put their money into savings accounts. GLB allowed insurance companies, brokerages, and banks to merge in order to provide both investment and savings opportunities legally. The economy in 1999 was booming, and as a result people put more money into investments. Investment companies and banks realized the increase in investment spending that parallels a booming economy, and began to combine in an attempt to expand the profits of their organizations.

In the early 2000's the United States entered a recession and the Fed lowered interest rates to help counter this recession. The low interest rates—including mortgage rates—fueled a demand driven housing bubble in the first half of the decade.

Along with the bubble and rapidly rising home prices came home loans that made little economic sense by historical lending standards. The first of these loans were "subprime," or high risk loans to borrowers deemed to have less than prime credit records. Because of the higher risks of default, rates on these loans were set high though many came with low initial ("teaser") rates that would adjust upward over time. The dynamic of the bubble depended on ever-rising housing prices which would permit borrowers, faced with higher mortgage payments, to refinance. As housing prices began to fall in 2007 and 2008, many borrowers defaulted on the loans and foreclosures became widespread in "subprime" markets.

Novel types of subprime debt instruments also began to appear. Lenders, failing to verify borrowers' incomes, made what were known as "ninja" loans, which stood for "no income, no job and no assets" loans. These loans had a high risk of default and of borrowers disappearing like "ninjas."

This leads us to the question: Why were these poor quality loans made in the first place? A major factor was the ability of firms to "securitize" them. Securitization means that firms could bundle or package the loans and sell them in secondary markets thus avoiding the risk of holding them in their portfolios. This permitted firms to make new loans while selling "subprime" loan paper in secondary markets.

Once securitized and sold in secondary markets, owners of the loans sought insurance against defaults. Insurance came in the form of derivative contracts called "credit default swaps," under which buyers of the swaps made periodic payments to sellers and in turn received revenue even if the underlying financial instrument defaulted. Essentially, this meant that buyers, even if they did not own the instruments, could be paid in the event of defaults. As we said earlier this involved taking huge risks. All of this is akin to taking out life insurance on your neighbor in the hope that if your neighbor dies, you will collect the insurance.

Surprisingly, credit rating agencies, such as Standard and Poors, gave these instruments high ratings. Often they were given AAA ratings, meaning that they were deemed very safe. Cost of insurance was low because of the perceived low risks. As the housing market started to crumble in 2007 and 2008, these mortgage-backed securities began to default and holders had to make payments to the owners of the swaps. Companies such as Lehman Brothers and AIG, who held much of this "toxic" debt paper, suffered huge losses.

Effects: How Quickly Markets can Change
The housing slump set off a chain reaction in the American economy. Individuals and investors could no longer "flip" their homes for a quick profit, adjustable rate mortgages (ARMs) adjusted skyward, and mortgages became unaffordable for many homeowners.

The thousands of mortgages that were defaulted left investors and financial institutions holding worthless debt. All this meant many firms bled money. In turn, there was then a glut of homes on the market and a sharp decline in housing prices. New home building declined dramatically and many home builders went out of business. Additionally, falling home prices caused many borrowers, unable to refinance, to default or simply walk away from their homes. This, in turn, caused many homeowners to suffer a sharp decline in their credit score and, thereby, to reduce credit for all purchases.

Massive losses in housing markets caused many financial institutions to tighten their lending requirements. For some institutions, though, it was too late and they went out of business. Others were forced to merge with stronger firms and still others received "bailouts" and continued to function. Credit markets became very tight, making it difficult to obtain consumer and commercial loans. The economy officially went into recession in December, 2007 and the housing market situation began to go through dramatic changes.

Waves of foreclosures during 2008-2011 led to rapidly falling home prices. This made housing more affordable and also encouraged homeowners, faced with falling interest rates, to refinance their existing mortgages. Financial institutions, however, became more restrictive in making credit available after their experience with subprime loans. In turn, this limited the expansionary effects of falling home prices and interest rates. In March of 2011 the median home price has dropped to $156,100; that is over a 25% decrease from its peak. By March of 2013 the median home price had increased to $185,100.

Effects on Governments
The effects of the housing market crisis have been widespread. Local governments have long relied on property taxes as a major source of revenue. Those revenues help to support a host of local activities including education. The financial crisis that began in housing markets, thus, is having effects throughout the American economy and society.

The Effects of the Crisis: A Philosophical Note
In an effort to minimize the effects of the crisis, the federal government, including both the Treasury and the Federal Reserve, responded with huge infusions of liquidity into the economy. This response involves loans to institutions, direct swap of bad debt for firms' stocks and many other approaches. As a result, the government began to "pick the winners and losers," as it rescued some firms while allowing others to fail. These choices have usually been made in markets, whereas government judgment became substituted in 2008 and 2009. In addition, these "bailouts" and federal loan guarantees often came with requirements about executive compensation, and the appointment of federal "overseers" or "czars" to superintend firms' decisions.

A fundamental question for us is this: Will these reactions to the financial crisis alter the basic nature of American capitalism, or will they prove to be a temporary reaction/solution to an economic emergency? We cannot, of course, yet answer this question, but its importance to our economic and political future, make it well worth consideration. There are also long standing and equally important questions that deserve attention: can we rely on unbridled markets to ensure that the excesses of some self-seeking individuals would not impose economic and hardships and social costs on many? Should market discipline be augmented by government regulations of the market? (See Chapter 4). Are the costs of inaction after a major crisis less or more than the costs of action by the government?

Application II: Has Government Stimulus Succeeded?

The deep crises in the housing and financial sectors that emerged in the late 2007 was soon followed by the most sever contraction in the level of economic activity since the "Great Depression" of 1929-33. Some factual aspects of this episode are worth reviewing. According to the Bureau of Economic Analysis data, the size of the U.S. economy real GDP (see Chapter 5) shrank by 0.3 percent in 2008 compared with a 1.9 percent growth in 2007. The magnitude of the accompanying job losses was horrific. The Bureau of Labor Statistics estimated that about 3.6 million nonfarm jobs were lost in 2008. The unemployment rate rose from 5 percent in December 2007 to 7.3 in December 2009. In January 2009 alone the economy lost another 818,000 jobs! The American Recovery and Reinvestment Act (ARRA) proposed by the Obama Administration was enacted by the Congress in February 2009 against the backdrop of an economy that was rapidly sliding downward. ARRA, commonly referred to as the "stimulus," was basically a multi-year package of tax relief (mostly to individuals) and spending hikes totaling $787 (later revised to $831) billion intended to provide fiscal relief to financially distressed state and local governments, promote economic recovery by boosting consumption and infrastructure and other investment spending, protect the vulnerable, and preserve and create jobs. The full impact of the recession was felt in 2009 during which real GDP contracted by 3.1 percent, job losses totaled approximately 5 million and the unemployment peaked at nearly 10 percent (October 2009). The "Great Recession" officially ended in the second quarter of 2009. The average growth rate in the twelve quarters since then was about 2.2 percent. The monthly unemployment rate fell with a lag from its peak to 7.8 percent in September 2012.

The stimulus stirred up debates among economists and non-economists alike. Some critics questioned the effectiveness of the stimulus's mainly "Keynesian" approach to encouraging growth and employment. The essence of this approach is managing the demand side of the economy to bring about more desirable economic outcomes (see Chapters 8 and 9). Being keenly aware of the role of human psychology and uncertainties in economic decisions, John Maynard Keynes argued that during recessions the "aggregate demand" for goods and services further falls after the initial negative shock to the economy as consumers and investors are unable or unwilling to spend as usual. This deficiency in aggregate demand pushes the economy down to a state characterized by low level of output and high unemployment. With the huge human and economic tolls exacted by the "Great Depression" in mind, Keynes argued that one cannot rely on the market's "self-correcting" mechanism to rescue the economy through adjusting wages and prices at least in the short-term. In this situation, Keynes suggested that the public sector needs to actively boost its demand to offset the fall in private demand, stabilize the economy, reverse the sentiment of private actors, and push the economy towards "full employment."

The slow pace of economic recovery and job creation is taken as evidence of failure of the Keynesian approach by its critics. They further point to some undesirable consequences of deficit spending that include the piling up of public debt, higher future taxes to repay the debt, and adverse effects of high taxes and "big government" on the private sector. Another controversial aspect of the stimulus emphasized by some critics has to do with "redistribution" from taxpayers/workers to those who benefit from the extended unemployment benefits and other provisions of the stimulus. Many critics of the stimulus favor a "supply-side" approach to counter recession and promote employment. This includes (permanent) lower taxes on income and capital gains and less government regulations. These measures along with more certainty about future public policy are argued to spur economic growth and job creation by improving the incentives of investors and employers.

Proponents of the stimulus contend that, given the size of the contraction, the size of stimulus package (approximately $831 billion over eleven years) was too small to begin with. Moreover, headwinds in the form of falling economic growth especially in China, India, and Europe along with domestic political paralysis further diluted the positive impact of the stimulus. Nonetheless, they contend that the stimulus achieved its major objectives: to arrest the economy's downward spiral and stabilize the macroeconomy at a positive rate of growth. Furthermore, a number of studies conducted by private firms concluded that the recession would have been deeper and longer without the stimulus. This suggests that the economic effects of the stimulus would be more pronounced if one also considers the negative consequences it helped to avert. In the words the Noble Laureate economist Paul Krugman:

> Without the recovery act, the free fall would probably have continued, as unemployed workers slashed their spending, cash-strapped state and local governments engaged in mass layoffs, and more. The stimulus didn't completely eliminate these effects, but it was enough to break the vicious circle of economic decline. Aid to the unemployed and help for state and local governments were probably the most important factors. If you want to see the recovery act in action, visit a classroom: your local school probably would have had to fire a lot of teachers if the stimulus hadn't been enacted.[3]

On the theoretical level, the proponents of the Keynesian approach counter its critics by noting that they miss an important point: businesses do not invest in capacity and hire more workers to produce more when there is weak for what they have already produced and a sense of fear that pervades the economy. While supply-side considerations (such as low tax rates) are favorable to long-term economic growth, addressing aggregate demand deficiency is a short-term priority. They further contend that critics conflate deficits and debt increases due to the stimulus with those that would have existed independent of it. The latter reflects the rising costs of popular programs such as Medicare, major tax cuts, and wars. Interestingly enough, public deficits and debt significantly increased under the "fiscally conservative" administrations of Presidents Reagan, Bush I, and Bush II and actually fell under the more "fiscally liberal" Clinton administration (see Chapter 10). Proponents note that relatively consistent and good fiscal and economic performance under President Clinton (1993-2001), when tax rates were relatively high and deregulations were not the order of the day, weakens the case of supply-siders. That period provides a reasonable blueprint for reducing deficits and debt in the medium to long term through a combination of higher tax revenues and spending cuts. They are opposed to sacrificing economic stability at the altar of fiscal austerity and balanced budget and risking another recession in the process (austerity induced recessions of 1937-39 in the U.S. and 2012 in the U.K. are offered as two examples).

---

3. Krugman, Paul, "Too Little of a Good Thing." The New York Times, November 1, 2009.

The jury is still out on the overall economic and social effects of the stimulus package. In this connection, Christina Romer, one of the chief architects of the stimulus, noted that:

> The ultimate verdict on the Recovery Act will depend in part on further studies. I believe that as more research occurs and the political rancor fades, the fiscal stimulus will be viewed as an important step at a bleak moment in our history. Not the knockout punch the administration had hoped for, but a valuable effort that improved the lives of many.[4]

A recent comprehensive study by two noted economists supports this assessment as it concludes that the recession would have been much more sever and lasted longer and the unemployment rate would have reached a peak of over 20 percent had it not been for the Recovery Act and monetary stimulus.[5]

Application III: Self-Interest, The Key to a More Productive Future?

The public is merely a multiplied "me."

Mark Twain

There is only one class in the community that thinks more about money than the rich, and that is the poor. The poor can think of nothing else.

Oscar Wilde

These quotations illustrate two points: (1) what happens to the economy as a whole depends on the economic actions of individuals, and (2) economic forces vitally affect and concern each of us. Economists and non-economists alike have long sought to understand the basic motivations that determine how we play our roles as consumers or producers on the economic stage. In this application we are going to examine some views on this subject.

Self-interest: Key to All Characters

One of the first people to theorize about economic motivation was Adam Smith, author of *The Wealth of Nations* (1776), who is often considered the founder of modern economics. Smith contended that people were not moved primarily by love of their fellow humans; they ordinarily acted in their own self- interest. Smith said, "It is not from the benevolence of the butcher, the brewer, or the baker that we expect our dinner, but from their regard to their own interest." This view of human nature led Smith to argue that the economic role the govern-ment should play is to create conditions under which the individual's pursuit of self-interest results in maximizing the public welfare. But Smith did not make it clear what kind of political system would best create such conditions. Moreover, one can legitimately ask what would prevent public officials from acting in their own self-interest rather than the public's? The problem of self-interested individ-uals making public choices within collective organizations such as government is the focus of the "public choice" area of economics. Public officials are argued to act like "political entrepreneur" (as opposed to business entrepreneur) who seek to maximize the votes and support they receive (as opposed to profits). They are, therefore, more likely to respond to the demands of special interest

---

4. Romer, Christina, "The Fiscal Stimulus, Flawed but Valuable," The New York Times, October 12, 2012.
5. Blinder, Alan and Mark Zandi, "The Financial Crisis: Lessons for the Next One." Center on Budget and Public Priorities, October 15, 2015.

groups that are well organized and financed than those of the average voter. This may lead to shortsighted policies and allocation of public funds to areas that benefit a few at the expense of general taxpayers. Such shortsightedness, however, may not be necessarily penalized by voters. This is because each individual voter may think that his/her vote is unlikely to change the outcome of an election and that the costs of casting an informed vote outweigh its benefits. Pursing self-interest, voters may act in a "rationally politically ignorant" manner undermining the disciplinary mechanism that elections provide.

Beyond Self-love

Was Adam Smith the guru of selfishness and advocate of unrestrained capitalism? Vulgar interpretations of Smith's writings may give one that impression. More careful readings of Smith suggest otherwise. Smith, a moral philosopher first, did not sanctify or even endorse selfishness and greed (out of bounds self-interest?) as natural. Moreover, the Nobel Laureate Amartya Sen[6] notes that Smith emphasized the role of self-interest in relation to what motivated market exchanges, but extensively discussed the role other motivations in influencing human behavior. He argued that while self-seeking advanced the interest of the *individual* "humanity, justice, generosity, and public spirit, are the qualities most useful to others."

According to Professor Sen, Smith was not a "free-market fundamentalist:" "He rejected market-excluding interventions, but not market-including interventions aimed at doing those important things that the market may leave undone." Poverty and inequality that might persist in an otherwise successful market economy were matters of deep concern to him. He defended public services such as free education and poverty relief and acknowledged the importance of interventions on behalf of the poor and the underdogs in the society: "When the regulation, therefore, is in favour of the workmen, it is always just and equitable; but it is sometimes otherwise when in favour of the masters." Perhaps the most unappreciated aspect of Smith's views is his belief in the importance of socially generated disparities, rather than differences in inborn talents and abilities, in explaining world inequalities. Many of Smith's concerns remain valid in modern economies and addressing them generally falls under the responsibility of the institution of government; although not without controversies. The point to keep in mind is that far from being a narrow- minded advocate of self-seeking and unbridled market forces, the father of modern economics was a "proponent of a plural institutional structure and a champion of social values that transcend the profit motive, in principle as well as in actual reach."

---

6. Sen, Amartya. "The Economist Manifesto." New Statesman, April 23, 2010.

"I wish all I had to worry about was the world,
not taxes, mortgages, rising prices, the cost of college..."

Homo Economicus

After Adam Smith, other philosophers continued to name self-interest as the dominant force moving people. Jeremy Bentham (founder of **hedonism**, or the philosophical school of self-satisfaction) carried this idea to new heights in his concept of **homo economicus**, or economic person, who was not only motivated by self-interest, but was literally a walking calculator of pain and pleasure. *Homo economicus* measured every action in terms of the amount of self-satisfaction that could be derived from it, precisely maximizing personal pleasure or minimizing pain.

Private Citizens Want Private Profits

Economists today no longer hold such an extreme hedonist view. They no longer believe that people either can, or always try to, maximize their pleasure or minimize their pain with precision. However, they do still believe that people are motivated by self-interest. Alfred Marshall, considered by many to be the originator of modern economic methods, put it this way in his path breaking book *Principles of Economics*:

> *The steadiest motive to ordinary business work is the desire for the pay which is the material reward of work. The pay may be on its way to be spent selfishly or unselfishly, for noble or base ends; and here the variety of human nature comes into play. But the motive is supplied by a definite amount of money; and it is this definite and exact money measurement of the steadiest motives in business life, which has enabled economics far to outrun every other branch of the study of man.*

In other words, Marshall, although admitting to a higher nature in humans, still argued that people's basic economic nature is one of self-interest, the desire for monetary gain.

Do Corporations Value Profits Above All Else?

Most orthodox economists today still accept the concept of the "economic man," especially as it relates to the decisions of business people. Some of them have attacked the idea that business firms seek to maximize profits. However, Nobel Laureate Robert Solow[7] defended the idea in these words:

> *Does the modern industrial corporation maximize profits? Probably not rigorously and single-mindedly, and for much the same reason that Dr.*

Hedonism
A philosophical school that argues that self-satisfaction is the primary goal of individuals.

Homo Economicus
A term meaning "economic person."

Johnson did not become a philosopher, because cheerfulness keeps break-ing in. Most large corporations are free enough from competitive pressure to offer a donation to the Community Chest or a fancy office building with-out a close calculation of its incremental contribution to profit. The received doctrine can survive if businesses merely almost maximize profits.

Solow also feels that consumers are more likely "almost" to maximize satisfaction than "almost" to do anything else and argues that the idea of firms maximizing profits comes closer to explaining and predicting their behavior than any other single assumption. His beliefs probably represent the position of most American economists.

The Radical View

One attack on economic self-interest has come from radical economists, who say that, in an industrial or capitalist society, *homo economicus* is at best an endangered species and at worst a myth.

Karl Marx argued that the concentration of power and ownership in private hands (which exists in a capitalist society) leads to alienation of workers and deprives consumers of their right to consume as they wish. It also deprives producers of their right to produce as they wish, because, according to the Marxists, it means that fewer and fewer people make decisions about production. Some radicals have argued that out of a Marxist society will evolve **homo communista**, communist man, in place of *homo economicus*. Homo Comunista would not rely on the profit motive to allocate resources nor incentives to material rewards to motivate effort or risk taking.

Homo Communista
Communist man

As we noted above, it appears in the twenty-first century that it is *homo communista* rather than *homo economicus* that is the endangered concept. Not only has Marxist economics been rejected in China, but Marxism itself has been rejected in the former Soviet Union and in many other formerly socialist societies. There are pressures in many other parts of the world to reform economic institutions in ways that recognize the need to appeal to the economic self interests of individuals. Few societies today are avowedly Marxist and fewer still are consistent in their practice of Marx's principles. On the other hand, many contemporary followers of Marx are quick to point out that many aspects of Marx's analysis of capitalist economies are still relevant: recurrent economic crises in these economies reflect the inability of workers to buy what they directly and indirectly produce due to a highly unequal distribution of income, mass unemployment and wages that do not reflect productivity improvements. This phenomenon, termed by Marx as "overproduction," can be delayed if the bulk of consumers can borrow and accumulate debt, but cannot be indefinitely sustained and end with crises.

The Psychology of Decision Making

Earlier we referred to the award of the 2002 Nobel Prize in Economics to Veron Smith[8] for his pioneering work in experimental economics. It should also be noted the prize was jointly awarded to Daniel Kahneman[9], a behavioral psychol-

---

7. In Dolan, Edwin G. and John C. Goodman. *Economics of Public Policy.* St. Paul, MN. West Publishing. 1989.
8. In "Nobel Recognizes Importance of Experimentation," *Wall Street Journal,* November 23, 2002.
9. In "Nobel Recognizes Importance of Experimentation," *Wall Street Journal,* November 23, 2002.

ogist whose work has focused on how people make economic decisions when faced with uncertainty.

In this text, we shall assume that individuals make equilibrium choices under conditions of certainty. While Kahneman's work questions whether consumers and producers will achieve the same choices under conditions of uncertainty, it does not, in the opinion of the authors, invalidate the basic microeconomic principles set forth in this text.

Application IV: Whither Social Security?

The Social Security Act was signed by President Franklin Roosevelt on August 14, 1935. On the 80th anniversary of the Act, a report by the Center for Budget and Public Policy ("Ten Facts About Social Security," August 2015) noted that "Social Security remains one of the nation's most successful, effective, and popular programs. It provides a foundation of income on which workers can build to plan for their retirement. It also provides valuable social insurance protection to workers who become disabled and to families whose breadwinner dies."

Some facts summarized in the report are worth briefly reviewing: (1) Social Security (retirement) benefits are not "means tested" and have almost universal coverage. About 97 percent of Americans aged 60-89 receive or will receive these benefits. In June 2015, for example, some 60 million people (more than one in every six U.S. residents) collected Social Security benefits. Among these, about three-quarters were retirees and elderly widow(er)s, while one-quarter received disability insurance and young survivors of deceased worker benefits. (2) Social Security benefits, while important to many, are modest: if you worked all your adult life at average earnings and retired at age 65 in 2015, Social Security benefits replace about 40 percent of your past earnings (the average payment is about $16,000 per year). This low "replacement rate" puts U.S. at the nearly bottom of the ranking of (relatively) developed countries (31st among 34). (3) Because Social Security has universal participation and does not use means-testing for paying benefits, its administrative costs are low (only 0.7 percent of annual benefits) and much less than those of private retirement annuities. (4) Social Security benefits are important tools in lowering the poverty rate. It is estimated the percentage of people of all ages living in poverty would be 21.5 percent without the benefits and 14.5 with them. This translates into over 22 million individuals lifted out of poverty by Social Security (March, 2014 data). Moreover, the effects of Social Security are particularly pronounced in the case of relatively vulnerable groups such as children, the elderly, minorities, and women.

The Social Security system, however, relies on payroll taxes paid by workers and employers to support current beneficiaries (currently, there are a Social Security tax of 6.2 percent of worker earnings and 1.45 percent Medicare tax which are both matched by employer contributions). Demographic changes have raised concerns as to whether the inflows of the Social Security Trust Funds will match the outflows and, therefore, whether it can remain solvent in the long run. Specifically, more and more of the oldest members of the baby-boom generation have reached the retirement age over time and they live longer than previous generations. (When Social Security was created, the average life expectancy was 61.7 years. Today's average life expectancy is over 77 years). These factors increase the size of the outflows. As for the inflows, when Social Security was created, there were about forty workers paying Social Security taxes for every person receiving benefits. Today, there are less than three workers for every beneficiary reflecting the significant decline in the U.S. fertility rate.

As a result of these changing conditions, it is projected that Social Security benefits paid out will exceed taxes collected by 2020 according to a Social Security Administration bulletin (Vol.75, No. 1, 2015). In this connection, a recent report by Social Security Trustees estimates that given current conditions, the trust funds will be exhausted in 2034. However, the report notes that "after 2034, Social Security could still pay three-fourths of scheduled benefits using its tax income even if policymakers took no steps to shore up the program. Those who claim that Social Security won't be around at all when today's young adults retire and that young workers will receive no benefits misunderstand or misrepresent the trustees."

Nonetheless, some proposals take possible future insolvency of Social Security seriously and campaigned to allow workers to invest (some portion) of their payroll taxes in personal retirement accounts. The amounts accumulated in those accounts would replace some of Social Security's benefits. Implementation of such plans has been called a "privatization of Social Security." The main rationale for privatization is to provide higher returns to future retirees and larger nest eggs upon retirement. Opponents of personal retirement accounts, on the other hand, argue that allowing individuals to invest their payroll taxes in the stock market is very risky. They contend that when even many "sophisticated" investors suffer huge losses due to the volatility in the stock market, it would be irresponsible to make workers put the bedrock of their retirement funds at the market's mercy. Another problem is the cost for the federal government to make the transition to a privatized system. They offer a far less radical approach focused on pushing back the "exhaustion year" far beyond 2034 through implementing modest changes in the current program. These changes include increasing the Social Security payroll tax above the current 6.2 percent rate, raising the maximum taxable earnings (set at $118,500 in 2016), extending the age required to collect full benefits beyond the current 67 years, and decreasing the cost of living adjustments (COLA) of the benefits by 1 percent.

Application V: Compound Interest and Why It Pays to Save

Applications, A Set of Brief Examples
Now let us look at some introductory examples of major economic problems and how they may be seen in the light of economic analysis.

What is the secret to becoming a millionaire? Well, one way is to inherit a million dollars. However, for most of us that is not likely. What most of us need to do is simply to spend less than we earn each year. This is a great starting place. What, then, prevents most people from ever becoming a millionaire? One major problem is procrastination. Procrastination is the most common cause of financial failure. The reason that avoiding procrastination is so important is found in the concept of "compounding." The "power of compound interest" takes us from today's values (present values) to future values. As long as interest rates are positive, a dollar in hand today is worth more than a dollar to be received in the future; if you had it now you could invest it and earn interest, thereby ending up with more than one dollar in the future. A Nobel Laureate, Edward Prescott, has argued for federally mandated savings accounts for individuals to overcome this procrastination. Prescott argues that this would not only begin savings earlier in the life cycle of workers but would also "turn our mandatory transfer system into a mandatory savings system."[10]

How does compounding work? Suppose, for example, you deposit $100 in a bank that pays 5 percent interest each year. At the end of one year you would have $105. However, at the end of 40 years the value would be over

10. Prescott, Edward C. "Why Does the Government Patronize Us?" *The Wall Street Journal.* November 11, 2004.

$700, due to compounding. Thus, what would it take to become a millionaire? Let's assume we invest in the stock market and can make 10 percent annually on our investment (this is about the average return for the stock market over the past 40 years). How much would we have to invest, one time, by age 25 to be a millionaire at age 65? The answer is just over $22,000. This may be a problem for many people so what is the alternative? Another suggestion that should be possible for most people is to save a specified amount of money each month. Just how much would we have to save every month for 40 years to reach our goal? The answer is $158 a month. By saving that amount for 40 years we would end up with $1,000,000.

The real secret to this compounding process is to start saving at an early age. If, for example, we wait until we are 35 years old before we begin to save, we would need to put aside over $442 a month to reach the same goal of $1,000,000. The moral of the "compound interest" story, then, is to start saving when you are young and your retirement goals could be well within your reach. Will it be necessary to mandate such saving to ensure that it begins in the early years of employment? Additionally, would that requirement be constitutional?

Application VI: Public Education: Will Vouchers Mean Improvement?

For many years individuals on all sides of the political spectrum have criticized the U.S. public education system, arguing that is has failed many of its students. One major problem facing the school system is how to deal with schools that consistently "under perform"- those schools that invariably have large numbers of students who score poorly on standardized tests and that have high "drop out" rates.

One widely-debated solution is the use of school vouchers. An education voucher is a certificate which enables parents to pay for their children's education at a school of their own choice, rather than the public school to which they would normally be assigned. These vouchers are to be paid out of tax dollars.

Proponents of this idea say that if parents are given a choice about where public money should go, they will pick the better performing schools, and underperforming schools will have to improve or lose their funding. These proponents of the voucher system believe, in other words, that school choice is a good way to improve public education at a low cost by forcing schools to perform more effectively. Many free-market economists believe that having competition between schools is a good way to improve the quality of schools. Critics of vouchers argue that tax breaks and vouchers will take money away from those schools that most need financial assistance, and that taking money away from them will make these schools' position even worse. Detractors of these changes believe that this choice might often result in the selection of a religious school, with public funds being given to a religious institution, thereby violating the separation of church and state. Opponents also believe the voucher system will cause a taxpayer-subsidized white flight from public schools in many large cities whose student bodies are predominantly non-white. Proponents counter that some of the strongest advocacy of vouchers comes from minority families in inner cities whose children disproportionately attend "under performing" schools.

The voucher system has been used in many countries including Sweden, Spain, the Netherlands, and Chile. In Chile, studies have found that private schools receiving voucher students show consistently better results on standardized tests than do state (municipal) schools.

At present it is hard to generalize about the successes or failures of the voucher system in the U.S. Time will tell if the benefits of such a system are great enough to cause its extension to many areas of the country, especially the inner cities.

A U.S. Supreme Court decision in 2003 invalidated the use of public funding for religious schooling. That decision apparently limits the extension of vouchers.

In 2010 the Federal government spent around $35 billion in a program to bring greater innovation to the public schools. The money was funneled to the states through competitive grants. This follows the Bush administration's "no student left behind" program of using testing to identify non-performing schools. It will be interesting to see how these efforts compare with the voucher program in improving student performance.

Application VII: Where is Health Care Headed?

A rising number of Americans say health care is one of the most critical domestic problems facing America today. Many say they are having trouble covering their health care costs. In 2003 health care ranked behind the economy as the top problem in the US, and in 2002 it was second only to terrorism.

To get a better picture of just how rapidly health care costs are rising annually, we can look at the historical trends in health care insurance costs. From 2000 to 2003 these costs increases rose from 8.2 percent, to 10.9 percent, to 12.9 percent, reaching 13.9 percent in 2003. During the same period, overall inflation and worker's earnings increased at only a 3 to 4 percent rate. From 2000 to 2004 health care costs increased approximately 49 percent. The high rates of health care cost increases have continued into 2013 and beyond; albeit at a slower pace.

Some reasons for escalating health care costs have been well publicized: expensive new life – prolonging medical treatments and technology, longer life spans with the elderly using disproportionate healthcare resources, more medical malpractice litigation, and new government healthcare mandates and regulations.

Given the fact that health care costs are skyrocketing, what are some ideas being suggested to slow their growth? First, insurers suggest a preadmission certification which basically requires individuals to receive approval from their insurers before entering the hospital for a scheduled stay. The hope here is to cut down on unnecessary hospital stays. A second suggestion is to require individuals to secure a second opinion for non-emergency procedures. This proposal would help ensure only necessary operations take place. Another cost-cutting proposal is to give the individual a choice between say, paying 80 percent of the cost of a brand-name pharmaceutical or receiving 100 percent reimbursement for its less expensive generic equivalent. These are just a few of the ideas being suggested to curb rapid increase.

Other proposals include a federally mandated cap on malpractice awards which some States, including California, have already enacted. Some economists argue for reducing costs, lowering the number of uninsured, and creating greater fairness by making health care expenses for individuals and families tax deductible. The argument is that this will cut unproductive health expenditures by relying on "gatekeepers" rather than deductibles and copayments. One estimate by the Rand Corporation is that this would reduce health care costs by $40 billion annually.[11]

Americans will continue to have to cope with rising health care costs in a variety of ways, and it seems clear these rising costs are causing, and will continue to cause financial pain to the American public. Some in the United States want to institute a "single payer" government-financed program of health insurance which, in essence, extends Medicare benefits to all. Such programs exist in many countries including nearby Canada. This is controversial in the U.S., not only on philosophical grounds but also because it contains no assurances that the real costs of health care would, thereby, diminish.

The Patient Protection and Affordable Care Act of 2010
In 2010, the Patient Protection and Affordable Care Act (PPACA), often dubbed "Obama care," was signed into law. The bill which was designed to make major changes in the American health care system remains highly controversial. PPACA expands insurance coverage to more than 32 million currently uninsured Americans by enabling them to purchase insurance through state-based "health insurance exchanges" (or insurance markets) at a subsidized price for the poor. These exchanges are supposed to increase competition among insurance providers and keep prices under control. Insurance reforms under PPACA include banning insurance companies from denying coverage based on pre-existing conditions and gender and dropping people when they get sick, allowing young adults to stay on their parents' health insurance plan until age 27, and including preventative care in new insurance plans. PPACA's costs are paid for by imposing the Medicare payroll tax on "unearned" (investment) income of families making more than $250,000 and a 40-percent tax on the high-end insurance plans, among others. Much of the provisions of PPACA are to be phased in over time. Perhaps the most controversial aspect of PPACA is insurance mandate for all Americans. Proponents of the mandate argue that it is necessary to get younger people and other uninsured to purchase insurance in order to reduce risks or diversify the risk pool of insured individuals. They note that uninsured individuals impose costs on the rest of the society through receiving emergency room care and other indirect channels and the health insurance mandate is essentially no different than requiring drivers to buy car insurance. Opponents argued that Congress exceeded its constitutional authority by forcing Americans to buy a product and imposing penalties on those who refuse to do so. A number of states challenged the legality of the mandate. However, in a 5-4 ruling in July 2012, the Supreme Court upheld the constitutionality of most provisions of PPACA.

Application VIII: The European Financial Crisis

The rising threat of default by heavily indebted European countries has spread fear across financial markets, caused rioting in several European countries and has weighed on economies worldwide. Banks along with investors have nervously watched Europe's political and financial leaders scramble to prevent the 17 nation euro zone from breaking apart. The problems in Europe are somewhat similar to ours in the United States, only worse. The European sovereign debt crisis has been created by a combination of complex factors which include the globalization of finance, easy credit conditions during the 2003-2008 period that encouraged high - risk lending and borrowing practices, international trade imbalances, real estate bubbles that have since burst, slow economic growth conditions since 2008, along with fiscal policy choices related to government

---

11.Cogan, John F., R. Glenn Hubbard, and Daniel P. Kessler. "Brilliant Deduction." *The Wall Street Journal,* December 8, 2004.

spending and revenues, problems have been caused by nations trying to bail out troubled banking industries and private bondholders.

It's not easy to pinpoint any one particular action stated above as the main culprit in the debt crisis. All of these actions played a part in the debt crisis. What we can say is that by the beginning of the 1990s, national debt growth along with annual budget shortfalls of numerous countries began to worry financial markets as they were turned into major political issues. In trying to maintain economic growth while at the same time cutting the deficit, both Washington and London dramatically deregulated the financial industries, leading to what some economists call "privatized Keynesianism". By allowing financiers to invent and market endless new forms of private debt. Governments in effect shifted the site of borrowing from sovereign states to companies and individuals who could now fund their own consumption, and speculation, by borrowing from their own future.

What ensued were two asset bubbles, the first in Internet stocks in the late 90s, and the second, far more devastating one, in American real estate and the financial instruments derived from it, so-called mortgage-backed securities, which brought down Lehman Brothers in 2008 and began the stages for the current financial crisis in Europe.

How each European country involved in the crisis borrowed and invested the money that caused them problems varies from country to country. For example, Ireland's banks lent the money to property developers, generating a massive property bubble. When the bubble burst, Ireland's government and taxpayers assumed private debts. In Greece the government increased its commitment to public works in the forms of extremely generous pay and pension benefits. In Iceland the banking system grew enormously, creating debts to global investors several times larger than its national GDP.

So the debt crisis came about differently in each country but because of the interconnection in the global financial system. If one nation defaults on its sovereign debt or enters into recession that places some of the external private debt at risk as well, which can cause the banking systems of the creditor nations to face severe losses.

By 2009 debt crisis problems were facing many countries. One of the first countries to show financial distress was Greece which had a debt amounting to 113% of GDP. By 2012 that number had risen to 157% of GDP - nearly two and a half times the euro zone limit of 60%. Rating agencies started to downgrade Greek bank and government debt. In early 2010 the Greek budget deficit was revised upwards to 12.7%, from 3.7%, and more than four times the maximum allowed by the EU rules. In February of 2010 Greece unveiled a series of austerity measures aimed at curbing the deficit. By mid-2010 concerns were building about all the heavily indebted countries in Europe particularly Portugal, Ireland, Greece, Italy and Spain. In May of 2010 the euro zone members and the IMF agreed to a €110 billion bailout package to rescue Greece. In November of the same year the EU and IMF agreed to a bailout package to the Irish Republic totaling €85 billion. At the start of 2011 the euro finance ministers set up a permanent bailout fund, called the European Stability Mechanism, worth about €500 billion. By April of that year Portugal admitted they could not deal with their finances and asked the EU for help. In May of that year the euro zone and the IMF approved a €78 billion bailout for Portugal. Two months later a second bailout for Greece is agreed upon. The euro zone agrees to a comprehensive €109 billion package designed to resolve the Greek crisis and prevent contagion among other European economies. In August of 2011 the European Central Bank said it would buy Italian and Spanish government bonds to try to bring down their borrowing costs, as concerns grow that the debt crisis may spread to larger economies such as Italy and Spain. In September of 2011 Italy passes a €50 billion austerity budget to balance the budget by 2013 after weeks of haggling in Parliament.

European Austerity - How will it Affect the U.S.?
In 2013, the five-year mark in the "Great Recession", the outlook across the developed world was mixed at best and dismaying at worst. The United States, one of the bright spots, is showing signs of slow but steady improvement. In Europe the outlook is more bleak. Germany stands virtually alone in terms of real economic growth, with most of southern Europe continuing to struggle. Greece especially struggles to keep its head above water. Portugal is trying to slow their downward slide on the same slope, and Cyprus races against a banking crisis. Meanwhile growth in France stalls and Britain tries to dodge a triple dip recession.

In the midst of all this is the policy of austerity that has been the rule across the European continent. It has been an unfortunate coincidence that severe debt crisis has coincided precisely with the general economic downturn. This has led to the unenviable situation of having to prioritize between growth and solvency. As bad as the recession has been in Europe, places like Greece and Cyprus have had to choose deficit cutting to avoid falling into bankruptcy. The latter would be even more catastrophic for their long-term health than the current economic decline. Adding to the fear is the nature of the shared euro currency, the value of which would be severely threatened if one or more of its members falls into bankruptcy and withdraw from the eurozones. A shrinking eurozone would cause strong economies such as Germany to face the burden of solving problems in other European countries.

The strong economies may be unwilling to continue to supply capital to the weaker economies for various reasons not least of which involve domestic political considerations. The Germans feared that simply handing other states their hard-earned money will paper over the ugliness of the recession and produce complacency towards real budgetary and structural reform in those countries. Strong economies hoping to shorten the financial crisis in southern Europe, have attached a number of strings to their aid. Countries seeking bailout funds have to reconfigure markets and seriously cut government expenditures as a sign of good faith toward the Germans, who preemptively did much of the same around 10 years ago.

Austerity is quite understandably unpopular. In places like Greece, which have laid off public employees for the first time in a century, it's a cause for protesting against both government taking away entitlements and foreigners like Germany supposedly imposing their will throughout the euro zone. In this regard the new president of France has indicated that austerity conditions in that country will be reduced. For its part Germany is becoming increasingly agitated about the failure of the Mediterranean states to enact real reform in budgetary matters. In Italy, voters last spring turned to Beppe Grilb, someone without political expereince to resolve the problems stemming from the difficult choice between austerity and bankruptcy. Greek politicians are struggling to make cuts without further provoking the wrath of the populace that has rioted repeatedly since the start of the recession and has seen their real incomes diminish greatly and rates of unemployment rise steadily. It seems everywhere austerity's grip on policy is tenuous.

Another major problem is that the consensus on austerity seems to be crumbling quickly on three fronts. First, the IMF has admitted recently that its projection for the cost of austerity has been higher than anticipated, with the multiplier effect of quickly cutting public expendatures being sharper than expected. Secondly, European commission President Jose Barros has begrudgingly acknowledged that austerity's viability is waning as European economies continue to struggle to meet both growth and deficit reduction targets.

Finally, it has become known that the data on which the IMF based its austerity recommendations are flawed. The Reinhart-Rogoff paper purported to show that a high degree of public debt (90% of GDP and up) was historically tied to low growth rates, and heavily implied that the former caused the latter. Unfortunately for the paper, numerous statistical problems undermined its results, not counting the apparently accidental loss of data between the spreadsheet and the final trends.

The effect of the report has been to strip much of the academic underpinnings for the pursuit of low indebtedness. To be sure, some countries had to cut deficits as a matter of necessity, having spent themselves past the point of continued solvency. However, for countries faced with noncritical high debt and a sluggish economy, the economic consensus is that shifting away from austerity would actually enhance growth.

A possible lesson to be taken from this is that austerity is a means, not an end. It is not an ideology, rather a tool with very specific uses not to be abused with overuse. This means that countries in debt crises should be as austere as needed to bring expenditures under control while remembering the serious negative effects it has on growth and setting realistic sights accordingly. Countries like the Netherlands, who are enduring a slow economy, not a debt crisis, need austerity less than they need a return to consumer spending that can be greatly aided by continued government expenditures. When one thinks about government policy and the Keynesian rule, austerity should be a policy for boom times, not down times. Whereas cutting back government spending might trim the top off of excess growth, it will better prepare the economy for the next recession and with much less pain than combining fiscal stinginess with slow business.

At the current time actions are being considered to decrease deficits and increase private - public labor market flexibility. Whether these actions will help the European countries hasten the end of their slow growth /recessionary problems is still up in the air.

One of the important lessons to be learned from the experiences of the EU policy makers during the "Great Recession" is the following: Attempts to formulate common economic policies are far easier during periods of economic growth and prosperity. During such periods, periods in which all member countries can agree that economic growth is a "positive sum gain" for all, common policies can be agreed upon. Contrarily in periods of economic crisis, periods in which some countries see economic growth and others see periods of economic declines, common policies tend to be much more difficult to agree upon.

As we enter the middle of 2015 we see that most of Europe continues to struggle with GDP growth. There are some positive signs that are happening at this time and now seven years past the middle of the "Great Recession" Europe may be making the turn towards more normal growth. There are certainly still problems in Europe and the possibility of Greece leaving the European Union still carries a heavy weight on the continent. Only time will tell what happens in the European Union.

Application IX: The Chinese Housing Market: A Bubble in the Making?

For the last few years the Chinese real estate market has been expanding almost uncontrollably. Is this a bubble? Many think the answer to this question is, yes. China is building 12 to 24 new cities each year with many of them basically "ghost towns" because no tenants have moved into them. This uncontrollable growth in the housing industry is partly due to government restrictions on investment. The rapidly expanding Chinese middle class are looking for places to invest. They're basically not allowed to make foreign investments, the Chinese stock market is unpredictable and risky, and Chinese banks don't offer interest rates that can keep up with inflation. As a result, the middle-class invest a substantial portion of their savings in housing projects, the prices of which they are convinced will continue to rise because China like the United States a century ago is rapidly urbanizing.

Concerns over China's seeming bubble continue to rise as result of troubling signs. In 2012, Shanghai property developers began cutting prices up to one third on their most recently sold luxury condos. As a result crowds of owners who recently purchased these condos converged on sale offices in the city, demanding refunds for their losses. Price reductions are predicted to occur throughout China. housing prices are likely to continue to decrease causing additional strain on the real estate market. According to Homelink, a property agency in China, in November of 2012 new home prices in Beijing dropped nearly 35%, from their peak. Falling prices alone cannot, howe a crash in the housing market. The biggest question, thus is whether investors who own the existing "ghost towns" will hold their investments despite the falling prices. Alternatively, they might join in a giant market sell off, which could severely disrupt the market. Many analysts conclude that as long as the Chinese continue to invest their money in housing, and the middle-class continues to increase their demand for housing, housing prices should reach a stable equilibrium.

If the bubble bursts, it would be the third wave of global crisis that began with the United States financial collapse in 2008. It could wipe out most anyone who has invested in the properties and hurt about 50 million Chinese construction workers. Since 13% of Chinese GDP in 2012 came from real estate investments, a bursting bubble could greatly slow the entire Chinese economy. As a result China could replicate the experience of the U.S. after 2007 and experience a recession.

The Chinese government has imposed severe restrictions on real estate in order to curb rising home prices in major Chinese cities. By March of 2013 Beijing limited single individuals to only buying one home in the city instead of two. There are also newly imposed higher capital gains taxes on homes. Also in early March of 2013 China's State Council released a statement calling for higher down payments for second homes in cities.

These new measures recently sent Chinese equities plunging and led to much commentary in the United States saying China could be the next economy to go down in the global system. In early March of 2013 Shanghai's stock exchange property index fell 9.25% in one day. It should also be noted that from early February until late March of 2013 the Shanghai composite index slumped 5.6%.

The consequences of a Chinese collapse would be severe for the United States and for the world. It would mean sharply cut Chinese purchases of U.S. Treasury bonds, far less revenue for companies like General Motors and far fewer Chinese imports of high-end goods from American and Asian companies.

This current Chinese housing bubble is quite different than that of the housing bubble in the United States. For example, home buyers in China always had to provide down payments of at least 20%. On average, owners have 40 to 50% equity in their homes. In the United States when US housing prices were rising, the government actively took apart in inflating the real estate bubble by allowing subprime loans, Alt-A loans, and ninja loans. US home buyers were able to get low interest loans with minimal down payments on these loans. The situation in China is nothing close to the mortgage-backed securities bubble that took place in the United States.

It will be interesting to see if the housing bubble bursts in China and causes a major negative economic impact throughout the world or if housing demand grows quickly in China and catches up with the current supply. Only time will tell what the final results will be.

Epilogue

Several decades ago, the famous English economist John Maynard Keynes wrote "Practical men, who believe themselves to be quite exempt from any intellectual influences, are usually the slaves of some defunct economist." However, as the applications above illustrated, economists, like other people, can look at the facts of an issue ("what is") and draw quite different conclusions regarding how it should be dealt with ("what ought to be"). For example, while some economists are "market fundamentalists" and subscribe to the view that "government is the problem," others may think that there is a government based solution for many problems. Between these two extremes, practical economists should find a place for themselves and try to better serve the interests of the society by not being slaves of some dogmas and rigid theories.

SUMMING UP

1. Economics has acquired the reputation of being difficult, abstract, and mathematical. This book attempts to make the difficult understandable, to give concrete examples to demonstrate the abstractions, and to de-emphasize the mathematics so that people without an extensive mathematics background can readily grasp the ideas.

2. In the nineteenth century, people referred to economists as "political economists." They also called economics "the dismal science," because of the pessimistic views of the future many economists held. We have come a long way in the past hundred years. Technology and improved economic organization have caused many modern economists to have an optimistic view of the ability of people to improve their material well-being.

3. Adam Smith, considered by many to be the founder of modern economics, argued that self-interest and acquisitiveness were the primary economic motivations of people. Smith thought that the appropriate economic role of government was to provide a system within which individual self-interest could be harnessed to accomplish the public good.

4. The *hedonists* (Benthamites), or self-satisfiers, thought that people were walking calculators who measured every act in terms of the pain or pleasure it would bring. Benthamites thought that people would always precisely maximize the amount of pleasure they could achieve. Most economists today no longer hold this view.

5. Most modern economists, beginning with Alfred Marshall, assume that people are motivated in their economic actions primarily by a desire for monetary gain and a desire to achieve maximum satisfaction. They are not able, however, to measure satisfaction or pain precisely, even though they can measure profit.

6. Most orthodox economists, regard the idea of the economic citizen (the profit- and satisfaction-maximizing person) as the most useful long-term view of human behavior, and believe that this view explains and predicts people's economic actions more accurately than any other single assumption.

7. Economists differ greatly among themselves about how to *solve* economic problems, but less about how to *study* them. While there is room for disagreement about alternative solutions to specific economic problems, there is increasing agreement that economic growth is enhanced by a system of incentives to individual initiative that encourages work, risk taking, and innovation.

8. *Economics* may be defined as the social science that deals with the analysis of material problems. Economists perform their functions by identifying alternative means through which people can provide for their material well-being.

9. Economics differs from physical science, in that physical science proves its principles by means of controlled and repeatable experiments. The laws of economics are derived from observations of human behavior. As behavior changes, so must economists' rules. Increasingly, however, work in Experimental Economics permits testing of hypothesis about the economic behavior of individuals.

10. When economists identify the alternative solutions to economic problems, they also point out the costs and benefits of each.

11. Economists are not necessarily more materialistic than other people. They do, however, insist that solutions to many noneconomic questions require material resources (land, labor, capital, and entrepreneurship). These solutions, thus, are based in economic reality.

12. Economic Analysis is done in three stages: (a) gathering facts, (b) theorizing and testing theory, and (c) making economic policy.

13. Gathering of facts is necessary to ensure that concrete information (not hearsay or superstition) is the basis for economic investigation and decisions. Theorizing is necessary to enable the economist to construct a systematic analogy to real life (a *model*), since reality itself is too complex to be described fully. Policy making, though frequently based on economic advice, is often out of the economist's hands.

14. This book is written with the following convictions: (a) people need to know economic principles in order to understand economic issues and these principles *can* be stated in a clear, understandable way; and (b) discussions about economic issues should be founded in logic and fact.

15. This book contains very little mathematics. However, it does use many graphs to help you visualize certain concepts. In a supply and demand graph, the vertical line represents the *independent variable*. The horizontal line represents the *dependent variable* (which depends on the independent one).

16. Graphical relationships come in four varieties: (a) the relationship between the dependent and the independent variables is inverse; (b) the independent variable does not change, but the dependent variable does change; (c) the relationship between the dependent and the independent variables is direct; and (d) the independent variable changes, but the dependent variable does not.

17. In *normative economics*, value judgments form the basis for choosing solutions to economic problems. Normative economics states what *should* be. *Positive economics* states what is; no value judgments are made. This book tries to avoid making normative statements. When they do occur, we have identified them, and the reader is free to agree or disagree.

18. The book makes a strong effort to avoid the use of "economese," or complex ways of wording economic principles. When more technical terms first occur, they are highlighted and defined in margin notes. They are defined again in the glossary at the end of the book.

KEY TERMS

Dependent variable
Direct relationship
Economics
Hedonism
Homo economicus
Independent variable
Inverse relationship
Macroeconomics
Microeconomics
Normative economics
Positive economics

QUESTIONS

1. The President proposes fighting a war on drug-related crime in the streets. Is this an economic question? If so, in what ways?

2. Is it possible to solve noneconomic problems without answering economic questions? Why or why not?

3. Consider the following statements and decide whether each is normative or positive:
>   a) There are too many homeless in the United States today.
>   b) Unemployment among black teenagers in the United States is too high.
>   c) A federally guaranteed annual income is a good idea.
>   d) Federally guaranteed annual incomes involve a transfer of income from one group to another.
>   e) The distribution of wealth in the United States is not equal.
>   f) The distribution of wealth in the United States should be equal.

4. Why is it that economists cannot conduct their experiments in controlled laboratory surroundings the way physical scientists do? Does this mean that economists cannot carry out experiments to better understand economic behavior?

5. What is an economic model? Why do economists construct models rather than just trying to describe reality?

6. Why do economists differ on solutions to specific economic problems when they differ relatively little on the way to analyze these problems?

7. Suppose that you are the personal assistant to the President of the United States on economic matters. The President calls you in and says: "For my main campaign strategy this year, I am going to promise to solve the nation's economic problems in my next term of office. I want your advice, though, on whether this is a realistic promise." What advice would you offer?

8. What do you think is the most desirable solution to the following economic problems?
>   a) Assuring the future of the social security program
>   b) Assuring that individuals save enough for future retirement costs?
>   c) Assuring that American children receive high quality educations?
>   d) Assuring that home ownership remains affordable in the US?
>   e) Assuring affordable quality health care is available to Americans?

Chapter 2: Scarcity and Economic Development

We have defined economics, related it to other subject areas, and talked about its methods of investigation. Now let us look at the overall operation of an economic system. At the outset, let us assume that the economy we are discussing is a free, private-enterprise capitalist economy. This means that most of the means of production, land, labor, capital, and entrepreneurship, are allocated as a result of many private decisions made by buyers and sellers in that economy's market-places.

Market System
A set of means through which buyer-seller exchanges are made.

Before moving on to look at this allocation process, let us define the term **market system**. All of us have had experience with markets. We tend to think of them as places such as stores or auction houses in which commodities are sold or exchanged. Although these places are markets, a market need not have a specific physical location. In fact, a market exists whenever buyers and sellers have the means to make exchanges. Thus a *market system* is the set of means through which buyer-seller exchanges are made. For example, today we can all make exchanges as readily by electronic means such as on-line exchanges as by going to an auction house. Whatever forms they may take, market transactions provide answers to vital economic questions in a capitalist society.

The Results of Market Exchanges: The Invisible Hand

Market processes can be viewed as games in some respects. Each team of players (buyers, sellers) is in the game to win. Each, in other words, is trying to maximize its own (self) interests. Buyers are presumably attempting to make choices that will yield them, individually, the greatest benefits possible. Sellers, likewise, are attempting to make choices about offering goods and services that will yield them, individually, the greatest return on the resources they are employing in their selling activities.

We often associate games with *both* winners *and* losers. In many games such as football, baseball, and the like, the association is correct since if one team wins the other must lose. A remarkable feature of "market games," however, is that *everyone* can be a winner. To see why, we need first to note that market transactions are voluntary rather than coercive. Buyers willingly exchange their income for the anticipated benefit or satisfaction of consuming goods and services. The fact that they do so voluntarily implies that these choices, as opposed to others, will make them better off. Sellers, too, voluntarily give up their ownership rights in these goods and services in the anticipation that the revenue they receive will make them (the firms and their owners) better off. Both parties, then, receive a net benefit. Viewed as a game, the market is a *positive sum game*, one in which all parties can improve their welfare.

It is important to note, however, that these net benefits are not created because buyers and sellers necessarily *intend* to make each other better off. Indeed, economists since Adam Smith (*The Wealth of Nations, 1776*) have assumed, as a fundamental presumption, that individuals ordinarily act in ways that serve their own interests rather than those of others. Smith observed that by these actions, and, "as if by an invisible hand," the larger interests of an economic society and its members are served. This has come to be known as the **invisible hand argument:** that self-interest decisions that involve voluntary exchanges can make everyone better off even if those decisions were not intended to accomplish that result.

Market exchanges occur, therefore, because individuals place different values on the things that can be traded. For example suppose you owned an automobile, which you value at $25,000 in terms of the satisfaction it provides you. What would induce you to exchange (sell) the automobile for money offered you by someone else? Presumably, there would have to be an offer of more than $25,000 since that would be necessary to make you feel better off. If someone sees your automobile and offers you $26,000 for it, that person is placing a higher value on it than you because he or she expects a larger benefit from its ownership. If you exchange the automobile, however, both you and the buyer are better off. The key point here is that voluntary exchanges occur because individuals place *different* values on exchangeable goods and services.

We will explore these benefit-creating results of market activities in more detail as we progress through the examination of a market economy and, in particular, we will see how the structure of an economic society affects those benefits. This will be especially important in the chapters on microeconomics that deal with the effects of competitiveness on the operation of a market economy.

Scarcity: Source of Basic Economic Questions

At all times, societies must create the means to answer some fundamental economic questions. Why do all societies need to find answers to these economic questions? For that matter, why do economic questions arise at all? To help understand the answers to these questions, consider two important facts:

Limited resources: at any given time, the resources available to a society are limited. There is only so much oil, gold, timber, or wheat; just so much capital, just so much labor. **Resources**, the inputs used to make consumer and producer goods, are limited.

Unlimited wants: people, individuals, families, or larger groups, have needs, wants, and desires which they would like to be satisfied, as much as they can be, by the goods and services produced by employing the society's limited resources. However, wants and desires, unlike resources, appear to be virtually unlimited. History and psychology show us that they may never be satisfied, since satisfaction of some wants only seems to lead people to acquire new wants.

As we move along, we shall look at each of these considerations in greater detail. For now, let's stress the fact that resources are *limited*, human

Invisible Hand Argument
The idea that self-interest based voluntary exchanges can make all those involved in the exchanges better off.

Resources
The inputs that are used to make consumer and producer goods.
Scarcity
The relationship between limited resources and unlimited wants which results in the inability to satisfy all human wants for goods and services.

wants are *unlimited*, and this means that each society, no matter how rich or how poor, has to face the problem of **scarcity**, the inability to satisfy all people's wants for goods and services. We can best see why this is so by considering the hypothetical case of a country without scarcity.

An Unreal World: No Scarcity

If there were no scarcity, there would be no need for social organizations (markets, planners, and the like) to allocate resources among competing potential users. But there always is scarcity, of course, so assuming a world of nonscarcity would not be a satisfactory basis on which to learn about economic reality.

If there were no scarcity, all wants could be satisfied. You and I would be able to choose among a vast number of **free goods**, goods in such abundant supply that they have zero prices, to satisfy ourselves. Free goods would exist in unlimited supply, and thus command no price. Air, under many conditions, is an example of a free good.

We certainly would not buy anything that existed in unlimited quantities. If beef, for example, were available in unlimited quantities, we would not pay today's prices for it. Indeed, we would not pay for it at all, since our nation would be giving up nothing to produce enough beef to satisfy our wants. Buyers and sellers of beef would not have to organize a market system. And if there were unlimited supplies of labor, no one would pay a wage for labor. Indeed, labor, in the traditional sense of the word, would be a free good too.

Back to the Real World: Basic Questions

But in the real world that we all know, there *is* **scarcity**, and social organizations are needed everywhere to allocate a society's limited resources. In the United States, a system of markets, established over several centuries, is mainly responsible for arbitrating the problem of resource allocation.

Consider the vast array of goods and services to be produced in the United States this year. Will there be ten or eleven million automobiles? How many color television sets? Will automobile production be even more automated this year than last? Who will "consume" the automobiles and television sets? These are the kinds of questions each resource-using society must ask. The basic questions that result from scarcity are:

What shall be produced? Out of all the combinations of goods that present technology makes possible, what combinations of cars, television sets, vacations, medical services, and so on, shall we choose?

How shall the goods be produced? There are many questions contained within this big question, which encompasses not only the technology of production, but also the *system* by which production is organized. Will markets be publicly or privately controlled? Will there be competition? How much consolidation of producers will there be? (That is, large firms, as opposed to smaller or even mom-and-pop production.)

For whom shall output be produced? In other words, who is going to have the satisfaction of consuming the goods? This is the basic *distributive* question. Will the income of the society be distributed relatively equally, or will there be a few who are rich and a majority who are poor? Or will there be some other pattern of distribution?

Are the solutions to these questions interdependent? They are. The technology and organizational structure of a society heavily influence who will receive satisfaction as consumers. When a society's industries tend toward monopolistic firms, the markets that result are likely to create a more unequal distribution of income. Why this is so will become clear later.

Free Goods
Those in such abundant supply relative to demand that they have zero prices.

Scarcity
Scarcity results in the following basic questions: 1) what shall be produced, 2) how shall goods be produced, and 3) for whom shall output be produced.

Is Scarcity Meaningful Today?

In many of the chapters, we'll talk about debates in the United States that involve scarcity and its effects on choice making. As we will see, in many ways the debates have centered on differences in definitions and ideologies. In spite of these differences of opinion, it is clear that, in the sense of unlimited wants, pursuing limited resources, scarcity exists even for supposedly well-off Americans, and that even this affluent society must make choices about how to use its limited resources.

Viewing the Choices: The Production-Possibilities Curve

At this point a numerical example should help. Suppose that a hypothetical society, Ruritania, must economize, that is, choose between producing two goods: beef and all-purpose machines. (These all-purpose machines do many things such as produce television programs, build roads, churn ice cream, dry wet hair, dig wells, light buildings, type letters, sew shoe uppers to soles, and drive people to work.) Obviously, this is a great simplification of choice making. In the real world, two things are clear: (1) choices are in *many* dimensions, with thousands of alternatives among which to choose, and (2) choices change almost continuously as technology changes. But in order to simplify the description of the process and make it easier to visualize what we mean by choices, we chose just two commodities. Let these two represent, in microcosm, the more complex process of choice making in the real world.

One way to visualize Ruritania's choices is to look at the *production-possibilities curve*, a useful device derived from the *production-possibilities function*, which is defined as follows:

Table 2-1
Production Possibilities for Beef Versus Machines, Ruritania, 2016

	Production Rates				
Product	A	B	C	D	E
Beef (thousands of tons)	0	2	4	6	8
Machines (thousands)	20	18	14	8	0
Marginal Rate of Transformation (MRT)		$\frac{2}{-2} = -1$	$\frac{2}{-4} = -\frac{1}{2}$	$\frac{2}{-6} = -\frac{1}{3}$	$\frac{2}{-8} = -\frac{1}{4}$	

Production-Possibilities Function Shows the combinations of goods that a society's resources can produce at full employment in a particular period of time (using the best technology).

*The **production-possibilities function** shows those combinations of goods that the full-employment use of a society's resources can produce during a particular period of time (using the best available technology).*

In other words, this represents for a society a kind of frontier, or outer limit to the capacity both to produce and to make choices among goods.

The Production-Possibilities Table

Suppose that Table 2-1 represents the various combinations of beef and all-purpose machines available to Ruritania at a given time (2016), within the limitations set out above (full employment and the best use of existing technology).

What does this table show? Let's look at it as a set of tradeoffs; that is, it's like a menu, except that the diner can't buy *all* the items on it.

Consider combination A. This shows that when Ruritania produces no beef, it can produce 20,000 machines. If it wants to use some of its resources to produce beef, it must give up (produce less of) machines.

This is illustrated at point B where it can produce 2,000 tons of beef, but only 18,000 machines. In the second case, it must give up 2,000 machines for 2,000 tons of beef; in other words, the marginal rate of transformation is $\frac{2}{-2} = -1$. These tradeoffs may continue until the situation evolves into combination E. At this point, Ruritania, employing all its resources and the best technology, can produce 8,000 tons of beef, but can't manufacture any machines.

Figure 2-1
Production-Possibilities Curve;, Ruritania, 2016

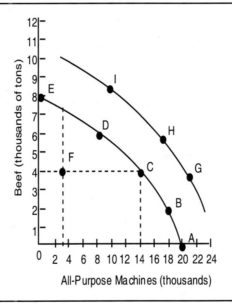

In making choice E, Ruritania gives up 8,000 machines for the additional 2,000 tons of beef and incurs an MRT of $\frac{2}{-8} = \frac{1}{-4}$. The key point is that the MRT continually decreases, reflecting a growing *opportunity cost*, which will be explained shortly.

Which of these various combinations will (or should) Ruritania produce? There is no way for us to find out from this table. Answering this question is complex, and the mechanisms by which societies make such choices vary greatly. Remember that we assumed that Ruritania is a private-enterprise capitalist society, and so the decision is largely made in its marketplaces. But we don't know which decision its producers and consumers will make. The data in Table 2-1 simply indicate the possibilities. (In some societies, these decisions might be made by both markets and government. In others, the decision may be made only by government fiat.)

Graphing the Production-Possibilities Curve

Graphs, being pictures, not only adorn, but also tell stories. For many people, a graph, in this case a picture of certain economic relationships, can be worth a thousand words.

For clarification, refer back to the basic data, which it portrays. Figure 2-1 is a visual image of the data in Table 2-1. Point C in Figure 2-1, for example, represents a combination that is a maximum attainable output: 4,000 tons of beef and 14,000 all-purpose machines. Each of the combinations, A, B, C, D, and E is possible for Ruritania. The curve that has been drawn through these points is the production-possibilities curve (PP curve).

Why are points F, G, H, and I not on the 2016 PP curve? Point F represents less production of *both* beef and machinery than some combinations that are on the curve.

In other words, F does not represent a maximum attainable output. To see this, follow the dashed line that goes through point F. If Ruritania chose to produce 3,000 machines (possible at F), it could produce approximately 7,400 tons of beef, much more than the 4,000 indicated at F. In other words, if Ruritania picked combination F, it would not be maximizing output, and it would not be employing its resources fully. We could apply the same logic to all such points (combinations) below or to the left of the production-possibilities curve.

On the other hand, points such as G, H, and I, lying beyond or to the right of the current PP curve, are by definition not attainable. They would involve Ruritania turning out more of *both* products than it possibly could, given its current technology and endowments of resources. Since we are assuming full employment and best use of existing technology, points G, H, and I are currently unattainable.

Economic Growth: Shifting the Production-Possibilities Curve

While points G, H, and I are not attainable for Ruritania in 2016, they may be reached if one or more of the following things happen:

1. Resources available to the nation (land, labor, capital, and entrepreneurship) increase, or

2. There is an improvement in the technology with which Ruritania employs its resources, or

3. Ruritania engages in trade with other nations, allocating its resources to their most productive uses and importing goods from Urbania and other nations who can produce them with greater efficiency. This means producing goods in which Ruritania has a *comparative advantage* and importing goods in which it does not have such an advantage. This very important source of growth will be explained more fully in chapters that deal with international trade and finance.

Any one or all of these three happenings will make it possible to produce more of both beef and machines. They will, in other words, shift the PP curve outward or to the right. We should note that although the two curves, (A, B, C, D, E) and (G, H, I), are parallel, it is by no means sure that the economic growth that the shift reflects will involve simply larger quantities of the same goods as before. As we shall see later in this chapter, economic growth is likely to change the composition of output (what can be produced, as well as what is produced) since it is likely to change both the costs of production and the tastes and preferences of those who consume it.

Employment, Full Employment, Unemployment, and Underemployment

In the upcoming section in this chapter on economic development, we will use concepts of employment, including full employment and underemployment. Therefore, we will first define some terms. The person in the street probably uses the word *employment* most often in connection with people's jobs.

Here, however, we want to relate employment to all the resources available to a society. So for our purposes, we define **employment** as that condition in which a unit of resource (labor, land, capital, entrepreneurship) is used in some economic activity. In other words, as soon as a resource becomes an *input* in a process that results in the *output* of economic goods, it is considered *employed*.

Now this means that **unemployment**, on the other hand, is the condition in which a unit of resource that would otherwise become an input is unable to find use as such. In the case of labor, this means that a person can't find a job. Land, capital, and entrepreneurship can also be unemployed.

Today all societies, especially in developed nations, give high priority to achieving an employment goal. Frequently, this goal is full employment of its labor force, or something near it.

In other words, the society seeks to ensure that each person who is looking for a job can find one (provided that he or she abides by certain institutional and legal restrictions, such as acceptable age of entry into the labor force or not working longer hours than the maximum work week). When a society attains full employment, it is reaching the maximum on its production-possibilities curve. That is, it is doing so if each unit of resource is not only employed, but is employed in conjunction with other resources to create the greatest output of goods and services possible at that time, with existing technology.

Achieving a full-employment (maximum-output) position, that is, reaching any point on the PP curve, is extremely difficult and unlikely. We will deal later with some of the reasons why. As we will see, the PP curve is a *limit*, an ideal benchmark against which the deficiencies of *actual* economic performance can be assessed.

What is likely to occur in any society is that there is **underemployment**, which means that some units of the nation's resources are not employed in their most productive uses. For reasons we shall explore later in this chapter, physicists may be tending shops and journeyman carpenters may be mowing lawns for a living. Although they are employed, these people would be more productive if used in more appropriate job opportunities; therefore, underemployment exists even though the nation may attain full employment.

A Word of Caution

Resist the temptation to read too much into a picture or graph. When we look at a Picasso painting, we may each read into it something different if we wish. On the other hand, what one may legitimately see in a graph is determined by the definitions and assumptions underlying the graph. In Table 2-1, we can see what the production alternatives are (at full employment and using the best technology). We do not, however, know which choice Ruritania will make. There are social, political, moral, cultural, and legal aspects to be taken into account.

Employment
The condition in which a resource is used to produce commodities or services.

Unemployment
The condition in which a resource is unable to find a use to produce economic goods.

Underemployment
The condition in which some units of resources are not employed in their most productive uses.

One thing is evident: What Ruritania produces today will influence what it can produce in the future. Now let us assume that Ruritania is a less developed (low-income) country. Ruritania, let us suppose, has a ten-year objective to increase productivity from point C (in 2016) to point H (in 2026). Refer again to Figure 2-1. This means that Ruritania has to shift its production-possibilities curve to the right. One way to do this, is to have more productive capacity, which means more all-purpose machines. Thus politico-economic objectives in 2016 may dictate more machines (at the cost of less beef) to increase capacity for tomorrow's output. We say that movement from C to H is Ruritania's planned growth path.

Increasing Opportunity Costs: Why Is The Curve Shaped That Way?

Refer again to Table 2-1. Each time Ruritania chose to produce more of one good (beef or machines) it had to produce less of the other (remember that it has no unemployed resources with which to produce more of the desired good).

Opportunity Costs
What is given up of other goods in order to produce more of one particular good.

We define what the nation gives up of the one good to produce more of the other as its **opportunity cost**. This is a very fundamental concept that underlies the entire study of economics. With all economic goods as opposed to free goods, there is a (positive) opportunity cost. Put another way, we shall assume that there is no free lunch" (zero opportunity cost) in using resources. The real or opportunity cost of using any resource, thus, is what we give up of other things in order to do so.

What Is the (Positive) "Cost of the Lunch"?
The PP curve we have made is concave to the origin of the diagram. This is so because there is a hidden assumption underlying the choosing of the numbers and the construction of the curve. The assumption is that of *increasing opportunity cost*. To define this concept, let us go back to Ruritania and its twin industries, beef and all-purpose machines.

Figure 2-2
Production-Possibilities Curve, Ruritania, 2016

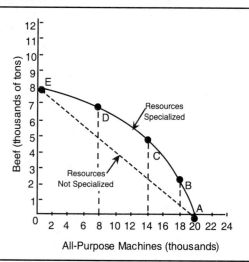

Figure 2-2 represents the production-possibilities curve for Ruritania in 2016. The solid line (A, B, C, D, and E) represents the full-employment choices available to the nation if resources are specialized in producing either beef or all-purpose machines. The dashed line (A and E) represents the choices that would be available if resources were equally productive in either employment. With A, B, C, D, and E the opportunity cost of producing more of either good grows larger. Along the A to E curve, the opportunity cost is constant.

We can illustrate *opportunity cost* by referring to movements along the PP curve. Suppose that the Farmer's Party gains power in Ruritania, and the government decides to produce fewer machines (producer goods) and more beef (consumer goods). It decides to move from the machine-beef ratio at point C on the PP curve to the ratio at point D. This means that Ruritania gives up 6,000 machines in order to get 2,000 more tons of beef. The machines it gives up (six thousand) are the *real opportunity cost* of the additional beef (two thousand).

Now suppose that Ruritania decides to produce *no* all-purpose machines and instead uses its resources to produce *only* beef. The effect is that Ruritania moves to point E from point D on the PP curve.

What has Ruritania given up? As you can see, the 2,000 additional tons of beef cost 8,000 machines. In other words, the real opportunity cost, as measured by the increasing slope of the PP curve, is becoming larger (the marginal rate of transformation is getting smaller). This would also be true if Ruritania chose to produce more machines instead of more beef. In moving down the PP curve, Ruritania would be forced to give up more and more beef for each additional machine produced, or would face **increasing opportunity cost**.

Increasing Opportunity Cost

The assumption that as a nation chooses to produce more of one good, it must (ultimately) give up increasing amounts of the other good.

Resources Are Specialized

The Ruritanian example we are considering is hypothetical. Consideration of opportunity cost as well as benefits is always important in reality in making private or public choices. Suppose that the United States is considering public choice involving lowered speed limits on its highways (as it did in the 1970s and again in the late 1980s). If a law is enacted lowering the speed limit to 55 mph, it will presumably have some social benefits, especially the saving of human lives as well as the saving of automotive fuels. What, though, are the (opportunity) costs? One such cost is the added cost of law enforcement, but this cost is relatively small. The most significant cost to both individuals and to society is the cost of people's time. Driving more slowly, of course, results in more time being used in transportation; that additional time could have been used to produce goods and services and their value is the major real opportunity cost of lowering the speed limit. Why does relative cost ultimately increase as a full-employment society chooses to reallocate its resources? Why aren't resources completely substitutable in all uses, so that the PP curve looks like the straight dashed line AE in Figure 2-2? There are complex factors involved. We shall examine some of these factors later in this chapter. For now the fundamental reason the PP curve is not a straight line is this:

Resources are relatively more productive in some uses than in others.

Imagine what would happen in Ruritania as it tried to produce more beef. Beyond some point, Ruritanian farmers would have to start turning their cows out into pasture land that is less well suited for cattle raising.

Marginal Rate of Transformation
The rate at which one good is traded off for another.

Diminishing Marginal Rate of Transformation
The rate at which one good may be traded off or transformed into another ultimately decreases. In other words, the real opportunity cost ultimately rises.

Of course, if resources were equally adaptable to any use, all land could be used just as well for one thing as for another, and the **marginal rate of transformation**, the rate at which the one good is traded off for the other, would be constant. In other words, it would be technically homogeneous in application. This means, the curve would be a straight line, such as the dashed line AE in Figure 2-2. But in real life this is not usually the case, though occasionally one does find perfect substitutability. In fact, sometimes resources gain in efficiency as they are reallocated from one use to another. However, we want our economic models to clarify reality. Therefore, if models are to help us analyze general economic problems, they must be based on valid assumptions. For this reason, we shall assume a **diminishing marginal rate of transformation**, which means that the rate at which one good may be traded off or transformed into another *ultimately* decreases, for a single firm, for an enterprise, or for an industry. In our illustration, this rate is shown as always decreasing (Table 2-1) from 1 (A to B) to $1/4$ (D to E).

Obviously, increasing efficiency, tied to growth, is an important aspect of economic development. Nonetheless, for the society as a whole, with existing technology, moving resources from one activity or industry to another (moving along the PP curve) ultimately decreases efficiency. This is so because, beyond some point (and with given technology and resources), people use inputs that are less and less well adapted to the new employment. Thus the industry will ultimately experience increasing relative cost. People will have to sacrifice more and more of one good to obtain a greater output of another.

Mental Reservations

You may have some mental opposition to these working assumptions about scarcity and increasing relative cost and may ask why you should accept them. In your own experience with producing something or your reading of economic history, you may have observed the following cases: (1) Sometimes, as a production process is speeded up or modernized, that is, as more inputs are used, output increases at a more rapid rate than input usage. Consider automobile production after 1914 and the emergence of the modern assembly line; (2) Throughout the twentieth century and the current century, U.S. resources have become much more productive, thus shifting the PP curve outward. Actually, both of these observations may be correct, and yet neither invalidates the law of increasing opportunity costs. The reasons why both factors above do *not* invalidate the concept of increasing opportunity costs are: (1) larger scale activities require new plant and equipment which can only be accomplished in a long run time frame *within* an industry not in terms of moving resources from one industry to another, and (2) most of the increase in resource productivity in the twentieth and twenty-first centuries has resulted from changes (improvements) in technology which are not incorporated into a particular production-possibility curve. Improving technology shifts the *entire* production-possibility curve to the right.

A Classical Explanation of Growth: Shifts in Production Possibilities

Consider case 1. Efficiency does increase as a result of specialization of resources and division of tasks, as markets expand and firms produce more and on a larger scale. This improvement of technique, which means more output from the same inputs, results in the shifting of the PP curve, not in movements along it. Economists have noted such growth in efficiency ever since Adam

Smith published *The Wealth of Nations* in 1776. Smith wrote about a pin factory in England in which, as specialization increased, labor became much more productive and output increased accordingly, just as it has in twentieth- and twenty-first-century automobile-assembly plants.

In the same way, steel output has increased. In the 1950s and 1960s the use of automation and improved techniques expanded greatly within the steel industry, resulting in increased production in the 1980s. Steel productivity throughout the world grew in the 1970s and 1980s as the result of new technology such as the oxygen process and continuous rolling mill.

As for case 2, the economic history of the last century showed this observation. Resources have indeed become much more productive since the early 1900s. On the other hand, the static assumptions of the PP curve about fixed supplies of resources and given technology clearly did not hold true. After 1900, the PP curve shifted dramatically to the right. Except during depressions, especially that of the 1930s, the shifts were fairly continuous. We can conclude from the assumptions of our production-possibilities model that the shifts have resulted from two factors:

Productivity growth: productivity increased as a result of technological changes (new tools, new processes, and larger-scale activities). These changes resulted, at least in part, from (a) increased economic integration, (b) market growth, and (c) specialization and division of use of resources.

Increasing resources: amounts and varieties of resources increased since 1900. Our producers today possess many resources not even considered potential inputs in 1900 (including a labor force that is much more productive, partly as a result of investment in education).

Institutions Play a Very Important Part in Decision Making

Economic Institutions
The social arrangements through which economic decisions are made.

Property Rights
Rights of ownership to use, to transfer, and to benefit from the employment of factors of production.

The *rate* at which productivity has grown has also been influenced by changes and refinements in **economic institutions**, the social arrangements through which economic decisions are made. Recent studies in experimental economics have shown how important institutions are through their direction of rules and incentives.

At the heart of resource usage lies the question of **property rights**: the rights to use, transfer, and benefit from the employment of factors of production. Institutional arrangements that efficiently assign and permit the transfer of such rights obviously enhance the productivity of resources. In addition, institutional arrangements may create incentives to resource owners to assume risks and make innovative uses of resources. Of course institutional arrangements may be such that resource owners take too many risks with prejudice to the interests of society. If innovative uses are the case, not only are resources used efficiently in a static sense, but they also are likely to be employed with increasing efficiency as time passes. As an example of a private institution, consider the modern corporation. Corporations today come in all sizes and forms, including the big multinational ones that cut across national boundaries and reach their roots into capital markets throughout the world. As devices for raising capital and spreading risk, such corporations have greatly enhanced the efficiency with which resources are used by business enterprises.

Let us sum up. Any changes in institutions such as these, whether for good or ill, can change the economic climate in which decisions are made. And naturally the pace of development, the shifting of the PP curve, can be altered as a result.

Economic development, such as that experienced by the United States, is a long-term, dynamic process, stemming from a complex set of economic, political, and social changes. Let's now look at that process.

As three distinguished economists have noted: "the efficient functioning of markets requires that some organization enforce contracts and property rights. Governments is usually that organization but they observe that any government strong enough to enforce contract and property rights is also strong enough presumably, to expropriate its citizens wealth..." [1] A balancing act is required, therefore, in which market reform occurs but in which political security of markets is attended to along with economic policies creating markets.

Economic Development: How Do Poor Countries Become Rich?

In this chapter, we have talked about scarcity and about the most difficult decision of all: How should one best use resources?

Through the device of a production-possibilities curve, we have examined the impact that both factors, scarcity and allocation of resources, have on economic growth. Now we can employ these concepts to examine what is perhaps every nation's most basic economic problem: **economic development**. It is one topic on which nearly everyone, expert and layman, has an opinion.

Interest in economic development was intense during the American Industrial Revolution in the nineteenth century, when people were losing their jobs to machines, but interest waned in the early twentieth century. Since World War II, the subject has generated interest again, not only for economists and other academicians, but also for politicians and the person on the street. It's easy to see why if we examine the definition of economic development.

Economic Development *The long-term process by which the material well-being of a society's general population is increased through a variety of economic and noneconomic changes.*

Why does the definition deal only with *material* well-being? Basically because, as students of economics, we are concerned with goods and services. We know that goods and services are necessary to help satisfy people's material needs and wants, although having more of them doesn't necessarily make people happier. On the other hand, people who are very poor, unless they can create the potential to produce more, cannot choose among alternatives. Their lives are hemmed in by necessity. They cannot choose whether they prefer more automobiles to more leisure, prefer more coal furnaces to cleaner air, or anything else. It is the freedom to make such choices that is a great value of economic development, and the main reason why we are concerned with it. The person who must toil for fourteen hours a day in order to live and the society that can barely keep this year's output the same as last year's small output have very little economic freedom. Without economic freedom, the freedom to choose among many alternatives, can there ever be much social and political freedom?

The above definition of development raises questions as well as answers them! How do you measure well-being? How long does the process of

Economic Development The long-term process by which the material well-being of a society's general population is increased through a variety of economic and noneconomic changes.

www.bea.doc.gov Visit this website for more information on economic growth.

---

1. Stephen Haber, Douglas C. North, and Barry R. Weingast. "If Economists Are So Smart, Why Is Africa So Poor?" *Wall Street Journal*, July 30, 2003.

economic development take? Let us deal with each of the questions in turn. As a generalization, however, our definition is broad enough to permit the study of the ***characteristics of development***.

Economic development is an evolutionary process, based on a set of interdependent actions. Economic development is associated with the creation of new products and processes. Consider the development of synthetic rubber. Prior to World War II, most developed countries had to import raw rubber from Malaysia and South America, because despite a hundred years of research, chemists had been unable to produce a synthetic rubber molecule. At the beginning of the war, enemy warships cut off U.S. supply lines of natural rubber, just as the United States was gearing up its war machine and desperately seeking rubber for truck, plane, and tank tires, for waterproof clothing and footwear for soldiers, and for hundreds of civilian uses. The U.S. government stepped in and combined forces with industry to search for the optimum combination of ingredients and for improved technology for making synthetic rubber. (The same thing was happening in Germany.) Finally, chemists abandoned the search for chemical equivalence and concentrated on trying to find materials with the same physical properties as rubber. And they succeeded. Today the world uses more than *twice* as much synthetic as natural rubber, and the United States is the largest world producer. If it had not been for the war and for the incentive created by the government, chemical engineers might not have made that all-out effort, and synthetic rubber might not have been developed until much later.

Actions resulting in development have multiple origins, both economic and noneconomic. For example, world food shortages and the population explosion led to the development of new strains of wheat, rice, and corn. Searching for a new wheat strain, Norman E. Borlaug, a plant breeder at the Rockefeller Foundation research station in Chapingo, Mexico, began in the 1950s to cross various strains of hybrid wheat until eventually he developed a new dwarf type that had much higher yields than the usual varieties and would flourish in many climates. This hybrid made possible year-round plantings in parts of the subtropics and tropics. Mexico was the first country to grow Borlaug's new wheat extensively. The results were astonishing. Until the mid-1950s, Mexico had been importing a large percentage of its wheat, but with the new dwarf wheat, Mexico was able, by 1964, to export a sizable amount of wheat, although in the 1980s, it again became an importer due to serious declines in agricultural productivity. Borlaug won a Nobel Prize for his accomplishment, the results of which have been termed the "green revolution."

The results of development are broad, and are both economic and noneconomic. For example, the success of the dwarf wheat strains led rice researchers at the University of the Philippines College of Agriculture (founded jointly by the Ford and Rockefeller foundations in 1962) to try to increase rice production in Asia. They used the same cross-breeding techniques as the wheat growers, and found a new dwarf variety of rice, IR-8, which grows approximately forty inches high (compared to seventy inches for the traditional Asian rices), yields 6,000 to 8,000 pounds of rice per acre (versus 4,600 for the older rices), and is ready to harvest only four months after it is sown (versus five to six months for the traditional rices). Where the weather is warm enough and water is plentiful, farmers can raise two or three crops of it a year. Thus, IR-8 has become known as the miracle rice, since it can double farmers' per-acre yields. Even tradition-bound Asian peasants were quickly won over to these new high-yielding varieties.

However, this rapid switch brought about problems. More labor is needed for more frequent planting, and there must be continuous weeding, frequent irrigation, and vastly increased storage and transportation facilities to store and market the greatly increased crops. In many cases Asian farmers have had to store their grain in open fields or in public buildings such as schoolhouses, which increased the demand for storage facilities that were in short supply. Another problem was consumer resistance. Many peasants didn't like the IR-8 rice because it doesn't stick together when cooked. Agronomists continuing their experiments in crossbreeding, managed to alter the grains to suit local preferences.

As a result of the development of IR-8 rice and Borlaug's dwarf wheat strain, many people who would have starved to death are now alive, and having more babies.

Economic Determinism

Our investigation of the problems of developing nations will naturally have to be very broad. We will emphasize people's economic motives, but also, of necessity, we will cover certain social and cultural factors bearing on the development process, factors that are not solely economic.

Pure Economic Determinism
The assumption that the actions of people are mere reactions to changing economic reality or opportunities.

If we were to examine the long-term evolution of a nation or people from a strictly economic standpoint, it would involve assuming **pure economic determinism**, assuming that the actions of people and institutions are mere reactions to changing economic reality or opportunities. Not only is such a notion simplistic, but also it ignores, for example, the relationship between social-cultural patterns and economic behavior.

Basic Questions About Economic Development

How Do You Measure Well-Being?
To some people, just having enough rice to fill their empty stomachs is material well-being. To someone else, owning a car that runs well enough to drive to work is material well-being. To a third person, having a chalet in a fashionable ski area is material well-being. Clearly, there is no single number or index that is adequate for this measure. However, many economists feel that growth in *real per capita product* (Y/P ÷ N, where Y = the value of national product/income and P = price level, and N = population) is the best approximation to *improved* material well-being.

To obtain this index, divide the total national product[2] (Y) by the prices existing in the country in question. To get "real" income figures we must, in other words, be sure to leave out of our accounting mere price increases. For example, if prices go up 8 percent this year and national product rises by 8 percent, then for a given population there is *no* increase in real per capita product. The resulting "real" national income (Y/P) is divided by population (N) to obtain per capita real national product as a measure of the average individual's purchasing power in the economy.

To sum up:

1. Total national product ÷ price level = real national product.

2. Real national product ÷ population = real per capita national product.

3. Growth in real per capita national product is currently the best single representation of economic growth (see Chapter 7). However, many other factors (such as the levels of education, health, civil liberties, political freedoms, and income inequality) are important to economic development. Thus, economic growth, while often a necessary condition for economic development, is not always synonymous with economic development.

How Large Is The Income Gap?

One measure of the difference in living standards between two countries (or country groupings and regions) is the gap between their real (or constant dollar) per capita gross domestic product (RPCGDP) levels (see Column 3 of Table 2-2) in a given period. This gap is known as the *absolute income gap*. It should be noted several factors introduce some biases into the process of comparing living standards across countries. One factor is the use of foreign currency market (or "regular") exchange rates, that do not reflect differences in cost of living, to express the income figures into the U.S. dollar. Another is the fact that RPCGDP is an average figure and may not represent the well-being of a typical citizen where income distribution is highly unequal. Finally, the values of nonmarket goods and services (such as food grown for own consumption) and activities in the "informal" sector of the economy (such as street vending and hawking) are not captured by the income figures (see Chapter 5). These and other biases mostly lead to an underestimation of the "poor" countries' actual income.

With these caveats in mind, Table 2-2 suggests that the size of the income gap between the high-income ("rich") and the low-income ("poor") countries was quite large as recently as 2014. The RPCGDP of the United States, for example, was roughly forty-six thousand dollars greater than that of Liberia! Similarly, rich countries as a group had RPCGDP that exceed poor countries' RPCGDP by more than thirty thousand dollars. The inescapable conclusion is that the average citizen is much better off in material terms in the rich countries than in the poor countries.

---

2. For reasons of definition, actual income value and actual product value are the same (see Chapter 5).

Table 2-2

Estimates of Per Capita Gross Domestic Product (PCGDP), 2014

Country	PCGDP Current U.S. Dollars	PCGDP Constant (2005) U.S. Dollars	PCGDP Purchasing Power Parity Adjusted Dollars
Luxembourg	116,613	82,924	98,460
Qatar	97,300	62,169	140,649
United States	**54,629**	**46,405**	**54,629**
Canada	50,231	38,255	45,066
United Kingdom	46,297	41,458	40,233
France	42,726	35,661	39,328
Chile	14,528	9,854	22,071
Brazil	11,727	5,881	15,893
Turkey	10,515	8,865	19,788
Mexico	10,326	8,522	17,315
China	7,590	3,863	13,206
Peru	6,541	4,124	11,989
India	1,582	1,234	5,701
Ethiopia	574	316	1,500
Liberia	458	227	842
Low income countries	640	422	1,591
High income countries	37,793	31,116	43,082

Note: U.S. serves as the basis of comparison in estimating the PPP exchange rates.
Source: Source: World Development Indicators, World Bank (2016)

Adjusting Per Capita GDP Comparisons for Differences in the Cost of Living

To what extent adjustment for the cost of living differences across countries would change the conclusion in the previous section? To see why such adjustment is necessary in the first place, let's use an illustration based on comparing the price of a Big Mac due to *The Economist* magazine (January 2016). Here, a Big Mac represents a bundle of goods that is produce in a virtually identical fashion in many countries. Suppose that the average price of a Big Mac in U.S. is $4.93 and 49 pesos in Mexico. Since $4.93=49 peso=1 Big Mac, it follows that $1=9.94 peso. This implied exchange rate is referred to as the "purchasing power parity", or PPP exchange rate, for at this rate a Big Mac would cost the same in both countries. Compare this rate with the actual (market) rate of $1= 17.44 peso. (The market rate reflects the demand for and supply of tradable goods and services, but not those that do not cross borders such as a Big Mac or a haircut. The nontradables, however, affect the local cost of living). The market exchange rate undervalues the Mexican peso relative to the PPP exchange rate by roughly 43 percent! (Why?) Thus, if the average income in Mexico equaled 100,000 pesos, the dollar equivalent of this using the market and PPP exchange rate would be $5,734 and $10,060, respectively. (Why?) This illustration underscores the importance of accounting for differences in the cost of living through the exchange rate.

The last column of Table 2-2 shows RPCGDP figures using the PPP exchange rates which are calculated based on a similar approach, but using a much larger basket than a Big Mac. Note that the income levels for many individual countries (and the low-income countries as a group) are adjusted upward to account for the fact that they have relatively lower cost of living than U.S. (which serves as the basis of comparison). This upward adjustment is particularly large for the countries at the bottom half of the table. (For more relatively expensive countries like Qatar the adjustment is downward). Thus, while the adjustment narrows the absolute income gap between the "rich" and "poor" countries it does not generally change the position of many countries in a significant way. The poor countries are still poor, but not as poor as what the unadjusted figures (Column 3) would suggest.

Will the Income Gap Close?

Given the large magnitude of the "rich-poor income gap" illustrated in Table 2-2, one may wonder if the gap will ever close and the "poor" countries catch up with the "rich" ones. There are two factors that determine the answer to this question. First, the *initial* level of RPCGDP matters, for the higher is a country's initial RPCGDP the narrower is the size of the gap to be closed. (Think of two marathon runners starting the race from different positions and the initial distance between these positions). Second, the *rate of growth* of RPCGDP over time matters a great deal. Since the "poor" countries are behind in terms of their initial level of RPCGDP, they have to make up for that by growing much faster than the "rich" countries if they wish to narrow and eventually close the income gap. (In terms of our analogy, the runner who is behind should run faster than the one who is ahead to catch up).

Figure 2-3
Per capita GDP (2005 dollars) of Groups of Countries in 1960 and 2014

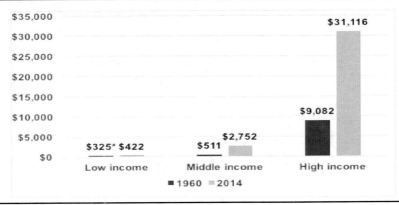

*1982 income level (first available year)
Source: World Development Indicators, World Bank.

Currently, the prospect of catching up for the "low income" and "middle income" countries as a group is rather bleak. As can be seen from Figure 2-3, the size of the income gap for each of these two country groupings has actually increased between 1960 and 2014. There are, however, several individual middle-income countries (China, Taiwan, Korea, Turkey, Brazil, Chile, and Mexico, for example) whose situation is more promising in that they may be able to catch up in several decades due to their relatively high income growth rates. Even these countries face a significant challenge, for they need to put themselves on a path of economic growth and development that is both *high* and *sustainable*.

Barriers and Resistances to Growth and Development

Economic growth is typically defined in terms of expansion of an economy's output/income over time. Economic development, however, involves changes that go beyond simply producing more output. These changes include reductions in the degree of inequality in income and wealth distributions, rural-urban disparities, and the proportion of people living below the poverty line. Economic development also involves modernization of all sectors of the economy including the agriculture and diversification of the economy's output and exports. These ensure that the fruits of economic growth (mainly, a larger economic pie) are distributed in such a way that it benefits the bulk of the population in a stable fashion. This distinction is important, for a country may experience economic growth which is not accompanied by economic development. Imagine a poor country with a corrupt elite and unaccountable government suddenly discovers vast oil reserves off its shores, or deposits of precious metals within its borders. Conceivably, economic growth in such a country can continue due of the newly generated revenues without improving the lives of ordinary people.

For countries to grow and develop on a sustained basis, they need to overcome a number of barriers and resistances which may be of cultural, social, demographic, technological, and/or institutional nature.

Attitudes towards women and their social status, accumulating wealth, and certain occupations may be considered as examples of cultural and social obstacles. In some Latin-American nations, middle-class families have for centuries clung to a culturally ingrained if declining bias against their children getting jobs in commerce or industry. Families wanted sons and daughters to enter the legal profession, the clergy, and the military because these professions were, and to some extent still are, considered more prestigious than working in business or trade. The importance of this sort of social resistance is that it is likely to affect the supply of *effort* in a society. Because bright and energetic people are needed to provide entrepreneurial and managerial skills for a nation's businesses, the social stigma attached to commerce may diminish both the amount and composition of entrepreneurial activity.

Entrepreneurship
The ability to organize resources into producing units.

Since **entrepreneurship**, the ability to organize diverse resources into producing units, is vital to technological change and development, such social foot dragging may retard growth in productivity or even prevent it entirely.

Population Growth
One of the greatest resistances to per capita income and product growth in less-developed countries is offered by rapidly increasing populations. The facts that women begin in their early teens to bear children and that families size tends to be large, make development all the more difficult. (You may wonder why, since in the twentieth-century United States, population growth has meant more prosperity because of dollars spent on everything from baby buggies to education.) Population growth that exceeds productivity growth, however, makes almost impossible the creation of a surplus from which saving and investment may occur. If a country sets aside only enough to take care of what is used up (*depre-*

ciated) in current production, future output is at best likely to be no greater than what it is now.

As Nobel Laureate W. Arthur Lewis[3] put it, the development of a nation depends on knowledge, capital, and the will to economize. A part of knowledge is that the future can be better than the present; this prospect induces people to save and form capital.

www.census.gov

For more information on population, visit this site and click on People.

Remember, however, that the United States, like other developed nations, has a large surplus. It does not consume everything it produces, while merely setting aside something to make up for depreciating plants and equipment. One of the basic economic questions is: How much of current output should one set aside to invest in machinery and other facilities with which to produce for the future? Now, suppose that a less-developed country, because of foreign aid or some internal "bootstrap" operation (a feat achieved by its own efforts), generates a surplus and uses this surplus initially to increase productivity. It may not necessarily maintain this surplus, or even expand it. Suppose that the higher productivity induces people to have larger families. Or suppose that the surplus is used to reduce the death rate. In either case there are more people of nonproductive (not in the labor force) ages to be fed, housed, and clothed. Supporting these people may literally eat up the surplus.

Therefore, the resistance to income growth may be so strong that development does not occur or is not self-sustaining. How serious is this kind of resistance? Table 2-3 indicates that it may be severe.

Table 2-3
Percentage Annual Growth Rate of Population (1920-2010)

Year	World	More Developed Regions	Developing Regions
1920-1930	1.0	1.2	1.0
1930-1940	1.0	0.8	1.2
1940-1950	0.9	0.4	1.2
1950-1960	1.8	1.3	2.0
1960-1965	2.0	1.3	2.3
1965-1970	2.0	1.0	2.4
1970-1975	2.1	1.0	2.5
1975-1985	2.0	0.7	2.5
1965-1980	2.0	0.9	2.3
1980-1990	1.7	0.6	2.0
1990-2000	1.6	0.5	1.8
2000-2010	1.17	0.4	1.7

Source: World Development Report, 2000 - 2010. More developed regions include North America, temperate South America, Europe, Japan, Australia, and New Zealand. Developing regions include Africa, East Asia (except Japan), South Asia, Latin America (except temperate South America, Melanesia, Polynesia, and Micronesia.)

----

3. Lewis, W.A. *The Theory of Economic Development*. New York, McGraw Hill, 1973.

Several things stand out in these data. Population throughout the world has grown since 1920, even in the depression years of the 1930s. It has grown much more rapidly since 1950 in the developing (low-income) regions than in the more developed regions, a trend that is expected to continue through 2010. This population boom has put heavier pressures on the ability to create and effectively use surpluses in the underdeveloped countries than in the developed nations. However, the economic backwardness of the less-developed countries cannot be attributed to this population increase alone, or even primarily to it. Indeed, not all such countries have high population-growth rates. And some, such as Mexico, have, until recent years, shown rapid income growth even while maintaining high rates of population growth. In most cases, however, a burgeoning population has exerted a negative effect on development.

Future Population Growth: Will the Pressures Diminish?
Many factors including medical improvements and technological revolution have fueled the population growth of the past 200 years. By 2003, reasons have arisen for cautious optimism about the population pressures on developing countries.

In its *2009 World Development Report*, the World Bank concludes that a "global demographic transition is well underway, even if it is not complete." That transition is represented in Figure 2-4.

Figure 2-4
Global population approaching stability: differing projections

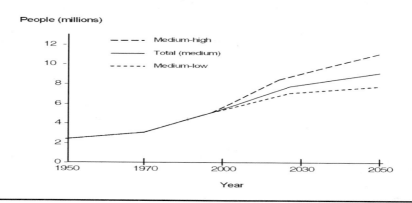

Source: World Bank Development Report, 2003

Note: Medium-high and medium-low variants based on U.N. projections of medium-high and medium-low scenarios scaled to World Bank aggregates.

There are three projections of population growth depending on projected income growth and other factors in Figure 2-4. The key conclusion is that population growth will diminish over the period 2000-2050 and, depending on which projection is realized, reach a maximum of 9 billion to 10 billion people by 2050. As of 2009 the world population growth rate has dropped to 1.17%. Economists at the World Bank believe that this scenario is due to many factors, among them 1) more educated working women and smaller families, 2) greater non-agricultural opportunities, necessitating better educated children, and 3) widespread rise in contraceptive technology which makes family planning easier.

Diminishing population growth will ultimately mean aging populations with resulting pressures on medical and other services. With a decreasing working age base to support those expenditures, financing them will be difficult.

In the meantime, however, developing nations will be able to spend less on children and the elderly. The savings, as the Bank reports, may be used to "generate economic growth." In turn, with appropriate investment criteria, this may be channeled in ways that "put development on a sustainable path."

Technological and Technical Resistances

Figure 2-5 shows the PP curve of two nations: one a developed country and the other a less-developed country. Shown are tradeoffs between present goods (such as beef in our earlier example) and future goods (such as the all-purpose machines used earlier). The curves in Figure 2-5 represent, for the same points in time, a country with a high per capita income (Sweden) and a country with a low per capita income (Ethiopia). Note that both curves reflect, in their slopes, *increasing opportunity cost*. In other words, each country's development comes not from the ability to substitute resources for various present uses, but from the ability to substitute future goods for present goods. If a country wants future capital, it has to forgo some consumption today. (This is hard to do if the country's populace is unable to read and write, and if many of them are half-starved.)

Clearly, the more a country moves out the future-goods axis, in other words, trades off present for future consumption, the greater its future stock of capital, including human capital, will be. More rapid diffusion of knowledge about technical change will shift the PP curve and development will take place. This is a major difference between the two curves.

The developing country (e.g.; Ethiopia) runs into the resistances we mentioned above and, in the absence of efficient markets, finds it harder to use its surpluses productively. Notice in Figure 2-5 that the slope of Ethiopia's supposed PP curve, in other words, the rate at which it may substitute future for present consumption, decreases quickly. This means that the underdeveloped country quickly approaches a zero rate of transformation, or a point beyond which no amount of giving up present consumption increases future output. The rate of substitution, or of giving up present consumption, is shown by the slope of the PP curve. In other words, in our example, it is equal to the *rate of change in present goods per unit change in future goods*.

Figure 2-5
Hypothetical Production-Possibilities Curves for Developed and Underdeveloped Countries

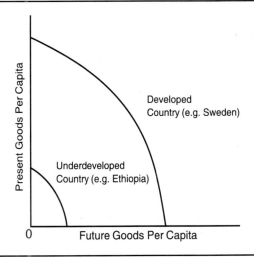

The developed country (Sweden) is able to substitute future per capita amounts. The developed country generates a larger surplus and reinvests more of it in future growth in productivity. Thus, the rich get richer while the poor get (relatively) poorer.

Some countries such as India and China are now growing rapidly. India's recent rapid growth seems to reflect a significant rightward-shifting production possibilities curve rather than a changing slope. What are the major technological barriers the developing countries must overcome? Indeed, is the argument for the existence of such barriers valid? Some students have argued that low-income countries actually have certain technological advantages over high-income parts of the world. Two of the principle building blocks of this argument are:

1. Progress is a matter of degree. Developing countries for the most part have relatively simple capital requirements. Introducing an inexpensive, manually operated irrigation pump may constitute a major technological leap forward in a low-income country, whereas to get the same degree of impact in an industrial nation, major changes in technology would have to be introduced. This amounts to saying that the developing countries have a relatively low ratio of additional capital needed to produce additional output (**incremental capital-output ratio**).

Incremental Capital-Output Ratio
The ratio of the additional capital to additional output.

2. Developing countries, unlike high-income nations, can import modern goods from the vast menu of technological choices developed in the industrial nations. They do not have to use their resources to develop sophisticated processes such as continuous-rolling steel mills, automated assembly plants, and the like. According to this reasoning, these developing countries stand to inherit the benefits of the historic labors of the industrial nations. We, however, specifically reject these two arguments, on grounds that the costs involved in realizing the benefits are likely to outweigh the benefits themselves. In many cases, the benefits are illusory; that is, they only seem to be benefits. Let us see why.

3. It may well be that developing countries need only (technically) simple changes in capital equipment. But how productive will these changes be? One economist[4] estimated that in the United States, between 1929 and 1957, about 43 percent of growth in real income was the result of (a) *increased education of labor* and (b) *advances in technical and managerial knowledge*. The study maintained that only 15 percent of such growth came from increased amounts of physical capital, such as factories and machines

Human Capital
Consists of improvement in the skills and knowledge of people.

Developing countries typically invest less in their **human capital**, that is, in the skills and knowledge of their people, than developed countries do. Poor countries typically spend much less than rich nations do on education, health care, and the like. The fact is that simple attainable capital improvements, such as the water pump, may not rapidly increase productivity, unless the country has already made major investments in its human capital.

Complementary Investment

Instances of such barriers abound in the developing countries. Some years ago, an American economist doing research in Central Mexico met a state planning official who told him of a program to distribute steel plows to the owners of

---

4. Dennison, Edward F. *Trends in American Economic Growth, 1929-1982.* Washington, The Brookings Institute, 1985.

small nonmarket farms in the region. The program was good in theory, but some time after the plows had been handed out, a team of officials, who had returned to assess the results, found that most of the steel plows were sitting in corners, unused. The native owners of the small plots said that they had not used the steel plows because the cold of the steel, as opposed to the warmth of the wooden plow, would offend the earth god. In other words, the steel plow, which had a strong positive effect on agricultural productivity growth in the United States in the nineteenth century, had no effect in this Mexican setting because there had been no prior investment in education. Nobody had come along before the plows were handed out and tried to overcome the peasants' religious-cultural bias against their use. This is an example of **interdependency,** an important principle in economics.

     In many cases, such **complementary investments**, those that increase the productivity of other investments, lie beyond the capacity of the developing countries, which often cannot substitute a present good (time and money spent on education) in favor of a future good (in the human capital form of a more educated populace).

     In part, the impact of importing advanced technology depends on the complementary investments outlined in reason 1. Will a modern oxygen-process, continuous-rolling steel mill built in Egypt have the same productivity (output per hour of labor employed) as one built to the same engineering specifications, but designed and built in Germany? Studies indicate that it will not, in the absence of the complementary investments discussed above, especially in education and infrastructure such as roads, railroads, harbors, and the like. There are also other reasons to believe that the advantages that imported technology offer to undeveloped countries are partly illusory. Modern technology is not completely divisible. Egypt cannot build *half* a modern steel mill. Even if it built a *whole* one, in order to use the mill's output to best advantage it would have to develop simultaneously metal-fabricating mills, a freight transport system, an automobile industry, and so forth. Thus, in order to internalize the efficiencies of modern technology, a nation must often adopt that technology in its entirety. So Egypt and other societies that are not *fully integrated* (using their resources in the most efficient manner) may not find the appropriate technology in the industrial countries. The cost of adapting advanced technology to the skill levels, market sizes, and degrees of economic integration in the underdeveloped countries may outweigh the seeming benefits.

     As a further point, consider that factor prices (wages, interest rates, land rents) differ throughout the world. The technological processes of industrial nations where wage rates are relatively high are almost always **capital-intensive**. That is, they use relatively more capital than labor or land. In most developing countries, *labor* is the surplus factor. (Exceptions are the oil-rich sheikdoms, such as Saudi Arabia, which we won't consider here because, although they have high per capita incomes, they have yet to demonstrate the kind of structural balance among agriculture, industry, and commerce that goes along with being developed countries.) In countries such as India, **labor-intensive processes**, those that use relatively more (relatively cheap) labor than capital or land, yield the greatest relative advantage.

     India however, provides an interesting case of finding relative advantages in unexpected places. While still relatively poor, this huge nation (population of over 1 billion) has many english speaking people with excellent technical skills. As a product of market interdependence in an increasingly globalized world economy, American and other firms have sought to remain cost competitive through utilizing these skills at lower than American or European wages. This process, which has come to be known as **outsourcing** has

Interdependency
A situation in which economic actions depend on each other.

Complementary Investment
One that increases the productivity of other investments.

Capital-Intensive Processes
Those processes that use relatively more capital than labor or land.

Labor-Intensive Processes
Those that use relatively more labor than capital or land.

Outsourcing
A term that refers to the substitution of less expensive factors of production including skilled labor available in developing nations.

increased the demand for highly skilled labor (an important part of India's human capital). As a result, a large, satellite service industry has arisen in the country.

Let us summarize: Technological advantages for poor nations are difficult to find. Transferring modern technology and adapting it to their peculiar problems and characteristics is likely to be a costly process and one that involves far more than merely using their surpluses to import technology.

What About Natural Resources?

Let us return to the production-possibilities model outlined in Figure 2-5. Remember that a shift factor, one that can move the curve to the right to reflect increased productive capacity, is an increase in the endowment of resources. Many poor nations are seemingly rich in resources. Why has the development of these natural resources not been effective as a device for accelerating their growth?

Basically, we may go back to the saying by the late Erich Zimmerman: "Resources are not, they *become*." Consider the example of oil. Prior to the late nineteenth century, oil was not a major resource for the United States. It became so with the rise of the automobile, a complementary development, and related changes in the American economy.

For Brazil, the riches of the Amazon basin fall into the same uncertain category. Without complementary investments in human capital and infrastructure, especially transportation, many of Brazil's mineral resources remain merely potential riches. It is worth noting that some of those resources may remain "untapped" because of ecological (environmental) concerns.

For most poor nations, exporting natural resources has failed to boost their economies to rapid growth. An exception would be the exports of cotton by the United States prior to 1860 (though it is arguable whether the U.S. was a poor nation at the time). However, in the case of the United States, much internal integration and investments in human capital and infrastructure accompanied that increase in exports of cotton.

The Importance of Income Distribution

www.imf.org
www.oecd.org
Visit these sites for more information on international incomes.

We should note that these comparisons across countries tell us nothing about the distribution of income and product *within* those countries. Does growth produce more equally distributed incomes? The World Bank concludes that in the period of 1960 to 1995, there was no systematic relationship between the two. In some countries inequality decreased, in others it increased, and in still others there was virtually no change. The factors that lie behind these differences are a "complex set of countervailing and reinforcing forces" according to the Bank. There are good reasons, however, to argue that it is the "nature" of the growth process that determines whether it is accompanied by more or less income (and wealth) inequality. If most of the benefits of economic growth accrues to a small segment of the population, then income inequality rises over time. Conversely, if the growth process is more inclusive it is likely to reduce income inequality.

Table 2-4 shows two measures of the extent of income inequality among countries at different levels of economic development. Consider, for example, the ratio of the share of income received by the richest 10 percent of population to the share of income received by the poorest 10 percent. When the gains of growth are concentrated, this ratio tends to be high. This seems to be the case particularly among the Latin American countries such as those in Table 2-4. In Bolivia, for example, the top 10 percent held an income share that was roughly 69 times as large as that held by the poorest 10 percent! Part of the reason for this glaring income inequality is a highly lopsided distribution of ownership of assets such as natural resources and land. On the other hand, (former) socialist countries including Hungary, Poland and Vietnam are characterized by the lowest income inequality reflecting the emphasis on equity by socialism. In between these two extremes lie countries of the "West" such as the United States, the United Kingdom, Germany, Canada, France, and Sweden. These countries, in varying degrees, rely on tools such as taxes, social spending, and regulations to modify their income distributions. Generally, where the government is more active and social norms favor more equitable economic outcomes (such as the Scandinavian countries) the degree of income inequality is significantly lower than that in countries with a more "free enterprise" orientation. The important point to keep in mind is that institutions (for example, private property rights, political system, land tenure arrangements, and government) make a difference in determining the way the economic pie is distributed.

Table 2-4

Income Inequality Across Countries: Income Share Ratios

Country	Richest to poorest 10 percent	Richest to poorest 20 percent
United States	NA	14.7
Bolivia	68.7	27.8
Brazil	53.5	20.6
Central African Republic	37.8	18.0
Chile	28.0	13.5
Colombia	51.1	20.0
Ecuador	34.5	14.8
Hungary	7.2	4.8
Mexico	21.4	11.3
Nigeria	21.8	12.2
Philippines	13.0	8.3
Poland	8.5	5.6
Vietnam	8.9	5.9

Source: World Development Indicators (2007-2009), World Bank.

Is There Hope For Developing Countries?

If by now you feel only mildly encouraged about the prospects of the poor nations, you have good reasons. We have argued that shifting the PP curve, sustained growth, in the developing countries will require a combination of the following factors:

> 1. Basic structural or institutional change, including the creation of secure property rights.
>
> 2. Economic integration.
>
> 3. Technological change through adaptation.
>
> 4. Specialization and division of resources.

Achieving these goals is obviously going to take a lot of doing. It will involve much more, as Simon Kuznets put it, than "merely borrowing existing tools, material and societal, or of directly applying past patterns of growth." The political and social changes the developing countries will have to make to achieve these goals will be traumatic and, in some cases, probably violent. Economic development involves basic changes, and since it alters basic social, political, and economic power relationships, it destabilizes a society. Any student of American history knows that this has been the case in the United States. Consider the redistribution of income away from landowners and in favor of owners of capital. This and many other changes in political and economic power create resistances and struggles. (Some believe that the American Civil War was, at least in part, the result of just such struggles.) It would be unrealistic of us to expect economic development to be otherwise in the less-developed nations.

One thing is clear, however. Recent experience demonstrates that economic development in the developing countries *is* possible, in spite of the disadvantages these countries face today in comparison with the way things were in Europe, the United States, Japan, and Australia when those countries were on the verge of *their* big climb in economic development.

When will this climbing process begin? And in which developing nations? Will it involve extensive economic planning, or will it involve, as it has in China recently, reliance on the incentives of a market economy? And will industrialization bring in its wake the problems as well as the benefits of urbanization?

As we have noted, most economists and political leaders now question the arguments for extensive central planning as a basis for economic development. There can be no question that most of the world's people want improved material well-being. As they realize more and more the gap between their own economic reality and what is socially and technically possible, pressure for the above four aspects of change will increase. It may well be that this pressure for change will overcome resistances, particularly in the face of the huge external debts of many developing countries and will be a primary fact of our international future. If so, the impact on the economic and social positions of all the developed nations will be intense.

How Long Will It Take?

There is no clear answer to the question of how long it will take because development, at least in the way we have defined it, is an open-ended process. Any society, no matter how affluent, is capable of further economic development. The less-developed countries will need to bring their population-growth rates down towards the level of the developed countries. Then, assuming debt problems can be solved and incentives to productive savings and investments created, the productivity in use of their surpluses will depend on the awesome power of compound interest. Assuming modern economic institutions to use it, a per capita income that has a 6 percent compound rate of growth will double in twelve years. In this sense, even supposing that the people in a given developing country begin with only $100 annual per capita income, that nation can significantly improve the material well-being of its people in a quarter of a century. And this, after all, represents but a brief moment in human history.

SUMMING UP

1. In a private-enterprise economy, owners and employers of *resources* determine the uses of resources. Thus, decision making about markets is a decentralized process.

2. A society has to decide which resources to use, and how to use them, because (a) at any given time, resources are limited, and (b) human wants for economic goods are virtually unlimited. The conjunction of these two factors gives rise to *scarcity.* This (relative) scarcity forces an economic society to choose among alternative uses of its resources.

3. Deciding what to do about resources involves answering the fundamental questions facing all economies: (a) *What* shall be produced? (b) *How* shall it be produced? (c) *Who* shall consume the output? We recognize that there are interdependencies among the first three questions and that answers to one heavily affect the answers to others.

4. A useful means of visualizing the resource dilemma is the *production-possibilities function and curve*, which reflect the maximum output choice and most productive technology of a society with full employment. In moving from one point (choice) to another on the curve, we incur an *opportunity cost*, what we give up of one good to obtain more of another. Drawing the curve usually involves assuming *increasing opportunity cost*. This is another way of saying that resources are partially specialized in their uses, and beyond some point, become less efficient as they are reallocated to other uses.

5. The production-possibilities curve derives from static considerations. Nonetheless, if we understand the basis on which it is built, studying it can provide insight into the problems of economic development connected with *employment, unemployment, underemployment*, and related factors.

6. The production-possibilities curve shows that a nation must give up some thing(s) if it is to produce other things. What the society forgoes in order to do so is called the *real opportunity cost* of production. The PP curve does not tell us which choice a nation will make in using its resources.

7. We can make the production-possibilities curve more useful as a device for explaining economic growth by bearing in mind the classical idea that as economic activities expand, growth depends on efficiency, which is tied to specialization and division of tasks.

8. To complete our model, we must recognize that changes in *economic institutions* engender more efficient decision making. This is especially true of institutions that create and permit the transfer of secure property rights. These changes in turn lead to both economic integration and faster growth, or shifting of the PP curve.

9. *Economic development* is the process by which the material well-being of a society's people is significantly increased.

10. The concern for material well-being derives, at least in part, from its relation to social and political well-being and to *economic freedom*, which enables people to choose among growing numbers of alternatives.

11. *Pure economic determinism*, the idea that *social* and *political* decisions depend only on changing *economic* opportunities, fails to reflect the interdependence of these three kinds of influences.

12. Currently the best single measure of economic development is growth in real per capita income. But this does not take into account public services and income redistribution, which also affect the material well-being of people.

13. Economic development in an developing country initially generates resistances, both sociocultural and technological. Sociocultural patterns affect the kinds and amount of effort needed to cause an economy to develop. Advanced technology is difficult to adapt to the peculiar conditions of the developing countries.

14. Population growth in developing nations is a major impediment to economic development. The beginnings of development brought about through the use of surpluses may be eaten up by a larger population in the form of food, clothing, and housing. Data indicate that population growth is a greater disadvantage to the developing than to the developed nations.

15. The developed nation with its more efficient markets can shift its PP curve by substituting future for present consumption much more effectively than the developing country can; that is, over a much wider range of its PP choices. This allows output to continue to grow in the future.

16. For a developing country, importing advanced technology is difficult, not only because of its indivisibilities, but also because technology is not as productive in the developing as in the developed countries. Statistics show that productivity brought about by technological improvements depends heavily on *complementary investments*, especially investments in *human capital*, achieved by education and health care. Also, many developing countries, in the absence of economic integration, constitute markets that are too small to use large-scale modern technology and for the benefits due to specialization to be economically feasible.

17. Natural resources are potentially abundant in many developing countries. The productivity of investments in these resources, however, depends again on complementary investments, especially in the formation of human capital.

18. Data suggest that recently the income gap between the developing countries and the rich nations has grown rather than diminished. With the exception of the Middle and Near East and a number of Asian nations including recently the Peoples Republic of China and India, most developing countries are not growing rapidly (in terms of economic development). More than half of the world's population lives in developing countries where the annual per capita income is very low.

19. Economic development for the developing countries is possible, in spite of barriers against it. However, basic structural changes in society within these countries will be needed to bring it about. Where such development does take place, it will be the power of compound interest that will make its benefits possible.

KEY TERMS

Basic economic questions
Capital intensive process
Complementary investment
Diminishing marginal rate of transformation
Economic development
Economic institutions
Economic integration
Employment, unemployment, underemployment
Entrepreneurship
Free goods
Human capital
Increasing opportunity cost
Incremental capital/output rates
Invisible hand argument
Labor intensive process
Marginal rate of transformation
Marginal rate of transformation
Market system
Opportunity cost
Outsourcing
Production-possibilities function
Property rights
Pure economic determinism
Resources
Scarcity

QUESTIONS

1. In what ways have modern communication and transportation changed the ways in which markets function?

2. Will scarcity, as economists define it, always be a part of the human condition? Why?

3. Why are resources not perfectly substitutable? Why, for example, can we not easily move resources from an industry that isn't employing them fully to an industry that is booming and that needs them?

4. What are some of the economic institutions that have changed or come into being in recent years?

5. Does economic dualism exist at all in the United States? If so, where?

6. Suppose that the Secretary of Labor says to you, "We're having a lot of trouble getting people in areas such as Appalachia and the urban inner-cities to seek and find jobs in commerce and industry. It seems as though these people are part of a different economy." In terms of economic integration, do you suppose that the Secretary's conclusion is correct?

7. Some, in the early 2000s, have argued for a return of the military draft. What is the opportunity cost or real cost to the American economy of the present all-volunteer armed forces of the United States? Would it be lower with a return to the military draft?

8. How does one define economic development? Would a broader definition be more useful? If so, what additional factors (or measures) do you think should be added?

9. Do you agree that pure economic determinism should not be used as the basis for explaining economic decisions and development patterns? Why?

10. Why is it important to subtract price increases from data on income growth in order to measure economic development in a given country?

11. What is an economic surplus? What factors do you think determine how large the surplus must be to permit economic development?

12. What are the basic resistances to economic development? Are they purely economic?

13. What role does the size of a nation's market play in the classical explanation of growth and development?

14. What are some of the countries that have had rapid economic growth since the 1970s, 1980s and 1990s? What are some that remain very low-income countries in the twenty first century?

15. How would you explain the fact that, after two hundred years of industrialization, more than half of the world's people are still very poor?

16. Construct an economic argument that industrialization is not necessary to the economic development of a country such as India, and that agricultural development may advance India's prospects just as well.

17. Why is investment in human capital so important to the economic development of a country such as Egypt? What advantages has it given to countries such as India?

18. What are the principal advantages of the developed nations in substituting future consumption for present consumption?

19. Given that many developing countries, such as the Democratic Republic of the Congo, are rich in natural resources, why have these nations not used them more effectively to bring about economic development?

Chapter 3: Supply and Demand Price Determination in Competitive Markets

The operation of an economic society necessarily involves making choices and these choices derive from three basic queries common to all societies: (1) *What* should be produced? (2) *How* should output be produced? (3) *For whom* should it be produced?

Let us now examine the means by which such choices, implicit in the production-possibilities curve, are made in a competitive private-enterprise system.

Economic reality is so complex that it cannot be described completely. What we can do, though, is establish principles and build models in order to draw analogies to reality. First, we are going to set forth some building-block principles that will serve to explain a few things about a competitive market economy. Who is in control? Who or what sends out the signals that determine how we are going to use our resources?

Any economy, including one based on competition, is complex. For the moment, we will not discuss the influence that big institutions, government, business, and labor, have on making economic decisions. We will focus on competition and then, as we go along, add in the complexities introduced by big institutions and measure their effects by comparing them to the effects of competition.

What Is Competition?

A single word can have many different meanings. Take the word *competition*. If you think of competition as a contest between rivals (as the dictionary defines it), then it describes how the rivals interact.

For economists, such a definition has two defects: (1) It is too general to use in analytical questions. (2) It contradicts real life, in which **price rivalry**, the contest in which sellers watch what prices others charge, and then react to those prices, *frequently is inversely related to the number of contestants*. If you are one seller among ten thousand others and you raise your prices, it affects the others little or not at all. If you are one seller among four and you raise your prices, the others may follow suit. Thus, for economists:

Competition; *is the market form in which no individual buyer or seller has influence over the price at which the product is sold.*

Unorganized single buyers bid for the available goods, and this determines demand. Unorganized single sellers make offers to sell, and this determines supply. While we will have much more to say about competition in the text, this general definition will permit us to set forth some basic concepts of supply and demand.

How Are Prices Set? Supply And Demand

If no single seller can set prices and no single buyer can either, how do prices become set, and how are resources allocated in competitive markets? The answer is that there are two independent influences, supply and demand, that determine prices in a competitive market. Let's look at these two components separately.

Demand

Demand; is another word that has many meanings. For one thing, demand is not desire alone, but desire plus the purchasing power to back up that desire. The newspapers may say that the demand for cars is expected to reach 11 million cars. A worried business executive may say that demand for the firm's product is "not good" or is "weak." Both of these statements mean something to the person making them. To economists, however, they lack one or both of the ingredients needed for analyzing markets: (1) the timing of the demand and (2) the range of prices for which the demand is expected to hold. The statement about automobile demand does not indicate the time period (e.g. this year) or the price range for which this estimate will hold. The worried executive, on the other hand, is summing up his or her judgment about the state of the market, rather than analyzing the general demand for the product. So let's define demand in a way that includes both necessary ingredients.

Demand *is a set of relationships showing the quantities of a good that consumers will buy at each of several prices within a specific period of time.*

Let's take as an example a good that most people consider desirable: pizzas. What will be the quantity of pizzas that you demand this year? You'll probably say, "That depends on what happens to the price of pizzas." Exactly! The price of a product, and changes in that price, are the main factors that determine how much of that product the public will buy. For example, an upswing in car sales followed the offer of low interest or interest free financing

Price Rivalry
The contest in which sellers watch what prices others charge and then react to those prices.

Competition
The market form in which no buyer or seller has influence over the price at which the product is sold.

Demand
A set of relationships showing the quantities of a good that consumers will buy at each of several prices within a specific period of time.

by car manufacturers in 2002. Similarly, the "cash for clunkers" program of the federal government lowered the effective price of new automobiles in late 2009 and resulted in an increase in new car sales.

Of course, there are other factors that influence an individual's demand:

1. Income of buyers.
2. Tastes and preferences of buyers.
3. Prices of other products, both **complements** (products consumed in conjunction with pizzas such as salad ingredients) and **substitutes** (products consumed in place of pizzas, such as hamburgers).
4. Consumers' expectations about future prices and market conditions.
5. Number of buyers.

Complements
Products used in conjunction with each other.

Substitutes
Products that may be consumed in place of each other.

These factors determine how many pizzas you or any other individual will buy or numbers bought by all buyers, within any given price range. So when you say that your demand for pizzas depends on what happens to the price, you are saying that this is true for your present income and tastes, given prices of other products and given your expectations about future prices and market conditions. In addition, there is a fifth factor that influences the total or market demand for a product, or for all products. That factor is *population*, or the number of consumers. (Remember that a problem of underdeveloped countries is that some have such small populations that there is inadequate demand to justify large-scale industries.)

Let's hold these factors (income, tastes, other prices, and expectations) constant and establish demand for pizzas in terms of the relationship solely between their price and quantity demanded. This amounts to the same thing as holding certain variables constant and permitting a *key* variable to change. This is called the **ceteris paribus** ("other things being equal") condition. It is an assumption that is common to much economic analysis, and in fact to analysis in other fields, too.

Ceteris Paribus The "other things being equal" assumption that involves holding other factors constant while permitting a key variable to change.

Table 3-1
Individual Demand Schedule for Pizzas

Price Per Pizza	Quantity Bought Per Week
10.00	0
9.00	1
8.00	2
7.00	3
6.00	4
5.00	5
4.00	6
3.00	7

An Individual Demand Curve

Let's take a week as the time period for which we're going to analyze your demand for pizzas. Table 3-1 is a demand schedule which shows the number you will buy at various prices (holding constant your income, tastes, prices of other products, and your expectations about the future). What do these data on demand tell us?

1. The quantity of pizzas you buy increases as the price falls and decreases as the price rises.

2. There is a price ($10.00) above which you will buy no pizzas; in other words, above that price you will be excluded from this market *(or you will exclude yourself)*.

When we plot the **demand schedule** in Table 3-1, we obtain the **demand curve** shown in Figure 3-1, which shows price on the vertical axis and quantity on the horizontal axis. (Remember that economists call a diagonal line of this sort a curve, even though it is a straight line.)

Point A (price = $10.00, quantity = 0) is the upper limit to your demand. For you, $10.00 is the price at which (or above which) you will stop buying. Point B represents three pizzas (price, $7.00); and point C, seven pizzas (price, $3.00). As price falls, quantity demanded increases.

Demand Schedule
Indicates the quantity demanded at each of several prices.

Demand Curve
Represents a demand schedule when plotted on a two dimensional graph.

Figure 3-1
Individual Demand Curve for Pizza

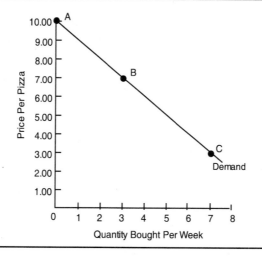

Law of Demand
Consumers buy more of a product at (relatively) low prices than at (relatively) high prices (ceteris paribus).

Substitution Effect
The change in quantity demanded of a good as its relative price changes and it becomes relatively less or more expensive leading to its substitution.

The fact that demand curve D in Figure 3-1 slopes down or to the right reflects the **law of demand**. *Consumers buy more at relatively lower prices than at relatively higher prices* (ceteris paribus). There are two reasons why:

1. As the price of a good falls, the purchasing power of your income increases, which ordinarily causes you to buy more of that good (the income effect). As the price of the good rises, your purchasing power declines, which ordinarily causes you to buy less of the good.

2. As the price of a good falls (other prices being unchanged), the good becomes relatively cheaper than other goods and you substitute the good for other, now more expensive, goods (the **substitution effect**). As the price of the good rises, you substitute other, now less expensive, goods for the one in question.

Each effect tends to reinforce the other. Under normal conditions, both tend to cause consumers to demand a greater quantity of a desirable good as its price goes down.

There are exceptions to this normal pattern. There maybe *Veblen goods* whose appeal to consumers increases with higher prices (perhaps Russian caviar, sable coats, large diamonds, and so on).

Income-Inferior Goods
Goods whose consumption decreases when income increases.

And then there are **income-inferior goods**, such as beans and rice, which people in poor countries eat at least in part because prices of these goods are very low and their cheapness permits people with low incomes to eat them. Compared to meat, milk, and other high-protein goods, beans (which are themselves high in protein) and rice are very cheap. When the prices of these income-inferior goods drop sharply, people may eat less of them and use their greater purchasing power (income) to diversify their diet, by buying meat, for example.

Normal Good
A good for which, other things being equal, an increase in income leads to an increase in demand.

Most goods are not income-inferior goods. In most cases, when one's income increases the demand for a product will also increase. If the demand for a good increases as your income increases, and falls when your income falls—this good would be considered a **normal good**.

Changes in Quantity Demanded Versus Changes in Demand

Change in Quantity Demanded
A movement along a good's demand curve that can be caused only by a change in the price of that good.

So far, we have been talking about a single demand curve, a curve charting the demand schedule for a desirable good and showing that *movements along* that curve are the result of changes in the price of that good. The only thing that can cause a **change in quantity demanded** (such as A to B in Figure 3-2), therefore, is a change in the price of the good. Remember that we are holding other factors constant: income, tastes of the consumer, prices of other goods, and the consumer's expectations of the future (plus population, for total demand). If even one of these factors changes, the entire demand curve will *shift*. There will be a **change in demand** itself (such as B to C in Figure 3-2).

Change in Demand
A shift of a good's demand curve that may be caused by a change in any factor other than the price of that good.

But people's incomes and tastes often do change, and so do the other factors. If we are to analyze the operations of markets and the pricing of goods and services, we must account for variations in these aspects, in addition to variations in price.

Figure 3-2 shows the difference between a change in quantity demanded and a change in demand. The movement from A to B along demand curve D_1 (caused solely by a reduction in price from \$8.00 to \$7.00) is called a *change in quantity demanded*. The shift from B to C is from demand curves D_1 to D_2 and may be caused by a change in consumers' incomes or tastes, prices of other goods, or consumers' expectations for the future (or all of these). This movement involves a shift in the entire demand schedule and is called a change in demand. First, let's see what effect a change in income will have on changing demand. In Figure 3-2, D_1 is a curve showing your original demand for pizzas. All points on it represent the original price-quantity relations. Now suppose you receive a raise in pay. Since we are assuming that pizzas are a good you want, your demand curve will shift to D_2. Now that you have more income, you buy approximately three more pizzas per week, at any price between \$3.00 and \$10.00. Of course, if you were to have a pay cut, your demand curve would shift to the left as your income decreased. If we now take your income increase away, we expect that you will buy approximately three fewer pizzas per week. In other words, your demand curve will shift back to D_1, unless, at the same time, your tastes or your expectations of the future, or the prices of other goods, change to offset the decrease in income.

Change in Other Prices. Suppose that the price of hamburgers doubles. Since pizzas and hamburgers are to some extent substitutes for each other, your demand for the now relatively cheaper pizzas will increase, perhaps to D_2. But if the price of hamburgers falls, your demand for the now relatively more expensive pizzas will decrease, perhaps from D_2 to D_1. The same thing might happen if lettuce and tomato prices rose, since these are a complement to salads, you might consume fewer pizzas along with fewer salads.

Figure 3-2
Individual Demand Curves for Pizzas

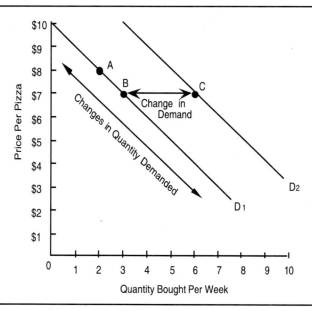

Change in Tastes. Suppose that your demand for pizzas is at D_2 and you develop a yen for hamburger, which weakens your taste for pizzas. Your demand for pizzas will shift to the left (perhaps to D_1).

Changes in Expectations About Future Prices. Suppose that you read in the newspaper that there is a consolidation in the pizza industry and that there will soon be big increases in pizza prices as a result of fewer firms. Your demand curve for pizzas may shift to the right to D_2 (you may decide to buy a dozen and freeze them). In other words, D_1 is your demand curve only as long as your current expectations about prices remain the same.

Individual Demand: Summing Up

There are four important concepts to remember about demand:

1. Demand curves slope downward, to the right. In other words, consumers buy more of a good at (relatively) lower prices than they buy at (relatively) higher prices (the *law of demand*).

2. Only changes in the price of a good can cause changes in the *quantity demanded* of that good. Such changes result in *movements along* a demand curve.

3. The only demand factor that *cannot* cause a change in the demand for a good is a change in its own price. This causes a change in quantity demanded, not a change in demand.

4. Factors that may singularly or jointly change an individual's demand for a good are changes in income or tastes, changes in prices of other commodities, and changes in expectations about the future. These factors shift the Table 3-1 entire demand curve and result in *changes in demand*.

Market Demand

Market Demand
The quantity demanded by all consumers in a market at each of several prices.

So far, we have looked only at one person's demand. But competitive markets are made up of many unorganized buyers expressing their individual demands. How, theoretically, do we figure the total **market demand**? We must add up the demand schedules of individuals, in the market for this product.

Figure 3-3 illustrates the principle involved, since it shows the sum of your and my demand curves at each price, which gives a picture of market demand. My demand schedule is plotted from the same kind of data as in Table 3-1. Thus, when pizzas are selling at $9.00, you buy three and I buy two. Let's assume for simplicity that we are the only two consumers who are buying them. Market demand at this price is then five pizzas per week. Similarly, when pizzas are selling at $4.00, you demand six per week and I demand five, making market demand eleven pizzas per week.

Figure 3-3
Market Demand for Pizzas

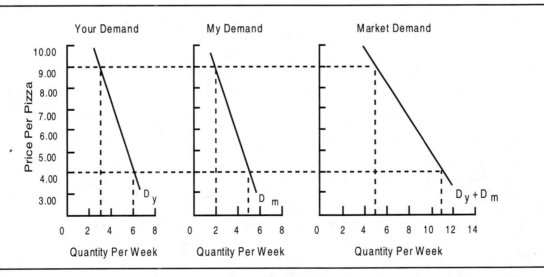

Here are some general things to remember about market demand:

1. Individual demand curves are not the same, since the individuals have different incomes, tastes, and expectations for the future.

2. Market demand curves, like the demand curves of individuals, slope downward to the right, since they derive their shape from the shapes of the demand curves of individuals. Of course, the market demand curve represents a larger quantity of a given item, because many people buy more items than one person would buy.

3. *Number of buyers* (market population) is a determinant of market demand. As the number of buyers increases, so does market demand.

Supply

As we know, there are two sides to a market: demand and **supply.** Now we want to set up the same kind of concepts for supply as we did for demand. We can use the same techniques.

You may think that the wellspring of a market economy's supplies, the business firm, has no objectives in common with the consumer who demands the output of the firm, but each, by assumption, *maximizes* (that is, builds up to the maximum) some aspect of self-interest. Consumers maximize satisfaction and business firms maximize profit. There will be more about those objectives in the microeconomics text.

What Is Supply?

Supply is a set of relationships showing the quantities of a product that a firm or all firms will offer for sale at each of several prices within a specific period of time.

We set up the picture of the supply situation on the assumption that certain other factors are constant or unchanged, the ceteris paribus or other-things-being-equal assumption mentioned earlier. The other factors, which if they did change could affect the firm's supply curve, are:

1. The technology of production.
2. The prices of inputs or resources.
3. The prices of other related goods.
4. The firm's expectations about future prices.
5. The objective of the firm. Will it maximize profit or does it have some other objective?
6. The *number of firms* in the industry will affect total or market supply.

Law of Supply
A firm will offer more for sale at (relatively) higher prices than at (relatively) lower prices (ceteris paribus).

Who is the source of supply? In our competitive market, many relatively small firms do the supplying. Enough firms participate in the market so that no one firm can influence the price of a good in the market as a whole.

To illustrate, let's go back to pizzas. Table 3-2, the supply schedule of the ABC Store, sums up the quantities supplied at each price for pizzas. See what happens to quantity as price goes down. The firm offers more for sale at (relatively) high prices than at (relatively) low prices (the **law of supply**).

Supply Curve
Represents a firm's or industry's supply schedule plotted on a two dimensional graph.

The **supply curve** of a firm or industry shows the relationships between the various prices of a product and the quantities of it the firm or industry offers for sale. A change in the price of a product is the only thing that can cause a change in the quantity supplied. Such changes are reflected in movements along the supply curve, as shown by the arrows parallel to S in Figure 3-4, which shows the relationship between price per pound and quantity supplied. Note that the supply curve slopes up, to the right.

Changes in Quantity Supplied
Movements along a supply curve that are caused only by changes in the price of that product.

Suppose that the price of pizzas goes up from $6.00 to $7.00. The ABC Store will increase the quantity it supplies from two to three pizzas per week. All such price changes are reflected in movements along a given supply curve, and are called **changes in quantity supplied**.

Table 3-2
ABC Store: Supply Curve of Pizzas

Price Per Pizza	Quantity Supplied Per Week
$10.00	5
9.00	5
8.00	4
7.00	3
6.00	2
5.00	1
4.00	0
3.00	0

Figure 3-4
ABC Store: Supply Curve of Pizzas

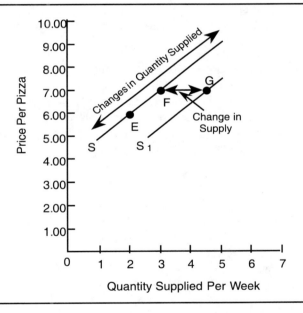

Changes in Supply
Shifts in a supply curve that may be caused by changes in any factor affecting supply other than a change in the price of that good.

What happens when there is a change in one or more of those "other factors" we mentioned? An improvement in the technique of production (a new meat-slicing machine), a lower resource price (price of feed grains goes down), a change in the firm's expectation (a rumor that meat prices may go down), or a change in price of other goods (a drop in the price of chickens), all these factors, or just one of them, can cause the *entire* supply curve to shift. For example, in Figure 3-4, the shift from F to G reflects an increase in supply from level S to level S₁. Such shifts are called **changes in supply**.

What Do Supply Data and the Supply Curve Tell Us?

1. The number of pizzas supplied per week rises as price rises and falls as price falls (the law of supply).
2. There is a price below which the firm will supply *nothing*. Reason: The firm that seeks to maximize profit likewise seeks to minimize losses. It will produce nothing if it cannot make a profit, or at least cover production expenses that cease if it ceases to produce.

3. Although, for a given firm with given physical facilities, the number of pizzas supplied rises as the price rises, the number of pizzas finally reaches a maximum, because the firm reaches its capacity.

Why Do Supply Curves Slope Upward?

There are two easily identifiable reasons why an individual firm's supply curve, unlike its demand curve, slopes upward or to the right. In the first place, a firm's input resources can be used to produce more than one good. If, for instance, the price of beef increases (ceteris paribus), it becomes relatively more profitable to use resources to produce beef than to devote those resources to some other product such as pork. The reverse occurs with price decreases; as a good's price falls, relative profitability declines and the firm reduces quantity supplied and shifts resources to other products. In addition, a firm producing larger rates of output will ultimately experience decreasing efficiency as it utilizes existing plant and equipment more intensively (the effect of bottlenecks, and the like).

Market supply or the supply curve of an industry is obtained by adding up the supply curves of individual firms, this market supply curve also slopes upward. An additional reason for variations in quantities supplied is that firms have *different* costs of production. As product price falls, those with higher costs may stop offering it for sale at all (industry quantity supplied will decrease). And, as the price rises, such firms will again offer it for sale (industry quantity supplied will increase).

Why Do Supply Curves Shift?

The factors discussed above explain why a firm or industry will have an upward sloping supply curve and also what *can cause a shift in supply or, in other words, cause supply to increase.* Quantity-supplied changes (such as the movement from E to F in Figure 3-4) vary directly with price. What, though, causes changes in supply, such as the shift from S to S_1 (such as the shift from F to G) in Figure 3-4? The factors that can cause such shift are:

Improvements in Technology: Technological changes increase productivity and reduce cost. Firms find it profitable to offer more of a product for sale at each price as a result.

Changes in factor prices: As factor (labor, capital, land) prices fall, costs to firms are lowered and, again, firms find it profitable to offer more of a product for sale at each price. If factor prices increase firms will supply less of the product.

Changes in the prices of other products: These prices determine the opportunity costs of a firm's resources. If the price of alternative products falls, the opportunity costs to ABC Store decrease and cause the firm to offer more pizza for sale at each price.

Figure 3-5
Market Supply of Pizzas

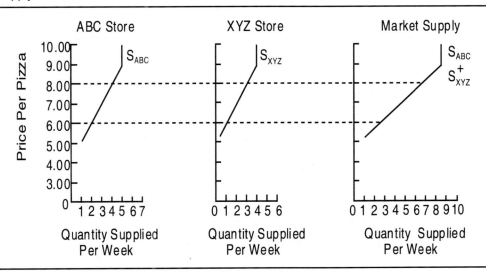

Changes in price expectations: If a firm expects its prices to fall in the future, it will offer more for sale at each present price. The reverse occurs for expected future price increases.

Changes in the number of firms in an industry: Industry or market supply, unlike the firm supply in Figure 3-4, also depends on the number of firms.

As new firms enter an industry, industry supply grows; as firms exit the industry, industry supply decreases or shifts to the left.

Adding Up To Market Supply

We can chart supply the same way we chart demand. Figure 3-5 shows the process of adding up, or *aggregation*.

For simplicity, we have assumed that there are only two firms operating in the market. But the adding-up process is the same, even if there are thousands of firms. When pizza is selling at $6.00, the ABC Store will supply two pizzas per week and the XYZ Store will supply one. Total market quantity supplied at this price is three per week. At $8.00, ABC will supply four pizzas per week and XYZ three; total market quantity supplied at this price is seven per week.

The market supply curve takes its shape from the supply curves of the individual firms, so it slopes upward to the right. Remember that the number of firms helps to determine market supply. Naturally, more firms tend to make a greater supply.

Before we go any further, let us sum up the distinctions between *movements along* demand and supply curves and *shifts in* them.

SUMMING UP: DIFFERENCE BETWEEN MOVEMENTS ALONG AND SHIFTS IN DEMAND AND SUPPLY CURVES

1. The only thing that can cause a *movement along* the demand curve for a product is a change in price of that product. Such movements are called changes in *quantity demanded*.

2. Factors that can cause a *change in demand* or *shift in* an individual's demand curve for a product are things other than the price of that product: (a) changes in consumers' incomes, (b) changes in prices of other related products, (c) changes in consumers' tastes, and (d) changes in consumers' expectations about future prices, (e) number of buyers.

3. The only thing that can cause a *movement along* the supply curve for a product is a change in the price of that product. Such movements are called changes in *quantity supplied*.

4. Factors that can cause a *change in supply* or *shift in* an individual firm's supply curve for a product are things other than the price of that product: (a) changes in techniques of production, (b) changes in prices of other related products, (c) changes in prices of inputs or resources, and (d) changes in firms' expectations about future prices and market conditions, (e) number of firms.

5. Changes in the number of consumers can also cause changes in market demand. Changes in the number of firms can also cause changes in market supply.

Equilibrium Pricing

Now let's return to our original question: How is the price of pizza, or of any product, determined? The answer is that their price tends toward an equilibrium price, one that clears the market.

Equilibrium Price
The price at which quantity demanded equals quantity supplied. It is a market-clearing price.

An **equilibrium price** or market clearing price is the price at which the quantity demanded is equal to the quantity supplied. It is the price that tends to prevail unless the forces (supply and demand) operating in the market change.

Let's see how such an equilibrium price comes into being in a competitive market through the joint influences of supply and demand. Table 3-3, shows price versus demand and supply for our minimarket, which, just to keep things simple, consists of only two consumers and two pizza markets.

Table 3-3
Market Demand and Supply Schedules for Pizzas

Price Per Pizza	Quantity Demanded Per Week	Quantity Supplied Per Week
$10.00	0	9
9.60	1	9
8.40	3	7
7.20	5 = Equilibrium = 5	
6.00	7	3
4.80	9	2
3.60	11	1
2.40	13	0

Figure 3-6
Market Demand and Supply: Equilibrium Pricing of Pizzas

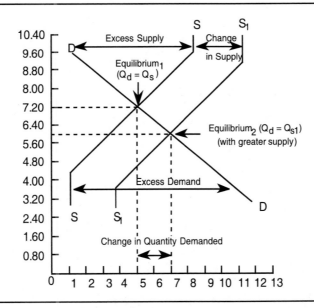

Table 3-3 shows that the equilibrium price, the price that prevails in this market, is $7.20 per pizza. It is at this price that quantity demanded equals quantity supplied, or the market is cleared. Because it is sometimes easier to understand relationships visually, Figure 3-6 shows these demand and supply schedules combined on the same graph. (D represents columns (1) and (2) in Table 3-3, while S represents columns (1) and (3).

As you can see, $7.20 is the equilibrium price, the price that clears this competitive market. This is so because any other price would create either a shortage or a surplus.

Suppose that for a while one of the pizza stores cuts its price to $4.80 per pizza. From Figure 3-6, we can see that the consumers would like to buy nine pizzas per week at that price, while the firms would supply only two. The difference, seven pizzas, is **excess demand**; or, from the consumers' point of

Excess Demand
The amount consumers are unable to obtain of a good at a non-equilibrium price.

view, a shortage of pizzas. (Other examples of excess demand are long lines of drivers waiting for gas when a small gas station offers gas at cut-rate prices and the rush to get cheap balcony seats for a concert.)

Since the demand curve (D) reflects consumers' tastes, incomes, and the like, it indicates that the consumers are willing to pay more than $4.80 to obtain more than those two pizzas they can buy at that price. As the consumers offer to pay more, the stores offer more pizzas for sale. Only when pizzas sell for $7.20 is there no difference between the two sets of interests, quantity supplied and quantity demanded. Neither of the consumers is willing to pay more than $7.20 to buy the additional pizzas that the pizza stores would supply if the price were higher.

What's the matter with prices higher than $7.20? At a price of $9.60, the stores will gladly supply nine pizzas per week. But at that price, one consumer will not buy *any* pizzas, and the other consumer will buy only *one*. The difference, eight pizzas, is **excess supply** or from the sellers point of view, a surplus of pizza.

Excess Supply
The quantity of a good firms are unable to sell at a non-equilibrium price.

Figure 3-7
Competitive Market Equilibrium With Equal Changes in Supply and Demand

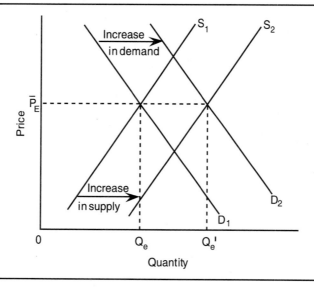

In Figure 3-7, the initial market equilibrium with demand, D_1, and supply, S_1, is with price, $\overline{P}_E$ and quantity, Q_e. When demand increases to D_2 and there is a proportional increase in supply to S_2, equilibrium price remains $\overline{P}_E$ and equilibrium quantity increases to Q_e'.

In order to sell pizzas and clear the market, the stores lower their prices until the market is cleared at $7.20. (Other examples of excess supply are new cars left on the showroom floor after a price increase and new textbooks left on a bookstore's shelves after a price hike.)

Equilibrium at a price of $7.20 lasts as long as the set of forces defining supply and demand holds. If supply changes (in Figure 3-6), as in the shift to S_1 (more supplied at all prices), a new market-clearing price (or equilibrium price) comes into being, in this instance at $6.00, where $Q_d = Q_{s1}$.

Note that a *change in supply cannot cause a change in demand, and a change in demand cannot cause a change in supply.* In a competitive market, demand and supply are independent of each other. Thus, a change in the supply from S to S_1 results in a change in quantity demanded (see the bottom of (Figure 3-6) from 5 pizzas to 7 pizzas on the horizontal axis).

It follows that (1) any change in supply or demand changes price, (2) any change in supply changes the quantity demanded, and (3) any change in demand changes the quantity supplied. The only exception occurs when equal and offsetting changes (either increases or decreases) of supply and demand occur simultaneously. We see this illustrated in Figure 3-7. In Figure 3-7, the competitive market initially tends toward price $\bar{P}_E$ with demand, D_1, and supply, S_1. A market-clearing equilibrium quantity of Q_e is established and there is neither excess demand nor excess supply. If there are equal increases in both demand (D_1 to D_2) and supply (S_1 to S_2), there is a larger market with equilibrium quantity increasing from Q_e to Q_e' but the equilibrating price remains $\bar{P}_E$. The reverse can happen with a declining market size. Had demand and supply both decreased (D_2 to D_1, S_2 to S_1), the equilibrium quantity would have fallen (Q_e' to Q_e) but the equilibrating price would have remained $\bar{P}_E$.

Conditions for Competitive Pricing

Let us summarize the conditions that are necessary for competitive pricing to exist.

Completely flexible prices: If the government (or some other agency) had set the price of pizzas at $4.80, there would have been excess or unsatisfied demand (a shortage). Black markets might have developed, as they did with many consumer products during World War II, to fill this unsatisfied demand at unregulated prices. In the following application, we will see the effect of inflexible prices in the case of price ceilings established by rent control laws.

Full information: In order for prices to be bid up or down to equilibrium, buyers and sellers obviously need to be aware of their alternatives, such as other prices.

Expectation of constant prices: If consumers think that today's $3.60 price will come down to $3.00 tomorrow, they may not buy any pizza today. If producers think the same way, they may want to supply more pizzas today than they would have otherwise.

Free entry to and exit from markets: Both buyers and sellers must be free to participate in the market or withdraw from it. In other words, there must be complete mobility of resources.

Maximization of satisfaction and profits: Buyers and sellers seek to maximize their satisfaction or profits, respectively, and always act to do so.

Absence of collusion: There must be no collusion between single buyers or sellers or between groups of buyers and sellers. Otherwise, prices might be pegged rather than being competitively flexible.

Application I: Should We Let Supply and Demand Work? Rent Controls and the Price of Housing

Friend and foe alike concede that market prices can be efficient devices for bringing the interests of buyers and sellers together and, ultimately, for making the two sets of interests consistent. The alternative in a world of scarcity, where resources must be allocated and products and services rationed, is for someone to set prices. The someone is *usually* (but not always) government.

We may presume that at times governments intentionally set prices at non-equilibrium, non-market clearing levels. There is no reason for governments to intervene in determining prices (other than an ideological reason) if prices are set at the same level as markets would tend to establish. As we have seen, actual prices can be above or below equilibrium levels and tend, *in free markets*, to create self-correcting responses to either excess demand (shortages) or excess supply (surpluses).

It is important to note that where governments, for ideological reasons, have not allowed markets to function through independent supply and demand influences, their efforts to set market clearing prices have almost always failed. A famous Nobel Prize winning economist, Friedrich Hayek[1], long ago pointed out that such government efforts cannot be informed by the same information as that generated *within* functioning markets. In this application, we are dealing not with such ideologically driven decisions to attempt to *mimic* market decisions but rather actions by governments to *constrain* movements of prices in private markets.

There are many examples of such government intervention in price determination in the history of the United States. Indeed, such controls go back as far as the American Revolution. Sometimes, as in that instance, these controls have occurred during periods of grave crisis and have consisted of direct establishment of "ceiling" prices. Such ceilings, for example, were created for many products (sugar, flour, gasoline, etc.) during World War II by the Office of Price Administration (O.P.A.). At times, intervention has taken the form of "floors" or efforts to keep prices from moving below pre-established levels or targets. After 1929, the federal government established target prices for a broad range of agricultural products (wheat, corn, sugar, etc.) and has undertaken various activities to achieve those prices.

Government Determined Prices: The Arguments

Throughout history, governments have expressed their dissatisfaction with prices established in markets either by setting prices directly or by mandating the limits within which prices are permitted to (legally) move. As we indicated above, this has happened even in private enterprise economies such as that of the United States. What is the main non-ideological argument for this kind of activity? Generally, governments, whether local or national, have assumed authority over prices because of a normative concern that markets would price and ration goods in a manner that is "unfair" or "inequitable." Concern, in other words, is over the availability of the good at the market price or over the effect on real income distribution of buying (or selling) it at that price. Here, let's concentrate on concerns of public officials that market prices will be "too high," and, as a result, decide to impose price ceilings. For the sake of specific illustration, we will focus on the price of housing and efforts especially at local government levels, to impose rent controls. Such laws have been enacted in many American cities and the question about them is not *whether* they work; rather, it is *how* do they work, *who* do they benefit, and *who* bears their costs. The question is especially meaningful given the numbers of people who can neither find nor afford housing and who show up in the data on homeless persons as the economy has moved into the twenty first century.

---

1. Von Hayek, Friedrich A. *The Constitution of Liberty*. Chicago, The University of Chicago Press. 1975.

Are Rent Controls Effective? (The Best Case)

Since we argued that there is always scarcity or, in other words, "no free lunch," you might suppose that the above question is needless. While that may be true, answering the question does illustrate the futility of trying to make resource allocation decisions without incurring opportunity costs.

In Figure 3-8, we see a hypothetical example of the imposition of rent controls in a situation in which the supply of housing (S) is $\bar{Q}_m$ and quantity supplied does not vary with housing prices. $\bar{Q}_m$ housing units, in other words, will be offered for rent at any of the prices represented on the vertical axis. With demand for housing, D, a free-housing market would tend to establish a market-clearing price, P_m, and the quantity demanded of housing (Q_d) would equal the quantity supplied (Q_s). All those looking for housing at that price would find it. Now let us suppose that a local government (New York City or one of the numerous others with rent control laws) imposes a ceiling price of P_c on housing units. The number of housing units offered for rent ($\bar{Q}_m$) does not change but there is a cost imposed on would-be renters.

Figure 3-8
Rent Controls When the Housing Supply is Fixed

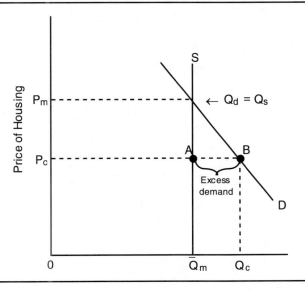

In Figure 3-8, the demand for housing (D) is downward sloping while the fixed supply of housing (S) is represented by a vertical line (from $\bar{Q}_m$) parallel to the axis on which the price of housing is measured. A market equilibrium price would tend to be established at P_m where the quantity demanded of housing equals the quantity supplied of housing at $\bar{Q}_m$. If government sets a price below equilibrium such as P_c (ceiling price), the equilibrium will still be at P_m but there will be excess demand of Q_c - $\bar{Q}_m$ or AB.

The quantity of housing demanded at P_c, $0Q_c$, is greater than the quantity supplied, $0\bar{Q}_m$. The difference ($0Q_c - 0\bar{Q}_m$), or the distance AB, represents excess demand, the number of units renters cannot find at the controlled price. The costs of searching for housing that is unavailable are a significant part of this burden.

The costs above are only a part of the reason why many economists are skeptical of the argument that rent controls are effective tools of public policy whose objectives (housing availability and equity) are accomplished at a low cost. Still, cities such as New York, which has had rent controls since World War II, show little inclination to repeal such controls.

Are Rent Controls Effective? (The Worst Case)

In the hypothetical case illustrated in Figure 3-8, renters didn't suffer a reduction in the number of housing units available because of rent controls. Instead, they incurred costs because at a below-equilibrium price, many searched fruitlessly for more housing than was available. The crucial assumption, upon which that conclusion rested, that housing units offered for rent do not vary with rental prices, seems unrealistic. In Figure 3-9, we see what economists would expect (and data suggest) is more likely, a housing market with an upward-sloping supply curve. A free housing market would tend to create a market equilibrium in Figure 3-9 with price P_m and quantity Q_m ($Q_d = Q_s$). Government now sets the ceiling price P_c with the following effects: (1) the quantity supplied of housing declines from $0Q_m$ to $0Q_{c_1}$, creating an excess demand of $(0Q_m - 0Q_{c_1})$ or the distance AB; (2) at the lower ceiling price, renters try to increase the quantity demanded of housing from $0Q_m$ to $0Q_{c_2}$ creating additional excess demand of $0Q_{c_2} - 0Q_m$ or the distance BC; (3) the total excess demand resulting from the rent control is the sum of the two effects, or $(0Q_m - 0Q_{c_1}) + (0Q_{c_2} - 0Q_m)$, or AB + BC = AC.

Figure 3-9
Rent Controls With a Variable Supply of Housing

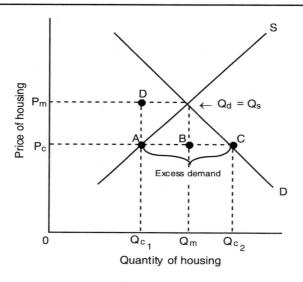

In Figure 3-9, the demand for housing (D) is downward sloping and the supply of housing (S) is upward sloping. A market equilibrium price would tend to be established at P_m where the quantity demanded of housing (Q_d) equals the quantity supplied (Q_s), or Q_m. If government sets a ceiling price such as P_c, the quantity supplied will be $0Q_{c_1}$, while the quantity demanded will be $0Q_{c_2}$; there will be excess demand of $(0Q_{c_1} - 0Q_{c_2})$ or AC.

Are *any* renters made better off by the rent control (as city officials apparently intended)? *Yes*. Those who are able to rent housing ($0Q_{c_1}$) at the legislated price, P_c. They expend on housing $0P_cAQ_{c_1}$ whereas to obtain that amount of housing at the market price (P_m), they would have had to spend $0P_mDQ_{c_1}$. The difference, P_mP_cAD, represents an income transfer to renters, which political decision-makers apparently intended.

Are renters as a *whole* made better off by the rent control? Economists are doubtful. Renters lose $0Q_m - 0Q_{c_1}$ of housing as a direct consequence of the price control because they have fewer units of housing that are offered for rent. Beyond this "supply effect," there is a "demand effect" as well; the quantity demanded of housing in Figure 3-9 increases from Q_m to Q_{c2} as the legal price ceiling of P_c is imposed. The legally contrived shortage of housing, thus, at the controlled price is $0Q_{c2} - 0Q_{c1}$ or the distance AC. While some people are made better off, others are made worse off, and it is by no means clear that, on balance, rent controls improve the welfare of the general populace.

The Dynamics of Rent Controlled Housing

The hypothetical housing market represented in Figure 3-10 is pictured at a point in time or in a static situation. Over time, or in a dynamic sense, the situation would likely get worse in terms of the costs of controlling housing prices.

Since resources are required to maintain or expand housing, fixing its price, below the market equilibrium, lowers the returns on housing relative to the returns on other (non-controlled) uses of resources. In New York City, for instance, prices of co-ops, condominiums, and expensive apartments are not controlled. Neither are the prices of most goods other than housing.

Figure 3-10
The Dynamics of Rent Controlled Housing With a Declining Supply

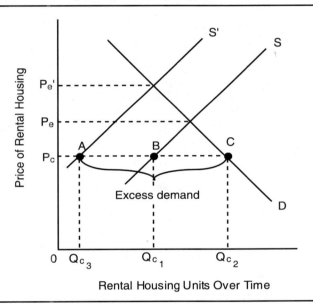

In Figure 3-10, a free housing market with demand D and supply S would be equilibrated at price P_e. If the supply of housing declined from S to S', the market would re-equilibrate at P_e'. In neither case would there be excess demand. If housing prices are controlled at P_c, the decline will increase the excess demand from BC to AC.

As the (relative) rate of return on housing for low and middle-income renters declines, buildings may no longer be maintained adequately. In fact, buildings may even be abandoned and/or converted to other uses. A leftward shift of the supply curve from S to S' shown in Figure 3-10 would normally result in housing prices rising from P_e to P_e'; since this cannot (legally) occur, the quantity supplied at P_c will continue to decline further. Whereas excess demand at the controlled price would have equaled BC, the excess (people searching and working for housing) increases to AC.

New York City has seen all of these effects. Landlords sometimes do not pay taxes on or adequately maintain buildings. There are entire blocks of buildings that stand vacant (at least for *legal* activities) and are unfit for housing. The city has, through tax arrears, become the owner of thousands of apartment buildings but is unwilling or financially unable to provide the housing that private landlords find unprofitable to provide. Finally, many buildings have been converted to condominiums or to other uses whose prices are uncontrolled.

Illegal or "Black Markets"
Faced with the shortage of housing shown in Figure 3-9, renters, who cannot wait for months or years to obtain housing at the controlled price, sometimes resort to bribes or "side payments." People who have apartments at controlled prices sublet them out for higher prices or landlords accept non-rental payments in lieu of rents. New York City and other cities with stringent rent-control laws not only have to spend resources enforcing the laws but also to revise them often in order to prevent the voluntary exchanges in which renters and landlords would otherwise engage.

The Future of Rent Controls
Economists, even those on opposite ends of the political spectrum, agree that rent-control laws have perverse effects on those they seek to benefit. Assar Lindbeck characterizes them as "the most efficient technique so far known for destroying cities." Why are such efforts to stymie the operation of free-housing markets (ones in which landlords and renters make voluntary and mutually beneficial exchanges) not repealed? It seems unlikely that their continuation results from ignorance of their effects. Economist Robert Thomas suggests instead that it is because the benefits of control are concentrated in the hands of a relatively small group (those who occupy rent-controlled housing) while the costs are spread over a much larger group (landlords, who are few, and many who seek better housing or who are new to the housing market). Says Thomas: "Politicians, attempting to win or to stay in office have found it necessary to pay attention to the private interests of tenants even at the cost of continued urban decay."

SUMMING UP

1. Studying the operation of a market system helps us to answer three basic questions about the use of resources: (a) *what* goods are produced (composition), (b) *how* goods are produced (technique), and (c) *for whom* goods are produced (distribution).

2. To understand the market system, one needs to begin with conditions of *competition*: the market form in which no buyer or seller has influence over the price at which the product sells.

3. Since each participant in a competitive market acts independently, *prices*, the signals for action in the market, are determined by independent movements of demand and supply.

4. There are two sides to every market: the demand side and the supply side. *Demand* is a set of relationships showing the quantities of a good that consumers will buy at each of several prices within a specific period of time.

5. One draws a demand curve for a good on the assumption of *ceteris paribus* (other things being equal). In other words, one assumes that the price, and only the price, of that good changes, not any of the other factors of demand.

6. We expect a demand curve to slope downward to the right, which means that people buy more of a good at lower prices than at higher prices (the law of demand).

7. The *law of demand* is based on (a) the income effect and (b) the substitution effect. The *income effect*: As the price of a good falls, the consumer has more purchasing power and ordinarily buys more of that good as a result. The *substitution effect*: As the price of a good falls, it becomes relatively cheaper than those goods for which it is a substitute. Thus, people buy more of it because it is relatively cheaper.

8. There are exceptions to the normal case, such as *Veblen goods* (perhaps diamonds, caviar, sable coats), and, especially in poor countries, *income-inferior goods* (certain basic staple goods, such as beans and rice).

9. For a given good, a *change in quantity demanded* is a movement along a demand curve. It can result only from a change in the price of the good. A *change in demand* is a shift of the demand curve, and can result from a change in any of the other factors affecting demand such as: income, tastes, the prices of substitutes and complements and expectations, and the number of consumers.

10. Basic factors that can change demand are (a) consumers' incomes, (b) consumers' tastes and preferences, (c) prices of other products, (d) consumers' expectations about future market conditions and prices, and (e) the number of consumers.

11. One can calculate the market demand curve by adding up individuals' demand curves, given that consumers buy independently of each other. Curves for market demand get their shapes from the demand curves of individuals, but measure larger quantities.

12. *Supply* is a set of relationships showing the quantities of a product that a firm will offer for sale at each possible price within a specific period of time.

13. Factors that can change supply are (a) changes in technology, (b) changes in prices of factors of production, (c) changes in prices of other related goods, (d) changes in firms' expectations about future prices, and (e) changes in the number of firms.

14. A *supply curve* shows that (a) firms supply more of a given product at higher prices than at lower prices, and (b) there is a price below which firms supply nothing to the market.

15. Supply curves that slope upward to the right are based on the assumption that ultimately firms run into decreasing efficiency and increasing costs as they expand output, either because of fixed physical facilities or difficulty in managing a larger operation. Also, the relative profitability of supplying a product increases as its price increases.

16. One can estimate the curve for market supply by adding up supply curves of individual firms, assuming that each firm behaves independently of the others. Changes in the number of firms cause changes in market supply.

17. Market prices, including competitive prices are *equilibrium prices*. That is, they are market-clearing prices. When there are equilibrium prices, quantity demanded and quantity supplied are equal and there is neither excess demand nor excess supply.

18. If prices are *above* equilibrium, there is *excess supply*, a market surplus or excess. If prices are *below* equilibrium, there is *excess demand*, a market shortage. In either case, demand and supply are not in equilibrium.

19. Conditions necessary to ensure competitive prices are (a) completely flexible prices; (b) possession of full information by both buyers and sellers; (c) expectation of constant prices; (d) free entry into and exit from markets; (e) consistent effort of firms to maximize profits and of consumers to maximize satisfaction; and (f) no collusion between buyers and sellers, all must behave independently of each other.

20. In a market economy, as long as resources are scarce, prices will be used to allocate resources and ration output. If markets are not permitted to establish equilibrium, prices must be set, usually by government, at non-equilibrium levels.

21. Non-equilibrium prices in competitive markets set in motion self-correcting movements of price and quantity that eliminate excess demand or excess supply. Non-market determined disequilibrium prices have no corresponding mechanisms of self-correction.

22. Governmentally established non-equilibrium prices may consist of price floors or price ceilings. There have been numerous examples of both in American history and there are many such examples today.

23. Government intervention in market pricing is most often based on "fairness" in pricing, rationing, and income distribution. In this application, the focus is on local government control over housing prices, which usually leads to rent-control ordinances.

24. Free housing markets will establish a market equilibrium price that equate quantity demanded and quantity supplied. Housing prices that are set below equilibrium will result in excess demand.

25. Even if the quantity supplied of housing does not vary as housing prices are lowered by rent controls, there will be an excess demand at the legal price ceiling. Those seeking housing will not be able to obtain all (including the quality of housing) they wish at the ceiling price (Figure 3-8).

26. Economists are skeptical of the argument that rent controls make housing available at equitable prices. This is especially the case with a downward-sloping demand curve for housing combined with an upward sloping supply curve for housing (Figure 3-9).

27. When rent controls are imposed, those who benefit are the individuals who obtain the amount and quality of housing desired at the controlled price. Those who lose include landlords, but also renters who see a decline in the quantity supplied of housing (the direct effect of rent control) and renters who seek more housing at the lower price than they would have sought at the equilibrium price (the indirect effect of rent control).

28. The indirect effect, plus the direct effect above, constitute the total excess demand for housing at the controlled price.

29. Over time, stringent rent controls are likely to result in a decline in both the quantity and quality of rental housing available. Incentives are created (through changes in relative prices and returns on resource usage) to convert housing units to other uses, to decrease maintenance outlays, and even to abandon buildings rather than pay taxes on them.

30. Rent controls continue in spite of the view of economists that they have unintended ill effects on those they seek to benefit. One explanation for their popularity is that their benefits are concentrated in politically active small groups, while their costs are spread over a much larger group (landlords but also those who suffer from urban decay and inability to find better housing.) One effect of rent controls is in the illegal housing markets they tend to create.

KEY TERMS

Ceteris paribus assumption
Change in demand
Change in quantity demanded
Changes in quantity supplied
Changes in supply
Competition
Complements, substitutes
Demand
Demand curve
Demand schedule
Equilibrium price
Excess demand
Excess supply
Income effect
Law of demand
Law of supply
Market demand
Market supply
Price rivalry
Substitution effect
Supply
Supply curve

QUESTIONS

1. Review the basic questions about use of resources, questions that are common to all societies. Be sure that you not only understand these questions but also realize why all societies must find answers.

2. Define *competition*, as economists use the word. How does the economist's way of looking at competition differ from your familiar usage of the word?

3. What is *demand*? Does the economist's meaning of demand differ from your usual meaning? If so, what do you think accounts for the differences? What is the *ceteris paribus* assumption?

4. Why do demand curves usually slope downward and to the right? What would it mean if one sloped *up* and to the right? List the five basic factors that influence demand. Which of these factors, in addition to price, do you think will be most influential in determining the demand for (a) cars? (b) safety matches? Why?

5. Define the *income effect* and the *substitution effect*. For a small change in the price of a good, which of the two effects would you expect to be more important? What are *inferior* goods? Can you think of some possible examples beyond those given in the chapter?

6. What is the *law of demand*? How is it explained? What can cause a change in demand? A change in quantity demanded?

7. How does one derive a market demand curve? What assumption(s) does one use to do so?

8. What is the *supply curve*? How do competitive suppliers behave toward each other? Why do supply curves usually slope up to the right?

9. What factors determine supply? What can cause a change in supply? A change in quantity supplied?

10. How does one derive a market supply curve? What assumption(s) does one use to do so?

11. How is *price* determined in a competitive market? What does *equilibrium* mean, in relation to the operation of a market? What conditions must exist in a market for competitive prices to be established? Are they hard to establish? Do you know any markets in which these conditions exist, or are closely approximated?

12. Suppose that you are chief economist for an automobile industry council. You are asked to forecast industry sales for next year. You know that in the coming year personal income is expected to rise by 3 percent, that mass transit is going to be heavily subsidized by government, and that the population and its average age are expected to remain fairly constant. What influences will each of these factors have on your forecast?

13. What determines the availability of housing to individuals in a free market?

14. What is meant in saying that there is no "free lunch" in imposing ceiling prices in housing markets?

15. Who benefits from rent-control laws? Who bears the costs?

16. How is the supply of housing related to the costs of rent controls?

17. Does the area in which you live have a rent-control ordinance? If so, what costs and benefits are created by its enforcement?

18. Why do rent-control laws tend to foster the development of "black" (illegal) markets?

19. Is it likely, in a dynamic sense, that rent-control laws accomplish their objectives of making housing generally available at "affordable" prices? Why or why not?

20. If your answer to (19) above is negative, why do we continue to see rent-control laws passed and enforced?

Chapter 4: Components of an Economic Society
Households, Business Firms, Governments, the Rest of the World

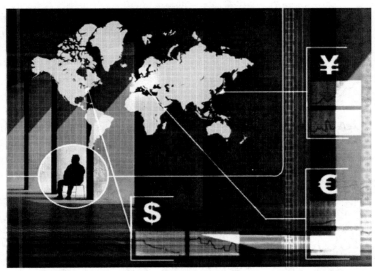

What are the basic parts of our economy, and how are they interrelated? One basic view is that the economy is made up of three sectors: (1) *households*, which provide all the factors of production and in return buy the output of the firms; (2) *business firms*, which employ these factors of production and produce goods and services; and (3) *governments*, which buy part of the output of firms, take away some of the income of households in the form of taxes, and make transfer payments to individuals. Governments also provide various forms of goods and services. These three sectors mesh in a system of flows of income and production called the *circular-flow model* of economic activity. The combined economic activities of these three sectors constitute a **closed economy**, one in which all economic flows occur within its boundaries. In this chapter we will see how this circular flow of economic activity works and then describe the characteristics of each of the three interrelated sectors. Finally, trade with the rest of the world is incorporated into our economic society. We see how exports and imports affect the flow of economic activity for a nation. This chapter concludes with an application on the important question: Are businesses committed simply to the pursuit of profits or do they also have a sense of social responsibility that transcends profits?

Closed Economy
An economy that does not trade with other economies. One in which all economic activity is domestic.

The Circular-Flow Model

The Simple Model
Let us begin by simplifying things, and assume for the moment that there is only a private sector in the economy we are examining. Thus, there are only two components of the economy: households (consumers) and producers (business

firms). Consumers *own* all the factors of production; that is, the resources necessary for production to take place. Firms *hire* all the factors of production, produce the goods and services consumers use, and pay a return (income) to the factors. Figure 4-1 illustrates this.

Households provide factors of production to business firms. In return, business firms pay households income for the use of those factors of production. Labor, as a factor of production, receives its reward in the form of wages and salaries. Owners of land receive their payments in the form of rent; owners of capital receive interest; entrepreneurs receive profits. Firms utilize the factors of production to produce goods and services for the use of the households. Households, with incomes obtained from firms' use of their factors of production, pay firms for goods and services. Firms now have incomes so they can pay the factors of production to produce more goods and services. And so the process continues.

The circular-flow model and the world of economic production have no beginning. You may start the analysis at any point. Only the amount of resources available (factors of production) limits the level of production. Firms use these resources because households use all the income they receive to buy the output firms produce by employing the resources.

The upper half of Figure 4-1, showing the flow of resources and the reverse flow of income, portrays the **factor markets**, in which the supply of and demand for factors of production interact to determine wages and other factor prices. The bottom half, which shows flows of product output and reverse flows of payments for goods and services, portrays the **product markets**. In these, the supply of goods and services, and the demand for them, interact to determine prices of goods.

Factor Markets
Those markets in which the supply of and demand for factors of production interact to determine wages and other factor prices.

Product Markets
Markets in which the flows of goods and services are established and in which the prices of goods and services are determined.

Figure 4-1
Simple Circular-Flow Model With Only a Private Sector

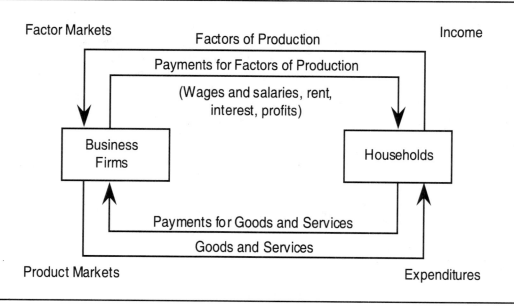

The flow of resources, products, and income between firms and households is circular in nature.

The Complex Model

Figure 4-1 is a simplification of our closed economic system. Let us now examine a more complex, more realistic circular-flow model of such an economy.

Figure 4-1 assumes that households spend all their income on buying the goods and services firms produce. This is not realistic, because people do manage to save some of their income, and also must pay some of their income to governments in the form of taxes, both of which reduce the demand for goods and services (see Figure 4-2). Since saving and paying taxes both mean *not* consuming, these two factors reduce households' demand for firms' output.

Figure 4-1also assumes that all output goes to households in the form of goods and services. Again, this is unrealistic. This more complete model includes two other sources of demand for firms' output:

1. *Other firms*. When firms demand output from other firms, this is not counted as part of the flow of goods and services to households, but as capital goods that aid in the production of other goods and services.

2. *Governments*. Federal, state, and local governments demand output from firms.

In both more complex and simple circular-flow models of the closed economy, the flow of income to households consist of wages, rent, interest, and profits. However, in the complex model, households spend their incomes not only on consumption, but also on savings and taxes. Governments enter the picture with spending for goods and services, and so do business firms themselves, with expenditures for investment. So the flow of funds is still circular. The money that taxes siphon from households' incomes becomes part of the purchasing power governments use for their expenditures. In addition, financial institutions make available for investment the money they obtain from people's savings. This keeps the money flowing. (By *financial institutions*, we usually mean commercial banks and other financial institutions including stock exchanges, though there are many other financial institutions.)

It should be apparent to you that the domestic American economy is a great deal more complex than even our so-called complex model shows. Not only do households save, but firms save also. Firms also have to pay taxes to various governments, especially if the firms are incorporated and have, so to speak, a life of their own. Governments also provide goods and services to households (for example, public schools). Governments, furthermore, provide households with income. By this, we don't mean just social security and welfare payments. Governments provide jobs and governments hire labor from households. And not only do firms invest (demand capital from other firms); so do households. The main form their investments take is home buying. (A house is considered an investment.) The list of activities that could be added to the model is endless. But the complex model gives us enough of a picture to approximate the vast complexity of reality.

What Does The Model Show?

The model in Figure 4-2 tells us that there are three sources of demand for the output of firms: households, other business firms, and governments. There are, therefore, as many different levels of demand as there are combinations of spending patterns by these three parts of society.

Figure 4-2

Complex Circular-Flow Model With Private and Public Sectors

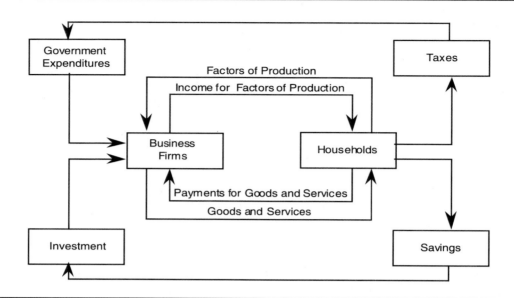

Savings and taxes drain off households' purchasing power and thus reduce their demand for consumer goods. Investment and government expenditures increase the demand for firms' output. These additions are also part of the flow, in that taxes become part of the government's purchasing power. And financial institutions such as banks make savings available for investment.

This more complex system of economic flows doesn't necessarily result in a socially desirable level of demand, one that creates full employment and a low rate of inflation. In subsequent chapters, we will examine the relationships between these flows and the overall level of income and employment and prices. At this point let us just note that households, because they have to set aside money for savings and for taxes, reduce their demand for consumer goods. Firms, by their investments, and governments by buying output of business firms, may take up some of the slack, but not all. So you may have a decrease in demand for goods and services and, eventually, unemployment. (The size of the circular flow decreases.)But if governments and business firms spend *more* than households have saved and have paid in taxes, then demand for products and services increases (the size of the circular flow increases) and inflation may result. While this is an oversimplification, you can get the general and important idea that as these flows change, the level of economic activity in a society increases or decreases with various effects on incomes, prices, and employment;. In the remainder of this chapter, we will look intensively at each of the three sectors in order to show what determines its pattern of demand for goods and services.

HOUSEHOLDS

www.bls.gov
For more information on wages and income visit this web site.

Three important questions about households and their role in economic flows are: (1) Where do they get their income? (2) How do they use it? (3) What is their share of total income?

Table 4-1

Percentage Functional Distribution of Income, 1929 – 2011

	1929	1941	1950	1960	1974	1988	1996	1999	2003	2011 *
Wages and salaries	60	62	69	71	75	73	71	71.2	73.0	69.2
Proprietors' income	17	16	13	10	6	8	8	8.8	8.8	9.3
Corporate profits	12	15	13	11	10	8	12	11.9	12.4	10.9
Rental income	6	3	4	4	2	1	2	2.0	2.0	2.8
Interest income	5	3	1	2	6	10	7	6.2	3.7	7.8

Source: Survey of Current Business, 2011
* 1st quarter

Answers to these questions will give you an insight into the probable effects of the economic decisions of households on total output and income and on the level and composition of output.

The Sources of Income: Functional Distribution

Functional Distribution of Income
The distribution of income that shows how each factor of production derives income according to its economic function(s).

When we talk about sources of income, we speak of the distribution of income as a **functional distribution**. Households, in other words, people receive their income from the wages and salaries they obtain from working; owners of land obtain theirs from rent; owners of capital obtain theirs from interest; businesses, both corporations and unincorporated firms, obtain theirs in the form of profits that are a result of their entrepreneurial activity. Economists look at these sources of income in terms of the functions they perform. It is convenient to view this functional distribution in relative terms, using percentage shares, as in Table 4-1.

Labor receives the largest portion of the money income, in the form of wages and salaries. Labor's share increased from 60 percent at the end of the 1920s to nearly 70 percent in 2011. Labor's increase is due mainly to the decline in the share that went to owners of unincorporated firms (proprietors' income), which fell by more than half during the same time span.

Corporate profits, which ran about 8 to 15 percent of total income during this period, vary according to the state of the economy. They go down in times of recession and go up when times are good. The share of income that comes from rent has been fairly steady (between 1 and 4 percent), while the share of income that comes from interest declined between 1929 and 1970 because of falling interest rates. However, in the 1970s and the late 1980s the share of interest income went up to 10 percent and more because of the revival of high interest rates. By the late 1990s, however, interest income had declined to less than 7 percent.

Many factors contributed to the changing ratios. Chief among them are changing market demand and supply for different resources, government's enlarged role in maintaining high levels of employment, efforts by unions to raise wages (at least for their members), growth in the number of corporations, and continued concentration of economic activity in corporate enterprise. You can see that both market and nonmarket forces play a role in determining the functional distribution of income.

Table 4-2

Allocation of Pre-Tax Household Income, 2015

	Billions of Current Dollars	**Percent of Total**
Personal Taxes	1,945	12.7
Personal Consumption	12,272	80.0
Personal Interest Payments	269	1.8
Personal Saving	678	4.4
Other	177	1.2

Source: Bureau of Economic Analysis

The Way Households Allocate Their Income

How do households spend their money? According to Table 4-2, in 2015, they spent about 80 percent their income on consumption and saved only 4.4 percent it. Householders paid about 12.7 percent of their income in taxes to the various levels of government, a figure that has grown in both absolute and relative terms from only 3 percent of their income in 1929. A substantial part of this increase has, until recently, been due to the increase in funding for government expenditures for military goods and services. There have also been big increases in government social services: social security, Medicare, aid to education and housing, welfare and unemployment relief, highway construction, expansion of the park service, the list is a long one. Many of these have continued to grow under the "stimulus" plans of 2009-2010.

Table 4-3

Distribution of Before-Tax Family Income in the United States for Selected Years

Families by income quintile	1929	1960	1970	1980	1992	2008	2011	2013
Lowest fifth	3.5%	4.8%	5.5%	5.2%	4.4%	4.2%	3.8%	3.2%
Second fifth	9.0	12.2	12.2	11.5	10.5	9.7	9.3	8.4%
Third fifth	13.8	17.8	17.6	17.5	16.5	15.4	15.1	14.4%
Fourth fifth	19.3	24.0	23.8	24.3	24.0	23.2	23.0	23.0%
Top fifth	54.4	41.3	40.9	41.5	44.6	47.5	48.9	51.0%
Top 5%	30.0	15.9	15.6	15.3	17.6	23.5	21.3	22.2%

Source: U.S. Census Bureau, Current Population Survey, Annual Social and Economic Supplements.

The Way Family Income Is Distributed

Lorenz Curve
The difference between the actual distribution of income and a perfectly proportional distribution as shown graphically.

How is income distributed throughout the United States? Who has much, and who has little? Table 4-3 gives us a general idea. It shows the unequal nature of the family income distribution before taxes are paid and without considering the effects of government transfer payments based on what is referred to as the "size distribution of income." In this way of looking at the division of income pie, families are first ranked according to their income levels from the lowest to the highest. They are then divided into equal-size classes (in our case "quintiles" or "fifths") and the relative income share of each class is calculated. Note that, unlike the functional distribution of income, the size distribution does not emphasize the source of income. According to the table, the richest and poorest 20 percent of families received 51 and 3.2 percent of total (pre tax and transfers) income in 2013, respectively.

When you convert the data on income distribution in Table 4-3 into a graph, you get a curve of the inequality of income. This curve has a special name. It is called a **Lorenz curve** (Figure 4-3). It shows the difference between the actual distribution of income and a perfectly equal distribution. If income were perfectly equally distributed, then 20 percent of all families would receive 20 percent of total income, 40 percent of all families would receive 40 percent of total income, etc. This puts us on the diagonal line, or the line of perfect equality. The actual distribution, however, is represented by the Lorenz curve. For example, in 2013, the poorest 20 percent of families received only 3.2 percent of income and the poorest 40 percent only 11.6 percent (3.2+8.4). The gap between the line of perfect equality and actual distribution is the shaded area. The Lorenz curve, therefore, enables us to visualize the extent of income inequality by focusing on the size of the shaded area.

Figure 4-3
Lorenz Curve and Gini Coefficient

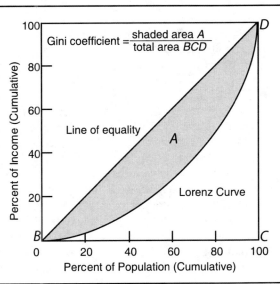

The straight 45 degree diagonal line shows what a perfectly equal distribution of income would look like. The difference between the actual (unequal) and the perfectly proportional distribution, represents the inequality of income.

The Lorenz curve, in turn, can be used to compute a summary measure of overall income inequality. This measure is know as the "Gini coefficient" which, as shown in Figure 4-3, is equal to the ratio of the shaded area A to total area BCD. Its value varies between zero (perfect equality) and 1 (perfect inequality). (Why?) In practice, observed Gini values in the 0.20-0.30 range signify low and in the 0.50-0.60 range high inequality level.

The Lorenz curves for different countries can be used to compare the relative inequality in their income distributions. However, before you draw any conclusions, remember that Lorenz curves frequently show before-tax money income only and not non-cash production, such as food that farmers grow for their own tables. Therefore, comparisons among countries, especially when non-cash incomes are significant, may be misleading.

Economic Implications of Inequality in Income Distribution

Although the ethical implications of inequality in distribution of income are fascinating, we will restrict ourselves to the economic implications.

In underdeveloped countries, the main problem is to increase the economy's output so that all citizens can have a higher standard of living. These countries need increased resources, especially capital, to shift the production-possibilities curve outward and increase economic growth. Forming new capital requires increased savings. Increasing savings withdraws resources from the production of consumer goods, thus making these resources available for investment, and the production of capital. So to increase the formation of capital and to foster more rapid economic growth, a higher rate of savings is needed. The rich save a larger percentage of their income than the poor because the poor spend all their income to maintain their standard of living. A more uneven distribution of income would increase the income of the rich and might increase savings. Thus, apart from other considerations, an underdeveloped country, in order to increase savings and the rate of formation of new capital, might require a less equal income distribution than it already has.

On the other hand, in a developed economy, a central problem is how to maintain full employment and keep the large industrial system growing. To do this, you want consumers to demand all the goods and services that business firms can produce. Here one may reverse the argument of the preceding paragraph and say that a developed country ought to have *its* income more evenly distributed. That way, the rich would get a smaller slice of the pie. Savings would be less and consumer demand higher. This view, though prevalent in the 1950s, '60s, and '70s, was challenged by supply-side economists beginning in the 1980s who have argued that increased savings are needed in developed economies too. Perhaps a reasonable way of reconciling these views is to note that while all economies need to save to accumulate capital in order to grow their economy's output of goods and services in the long term, many may have to be mindful of the adequacy of the demand for that output in the short term. In other words, demand-side considerations may become more important over a short time frame (see Application II for a discussion of this point in the context of the U.S. economy).

Two qualifications are necessary to the above. The problems of economic growth and full employment are much more complex than the above brief sketch indicates. Second, economic *efficiency* (maximizing output with a given set of resources) is not the same thing as economic *equity* (what we think, normatively, is right or wrong in a moral sense). The implications for distribution of income may differ, depending on whether our goal is efficiency or equity and on what weight we give to each.

BUSINESS FIRMS

Today there are more than 10 million companies in the United States, from the corner grocery store to such corporate giants as AT&T. We can classify business firms primarily under three legal headings: (1) *Sole Proprietorships*, (2) *Partnerships*, and (3) *Corporations*.

Sole Proprietorships

Sole Proprietorship
A business firm owned by one individual who has full responsibility for it.

The most common form of business organization is the **sole proprietorship**, an enterprise owned by one person, who is solely responsible for it. There are more than 9 million sole proprietorships in the United States, chiefly in agriculture, retail trade, pharmacy, law, and medicine. They are usually small in scale and have an average life span of five to seven years. Although hundreds of thousands cease production each year, even larger numbers begin each year.

Advantages of a Sole Proprietorship
1. You can easily form a sole proprietorship; it doesn't take much cash. In many areas, just the act of beginning production is all that is necessary.

2. The sole proprietor is the only one to receive benefits when the firm succeeds, and is the only one responsible for its activity, so there is a close correlation between effort expended and reward. Thus, the incentives for efficiency are great.

Disadvantages of a Sole Proprietorship
1. The sole proprietorship has **unlimited liability**. This means that there is no differentiation between the assets of the business enterprise and the personal wealth of the proprietor. If the business incurs losses, the proprietor is responsible for them.

2. Sole proprietors must rely on themselves for all management skills, and since no one person can be a specialist in all managerial functions, the business may suffer. Inadequate management is one of the chief cause of failure in small, sole-proprietor businesses.

3. The sole proprietorship often has limited capital, since the proprietor has to depend primarily on his or her own resources, and since an individual's borrowing capacity is limited. Sole proprietors also tend to have lower credit ratings than partnerships or corporations.

4. The sole proprietorship has *limited life*, in the sense that the lifetime of the business may be limited to the working lifetime of the proprietor.

Partnerships

Partnership
A form of business organization in which two or more individuals combine to operate an enterprise.

A second form of business organization is the **partnership**, in which two or more individuals combine to operate a business enterprise. There are several kinds of partnerships, but the following is a general description.

Advantages of a Partnership
1. Because there are two or more people involved in the ownership, the partner-owned business has access to more capital. The enterprise can draw on the wealth and borrowing power of its several partners.

2. A business with more than one owner can count on specialized skills in management. One partner can be in charge of production; another of accounting; a third, of sales; and so on. Specialization of management functions strengthens a business greatly.

Disadvantages of a Partnership

1. A partnership, like a sole proprietorship, has unlimited liability. Each individual partner's personal wealth can be tapped to pay debts. Each partner is responsible not only for his or her own mistakes, but also for the mistakes of all the rest of the partners.

2. Partnerships have limited life, which fosters instability. Partnership agreements are automatically dissolved whenever a partner dies, or whenever one withdraws from the partnership because of a disagreement. The remaining partners may draw up a new partnership agreement, or they may not.

3. Partnerships have limited access to capital. Various devices that the corporation can use to raise financial capital are not available to the partnership.

Corporations

Corporations
Business firms whose existence and function is apart from that of their owners.

Corporations are legal entities that function separately from their owners. There are fewer corporations by far than there are sole proprietorships or partnerships, but corporations produce more, employ more people, and have more assets than all other business forms combined.

Limited Liability
In a corporation, the fact that individual owners are responsible only for the value of their shares purchased and not other debts.

Advantages of a Corporation

1. A corporation's owners have **limited liability**. This means that the people who own it, the stockholders, are not responsible individually for its debts. They can lose only the money they paid for their stock. The risks of the firm, thus, are not only spread over a larger group of owners but limited to the value of the individuals' shares.

Obviously, the situation is not that simple. The owner-manager of a small corporation may very well have to pledge her or his own credit and take on a personal liability. For example, in order to raise additional funds, the manager may become personally liable by signing a personal note for a loan for the corporation. The discussion that follows, however, relates more to the larger corporation than the smaller.

Bonds
Debt instruments issued by corporations.

2. Because a corporation is a legal entity, it can be sued (or it can sue) without the owners, the stockholders, becoming involved.

Preferred Stock
Stock issued by a corporation that has no voting rights but has a preferred right to dividend payments.

3. A corporation has **unlimited life**; it can continue to exist no matter who owns stock in it. Stockholders continually buy and sell their ownership instruments (shares of stock) with no effect on the life of the company.

Common Stock
Stock issued by a corporation that has voting rights but no preference in the distribution of dividends.

4. A corporation has easier access to financial capital because of its ability to use a variety of financial instruments: bonds, preferred stock, and common stock. **Bonds** are instruments of debt; the corporation has to pay interest on them regularly, and counts this as a cost of production. Stocks, on the other hand, are equities or instruments of ownership, and the company is not required to pay dividends on them regularly. **Preferred stock** is called preferred because the company has to pay dividends on it *before* it pays dividends to holders of **common stock**. Owners of preferred stock have no voting privileges, however, and

usually there are limits on the amount of dividends the company can pay to them. Owners of common stock have full voting rights and no limitations on the amount of dividends that the company can pay them.

5. Because stockholders need not be managers of a corporation, and because the corporation can raise large amounts of financial capital, it can afford to hire efficient managers, capable of taking on very specialized management functions.

Disadvantages of a Corporation

1. Forming a corporation may take a long time and be very expensive, depending on the nature of the proposed firm. People involved in the formation of a new corporation have to follow state and federal laws, pay fees of incorporation, and pay lawyers' fees and other expenses.

Double Taxation
The fact that a corporation pays taxes on its gross earnings and its shareholders pay taxes again when corporate earnings are distributed as dividends.

2. A corporation has to pay taxes to both the state and federal governments (corporate income taxes, property taxes, and so on). This leads to **double taxation**, which means that the corporation pays taxes on the gross income it earns, and distributes parts of the remaining income as dividends to stockholders; then the stockholders have to pay taxes on the dividends, since this money constitutes personal income.

3. State and federal governments pass laws that restrict the behavior of corporations. Some of these restrictions do not apply to sole proprietorships or partnerships.

4. The larger the corporation, the more ownership may become separated from control, and the greater the possibility of conflict of interest between managers and owners. Large corporations may have thousands of stockholders. The largest corporations, such as AT&T, General Motors, and Exxon/Mobil, may have millions. Stockholders who hold only a few shares have neither the time nor the incentive to take an active part in controlling the corporation by their votes.

When management sends out its annual report, containing a glowing description of what it has done for the stockholder this year, it includes a proxy card. This proxy card, if the stockholder signs and returns it, gives the company's management the right to vote his or her stock. If the corporation has paid the usual dividend, the stockholder generally mails the proxy card back. In this way management tends to become self-perpetuating and often may regard its stockholders as being, in a sense, the recipient of corporate welfare (after all, they get their regular dividend checks). Stockholders, busy people placated by regular payments of money, may become lethargic and uncritically accept the policies of management. Management may orient its policies first and foremost toward its own continued control of the corporation. In brief, we are implying that, in many large corporations, the stockholders may find it hard to control the management. If this occurs, the self-interest of these independent managers may conflict with the self-interest of the stockholders.

Readers will note that even when management policies diverge from the interests of stockholder-owners, market discipline may occur in the form of takeover bids. Should management decisions result in lower profits and reduced prices of a firm's stocks, financial entrepreneurs may initiate a "takeover" of the firm in the belief that present share prices "undervalue" the firm, and that with new management, the firm can be made more profitable.

Big Business and the American Corporation

Americans have a long history of concern about firms that engage in monopolistic behavior. This concern is evidenced by U.S. acceptance of the antimonopoly provisions of English Common Law and by the many antimonopoly or antitrust laws that Congress has passed since the Sherman Antitrust Act of 1890.

People have feared that large monopolistic firms would interfere in a competitive economy and even try to subvert the democratic political system, and that these firms would increase prices while reducing output, and slow the rate of adoption of improved technology. In addition, some people have been afraid that firms of great size and wealth could encourage decisions by government that would be unduly favorable to them, and that would ignore the public good.

www.whitehouse.gov/fsbr/ esbr.html

For more information on production visit this web site.

Although corporations are a minority of business firms, they are the dominant form of business organization. Table 4-4 shows that the four largest automobile corporations had around 87 percent of the sales of the industry, not including imports, in 2007 alone. Concentration, though, becomes much smaller in other industries such as food preparation in which the four largest firms made 34 percent of sales. We will consider the implications of such concentration in later sections of this book. Figure 4-4 shows how dominant the corporate form of business is in the modern American economy. Although accounting for only 21 percent of the number of firms, corporations accounted for over 90 percent of sales in 2008. On the other hand, single proprietorships dominated the number of firms (69 percent) but accounted for only 6 percent of sales. Partnerships made up the remainder in both categories (10 percent of firms, only 3 percent of sales).

Table 4-4

Concentration of Manufacturing Production: Sales Ratio for Selected Industries, 2008

Industry	Percentage of Sales by Four Largest Firms
Motor vehicles	87
Malt beverages	77
Aircraft engines and parts	70
Soap and detergents	55
Metal cans	41
Food Preparation	34

Source: U.S. Bureau of the Census, Census of Manufactures, 2008 (data are for 2007).

Figure 4-4
Number of Firms and Percent of Sales by Types of Firms, 2007

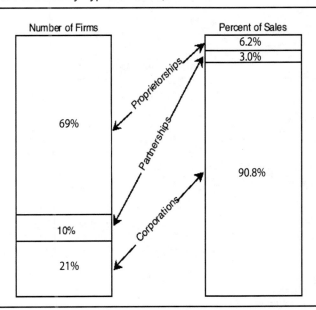

Source: Statistical Abstract of the United States, 2008.

Some critics, as we noted earlier, have criticized corporations for their dominance of the economy and feared their ability to exert undue influence both politically and economically in American society. As we have seen, though, this form of business organization offers great advantages in its ability to raise capital and bring together the larger quantities of resources, including organization and management, that modern technology dictates for the sake of efficiency. Critics mistakenly equate bigness with the ability to restrict competition or to exercise monopolistic influences over both the economy and its political processes. There will be much more about these subjects in the microeconomics portion of your principles of economics course.

It is worth noting that many modern corporations have crossed national boundaries in this century. Indeed, since World War II, there has been a major growth of **multinational corporations,** those that buy resources as well as produce and sell products in many countries throughout the world. Though fear was expressed early on that such corporations would lie beyond the control or oversight of individual nations, and thus potentially destabilize economic relations, international competition and growth in market sizes seem to have greatly diminished that concern. Clearly, the multinationals have performed a useful role in enhancing the movement of resources as well as goods and services throughout the globe. In other words, they have helped to create a more integrated international economy. On the other hand, critics note that multinationals, to varying degree, have corrupted the domestic political system through their undue influence on elections and the legislative processes. Moreover, in an attempt to expand their markets and profits, they teamed with the corrupt elites of authoritarian governments overseas to gain lucrative contracts and violated international labor laws and environmental standards.

Multinational Corporations
Those that buy resources as well as produce and sell products in many countries and throughout parts of the world.

Table 4-5
Expenditures of the Federal Government, 2015

Major Category	Expenditures (Billions of Dollars)	Percentage of Total
Defense (military)	589.6	16
Medicare & Health	1,028.4	27.9
Income security	508.8	13.8
Social security	887.8	24.0
Net interest (public debt)	223.2	6.5
All other	402.0	9.8
Total	3,688.3	100.0

Source: Economic Report of the President, 2016.

Table 4-6
State and Local Government General Expenditures by Function, 2012-2013

State and Local		
Major Functional Category	Expenditures (Billions of Dollars)	Percent of Total
Education	876.5	33.2
Public welfare	516.4	19.5
Health and Hospitals	247.8	9.4
Transportation	275.3	10.4
Public Safety	234.7	8.9
Environment and housing	202.6	7.7
Government administration	233.3	8.8
All other	240.9	9.1
Total	2643.0	100.0

Source: State and Local Government Finance, Census Bureau.

GOVERNMENTS

Governments, federal, state, and local, affect economic activities through many means: (1) expenditures, (2) taxation, (3) enactment of laws, and (4) regulatory activities.

Expenditures: What Do They Spend All That Money On?

The expenditures of the federal government for all sorts of things, from guns to butter, stimulate output in the economy, both directly and indirectly. These expenditures stimulate output directly by creating a demand for goods and services; they stimulate it indirectly by income transfers that do not require an immediate good or service in return, such as educational grants, social security, and interest on the national debt.

When you look at Table 4-5, you will notice the figures for income security, Social Security, and Medicare, which together accounted for about 62 percent of expenditures in 2015. Defense expenditures accounted for nearly 16 percent. Since the three income transfer categories and defense combined constitute nearly 78 percent of the federal spending, no attempt to reduce the size of the federal budget deficits can succeed if it does not involve cuts in these categories. This, however, is easier said than done, for the income transfers, as components of a "social safety net," are quite popular among the middle-class households. Also, cuts in the defense budget often encounter stiff resistance by the military, defense contractors and politicians whose states will be adversely affected by the cuts.

Table 4-6 shows how subnational (state and local) levels of government allocated their expenditures in 2012-2013. Education was the top spending category receiving nearly one-third of the total (state governments fund higher education and local governments K-12). The next two categories were "public welfare" (mostly vendor payments and relatively small cash assistance) and "transportation" (highways).

Generally speaking, expenditures by various levels of government reflect government roles in providing "public goods" (such as national defense), goods that benefit the society due to their beneficial spillover effects (such as education and health, and police and fire protection), and improving income security and distribution (through, for example, social security and welfare programs).

Taxation

Taxes drain off; (that is, consumes) purchasing power that households could otherwise use to buy consumer goods. Thus, taxation reduces consumer demand. Let us look briefly at the way taxation affects this demand.

Principles of Taxation

Who should pay for government services? And how much should they pay? There are two ways of looking at this problem: (1) benefits received and (2) ability to pay.

Benefits Received: According to the **benefits-received principle**, people should pay taxes commensurate with the benefits they receive from government services. School taxes are a hypothetical example: a family with two children in public schools would pay twice as much as a family with only one in public school, and a family with no children in public school would pay no school taxes.

This view looks at government services as services that the taxpayer buys, much as she or he buys shoes or tomatoes in the market. It reverses the old adage that "you get what you pay for" to "you pay for what you get." The people who receive government services pay for them with taxes. By this reasoning, the more services you receive, the more taxes you should pay.

In reality, there are limitations to applying the benefits-received principle. First, it is practically impossible, in many cases, to figure out a fair basis for taxes by this principle. For example, how could national security expenditures be distributed on the basis of benefits received? Even the distribution of school taxes is not simple, because a person who never has

Benefits-Received Principle

That argument that tax payments should be commensurate with the benefits received from government services.

children benefits from living in a society of better-educated citizens. Second, if one applied the benefits-received principle strictly, it would place heavy burdens on the poor and disadvantaged members of our society, who would be denied access to most government services because they could not pay for them. The point is that the benefits-received principle may be more appropriate in some areas than others, and in some areas it may not be appropriate at all.

Notwithstanding these two drawbacks, the government has sources of tax revenue based substantially on benefits received:

1. *State and federal excise taxes on gasoline.* These taxes are frequently earmarked for construction and maintenance of highways; the more you use the highways, the more gasoline you must buy and the more taxes you must pay to maintain the highways. It is true, however, that tax revenues are increasingly being used to fund mass transit systems that are not based on the benefits-received principle.

2. *Payroll taxes.* These are put into various funds, out of which social security, Medicare, and other benefit payments are made. As the social security program is expanded and as the average age of Americans increases, the government increases these taxes to pay for the added benefits, and to compensate for inflation. (Although social security benefits do vary somewhat, according to variations in how much one has paid into the program, these differences are fairly limited and thus weaken this example.) In fact, recent studies suggest that there is little relationship between social security benefits and taxes paid by individuals.

Ability-to-Pay Principle
The argument that, as peoples' incomes grow, they can afford to pay a larger part of their incomes in taxes.

The **ability-to-pay principle** of taxation assumes that those who have a larger income are capable of paying not only a larger tax, but also of paying a larger percentage of their income in taxes than those who have smaller incomes. According to this argument, when a person has a very low income, all of it goes to buy necessities. As the person's income increases, some of it can be devoted to non-necessities. The higher a family's income, the more it can afford to spend on nonessentials and the larger percentage of its income it can pay in taxes, while still being able to buy essentials.

One tax based on the ability-to-pay concept is the graduated income tax. The taxpayer, after deducting for size of family and for certain expenditures (health-care expenses, interest payments, charity, and so on), pays a percentage of net income in taxes. The higher the net income, the higher the percentage. A real flaw in this system is the near impossibility of enacting tax laws that are equitable to all and of arranging the deductions in such a way that families are taxed at a comparable rate. For a long time there has been controversy about these deductions and about other rules relating to what is considered taxable income. Many people charge that tax loopholes benefit higher-income groups. One big loophole which you have probably heard discussed, is the **capital gains tax**. It used to work this way: If you bought an asset and held it for at least one year and sold it for a gain, only 25 percent of the difference, or capital gain (that is, the increase in value of the asset), was considered taxable income. In 2003, capital gains taxes were again treated differently. The gains in asset values are now taxed at a rate of 15 percent. Proponents argue that this will lead to increased saving and investment while opponents say that the change simply reinstates a loophole that primarily benefits those with high incomes.

Types of Tax Rates

Tax Rate
The percentage of income paid in taxes.

Progressive Tax
A tax in which the rate increases as income increases.

Regressive Tax.
A tax in which the rate decreases as income increases.

The **income tax rate** is the percentage of income a person pays in taxes. We can classify taxes in relation to the tax rate and what happens to it as our income increases. From this point of view, taxes are either progressive, regressive, or proportional.

A **progressive tax** is one in which the rate increases as income increases. The best example of it is federal income tax. As a person's taxable income gets larger, the rate of taxation increases also.

A **regressive tax** is one in which the rate declines as income increases. A sales tax is an example: When you pay a sales tax on clothes, you pay it on the basis of how much you buy. The *rate* does not change as the amount you buy increases. However, the higher your income, the larger the percentage of income you put into savings, and the smaller the percentage of income you put into clothes. So the percentage of your income that the government takes for sales taxes declines as your income increases.

Here is how this works in figures. Suppose that the sales tax is 5 percent. Adams has an income of $100 a week and spends all of it on taxable items. Thus Adams spends 5 percent of income on sales tax. However, Bloggs makes $200 a week. Being "richer," Bloggs saves $50 and spends only $150 on sales-taxable items. The sales tax Bloggs pays, as a percentage of income, is only 3.75 percent. *Note:* Some sales taxes have a stronger impact on low-income groups than others. A sales tax on bread would be much more regressive than a sales tax on swimming pools. In fact, if a sales tax is properly selective, it need not be regressive at all.

Figure 4-5
The Three Types of Tax Rates

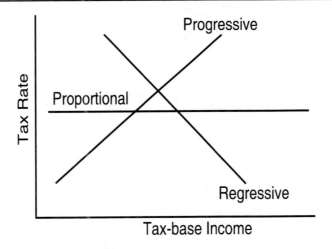

Proportional Tax
A tax in which the rate remains constant as income changes.

A **proportional tax** is one with a rate that remains the same as the taxpayer's income changes. Social Security taxes fit this concept. The percentage tax rate (6.2 percent) stays the same up to the cap of around $118,500 (as of 2016). Beyond this limit the tax becomes regressive since you continue to earn more income and pay no additional taxes. Some states have proportional taxes on incomes[1].

Figure 4-5 shows that the progressive curve slopes upward, so that the tax rate increases (up the vertical axis) as the tax-base income increases (out the horizontal axis). The regressive curve slopes downward, so the tax rate decreases (down the vertical axis) as the tax-base income increases (out the horizontal axis). The proportional curve is horizontal, since the tax rate remains unchanged as the ax-base income increases (out the horizontal axis).

Table 4-7
Federal Government Revenues by Source, 2015

Source	Amount of Revenue (Billions of Dollars)	Percent of total
Individual income taxes	1,540.8	47.4
Corporate income tax	343.8	10.6
Social insurance receipts	1,065.3	32.8
Other	300.0	9.2
Total	3,249.9	100.0

Source: Economic Report of the President, 2016

Table 4-8
Sources of State and Local Revenues, 2012-2013

Source	Amount of Revenue (Billions of Dollars)	Percent of total
Property taxes	455.4	16.9
Sales and gross receipts taxes	496.4	18.5
Individual income taxes	338.5	12.6
Corporation net income taxes	53.0	2.0
Revenue from Federal Government	584.6	21.7
All other	762.4	28.3
Total	2,690.5	100.0

Source: Economic Report of the President, 2016

Composition of Taxes

Table 4-7 shows where the federal government obtains its revenues. As you would expect, personal income taxes are the most important source, bringing in 47.7 percent of the total in 2016. Payroll tax dollars (social insurance receipts), which mostly go to pay for social security and Medicare, are next, with 32.8 percent. Corporate income taxes account for slightly over 10 percent of the total federal government revenues. This relatively small share, in part, reflects the fact that effective corporate marginal tax rates are lower than the statutory rates (the top rate being equal to about 35 percent) due to the existence of a variety of tax exemptions and loopholes. Moreover, many corporations have been reduc-

---

1. The definitions used in this section are followed by most economists. These definitions of progressive, regressive and proportional taxes are slightly different from the definitions one would find in a dictionary.

ing their tax liability through "tax inversion" which basically means that a corporation relocates its legal domicile to a low-tax country to shelter its profits.

Table 4-8 gives the same information about state and local governments combined. Note that these governments typically get a large percentage of their revenues from sales taxes. This category accounted for 18.0 percent of total during the 2012-2013 survey period. Property taxes also constitute a major source of revenue especially for local governments. This category had a 16.9 share of total revenues. Only about 12.6 percent of state and local revenues came from personal income taxes. Corporate taxes were almost negligible (about 2 percent). Transfers ("grants") from the federal government have been growing as share of total state and local revenues over time. The "stimulus package" implemented beginning 2009 to mitigate the effects of the "Great Recession" (see Chapter 1) significantly increased the share of this category to 22.2 percent.

Who Pays the Tax?

Usually, you cannot shift the responsibility for paying your personal income taxes to another person. Most of us lack the economic power to pass on these taxes by making others pay higher rates for our service or products. Property taxes are, in effect, paid by those who use the property. For example, renters usually pay the property tax, indirectly, as part of their rent unless their building has many vacancies, in which case the landlord may not be able to charge high enough rents to shift all the tax to the renters.

But what about corporate income taxes? Does the corporation pay them, or can they pass these taxes along to their customers through higher prices? If the corporation is operating in a field in which there is a lot of competition, the competition prevents it from passing the tax along to customers. If a corporation is in an industry in which there is little competition (for example, large firms that make a product for which there are few good substitutes), the firm may be able to shift at least part of the burden of the tax to the customer.

Is the tax structure as a whole, federal, state, and local, progressive or regressive? Federal income taxation, because of the large share coming from personal income taxes, is probably somewhat progressive. Tax loopholes (such as the exemption from taxes of the interest from tax-free municipal bonds) cancel some of the progressiveness of the personal income tax. State taxes, because of the predominance of sales taxes, are probably regressive, whereas local taxes are probably closer to proportional, because of the predominance of property taxes.

Government and the Rules of the Game

Governments, by enacting and enforcing various laws, set the rules for economic activity. To begin with, the Constitution itself sets some of the rules, and the Supreme Court has backed these up through its interpretations of the Constitution. Also there have been many statutes passed, plus countless laws relating to contracts. Virtually every business transaction involving a contract is limited by these laws. The many antitrust laws indicate how anxious Congress is to keep large corporations from exercising monopoly power. Bear in mind that labor unions, and the government itself, also have monopoly power, though labor unions are exempted from the provisions of the antitrust laws.

Government and Regulation

To set limits for the nation's industries, many federal and state commissions regulate economic activities to varying degrees. For example, in every state, there are public utility commissions that set prices and set other guidelines for telephone, electricity, gas, water, and transportation services. Some argue that these utility commissions are politically biased and even in some cases have anti-competitive effects. Perhaps so, but their intended purpose is to prevent the utility companies from taking advantage of the public through their power over prices.

Some of the principal federal government agencies charged with economic regulations are:

1. *The Interstate Commerce Commission.* Established in 1887, it was responsible for overseeing rail, bus, and truck transportation; sets rate schedules, routes, and various conditions of competition. Its powers have diminished with the substantial deregulation of recent decades.

2. *The Federal Trade Commission.* Established in 1914 to prevent unfair practices by firms (such as false and misleading advertising).

3. *The Food and Drug Administration.* Acts as watchdog against harmful or disease-carrying foods, cosmetics, and drugs; also checks the efficacy of drugs and the validity of drug advertising.

4. *The Federal Communications Commission.* Regulates TV and radio; grants and revokes licenses to broadcast.

5. *The Securities and Exchange Commission.* Supervises the stock exchanges, the over-the-counter stock market, and the issuance of new securities; tries to prevent manipulation of stock prices; tries to ensure truthful and adequate information on stocks to stockholders, both present and potential.

6. *The Departments of Agriculture; Housing; Transportation; and Health and Human Services* have branches that perform overseeing and regulatory functions.

With all these agencies to help protect consumers and businesses, is the public well protected? There is doubt; many people feel that in spite of this network of regulatory agencies, the consumer is often short-changed. Some people charge that many of the people serving on the commissions, in fact, are "captured," that is, they favor the industries they're supposed to regulate, a case of the wolves guarding the sheep. This may be true, at least in some cases, since many of them were executives in these very industries before they were appointed, and many of them, after their term of office, become executives in the same industries they have been regulating. On the other hand, the agencies are sometimes so "captured" by consumer interests that they fail to leave firms with revenues that permit them to compete for capital. Again, these are subjects that will be treated more extensively in the microeconomic principles of economics course in which the regulatory functions of governments are examined in more detail.

The Rest of the World

In the absence of trade with other nations, the components of an economic society would consist of its households, business firms, and its government(s). Throughout history, however, societies have exchanged goods and services as well as resources with each other. In doing so, an economic society becomes an open economy, one whose levels of income and product are influenced both by domestic and foreign economic activities.

Open Economy
One whose levels of income and product depend on both domestic and foreign economic activities.

In an **open economy**, the circular flow diagram shown in Figure 4-2 must be modified to incorporate the effects of (1) exports, those goods and services sold to other nations, and (2) imports, those goods and services purchased from other nations. Business firms, households, and governments are all involved in these flows. Businesses export goods and services and earn incomes from factors of production such as capital investments abroad. Conversely, foreign businesses export goods and services to our domestic economy and earn factor incomes from factors such as capital employed in the domestic economy. Households buy imported goods and sell factors of production such as financial capital. Governments not only regulate these international flows but also collect import tax revenues and, through domestic international financial institutions, influence the monetary flows and currency exchange rates that play an important role in the open economy's international transactions. Much more will be said about these activities and their importance to the domestic economy in the chapters on international trade and finance.

Application I: Business Firms, Profit Maximizers or Agents of Social Responsibility?

The Effect of Competition on Business Morals

In Western Europe in the Middle Ages, the moral prescriptions of the church affected the economic behavior of merchants. The concepts of a just price and a just wage, plus the widespread idea that anyone who charged interest on money was guilty of usury, were intended to limit employers and merchants in setting prices.

By the time Adam Smith[2] wrote *The Wealth of Nations*, in 1776, the dictates of the church that restrained merchants were replaced by the dictates of competition, which surprisingly enough exerted an even stronger effect, and in the same direction. Adam Smith's "Invisible hand" was *competition*. According to Smith, businessmen (as well as consumers) were selfish and concerned primarily with their own personal gain. Self-interest ruled economic behavior, but competition restrained this behavior, this desire to maximize one's own economic good, and channeled it into maximizing the public good. Why?

Each firm had such a small part of the total market that it could not control the price of a given product and thus gain an advantage over others. Each small firm seeking customers had to produce at the most efficient level, turn out the kinds of products and services the consumer wanted, and sell them at the lowest price commensurate with staying in business. The selfishness of these small producers was guided, as if by an invisible hand (competition), to maximize the welfare of society at large.

However, today, although many industries do have to cope with fierce competition, many others are dominated by a few giant firms (though even these

---

2. Smith, Adam. *An Enquiry into the Nature and Causes of the Wealth of Nations*. London, Metheun and Co. 1904. Fifth Edition.

may be restrained by foreign competition or by competition from firms in other industries). So the tenets of the medieval church no longer exercise the force of law over the people, and monopoly power may have weakened Adam Smith's invisible hand of competition.

How should corporate producers behave? Should they produce goods and services and price them with only the goal of maximizing their own profits, using every advantage their size and market dominance affords? Or should the corporation, like a good citizen, consider the social and economic needs of the society as a whole? In other words, what are the social responsibilities of business?

Responsible to Whom?

Business decision makers, including corporate managers, have many responsibilities. In recent years, the notable corporate scandals involving firms such as Enron and Worldcom have reinforced the importance of reexamining these responsibilities. The financial crisis of 2008 - 2011 has exposed extensive risk taking and its impact on the economy as indications of a lack of social responsibility as well. Among these are responsibilities to stockholders, to employees, and, of course, to their own self-interests. An interesting and important question to ask is: Does the pursuit of profit by firms, especially in a competitive market environment, necessarily lead to the serving of the broader interests of society? Adam Smith clearly believed that this coincidence of interests (those of individuals and society) would occur through the invisible hand of competitive pressure even though it was through "no intent" of those making the business decisions. In more recent times, however, questions have been raised about whether and under what conditions the coincidence occurs. Further questions have arisen as to whether firms *should* act out of a sense of social responsibility as well as one of responsibility to shareholders. In a fundamental sense, these two sets of questions (*are* society's interests served by individual firm decisions, and *should* firms try to serve social interests) are bound up together. Let's look at the arguments on both sides.

Maximizing Profits: Serving Private or Public Interests?

Corporate directors and the managers who report to them have a responsibility to the firms' owners, its stockholders. That responsibility to enhance the value of their shares is consistent with making decisions that maximize the firms' profits (the difference between its revenues and costs). Critics of decisions made on this basis say that while it satisfies one narrow set of (stockholder) interests, it can result in actions that are socially irresponsible or that impose costs on many others in society. While it may, for example, be possible to produce a passenger vehicle at lower costs by failing to make it "crash-safe," or to equip it with tires or other systems that are unsafe, the extra profit gained merely transfers costs to others and, in the judgment of such critics, is unethical or immoral. More to the point, say critics, it creates a need for government regulation to ensure that public health and safety standards are adequately represented where profit maximizing decisions do not lead to those results.

Critics of profit maximizing decisions frequently argue, thus, that the public's representatives (government) should constrain profit maximizing decisions by (1) limiting how products can be produced (e.g., crash resistant construction of cars, non-polluting insecticides) and (2) What products can be marketed (e.g., banning such "noxious" products as marijuana, cocaine, asbestos, and the like). Also government has a responsibility, say critics, to regulate the behavior of the firm not only in producing its products, but also in marketing them. While deceptive advertising, for instance, *might* be profitable for a firm, government agencies (e.g., the Federal Trade Commission and the Securities and Exchange Commission) help prevent consumers from being misled by narrowly focused profit-seeking firms.

Of course, there are many others who say that many business firms, while concerned with profits, also *do* act out of a sense of social responsibility. Why else, say proponents of this view, would corporations sponsor medical research or make donations to public broadcasting or voluntarily recall defective products. If nothing else, say those with this view, the "immoral" and abusive actions that profit maximizing firms might undertake would be deterred by the fear of a reaction from the public. Such corporate actions might lead to public insistence that governments strictly regulate firm behavior and do so in a way contradictory of the firm's and its stockholders' interests.

Cartoon Feature Syndicate

"I figure someone has to hold the line."

Maximizing Profits: Competition and the Invisible Hand

There is evidence that the American economy has become substantially more competitive in recent decades. According to an important study in the 1980s by William Shephard[3], increased competitiveness has been due to (1) deregulation (removal of government controls) of several industries, (2) increased competition from other countries (imports), and (3) antitrust (antimonopoly) legal actions by governments. Thus, although market power remains significant in some U.S. industries (e.g., computers, soups, cereals, drugs, and the like) there has been a major resurgence of competitive forces in almost all others. While these are subjects that you will explore more fully in the microeconomic principles course, for our purposes, it suffices to ask: How is competition related to socially responsible behavior by firms?

The answer to the above question turns heavily on the kind of business behavior considered. Firms in a competitive industry all sell at the same price. We would not, therefore, expect a single firm to make production decisions that raise its costs above those of other firms for to do so would lower the firm's

---

3. Shepherd, William G. "Causes of Increased Competition in the U.S. Economy, 1939-1980." *Review of Economics and Statistics* 64. November, 1982.

profit. The market, in other words, would punish such behavior. On the other hand, the competitive market will also punish firms that produce inferior or unsafe products for such firms will lose customers to the many other firms whose (superior or safe) products are very good substitutes for those of the "greedy" firm.

Where monopoly exists, that is where consumers do not have good alternatives to buying from "greedy" firms or those that produce unsafe or inferior products, markets may not punish or at least may not punish as quickly or surely a firm's "profits at any cost" strategy. Under these market circumstances, many argue for government regulations that may take such forms as product safety standards or even government licensing of products. Even in many of these cases, however, it may be more advantageous for government policy to encourage competition than to engage in regulation.

When May Markets Punish Socially Responsible Behavior?

Even competitive markets will not necessarily encourage socially desirable behavior or punish undesirable behavior in all cases. One of the clearest examples is the case of environmental pollution. A firm that voluntarily undertook costly pollution reduction decisions (e.g., smokestack scrubbers) in producing its products while other firms did not would see its relative profit fall. The market, in other words, might well punish socially desirable behavior. To ensure that such behavior is forthcoming, therefore, may well require government action or intervention. As environmental problems have become more apparent and in many instances more severe, pressure for government intervention to cause firms to use scarce environmental resources (e.g., air, water) in ways compatible with social goals has increased. As a result, air quality goals and standards have been developed in many areas. Emissions controls have been mandated and other actions taken that affect products produced and the techniques used to produce them. While these actions have not changed the basic nature of profit maximizing decisions by firms, they have altered the constraints within which those decisions are made. In the twenty-first century, there are calls for government to engage in regulatory and other programs that will reduce the environmental effects of "greenhouse" emissions. This may result in effects that change production processes and prices, although how and to what extent is not clear yet.

Can or Should Firms Decide What is in Society's Interest?

The idea of Smith's invisible hand was not that business people either intended to promote the public's interest or, in fact, even *knew* necessarily what that interest was. Doubtless, there are instances in which decision makers realize that certain actions would even be counter to the interests of many other citizens. Selling products that are known to be harmful and deceiving consumers into believing them to be beneficial falls into this category. In other cases, though, firms may simply not have either the information or the perspective to judge what is or is not in society's interest as opposed to their own (profit maximizing) interest. A single competitive firm in Los Angeles, for example, may have no idea what *its* production technology contributes to the environmental pollution of that "air shed." As a result, it could make no rational choice, even if it wanted to act in a socially responsible manner, about how much it should spend on modifying its plant. All firms acting in this same manner, though, may significantly pollute the air. A decision about socially desirable air purity standards, thus, must be made socially rather than privately. The main point here is that, in instances such as the hypothetical one above, it is not always greed or selfishness that creates the lack of correspondence between private and social interests; rather, it is at least sometimes the lack of information or perspective that creates the problem. Where those circumstances exist, society must, through some means, create the perspective and provide the information upon which firms are expected to act. In 2009, the federal government assumed much larger responsibility for circumscribing private firms behavior. Its actions included limiting cooperate salaries for executives whose firms received "bailout" funds and even determining which executives would be retained and which fired.

Application II: The Distribution of Income in the United States

The distribution of income has become a major issue in American economic and political life. In the early 2000s, the distribution discussions focused on "two Americas, one rich, one poor." After the financial crisis of 2008 that lead to tremendous economic hardship for millions, concerns about income (and wealth) inequality manifested themselves in protests against the "Wall Street." The "Occupy Movement" was born in 2011 and adopted the slogan "We are the 99%." The following is a brief review of the evolution of the extent of income inequality and some of its causes and consequences in the United States.

As Figure 4-6 shows, the value of the Gini coefficient began to rise from approximately 0.35 around the late 1960s to 0.45 in 2015 suggesting a significant deterioration in the (before tax) distribution of family income (the distribution of wealth is even more unequal).

Figure 4-6
The Gini Coefficient of Before-Tax Family Income

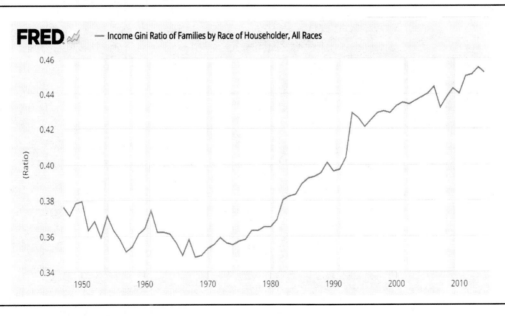

Source: The Federal Reserve Bank of St. Louis.

The cause of this deterioration was the very unequal manner in which gains from economic growth benefited different income group during much of this period. As shown in Figure 4-7, the richest 1 percent of families saw its income (on an inflation adjusted before tax basis) grow by two hundred percent. This dwarfs the income growth rates of the middle sixty percent and the poorest twenty percent which were merely 48 and 40 percent, respectively. Note that those at the bottom and middle segments of the family income distribution heavily rely on their labor (wage) income and, as the functional distribution in Figure 4-1 shows, this form of income has been losing share over time to other forms of income. A major reason for this phenomenon is "wage stagnation" which have been attributed to globalization (offshoring) and technological progress that reduce the demand for unskilled and semi-skilled labor in the U.S. However, Figure 4-8 suggests perhaps a more important contributing factor: the decoupling of hourly labor compensation (wage and benefits) and productivity growth rates since the early 1970s. More specifically, over the period 1948-1973 improvements in labor productivity translated into roughly equal improvements in hourly labor compensation. In the post 1973 period, however, the compensation growth rate was less than half of the corresponding productivity growth rate. In other words, workers were significantly undercompensated despite the fact that they became much more productive!

Figure 4-7

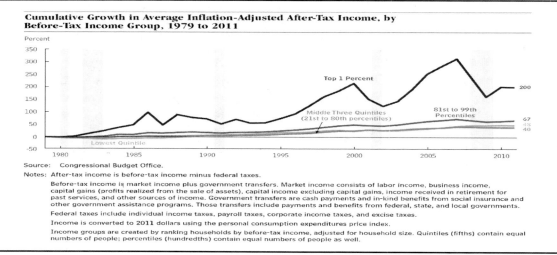

Cumulative Growth in Average Inflation-Adjusted After-Tax Income, by Before-Tax Income Group, 1979 to 2011

Source: Congressional Budget Office.

Notes: After-tax income is before-tax income minus federal taxes.

Before-tax income is market income plus government transfers. Market income consists of labor income, business income, capital gains (profits realized from the sale of assets), capital income excluding capital gains, income received in retirement for past services, and other sources of income. Government transfers are cash payments and in-kind benefits from social insurance and other government assistance programs. Those transfers include payments and benefits from federal, state, and local governments.

Federal taxes include individual income taxes, payroll taxes, corporate income taxes, and excise taxes.

Income is converted to 2011 dollars using the personal consumption expenditures price index.

Income groups are created by ranking households by before-tax income, adjusted for household size. Quintiles (fifths) contain equal numbers of people; percentiles (hundredths) contain equal numbers of people as well.

Figure 4-8

Workers produced much more, but typical workers' pay lagged far behind

Disconnect between productivity and typical worker's compensation, 1948–2013

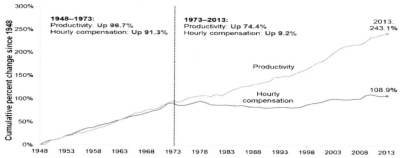

Note: Data are for compensation (wages and benefits) of production/nonsupervisory workers in the private sector and net productivity of the total economy. "Net productivity" is the growth of output of goods and services less depreciation per hour worked.

Source: EPI analysis of unpublished Total Economy Productivity data from Bureau of Labor Statistics (BLS) Labor Productivity and Costs program, wage data from the BLS Current Employment Statistics, BLS Employment Cost Trends, BLS Consumer Price Index, and Bureau of Economic Analysis National Income and Product Accounts

Why does any of these matter? A major economic reason is that the bulk of consumers in the U.S. economy are wage earners. If wages do not sufficiently rise over time, then consumption expenditures cannot be supported by relatively small groups whose incomes are in the form of capital gains and dividends, interest income, and rent. This means that families typically have to borrow and/or increase work efforts just to sustain their level of consumption. During sever economic contractions, however, many jobs are lost and access to credit becomes harder. This puts downward pressure on consumption and, subsequently, investment spending (businesses have no incentive to expand capacity if they cannot sell what they have already produced). The economy then further contracts due to additional layoffs, loss of incomes, and spending cuts. Accordingly, it is desirable to prevent the distribution of income from becoming highly unequal, for it can cause insufficient demand for goods and services produced and, consequently, intensify the magnitude and increase the duration of economic recessions.

Figure 4-9

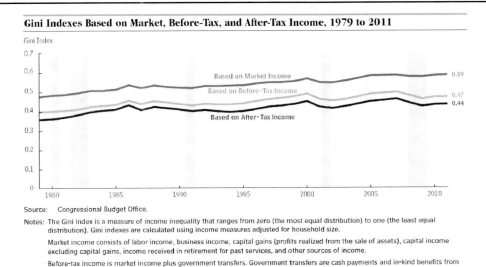

Gini Indexes Based on Market, Before-Tax, and After-Tax Income, 1979 to 2011

Source: Congressional Budget Office.

Notes: The Gini index is a measure of income inequality that ranges from zero (the most equal distribution) to one (the least equal distribution). Gini indexes are calculated using income measures adjusted for household size.

Market income consists of labor income, business income, capital gains (profits realized from the sale of assets), capital income excluding capital gains, income received in retirement for past services, and other sources of income.

Before-tax income is market income plus government transfers. Government transfers are cash payments and in-kind benefits from social insurance and other government assistance programs. Those transfers include payments and benefits from federal, state, and local governments.

This leads us to the (controversial but necessary) role of government in modifying the distribution of income using progressive taxes and transfer payments, among others. Figure 4-9 shows that the Gini coefficient (index) of family income dropped, for example, from 0.59 to 0.47 in 2011 after accounting for transfer payments (see notes to the table). It further dropped from 0.47 to 0.44 allowing for the effect of progressive taxes (such as those on income and corporate profits).

Finally, we should keep in mind that there is an important difference between a "fair" or "equitable" distribution of income (a normative concept) and an equal distribution of income. If the distribution of income is initially lopsided, reducing the degree of income inequality will make the distribution more equitable. However, the objective of modifying the distribution of income should not be an equal distribution, for in view of differences among individuals in terms of their skills and talents, willingness to work, save, invest and take risk an equal distribution of income would itself be unfair or inequitable.

SUMMING UP

1. In the basic circular-flow model of the national economy, households provide firms with all the factors of production. Firms, in turn, pay to employ these resources, which they use to produce goods and services for the households. To complete the circle, households use the income from selling their resources to pay for the goods and services. Firms using the income from the sale of goods and services pay for still more factors of production to produce still more goods and services. And so on.

2. The more complex model of the national economy takes into account the fact that people do not spend all of their incomes. They save some and pay some out to governments as taxes. This reduces the public's demand for business firms' goods and services. The household's savings go to financial institutions, which make them available for investments. The household's tax dollars go to the government, which uses them to buy goods and services, and thereby becomes industry's biggest customer. However, these flows of money from investment and from government to business firms, to buy industry's goods and services, are not always at a level that make possible full employment and stable prices.

3. The concept of *functional distribution of income* has to do with the sources of income. In 2011, 69.2 percent of income in the United States came from wages and salaries; about 10.9 percent was corporate profits; about nine percent was proprietors' income; eight percent was interest income; and three percent was rental income.

4. The distribution of income in the United States is unequal. When one diagrams the data on income distribution for a given period, one sees that the resulting curve which economists call a *Lorenz curve*. The distribution after taxes and transfer payments, if drawn, is less unequal.

5. The advantages of a *sole proprietorship* are that (a) it is easy to form, and (b) there are high incentives to succeed. The disadvantages are that (a) its owner has *unlimited liability*, (b) it is difficult for a person working independently to specialize management functions, (c) access to capital is limited, and (d) it has limited life.

6. The advantages of a *partnership* are that (a) it has increased access to capital, and (b) it offers management more chances to specialize functions. The disadvantages are that (a) its owners have unlimited liability, (b) it has limited life, and (c) its access to capital is less than that of a corporation.

7. The advantages of a *corporation* are that (a) its owners have *limited liability,* thus the risks of the firm are spread over a larger group of owners, (b) it constitutes a legal entity, (c) it has *unlimited life,* (d) it has greater access to capital than a sole proprietorship or a partnership, and (e) its management can specialize functions because of its larger size. The disadvantages are that (a) the process of forming a corporation takes a long time and is expensive, (b) corporate profits are double-taxed, (c) there are special laws directed at corporations, and (d) there is a danger of separation of ownership and control.

8. Many industries in the United States are dominated by corporations. Some people charge that these large firms prevent competition and bias political decision-making although large firms, including multinational firms, are an efficient means for raising capital and enhancing resource mobility.

9. The dictates of the church, about just prices and wages, in the Middle Ages were intended to restrain business pricing. These dictates have been replaced in recent centuries by the "invisible hand" of competition has caused the private pursuit of self-interest to result in socially desirable outcomes. Development of monopoly power in some markets, though, may have limited the effect of the "invisible hand."

10. A firm's decision makers have responsibilities to the owners of the firm and profit-maximization is consistent with serving the owners' interests. Adam Smith argued that competition would make selfish (profit-maximizing) decisions by individuals consistent with the interests of society.

11. Arguably, efforts by firms to minimize cost and maximize profit may lead to the production of products that are harmful and that impose costs on many members of society. This has led critics of profit-maximizing decisions to argue that government should constrain such decisions by limiting how some products may be produced and even, in some instances, *which* products may be marketed.

12. Some say that business firms *do* act with a sense of social responsibility, which tempers their profit-maximizing decisions. If nothing else, according to proponents of this view, strict profit maximizing decisions are not always undertaken because of a fear that public insistence would lead to government strictly regulating firms' decisions.

13. Evidence suggests that the American economy has become substantially more competitive in recent decades, though market power continues to exist in some industries. The way in which competition is related to firm behavior depends on the type of behavior considered.

14. Competitive markets will punish firms that incur costs not incurred by other firms since all sell at the same price. Competitive markets also will punish firms that produce inferior or unsafe products. Monopolistic markets are not as certain to punish the latter type of behavior.

15. Socially desirable behavior, such as reducing the environmental pollution effects of production, will not likely be undertaken by competitive firms. To insure such behavior probably requires government intervention and constraining profit-maximizing behavior. That intervention may result from increasing calls to fight the environmental effects of "global warming."

16. In some instances, the invisible hand may not lead to socially desirable behavior by firms not because of greed, but because of lack of knowledge of what is socially desirable and also because of lack of social perspective.

17. There are two main principles of taxation: (a) benefits received, and (b) ability to pay. According to the *benefits-received principle*, one should pay taxes on the basis of the amount of benefits one receives from government expenditures. According to the *ability-to-pay principle*, the tax rate should be higher percentage for higher incomes.

18. A *tax rate*, the percentage of income one pays in taxes, can be either *progressive*, *regressive*, or *proportional*. When a tax is *progressive*, the tax rate increases as income increases (for example, the graduated federal income tax). When a tax is *regressive*, the tax rate decreases as income increases (for example, some sales taxes). When a tax is *proportional*, the tax rate remains unchanged as income increases (for example, property taxes).

19. Governments, by passing laws, set the rules for economic activity. Two important areas of law are those that deal with (a) contracts, and (b) antitrust legislation. Governments also affect economic activities through various regulatory commissions and agencies.

20. Closed economies, those that do not engage in trade with other nations, have their economic flows determined exclusively by domestic activities of households, firms, and governments.

21. Open economies, those that do engage in trade with other nations, have their economic flows determined not only by domestic activities, but also by the effects of exports, sales to other nations, and imports, purchases from other nations.

KEY TERMS

Ability-to-pay principle
Benefits-received principle
Closed economy
Corporation
Factor markets
Functional distribution of income
Lorenz curve
Multinational corporations
Open economy
Partnership
Product markets
Progressive tax
Proportional tax
Regressive tax
Sole proprietorship
Tax rate

QUESTIONS

1. Using the complex circular-flow model, show how changes in (a) efforts to save, (b) efforts to invest, (c) payments of taxes, and (d) spending by government all affect total output and employment. Show these changes in factors one at a time.

2. How has the functional distribution of income changed since 1929?

3. How do Lorenz curves permit comparing a number of countries in terms of the level of equality in their respective distributions of cash income? What effect(s) may taxes and transfer payments have on the equality of income distribution?

4. If you were in charge of a firm, what would be the advantages and disadvantages of operating as a sole proprietorship, as a partnership, or as a corporation? What are the disadvantages of each form of operation?

5. What is meant by saying that the "invisible hand" leads self-interest serving private individuals to make decisions that are "through no intent of their own" consistent with society's interests?

6. What are some types of profit maximizing behavior by firms that may be socially irresponsible? Should governments intervene where such behavior takes place?

7. If governments do intervene to constrain private business decisions in (6) above, what types of constraints may be imposed?

8. Even if firms are tempted to engage in narrowly "greedy" behavior, what fear might cause them not to maximize their narrow self interests?

9. What has happened to the competitiveness of the American economy in recent decades? What factors has contributed to this change?

10. What types of behavior by firms will competitive markets punish? Reward?

11. Can a society rely totally on the "invisible hand" to solve its environmental problems including "global warming?"

12. Why may it be difficult for firms that seek to behave in a socially responsible way to do so?

13. In general, which principle of taxation do you prefer: benefits received or ability to pay? Why?

14. Look at the taxes listed in Tables 4-8 and 4-9 and decide which are progressive, which regressive, and which proportional. What determines who ultimately pays each of the taxes?

15. "Economic activity is heavily influenced by the way governments define the rules of the game." Do you agree? Why?

16. "With all the government regulatory commissions and agencies, the consumer is amply protected from improper business activity." Do you agree? Why?

17. You are the economic adviser for a federal commission studying taxes. You have been given the task of recommending comprehensive changes in the composition of taxes. What recommendations on tax changes would you make? Since any changes in the composition of taxes would shift the incidence of taxes (change the people who would be paying taxes), clearly state what changes in the incidence of taxes would occur. Explain your recommended changes from an economic point of view; from a moral or ethical point of view.

SECTION II:

The Basics of the Macroeconomy

SECTION II

The Basics of the Macroeconomy

Section I gave you an introduction to the workings of a market economy including the fundamental ways in which markets work to allocate resources. It also introduced you to the economy's players, that is, its consumers, producers, and governments.

With that background in mind, we are going to shift focus in Section II to begin building an understanding of macroeconomics, or of the economy operating at its highest level of aggregation. In Chapter 5,we will first build the empirical basis for understanding the macroeconomy by measuring the size of its output and income flows. In Chapter 6, we will begin by explaining some of the reasons causing short-term fluctuations in the level of overall economic activity. These fluctuations generate deviations from the trend level of output and are referred to as economic "booms" and "busts." We will then discuss unemployment and inflation as two major by-products of these fluctuations. Chapter 7 shifts the focus from short-term fluctuation in the level of aggregate economic activity to some of the factors that contribute to its long-term growth. Chapter 8 will develop an analytical framework known as the aggregate demand-aggregate supply model. We will present some of the factors that affect the aggregate demand and supply schedules. We will then show how they interact to determine the equilibrium levels of aggregate price and real output/income and how these levels change in response to changes in economic and noneconomic conditions. Chapter 9 will present some major differences between two major macroeconomic schools of thought known as the "classical" and "Keynesian" schools. This chapter lays the foundation for discussing different views regarding the extent to which the market mechanism or government interventions can be relied upon in dealing with macroeconomic instability.

Chapter 5: Measuring Domestic Income and Product

Gross Domestic Product: The market value of all final goods and services produced in any particular year within a country.

For reasons you will examine closely in this course, it is extremely important to measure (or estimate) how much the American economy is producing in any particular period of time. The largest such measure now in common use is called the **Gross Domestic Product (GDP)** or the market value of all final goods and services produced in any particular year within a country. All attempts to estimate national income flows go back to the 1930s and are regarded as indicators of the nation's economic health, they are also vital information in the making of national economic policy and the policies of firms throughout the economy.

In this chapter, we will look at a broad range of these estimates and also at ongoing efforts to coordinate them across the many different national economies. As we will see, changes in our national income accounting system have been made, and more changes seem likely to come as the world's economies become increasingly interdependent.

As you read, it is important to remember that GDP and the other concepts contained in this chapter are *estimates*, not precise measures. The following anecdote illustrates some of the reasons why this "caution" is necessary.

Way back in 1971, President Nixon unveiled the GNP[1] (Gross National Product) clock in the lobby of the Bureau of the Census building. The machine had been preset, according to the predictions of statisticians, to tick off the value of output produced. When the President showed the clock to reporters, it was recording a $1-trillion GNP. It didn't seem to bother anyone that (1) the machine had been running for some time, waiting for the proper moment to be revealed, (2) actual GNP was a good bit less than the $1 trillion predicted at the time, and (3) the $1-trillion GNP was in part achieved by increased prices rather than by increased output.

But despite the gadgetry and the "slight" distortions of politicians, GDP and the concept of national income accounting are important to a better understanding of the economy. Changes in the amount of the output of an economy can affect the material levels of well being of everyone within that

---

1. The difference between Gross Domestic Product and Gross National Product is small and is explained in the next few pages.

economy. In this chapter we shall discuss some of the most important concepts and estimates of economic performance.

An important question is: Even if the level of output in the economy increases, does it really mean that the individual member of the economy is better off? With all these urgings for increases in GDP, do such increases really improve material life? The application in this chapter will discuss that question. But first we need some basic understanding of the national economic accounts.

Background: Why is National Economic Accounting Important?

Although most of these concepts were, as indicated before, worked out during the depression of the 1930s, especially by Nobel Laureate Simon Kuznets, economists greatly improved and expanded the national economic accounts during World War II to meet the government's needs for wartime planning. Government agencies had to have measures of economic performance in order to make the best allocation of output and to formulate policies that would keep the economy stable. A British economist, Richard Stone, who made a major contribution to this effort, was also awarded the Nobel Prize in Economic Science for his efforts. A difficult problem for the United States was how to shift all those resources to fight the war and still minimize inflation. Data provided by the national economic accounts gave information about how much production could be used for consumption and how much income people would have for consumption. Now, knowing how much excess income people had, the government could estimate the size of government programs, taxes, savings, and government bond sales. The government needed to soak up consumers' excess income and reduce demand, so that prices could be kept down. Sales of government bonds were an important way to keep people from spending their incomes on the reduced supply of consumer goods available during the war.

The national economic accounts, like a family's account books, give government policy makers the information necessary to formulate economic policies that are appropriate to prevailing economic conditions as well as those that are expected. This information is also important for business groups and consumers, who also have to make economic decisions. Do you buy your house now or next year? What you think the economy is going to do next year is important because, along with many other things, it not only affects your own income, but also the income of others, and *their* level of demand and prices. The totals of these accounts, especially when we compare one year with another, give us all indications as to whether the economy is changing, and if so, how.

The Expenditure and Income Approaches

Expenditure Approach
An approach to national income accounting that measures the goods and services people buy, or the expenditures they make.

Income Approach
An approach to national income accounting that measures the incomes generated in producing the national output.

The National Income and Product Accounts (NIPAs) framework suggests two approaches to measuring the size of the economy: (1) the **expenditure approach**, which measures the value of the goods and services that people buy, that is the kinds of expenditures they make and (2) the **income approach**, which measures the incomes that are generated by the output of the economy. To sum it up, the expenditure approach deals with kinds of output, while the income approach deals with kinds of income generated in the production of that output.

The circular flow models of income discussed in the previous chapter suggest that, in effect, the two approaches are two sides of the same coin, and the statistical results of each are (indeed *must be*) equal. Suppose that the only output of an economy were one car, one machine to produce the car, and one schoolhouse. The expenditure approach to measuring economic performance would entail totaling the value of those three items of production. But the value of that output would be apportioned to the factors of production as income. The income approach would entail recording how much of that income is apportioned to each of the different factors of production. The two results, that obtained from the expenditure approach and that from the income approach, must be equal. *The value of what is produced is equal to the income distributed.*

We see how these two approaches lead to the same result in Table 5-1. The expenditure approach is concerned with what is produced. In Table 5-1, the total value (column (4)), the value of the labor and other costs, is $19,000. The income approach is concerned with the income generated. The total income, the sum of columns (1), (2), and (3), is $19,000. The two approaches lead to the same numerical results. In each case, the income generated must be equal to the value produced.

Cartoon Feature Syndicate

"Remember when one billion was such a frightening figure?"

Table 5-1
Income and Expenditure Approaches

Income Approach	Expenditure Approach			
	(1) Car	(2) Machine	(3) Schoolhouse	(4) Total Value
Labor	$10,000	$3,000	$6,000	$19,000
Interest	5,000	750	1,000	6,750
Rent	2,500	400	750	3,650
Profits	7,500	500	1,000	9,000
Depreciation	2,500	250	1,150	3,900
Indirect business taxes	2,500	100	100	2,700
	$30,000	$5,000	$10,000	$45,000

Gross Domestic Product and Gross Domestic Income

Gross Domestic Product (GDP)

Gross domestic product, as mentioned earlier, measures the total dollar value of all final goods and services produced in a particular period, in a given economy. Two elements of that definition need explaining.

1. When we say that only the value of *final goods and services* is included in the GDP, we avoid the possibility of counting output more than once in the GDP statistic. Most manufactured products use materials from several firms. These intermediate products become part of the final product, so the value of the final product also covers the cost of these intermediate products. To include the intermediate products separately would mean that we would be counting them twice, once when we included them separately and again when we listed the final product.

For example, suppose that the intermediate products that go to make up our $30,000 car in Table 5-1 include $500 worth of steel and $100 worth of rubber, which the automobile producers buy and then incorporate into the car. When the manufacturer sells the car, the price must be high enough to cover the cost of all the intermediate products. Economists, to avoid counting a unit of output twice in the GDP, therefore list only the final value of the car, the price to the ultimate user.

This policy, however, creates a problem. Work in progress and inventory on hand at the end of the year represent output for that year, and should be included in the GDP for that year. At the same time, work that was in progress the year before and inventory that was produced the year before are also included in the final product, and they should not be included in the current year's output. Economists resolve this by subtracting from the GDP the inventory at the beginning of the year and adding to the GDP the inventory at the end of the year. Formally, this is accomplished by including in investment a net inventory figure (beginning inventory subtracted from ending inventory).

Let's look at our car again. At the beginning of the year, it was only partially completed and was worth about $10,000. That was output from last year, which should not be included in this year's GDP. But the car is completed this year, and sold to a consumer. Also, this year, more than just one car is produced. Half of the second car is made, say, $15,000 worth. That $15,000 in partially completed car should be counted as part of this year's output. Solution: Subtract the $10,000 work-in-progress car that was on hand at the beginning of the year (beginning inventory) from the $15,000 work-in-progress car that is on hand at the end of the year (ending inventory). Net inventory (part of the investment) is +$5,000.

2. The GDP contains the total dollar value of goods and services for a specific time period only, usually one year. Only output for that year is included, and none from any prior period.

The three major groupings of expenditures on goods and services that are counted in the gross domestic product are (1) expenditures for personal consumption, (2) expenditures for investment, and (3) expenditures by the government.

Personal Consumption Expenditures (C)
Expenditures by consumers for durable goods, nondurable goods, and for services.

When we talk about **personal consumption expenditures** (C), we're actually talking about three kinds of expenditures: (1) When you buy a refrigerator or a car, you're buying *durable goods* (durable because is takes a long time to use them up). (2) When you buy food or clothes, you're buying *nondurable goods* (they are used up quickly). (3) When a barber cuts your hair or a waiter brings you a pizza, you're buying *services*. But remember that although the waiter who brings you that pizza is giving you a service, the pizza itself is a nondurable good. Note that, strictly speaking, C includes purchases of goods and services by households and nonprofit institutions that serve them. It also includes imputed expenditures on items such as the "services of housing by a homeowner (the equivalent of rent), financial and insurance services for which there is no explicit charge, and medical care provided to individuals and financed by government or by private insurance."

Gross Private Domestic Investment (I_g)
Capital creating activities that are private (nongovernmental) in a domestic economy.

Investment expenditure is really a simplified way of referring to **gross private domestic investment** (I_g). *Gross* means all investment output is counted, including investment that replaced depreciated and obsolete capital. *Private* means that only *non government* investment is counted. *Domestic* means that only investment made within the United States is counted. So, when General Motors builds a new plant for its Chevrolets in Michigan, this is included in investment because it represents output of U.S. resources. However, when GM builds an assembly plant in Mexico, it is not part of our GDP. It may be owned by a company based in the United States, but the employment generated and production capacity created directly benefit the Mexican economy, not the U.S. economy. *Investment* is the act of creating capital, manufactured producer goods that aid in the production of other goods and services.

Gross investment is divided into (1) fixed assets (such as equipment, tools, and machinery) and intellectual property products that contribute to production and have a useful life longer than on year, (2) business and residential construction, and (3) net changes in inventory. Remember that one subtracts beginning inventory from ending inventory to get the net change. The balance is part of investment.

Government Expenditures (G)
Purchases of goods and services by all levels of government.

Government expenditures (G) include only government purchases of goods and services. These are divided into three types: services, goods, and investment. *Services* include the salaries the government pays to its employees, such as soldiers and county agents. *Goods* are products used up in the operation of the government (paper, gasoline used in government cars, and so on). Government *investment*, like private investment, is the creation of physical things that aid in the production of goods and services and exist for at least one year (computers, school buildings, and so on). Of course, when we say government, we mean *all* levels of government: local, state, and federal. GDP measures only the output of the economy, and therefore, includes only those expenditures for goods and services (these are output of the economy) by the government. However, the government also spends money for things other than output that it buys, and these are not included in GDP for example people receive government transfer payments without an immediate obligation to do something in return. The secretary taking dictation in the Department of Commerce provides a service (labor) for a paycheck. The secretary's salary *is* included in GDP. The family on welfare does not give goods or services in return for its check, nor does the jobless worker who receives unemployment compensation, nor does the wheat farmer from Kansas who receives agricultural subsidy payments. These government expenditures, since they do not involve concurrent production of either goods or services, are not included in GDP.

However, several adjustments still have to be made. Imports are included in these expenditures, and since imports were produced outside the United States, we must subtract them from GDP. Also, the United States produces goods that are not included in our expenditures for   consumption, investment, and government; our exports. Exports, however, represent output of the U.S. economy, so we must add them to GDP. The plus exports and minus imports can be shortened to **net exports** (Xn). In other words, we subtract imports from exports. If exports are larger, net exports are positive; and if imports are larger, net exports are negative. For example, the United States imports Toyota Corollas from Japan. They are part of our consumption, because Americans buy them. But the Corollas are not part of our output. Therefore, they must be subtracted from our GDP. On the other hand, we export wheat to Japan. It is not part of our consumption, because we do not consume it, the Japanese do. But it *is* part of our output and must be added to our GDP. In other words, we subtract the imports (Toyota Corollas) and add the exports (wheat sold to Japan).

Table 5-2 contains a breakdown of the GDP for 2015. The formula for GDP is thus:

$$GDP = C + I_g + G + Xn.$$

Net Exports (X_n)

The difference for an economy between its exports and its imports. Net exports are positive when exports > imports, negative when exports < imports.

Table 5-2

The Expenditure Approach: Gross Domestic Product (GDP) for 2015 (billions of current dollars)

Personal consumption expenditures (C)	12,271.9
Gross private domestic investment (Ig)	3,020.6
Government expenditures (G)	3,183.4
Net exports of goods and services	-528.9
Gross domestic product (GDP=C+Ig+G+Xn)	17,947

Source: Bureau of Economic Analysis

Gross Domestic Income (GDI)

Gross domestic income measures the total income (and costs incurred) at market prices generated in the production of all final goods and services during a given period, in a given economy. The term *at market prices* simply indicates that we compute the measure at the market level for goods and services and that this measure must cover all costs incurred through that market. You can keep this straight if you remember that GDP shows total output, while GDI shows how the income generated by that output is distributed. The two are conceptually equal since spending and income are two sides of the same coin as we noted in our discussion of the circular model of income in Chapter 4.

Table 5-3

The Income Approach: Gross Domestic Income (GDI) for 2015 (billions of dollars)

Compensation of employees (wages, salaries, and supplements paid) (W)	9,667
Plus: Proprietors' income and corporate profits with inventory valuation and capital consumption adjustments (P)	3,397
Plus: Net interest and miscellaneous payments on assets (INT)	524
Plus: Rental income of persons with capital consumption adjustment (R)	657
Equals: Net national factor income	14,244
Plus: Consumption of fixed capital or "depreciation" (D)*	2,821
Plus: Taxes on production and imports less subsidies (IBTX)*	1,177
Minus: Misellaneous items **	89
Equals: GDI	18,154
Minus: Statistical discrepency (SD)	207
Equals: Adjusted GDI (=GDP)	17,947

* A nonincome expense/charge item
** Include current surplus of government enterprises and net current business transfer payments.
Source: Bureau of Economic analysis

Compensation of employees (W) All income payments to labor (wages and salaries and their supplements)

Interest (INT) The income payments to owners of capital

Rent (R) The income payments to owners of land.

Profit (P) The payments to entrepreneurship in incorporated and unincorporated firms.

Table 5-3 shows the estimates of GDI and its components in 2015. The first four components are forms of incomes earned by factors of production (labor, capital, land, and entrepreneurship) in the process of producing GDP. All income payments to labor is referred to as **compensation of employees** (W). It includes wages and salaries and but also supplements such as employer contributions for employee pension, insurance funds, and government social insurances. **Interest** (INT) is the income paid to owners of financial capital. Only interest paid by private business is included; the interest on government debt and on consumer debt is not. **Rent** (R) is the income payments to owners of land; this figure includes an estimated rent for homes occupied by their owners. **Profit** (P) is the payment to entrepreneurship for the function of organizing and taking the risks of business. It consists of the profits of owner-operated (unincorporated) businesses or "proprietor's income" and corporate profits.

Capital Consumption Allowance, or Depreciation (D): **A** measure of the wearing out of capital through use or obsolescence.

Indirect Business Taxes (IBTX): Taxes on goods and services that are passed on to consumers.

Besides the four income items listed for GDI in Table 5-3, there are two costs that must be covered by the final value of the product, but cannot be apportioned to the factors of production. **Capital consumption allowance**, or **depreciation** (D), is a legitimate expense, since it measures the wearing out of capital each year, either through use or obsolescence. The other non-income cost in **indirect business taxes** (IBTX), or taxes on goods and services that are passed on the consumer. Two main forms of these are excise and sales taxes. The firm pays excise taxes (for example, cigarette and liquor taxes) and passes them on to the consumer in the form of higher prices. These taxes are covered by the final value and must be listed separately in gross domestic income.

As noted before, in principle GDP and GDI should be roughly equal for they are both measures of the size of the economy. However, since the sources of data for GDP and GDI are different, the estimated values of these two measure often diverge. The item termed statistical discrepancy (SD) is, therefore, used to reconcile the difference between the two estimated values. SD reflects errors, for example, in measurement recording and reporting of the components of GDI.

Changes in U.S. Income Accounting: From GNP to GDP

System of National Accounts (SNA) A system of measuring national income and product that is standardized across nations.

For many years, the United States used a system of income accounting different from that of most other nations. Gross National Product was the focal measure of overall economic activity in this country. Most other nations, however, had shifted to a **System of National Accounts (SNA)** devised by the United Nations, and intended, in part, to standardize such measures across a vast range of economies. The range is from those with extensive central planning and government ownership of resources to market economies with an emphasis on market allocations of resources and private ownership.

In 1991, the United States began shifting to the SNA framework. As a result, changes have occurred in the reporting and measuring of national income and product. The most important such change is to move away from the use of GNP as the primary measure of U.S. economic output. The new measure, instead, is GDP.

Gross Domestic Product Contrasted with Gross National Product

Although we have, as a nation, moved largely to use of GDP data, GNP continues to be useful for some purposes. Thus, it is useful to explain briefly differences between the two concepts. Gross National Product (GNP) is a measure of the current value of output from the use of factors of production owned by a country's residents. Even if production occurs outside the borders of the U.S., it is included in our GNP as long as the output occurs from the use of U.S. owned resources. As we have seen, Gross Domestic Product (GDP), on the other hand, is a measure of the value of output that occurs *within* a nation's borders. The GDP of the U.S., thus, is a measure of economic activity occurring in this country, regardless of who owns the domestic resources that give rise to the output. Since part of U.S. output is from foreign-owned resources, GDP includes income payments to foreigners, but does not include payments to U.S. residents from abroad. GDP, thus, is conceptually different from GNP.

Table 5-4

Gross Domestic Product (GDP) and Gross National Product (GNP) for 2015 (billions of dollars)

Gross domestic product (GDP)	17,947
Plus: Income receipts from the rest of the world	830.5
Minus: Income payments to the rest of the world	616.9
Equals: Gross national product (GNP=GDP + net factor income from abroad)	**18,160.6**

Source: Bureau of Economic Analysis

The difference thus between gross domestic and gross national product or income is the net difference between receipts and payments of factor income from or to the rest of the world. As can be inferred from Table 5-4, this difference, called net factor income from abroad, was approximately 213.6=830.5-619.9 billion dollars in 2015.

Which is More Helpful: GDP or GNP?

As noted above, GNP includes net incomes earned by U.S. owned resources worldwide. Given the fast pace of globalization, a measure like GNP that emphasizes ownership of factors of production and de-emphasizes geography is more helpful than GDP in representing the economy's income. This is especially true in countries the net factor income from abroad is substantial.

Current, Constant, and Per Capita Real GDP

Back in the 1960s a Republican Senator (Barry Goldwater) and a Democratic Secretary of Labor (Arthur Goldberg), debated on educational TV with each using extensive statistics concerning the national economic accounts. With these statistics, each of the speakers proved that the only time Americans were well off was when his own party was in power. Who was lying, the statistics or the statisticians? In a sense, neither, because the debaters were using different measures, sometimes including, sometimes excluding the effects of prices on GDP. It would have been "fairer" if they had made clear to the onlookers what measures they were using. When statistics are being bandied about, much skepticism is needed, especially concerning whether prices are or are not included. As Disraeli said, "There are three kinds of lies: lies, damn lies, and statistics." With our new emphasis on GDP, let's see what the differences are between nominal or money GDP, and real or constant GDP.

Money (Current) GDP
The value of final goods and services produced expressed in the prices of the period in which they are produced.

Gross domestic product may change because of changes in (1) prices and (2) level of real output. But only the changes in real output (that is, in number of products produced) affect material well-being. To obtain GDP data for comparative purposes, therefore, you need to do away with price changes. Here's how you do it:

Statistics on GDP before the data are adjusted for price changes are called **money** or **current GDP**, which is the output of a given year valued in the prices of that year. (In 1940 you could buy a brand-new Oldsmobile for less than $1,000. But at that time many people were paid only $25 a week, and the best hamburger was 25 cents a pound.)

Real (Constant) GDP
The value of final goods and services produced expressed in terms of a base year's prices.

Real or **constant GDP** is the output of a given year adjusted for price changes. Converting money to real GDP involves the use of a particular price index called the implicit GDP deflator. The latter may be thought of as an indicator of the general price level in the economy.

There are various kinds of price indexes, depending on what you're measuring. Two well-known indexes are (1) the *consumer price index*, compiled and published by the Bureau of Labor Statistics, which measures price changes for a certain market basket of goods purchased by a family of four in an urban area, and (2) the *wholesale price index*, or now often called the producer price index, which measures changes in wholesale prices. In addition, the national income division of the Commerce Department has developed an index called (3) the *general price index* (or more formally the *GDP implicit price deflator*), by which you can convert current to constant GDP.

Now let's see how this works. Pick a specific year as the base year, and assign the value 100 to the price level in it; then compare the prices that prevailed in all other years to the prices that prevailed during the base year. Let's say that in year 2, prices increased by 20 percent over the base year, so, the price index for year 2 is 120. Let's say that in year 3, prices were 10 percent lower on the average than prices in the base year. Then the price index for year 3 is 90.

To convert nominal GDP to real GDP for year t, we use the following formula:

$$(RealGDP)_t = (NominalGDP)_t \times \frac{(\text{Price Index})_{base}}{(\text{Price Index})_t}$$

Note that the value of the price index in the base year is conventionally set at 100. To understand the logic of this formula, suppose that in year t the price index is less than 100. In this case, the nominal GDP is inflated (as it is multiplied by the ratio of the price indexes which is greater than one) to give us real GDP. Now suppose that in year t the price index is above 100. In this case, the nominal GDP is deflated (as it is multiplied by the ratio of the price indexes which is less than one) to give us real GDP. Thus, real GDP in year t can be greater or smaller than the corresponding nominal GDP depending on how the price index in year t compares with the base year price index. Only when year t and the base year are the same, nominal GDP is equal to real GDP (why?).

Table 5-5 shows the values of nominal GDP, the GDP price index, and real GDP in Columns 1, 3, and 5, respectively, for the period 2006-2015. With 2009 as the base year, the estimated value of real GDP in 2015, for example, was $16,348.9 = ($17,947.0)(100/109.8). It is important to keep in mind that real GDP provides a more accurate picture of changes in economic activity as it purges the effect of price changes relative to a fixed time period (the base year). For this reason, when prices are rising, the real GDP growth is lower than corresponding nominal GDP growth rate (see Columns 3 and 7). For example, in 2008 when the economy began to slow down, nominal GDP grew at a rate of 1.7 [= ($14,291.5-14,028.7) ÷ (14,028.7) X 100] percent while real GDP actually shrank by 0.3 percent. In 2009, when the full impact of the economic downturn hit the economy, the growth rate nominal GDP was -2.0 percent. This indicates a significant decline in the size of the economy. On an inflation adjusted (real) basis, however, the contraction was much worse as the economy's size fell by -2.8 percent!

Table 5-5
Nominal GDP, Price Level, and Real GDP (GDP in billions of dollars)

1	2	3	4	5	6	
Year	Nominal GDP	Percent change in nominal GDP	Price index (base year: 2009)	Percent change in price index	Real GDP	Percent change in real GDP
2006	13,855.9		94.8		14,613.8	
2007	14,477.6	4.5	97.3	2.7	14,873.7	1.8
2008	14,718.6	1.7	99.2	2.0	14,830.4	-0.3
2009	14,418.7	-2.0	100.0	0.8	14,418.7	-2.8
2010	14,964.4	3.8	101.2	1.2	14,783.8	2.5
2011	15,517.9	3.7	103.3	2.1	15,020.6	1.6
20012	16,155.3	4.1	105.2	1.8	15,354.6	2.2
2013	16,663.2	3.1	106.9	1.6	15,583.3	1.5
2014	17,348.1	4.1	108.7	1.6	15,961.7	2.4
2015	17,947.0	3.5	109.8	1.0	16,348.9	2.4

Source: Bureau of Economic Analysis

What explains these differences? The answer is the growth rate of the GDP price index or the overall inflation rate as shown in Column 3. One can think of real GDP growth rate as being approximately equal to portion of the nominal GDP growth rate which is not due to inflation. More formally,

$$\%\Delta \text{ (real GDP)} \approx \%\Delta \text{ (nominal GDP)} - \%\Delta \text{ (price level)}$$

Where %Δ denotes percent change or growth rate. Substituting the relevant growth rates for 2008 and 2009 from Table 5-5 in the above relationship, we get -0.3 ≈ 1.7-2.0 and -2.8 ≈ -2.0-0.8 as *approximate* real GDP growth rates for the two years, respectively. A major lesson that can be drawn is that when we have rising (falling) price level, the rate of growth of nominal GDP overstates (understates) the rate of growth of real GDP.

Output Excluded from GDP

The national economic accounts are *definitional* concepts. The people responsible for computing the accounts define what will be considered output, and, for various reasons, including the difficulty of computation, they do not include everything produced. By definition, they exclude the following kinds of output from the national income accounts.

1. *Services by homemakers*. If one had to buy these services on the market, children's nurses, house cleaner, cook, chauffeur, companion, the cost would be high. The services of a homemaker, for example, would cost hundreds of dollars per week if bought in market. National income accountants, though, exclude

these services when they are figuring the national income because homemakers don't get paid in money.

2. *Illegal goods and services*. These illegal activities involve production, supply, demand, and market prices. Economists exclude them, however, because it is impossible to estimate their monetary value. You can't ask the local pushers how much heroin or cocaine they sold last year, or the owners of gambling establishments what their takings were. (Imagine a president analyzing the way GDP had increased in the nation because drug sales had increased 10 percent.)

3. *Labor of children in the household*. If your daughter or son mows the lawn, it doesn't add to the GDP. But if he or she mows the *neighbor's* lawn and is paid $20.00, economists count it in (or at least attempt to).

4. *The labor in do-it-yourself projects*. When you buy wood and brackets to build bookshelves in your living room, economists include the materials you bought in GDP. But the labor it takes you to build them doesn't count.

5. *Volunteer help to nonprofit organizations*. For example, the Red Cross has a paid staff; their wages *are* counted. But if you donate your services, even though you work very hard for long hours, this volunteer help isn't counted in the GDP.

Economic Transactions Excluded from GDP

Just as economists exclude certain types of production, they also exclude the following types of economic transactions:

1. *The buying and selling of intermediate products*. This is excluded because intermediate products are included in the final value of the products. This exclusion prevents counting them twice.

2. *The buying and selling of used items* such as cars and homes. This is excluded because the production of these items took place and was included in a prior time period. Their resale now constitutes only a change in ownership, not an increase in production of goods and services.

3. *The buying and selling of financial securities such as bonds and stocks*. This is excluded because production has not taken place, only the transfer of ownership of debt (though the value of the services involved in the transfers are counted).

Other Components of the National Income and Product Accounts (NIPAs)

In this section, we introduce a number of other measures that are reported by national income and product accountants. These estimated values of these measures for 2015 are shown in Table 5-6.

Net National Product (NNP)

GNP includes depreciation or the amount of capital used up in producing output. Because economists find it useful to have a measure of output that does not include this depreciation, so that they can measure only net additions to total production, they use the expenditure approach to compute **net national product**, which is the net dollar value of all final goods and services produced during a given period. We speak of GNP as being; "total value," indicating that depreciation is included, while we speak of NNP as being "net value," indicating that depreciation is *not* included.

Your car is not considered an investment, but part of consumption. (A salesperson's car would be an investment.) However, to give you an understanding of what is meant by depreciation, let us think about your car as an investment. After your new car is one year old, it is less valuable than when it was new. Its value has gone down for the following reasons: (1) It has been driven, and there is only just so much mileage one can get out of the car. Let us say that you can get 100,000 miles of driving out of the car. If you drove 20,000 miles the first year, the car is one-fifth used up. (2) The car is no longer new, styles have changed, and, most important, manufacturers have made improvements in cars since this one was made. This aspect of depreciation is called *obsolescence*.

Just as a car, a consumer durable, decreases in value over time, investment goods, the capital people produce to aid in production, such as machines and factory buildings, depreciate by being used up and becoming obsolete, unless they have the most up-to-date improvements. One can say that depreciation is excluded in calculating the net national product because to count the value of capital used up in the process of current production would be to count something made in previous income periods.

Table 5-6

Other Components of the National Income and Product Accounts (NIPAs) for 2015 (billions of dollars)

Gross national product (GNP)	18,160.6
Minus: Consumption of fixed capital or "depreciation" (D)	2,821.3
Equals: Net National Product (NNP)*	15,339.3
Minus: Statistical discrepancy (SD)	-207.0
Equals: National income (NI)	15,546.2
Minus: Indirect business taxes, net (IBTX)**	1,177.3
Minus: Corporate profits***	2,008.9
Minus: Contributions for government social insurance ("social security taxes")	1,204.0
Minus: Net interest and miscellaneous payments on assets	523.8
Minus: Business current transfer payments (net)	141.2
Minus: Other minor items	-16.5
Plus: Personal income receipts on assets (personal interest and dividend incomes)	2,180.5
Plus: Personal current transfer receipts from government and businesses	2,662.7
Equals: Personal income (PI)	15,350.7
Minus: Personal current taxes	1,947.4
Equals: Disposable personal income (DPI)	13,403.2
Minus: Personal consumption expenditures (C)	12,271.9
Minus: Personal interest payments	268.5
Minus: Personal current transfer payments	177.1
Equals: Personal saving (S)	685.7

* Similarly, net domestic product or NDP=GDP-D=C+In+G+Xn = 13,138.9

** IBTX is conventionally subtracted from NNP. However, following the Bureau of Economic Analysis practice, we subtract it from NI.

*** Net of inventory valuation and capital consumption adjustments

Source: Bureau of Economic Analysis

Note:
When gross investment exceeds depreciation, net investment is *positive*.

Note:
When gross investment is less than depreciation, net investment is *negative*.

In the definition of NNP, net private domestic investment (In) replaces gross private domestic investment (Ig). The difference between gross and net is measured by the amount of depreciation, or capital consumption allowance (D). More formally,

$$Ig=In + D \text{ and } GNP - NNP = Ig - In = D.$$

(Note that the same applies to the domestic counterparts of these concepts : GDP-NDP= Ig-In=D).

The distinction between gross and net investment is important, because net investment measures only the additions to the capital stock of the economy. If the value of gross investment is greater than depreciation, then more capital is being created than is being lost through depreciation. Net investment is then *positive*, and the economy generally expands because its stock of capital is expanding. Depreciation may be greater than the value of gross investment. If so, net investment is *negative*. In this case, the stock of capital is contracting because more capital is being lost than is currently produced. Capital stock, and thus the ability of the economy to produce, is contracting. This situation of a negative net investment has occurred during severe depressions (1929-1933) and during wars (World Wars I and II) when the need to produce war goods was greater than the need to produce investment. During the years 1917-1918, while the United States was fighting in World War I, total real output declined because the United States was at full employment when it entered the war. But during World War II, in 1942, 1943, and 1944, real output increased substantially (despite a negative net investment) because of the large amounts of unemployed labor and unused plant capacity remaining from the depression of the 1930s, and because employers used both labor and plants more intensively through the device of overtime.

National Income (NI)

National Income (NI)
For an economy, the net income at factor prices generated in the production of all final goods and services.

The third major measure of the value of economic output is **national income**, which is a measure of income generated only by the factors of production (labor, land, capital, and entrepreneurship). National income is net income at factor prices generated in the production of all final goods and services in a given time period. As before, *net income* means that depreciation is not included. *At factor prices* means prices obtained in the factor market for the factors of production, and therefore we are excluding indirect business taxes (IBTX), which are paid as a part of market prices. For example, an excise tax is levied on cigarettes by the federal government and is collected not at the retail level, as with a sales tax, but at the manufacturing level. The market value for cigarettes for inclusion in GDP and NNP includes the excise tax. The income generated by the production of cigarettes at the factor market does not include excise tax.

Personal Income (PI)

Personal Income (PI)
For an economy, all incomes received by individuals in the production of final goods and services as well as from transfer payments.

Our fourth measure of a nation's economic performance is **personal income**. Personal income consists of all income received by *individuals*, whether from production or by transfer payments. It is computed by deducting from national income those income flows that do not accrue to individuals, as distinct from corporations and governments, and by adding those income flows to people that are not included in national income.

First, to compute personal income, subtract that part of national income that does not accrue to persons. Corporate profits consist of corporate taxes, the savings of corporations or retained earnings, and dividends. Dividends are distributed to the stockholders (persons) and are retained in Personal income. Corporate taxes and retained earnings (undistributed corporate profits) are not income to persons and are subtracted from national income. Social security taxes are included in wages and salaries. These are transfer payments to the government and must also be subtracted from national income to derive personal income

Second, add income persons receive that is not included in national income. These are personal interest income and personal dividend income. Transfer payments *from* the government include such things as unemployment compensation, welfare payments, social security payments, and interest on government debt. Although interest on government debt is not really a transfer payment, since it is a payment for the use of borrowed funds, we included it here by definition. Also included as an addition to personal income are business transfer payments to persons. (Remember that the accounts are definitional concepts, depending for their definition on ·the decisions of the authority responsible for computing the accounts.)

Disposable Personal Income (DPI)

Disposable Personal Income (DPI) For an economy, those personal incomes over which individuals have control as to their uses.

The fifth and last measure of economic performance is personal **disposable Personal income**. This is the portion of people's incomes that they have control over; that is, they can control where and how this portion is spent. People do not have control over the part of their income paid to the government in taxes, such as personal taxes and property taxes. So *disposable* personal income is personal income less personal taxes. One can also look at disposable personal income from the point of view of how people apportion it. They can either spend it (consumption), save it (personal saving), or use it to pay interest on consumption loans. Disposable personal income is an important measure in the national economic accounts. It is, in effect, the measure of purchasing power of the consuming public. Changes in DPI result in changes in total consumer demand. Government economic policy must keep a close eye on this measure. How would tax changes affect it? How would changes in government expenditures affect it? The federal government made tax cuts for the 1974 and 1975 tax years precisely for the purpose of increasing personal disposable personal income to stimulate consumer demand.

Final-Value and Value-Added Methods

Final-Value Method A method of computing the GDP in which only the prices of goods sold to final users are added.

We have been defining the various national accounts and what goes to make them up. But how does one compute the values for domestic product? By two methods: the final-value method and the value-added method.

1. *The **final-value** method*. The sum of prices to the ultimate users of goods and services produced. These final values include all values added at substages of production. To avoid double counting, one does not list intermediate products.

Value-Added Method A method of computing the GDP in which the values added at each stage of production are summed.

2. *The **value-added** method*. Commodities go through many stages of production. As an unfinished product moves from one firm to another, it is changed in form or location or is stored. Each of these functions adds value. The sum of these additions to value equals the final value of the product.

Let us examine Table 5-7 where we have used a desk as an example. *Stage 1*: Lumbermen cut down a tree and transport it to the sawmill. By the time the tree arrives at the sawmill, it is worth more than when it stood in the forest. Value has been added to it, say, $2.50, because of the expenditure of labor, land, capital, and entrepreneurship. *Stage 2*: The sawmill cuts the tree into lumber. Again, value is added, say $2.00, and again it is equal to the cost of the factors of production used at that stage. At each succeeding stage (the furniture factory and the retailer) the expenditure of resources means that value is being added. The furniture factory takes $4.50 worth of materials, applies resources, and sells the resulting product for $10.00. Value added was $5.50. The values added at each stage are equal to the final value, or the price to the ultimate user ($20.00).

Table 5-7

Stages of Production of a Desk

Stages	Value of Product Sold	Value Added
1. Lumbering	$2.50	$2.50
2. Sawmill	4.50	2.00
3. Furniture factory	10.00	5.50
4. Retailer (the final value)	20.00	10.00
Final value		$20.00

Note: The value added does not include values from prior stages. When one adds all of the values at each stage, the total equals the final value.

Table 5-8 shows how this value-added method of computation works. The left-hand side shows how the income produced by the added value was distributed during production by the furniture factory, Atlas Furniture Company. Labor (one factor of production) received wages plus social security taxes, or $865,000. Land ownership received rent, or $250,000. Corporate profits earned were $150,000. However, the factors of production are not the only contributors to value added. Depreciation and business taxes also contribute, $300,000 and $150,000 respectively, because the company has to count these costs into the expense of making furniture.

Table 5-8

The Atlas Furniture Company, Statement of Value Added

Income Generated by Value Added		Sources of Value Added	
Wages	$850,000	Net sales to U.S. government	$600,000
Social security taxes	15,000	To Smith Company	600,000
Rent	250,000	To Jones Company	800,000
Interest	200,000	To business firms	400,000
Depreciation	300,000	To exports	250,000
Taxes other than corporate income taxes	150,000	Inventory increase or decrease	
Corporate profits	150,000	Inventory decreased	−100,000
Income generated by value added	$1,915,000	Value of production	$2,550,000
		Cost of raw material	−635,000
		Value added	$1,915,000

Because ending inventory was less than beginning inventory, the total production figure must be reduced by that difference (-$100,000). Last, and most important, not all the value was created at this stage of production (the fashioning of wood into furniture). The raw materials bought by the firm acquired their value at prior stages of production. Value added, according to both the final-value method and the value-added method, was thus $1,915,000. The British (and several other European countries) use *value-added taxes* to raise tax money although the tax rates vary from one nation to another. The British call it the VAT. The French have a similar tax, which they call a *turnover tax*. Thus far the United States does not have a value-added tax, although a proposal to enact one has been discussed in Congress in recent years.

Application I: Does GDP Growth Measure Improving Human Well-being?

In the years 2007 through 2011, as we have seen, America has experienced recessions or periods of slow GDP growth together with continued higher rates of unemployment and underemployment. It is probable that most Americans regard faster GDP growth as not only desirable but necessary to reduce the countries unemployment rate.

There is a temptation to view the various measures of national income as measures also of material well-being. Many people, economists among them, view increases in per capita real GDP as evidence for widespread improvement in people's well being. Until a few years ago, most people went along with this idea. But since then, we are less certain of the relationship between income growth and human welfare. You may well ask, "Am I *really* better off as GDP increases?" If the nation increases the annual output of cars and flat screen television sets, will we all be happier for it?

Setting aside the problem of measuring human happiness, the attack on the use of GDP growth as a measure of human well-being is threefold. First, since GDP doesn't include *all* output and costs, it is not as accurate a measure of output contributing to well-being as we would like. Second, there is a large amount of counted output that may not contribute to material well-being, and may even detract from it. Third, the very process of increasing GDP may possibly decrease well-being.

What GDP Does Not Include

As we have noted, not all output is included in GDP. Remember that the labor of homemakers, illegal production, labor on do-it-yourself projects, labor by children in the household, and volunteer labor are all excluded from GDP. But when comparing the *change* in output from one year to the next, one tends to think that these exclusions don't really matter or that these exclusions don't vary.

The women's liberation movement has long argued for concrete recognition of work in the home by placing dollar values on household chores. However, the amount of housework as a percentage of GDP does not *change* much from one year to the next.

As for illegal production, such as gambling (where illegal), prostitution and dope peddling, who is going to convince anybody that this sort of thing adds to the well-being of the public or that the level of it changes from one year to the next?

As for the other excluded items, do-it-yourself work, children's work in the household, and volunteer work, no one can measure them accurately enough to give us statistics, so they are excluded in the measurement of GDP for very practical reasons.

Cost of Pollution

In addition, GDP statistics fail to take into account many costs outside the realm of the marketplace itself, such as pollution. The air, the rivers, the oceans, and the land can be, in many circumstances, free dumping grounds for the wastes that are by-products of the production and consumption of goods. This pollution, however, does cost society something, because pollution affects the aesthetic quality of the environment, causes physical discomfort, threatens health, disrupts the food chain, and unbalances the atmosphere.

The cost of all this pollution is not borne by either the producers or consumers of the products that create the pollution, but by those who are hurt by it. Since this kind of cost is not reflected in GDP or in the cost of specific products, we cannot make completely informed choices in the marketplace about what to produce and how much to produce. If the costs of pollution were reflected in the price of the products we buy, the composition of our output would probably be quite different from what it is now. This in spite of efforts to include the effects. Ongoing efforts to incorporate these costs into the price of production may lead to significant future changes in the composition of output.

The problems of estimating the costs of pollution are hard to overcome. It would be much like subtracting depreciation from gross investment to get net investment. After one had subtracted the external costs from the final value, one would have "net economic product," a phrase coined by Nobel Laureate Paul Samuelson.

If you measured the net economic value of production in these terms, some products would add less to the country's well-being than their value. In fact, some kinds of output might even detract from the country's well-being. How much do people benefit from the output of a chemical plant in Cincinnati after you deduct the destructive effects of the millions of gallons of waste the plant pours annually into the Ohio River? What is the contribution to public well-being of a new car after you deduct the car's pollution of the air with hydrocarbons and carbon monoxide?

What Does Contribute to Well-being?

One can also attack GDP as a measure of well-being by challenging the contributions to social welfare of some parts of output that are included in GDP figures. Does the flood of advertising to which we are all exposed make us healthier, happier, or wiser? We don't have space here to go into the pros and cons of advertising. There seems little doubt, however, that some of the resources spent on advertising are wasted, as far as material improvement is concerned. Advertising that does not give information on which to base an economic decision or that actually gives wrong information is not a benefit to consumers.

And then there are defense expenditures. While such expenditures do add to security, or the protection of our lives and property, there is an optimal outlay on this as well as other activities. We may sometimes exceed this level. For example, do expenditures that make it possible for U.S. military forces to kill each human being on earth several times over increase security or well-being.

The forms of output that increase GDP but not human well-being, and certainly you can add more to the few mentioned here, use up resources of the economy that could have been used to produce other things that do add to material well-being. In other words, the opportunity costs of these "wasted" resources are the goods we could have produced by using the resources in other ways.

Is Further GDP Growth Desirable?

In an article written in the 1970s, Robert Heilbroner[2] seemed to take the view that continued growth would lead not so much to the exhaustion of the earth's natural resources as to the destruction of its environment. He said that the exponential curves of growth, human and industrial "would sooner or later overtake the finite capabilities of the biosphere," and bring about a terrible reduction in the quality of life. Heilbroner's recommended solution was public (government) control over family size and consumption habits and over the volume and composition of industrial and agricultural output.

There are probably few today, including few economists, who concur with this extreme or "doomsday" view. Our space here is too limited to permit us to survey the large amounts of literature on the economics of pollution. However, we do not believe that growth per se causes pollution. The problem lies in the signals by which production and consumption take place. We believe that industry can control pollution by various devices and incorporate the cost of controlling it into the market price of the products. How to eliminate pollution or even *how much* of it to eliminate (the question of opportunity cost enters in) are the questions. But it is highly probable that we *can* control pollution and still maintain growth. In fact, we need continued growth to be able to create the resources necessary to control pollution.

Measures of Economic Welfare: A Caveat

There is likely no measure of economic welfare that will not be highly controversial. Nonetheless, such attempts are not only interesting but useful. If nothing else they focus our effort to relate economic production and human well-being. A noted economist, Arthur Okun[3], once observed that caution is advisable in these regards. According to Okun:

> *I know you will not ignore the GNP[4]. I urge that you not try to "fix" it, to convert GNP into a purported measure of social welfare. You are doing your job so well that people are asking you to take on a different and bigger job. Resist at all costs, for you can't do that job; indeed, nobody can. Producing a summary measure of social welfare is a job for a philosopher-king, and there is no room for a philosopher-king in the federal government.*

---

2. In Passell, Peter and Leonard Ross, *The Retreat from Riches*. Viking. 1972

3. Okun, Arthur, "Should GDP Measure Social Welfare?" *Survey of Current Business*, July, 1971

4. Recall that GNP was the preferred measure of total national output before GDP.

SUMMING UP

1. The National Income and Product Accounts (NIPAs) provide measures of economic activity. They are definitional concepts, and in each country the economists who compute the accounts define what is to be included and what excluded.

2. The *expenditure approach* to economic accounts analyzes the kinds of output the economy produces. The *income approach* looks at the kinds of income generated in the process of producing the economy's output.

3. There are five main yardsticks used to measure national economic accounts. The first consists of *gross national product*, computed by the expenditure approach, and *gross domestic income*, computed by the income approach. The second is *net national product*, the third is *domestic income*, the fourth is *personal income*, and the fifth is *disposable personal income*.

4. In NIPAs, the word gross typically is used to mean including depreciation and net excluding it. Moreover, domestic emphasizes geography/location (regardless of ownership of factors of production) and national focuses on ownership (regardless of geography/location).

5. Economists use two methods, the *final-value method* and the *value-added method,* to compute the values of the gross domestic product. When they use the final-value method, they add all the prices paid by the ultimate consumers of all goods and services produced. When they use the value-added method (the second method), they first compute the value added at each stage of production, and second, total all the values added.

6. The U.S. is switching its reporting of national output to the System of National Accounts (SNA) devised by the United Nations. GNP is no longer the main measure of output. Rather, Gross Domestic Product (GDP) is now used. GDP measures the current value of output that occurs within a nation's borders. It includes income payments to foreigners but excludes payments to U.S. residents from abroad.

7. *Money* or *current GDP,* for a given year is GDP valued in the prices of that year. *Real* or *constant GDP* is the output of a given year adjusted for changes in prices. One computes real or constant GDP by dividing money GDP, by the *price index* and multiplying by 100. However, currently, the best single measure of comparative well-being is *per capita real GDP*, which one finds by dividing the real or constant GDP by the total population.

8. The following output is excluded from gross domestic product: (a) services by homemakers, (b) illegal goods and services, (c) labor of children in the household, (d) labor on do-it-yourself projects, and (e) volunteer help to non-profit organizations.

9. The following transactions are excluded from gross domestic product: (a) the buying and selling of intermediate products, (b) the buying and selling of used items, and (c) the buying and selling of financial securities.

KEY TERMS

Capital consumption allowances
Disposable personal income
Expenditure approach
Final value method
Government expenditures
Gross domestic income (GDI)
Gross domestic product (GDP)
Gross national product (GNP)
Gross private domestic investment
Income approach
Indirect business taxes
Interest
Money (current) GDP
National income
Net exports
Net factor income from abroad
Net national income
Net national product
Personal consumption expenditure
Personal income
Profits
Real (constant) GDP
Rent
System of National Accounts (SNA)
Value added method
Wages and salaries

QUESTIONS

1. Economists in the Soviet Union did not include services as output when they computed national income accounts. If you were creating an income accounting system, would you include services as part of the national income accounts?

2. From the following data for a hypothetical nation, compute:
    a. gross domestic product.
    b. net national product.
    c. national income.
    d. personal income.
    e. disposable personal income.

3. Gross domestic product must be equal to gross domestic income, and net national product must be equal to net national income. Why?

4. Of the two methods of computing the national economic accounts, the final-value method and the value-added method, which do you think is easier to use? Why?

5. If you were listening to a politician quote income statistics, what role would price changes play in helping you to understand the statistics?

	Billions of Dollars
Consumption	300
Gross private domestic investment	150
Government expenditures	200
Imports	35
Exports	30
Capital consumption allowances (depreciation)	50
Indirect business taxes	25
Social security taxes	20
Transfer payments from the government	35
Corporate taxes	20
Retained earnings	10
Personal taxes	100

6. What is the difference conceptually between GNP and GDP? What are the advantages of GDP as a measure of national output?

7. Compute the *real* GDP of a hypothetical nation from the following data:

Year	Money GDP	Price Index
1929	103.1	50.6
1940	99.7	43.9
1950	284.8	80.2
1960	503.7	103.3
1980	974.1	135.3
2000	1075.0	150.7

8. The national economic accounts are definitional concepts and do not include all output or economic transactions. What kinds of output and transactions are excluded from the national economic accounts? Why?

9. What is the basis for the argument that GDP measures fail to include many things that are part of human welfare?

10. Do GDP measurements correct for the social costs of environmental pollution?

11. Why are economists skeptical of the argument that continued GDP growth will lead to the exhaustion of non-reproducible resources?

12. How is the Nordhaus-Tobin calculation of *measured economic welfare* made? What is the fundamental problem with all such measures?

Chapter 6: Economic Fluctuations, Unemployment and Inflation

During its more than two centuries of existence, the United States has achieved an enviable record of economic growth as we noted in the introduction, the nation was probably never "poor," except for the earliest year if its colonial period. It has evolved from a small agricultural nation into the largest economy in the world. Today, its people enjoy one of the globe's highest standards of living.

This impressive record of growth by America's market economy has conveyed widespread benefits for almost all Americans in terms of real income and economic well-being. Nonetheless, the upward tide of growth has not been smooth. Throughout our history, there have been 13 sharp and sometimes lengthy periods of growing unemployment and declining real incomes. At other times, growth has been so rapid in nominal terms that it has been accompanied by the effects of large price increases or inflation.

This chapter will assay the causes of these deviations from the trend of rising real growth. The deviations from the smooth historical trend of 3 percent real growth per annum are called economic fluctuations or business cycles. We will examine not only the causes of these fluctuations but also look at what can be done to reduce or avoid the costs they impose upon this nation's people. In an extended application, we will look at how far we can push down unemployment without triggering the costs of inflation.

First, though, let's look at the characteristics of these fluctuations.

Fluctuations: Characteristics and Clues

Types of Economic Fluctuations
Economists identify four types of fluctuations in economic activity. We see these phases represented in Figure 6-1.

Figure 6-1
Phases or Fluctuations of Economic Activity

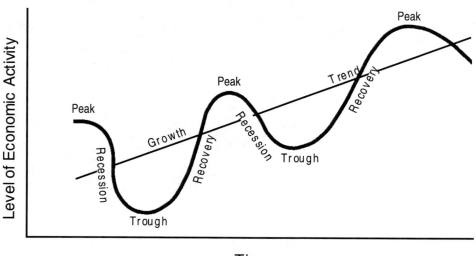

Economists distinguish four phases of economic activity: Peaks, Recessions, Troughs, and Recoveries. Although these phases are represented here as smooth deviations from the long-term upward trend of growth in economic activity, we must recognize that each phase is unique in its length, severity, amount of unemployment, and degree of inflation.

Secular Trend
The long-term expansion or contraction of an economy's business activities.

1. The **secular trend**, represented by the upward sloping growth trend line in Figure 6-1, represents the expansion of an economy over very long periods of time. These trends may occur over fifty to a hundred years. Within these long-run trends, shorter fluctuations occur. These are called business cycles.

Business Cycles (or fluctuations)
Recurring non-periodic fluctuations in economic and business activities.

2. **Business cycles (or fluctuations)** are recurring non-periodic fluctuations in economic and business activities. They happen over and over again, but not necessarily in any regular or periodic way, and take place over a period of six to eight years. These business cycles will be the main topic of this chapter. Within these business cycles, regular seasonal variations occur.

Seasonal Variations
Regular variations in economic activity that occur within a year.

3. **Seasonal variations** are fluctuations that occur regularly within each year. For example, employment in agriculture increases in the summer as harvest time approaches, and retail sales increase just before Christmas and Easter. To judge the significance of these seasonal increases or decreases in economic activity, you must compare them to the levels of activity at the same time in other years. In other words, to analyze various other influences on business activity, you must make allowances for seasonal activity and "filter out" the seasonal effects.

Random Variations
Irregular variations in
economic activity that
cannot be accounted or
planned for.

4. **Random variations** are irregular variations that one can't account or plan for, since they don't follow any regular pattern. Examples of random variations are the depressed agricultural output caused by the drought of 1936; the steel strike of 1959; and the stock market downturn when President Reagan was shot in 1981.

Phases of a Business Cycle

In the beginning of the **recession phase** of a business cycle, the level of economic activity begins to fall. (See Figure 6-1). Output and employment start to sag, and investment and consumption start to shrink. Inflation tends to creep downward. As the recession continues, unemployment may become high, investment and consumption low and sluggish. A great deal of plant capacity sits idle, and price drops may occur. Profits fall. By definition, a recession is a downturn that lasts at least six months.

Recession Phase
That downward part of the
business cycle in which
output and employment
fall for at least six months,
and inflation tends to
decrease.

In the **recovery phase**, unemployment begins to diminish and unused plant capacity begins to be put into operation again, while income, output, and consumption rise. At this stage, prices may stay relatively stable. As the recovery continues, the nation approaches full employment and full utilization of capacity. Investment and consumption rise, and because of high levels of demand, so do prices. Profits typically rise.

Recovery Phase
That upward part of the
business cycle in which
output and employment
rise and ultimately, as
capacity approaches,
prices tend to rise.

Do Business Cycles Follow a Regular Pattern?

The very word *cycles*, the concept of phases, and such as those in Figure 6-1 seem to imply regularity or uniformity. However, history shows that although business cycles do recur, there is little or no regularity or uniformity to them. Because of this lack of uniformity, many economists say that the terms *business fluctuation* or *economic instability* are more appropriate than *business cycle*.

Durable- Versus Nondurable-Goods Industries

Not only do the cycles differ from one to another, but also each cycle differs in the way it affects various kinds of economic activity. The biggest differences are those in price and output in industries that produce durable goods and industries that produce nondurable goods. Over the whole cycle, in the durable-goods industries, output varies widely. Prices vary much less. In the nondurable-goods industries, prices vary, but output tends to be more stable.

www.nber.org
For more information on
business cycles visit this
web site.

In the durable-goods industries (heavy equipment and machines, major appliances), the main effect of declining demand during the recession and depression phases is reduced output and employment. In the nondurable-goods industries (food, clothing, furniture), the main impact of declining demand is on prices. To learn why this variation occurs, let's think about the differences between durable and nondurable goods, and the differences between these industries in the nature of competition.

1. People can postpone buying new durable goods for a long time. When times are bad, the consumer repairs the old car or washing machine rather than buying a new one. A manufacturer faced with falling demand and dwindling profits repairs the machines on hand rather than buying new ones. And, with plenty of idle plant space, the manufacturer sees no point in building a new plant or a new wing on the old one.

2. Industries that make consumer and producer durables (cars, steel, electrical equipment) tend to be more concentrated industries, with just a few large companies and less competition than in other industries. Various forms of monopoly power are manifest, so the big firms tend to protect their prices. Unless faced

with intense international competition, they sometimes react to decreases in demand by cutting back on the quantity they produce.

During a recession, when decreased consumer buying is combined with decreased production by the large durable-goods companies, supply decreases. Prices may also go down, but at a slow rate. In the recession of 1958 and the ones in 1969 and 1970, prices rose rather than fell. The likely reason is that the concentrated durable-goods industries prevented their own prices from falling.

3. People can't easily postpone buying nondurable goods (food, clothing, furniture) because there is a recession. Thus the demand for the output of these industries is more stable. But it still falls off in a recession.

4. In the nondurable-goods industries, there are many small companies and more competition. These firms can't stabilize prices by cutting supply because they lack power. Their prices, thus, fluctuate more with the business cycle.

Some Causes of Economic Fluctuations: A Preliminary Look
Many economists have advanced theories about the causes of the irregular fluctuations in economic activity that have occurred throughout our history. We will devote much of the chapters that follow to these theories. As an introduction, however, it is useful to summarize some of the more important arguments:

1. *Innovations.* Some economists have focused on the role of innovations (new products, new technologies, new supplies of resources, new markets, and the like) in economic growth and development. A famous economist at Harvard, Joseph Schumpeter, is especially associated with this line of thought. Though innovations ultimately result in rising productivity and economic growth (a movement upward along the growth trend line in Figure 6-1), they occur irregularly and in "swarms." Throughout our history, major innovations such as the railroad, the automobile, and micro-chips and processors have caused bursts of economic activity pushing the economy to a new peak. But as their effects ultimately diminish, firms fail and a recession moves the economy toward a new trough. Thus, the theory suggests that fluctuations are an inherent part of the dynamic of economic progress in a market economy.

2. *Political and Random Events.* Many peaks and troughs in American history have been associated with political events, especially wars. The Civil War, World Wars I and II, and the Vietnam War are all examples of this association. Some wars have been associated with severe inflation or with wage and price controls and with inflation that followed their removal. Some economists believe there is a "political business cycle" in the sense that government expenditures may be timed to maximize re-election prospects of incumbent politicians and thus timed irregularly to produce or at least accentuate peaks and troughs. Still others believe that government monetary policy and its irregularities are largely responsible for economic fluctuations.

3. *Aggregate Demand.* Many economists believe that, at least in the short term, the most important influence on the level of economic activity in a market economy is aggregate spending. Firms produce goods and services in order to obtain profit. We presume that they produce what is expected to be the most profitable amounts of these goods. When aggregate demand or expenditure is low, firms produce less and employ fewer resources, including labor. In reverse, when aggregate spending increases, firms find it profitable to employ more resources

and hire more labor. As we will see in this and in upcoming chapters what happens to overall prices is also related to aggregate spending. If, beyond some point, spending rises and little or no additional output can be produced, because output is at or near capacity, prices rise sharply and inflation will result.

4. Constancy of government policy. Nobel-prize research has led to the conclusion by many economists that the lack of constancy in government policy (especially monetary policy) and failure to commit to rules rather than short-run variations in policies has led to failures of the economy to respond in the desired ways to those policies! This has contributed to "boom and bust" periods[1].

Leading Economic Indicators

As we have seen, the general level of economic activity moves with the business cycle. However, there are exceptions. In 1974, for example, real GDP fell by about 5 percent. Inflation increased at a two-digit rate and business profits in some industries were high, yet unemployment increased. In the recession phase, the general level of activity goes down. With the recovery phase, it goes up. Changes in output and price vary in degree as well as timing in different kinds of activity. Some measures of economic activity, called **leading indicators**, lead the business cycle by decreasing or increasing before the rest do. They are, thus, commonly used as tools for forecasting changes in economic activity.

A frequently employed measure is the Conference Board Leading Economic Index (LEI) which is a composite, or weighted average index, of several indicators. The components of LEI change from time to time. The most recent list includes the following ten indicators:

1. *Average weekly hours, (manufacturing.* Employers usually adjust work hours before adjusting the size of their workforce. So, if the average number of hours worked per week by production workers falls, policymakers expect future reductions in GDP and employment by manufacturing firms.

2. *Average weekly jobless claims for unemployment insurance.* The number of first time claims filed is typically more sensitive to changes in overall business conditions than total (un)employment. Consequently, a rise in this number signals future reductions in jobs and GDP.

3. *Manufacturers' new orders for consumer goods and materials.* If manufacturing firms receive fewer new orders for goods primarily used by consumers, then the actual production is expected to fall as unfilled orders decline and inventories build up. Thus, GDP and employment level are expected to subsequently decline.

4. *The Institute of Supply Management (ISM) New Order Index.* This index reflects the number of increased orders compared with the number of decreased orders reported by participants in the ISM monthly survey. An index value below 50 indicates that orders have declined on a net basis during the previous month. This tends to lead a contraction in future investment and GDP.

---

1. "American, Norwegian Win Nobel" The Wall Street Journal. October 12, 2004

5. *Manufacturers' new orders (nondefense capital goods excluding aircraft orders)*. This indicator may be considered as the producers' counterpart to number 3 above.

6. *Building permits (new private housing units)*. Home building is a major form of investment and the construction industry is a bell weather of the economy. A significant decline in the number of permits to build new houses portends a likely fall in GDP

7. *Stock market prices (Standards and Poor's 500 stock index)*. Falling prices of a broad selection of common stocks reflect deterioration in the general investors' sentiments and several associated changes such as expected falling profits, reductions in consumers' wealth, and less attractive opportunities to issue new stock. A sharp decline in the S&P 500 index, therefore, may lead a fall in GDP.

8. *Leading credit Index (LCI)*. This is a composite of six financial indicators that tracks financial conditions (basically, the availability and cost of credit and the willingness of economic actors to borrow and lend) of the economy. Deterioration in financial conditions signals an economic downturn. (It should be noted that LCI has recently replaced a measure of the real stock of money in circulation- known as M2- due to unsatisfactory performance of the latter).

9. *Interest rate spread*. This spread is defined as the difference between the interest rate on the 10-year Treasury bonds (a measure of long-term interest rate) and the federal funds (a short-term interest rate charged on interbank loans). Under normal circumstances, the spread is positive as long-term lending is associated with a higher return than the short-term one. However, a negative assessment of future economic conditions by bond investors may narrow the spread or even make it negative (this is known as the "inversion" of the rate spread) signaling a recession.

10. *Average consumer expectations for economic and business conditions index*. This indicator is a simple average of consumer expectations about economic conditions 12-month ahead (based on the University of Michigan's survey) and consumer expectations for business conditions 6-month ahead (based on the Conference Board's survey). A sharp fall in this index indicates erosion in consumer confidence, a likely future decline in consumer spending and, ultimately, a contraction in GDP.

We have discussed each of these indicators as predictors of recession. The direction of prediction can exactly be reversed to see how each might contribute to a prediction of recovery. Each of the ten indicators is assigned a weight which may change with the changing structural characteristics of the economy. It is important to note that it is the *composite* or *weighted average* index that is the forecasting indicator rather than any individual component. As a rule of thumb, when the index moves in a particular direction for three consecutive months, the economy tends to soon turn in that same direction.

The index, however, is not infallible. While its movements have correctly forecast several recessions, as well as recoveries, it has also incorrectly forecast both on occasion. (For example, between 1959 and 2012 changes in LEI predicted ten recessions eight of which actually materialized). As a macroeconomic policy tool, it is useful only when its forecasts are correct and timed such that policy adjustments can be put into effect. On a few occasions, the LEI has forecast recessions that occurred so quickly thereafter that policy adjustments could not be made in time to mitigate the effects of the recession.

Nonetheless, the LEI is a useful tool in forecasting cyclical downturns and upturns. It is useful not only to the executive and legislative agencies of the government but also to private firms and research institutes. A major reason for making such forecasts is because of the effects of cyclical changes in economic activity on the level of employment and unemployment. In the next section we will examine the various concepts and definitions of employment and unemployment.

Unemployment

Unemployment is one of the by-products of variations in the level and composition of economic activity (as measured by GDP) and changes in technology. As an indicator of labor force underutilization, the unemployment rate is widely publicized and discussed. How is the **unemployment rate** measured? The Bureau of Labor Statistics (BLS) of the U.S. Department of Labor publishes an estimate of the U.S. unemployment rate using information from a monthly sample survey called Current Population Survey (CPS). The sample is selected so as to be representative of the country's entire population. It includes about 60,000 households (approximately 110,000 individuals) and covers 2,025 geographic areas. Since the sample size is quite large, the margin of error in estimating the national unemployment is relatively small (with a 90 percent probability, a sample based estimate is within about 290,000 of the figure resulting from a national census). About a quarter of the households in the sample are changed every month so that no household is interviewed four months in a row.

The BLS employees ask sample members a series of questions during their face-to-face or telephone interviews. Depending on the answers, individuals are classified as *employed*, *unemployed*, or *not in the labor force*. The BLS uses the following criteria for its classifications:
Employed persons are:

> All persons who did any work for pay or profit during the survey week.
> All persons who did at least 15 hours of unpaid work in a family-owned enterprise operated by someone in their household.
> All persons who were temporarily absent from their regular jobs because of illness, vacation, bad weather, industrial dispute, or various personal reasons, whether or not they were paid for the time off.

Unemployed persons are:

> All persons who did not have a job at all during the survey reference week, made at least one specific active effort to find a job during the prior 4 weeks, and were available for work (unless temporarily ill).
> All persons who were not working and were waiting to be called back to a job from which they had been laid off (they need not be looking for work to be classified as unemployed).

Basically, individuals who have jobs are employed, individuals who do not have jobs and are (actively) seeking jobs are unemployed, and those who do not fall into either of these two categories are considered as not in the labor force. Among those who are counted out of the labor force are "**discouraged workers.**" These workers are marginally attached to the labor force in the sense that they have looked for work in the past 12 months (or since they last worked), but have been unable to find work for a variety of reasons. (Reported reasons include no jobs being available to the workers in their line of work or area, lack of skills, education, or experience and discrimination). However, while they have given up actively looking for a job they currently want to have a job.

Figure 6-2 shows estimates of the U.S. unemployment rate and a few other labor market indicators for December 2015 obtained based on the procedure explained above. As can be seen, out of the relevant population size of over 252 millions (see NACP), roughly 62.6 percent participated in the labor force. The **unemployment rate**, defined as the fraction of the labor force that did not have a job but actively looked for one, was 5.5 percent. In interpreting the national unemployment rate, it is important to keep in mind the following points:

Figure 6-2

Measuring the Adult Civilian Unemployment Rate (December 2015, Seasonally Adjusted Numbers in Thousands)

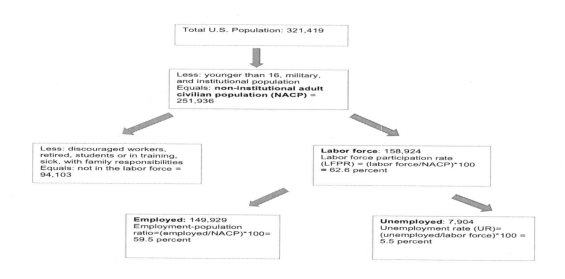

Source: Bureau of Labor Statistics

First, there are usually significant variations in the unemployment rates across regions of the country, sectors of the economy, and socio-economic groups. The national rate, as an average, masks these variations and may give the wrong impression that the burden of unemployment is equally distributed.

Second, the national unemployment rate does not reflect the existence discouraged workers, account for the fact that many part time workers who like to have full time jobs, and adjusts for the duration of the unemployment.

Third, the unemployment rate as defined is sensitive to movement in and out of the labor force. Its changes, therefore, do not necessarily reflect the health of the economy. For example, as signs of an economic recovery emerge, more people enter the labor force and begin to actively look for work. As a result, the unemployment rate goes up even if the economy creates many new jobs! This explains why the employment-population ratio which insensitive to such movements is calculated.

Full Employment
A concept of the employment goal to be attained in an economy. As such, it must be defined and redefined as the structure of an economy changes.

Full employment is a main goal of any country's national economic policy. Though it may seem an obvious concept, defining and measuring it is, in fact, fraught with difficulties. *Full employment* doesn't mean that every person in the nation has a job. The term refers to the labor force in general, which, by definition, includes anyone in the United States age sixteen or over who is permitted to work and who has a job or is actively seeking one. In 2015, the civilian labor force of the United States comprised almost 159 million people. Full employment doesn't even mean that all the labor force is employed. Allowances are made for people who are temporarily between jobs or are in the process of changing jobs. In other words, some amount of unemployment is a normal condition in a market economy that is continually reallocating its resources.

Cartoon Feature Syndicate

"Merry Christmas, Staff!"

Kinds of Unemployment

You may think that unemployment is unemployment, and that's that. But economists have identified different *kinds* of unemployment:

Frictional Unemployment
The measure of unemployment of those who are moving from one job to another (also called transitional unemployment).

      Frictional or Transitional Unemployment occurs among those people who are unemployed for a while as they search for new jobs or await taking new jobs. There are imperfections in all labor markets that necessarily result in *frictional unemployment*:

1. Labor immobility of one kind or another, such as inability or unwillingness to commute or relocate.

2. Workers' inadequate knowledge of the job market.

3. The impossibility of instantly matching job-hunting people with job vacancies.

      The amount of frictional unemployment depends on the degree of these imperfections. As we noted before, it may be desirable to the extent that it reflects labor mobility in moving from less productive to more productive employment. When everybody in the labor force is employed except for people who are frictionally and structurally unemployed, we say that full employment exists.

Cyclical Unemployment
The amount of unemployment associated with deficiencies in aggregate demand during recessions and troughs.

Cyclical unemployment. During recessions and business cycle troughs, the aggregate demand of the public for goods and services may not be enough to create a full-employment demand for members of the labor force. We sometimes refer to the resulting unemployment as "demand-deficient unemployment." Although frictional unemployment is a fact of life in all phases of a business cycle, unemployment due to lack of demand is a direct result of the "downward" phases of business cycles. Consequently, to get rid of this kind of unemployment, a government will try to achieve economic growth or at least stability and to reduce business fluctuations.

Structural Unemployment
Unemployment due to changes in technology or in the composition of output caused by changes in consumer demand.

Structural Unemployment. Changes in the structure of the economy are what cause *structural unemployment*. These changes in structure may come about because of changes in technology or because of changes in the composition of consumer demand and output, which lead to shifts in the pattern of demand for labor. Such structural changes affect both skilled and unskilled workers. In the 1950s and early 1960s, the shift from coal to oil for heating homes left massive unemployment in the anthracite coal mines in eastern Pennsylvania. In Minnesota, many workers became jobless when iron ore deposits in the Mesabi Range were exhausted. On the West Coast, in the late 1960s, large numbers of engineers who worked in the aerospace industries lost their jobs because of the government's cutback in its aerospace program when the Vietnam War caused reallocation of defense expenditures. All these events are examples of structural unemployment. In the 1990s, we saw major changes in employment as defense spending was reduced and as firms "downsize" and adopted new technology to increase their "competitiveness" in international markets. To these we can add more recent advances in robotics, communications, and information technology that have rendered a number of skills obsolete. Workers who are structurally unemployed need to retrain to learn new skills and/or relocate. However, this is often challenging and costly and may require subsidizing displaced workers to ease their burden.

Seasonal Unemployment
Unemployment that occurs during specific seasons of the year.

Seasonal Unemployment. Unemployment caused by seasonal shifts in labor supply and demand during the year is called *seasonal unemployment*. It often occurs in industries such as construction, agriculture and tourism, where the weather affects the demand for labor. When the unemployment data are reported on a "seasonally adjusted basis," the effects of these seasonal variations are statistically filtered out.

Problems That Accompany Unemployment
A particularly disturbing aspect of structural unemployment involves low skilled workers. Since World War II, with the advent of computers and countless technologically sophisticated gadgets, the demand for low skilled labor, as a percentage of total demand for labor, has dropped greatly, even though the percentage of low skilled laborers in the labor force has remained constant. Many jobs for the less skilled have disappeared entirely. One problem of the last forty years, is that our educational system has failed to impart to some students the skills they need to make them employable. The needs of inner city minority groups, in particular, are not adequately met.

Unemployment due to lack of demand is a serious problem. However, if we can maintain economic growth or at least greater stability in the business cycle, we seem to have some tools to control it. Structural unemployment, though, is much more difficult to control. We must find ways to ensure that the hard-core unemployed obtain the new skills they need to survive in today's internationally competitive economy. Job-training programs, in the last thirty years have, for the most part, fallen short of their goals. Minimum-wage laws, originally introduced to help unskilled workers and young people entering the job market for the first time, may actually be hurting them, although the magnitude of the job loss is disputed by some economists. These laws have caused wages to rise beyond the productive ability of some low skilled workers and some teenagers. Some people argue that a reduction in these minimum-wages, at least for certain categories of workers, especially the young entering the labor force, would increase employment among teenagers. The minimum wage law that went into effect in 1990 provided for a training wage for several months and its effects were a source of controversy, the most recent increase in the Federal minimum wage was enacted in 2009.

We should also mention the discouraged-worker effect. Workers who have been rendered unemployed by so-called structural changes may eventually give up seeking work and just drop out of the labor force. Teenagers especially suffer from this discouragement. Those who never find jobs in the first place, disappear from the labor force and from our GDP statistics, as if they had become invisible, and form a hidden cost of unemployment.

The continuously high unemployment rate among minority groups, and among teenagers indicates the magnitude of our failure to deal with structural unemployment among those who are least skilled.

Economic Costs of Unemployment: The GDP Gap

The costs of unemployment to society are both economic and psychological. Obviously we can measure the economic costs in terms of goods and services the unemployed could have produced if they had jobs. One economist, Sherman Maisel, in a book called *Fluctuations, Growth, and Forecasting*, estimated that unemployment in the depression of the 1930s cost the economy $650 billion in foregone product (using 1957 prices as a basis). This was more than enough to pay for World War II, to provide every family in the United States with a new home and two cars, or to give all who qualified a college education.

We can also measure economic costs of unemployment as the difference between actual GDP achieved and potential GDP, or the GDP that could have been obtained with full employment. The difference between the two is called the **GDP gap**. It measures the opportunity cost or foregone output that is forever lost when all who are able and willing to work do not find jobs. When actual GDP falls short of potential GDP (that is, when the economy underachieves), the GDP gap is negative. When actual GDP exceeds its potential level (that is, when the economy overachieves) the GDP gap is positive. Figure 6-3 shows that the U.S. economy significantly underachieved during the Great Recession and subsequent years. It paid a hefty price in terms of loss of output (negative GDP gap) estimated to be equal to 868 billion dollars in 2013.

www.bls.gov
For more information on unemployment visit this Bureau of Labor Statistics web site.

GDP Gap
The difference between actual GDP achieved and potential (or "full employment") GDP.

Figure 6-3

GDP Gap (Actual GDP-Potential GDP)

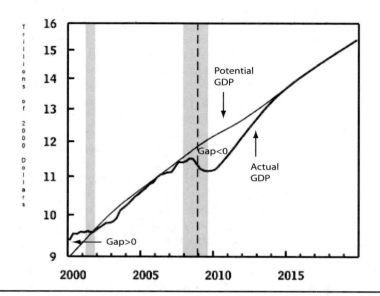

Source: The Congressional Budget Office.

Okun's Law
The rule that for each 1 percent that the actual unemployment rate exceeds the natural rate, a 2¹/2 percent GDP gap results.

One way to quantify the opportunity cost of "above-natural" unemployment rate in terms of loss of output is **Okun's law** (or, more accurately, Okun's rule of thumb). A popular version of the law is given by the following formula:

$$\%\Delta \text{ (GDP gap)} = (\text{GDP} - \text{GDP*}) \div (\text{GDP*}) = -2 \, (\text{UR-UR*})$$

where GDP and GDP* are actual and potential GDP, respectively and UR and UR* are actual and natural unemployment rate, respectively. Accordingly, for each 1 percent that the actual unemployment rate exceeds the natural rate, a 2 percent GDP gap results. For example, if the natural rate of unemployment is 5 percent and the actual rate is 8 percent, then the actual GDP is estimated to fall below potential GDP by 6 percent. Note, however, that Okun's law is an *average* relationship between the unemployment rate and output and deviations from the average may yield incorrect results.

Psychological and Social Costs of Unemployment
In a society basically still ruled by the work ethic, to be out of work, especially to be unemployed for a long time, causes acute mental suffering. Two extreme examples, which appeared in the newspapers in the mid-1980s, are the cases of two individuals, one who lost his job and shot himself, and another who hung himself in the steel mill from which he had become unemployed.

In addition to mental anguish, prolonged unemployment causes insecurities about one's self-worth. It creates family strain that goes beyond economic privation. In the past, and even more so today, prolonged unemployment has placed the individual psychologically, as well as economically, beyond the pale of normal society.

High levels of unemployment also put social and political stress on society at large. In a very real sense, a less affluent group may become pitted against a more affluent group. To paraphrase Abraham Lincoln, a society that is half affluent and half deprived, cannot long endure, or, at least, cannot expect to have social tranquility.

Prices and the Problem of Inflation

Inflation
A general rise in the level of prices.

During various phases of a business cycle, the level of employment changes. Thus a nation must not only maintain economic growth but also try to maintain full employment. Another serious problem an economy faces is **inflation**, or a general rise in the level of prices. During various phases of a business cycle, the level of prices changes. Since World War II, prices have primarily been rising. This, as we know, is inflation.

As prices of goods and services increase, the amount of these goods that a dollar will buy decreases. Thus, inflation causes a decrease in the purchasing power of the dollar. This and other adverse consequences of inflation explain why the inflation rate, along with the GDP growth and the unemployment rates, is considered a key economic indicator.

The Consumer Price Index (CPI)

How is the inflation rate measured? The first step is to define a price index to represent the general price level in the economy. A price index is a summary measure, or a composite of individual prices. As we have seen in Chapter 5, a price index that represents the prices of all goods and services included in GDP is used to convert nominal GDP to real GDP. However, households directly buy and consume only a small subset of the goods and services in the GDP basket. The Bureau of Labor Statistics of the U.S. Department of Labor constructs a price index that is called the "All Items Consumer Price Index for All Urban Consumers (CPI-U) for the U.S. City Average." This is the index that receives a lot of attention by the public and the media, for about 87 percent of the U.S. population lives in urban areas. The items included in the CPI-U basket are identified based on a detailed survey of the spending habits of 7,000 households around the country. All the expenditure items are then classified by the BLS into 211 categories. These categories are further arranged into the following eight major groups: food and beverages, housing, apparel, transportation, medical care, recreation, education and communication, and other goods and service. The relative importance (weight) of these groups in the market basket is not the same. For example, in the 2007-2008 Consumer Expenditure Survey "housing" had a weight of 42 percent while the weight of "apparel" was only 3.7 percent.

Having defined the "market basket" purchased by the average (or typical) household, the BLS data collectors record the prices of 80,000 items (representing a scientifically selected sample of prices paid by consumers on a variety of products available within each category) from thousands of business establishments each month. Prices include sales and excise taxes paid by consumers and government-charged user fees. (Prices of investment items such as stocks and bonds are excluded). The newly recorded prices make it possible to measure changes in the cost of the market basket relative to a base period (1982-1984 is currently used as the reference base).

To better understand this, let's first more formally define the CPI:

$$CPI = \frac{\text{Cost of the market basket at the current-year prices}}{\text{Cost of the market basket at the base-year prices}} \times 100$$

The inflation rate between two years (1 and 2) is computed by calculating the percentage change in the CPI value between the two years:

$$\text{Inflation rate (INFR)} = (CPI_2 - CPI_1 / CPI_1) \times 100.$$

Now consider a simple example presented in Table 6-1. The market basket consists of only two items (gasoline and computer). The quantity of each item was determined in the base year (2000) and item prices were recorded for the base year and the current year (2015).

The CPI value for the year 2015 is equal to 125.7 = ($2,200/$1,750) X 100. The CPI value for the year 2000 is equal to 100 (why?). The inflation rate between the two years is equal to 25.7 percent = (125.7-100/100) X 100. This means that the *same* basket costs roughly 26 percent more to buy relative to the base year.

Note that the inflation rate for the entire basket and individual item price changes (see the last column of the table) are not the same. This leads us to an important point: inflation does not mean that all individual prices must be rising. Some individual prices (computer price) may be actually falling; some may rise at a different rate than the inflation rate (gasoline); and some prices may remain unchanged. Inflation results if enough individual prices rise enough to pull up the general price level. How do we then reconcile the inflation rate for the whole basket with individual item price changes?

The answer is that each individual item contributes to the basket inflation rate in the following way:

$$\text{Item's contribution} = (\text{item's weight}) \times (\% \text{ change in item's price})$$

Table 6-1
Calculating the Consumer Price Index (CPI)

Item	2000 (Base) Market Basket Quantity	2000 Price per Unit	Cost of Market Basket item in 2000	2015 Price per Unit	Cost of Market Basket item in 2015	Item Price Change
Gasoline	500 gallons	$1.50	$750	$2.80	$,1400	86.6 percent
Computer	1	$1,000	$1,000	$800	$800	- 20 percent
Total basket cost			$1,750		$2,200	

The item's weight (reflecting its importance in the consumer's budget) is represented by the relative share of the item in the total spending in the base year. In our example, the weights for gasoline and computer are equal to 0.428 (=$750/$1,750) and 0.57 (=$1,000/$1,750), respectively. We can now calculate each item's contribution and then add them up as follows: (0.428) (86.6%) + (0.571) (-20%) = 37.06 -11.42 ≈ 25.7. This exercise suggests that the inflation rate is not a simple average of individual item's price changes; rather it is a *weighted average* of those changes.

How good is the inflation rate based on the CPI as an indicator of increase in the cost of living? The answer is not simple. The cost of living depends on what households actually spend to maintain a given standard of living, or well being. The latter is affected not only by prices of what households directly buy and consume, but also by government policies and environmental factors. Caution must be exercised even if we more narrowly define the concept of cost of living. Critics have argued that the CPI-based inflation rate may *overstate* the actual increase in the cost of living. One reason is that the CPI uses the base-year quantities to construct the weights. These "fixed weights" assumes that consumers do not respond to changes in prices between two points in time (this is know as the "substitution bias.") Note, for example, that the number of gallons of gasoline purchased in Table 6-1 is assumed to be 500 in both years even though the gas price significantly rose. Another reason offered is that components of the basket do not change frequently enough to reflect new products purchased by consumers in a timely manner (this is known as the "new products bias."). Often new products embody a new technology that reduces the cost of living Cell phones, for example, have reduced the cost of communications and digital cameras lowered the cost of taking and storing pictures. Finally, the CPI may not adequately account for qualitative changes (this is known as the "quality change bias.") Medical care prices, for example, are widely reported to be rising rapidly and significantly influence increases in the CPI. Failure to account for improvements in the quality of medical care, however, causes this medical price (and cost-of-living) increase to be overstated. What is the extent of the overstatement? The "Boskin Commission" formed in 1995 estimated the average magnitude of the total bias to be roughly equal to 1.1 percent with a plausible range of 0.8-1.6 percent.

Why does this purported overstatement of inflation by the CPI matter? First, it contributes to inflation itself. Many wage contracts as well as social security payments to millions of Americans are tied to the CPI as part of cost-of-living adjustments, or **COLAS**. If inflation is overstated, overpayments by employers and the government increase the aggregate demand for goods and services and, thereby, inflationary pressure on prices. Secondly, beginning 1985, income tax brackets and standard deductions are adjusted for inflation to prevent a phenomenon known as the "bracket creep." This happens when taxpayers are pushed to higher tax brackets when inflation increases their nominal income levels. If inflation is overstated, then the government over-adjusts and, consequently, takes in less in tax revenues than would have otherwise been the case. Finally, the interest cost of the government debt increases as lenders demand higher interest rates to compensate for inflation. A combination of less tax revenues collected by the government and more outlays (social security and interest payments) increases the size of the budget deficit and, subsequently, the stock of the public debt as the government borrows more.

COLAs
Cost of living Adjustments

Theories of Inflation

There are two basic types or causes of inflation.
1. ***Demand-pull inflation***. Remember that in our discussion of supply and demand, we said that when demand increases (for a given supply of a good), the price of that good will increase. The same sort of phenomenon occurs for the entire economy. When the economy is at full employment, output, over a short period of time, cannot increase because there are no resources (especially labor) available to increase it. When demand for goods and services increases, there are not enough productive facilities to increase output in order to meet this increased demand. Consequently, markets ration out their goods or services, causing increased prices.

Demand-Pull Inflation
The rise in aggregate prices that occurs when demand increases more rapidly than supply.

www.bls.gov
For more information on
inflation visit this web site.

Let's look at an example of a demand-pull situation: In 1966, President Johnson escalated the war in Vietnam by increasing our troops there to more than 500,000 men. To maintain these troops in combat half a world away, the U.S. government had to buy billions of dollars worth of equipment and supplies. The government had also sharply increased its expenditures on antipoverty programs, and there had been tax cuts in 1964 and 1965. As a result of this combination of events, the economy had reached full employment. Unemployment had actually dropped below 4 percent. Thus, the economy was able to meet the increased demand for armaments only by drawing resources away from the production of other commodities.

It did this by increasing the prices of resources used to make nonmilitary goods. Then prices of resources used to make armaments increased, which increased the price of the finished products. At the same time, the supply of resources to other markets declined, decreasing supply and increasing prices. That is what we mean when we say that the marked inflation of 1967-1969 was primarily due to demand-pull inflation.

In brief, then, demand-pull inflation occurs when an economy's demand exceeds the ability of that economy to supply at existing prices. Too many dollars are chasing too few goods. The effect is to pull prices up.

Cost-Push Inflation
The rise in aggregate prices that occurs when resource prices and costs increase more rapidly than factor productivity.

2. *Cost-push inflation*. When the suppliers of resources increase their prices faster than their productive efficiency increases, cost-push inflation occurs. When resource costs go up faster than increases in productivity, a company's production costs per unit increase. These increased production costs are ultimately reflected, at least in part, in higher prices.

The usual example people give of cost-push inflation is that of wage push. When unions force industry to give workers wage increases and the workers do not produce correspondingly more output, cost-push inflation occurs. Suppose that workers in the carpet industry increased their productivity 3 percent and the union obtained wage increases of 4 percent. You can see that the carpet manufacturer's labor costs per yard of carpet go up. (Increased productivity reduces labor costs per unit by 3 percent, while wage increases raise costs per unit 4 percent; net cost increase is 1 percent.) Right after World War II (between 1945 and 1949), labor unions staged a real drive to increase wages. They argued that wage rates had stayed at about the same level during the war, while both productivity and company profits had risen dramatically.

The labor unions naturally wanted workers' wages to catch up. On the whole, industry leaders did not fight this move to increase wage rates, because a strong demand-pull inflation was already under way because of the ending of the depression and war-postponed consumption. It was easy to pass the wage hikes on to the consumer in the form of higher prices.

In the 1970s, the whole world experienced two singularly agonizing cases of cost-push inflation through supply shocks. At the beginning of the 1970s, the world's major oil-producing and oil-exporting countries formed an association: OPEC. Among them, the OPEC countries control the bulk of the world's oil. And between 1971 and 1974, they quintupled the price of their crude oil. The industrialized world is heavily dependent on oil. It is primarily oil that keeps the wheels of industry turning, that generates electricity for our power plants, that gets most of us to work. Therefore, the OPEC countries' two increases in oil prices quickly increased the costs of production generally and set off a worldwide inflation and economic crisis. We will examine the effects of this inflationary experience along with the deflationary experience of falling oil prices in the mid-1980s in another chapter.

Effects of Inflation and Deflation

When prices go up or down, this movement has a financial effect on all of us. It affects the economy in three ways: (1) by redistributing real income, (2) by redistributing real wealth, and (3) by changing the level of output.

Money Income
The current flows of money incomes to individuals.

Real Income
The current flows of money incomes to individuals expressed in terms of purchasing power.

1. *Redistribution of real income.* First, we should make a distinction between *money* and *real income*. **Money income** is the number of dollars a person receives in income, or the number of dollars in the paycheck, for most people. **Real income** is what can be bought with money income. You can see that your real income can change when there is either (a) a change in your money income, or (b) a change in the general level of prices and the purchasing power of your dollar. In the following discussion, we shall assume that the total pie (the level of output) remains constant; that is, that the total level of output is unaffected by changes in prices.

In terms of income, there are two broad classes of people: people whose incomes are fixed, or semifixed, and those whose incomes are variable. When there is inflation, the people with fixed or semifixed incomes suffer because their money income does not increase as fast as prices do; their real income, therefore, declines. People with fixed incomes are usually nonunion workers, those living on welfare or pensions, and those with income based on interest; that is, the widows and orphans, the elderly and the poor, and the unorganized.

The money incomes of people with variable incomes often increase faster than prices go up, for example, the incomes of the people whose earnings come from the profits of a business. Some elements of cost for the business may tend not to increase as fast as prices. In industries where this occurs, profit margins increase. In general, (although there are exceptions), the money incomes of those who obtain their incomes from profits tends to increase faster than prices increase.

Historically, organized labor generally has had enough clout to increase wages at least as fast as prices rise, and often more so, so organized labor usually has enjoyed increased real income, at least for a time. This is particularly true when unions make their contracts for short periods and adjust them quickly to inflation rates.

Real Interest Rate
The nominal interest rate minus the rate of inflation.

Savers are frequently hurt by unanticipated inflation. To begin with, the real value or purchasing power of accumulated savings will decline as prices rise. This is true of savings accounts, fixed value paper assets and a wide variety of other forms of savings. Additionally, rising interest rates on savings often lag the growth in other prices, so that the **real interest rate** (nominal interest rate minus the rate of inflation) may become negative. As the experience of the late 1970s and early 1980s shows, this results not only in a redistribution of real income but is also a powerful disincentive to saving.

Deflation
A general fall in the level of prices.

During a **deflation**, when prices fall, those with fixed incomes temporarily enjoy increases in their real income, because a dollar buys more. This often does not apply to unorganized labor, because unorganized labor does not have enough economic power to prevent wage cuts. ("Times are hard. You will just have to take less per hour.")

"You've no idea what's happened to prices, you'll have to pull a really big job the first thing when you get out!"

What happens to people with variable incomes during a deflation? Those with income from profits tend to suffer losses in real income. Suppose you are living on the income from stock you own in one company. The company has to lower its prices because of the deflation. But the company still has to pay for resources (labor and materials), and the costs of these resources lag behind the fall in prices. Thus, the margin of profit gets narrower and narrower, and presently the company is unable to pay dividends to its stockholders.

Often for organized labor in a deflation, it has the economic power to keep employers from cutting back wages, (though not jobs) in spite of falling prices.

2. *Redistribution of real wealth.* In terms of real wealth, there are three categories: debtors (who borrow money), creditors (who lend it), and savers (who save it).

www.cbo.gov
For more information on interest rates visit the Congressional Budget Office at the web site listed above.

During an inflationary period, debtors benefit. But creditors and savers lose real wealth; that is, their wealth does not buy as much as it used to. In our example, suppose you are the debtor. Let's say that you borrowed $100 from your brother a year ago and he is not charging you interest, and suppose that there has been a 10 percent inflation during the year. Prices in general were 10 percent lower a year ago, and thus purchasing power of each dollar was 10 percent higher. If you repay the loan today, you're 10 percent richer, assuming that you didn't pay interest. But your brother, the creditor, is 10 percent poorer. He lent you the money when prices were lower and purchasing power higher. If he spends that $100 today, he'll get 10 percent less for it than he would have a year ago.

Now suppose that your brother had saved the $100 instead of lending it to you. Unless he earned interest on it, he would still have lost 10 percent, because a year ago when he saved the money, its purchasing power was 10 percent higher than it is today. (The creditor and saver would not be hurt by inflation if the rate of interest increased enough to compensate for the inflation and to pay them back for the risk, for the loss of liquidity, for the fact that they could not use the money themselves, and for all the other sacrifices people make in order to earn interest on their money.)

During a deflationary period, just the reverse holds true: Creditors and savers benefit, and debtors lose real wealth. Creditors lent money when prices were higher and each dollar was worth less, but they are paid back when prices are lower and thus the dollar's purchasing power is greater. Savers, too, are better off. They saved money when prices were higher and each dollar bought less. But now that prices have come down, their savings have higher purchasing power. Debtors, on the other hand, are hurt, because they borrowed money when prices were higher and purchasing power lower, but now they have to pay it back when prices are lower and dollars have greater purchasing power.

3. *Changed level of output due to changed prices.* We have been assuming that the economy's output was unchanged as prices changed and that as prices changed, some groups gained at the expense of others. What happens, though, if the total output changes? Relative redistribution of wealth still takes place, but its adverse effects may be lessened or accentuated. Let us see why.

A strong inflation can lead to recession and unemployment for a number of reasons: (a) Since all prices do not increase at the same rate, a sharp inflation may quickly cause structural distortions. Some firms' costs rise faster than they can raise prices of their output, so their profits are reduced. They could possibly take losses. They reduce their output, they lay off workers, and they may even go bankrupt. (b) Rapidly rising prices confuse both producers and consumers, so that people hesitate to make decisions. This causes a decrease in demand for output. On the other hand, rapidly rising prices may lead to **inflationary expectations**, or the belief that prices will continue to rise and cause decreases in real income. This may lead to increased current demand and further inflationary pressure. (c) Consumers may revolt against rising prices and refuse to buy. This again causes a decrease in demand. (d) People who are hurt by the redistributive effect of higher prices have to cut back on their buying, again decreasing the demand for output. The lucky ones who actually benefit from higher prices may step up *their* buying, but their increased demand may not compensate for the decreased demand on the part of those who are caught in the squeeze of higher prices.

The net effect of all this is a decrease in total demand for the economy's output, which means that output falls off and so does employment. The result is *recession.*

We have been discussing sharp increases in prices. But some economists argue that *moderate* increases in prices can actually be beneficial to output, for the following reasons: (1) When inflation is slight, business and industries can see in advance that the costs of their resources (labor and materials) are going to go up by a certain amount next year, so they can raise their own prices slightly and thus counter the structural effects of varying rates of price changes. (2) The prices of products may increase faster than the prices of resources, so that the profits of business and industry actually increase. When business people are making high profits, they are more inclined to invest. Thus, more jobs open up, employment rates rise, and the rate of economic growth increases.

However, if a moderate inflation continues for a long time, it may accelerate and become built-in or what is called *creeping inflation.* This may become a threat to the economy for three reasons: (1) Creeping inflation can accelerate until it becomes a severe inflation, with all its potential for causing recession. (2) Creeping inflation can generate inflationary expectations and lead to a wage-price spiral, resulting in serious inflation. Unions demand wage increases to compensate for past inflation and often add an extra margin for anticipated future inflation. During a prosperous period, business people are

Inflationary Expectations
The belief that inflation is inbuilt and will continue, thus, leading to falling real income.

reluctant to face a strike, so they agree to grant the unions their wage hikes, which in turn, increase the costs of production. Businesses pass these higher costs on to consumers through higher prices, which often reflect an extra profit margin for the firms. (3) In due course, creeping inflation results in redistribution of wealth and puts serious economic strain on disadvantaged groups. The result may be *recession*.

A moderate deflation, bringing about a gradual fall in prices, may also contribute to increases in output. Deflations in the twentieth century, however, have been rare, especially since World War II. During the prosperous part of the 1920s (1922 to 1929), prices sloped gently downward because of increases in productivity without corresponding increases in workers' wages. (The unions had a hard time surviving during the 1920s.) The general population enjoyed increases in their real income as prices fell. At the same time, businesses had larger profits, since productivity increased faster than prices fell. Both factors kept the demand for capital goods high. More recently, there was a moderate slowing of inflation in 1982-1983, when, in the face of restrictive monetary policy, prices slowed down.

But deflation, too, can create problems. When the decrease in prices is very rapid, it tends to reduce the level of output. The following sequence occurs: (1) Retail prices fall faster than prices of *factor inputs* (the resources an industry uses to manufacture things). This squeezes out profits and introduces losses. (2) Since prices do not fall uniformly, the structure of prices becomes distorted. Some firms have their profits wiped out entirely. (3) Business people, when faced with falling prices, become very pessimistic and tend to withhold further investment. All these conditions lead to decreases in output. The result is *recession*.

The Misery Index

As we have seen, both unemployment and inflation can impose significant economic as well as social costs on members of the society. For this reason, some refer to them as "social evils." With this in mind, Arthur Okun, an economist and an adviser to President Lyndon Johnson in the 1960's, constructed a simple index to measure the extent of economic discomfort in the country due to unemployment and inflation. Figure 6-4 shows the rates of unemployment and inflation in the United states between 1948 and 2015. Note that the overall unemployment rate spiked during economic downturns (for example, during the Great Recession of 2007-2009) and fell afterward reflecting changes in its cyclical component. Also note the spikes in the inflation rate during the 1970s reflecting the sharp increase in the price of crude oil and monetary expansion.

Figure 6-4
Civilian Unemployment Rate (Seasonally Adjusted, 1948-2015)

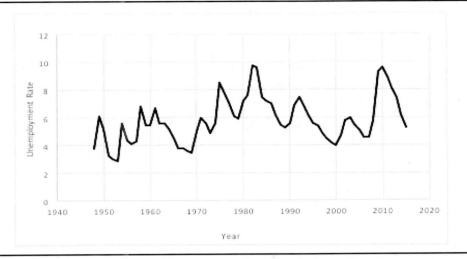

*Percent of adult civilian population, seasonally adjusted (Current Population Survey)
Source: Department of Labor, Bureau of Labor Statistics

Inflation rate (All Urban Consumers, Seasonally Adjusted, 1948-2015)

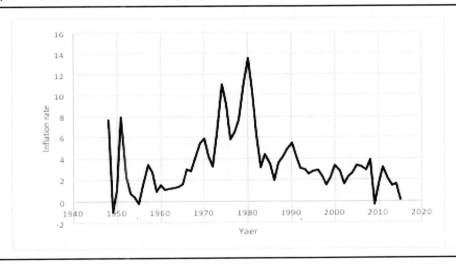

* Percent change in the Consumer Price Index-All Urban Consumers, not seasonally adjusted
Source: Department of Labor, Bureau of Labor Statistics

This index is called the "misery index" and is obtained by simply adding the unemployment and inflation rates:

Misery index = Unemployment rate + Inflation rate.

Figure 6-4 shows changes in the degree of economic discomfort during the period 1948-2015. The misery index reached its peak of 20.76 (= 7.18+13.58) in 1980. The lowest index value was 3.74 (= 2.92+0.82) which was observed in 1953. To put the more recent economic situation in perspective, the misery index stood at 12.01 percent in March 2010. This reflects a substantial increase in the unemployment rate due to a sharp economic downturn that began in the 2007.

Figure 6-5
Arthur Okun's Misery Index (1948-2015)

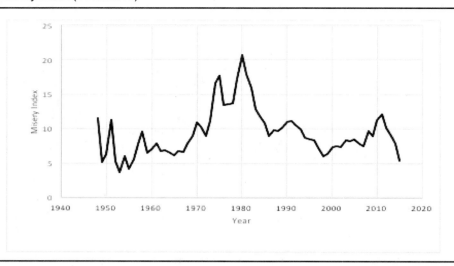

Employment and Prices

To prevent the economy from continually plunging down and climbing up, governments try to initiate policies of stabilization, aimed at maintaining full employment and stable prices. It is difficult to attain both objectives at the same time, since they are sometimes contradictory.

Figure 6-6 shows that as output increases, more people get jobs, so unemployment is reduced while prices remain stable. At this stage, there is still some unused space and unemployed labor that industry can use without raising its prices. However, as output reaches point A, industry can achieve further increases in output only by raising its prices. Although point A is reached before there is full employment of all labor, certain categories of skilled labor and other resources may be in short supply. Beyond point A, the ever expanding output creates an ever greater demand for resources, which means that the prices of these resources will increase still further and inevitably the general level of prices will also rise. At point B or full employment), any further effort to increase output will result in continued demand-pull inflation; prices increase but real output cannot. In other words, demand-pull inflation occurs before the economy reaches full employment because some forms of labor and resources are in shorter supply than others. More expensive resources force up the prices of products before full employment is achieved.

Figure 6-6
Prices and Employment

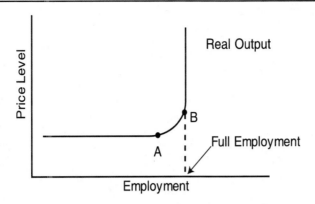

As output increase, industry starts using resources that were formerly unemployed, and prices remain stable. At point A, some resources start to be in short supply; this forces prices up. At point B, there is full employment. Further increases in demand only result in still higher prices.

Phillips Curve
A function that depicts the tradeoffs between unemployment and inflation.

From this we can see that there is a tradeoff between employment and prices. Beyond some point of resource use, if you want to reduce unemployment you most likely will have to accept some increases in prices. We can diagram this tradeoff between employment and prices. The resulting curve, called a **Phillips curve** after A. W. Phillips looks like the one in Figure 6-7.

When we examine Figure 6-7, which covers the period since World War II, we see a Phillips curve representing a relationship that many considered politically acceptable until the 1970s: unemployment at 4 to 4.5 percent, inflation at 4 to 5 percent. If the government then had tried to force the unemployment rate below 4.5 percent, prices would have increased too much. According to this Phillips curve, before the 1970s, the tradeoff between inflation and unemployment was a politically acceptable one.

Figure 6-7
A Phillips Curve

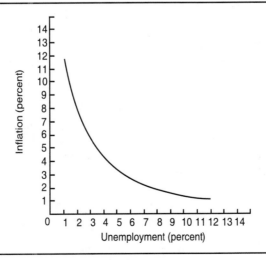

The horizontal axis is the percentage of unemployment; the vertical axis, the percentage rate of inflation. The Phillips curve shows the relationship between the two.

Now lets see what has happened to the Phillips curve since 1970. During the recession of 1970-1971, unemployment of about 6 percent was coupled with an inflation rate of about 7 percent, making the government's policy of economic stabilization much harder to carry out. The economy seemed to be in a period of **stagflation**, or a combination of inflation and economic stagnation. In other words, the economy seemed unable to move down the Phillips curve. In the recession of 1974-1975, the tradeoff was even less acceptable. In 1974 unemployment reached 9 percent, while inflation was nearly 12 percent. Our experience with unemployment-inflation in the late 1970s and early 1980s did not seem to invite optimism about the prospects of achieving lower rates of unemployment and inflation at the same time. The period since 1982, however, has seen relatively low rates of inflation and unemployment compared to the 1970s. Some, though, continue to worry about a resumption of stagflation.

Other economists doubt that stagflation will recur. Nonetheless, if stagflation resumes, whenever the government tries to reduce unemployment, it will have to stimulate output, which increases demand, which in turn might increase prices. On the other hand, whenever the government tries to reduce inflation, it will have to reduce demand, which reduces output, which can increase unemployment. When the tradeoff between inflation and unemployment is politically unacceptable, any effort the government makes to reduce unemployment just increases an already politically unacceptable level of inflation and vice versa.

Application I: Defining Full Employment

What is the "Natural Rate" of Unemployment for the U.S.?

The rate of unemployment in the first few years of the twenty first century was around 4 to 6 percent though in 2011, it was over 9 percent. In the early 1980s it was just under 10 percent, the highest since 1941. Since World War II, and especially since the Employment Act of 1946 and the Humphrey-Hawkins Act of 1978, various efforts have been undertaken to spell out a national employment goal. Humphrey-Hawkins asserted that goal to be 4 percent unemployment. Can we construct a set of macroeconomic policies that will permit us to reach that goal? As you will learn in this course in macroeconomic principles, there are various policy tools available to government that permit it to try to influence the level of employment. One problem or constraint in executing employment policy, however, is the set of tradeoffs between unemployment and inflation that we have observed and which is represented in the Phillips curve.

How far, then, can economic policy move the economy in the direction of full employment without causing an unacceptable rate of inflation? What, in other words, is a reasonable definition of full employment and a target for policy makers to attempt to reach?

For many years, it was thought that unemployment could not be pushed below the rate of *frictional unemployment*. Since that rate was widely assumed to be about 4 percent, policy goals (such as Humphrey-Hawkins) centered on that figure. As a result of the experience of the 1970s and 1980s, there is, today, less concern for frictional unemployment (indeed, economists rarely focus on the term now) and more concern for identifying a **natural rate of unemployment**, a rate at which the economy tends to produce neither an acceleration nor a deceleration in inflation (i.e., the inflation rate is stable).

A major problem with identifying the natural rate of unemployment for the American economy is *shifting inflationary expectations*. The Phillips curve

Stagflation
A combination of inflation and economic stagnation.

Natural Rate of Unemployment
The rate of unemployment at which inflation neither accelerates nor decelerates (i.e., the inflation rate is stable).

tradeoffs between unemployment and inflation, even if identifiable, are unstable. We see this instability in Figure 6-8. In this hypothetical example of the natural rate argument, the economy is initially in equilibrium at point A on a short-run Phillips curve that is based on an expected inflation rate of 3 percent. The natural rate of unemployment is assumed here to be 6 percent. Point A is stable because there is no tendency for inflation or deflation to occur. Now, suppose that a public policy decision is made to lower the (unacceptable) rate of unemployment below 6 percent at point A. By whatever set of means (government expenditures, tax changes, money supply changes), the economy is stimulated and total spending rises. Employers, facing a growing demand for output, try to hire more people and other resources and, in doing so, bid up resource prices (wages, etc.) and, thereby, cause firms' costs to rise.

In the short run, the response to the stimulation of the economy is to move to point B with a lower (4 percent) rate of unemployment and a higher (5 percent) rate of inflation as prices rise in response to cost increases. Some workers, though, whose wage agreements were based on an expected inflation rate of 3 percent, see a decline in their real incomes. As those agreements expire, new wage agreements, based on a new higher expected rate of inflation are negotiated. These new higher wage cost agreements, though, lead to a new round of inflation and a higher *expected* level of price increases. The Phillips curve, in other words, shifts to a new (6 percent) expected inflation rate and equilibrium is restored at point C with the economy again at its natural unemployment rate of 6 percent. The long-run Phillips curve is a vertical line parallel to the inflation rate axis from the natural rate of unemployment. Points A and C are on this vertical Phillips curve. That is, they consist of points at which (at different inflation rates) there is no tendency for further inflation or deflation.

Figure 6-8

A Hypothetical Example of the Short-Run and Long-Run Tradeoffs Between Inflation and Unemployment: The Natural Rate Argument

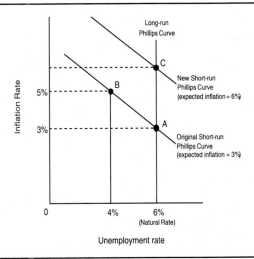

Source: From Stuart Weiner "The Natural Rate of Unemployment: Concepts and Issues." *Economic Review.* Federal Reserve Bank of Kansas City. January, 1986.

The key points of the natural rate of unemployment argument are, (1) It is difficult, if not impossible, to push the actual unemployment rate of an economy in the long run below its natural rate, and (2) attempts to do so merely result in higher rates of inflation rather than lower unemployment.

Chapter 6: Economic Fluctuations, Unemployment and Inflation 177

What is the Natural Rate for the U.S.?

According to research done by macroeconomist Robert J. Gordon, the U.S. has rarely been able to lower unemployment to its natural rate since 1945. More importantly for this application, the natural rate trended upward from less than 5 percent to about 6 percent in the forty years between 1945 and 1985. A major reason for this rise in the natural rate appears to be the change in the composition of the American labor force. In 1945, men comprised the overwhelming part of the labor force, whereas in recent years, women and teenagers have constituted a large and growing portion. The latter groups have higher structural as well as frictional rates of unemployment. Thus, as Economist Stuart Weiner[2] notes, the "overall unemployment rate consistent with constant inflation has risen." Weiner estimated the natural rate in 1994 was 6.25 percent and could go higher in the next twenty-five years.

Can We Lower the Natural Rate?

Can we find ways to lower the natural rate of unemployment? Can we, in other words, shift the long-run Phillips curve in Figure 6-8 to the left so that points such as B involve stable relationships with a 4 percent unemployment rate as well as acceptable inflation rates and lower inflationary expectations? Weiner argues that doing so will involve making labor markets work more perfectly and will involve some combination of the following:

1. Creating a better match between skills of available workers and job openings (better educational and vocational programs).

2. A better match between locations of jobs and available workers (worker relocation subsidies and a more efficient national employment service). Also, programs such as "enterprise zones" in cities to keep firms from leaving urban areas.

3. Eliminating or reducing institutional barriers. (Laws and practices such as minimum wage laws, union membership restrictions, and racial or sexual discrimination are examples).

Weiner also notes that lowering the natural rate below the currently estimated range of 5 to 6 percent is desirable. Opportunity costs to society of having such a large part of its labor force unemployed are very high. It is not desirable to eliminate all unemployment for we need the labor mobility of people *moving* from less productive to more productive employment that is reflected in *transitional* unemployment. Nonetheless, a 4 percent natural rate is far more desirable, socially, than a 5 to 6 percent rate.

Did the Natural Rate Fall in the 1990s?

In 1995, the natural rate estimates were under attack. The estimate is increasingly important because it influences monetary policy as well as in other ways. With unemployment rates falling in 1994 from 6.7 percent to 5.4 percent, inflationary pressures should be building according to Gordon's earlier estimate. Today, Gordon says, the natural rate could be as low as 5 percent. Caution remains, however, as some fear that a lengthy lag may exist between declining unemployment and a rising rate of inflation.

---

2. Weiner, Stuart E. "The Natural Rate of Unemployment: Concepts and Issues" *Economic Review*. Federal Reserve Board of Kansas City. January, 1986.

Application II: The Modern U.S. Economy: A Record of Growth, Recession, and Depression

Below, we shall briefly explore the history of economic fluctuations in the United States since the 1920s, in order to gain a better insight into the factors that cause the irregular cycles of economic growth and recession in the last 75 years.

The Roaring 20s

From 1922 to 1929, the economy expanded rapidly from a low of $70 billion in money GDP in 1921 to a high of $104.4 billion in 1929. This expansion was marred by two mild recessions, one in 1924 and the other in 1927. Even so, there was less than 5 percent unemployment in these downturns. Prices declined somewhat between 1921 and 1929, from a price index of 52.8 in 1921 to an index of 51.3 in 1929. (1967 is used as a base year. In other words, in 1967 the index was 100.)

The two main bases of the prosperity of the 1920s were (1) the expansion of the construction industry and (2) the increase in output of a number of "new" industries, especially the automotive industry. Both residential and business construction expanded through 1926, but then residential construction began to fall off. Further expansion in business construction, however, maintained the increases into 1927, at which time they began to decline.

This development of new industries in the 1920s seen in Keynesian terms was a main cause of high aggregate demand. Radios, electric power, chemicals, telephones, motion pictures, durable consumer appliances, and cars, especially cars, contributed to the boom. Although most of these industries were not new in the 1920s, they grew up in that decade. **Primary demand** (that is, demand by those who had never owned certain goods before) was large. Automobile production went from 2.2 million per year in 1920 to 5.5 million by 1929, more than double in nine years.

Primary Demand
Demand for products created by first-time buyers.

The direct effect of this expansion was that people began to demand these new products in increasing numbers. ("I'd give anything to have a refrigerator. You never have to empty the drip pan, and you don't have to stay home to let the ice man in.") Many industries supplying goods to manufacture new products were stimulated as well. Car makers had to have vast quantities of raw materials and semifinished parts. Their needs stimulated booms in the steel, rubber, glass, textile, and petroleum industries and created a new service industry: gasoline retailing. Governments (mainly local and state) built $10 billion worth of roads for these new machines. But most important were the capital investments that auto makers had to make for plant and equipment to expand their production capacity.

Despite the general prosperity, there were some weak spots in the economy. The agricultural sector was semi-depressed throughout the decade due to many factors.

A problem that soon became more serious than the rest was developing over the international means of payments. After World War I, the German government owed huge sums of money (reparations) to the Allies. The U.S. treasury encouraged private individuals and institutions to lend more to the German government, so that Germany might pay war reparations to England, France, and Italy, so that in turn these countries could pay to the United States the money they borrowed during World War I. This was a very circular process and in the long run dangerous to the economy. (We shall say more about this later.)

The Great Depression: Phase I

In 1929 the U.S. economy, and for that matter, the world economy, entered a recession that became the worst depression in history. Money GDP in the United States fell from about $104 billion in 1929 to about $56 billion by 1933. Unemployment in 1933 increased to the highest level ever: 25 percent of the labor force was unemployed and another 25 percent was partially employed. Prices dropped by about 24 percent. Oddly enough, the very factors that led to the prosperity of the 1920s laid the foundations for the depression.

Secondary (Replacement) Demand Demand that is created when consumers replace products.

The large primary demand for automobiles (demand by those who had never had cars before), and for the products of the other new industries, was beginning to drop off by 1929. There was a time lag before the onset of **secondary (replacement) demand** (demand for products to replace consumer goods), which was needed to prop up demand to the levels of 1929.

To see this, look at Figure 6-9, which is an idealized version of the life cycle of the automotive industry. During Stage I (1895-1920), people invented the automobile and worked to improve it. This stage is referred to as *the perfection of the innovation*. Note that the rate of growth of demand is relatively slow. In Stage II (1920-1929) the perfected innovation enters the primary market, and it catches on quickly. In Stage III (beginning in 1929) primary demand has become saturated.

Figure 6-9
Growth Curve of the Automobile Industry

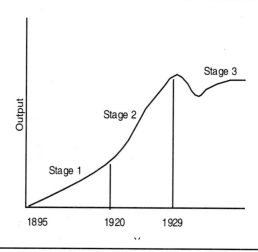

While the shift to replacement demand is going on, excess capacity develops. Output falls from its 1929 high. As the demand for the products of the new industries fell, a negative accelerator effect appeared, and there was a fall in induced investment, both in the new industries themselves and in those industries that had been stimulated by them. By June of 1929, there was excess capacity, so people decreased their investing. Manufacturing output declined. The construction industry, the second major stimulator of the 1920s economy, had been hit by excess capacity and falling output as early as the middle of 1927. By the end of 1929, it had collapsed.

To put it in Keynesian terms: As demand fell toward the end of 1929, investment fell also. The large savings caused by the widening of the profit margins reduced consumption demand. Aggregate demand fell, and so did income.

For a year the stock market had been going up. Prices of stocks rose rapidly in relation to potential earnings. In October of 1929 the market simply collapsed. Another key function of the stock market is to mirror the psychological view of investors and during the year before the crash, it mirrored such optimism that few noted the signs of decline. After the crash, pessimism ruled and many people felt there was no hope.

From 1929 to 1933, the U.S. banking system also came close to complete collapse. When the stock market crashed, it crashed so quickly that banks were left holding large amounts of corporate stock, a huge capital loss. In addition, banks owned large numbers of mortgages. When mortgage holders could no longer make their monthly payments and real estate values plummeted, the banks were left holding innumerable chunks of illiquid property. All these factors eroded their asset position, and banks began to fail. People panicked. Long queues of frantic people lined up outside banks, waiting to withdraw deposits. This caused even secure banks to fail. By 1933, when Roosevelt took office, the banking system was in a desperate position.

As the U.S. banking system deteriorated, so did international trade, and quickly, too. The shift from government ownership to private ownership of war debts meant that private means of international payments became linked to reparations and war-debt payments. When the market collapsed in 1929, the structure of repayment of war debts crumbled also, bringing down the private system of international payments. A further blow to international trade came in 1931, when the United States started a round of retaliatory tariff increases that further reduced exports and put a damper on world production.

Weak Recovery: 1933-1937
When Roosevelt became president in 1933, government spending rose and this had the effect of creating what were, for that time, large deficits. Congress also passed a series of laws aimed at correcting weaknesses in the economy, though some, by encouraging monopoly, would be seen by many economists as counterproductive.

The national debt jumped from $19.5 billion in 1932 to $36.5 billion by 1937, an increase of $17 billion in five years. This stimulated an increase in GDP of $35 billion between 1933 and 1937. Private investment remained low, however. (In 1929 net private domestic investment was $8.3 billion. By 1933 it had dropped to *minus* $5.6 billion, and in 1937 it was still only $4.6 billion.)

The Recession of 1937-1939
President Roosevelt, concerned about the increasing federal deficits, decided that private investment should shoulder more of the task of coping with the continued depression. So in 1937 the federal government reduced deficit expenditures. At the same time, monetary policy was tightened. In the face of higher interest rates and weak demand, private investment, however, failed to take up the slack and continue the expansion. As a result, output declined and unemployment increased from about 14 percent to 18 percent. In 1938, the Social Security system went into effect. The taxes associated with this system reduced disposable incomes and probably contributed to the recession. For the first time in the history of U.S. business cycles, a second recession came along before the economy had recovered from the first.

The Early Forties and World War II
During 1940 and 1941, as the United States increased its military expenditures and its exports to its allies, who were already at war, the recovery began to

quicken. Keynesians saw in this the multiplier and accelerator effects of this increased output in the form of increases in both consumption and investment.

When the United States entered the war, on December 7, 1941, the economy went all out in the war effort. However, because there was so much unemployment left over from the depression of the 1930s (unemployment was still at 10 percent in 1941), the economy did not reach full employment until the beginning of the third quarter of 1942. Until then, there had been sharp increases in output of military goods, consumer goods, and investment goods. Once full employment was achieved (the vertical range of aggregate supply), the economy had to cut back on the production of investment and consumer goods in order to continue to increase output of goods needed by the military.

Since there was full employment and plenty of overtime work, people had higher personal incomes. Yet the nation's need for more and more military goods reduced the availability of consumer goods. The government prevented excess demand by imposing higher taxes and price controls and by encouraging people to save and to buy government bonds. Thus large amounts of personal savings, plus price and wage controls and rationing, kept inflation within reasonable bounds.

The Postwar Boom: 1945-1948

At the end of the war, there was a slight dip in the economy as the United States shifted from military production to civilian production. Then, despite many people's fears that there would be a repeat of the 1930s, the economy began to expand rapidly. Even though the government cut back its military spending by more that $55 billion, the demand for consumer goods, investment, and export goods created a boom.

Because of the depression and then the war, both business investment and consumer demand had been kept low for fifteen years. After the war ended, businesses rushed to invest in plant and equipment, because of depreciation, obsolescence, and the need to reconvert to peacetime production.

Americans were not alone in their headlong rush to achieve the good life, to gratify demands they had postponed for so long. They were joined by the rest of the world. Exports rose to new highs as a war-ravaged world turned to the United States for consumer goods and for investment to rebuild the world's economy. Unfortunately, under the impact of all this demand, inflation developed.

The Recession of 1949 and the Expansion of 1950-1953

In late 1948 the economy had its first postwar recession, a short, mild downturn caused primarily by excess inventory that businesses accumulated as output temporarily outstripped demand. In June of 1950, war broke out in Korea, and the recovery from the 1949 slump accelerated and became another boom. Consumers, fearing another round of inflation and also fearing that the government would again put on controls, increased their purchases. As the Cold War became hotter, the government increased its military expenditures, both to fight the war and to increase U.S. military strength in general.

The Recession of 1954 and the Expansion of 1955-1957

When the Korean War ended, consumers stopped buying so much, and so did the government; inventories piled up. In 1954 along came a recession. This too was mild and short, however, because the government took prompt fiscal and monetary steps to ease the situation. A tax cut plus an easy money policy softened the downturn.

In 1955 a boom in residential construction and in demand for consumer durable goods, especially cars, caused U.S. national output to expand quickly. But in 1956 and 1957, the market for consumer durables, saturated by the sales of 1955, again sagged. However, the economy held steady because of increases in producer durable goods and in nonresidential construction.

The Recession of 1958

By the end of 1957 the investment boom slacked off. Demand for consumer durables was still as a low point after the saturation of the 1955 boom. And the government further restricted demand, both by cutting its expenditures and by following what many people considered a too tight money policy. The result was the most severe recession to come along since the war.

Light Ahead

Weak Recovery in 1960-1961 Followed by the Expansion of 1962-1969

Although the recession of 1958 was severe, it was short, less than one year. Business recovered, consumer demand picked up, and so did government demand, so that 1959 saw a renewed expansion. However, this recovery was not strong enough, and the economy went through another recession in 1960 and 1961, a mild one this time.

Between 1962 and 1969 the economy expanded without interruption, the longest expansion in U.S. history until the 1980s. Yet, early in the sixties Presidents Kennedy and Johnson were both concerned about the slowness of growth, the high unemployment rates (between 5 and 6 percent between 1962 and 1964), and the perception of a problem of chronic poverty.

The government used deliberate economic policy to combat these problems. To attack chronic poverty, there was Johnson's (largely unsuccessful) "War on Poverty." The government stepped up its expenditures, which in Keynesian terms gave some stimulation to the economy. The real stimuli, however, were the Johnson tax cuts in 1964 and 1965. The 1964 tax cut alone amounted to $11 billion, which had a marked effect on the economy: Unemployment fell from 5.2 percent in 1964 to 4.5 percent in 1965. As the tax cut worked, the economy moved toward full employment.

The 1965 escalation in Vietnam compounded our problems, as defense expenditures increased from $50 billion in 1965 to $80 billion by 1968.

Government, all levels of government, increased spending during this period, pouring out money, especially on schools and highways. Then, too, people's demand for consumer goods continued to be enormous, which caused a spurt in the growth of the GDP. Unemployment fell to 3.5 percent by 1969.

Excess aggregate demand, however, soon lead to substantial inflation. The consumer price index rose from 92.9 in 1964 to 109.8 in 1969, 17 points in only five years, in large measure caused by the overheating of the economy; that is, by demand-pull inflation on an economy operating near capacity.

Inflation and Unemployment in 1970-1971: Wage and Price Controls in 1971-1973;

Stagflation
A term used to describe the combination of high unemployment and a high rate of inflation.

Toward the end of the sixties there was such a high rate of inflation that in 1969 the government, in alarm, adopted some restrictive policies. The effect was only to increase unemployment. It was a repetition of 1958. The economy suffered from the worst of conditions, **stagflation**: high unemployment and high inflation.

In 1971, although the economy was beginning to recover and GDP was expanding, prices were still rising. The balance of payments was worsening, and unemployment was still high. Existing fiscal and monetary policy seemed inadequate to policy makers to deal with all these problems at the same time. So in August of 1971 President Nixon took several steps, announcing fiscal programs designed to increase demand and employment, a 90-day wage and price freeze, and the first of a number of "phases" to control prices. Also, to help the balance of payments, Nixon floated the dollar in international exchange markets. All this took everybody by surprise. A few weeks before, Nixon had said that he did not believe in controls and that he would never devalue the American dollar.

In 1972 price increases were noticeably less, and so was unemployment. Our balance of payments improved, and GDP increased sharply. As a result, in Phase II and Phase III, Nixon loosened price controls. But in 1973 prices went up again, by about 8 percent, and the dollar depreciated by 12 percent on the international market. So one might say that Nixon's medicine did not work in the long run.

Inflation and Unemployment Again: 1974 to 1976

From 1974 to 1976 unemployment rose rapidly to more than 8 percent. Inflation passed 12 percent, for 1974, and real GDP rose very slowly after first falling. Stagflation seemed to many to have become built into the economy.

In the mid-1970s, the central problem seemed to be how an economy could combat at the same time high unemployment, falling or very slowly growing real GDP, and significant inflation. Simply using fiscal and monetary policy to expand the economy, to reduce unemployment, and to contract the economy in order to control inflation was not feasible.

Recovery: 1977 to 1979

The stagflation concerns subsided somewhat as favorable monetary policies and continuing federal deficits stimulated the economy. As unemployment fell from 7.1 percent to 5.8 percent, real GDP grew by about 8 percent. A continuing high rate of inflation (almost 20 percent growth in the CPI) led many to conclude that productivity and supply were not growing rapidly enough in the United States.

Recession Followed by Growth and Deficits: 1980-1989

The supply shocks of sharp energy price increases from OPEC II led to rising costs, declining aggregate supply and rising unemployment. Unemployment reached almost 10 percent and the economy entered double digit inflation (13.5 percent from 1979 to 1980). A change of administration in 1981 led to tax cuts and efforts to stimulate both aggregate demand and aggregate supply. Supply-side economic policies became the focus of public macroeconomic policy. To combat inflation, restrictive monetary policies were pursued with a sharp recession resulting in 1982-1983, and unemployment peaking at 9.7 percent in 1982. Thereafter, the stimulative effects of easier monetary policies, tax cuts, investment tax credits and large federal budget deficits combined to reduce unemployment (to 5 percent in late 1989) and cut inflation rates (the CPI rose only about 2 percent annually from 1985 to 1986 and at rates of 3 percent to 4 percent from 1986 through 1989). Large trade deficits to be financed and very large budget deficits remained key problems.

1991-2004

The economy lapsed into recession in 1991. By now, there was little sympathy for an incomes policy and in view of the large national debt and federal deficits, little ability to employ Keynesian stimuli to the economy. By late 1994, and following a period of cost reducing measures by firms, the economy began to grow substantially and with little evidence of inflation.

That growth continued to 2001 and the result was the longest period of such expansion in the nation's history. By late 2001, the economy slowed with a brief recession followed by slow growth. In 2004, the economy returned to its historical growth path.

2008-2011

In December, 2007, the American economy moved into recession. That recession continued into mid 2009 and was quite sharp. By 2010, the economy experienced very slow growth and was out of the recession and into very slow growth. Some have compared this recession with the "Great Depression" of the 1930s which, as we saw earlier, did not end until 1940-1941. In 2009 and 2010, there were massive interventions by the federal government to arrest the downward movement of the economy. As it turned out, these interventions were generally successful; although the economy continued to perform below its potential much longer than most observers expected. See Applications I and II in Chapter one for details.

A Judgment About Stability

Is American capitalism inherently unstable? You can see from this short record of the past sixty years that the U.S. economy is subject to oscillations in levels of output, employment, and prices. We have even seen that many combinations of these three can exist at the same time.

The U.S. economy can experience severe drops in prices, income, and employment (the recessions and depressions prior to 1945). It can also have stable or near-stable prices, low unemployment, and expanding output (as in the 1920s and the mid to late 1980s and the 1990s). It can have expansions accompanied by substantial inflation (1945-1948, 1950-1953, 1955-1957, 1965-1969, 1972-1973, 1977-1979). Finally, recession, with falling real incomes and high unemployment, can occur at the same time as sharp increases in prices (1958, 1970-1971, and 1974 to late 1975).

Let us sum up this overview with the following: The American economy clearly is growth oriented. Its long-term trend in terms of real income and employment has been upward. Standards of living have risen secularly and by the late 1980s, a larger percentage than ever of the potential labor force was employed. In 2004, the unemployment rate was as low as 5.4 percent and has continued at 4 to 5 percent in the years since. Yet, the nation, historically, continues to be plagued by cyclical variations that sometimes are sharp. Is there a way to have long-term growth without these cycles? Unfortunately, at this point in time, economic theory provides no clear answer to this question.

SUMMING UP

1. There are four types of economic fluctuations: (a) The *secular trend*, which is the expansion or contraction of the economy over very long periods of time; (b) *business cycles*, which are repetitive but not regular variations in general economic activity; (c) *seasonal variations*, which happen regularly at the same time each year; and (d) *random variations*, which have no regular pattern or recurring cause.

2. The two phases of the business cycle are: (a) the *contraction phase*, often leading to a recession, when unemployment and unused capacity are high and investment and consumption are low; and (b) the *expansion phase*, when investment, consumption, and employment are high and prices may be rising.

3. In business cycles, there is no regularity in the length of the cycle or any of its phases, nor is there regularity in the intensity of activity. Many consider the term *business fluctuation* more descriptive than *business cycle*.

4. Prices in durable-goods industries tend to be more stable over a given business cycle than prices in nondurable-goods industries. (a) During a contraction in economic activity, people postpone buying new durable goods such as automobiles and washing machines; they tend to repair and keep using the goods they have. But they must continue to buy nondurable goods, such as food and clothing. (b) Nondurable-goods industries are more competitive than durable-goods industries; thus individual firms cannot limit the drop in their own prices.

5. *Leading economic indicators* are measures of economic activity that point the way to coming increases or decreases in economic activity shortly before there is an actual rise or fall. Economists use these leading indicators (stock-market prices, building permits, average workweek, and so on) as tools with which to forecast economic activity.

6. There are several kinds of unemployment: (a) *Frictional unemployment* includes people who are unemployed only for short periods of time as they move from one job to another. (b) *General Unemployment* or *Unemployment due to lack of demand* occurs when there is not enough total demand for industry's output for full employment to be attained. (c) *Structural unemployment* which is due to structural changes in the economy, which take place because of changes in technology and the composition of output, with resulting changes in the pattern of demand for labor. (d) *Seasonal unemployment*, which reoccurs regularly during the same time of the year.

7. The *GDP gap* reveals the economic costs of unemployment by showing the difference between potential and actual gross domestic product. The cost of unemployment in economic terms may be high, but the individual psychological and social costs, plus social and political tensions, may be even higher. According to *Okun's Law*, for each one percent that the actual unemployment rate exceeds the natural rate, a 2 percent GDP gap results.

8. There are two types of inflation: (a) *demand-pull inflation*, in which total demand for an economy's output exceeds the ability of the economy to supply at existing prices, and prices rise to ration the scarce supply; (b) *cost-push inflation*, in which suppliers of resources increase their prices faster than workers increase their productivity, which pushes cost of production up, forcing companies to increase their prices.

9. Cost-push inflation and administered-price inflation exist because of the dearth of competition in certain industries and can interact to cause an upward spiraling of prices.

10. During periods of inflation, *redistribution of real income* occurs, because those with fixed or semifixed incomes cannot increase their *money income* to compensate for rising prices. Those with variable incomes can usually increase their real incomes, since their money incomes might go up faster than prices do. The reverse occurs during a period of *deflation*, when prices fall.

11. There is also redistribution of real wealth during a period of inflation, as debtors benefit from inflation because they borrow high-purchasing-power dollars and pay back low-purchasing-power dollars. Creditors and savers lose in an inflation because they lend (or save) high-purchasing-power dollars and are paid back low-purchasing-power dollars. The opposite occurs during a deflationary period, when prices fall.

12. A strong inflation may ultimately lead to recession, as cost distortions put pressure on some firms, confuse both producers and consumers, and weaken the consumer's willingness and ability to buy. Moderate inflation may increase output and income by stimulating investment. *Creeping inflation* (or moderate inflation over a fairly long period) may eventually have bad effects on the economy. Savers may be hurt during inflation as real interest rates (nominal rates minus the rate of inflation) may even become negative.

13. It is difficult for a government to readily achieve both full employment and stable prices at the same time, especially in a noncompetitive economy. As the economy increases its output, some resources run out before full employment is attained. The prices of these resources will increase, and prices in general will increase, before full employment is reached.

14. A diagram of the tradeoff between unemployment and higher prices is called a *Phillips curve*. Some economists question whether a valid Phillips curve tradeoff may be established. To the extent that it is a valid concept, the Phillips curve for the pre-1970 period appeared to be stable and had politically acceptable levels of tradeoff between unemployment and inflation. After 1970, the Phillips curve reflected higher levels of tradeoff between unemployment and rising prices. In recent years, however, the economy has achieved relatively low rates of inflation consistent with relatively small GDP gaps.

15. Unemployment in the U.S. as we entered the mid-1990s was about 6 percent. Most national goals or targets have set 4 percent as the desirable rate. Macroeconomic policies can influence the actual rate of unemployment.

16. There are tradeoffs between unemployment and inflation (or price instability). Economists, in assessing these tradeoffs, have sought to define and measure a *natural rate of unemployment*, one in which inflation tends neither to accelerate or decelerate (the inflation rate is stable).

17. Phillips curve tradeoffs have been unstable in the short run because of changing inflationary expectations. As macroeconomic policies are applied to lower the actual unemployment rate below the natural rate, inflation rises and there is a shift upward of inflationary expectations.

18. Rising inflationary expectations cause rising wage and other resources costs that become reflected in higher prices and increasing inflation. As a result, the economy returns to its natural rate of unemployment but with a higher rate of inflation than before.

19. The natural rate argument leads to the conclusion that (1) in the long run, an economy cannot be pushed below its natural rate of unemployment, and (2) attempts to push unemployment below that level simply raise inflation.

20. Studies indicate that the natural rate of unemployment in the U.S. has (1) rarely been reached since 1945, (2) tended upward since the 1960s time period, and (3) is currently somewhat more than 5 percent.

21. A changing composition of the labor force is thought to be the major reason for the increase in the natural rate of unemployment (more women and teenagers participating in the labor force). The labor force now exhibits more structural as well as frictional unemployment.

22. Lowering the national rate of unemployment is desirable. Doing so will require changes in labor markets that include (1) better matches between skills and job vacancies, (2) better matches between job locations and available workers, (3) eliminating institutional barriers in labor markets.

23. Transitional unemployment remains desirable because the economy needs the labor mobility that is reflected in people moving from less productive to more productive jobs.

KEY TERMS

Business cycle
Contraction phase
Cost-push inflation
Cyclical unemployment
Deflation
Demand-pull inflation
Expansion phase
Frictional unemployment
Full employment
GDP gap
Inflation
Inflationary expectations
Leading indicators
Natural rate of unemployment
Okun's Law
Random variations
Real interest rate
Seasonal variations
Secular trend
Stagflation
Structural unemployment

QUESTIONS

1. Some economists have said that the term *business cycle* is not accurate, and they advocate using such terms as *business fluctuation* or *economic instability*. What is the basis of their objection? Do you agree with them?

2. Define the following terms:
        a. Secular trend
        b. Concentrated industries
        c. Leading Economic Index (LEI)
        d. Frictional unemployment
        e. Structural unemployment
        f. The GDP gap
        g. Inflation
        h. Demand-pull inflation
        i. Cost-push inflation
        j. Administered-price inflation
        k. Stagflation
        l. Inflationary expectations

3. Compared to clothing prices, washing machine prices tend to be stable, although there are wide variations in production over a given business cycle. Why is that?

4. Unemployment due to the public's lack of demand for industry's output fluctuates as business activity fluctuates, while structural unemployment may not. Why is this so?

5. How does the existence of monopoly power affect the level of prices?

6. How does the level of prices affect the distribution of real income? The distribution of real wealth?

7. What are real as opposed to nominal interest rates? What effects result from negative real interest rates?

8. In a market economy, some argue that it is difficult to have full employment and stable prices at the same time. What is the argument?

9. The natural rate of unemployment seems to be higher than previously. What implications does this have for an economic policy that will stabilize the economy? Why did this change occur?

10. You are a member of the President's Council of Economic Advisers in 1994. You have just told the President that the country cannot have full employment and stable prices at the same time. Furthermore, inflation in 1994 is 7 percent and unemployment is just over 6 percent. The President charges you to advise him which should be decreased: inflation or unemployment. Which would you counter with government policy: inflation or unemployment? Give *economic* justification for the one you've chosen. Since some groups are hurt by inflation and others by unemployment, your decision hurts some and helps others. Give ethical and moral justifications for your decision.

11. What is meant by the term "natural rate of unemployment"?

12. What is the difference between identifying the natural rate and the actual rate of unemployment for an economy? Which has typically been higher in the American economy?

13. What may cause the tradeoffs between inflation and unemployment shown in a Phillips curve to be unstable?

14. Why, according to the natural rate of unemployment argument, is it difficult to keep an economy below its natural rate of unemployment? What happens, according to this argument, when efforts are made to push the unemployment rate below the natural rate?

15. What has happened to the natural rate of unemployment in the U.S. since 1945? What seems to have caused this effect?

16. Is it desirable to lower the natural rate of unemployment in the American economy? Why?

17. Of the various things necessary to lower the natural rate of unemployment, which do you favor? Which will probably be most difficult?

Chapter 7: Economic Growth

Except for the earliest formative years of its colonial period, the United States has enjoyed one of the most impressive economic growth records among the world's nations. A small but prosperous nation in the late eighteenth century, it had, by the early twentieth century, become the world's leading industrial society. That process of industrialization, which came to be called the "American system of manufactures," produced a rate of growth in output that, even in the face of very rapid population growth, assured that each new generation of Americans enjoyed a higher standard of living than its predecessor. Indeed, each generation came to think of economic growth as the norm and to assume, justifiably, that its children would be better educated and more prosperous than themselves. Now, in the early twenty first century, troubling questions have arisen as to whether that long growth trend will continue and whether the resulting sanguine view of the future is still warranted. While we cannot forecast with precision the future of the nation's economy we examine topics such as what constitutes economic growth and what were the factors that contributed to America's successful growth record. In doing that, we may gain some insights into what will be necessary to insure that the long-term trend is maintained.

Statics versus Dynamics

Until now, we have dealt with economic analyses and discussions that are primarily *static*. That is, they are like a snapshot of a situation at a point in time, rather than like a motion picture showing the situation changing with the passage of time. Static principles of economics, such as supply and demand and national income determination, have helped us analyze problems as diverse as how to view the effects of rent control laws, and whether monetary policy is an effective tool against inflation.

Dynamic Framework
A framework that explains how things change over time.

We are about to explore some problems that, at least in some of their aspects, require a **dynamic framework**, one that explains how things change over a period of time. We will examine, for example, the growth record of the U.S. economy and its prospects for the future. In this chapter we will discuss several theoretical explanations of economic growth, and in the second application, we will present the following related problem: Do we have to choose between more growth and a clean environment?

Let's begin by making a distinction between expansion and growth. We'll use **extensive growth** to refer to the process by which the output of an economy grows as it uses more and more resources. **Intensive growth** refers to the process by which productivity, output per hour of labor (or income per capita), increases.

Extensive Growth
The process by which the output of an economy grows through the use of more resources

Intensive Growth
The process by which productivity, output per hour of labor increases.

Sources of Extensive Growth

Extensive growth can be thought of as an outward shifting of a nation's production-possibilities curve. An economy can achieve such growth by using more resources. First, it might achieve extensive growth because of an increase in the supply of total resources (land, labor, capital, and entrepreneurship). Let's look at each of those resources to see how, and how much, each might contribute to expansion.

1. *Land* represents all the natural resources of a nation, not only the surface soil but the subsoil minerals, the timber, and the water. It is tempting to think of all resources as being fixed: so many acres of land, so many acre-feet of water, tons of minerals, and so forth. Although it is useful to know (or estimate) the economy's resources at a particular time, you should realize that they can and do change as time and technology change the ways of producing things as well as the things that can be produced. It is very important, also, to remember the role of prices in defining the supply of natural resources. At a price of $10 a barrel a nation may have so many billions of barrels it is profitable to use as a resource (to produce goods and services). At $65 a barrel, the amount that is profitable to recover and use will certainly be greater.

Consider the case of offshore oil, under the continental shelf: A few decades ago no one was even sure it was there and even if knowledge of it existed, at then-existing oil prices, it was not profitable to explore and recover it. Even after geologic surveys confirmed its existence, it was still only a potential resource that might be tapped someday. Now, technology and price changes have made a difference. With new oil-drilling technology, and with world oil prices much higher than in 1971, offshore oil, as well as oil in Alaska and other places, has become a resource, something available to use in producing goods.

Another example of technology creating a resource occurred in iron mining. In the Mesabi iron range, the richest iron ore was mined and the second-grade ore, called *taconite,* was thrown aside because it was too expensive to refine. Now, with new technology, the mining companies are working the Mesabi range again, this time getting iron from the taconite. The price of iron makes it economical, definitely worth the trouble.

We should note here that technology and changes in technology affect not only extensive growth, through making resources out of previously unusable potential resources. They also, as you shall see shortly, increase the productivity of resources that are employed and, thereby, are themselves a major source of intensive growth.

2. *Labor* represents the human resources of a society. In a sense, labor is the most basic of all resources. Without labor, nothing happens. The whole process of intensive and extensive growth depends on human motivations, work, aspirations, and skills. An increase in population or an increase in participation in the labor force (for example, labor force participation by women during and since

World War II) increases a society's total output (that is, it creates extensive growth).

3. *Capital* is the physical result of investment. Capital consists of the plant and equipment and tools with which people work. Capital's productivity rises with specialization, and specialization is limited by the size of the market. In a small town in a largely rural (perhaps low-income) area of the United States, there's not much specialization of either labor or capital. If you get sick, you go to the town doctor, who is almost certainly a general practitioner. If you have a leaky roof, you go to the town's general handyman, a jack-of-all-trades. If your car's engine is idling badly, you take it to the town mechanic, no matter whether the car is a Chevy or a Nissan.

Now, what happens if you live in a city and have the same problems? If your medical problem is a skin rash, you go directly to a dermatologist or you are referred to one. If you have a roof leak, you call in a firm of roof specialists. If you have car trouble, you probably find a garage that specializes in that particular make of car.

Whether in small town or city, the kind and amount of capital that people have to work with has a lot to do with their productivity. The more capital, and the more sophisticated the capital available to workers, the greater their output.

The differences in these two earlier situations are due to *different market sizes*. The small (poor) town has few consumers and relatively little aggregate demand. The city has many consumers and much more aggregate demand. In the city there are enough people with enough purchasing power to warrant the investment that results in specialized tools, machines, and plant facilities. Without this capital, jobs for those in the (increasing) labor force will not be created and the society will not be able to use its (potential) natural resources.

4. *Entrepreneurs* (enterprisers) constitute a critical resource to any society. Indeed, entrepreneurial activities involve seeking out the best opportunities, especially *new* opportunities for using resources to produce goods and services. Often, such activities involve *innovation*, the creation of new firms, new products, new markets, as well as applying new technology to produce existing products in more efficient ways. In doing these things, entrepreneurs take differential risks and, when successful, not only shift the production-possibilities curve outward, but also raise productivity. They decisively influence, thus, not only extensive growth but also intensive growth.

Increasing Productivity and Growth

There is a link between productivity and growth. As more and more resources are used in production, growth may occur because as productivity increases the cost per unit of output goes down. As the economy uses existing plants, or builds more plants, and as it employs more people and uses more land (natural resources), output may increase more rapidly than input. In other words, a five percent increase in the use of inputs may generate more than a five percent increase in output. Let's examine the reasons for this.

According to Adam Smith and other early classical economists, *specialization* is a major reason for such increases in output. In an economy whose market size is growing, there is more and more specialized use of labor and capital, which leads to more and more output. In fact, large market size, as we mentioned a bit earlier, is necessary if specialization is to become widespread in an economic society.

Technological Change
The growth in knowledge or advances in techniques that result in more productive capital goods and more efficient organization.

Technological change, the growth in knowledge or advances in techniques that result in more productive capital goods and more efficient organization, is perhaps the main thing that holds out hope for future growth. If all our prospects for growth depended on the static benefits of specialization, the future might prove as gloomy as the classical economists (Adam Smith, David Ricardo, and others) predicted. Their dismal view prevailed through much of our industrial history. To see why, examine Figure 7-1.

Let's suppose that the economy shown in Figure 7-1 has met various preconditions for growth: attitudes favorable to growth, financial institutions to receive and channel savings into productive investments, a government to establish and enforce commercial rules, people drawn into the market system, all the things we have discussed in previous chapters. Suppose also that it has at least one industry that has a high growth potential whose effects seem likely to spread throughout the economy.

What will happen first as the economy starts to grow and expand? In the early years, its productivity and per capita income may rise rapidly. The part of the growth path (Y/P) from zero up to time t_0 represents this period. As the size of its market gets larger (as reflected in its growing per capita income), it begins to enjoy all the efficiencies of increased specialization. The slope, or rate of change, of (Y/P) increases, indicating that real per capita income is growing faster and faster.

Then, after time t_0, the slope of (Y/P) becomes less steep, which means that if the economy remains on this growth path (even at full employment), growth will be slower. (As time passes, the increments in growth will get smaller and smaller.) This implies that there are barriers or resistances to rapid growth. What are they? Why can't the economy simply keep on growing at the same rate?

Decreasing Productivity and Growth

Let's answer the question of why there has been a slowdown in the growth rate:

1. In the short term, some resources may be relatively fixed in usage. For example, the Atlas Company makes stereo sets, for which plant and equipment are the fixed inputs. Now it naturally takes longer to put new plant and equipment into use than it does to vary the use of other inputs (labor, land, and materials). So if Atlas wants to make more stereos, and if it starts using more labor and land without increasing its use of capital (plant and equipment), then its productivity (output of stereos per unit of additional input) will ultimately decline. Why? Basically, because of overcrowding. With a fixed number of machines and a fixed amount of plant space, workers may start having to wait to use machines. They may finally get in each other's way and disrupt the specialized routines of the plant.

2. As an economy begins to suffer diminishing productivity growth, the rate at which per capita income grows slacks off. At some point (t_0 in Figure 7-1), diminishing efficiency (due to the slowness of increase in plant and equipment) begins to more than offset the increased amount of efficiency resulting from specialization. The slope of the (Y/P) curve becomes less and less steep. When it reaches zero (past t_1), the society is in a *stationary state*. Real per capita income is at a maximum and will not grow further until something in the economy changes.

Figure 7-1
Growth Paths of an Economy

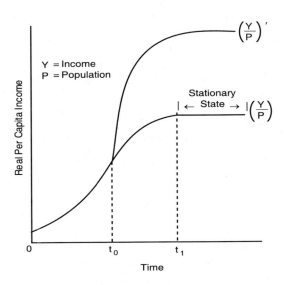

The Classical View

The classical economists (Adam Smith, et al.) who talked about the stationary state disagreed about how high the upper limit to (Y/P) might be. Smith was among the most optimistic. Unlike others, Smith refused to look upon technology as containing a fixed number of choices. Some classical economists gloomily predicted that a society would use techniques that added less and less to productivity as time went on and that it would finally run out of new technological choices. They felt that this gradual disappearance of new technology, combined with the need to produce more and more food for a growing population on a fixed supply of land, would ultimately produce the stationary state at a fairly low level of real per capita income. But Smith had slightly more optimistic hopes for the future. He believed that population growth might be held in check because as people become accustomed to more goods and services, they might develop a taste for more goods rather than more children.

Malthusian Specter
The view of Thomas Malthus that because of slower growth in food supplies than in population, starvation, wars, plagues, and famines would result.

The most pessimistic of the classicists was the English economist, Thomas R. Malthus. Parson Malthus (he was a preacher) originated what has become known as the **Malthusian specter**. His grim view of the future derived from two influences: the supply of people and the supply of food to maintain them. Malthus argued that the supply of people (the population) will increase at a geometric rate (1, 2, 4, 8, 16, and so on), that is, double each generation, or every twenty-five years. On the other hand, the food supply will increase only at an arithmetic rate (1, 2, 3, 4, 5, and so on). Finally, widespread starvation will result unless people are able to restrict the population. According to Malthus, there will be wars, plagues, and famines that ultimately will bring population into line with the means of sustaining people.

Has the Malthusian Nightmare Occurred in Some Places?

We said in an earlier chapter that a small but growing part of the world's population lives in high-income countries. For this lucky minority, the ominous predictions of the classical economists have obviously not come to pass. For the majority, however, the scenario, especially Malthus's version, has real meaning. Everyone reads about starvation, plague, famine, and war in such countries as Congo and Somalia. The photographs from those areas are heart-rending. Real per capita income in such countries is extremely low. For example, in India, each year population growth presses ever harder on the means of sustaining India's more than one billion people. In spite of the green revolution (that is, the growth in agricultural productivity), countries such as Bangladesh and Rwanda sometimes need foreign relief in the form of massive shipments of grain and other foodstuffs to prevent widespread starvation. For such countries, the low-level stationary state is a grim reality.

But what about that one-third of the world's people who live in Europe, North America, Australia, Japan, and the newly industrializing nations such as Taiwan and Korea? Why have they escaped? Look again at Figure 7-1, and let's use the United States as an example. The United States has experienced, at least over the last 25 years, a continuous shifting of Y/P, our growth path. In fact, real growth over that period has averaged 3.25 percent per annum. Each time, before the economy actually reached a point of declining growth (such as t_0), it has moved into a higher growth path, such as $(Y/P)'$. A series of such shifts has kept the U.S. economy from entering a stationary state. A study of our industrial history suggests that there are two major reasons for this: technological change and population increase.

Technological Change

A large part of U.S. productivity growth and increase in real income is due to the fact that U.S. industry has constantly changed the techniques by which it produces things. There is an old but true story about the clerk in the U.S. Patent Office who resigned, in the early nineteenth century, because he was sure that most of the important inventions had already been made. But Americans as a rule are optimistic about the future and count on technological change to increase their incomes and their productivity. To a great extent, their optimism is justified. Except for cyclical variations in investment in new forms of technology (such as the depression of the 1930s), U.S. industry has kept pushing ahead, using new methods as fast as people invent them. Beginning with the cotton gin in the late eighteenth century and continuing through the glamorous devices made possible by the aerospace technology and computer technology of the last three decades or so, U.S. industry has employed better and better machinery and tools, which have raised the productivity of American laborers right into the twenty first century. The United States has also made larger and larger investments in people themselves, spending billions on such things as education, health programs, and slum clearance, all of which have helped raise the productivity of the American worker.

Technologicial change can be thought of as improvements in the *quality* of capital. A new, faster computer, for example, raises the productivity of labor because it embodies the latest technology. Not all technological change however, is so embodied. A second form of technological change is through **disembodied technological change**, or change that is only partly, if at all, embodied in the quality of labor or capital resources. For example, a new transportation or communications network may lower the costs of many firms even if those firms continue to use the same capital and labor resources. Supply of the firms, thus, may increase without any embodied technical change.

Disembodied Technological Change
Technological change that is not completely reflected in improved quality of labor or capital.

Population Increase

In 1930 there were 123 million Americans. In 2015 there are about 320 million, more than a two-and-a-half-fold increase. This increase in population has been favorable to growth in the United States. Until people began to question the idea in recent years, Americans believed that growth in numbers would make them better off in the long run, which naturally influenced their willingness to have children. During the nineteenth century, when we were an agricultural society, large families were like money in the bank. Children started working on the farms at an early age and were active producers.

Likewise, when the United States was becoming an urban industrial society in the late nineteenth and early twentieth centuries, large families (together with waves of immigrants) were a good thing because they produced the labor force needed to build and operate mass-production factories.

But now that the United States is a mature industrial, or post-industrial, society, large families are no longer an *economic* asset (at least to individuals), although we continue to benefit from a large influx of immigrants. Children are consumers, not producers. So now, in the early years of the twenty first century, America has a relatively low rate of natural population growth. Though controversial to many, birth-control information is free in most states, and the advent of the Pill, plus the passing of laws and court decisions to legalize abortion (which are even more controversial) have combined to reduce the number of births from 27.7 live births per thousand in 1920 to less than 12 live births per thousand in 2000, a drop of more than 50 percent in eighty years.

©Punch (Rothco)

"Now will you have the vasectomy?"

Capital-Intensive
Techniques that use relatively more capital than labor or land.

Labor-Intensive
Techniques that use relatively more labor than capital or land.

Capital Deepening
When the capital/labor ratio rises for the economy.

Capital Broadening
When capital grows at the same rate as labor and the capital/labor ratio remains constant.

Instead of trying to expand its labor force, the United States is trying to expand its capital. This means that industry produces things through techniques that are ever more **capital-intensive** (using relatively more capital than labor or land) rather than through techniques that are **labor-intensive** (using relatively more labor than capital or land). As this is done generally, **capital deepening** occurs, that is, relatively more and more capital is used (raising the capital-to-labor ratio for the economy).

By contrast, **capital broadening** occurs when capital instruments (tools, plant, and the like) grow at the same rate that labor grows.

There is a lesson to be learned from the economic history of the U.S. and other industrial nations: The Malthusian nightmare need not come true at all. Technological change, both that which is embodied as well as that which is disembodied, can rapidly increase a nation's ability to produce all things, including food. Population increase need not be a drag on industrial growth. In fact, an educated populace *can* slow population growth to zero.

But the extent to which the experience of the United States (and other industrial nations) will be repeated in other nations as they attempt to industrialize, or whether the grim Malthusian scenario will indeed come to pass for some of the world's poorer countries, remains to be seen.

The Importance of an Educated Populace: Human Capital Formation

Beginning with Nobel Laureate Theodore Schultz, economists in recent decades have identified and focused on the growth impact of a fifth factor of production, **human capital.** Recall that it is defined as the improvement in labor skills attributable to investment in education. Michael Walden[1] puts the impact this way, "Clearly, better educated and skilled workers are more productive workers, and more productive workers increase the long-run economic growth rate." Robert Barro[2] estimates that a 10 percent increase in educational levels of the labor force is associated with a 0.2 percent increase in the annual long-run growth rate. Remember that increase, while it may seem modest, is a *permanent* increase. Robert Barro has compared the long-run rates of economic growth across many countries, rich and poor. A fundamental conclusion of Barro is that it is underinvestment in human capital, rather than physical capital that explains the failure of poor countries to catch up with the rich ones.

Human Capital
The improvement in labor skills attributable to investment in education.

These are but a few of the important options to the United States if, in the early twenty first century, it decides to consider ways to enhance its long-run growth rate and projected standards of living.

Slowing Productivity Growth in the United States?

Edward Denison[3], a leading authority on productivity in the American economy found that the growth of potential output (shifting of the American production-possibilities frontier) declined between 1948 and 1983. For the period 1948-1973 this potential grew at an annual rate of 3.9 percent per year. Between 1973 and 1979, this rate fell to 3.0 percent. From 1979 to 1983, it fell dramatically to

1. Walden, Michael. *Economic Issues: Rhetoric and Reality.* Englewood Cliffs, N. J. Prentice Hall. 1995.
2. Barro, Robert. "Economic Growth in a Cross Section of Countries." *Quarterly Journal of Economics,* 106. 1991.
3. Dennison, Edward. *Trends in American Economic Growth, 1929-1982.* Washington, The Brookings Institution. 1985.

1.8 percent, less than half of the 1948-1973 rate. Growth in output per worker fell over the same period from 2.3 percent per year to zero or less. Why the dramatic slowdown or virtual elimination of the shifting of the production-possibilities curve? At least five basic explanations have been offered:

1. **A change in the composition of the American Labor Force**. People who have had years of on-the-job experience have higher levels of productivity than new entrants. As the proportion of the labor force made up of new entrants has risen, productivity growth has slowed. This change, however, does not appear to be a major explanatory factor.

2. **The Composition of Output in the American Economy Has Changed**. As America's demand for output shifts more and more to labor-intensive services, productivity will grow more slowly than it did when a larger part of the GDP was produced by more capital-intensive manufacturing industries. Almost all students of the productivity growth problem agree that this factor has contributed to the slow down. Some say it has had little effect, others say almost half of the slow down can be explained by this change.

3. **Growth in Government Regulation:** Costs to firms of complying with government regulations fell in the early 1980s but rose again in the late 1980s and 1990s. Resources are required not only to regulate industries but also to meet standards of compliance with regulations. Neither of these resource usages is directly productive. While such diversions of resources may improve our quality of life or standard of living, as in the case of much environmental regulation, they reduce the (full-employment) growth of our productive potential. Thomas Hopkins[4] has shown that as regulatory costs rise, long-run economic growth declines. Milton Friedman[5] argues that, "dismantling the regulatory state would foster a return to the long-run capacity of the U.S. to grow at roughly 4 percent a year...."

4. **Rising Resource Prices**. Some have particularly suggested that OPEC I and OPEC II made fuel inefficient capital less productive to use and encouraged the substitution of labor for capital. Denison found, however, that rising prices for energy in the 1970s accounted for only about one-tenth of one percent of the reduction in productivity growth. If so, we might have expected little positive effect in this regard from falling real energy prices after 1987. Since 1995, energy prices have risen substantially.

5. **A Decline in the Rate of Capital Formation.** Capital formation and productivity growth are closely related. Economies that use relatively more capital have higher levels of productivity. Imagine a choice between solving data processing problems with (1) pen and paper, (2) mechanical calculators, (3) modern computers. Obviously (3) is the most capital intensive and also the most productive. Denison found, however, that only a small part of the productivity growth slowdown could be explained this way.

---

4. Hopkins, Thomas. *Cost of Regulation*. RIT Working Paper, Rochester Institute of Technology. 1991.
5. Freidman, Milton. "Getting Back to Real Growth." *The Wall Street Journal*, August 4, 1995.

What is the Implication: A Contrary View

A leading American economist, William Baumol[6] of Princeton, argues that the U.S. economy is *not* losing its productivity edge. Writing in the *Wall Street Journal* in March, 1990, Baumol cited the following: (1) Although the productivity growth rate has fallen, it has simply adjusted back to its historic rate (the 1950s and 1960s, with U.S. dominance of the world, were abnormal, says Baumol), (2) the productivity growth rate has slowed in all industrial nations (That of Japan has decreased as much as that of the U.S.), and (3) the "absolute productivity level of U.S. labor in general, and manufacturing in particular continues to be the highest in the world".

U.S. domination of manufacturing output, says Baumol, is growing along with that of Japan and in contrast to the European economies. Between 1975 and 1988, the share of the U.S. in world manufacturing output rose from 25.5 to 27.0 percent (Japan's from 11.5 to 17.5 percent). Service sector employment ("flipping the hamburgers") has grown because of rapid population growth between 1962 and 1985. U.S. labor is moving into services less rapidly than that of any U.S. trading partner except New Zealand. That the U.S. has become increasingly a service economy has resulted from "the outstanding productivity achievements of both industrial and agricultural section, there is nothing disturbing about the U.S. record."

While conceding that some U.S. industries have lost their competitive edge (including consumer electronics, automobiles, and such), and that this has created tragedies, especially for older workers, this process of rise and decline in industries, has been, according to Baumol, a "hallmark of technological progress accompanied by international competition". Views to the contrary, he says, are "a melange of half-truths" and the implications drawn from them false.

Technological Change Again: The Answer to Faster Growth?

A Nobel Laureate, Simon Kuznets[7], said that about 90 percent of growth came from a qualitative improvement in resources or from technological change. For this reason, many feel that more should be done in America to stimulate research and development activities (R&D). While R&D by private firms has been fairly constant since the 1960s, government support fell although it partially recovered in the 1980s. The repeal of investment tax credits in the 1987 law was regarded as unwise by some economists who believe that a government subsidization is warranted in view of the declining rate of growth in productivity. Still, high-tech industries have grown in the U.S. In 1980, they produced 20 percent of U.S. manufacturing output; in 1990, they produced 30 percent of that output. Real expenditures by U.S. firms on R&D increased in the same period from 1.7 percent of GDP to 2 percent in 1989. Thus, many other economists believe that investment tax credits are unnecessary and simply distort resource usage.

Has the U.S. Growth Rate Really Fallen?

We began this chapter by noting that troubling questions have arisen about the long-term growth rate of the American economy. Yet, as Baumol notes, Ameri-

---

6. Baumol, William J. "Americas' Productivity "Oasis: A Modest Decline Isn't All That Bad." *New York Times*, February 15, 1987.
7. Kuznets, Simon. "Economic Growth Explaining the Mystery." *The Economist*, January 4, 1992.

cans have not lost their productivity edge. Recent data show that American workers are still the most productive in the world. If productivity is measured by economic output per full-time employed person, U.S. workers in 1988 were 10 percent more productive than French workers, 16 percent more productive than German workers, 30 percent more productive than British workers, and 39 percent more productive than Japanese workers. While these "edges" are not uniform across all industries, they do not suggest an American manufacturing economy that is in decline.

Growth Rate Implications

Many studies of American economic growth have focused on recent performance in comparison to that of the 1950s and 1960s. DeLong, and Summers[8] say that on that basis, the average long-run growth rate in the 1970s and 1980s was only 0.9 percent whereas it was 2.3 percent on average during the 1950s and 1960s. Michael Walden[9] argues, however, that this comparison is not valid for two reasons: (1) all industrialized nations have witnessed a long-run growth rate decline in the 1970s and 1980s, and (2) the U.S. is one of only two industrial nations (Canada, the other) to witness an increase in its long-run growth in the 1980s over the 1970s..

Table 7-1
Long-Run Per Capita Economic Growth Rates in the United States

Period	Real Average Annual Growth Rate (%)
1840 – 1860	1.8
1860 – 1880	3.3
1880 – 1900	1.1
1900 – 1920	1.9
1920 – 1940	1.1
1940 - 1960	1.7
1960 - 1980	2.0
1980 – 1990	1.6
1990 - 2002	1.9
2001 - 2005	1.46
2006 - 2010	.07
2011 - 2014	2.1

Source: The World Bank, 2014.

---

8. DeLong, J. Bradford and Lawrence Summers. "Macroeconomic Policy and Long-Run Growth." *Economic Policies for Long-Run Economic Growth.* Kansas City, MO. Federal Reserve Bank of Kansas City, 1992.
9. Walden, Michael. *Economic Issues, Rhetoric and Reality.* Op. Cit.

Robert Barro[10] says that there are two reasons for skepticism about the studies that purport to show a decline in America's long-run growth rate beginning in the 1970s: (1) they focus on aggregate rather than per capita growth, and (2) they assume that the 1950s and 1960s are the appropriate time frame for comparison. Barro corrects for this by measuring average growth rates on a per person basis and takes an historical (1840 – 1990) time period as the basis of comparison.

You can see that there have been fluctuations in the long-run per capita growth rate of the U.S. economy since 1840 (as far back as we can go using census data). Barro concludes that there has been no significant decrease in the growth rate since the 1970s. Barro estimates the average growth rate for the entire period since 1880 at 1.6 percent per annum. The growth rate in the 1980s was exactly equal to the long-run post-1880 average. The 1950s and 1960s may have been abnormally high for two reasons: (1) an unusually high population growth rate, and (2) the recovery of the American economy from the depression of the 1930s and World War II.

What Could We Do to Increase the Growth Rate?

The research of Robert Barro suggests that there has been no long-term slowing of this country's growth rate. That does not mean, however, that an increase in the growth rate is undesirable or that it would not convey great benefits. Remember that the growth rate of the 1980s was about 1.6 percent. Suppose it could be raised by 50 percent to 2.4 percent per annum. While an enormous task, the increased rate of growth would mean that Americans thirty years from now would have more than 75 percent more goods and services than they would with the (historic long-term) rate of 1.6 percent! What could be done to raise America's growth rate? Here are just some of the suggestions that have been made in recent years.

1. *Increased savings and investment* in R&D, implementing new technologies, and building "state-of-the-art" plant and equipment. While the U.S. does have a relatively low rate of savings (especially by comparison with Japan), spending on plant and equipment has not declined; in fact, it rose in the 1980s.

2. *Increased investment in human capital*,– We looked at this earlier and know of the contribution it can make to a faster growth rate. There are major concerns about the nation's educational system in the early twenty first century. Additional effort to reform are being undertaken, though it is not clear how much of the problem is due to underinvestment.

3. *Regulatory and tax reform* – We mentioned earlier that recent research shows a negative effect of increased regulatory cost on the long-term growth rate. A proposal in the Congress in 1995 to require that cost/benefit analyses be applied to government regulatory programs was defeated. We may find that both direct and indirect regulation has exceeded the optimal level in terms of its effects on long-term growth.

4. *The size of government* – Robert Barro and others have found that larger government spending, especially on transfer programs that redistribute income,

---

10. Barro, Robert. "Economic Growth in a Cross Section of Countries." *Quarterly Journal of Economics* 106, 1991.

tends to lower the long-run growth rates of countries. It does so through lowering incentives to individuals to work.

Proximate Causes of Economic Growth: A Review

Figure 7-2 is a simple diagram showing how the factors discussed in this chapter affect output growth as measured by the percentage change in per capita real GDP (%ΔRPCGDP). It suggests that real per capita output growth rate is approximately equal to the difference between the rate of grow of real output (%ΔRGDP) and the rate of growth of population (%ΔPOP). That is, the growth rate of the "average slice" depends on how fast the size of the "economic pie" grows versus how fast the number of people who share that pie grows. The real output growth rate in turn is determined by growth rates of quantities of factors of production (for example labor or L and physical capital or K) and their productivity (P). That is, the larger the quantities of factors of production and the more productive they are, the higher is the rate of growth of real output. Continuing to move from right to left, we can further identify "proximate causes" of economic growth. The rate of growth of labor (%ΔL) reflects past rate of growth of population augmented by the growth of net inflows of migrants as well as norms and customs about the number of hours worked per year.

Figure 7-2
Proximate Causes of Economic Growth

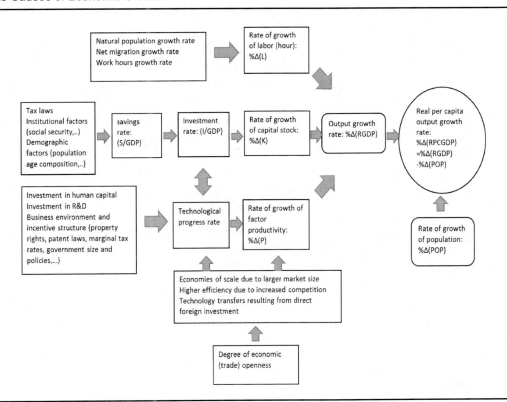

The rate of growth of capital stock (%ΔK) is a function of the share of GDP set aside for investment (I/GDP). The investment rate in turn reflects the share of GDP saved (S/GDP), as opposed to consumed, and therefore available for supporting the economy's investment needs. A host of factors such as our tax laws and the age composition of the total population affect saving decisions.

Productivity growth rate (%ΔP), which is becoming an increasingly more important driver of economic growth, is heavily influenced by the rate of technological progress; or how the new knowledge that we accumulate, through inventions and innovations, translates into new ways of doing things including production. The drivers of technological progress include investment in people through (formal and informal education) and training, investment in research and development (R&D), and a business environment that is conducive to innovation.

Application I: Economic Growth and the Power of Compounding

As discussed in Chapter 2, there are huge income gaps between poor and rich countries of the world both individually and as a group (see Table 2-2 and Figure 2-3). The rich countries of North America and Western Europe as well as a few others like Japan did not achieved their current economic status overnight. Rather, they relied on educated workforce, superior institutions, improvements in technology, and other factors (such as access to rich domestic and/or foreign natural resources) to grow their economies over a period spanning many decades. Our brief discussion of "income convergence" in Chapter 2 also highlighted a very important point: for poor countries to be able to narrow the income gap and eventually close it, they need to grow at faster rate than rich countries and do so on a sustained basis for a long period. This is a tall order for many low-income countries as we noted before.

This application illustrates the importance of the magnitude of the growth rate and the length of the period over which growth takes place using two quantitative approaches. The first one is based on the concept of "compounding." To understand what compounding means, suppose that you put $1 in a bank account which pays you 10 percent interest at the end of each year. Your dollar will grow to:

$1.10 =($1)+(0.10)($1) at the end of the first year

$1.21=($1.10)+(0.10)($1.10) at the end of the second year

$1.33=($1.21)+(0.10)($1.21) at the end of the third year, and so on

Compounding refers to this snowballing effect due to the fact that the amount to which the interest applies gets larger over time. Figure 7-2 shows to what value a dollar grows (the "future value") under different interest (growth) rates and time periods. As can be seen, the future value of the dollar will be larger the higher is the interest rate and the longer is the length of time that the interest income accumulates.

Table 7-2
The Power of Compounded Growth

Number of Years	Interest Rate 3%	Interest Rate 4%	Interest Rate 5%	Interest Rate 6%	Interest Rate 8%	Interest Rate 10%	Interest Rate 20%
1	1.03	1.04	1.05	1.06	1.08	1.10	1.20
2	1.06	1.08	1.10	1.12	1.17	1.21	1.44
3	1.09	1.12	1.16	1.19	1.26	1.33	1.73
4	1.13	1.17	1.22	1.26	1.36	1.46	2.07
5	1.16	1.22	1.28	1.34	1.47	1.61	2.49
6	1.19	1.27	1.34	1.41	1.59	1.77	2.99
7	1.23	1.32	1.41	1.50	1.71	1.94	3.58
8	1.27	1.37	1.48	1.59	1.85	2.14	4.30
9	1.30	1.42	1.55	1.68	2.00	2.35	5.16
10	1.34	1.48	1.63	1.79	2.16	2.59	6.19
20	1.81	2.19	2.65	3.20	4.66	6.72	38.3
30	2.43	3.24	4.32	5.74	10.00	17.40	237.00
40	3.26	4.80	7.04	10.30	21.70	45.30	1,470.0
50	4.38	7.11	11.50	18.40	46.90	117.00	9,100.00

This point is more formally presented in the formula $FV = (PV)(1+g)n$ where FV is the future value, PV is the present value, g is the growth (interest) rate, and n is the number years. For example, if you deposit one dollar in a bank and earn 5 percent interest at the end of the year for the next 20 years that dollar grows to $2.65= ($1) (1+0.05)20 at the end of the twentieth year. Note that the values in the table are simply the calculated compounding factor $(1+g)n$. (Try to see why by plugging different interest rates and years from the table in the formula).

A second approach to illustrating the importance of growth rate and time frame is based on a rule of thumb known as the "rule of 72." It gives you the approximate number of years for a variable that is growing at g percent per year to double in size. More specifically, we have doubling time (years)= 72/g. So, if real per capita income is growing at 2 percent per year, then its size doubles in about 36 years (=72/2). However, if the rate of growth increases to 3 percent, then it takes only 24 years (=72/3) for income to double. With a 10 percent growth rate (something close to China's growth performance in the past couple of decades) the doubling time is merely 7.2 years!

The main lesson of this application is that even a small increase in the growth rate makes a significant difference in the long term due to compounding. Stated differently, no increase in growth is too trifling to bother with!

Application II: Must We Sacrifice Growth to Have a Clean Environment?

More than a century has passed since the era of the "dismal science" and its grim Malthusian predictions. Optimism about the material future of human beings has grown even in the recession of 2008-2009. Improved technology and better organization, plus growing supplies of resources (including labor), have caused more and more countries to follow Britain and the United States toward ever higher levels of real income and better standards of living. Evidently the economist's assumption about growing output chasing rising aspirations was correct.

In the 1970s, however, the optimists began to qualify their optimism. (As Don Marquis said, "An optimist is a guy who has never had much experience.") Some argued that growth was inconsistent with environmental quality.

The Economists' View

Economists in general will not concede that pollution of the environment is the result of economic growth *per se*. Many also believe that the market system can offer solutions to the problems of pollution. In addition, many economists believe that continued growth is necessary, not as an end in itself, but as a means of solving a Pandora's box full of economic problems. Walter Heller[11] (chairman of the council of Economic Advisors during the Kennedy and Johnson administrations) summarized these views as follows:

> *In the starkest terms, the ecologist confronts us with an environmental imperative that requires an end to economic growth, or a sharp curtailment of it, as the price of biological survival. In contrast, the economist counters with a socioeconomic imperative that requires the continuation of growth as the price of social survival....Like it or not, economic growth seems destined to continue.*

Heller goes on to say the following: (1) Ecologists disagree with economists about whether real growth (improvement in the quality of life) has occurred, considering negative externalities. (2) Ecologists envision absolute bans and absolute limits to growth: economists envision marginal trade-offs and cost-benefit relations. (3) Ecologists want to rely on government to solve ecological problems; economists would rely on the price system to create solutions. Walter Heller says that growth could be checked, but that this "would throw the fragile ecology of our economic system so out of kilter as to threaten its breakdown."

Most economists would probably agree with Heller that it is the *pattern* of growth of the U.S. economy, not growth itself, that has created environmental pollution. Heller makes the point that scares about the environment (based on a static view of resources) occur periodically. He also

---

11. Heller, Walter W. "Economic Growth and Ecology, an Economist's View." In *Economics Mainstream reading and Radical Critiques,* 2nd ed. Random House, New York, 1973.

says that our attempts to solve problems such as adequate defense, poverty, discrimination, and pollution have so mortgaged future GDP growth that there is no choice left; the economy *has* to grow.

Economists generally agree that good environmental quality is a scarce commodity. Most of them acknowledge that the market system does not adequately incorporate externalities, such as pollution of the nation's water supply by industry, into its pricing system. However, this problem cannot be solved by limiting growth or by eliminating it.

Let's examine the problem of water. The world is running short of clean water, yet our need for it is growing with each passing year. Industries use millions of gallons of it hourly, for quenching steel ingots, for washing paper pulp, for cooling nuclear power plants, for cleaning newly slaughtered animals being readied for market, for washing away the chemicals from textile mills, and for thousands of other uses. The *effluent*, that is, the used water that flows out of factories, is often dumped into nearby rivers or streams. The water itself is not used up in this process. Rather, we have to clean it so that we can use it again, for bathing, swimming, cooking, and drinking.

To solve this problem, we could do several things: (1) *set minimum standards for industrial effluents* (though this would circumvent the market, and create large bureaucratic costs), (2) *tax industrial effluents* (this would make firms, and ultimately consumers, internalize the costs of pollution) or (3) Sell the rights to pollute water and raise the revenues to clean it up.

How Population Enters the Picture

Both economists and ecologists point out that the problems of economic growth are inextricably tied in with the problems of population growth. However, as industrialization and urbanization take place, population growth tends to level off, even to decline. Families that live in urban, industrial societies acquire education and realize that children are consumers, not producers. Also, since a pollution-free environment is a "luxury" good, demand for it rises with income. As the economy continues to grow, people may be expected to demand more of this luxury (income superior) good and substitute it for the relatively less desirable (income inferior) good, in other words, more children.

It is mainly ecologists who present the anti-growth view, but some economists join in. Fundamentally, the arguments are founded on the belief that it is nature that imposes the limits to growth. As the distinguished historian Arnold Toynbee[12] put it:

> *More and more people are coming to realize that the growth of material wealth, which the British industrial revolution set going, and which the modern British-made ideology has presented as being mankind's proper paramount objective, cannot in truth be the "wave of the future." Nature is going to compel posterity to revert to a stable state on the material plane and to turn to the realm of the spirit for satisfying man's hunger for infinity.*

Economist Kenneth Boulding[13] has argued that we must move from viewing the economy as an open system, with unlimited resources and growth

---

12. In Hailstones, Thomas J. and Frank V. Mastriana. Contemporary Economic Problems and Issues. Cincinnati. Southwestern Publishing Co. 1988.

(the cowboy economy"), to a "spaceship earth" closed economy (the "spaceman economy"). Boulding says that in the latter system, consumption and production that use up finite (nonreproducible) resources is not "good." Society must distinguish between reproducible and nonreproducible resources.

As Some Ecologists Have Seen It

Others, such as Herman Daly[14], argued for many years that "growthmania", the insistence that growth is the solution to economic problems, had outlived its usefulness. This view was reinforced by certain famous computer studies (the 1971 Club of Rome study is the most famous one) that predicted disaster unless growth trends were reversed. Daly and others argued not only for **zero economic growth (ZEG)**, *no* increase in GDP, but also **zero population growth (ZPG)**, no increase in population. To alleviate any hardships that this reversal of industrial history would cause, they wanted to see constant controls on physical wealth and distribution of income.

Such ecologists reject the market solution, which would entail forcing industries to internalize the externalities. Two observers, Richard England and Barry Bluestone, maintained, however, that this would require *total recycling* of wastes, with an accompanying "astronomical cost."

As Many Economists Have Seen It

Few economists have favored ZEG. Those that have argued that using selective means, such as tax cuts, to stimulate consumer spending is *not* necessary to maintain full employment. They say that a guaranteed annual income can maintain a full-employment level of spending just as well, and accomplish many of the same objectives.

In rebuttal, economists who oppose ZEG generally (1) attack the idea (which is implicit in the computer models) that the supply of resources is static, that the world will soon run out of oil, coal, and other essentials; (2) argue that leaving resources unused so that future generations may use them may not be as important as the capital and technology that would result from using them in the present; (3) feel that the ZEG and ZPG groups underestimate the ability of the price system to ensure efficient use of resources, to cause substitutes to be developed, and to force industry (when required to) to internalize the externalities that may have been ignored in the past.

Growth and the Environment: A New Consensus?

As America enters the twenty first century, concerns for achieving an acceptable level of environmental quality seem to be growing. At the same time, few people now seem inclined to advocate stopping economic growth to solve problems such as acid rain or the greenhouse effect. Indeed, as political scientist Robert Slavins has argued: "A new environmentalism has now emerged that embraces market-oriented environmental-protection policies." Both economists and ecologists now see that there are major environmental problems and, unlike the earlier era, many ecologists now believe market forces can be harnessed to help solve these problems in ways consistent with maintaining economic growth.

Zero Economic Growth (ZEG)
The argument that GDP growth should be stopped.

Zero Population Growth (ZPG)
The argument that population growth should be stopped.

13. Boulding, Kenneth E. "The Economics of the Coming Spaceship Earth." In *Environmental Quality in a Growing Economy*. Baltimore, Johns Hopkins, 1966.
14. Daly, Herman E. "The Steady State Economy: Toward a Political Economy of Biophysical Equilibrium and Moral Growth." In *Toward a Steady State Economy*. Freeman, San Francisco, 1973.

SUMMING UP

1. The United States has enjoyed a long-run economic growth rate that, including growth by the 20th century, made it one of the most prosperous of the world's nations. In order to be able to analyze many economic problems, one needs a *dynamic* rather than a *static* framework, that is, a structure that shows change through time.

2. *Extensive growth,* a process by which total output increases, comes about through the use of more resources, land, labor, and capital. *Intensive growth* is a process by which productivity, output per hour of labor (or income per capita), increases and becomes more complex.

3. According to Adam Smith and other classical economists, growth takes place because of the increased productivity that accompanies specialization in the uses of resources. This specialization is limited by the size of the market. As the market grows, more and more specialization takes place. But because of limited supplies of land and, ultimately, diminishing efficiency (diminishing returns), an economy's growth will diminish beyond some point and will ultimately reach a *stationary state.*

4. The stationary state may be high or low in terms of real per capita income. Smith envisioned it as becoming high, since with the development of better technology, people might prefer more goods to more children. Malthus thought it was likely to be low, since population increase would outstrip the food supply, and famine, plagues, and the like would result.

5. The classical scenario (the Malthusian version in some cases) has come true in many poor countries, whose growth has been very slow, or nonexistent, and whose investment in education has been slight.

6. Industrial nations and newly industrializing nations have escaped the stationary state, for two reasons: (a) Technological change has shifted their growth paths upward and overcome the long-term tendencies toward stagnation. (b) As growth has occurred, the rate of growth of their populations has tapered off.

7. Even a growing economy's growth is not necessarily accompanied by full employment. Therefore, a society's *actual growth path*, the change in its real per capita income as time goes by, may be less than its full-employment potential.

8. The *aggregate production function* is the relationship between total output and the labor force employed. It tells us how much output an economy produces at various levels of employment.

9. According to Edward Denison, productivity growth in the United States slowed over the period from 1948 to 1983, especially from 1979 to 1983. Some of the reasons for this slowing appear to be: (a) A change in the composition of the American labor force, (b) A change in the composition of the output of the economy, (c) Growth in government regulation, (d) Rising resource prices, (e) A decline in the rate of capital formation.

10. An important ingredient that contributes to economic growth is investment in *human capital*, the improvement in labor skills due to investment in education.

11. Most productivity growth is due to improvements in the quality of resources or to technological change. There are calls in the United States to create greater incentives to research and development and the resulting improvements in applied technology. Technological change represents an improved *quality* of capital. It may be embodied in better plants and equipment or it may take the form of *disembodied* technological change, that which is not completely reflected in an improved quality of labor or capital.

12. The United States has a long record of growth. Over the last one hundred years its output has increased at a compound annual rate of 2.1 percent. But it has had long periods of less than full employment, and therefore its growth path has often been below the full-employment level. Thus, the United States has lost a great deal of per capita income.

13. According to William Baumol, a slowing rate of growth in productivity is not a reflection of economic failure. For the U.S. this slowing reflects what has happened in most other industrial nations. Growth in services was caused by rapid population growth and, though severe dislocation have resulted in some industries, this has been so throughout modern U.S. history.

14. Americans are still the world's most productive workers. They are more productive than French, German, British or Japanese workers, though not uniformly so across all industries.

15. Some studies have concluded that there was a slowing of America's long-term growth rate in the 1970s and 1980s. Michael Walden argues that (a) this was true of all industrial nations, and (b) America's growth actually rose in the 1980s above that of the 1970s.

16. Robert Barro's research on America's growth rate focuses on (a) per capita growth and (b) a very long-term (1840 – 1990) historical view of growth. Barro concludes that there has been no significant decline in that growth rate. The 1950s and 1960s were higher because of (a) high population growth, and (b) recovery from World War II and the depression of the 1930s.

17. Increasing the nation's growth rate would convey significant long-term benefits in terms of the real standard of living.

18. Some ways by which the country's growth rate could be increased include (a) increased savings and investment in R&D, implementing new technologies, and building "state-of-the-art" plants and equipment, (b) increased investment in human capital, (c) a reassessment of the *costs and benefits* of government regulation, and (d) assessing what the trade-offs are between government size and the country's long-term growth rate.

19. Some economists, including Douglas Dowd, have argued that defense spending since World War II has been the key to growth and stability in the American economy. Other economists, however, dispute that connection.

20. The economic record for the 1950s and 1960s seems to show that (1) *variations* in defense spending were not used to reduce unemployment, and (2) that military spending was a large but stable portion o aggregate demand.

21. Even a small change in the rate of growth of an economy's output can make a big difference in the long run due to the compounding effect.

22. Until recently, twentieth-century economists, unlike their nineteenth-century forerunners, generally held an optimistic view of economic growth and its potential for solving economic problems. In the early twenty first century, optimism is tempered by the need to maintain environmental quality.

23. Certainly it is not economic growth alone that is responsible for polluting the environment. In fact, many economists believe that economic growth and the free market can solve the problems of the environment in the future.

24. Walter Heller said that economic growth seems destined to continue and that (a) economists and ecologists disagree over whether the quality of life has improved in recent years; (b) ecologists see absolute limits to growth and to resources, while economists do not; and (c) ecologists want government to solve environmental problems, while economists rely heavily on the market system.

Cartoon Feature Syndicate

25. The market system does not fully incorporate externalities, such as pollution of the nation's water supply by industry, into its pricing system. The solutions to this might be (a) to set minimum standards for industrial effluents, or (b) to tax industrial effluents so that producers (and ultimately consumers) would have to pay the full social costs of polluting the water.

26. Economic growth is inextricably intertwined with population growth. However, population growth declines with economic growth, since children in an urban, industrial society are nonproducers and people begin to prefer higher *per capita* income as well as environmental improvement to more children.

27. Arnold Toynbee argued that growth is not the wave of the future, but that natural forces will force the world's people to revert to a stable state, that is, no growth.

28. Some economists and ecologists have decried "growthmania" and argued for both *zero economic growth* (ZEG) and *zero population growth* (ZPG). They argued that obtaining these would necessitate government controls over physical wealth and distribution of income.

29. Some ecologists rejected for many years the idea of the free market offering the solution to environmental pollution, on the grounds that the cost of total recycling of wastes would be astronomical.

30. The few economists who favor ZEG say that a guaranteed annual income (with its income redistribution effect) would be a good substitute for economic growth. A guaranteed annual income, they say, would sustain consumption demand and thereby keep employment at an acceptable level.

31. In rebutting the gloomy arguments of the ecologists, most economists oppose ZEG on the grounds that (a) resources are not static, (b) it is better to leave capital, technology, and productive capacity to posterity than to leave unused resources to posterity, (c) proponents of ZEG and ZPG underestimate the ability of the price system to change patterns of resource use and to induce people to use and find substitutes for nonreproducible resources.

32. In the early 2000s, there appears to be a growing consensus among economists and ecologists that environmental problems are severe and that market solutions to many of these problems are possible without sacrificing economic growth.

KEY TERMS

Capital broadening
Capital deepening
Capital intensive
Disembodied technological change
Dynamic framework
Extensive growth
Human capital
Intensive growth
Labor intensive
Malthusian specter
Technological change
Zero economic growth (ZEG)
Zero population growth (ZPG)

QUESTIONS

1. Why is a dynamic framework more useful than a static one for analyzing growth relationships and problems?

2. Is extensive growth or intensive growth more important to improving the material well-being of people? Why?

3. What are resources? What is the role of prices in creating and identifying the resources of a nation?

4. What is entrepreneurship? What is its important role in long-run economic growth?

5. What is the impact of technological change on growth? What is meant by dis-embodied technological change?

6. What was the classical view of long-run economic growth for a nation?

7. Why is investment in human capital so important to long-run economic growth?

8. To what did Edward Denison attribute the slowing of America's growth rate?

9. What does William Baumol conclude about the causes and effects of a slowing rate of growth in productivity?

10. Is 1950 – 1970 the appropriate base period of determining whether America's growth rate has slowed? What period does Robert Barro use and what are his conclusions?

11. What are some of the important ways through which America's growth rate could be increased?

12. Suppose that you are chairman of a special task force on employment. The President of the United States calls you in and says that he is going to propose an extraordinary increase of $50 billion in federal spending in order to create one million new jobs. He can't decide, though, whether to increase the spending of the Defense Department (which maintains that it needs a new manned bomber system) or the Department of Health and Human Services (which wants to expand educational benefits, medical care benefits, and other such programs). The President wants to know whether there will be different aggregate demand effects from the two types with expenditures of equal size. What would you tell the President?

13. The long-run growth future of the American economy depends as much on stimulating aggregate supply as on stimulating aggregate demand. Do you agree? Why?

14. What is the relationship between economic growth and the solutions to such ills as poverty, discrimination, and the welfare situation?

15. Is pollution of the environment *necessarily* the result of economic growth? If not, what else might it result from?

16. How may the market system, either with or without additional government control, develop solutions to problems of pollution?

17. What does Boulding mean by the "spaceship earth" concept?

18. State what you think of the arguments for and against ZEG.

Chapter 8: Aggregate Demand and Aggregate Supply

We have seen that, in spite of long-term real economic growth, price levels, employment-unemployment rates, and real income levels have varied greatly in uneven cycles of American history. In this and succeeding chapters we will build a framework for determining what creates not only aggregate price levels, employment levels, and growth rates but also how we may understand and explain the fluctuations in those key macroeconomic variables that were examined in the chapter covering supply and demand.

Let us begin with an explanation of the aggregate price level and changing levels of price. First, however, remember that we are not talking about a single price, like that of a particular good. Rather, we seek to explain the average level of all prices in an entire economy. In the chapter on supply and demand, we saw that in individual markets for commodities and services, prices are established by equilibrium forces that clear markets at levels that equate quantity demanded and quantity supplied.

The single product equilibrium-price model of chapter three on supply and demand are very useful for understanding and predicting how the price of a good such as personal computers is determined. It is also useful for explaining relative prices such as those of diamonds and water, or oil and gasoline. In addition, the model is helpful in explaining large changes in relative prices such as the change in gasoline prices relative to microcomputers in the early twenty first century.

Figure 8-1
Aggregate Level of Prices and Real Income for the Entire Economy

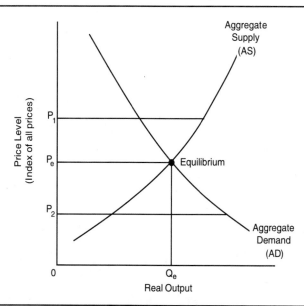

Aggregate demand and aggregate supply determine, in equilibrium, the level of prices and the level of real output for the economy. Aggregate demand is negatively sloped; as the price level falls, quantity demanded increases. Aggregate supply is positively sloped; as the price level rises, quantity supplied increases. Equilibrium national income and the equilibrium price level are where aggregate quantity demanded = aggregate quantity supplied or at equilibrium quantity Q_e and price level P_e. At any disequilibrium price level, (such as P_1 or P_2), there would be excess supply or excess demand forcing prices downward or upward to eliminate shortages or surpluses.

Useful as it is, the single-good supply and demand-based pricing model does not provide insights into important macroeconomic questions. Why are overall prices in the early twenty first century rising so slowly? What conditions might trigger a return to the double digit inflation of the late 1970s and early 1980s? These are but two of many aggregate price questions which require a different framework for their understanding. This framework is called an aggregate demand- aggregate supply model of the overall level of prices and real output in an economy. We see in Figure 8-1, a picture of an economy's price level using this model.

On the vertical axis of Figure 8-1 are the economy's various possible price levels or indexes of prices. Later in this chapter, we will explain how such price indexes are constructed and measured. For the moment, think of the index as a measure of the weighted average of the prices of all important commodities and services being traded in the economy. On the horizontal axis, we measure the various levels of real output for the same economy. The model explains how the equilibrium level of prices and the equilibrium level of real output is established. Equilibrium here has the same meaning as in the chapter on supply and demand; it is the level of prices and real income toward which the economy is moving given the aggregate demand for and the aggregate supply of its commodities and services.

Aggregate demand and aggregate supply determine, in equilibrium, the level of prices and the level of real income for the economy. Aggregate demand (AD) in Figure 8-1 is negatively sloped; as the price level falls, the quantity demanded of real output increases. Aggregate supply (AS) is positively sloped; as the price level rises, the quantity supplied of real output increases. We will shortly examine the reasons why AS is positively sloped and AD negatively sloped.

Equilibrium national income and the equilibrium price level are established where aggregate quantity demanded = aggregate quantity supplied or at income Q_e and price level P_e. We should note again, for emphasis, that this equilibrium real income is simply the level toward which the economy tends given the underlying AD and AS schedules. It is not a target or even necessarily a desirable level of real income. Q_e might be a level associated with severe recession and high unemployment or it might be associated with over- full employment and a high rate of inflation.

At any disequilibrium price level (P_1 or P_2) there would be excess supply or excess demand causing producers to adjust prices downward or upward to eliminate shortages or gluts.

Equilibrium Level of Prices and Equilibrium Level of Real Output
A level that is established where aggregate quantity demanded equals aggregate quantity supplied.

*The **equilibrium level of prices** and the **equilibrium level of real output** is established where the aggregate quantity demanded equals the aggregate quantity supplied.*

Only at P_e, in Figure 8-1, the equilibrium level of prices, are the plans of producers to offer commodities and services for sale made equal to the plans of buyers to purchase commodities and services.

Aggregate Demand: Its Definition and Determinants

Aggregate Demand
A measure of the entire planned spending on final goods and services at different price levels.

Aggregate demand (AD) is a measure of the entire desired or planned spending on final goods and services at different price levels. As there are four sources of such planned spending, there are four corresponding determinants of AD. When we examine the "Keynesian" model of income determination, we will see that managing or influencing AD involves influencing one or more of these four components.

Consumption Expenditures
The largest element of AD, consumption spending and variations in consumption spending, are subject to determination and variation by the many things that influence consumer behavior. Economists believe that the major elements or components which influence that behavior are:

1. ***Disposable income***. Disposable income may be used for consumption or saving. From our individual gross incomes, what we may dispose of in these ways depends on taxes, and private and public transfer payments. If, for example, social security payments are taxed, disposable incomes of retired persons will decline and so will the contributions of such households to AD.

2. ***Cost and availability of credit***. Durable, often expensive, consumer goods are usually purchased with loans. The cost of this credit and its availability heavily influence consumer expenditures on automobiles, housing, and other such goods. If the (interest rate) cost rises, the availability of such credit diminishes and this important component of AD will fall. Of course, if the cost of credit falls as it did during much of the early 1990s, aggregate demand will rise.

3. ***Expectations***. All of us have expectations about future economic events that will affect us. Will we have a job? If so, will our incomes rise? These expectations are influenced by both public and private actions. If our expectations worsen, if we expect declining income or even unemployment, our purchases of

many goods will decline. Consumer confidence surveys are often taken as a measure of these expectations.

Investment Expenditures

The most volatile element of AD is investment spending on plant and equipment, inventories, and research and development. Firms' investment decisions appear to be influenced by the following four factors:

1. *Interest rates*. Whether investments are financed by borrowing in capital markets or by the use of retained earnings, firms use interest rates as the benchmarks against which to measure the expected profitability of an investment. Thus, if interest rates rise, the profitability of an investment must be higher to induce a firm to make the investment, and fewer investments will be made.

2. *Government policy*. Present government policies as well as expected future policies influence investment choices. Will there be investment tax credits? Will tax breaks be given to firms that locate in a particular area? These and many other aspects of government policies affect the profitability of an investment strategy.

3. *Expectations*. Many investments have long-term payoffs. While the future is uncertain for firms as well as for consumers, both groups must establish expectations about future market conditions as well as future public policies. Present investment decisions, therefore, are partly a function of expected future events.

Government Expenditures

The second largest element of aggregate demand in the United States, government spending, is quite variable but difficult to ascribe to a simple set of influences since it is the result of a complex political process. There are various levels of government and various factors that seem to influence the expenditure policies of each. Among the factors which may be influential are efforts to secure re-election by public officials, automatic stabilizer programs which are tied to varying economic conditions, changes in political philosophy (the proper role of government), and national emergencies such as war and depression.

Net Exports (Exports Minus Imports)

Currently, the smallest element of aggregate demand; net exports has nonetheless become increasingly important in recent years. Net exports can be positive or negative. If positive, net exports add to aggregate demand. If negative, net exports decrease aggregate demand. Net exports are most influenced by three basic factors:

1. *Trade policy*. If Japan "voluntarily" limits its exports of cars to the United States, Americans will probably spend less on Japanese cars and the net imports of the United States will tend to fall. If nations impose or raise tariffs on U.S. goods, our net exports will tend to decrease as a result of the decrease in the quantity demanded of our exports.

2. *Exchange rate changes*. If, for example, the dollar buys fewer yen, Japanese imports tend to cost more in the United States, and U.S. exports to Japan tend to become cheaper. Rising U.S. sales to Japan and decreasing Japanese sales to the United States tend to increase our net exports.

3. *Politics*. Politics always plays an important role in trade between nations. If the government of Japan will not allow U.S. firms to bid for construction contracts in Japan, then our net exports tend to decrease. On the other hand, if Japan opens its markets to free trade, our net exports will tend to grow.

AGGREGATE DEMAND: A SUMMARY

Aggregate demand is the sum of intended spending on consumption expenditures, investment expenditures, government expenditures, and net exports at each overall price level. AD thus may be expressed as the sum of consumption expenditure (C) + investment expenditure (I) + government expenditure (G) + net exports (X_n).

$$AD = C + I + G + X_n$$

Why Does the Aggregate Demand Curve Slope Downward?

The aggregate demand curve shown in Figure 8-1 has a negative slope. That is, the lower the price level, the higher the quantity demanded, the higher the price level, the lower the quantity demanded. It may be tempting to think that this is simply a restatement of the law of demand. However, that is not so! Recall that the law of demand dealt with the effects of a change in the price of a single good, holding other prices (and income, taste, etc.) constant. Clearly such a *ceteris paribus* assumption cannot be made in the case of the aggregate demand curve which deals with changes in the (weighted average) prices of all goods on the level of real national income. If the aggregate price level falls, substitution effects will explain nothing for there are no substitutes for all goods and services (including savings).

Basically, there are *three reasons* why AD in Figure 8-1 has a *negative slope*. Although we will develop each more fully in other chapters, let us summarize these three causes:

1. *Effects of interest rate changes* on aggregate spending. Consider what happens when the price level rises. Households and firms need to hold more money to cover their transactions between receipts of income, thus increasing the demand for money. The increased money demand will cause interest rates to rise. As these rates rise, the demand for both consumer goods and non-consumer goods decreases, causing a decline in the quantity demanded of the economy's output.

2. *The effects of changes in wealth* on aggregate spending. Asset values are expressed in monetary (dollar) terms. When the price level changes, the real purchasing power of these assets, such as bonds and balances in banks, moves in the opposite direction. If prices double, for instance, the value of a $10,000 bond is halved. Therefore, if prices go up, individuals will have to save more to restore their real wealth positions. The increase in savings will tend to reduce the quantity demanded of current output.

3. *Relative price changes between foreign and domestic goods*. An aggregate demand curve includes all sources of demand for domestically produced goods, including foreign sources. When the price level in the United States increases (*ceteris paribus*), American goods become more expensive relative to foreign

goods. Americans substitute foreign goods for those domestically produced and foreigners substitute their own domestically made goods for American goods. Both substitution effects tend to decrease the quantity demanded of U.S.-made commodities and services.

For all three reasons, we may assume the following:

As the aggregate price level rises, the quantity demanded of the output of an economy decreases; as the price level falls, the quantity demanded of the output of an economy increases.(Aggregate demand curves slope downward.)

Aggregate Supply: Its Definition and Determinants

Aggregate Supply
A measure of the entire desired output of final goods and services at different price levels.

Aggregate supply (AS) is a measure of the entire desired output of final goods and services at different price levels. All of the things that may influence business decisions about production rates are potential determinants of aggregate supply. Included in such a list would be the following six basic factors:

1. *Cost and availability of resources*. Firms making profitable supply decisions consider not only revenue but also cost in deciding what and how much to produce. If resource prices rise, firms' costs do as well and AS tends to decrease. In this chapter's application, we will look at what sharp increases and decreases in oil prices in the 1970s and 1980s did to output decisions as well as real income and price levels. As oil prices rise in the early 21st century we should remember that increases in resource prices work their way through the economy and its supply of goods quickly in comparison with other determinants of aggregate supply.

2. *Capacity and investment plans*. In any short-run period, an economy has only so much *capacity*; its stock of plants and equipment, skilled laborers, and other resources. Naturally, the economy cannot produce beyond the limits imposed by this stock. Investment spending, however, will in the long run result in a shift of, or increase in, this capacity and a greater aggregate supply. Since investment also creates jobs and income, it will stimulate aggregate demand.
Most investment spending is undertaken by private firms. Government spending, however, may directly or indirectly raise the capacity of the economy. In wartime, governments may actually build plant and equipment. Ordinarily, though, the effects are indirect; government spending on activities such as roads, ports and airport facilities increases the productivity of private investment and results in a larger capacity.

3. *Technology*. Technological change raises the productivity of all resources and increases aggregate supply. As an example, the U.S. automobile industry founding itself threatened by the inroads of Japanese cars in recent times, has invested billions of dollars in developing and implementing new technology including robotics.

Technological changes not only result from investments, they also cause new investments. While much technological change is gradual, the big changes, such as microchips in the 1970s, come from intensive processes of research and development. These changes occur with significant time lags before implementation and are often subsidized by government.

4. *Productivity*. The *productivity* of resources, the output produced by each unit of input, depends on many things. The productivity of labor, for example, depends on the productivity of the capital with which it is employed. Labor's

Investment in Human Capital
Expenditures made on training, education, and increasing the skill levels of individuals

productivity also depends heavily on training, education, and on increasing skills. Economists refer to these three factors as **investment in human capital**.

Productivity growth has become a major issue in the United States in recent years, particularly since it has been growing at a faster rate in some other industrial nations than in this country. There have been calls for more investment in human capital as well as in new plant and equipment to raise the joint productivity of labor and capital and thereby increase the aggregate supply of commodities and services.

5. *Expectations*. Firms, like consumers, form expectations. Payouts on many investments is often long term. In making investment and production decisions, firms must form expectations about prices for their products as well as expectations of future overall price levels in order to assess the present value of such decisions. If expectations change, we would expect firms to re-evaluate their decisions and alter both the mix and amount of investments and planned production rates.

www.commerce.gov
For more information on commerce policies visit the Department of Commerce at the web site listed above.

6. *Government policies*. Government policies affect aggregate supply decisions in numerous ways. Such policies affect the availability and cost of resources. Will the United States allow exploration for oil in offshore sites? The policy decision will likely affect the price of oil and energy costs of firms. Will government policy tend toward further deregulation of transportation? The result will certainly affect the transport costs of firms in producing and distributing goods and services. These are merely illustrative of the myriad of government policies and changes in policy that influence firm's supply decisions.

Why Does the (Short-Run) Aggregate Supply Curve Slope Upward?

The aggregate supply curve in Figure 8-1 is positively sloped. Indeed, we will assume the following:

As the aggregate price level rises, the quantity supplied or produced will rise; as the aggregate price level falls, the quantity supplied or produced will decrease. (Short-run aggregate supply curves slope upward.)

Recall that we assume that the supply curve of a firm is based on cost and that in the short run, rising costs associated with ultimately diminishing productivity result in firms offering more for sale, only at higher prices. The AS curve for the entire economy in Figure 8-1 is based on the same assumption. In the short run, it is reasonable to assume that input prices (wages, interest rates, etc.) are constant and that it is rising real cost that explains the upward-sloping (short-run) aggregate supply curve. Of course, the process works in reverse. If private firms reduce output rates, they will lay off less efficient resources, and their (unit) costs will fall, making them willing to offer smaller rates of output for sale at lower prices.

It will be important to the reader to know that if the overall price level rises, there will ultimately be pressure to increase factor prices, including wage and salary rates as well as interest rates. The ultimately increasing costs associated with rising factor prices create supply shocks and affect equilibrium income and price levels. This interaction will be addressed more fully in another chapter.

Figure 8-2

Equilibrium Income, Actual Income, and the GDP Gap

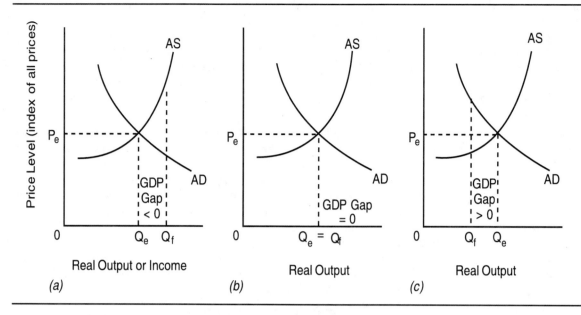

In *(a)*, the equilibrium level of income, Q_e, is less than the potential or full employment level of output, Q_f. The GDP gap Q_e - Q_f is negative. In *(b)*, the equilibrium level of income, Q_e, equals the potential or full employment level of output, O_f. The GDP gap is zero, the economy is producing at its potential with only a natural rate of unemployment. In *(c)*, the equilibrium level of income, Q_e, is greater than the potential or full employment level of income, Q_f. The GDP gap Q_e - Q_f is temporally positive.

Equilibrium and Full Employment May Not Be the Same

We have seen that there is a potential or capacity GDP that a nation is capable of producing if it fully employs its resources, especially its labor force. We also have seen that the full employment level, though rarely reached, does not correspond to zero unemployment. The actual level of unemployment is the one that the current economy produces. The natural rate is the one at which inflation tends neither to accelerate or decelerate. (Explained by frictional unemployment or people seeking to move to new jobs.) In recent times, this natural rate has been estimated to be about 5 to 6 percent of the labor force, though recent estimates suggest it may be lower.

Equilibrium income, therefore, may be greater than full employment, less than full employment, or correspond to full-employment income. We see all three of these possibilities represented in Figure 8-2. In *(a)*, the equilibrium level of income, Q_e, is less than the potential or full employment level of output, Q_f. The GDP gap Q_e - Q_f is negative. In *(b)*, the equilibrium level of income, Q_e, equals the potential or full employment level of output, O_f. The GDP gap is zero, the economy is producing at its potential with only a natural rate of unemployment. In *(c)*, the equilibrium level of income, Q_e, is greater than the potential or full employment level of income, Q_f. The GDP gap Q_e - Q_f is temporally positive.

When Real Income and the Price Level Change

What we have seen is that aggregate demand and aggregate supply determine, in equilibrium, the level of real income together with the level of prices. Now let's see what happens when either aggregate demand or aggregate supply changes.

Shifts in Aggregate Demand and Aggregate Supply

Aggregate Demand Shift
The term used to describe an increase or decrease in aggregate demand.

Aggregate Supply Shift
The term used to describe an increase or decrease in aggregate supply.

Aggregate Demand Shift is the term used to describe an increase or decrease in aggregate demand. A shift to the right is called an increase in aggregate demand and means that more real income will be demanded at each price level. A shift to the left is called a decrease in aggregate demand and means that less real income will be demanded at each level of prices.

    Aggregate Supply Shift is the term used to describe an increase or decrease in aggregate supply. An increase in aggregate supply means that more real product will be supplied at each price level. A shift to the left, on the other hand, means that less real product will be supplied at each price level.

    The most important point to remember about this is:

When either an aggregate demand or an aggregate supply shift occurs, there will be a change in the equilibrium level of income and product for an economy as well as a change in its level of prices.

Figure 8-3
The Effects of Aggregate Demand Shifts

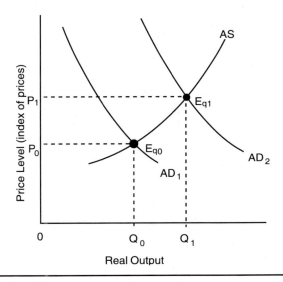

An increase in aggregate demand shifts the AD curve to the right from AD_1 to AD_2. Equilibrium output increases from Q_0 to Q_1 in a movement along the upward sloping short-run aggregate supply curve, as the price level from P_0 to P_1. The reverse occurs with a decrease in aggregate demand, decreasing equilibrium output to Q_0 and the price level to P_0.

Aggregate Demand Shifts: Their Effects and Some Causes

We see in Figure 8-3 the effects of aggregate demand shifts. If AD increases, as from AD_1 to AD_2, both income and the price level increase as well (from Q_0 to Q_1 and from P_0 to P_1). If AD decreases, as from AD_2 to AD_1, both income and the price level decrease (from Q_1 to Q_0 and from P_1 to P_0). Both directions of change involve a movement along the short-run aggregate supply curve. For example, in the early 1980s, the United States faced "double-digit" inflation which was perceived to be a serious problem threatening the growth and stability of the economy. In response, the monetary authorities contracted the money supply sharply, reducing AD_1 and helped create a severe recession with almost 10 percent unemployment and sharply falling inflation rates. In 1983, AD increased in the face of tax cuts, budget deficits, and increased confidence. This resulted in growing income and declining unemployment, which fell to less than 4 percent by 2000. Anything which causes households and firms to spend more at all price levels can shift AD to the right. Conversely, anything that causes households and consumers to spend less at all price levels can shift AD to the left.

Figure 8-4
The Effects of Aggregate Supply Shocks

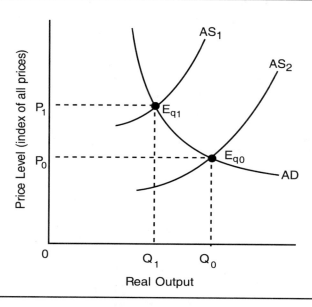

A decreasing aggregate supply shifts the AS curve to the left as from AS_2 to AS_1. Equilibrium income decreases from Q_0 to Q_1 and the level of prices increases from P_0 to P_1. The movement from Q_0 to Q_1 is a movement along the aggregate demand curve, AD. An increasing aggregate supply shifts the AS curve to the right as from AS_1 to AS_2. Equilibrium income increases from Q_1 to Q_0 and the level of prices decreases from P_1 to P_0. The movement from Equilibrium (Q_1) to Equilibrium (Q_0) is a movement along the aggregate demand, AD.

Aggregate Supply Shifts: Their Effects and a Cause

In Figure 8-4, we can see the effects of aggregate supply shocks. If AS decreases, as from AS_2 to AS_1, equilibrium income decreases from Q_0 to Q_1 and the price level rises from P_0 to P_1. If aggregate supply increases, as from AS_1 to AS_2, equilibrium income rises from Q_1 to Q_0 and the price level declines from P_1 to P_0. Both directions of change in AS result in movements along the aggregate demand curve, AD. As we have seen, there are many things that can cause changes in aggregate supply.

In the early to mid-1970s, there was a dramatic and largely unexpected increase in energy prices, especially in the price of imported crude oil. As a result, the costs of producing virtually all commodities and services increased. This influence shifted aggregate supply to the left and contributed to reduced income, rising unemployment, and rising prices, a condition that came to be known as stagflation. We will look at this in more detail in the application to this chapter for this shift came about because of influences outside the domestic economy.

By the early to mid-1980s, oil export prices began to grow more slowly and then to decline in absolute terms. Falling energy prices reduced the costs of supplying commodities and services, shifting aggregate supply to the right and contributing to rising real income and a declining price level. (Inflation rates actually became negative for a very short period in 1987.)

Ranges of Aggregate Supply

The aggregate supply curves seen in Figure 8-1 through Figure 8-4 were all upward sloping, showing that increasing quantities of commodities and services were associated with rising levels of prices. Clearly, however, the general state of the economy will determine whether production costs rise and how sharply they rise as output expands. We can identify three possible ranges of aggregate-supply price-level relations. These three sections of aggregate supply we will call (a) unemployment, an economy with large quantities of unemployed resources, (b) bottlenecks, the economy approaching full employment, and (c) full employment, the economy at capacity. We see all three conditions represented in Figure 8-5.

Figure 8-5
Ranges of Aggregate Supply

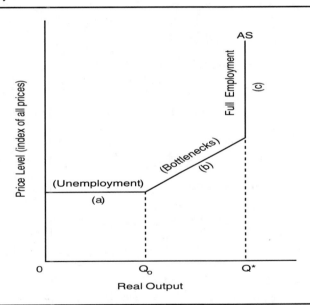

Range (a) represents an economy with large quantities of unemployed resources, an economy in recession or even depression. Range (b) represents an economy moving toward full employment and bidding less efficient resources into use as output grows; i.e., an economy with bottlenecks in supply responses. Range (c) represents an economy at full employment income (Q^*); i.e., an economy that cannot increase real output, only prices.

In Figure 8-5, we see that in range (a), the economy's real income can grow in response to changes in aggregate demand, and this growing income can be accomplished without an increase in overall prices. This stable price level growth can be maintained up to income level Q_0. In range (b), the economy's real income can grow but presumably only with the rising costs associated with bottlenecks and drawing less productive resources into use. This growth with rising prices can be maintained up to income level Q^*. In range (c), at full employment, Q^*, the economy can respond to further increases in demand only with rising prices. The economy at Q^* has reached its production-possibilities frontier and until that frontier shifts outward from increasing endowments of resources or from improvements in technology, real income cannot grow.

The most important implication of these ranges is that efforts to increase real income, reduce unemployment and maintain stable price levels through changes in aggregate demand are crucially influenced by aggregate supply responses. If, for example, taxes are cut and disposable incomes increase, we would expect aggregate demand to increase. If the responding economy is in range (a), real income will grow with stable prices. In range (b), real income will grow but there will also be rising prices. In range (c), real income cannot grow and the consequence of an aggregate demand increase will be inflation.

Supply-Side Economics

From the end of World War II to the early 1980s, national policies, including monetary and fiscal policies, focused on trying to change aggregate demand in the appropriate direction and amount necessary to create acceptable levels of employment and real income in the United States. Such efforts were designed to create growing real income at relatively stable price levels. All such efforts seemed to grow, at least in part, from the commitments in the Employment Act of 1946, but stopped short of a commitment to full employment such as that in the Humphrey-Hawkins Act of 1978. The implicit assumption in all these efforts seemed to be that changes in aggregate quantities supplied would adjust to whatever level was required to create stable prices in the face of growing aggregate demand. In other words, the assumption seemed to be that the economy's supply responses would occur in range (a).

In the early 1980s, we began to hear from "supply-siders" who said that tax cuts and other incentives to increase aggregate supply were the recipe for economic growth with acceptable price stability. Some even argued that cutting tax rates could not only shift aggregate supply to the right and increase income at lower prices levels but also produce increases in tax revenues with which to deal with budget deficit problems. Supply-side advocates and supply-side skeptics are far from resolving their differences and we shall have much more to say about these arguments in another chapter.

Measuring the Aggregate Price Level: The GDP Price Index or Deflator

As you may recall from our discussion of the Consumer Price Index (CPI) in Chapter 6, a price index is a number that represents individual prices of goods and services in a basket. Throughout this chapter, we have also used a price index to represent the general level of prices along the vertical axis of our AD-AS graphs. This particular price index, referred to as the GDP price index or deflator, is the same as the one that was employed in Chapter 5 for converting nominal GDP into real GDP. It differs from the CPI in two important respects: First, it corresponds to the prices of goods and services that compose GDP. The GDP basket is much larger than the basket that corresponds to the CPI. Secondly, since 1996, the GDP price index has been constructed based on a methodology (called "chain-type" index) that allows for the effects of changes in relative prices and in the composition of output over time. In this way, it is not subject to the "substitution bias" that plagues the CPI and other indexes using a fixed-weighted formula (see Chapter 6). Given its much larger scope of coverage and flexibility, some economists consider the GDP price index as a superior and comprehensive indicator of inflation in the macro economy.

Application I: Demand and Supply Shocks: OPEC in the 1970s and 1980s, A War on Terrorism in the 21st Century

In the preceding chapter, we learned that the equilibrium level of real income and the aggregate price level associated with that equilibrium are determined by aggregate demand (AD) and aggregate supply (AS). Changes in either AS or AD or simultaneous changes in both can change the equilibrium and produce a new level of prices and real income for the economic society. Such variations occur internally and arise from changes in the internal factors affecting AS and AD which we also examined in the preceding chapter. Almost continual variations in AD and AS produce new levels of income and prices. Also, cycles of expansion and contraction together with varying levels of employment and unemployment that we examined in chapter 6 result from these variations.

External Aggregate Demand and Supply Shocks
Factors external to the macroeconomy that change its equilibrium levels of income, employment, and prices.

At times, the macroeconomy, whatever are it's AD and AS driven internal equilibrium tendencies, is "shocked" by external factors, factors that can affect either AS or AD or both simultaneously. These shocks, called **external aggregate demand and supply shocks** may have important effects on equilibrium levels of income, employment, and prices.

In this application, we will examine several external shocks to the American economy that have occurred in recent decades. Those shocks in the 1970s and 1980s related to the efforts of OPEC (Organization of Petroleum Exporting Countries) to increase petroleum prices thereby enhancing foreign exchange earnings of its member nations. We will also examine the effects of a reverse shock from falling petroleum prices in the late 1980s and early 1990s when OPEC lost control of those prices. Finally, we will look at the possible effects of an ongoing shock to the American economy, that arising from the terrorist attacks of 2001 and the ensuing "war on terrorism" waged by the United States and it's allies.

The OPEC Shocks

The 1970s and 1980s were periods marked by wide variations in economic activity. Vietnam War spending, substantially financed by deficit spending, resulted in inflation and price controls. The end of the war and demobilization accompanied by falling military expenditures caused a decline in Aggregate demand. Dramatic increases in oil prices (OPEC I in 1973–1975) reduced aggregate supply and resulted in a sharp recession in 1975–1976. In the late 1970s, continued inflation combined with a second sharp increase in oil prices (OPEC II) produced slow growth. In five years, the real (discounted for inflation) price of oil increased by about 600 percent.

To illustrate the effects of a supply shock, let's look at OPEC II in 1979–1980. Remember that aggregate supply curves are based on costs of production and that they slope upward because of rising costs of larger quantities supplied from existing plant and equipment.

When costs rise – in this case because of a rapid rise in oil prices – the AS curve shifts upward or to the left. As this happens, we expect the equilibrium level of real output to decrease and the price level (index of all prices) to rise. How great these effects will be depends in large measure on how much production costs have been raised. In the case of oil prices, the two shifts appear to have been quite significant. By one estimate, almost 5 percent of the world's gross product is composed of the value of oil production.[1] Putting this in perspective, it is likely that no other energy price, indeed no other   resource price, reaches that level of significance. Thus, the shift in aggregate supply costs from a major change in such a price should be expected to be large.

We see the outlines of such a process in Figure 8-6. The very large increases in oil prices from OPEC II increased short-run production costs and shifted aggregate supply from AS (1979) to AS (1980). With a smaller supply, aggregate quantity demanded decreased and real income (GDP) declined with the economy spiraling into a major recession. The recession was accompanied by a strong inflationary pressure with the consumer price index (including the price of gasoline and heating oil) rising from 217.4 to 246.8 or by 13.5 percent. America experienced "double digit" inflation for only the second time in its modern history. With a smaller aggregate supply, the demand for labor decreased and the unemployment rate among civilian laborers rose from 5.8 percent to 7.1 percent.

Figure 8-6

Aggregate Supply Shifts Resulting From Cost Shocks of Oil Prices in 1979-1980

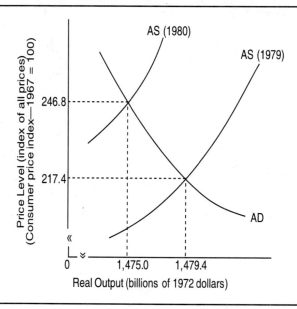

In 1979 OPEC announced major increases in oil export prices. The aggregate supply costs shifted upward (leftward) from AS (1979) to AS (1980). As a result, real output declined from 1,479.4 billion to 1,475.0 billion and the consumer price index rose from 217.4 to 246.8.

Was the entire set of macroeconomic effects attributable to the supply shock? Probably not, but the majority of the independent causality appears traceable to this major price-cost-supply shift. The main point is that employment, price levels, and real income can be affected dramatically not only by changes in aggregate demand, about which we will say much more in the ensuing chapters, but also by changes in aggregate supply. This introduces a very troublesome element in national economic policy when such supply changes may be caused by forces difficult or impossible to effect with domestic policy measures.

We have chosen the 1979-1980 supply shock because it was a "pure price effect," one unaccompanied by other types of external shocks. The same effects might have been shown through OPEC I (the oil price change in 1974).

1. Fried, Edward R., "World Oil Markets New Benefits, Old Concerns," in McClelland, Peter D., *Readings in Introductory Macroeconomics*. New York: McGraw Hill, 1988

In that instance, though, there was also an embargo with its own price and other supply effects.

Minimizing the Supply Shock

Many economists were surprised that income and price effects of OPEC II were not more dramatically adverse than they were. On reflection though, this should not be so surprising. Naturally, when the price of something as basic as energy increases sharply, consumers, including nations and firms, look for ways to minimize the costs to themselves. As Edward Fried has shown, in the case of OPEC II, the 1980s witnessed the following:

1. Energy use efficiency increased after the 1973-1974 shock. Energy was conserved as an input in production as well as in households.

2. Oil became less important as a source of energy. Oil became a relatively expensive source of energy; as a result, it declined from 55 percent to 45 percent of primary energy use.

3. At higher oil prices, many non-OPEC producers expanded output. For example, the fields in Mexico, the North Sea, and the coast of Alaska expanded output.

4. OPEC, as a cartel, found it increasingly difficult to maintain its monopoly prices. Lacking an effective means to discipline its members, it tried production quotas but the incentive to cheat on prices and quotas was intense.

5. Saudia Arabia, the lowest cost producer which then held 40 percent of the world's reserves, found its ability to maintain prices through adjusting its output increasing untenable.

As a consequence of the above, the quantities demanded of (OPEC and non-OPEC) oil proved to be smaller than anticipated. Quantities supplied, on the other hand, proved much larger. As a result, by the mid-1980s, downward pressures on oil prices became irresistible.

A Reverse Supply Shock:

Oil Prices in the Late 1980s? The 1990s? The Twenty First Century?

Between late 1985 and April 1986, average oil prices fell from $28 to $14 a barrel (a kind of *unintended* OPEC III). Go back to Figure 8-6, but reverse the direction of change in aggregate supply. Even though oil had become less influential as a source of energy, it was, and remains, very important in that regard. A major reduction in costs and a shift downward or to the right of AS occurred tending to reduce the GDP price index or at least its rate of growth. From 1985 to 1987, these prices rose by less than 6 percent. At the same time, the aggregate quantity demanded rose as price pressures diminished and   real GDP rose by 6.2 percent. It would be wrong to think that both events were caused entirely by the reverse (positive) supply shock of dramatically falling oil prices. Indeed, other things (e.g., budget deficits) were happening to stimulate aggregate demand. The point, though, is that supply shocks can have positive as well as negative effects on inflationary pressures and growth in real income. They can, in other words, help to solve problems as well as create them.

In the early 1990s, the U.S. and its allies fought a war in the Persian Gulf that was at least partly undertaken to keep oil supplies and oil prices stable. Another oil price "shock" of the sort experienced earlier could, however, again reduce aggregate supply, cause inflation and plunge the nation into serious recession. However, in 2001, oil prices again fell sharply. This time, through, the "shock" occurred against a different economic setting.

2001: The Economics of a War on Terrorism

As we have seen, aggregate demand and aggregate supply shocks can, at times, be positive in their effects on the macroeconomy. Earlier we saw an example of a dramatic decline in petroleum prices-driving energy prices down in 1985–1986. A similar decline began occurring in 2001. The former occurred against a backdrop of a growing economy and, by reducing supply costs, increased AS and real income, while restraining upward pressure on prices. The latter decline however, occurred in an economy that had been slowing for months. In March, 2001, the American economy entered a recession (two consecutive quarters of decline in GDP).

A War Economy

In September 2001, America and its economy were shocked by terrorist attacks which quickly led to military mobilization and efforts to seek out and eliminate further terrorist threats to the nation. Although the outcome of those efforts is yet to be determined, they will certainly have effects on the nation's macroeconomy. Let's sketch out what (in Figure 8-7) the effects may be:

Figure 8-7

Possible Unfavorable Effects of the War on Terrorism and Declining Consumer Confidence

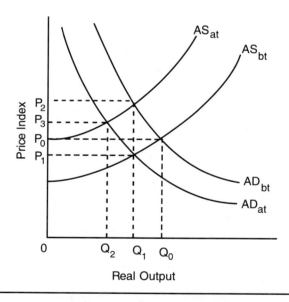

In Figure 8-7, the possible unfavorable effects associated with the period following terrorist attacks are illustrated. The pre-terrorist attack equilibrium with aggregate supply before terrorist attack (AS_{bt}) and aggregate demand before terrorist attack (AD_{bt}) is with price level P_0 and real output Q_0. As a result of rising costs of production and distribution due to counter terrorism measures, AS shifts upwards to AS_{at} and the (aggregate supply after attack) and prices rise to P_2 with real output falling to Q_1. As a result of declining Consumer Confidence, however, AD falls to AD_{at} and together with AS_{at} causes prices to fall from P_2 to P_3 and real output to fall from Q_1 to Q_2. The net effect is slightly rising prices and falling real output.

Negative Economic Effects

Those who argue that efforts to combat terrorism will have a negative effect on an economy already in recession cite the following:

a) The costs of production and distribution will increase to reflect the higher costs of added security. In December 2001, the International Monetary Fund estimated the direct costs to the U.S. at $21 Billion; at the same time it lowered its estimates of the 2002 growth of the American economy from 2.7 percent to 2.2 percent. These higher costs include such things as airport security and security of the mails; higher costs, in turn, will reduce aggregate supply. We see this in Figure 8-7, where AS shifts from AS_{bt} (Aggregate supply before terrorism) to AS_{at} (Aggregate supply after terrorism). Real income falls from Q_0 to Q_1 and prices rise from P_0 to P_2.

b) Declining Consumer Confidence causes Aggregate demand, to decline, in Figure 8-7, before terrorism (AD_{bt}) shifts to the left to AD_{at}. With a reduced Aggregate supply (AS_{at}) a new lower level of aggregate demand (AD_{at}) produces a new macroeconomic equilibrium with real income Q_2 and price P_3.

The overall impact of the War on terrorism according to this argument is to reduce real income from Q_0 to Q_1 and to increase prices from P_0 to P_3. In other words, the war on terrorism increases the recessionary pressure on an that may be experiencing those pressures.

Figure 8-8
Possible Favorable Effects of the War on Terrorism and Declining Consumer Confidence

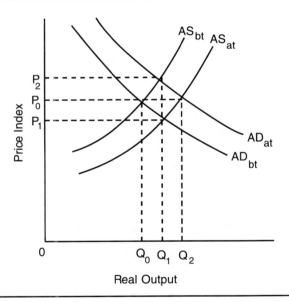

In Figure 8-8, the possible favorable effects associated with the period following terrorist attacks are illustrated. The pre-terrorist attack equilibrium with aggregate supply before terrorist attack (AS_{bt}) and aggregate demand before terrorist attack (AD_{bt}) is with price level P_0 and real output Q_0. As a result of declining energy prices, AS shifts outward to AS_{at} (aggregate supply after attack) and the price level falls to P_1 with real output growing to Q_1. Expenditures on combating terrorism increase aggregate demand to AD_{at} (aggregate demand after terrorism) and prices rise to P_0 but income rises further to Q_2. The net effect is stable prices and growing real output and employment.

Positive Economic Effects

Those who argue that efforts to combat terrorism will have a positive effect on an economy already in recession cite the following:

a) Aggregate demand will rise because the federal government, free of the pressure to run budget surpluses and pay down the national debt, will increase both direct military expenditures and those related to international security. As a result, aggregate demand shifts upward to right as in Figure 8-8 from AD_{bt} to AD_{at}. This causes real incomereal income to increase from Q_0 to Q_1, and prices to rise from P_0 to P_2.

b) Falling oil and other energy prices will cause costs of production to decrease which increase aggregate supply from AS_{bt} to AS_{at} in Figure 8-8. This increased supply, in conjunction with increased aggregate demand (AD_{bt} to AD_{at}) creates a new equilibrium with real income rising from Q_1 to Q_2.

The combined effects of increased aggregate demand (AD_{at}) and increased aggregate supply (AS_{at}) are to increase real income with a stable level of prices. The net effect in other words, is to reduce recessionary pressure on the macroeconomy.

What Really Happened: Summing Up and A Few Caveats

External shocks to the economy, as we have seen, can have major effects on its equilibrium levels of real income and prices. A major derived effect may be on job creation or the level of employment. A negative shock not only causes lower real income, it also reduces the demand for labor. A positive shock, on the other hand, not only causes real income to grow but also increases the demand for labor.

A few caveats

1. The long term effects of favorable shocks such as falling energy prices will depend on how long they last. Expectations of consumers and producers which, as we have seen, influence both demand and supply, are formed out of recent experience and expectations of the future.

2. The arguments about government spending to fight a "war on terrorism" are controversial. That war, like others in American history is likely to increase aggregate demand. This increase, if large may have major effects on an economy in recession. For example, some economic historians argue that military spending in 1942-1945 finally ended the great depression. Robert Higgs[2] points out however price controls during the war make it difficult to assess the increase in real income during that period. Higgs argues that war output satisfies no consumer demands and that such output should be excluded from measures of increasing product. David Henderson[3] adds that wars lead to increased government control over the economy, and that Higgs is right in labeling war expenditures an "opportunity cost" rather than a benefit. On the other side of this argument, many economists say that war expenditures do create jobs (as they did between 1942 and 1945.)

3. Finally, it is important to remind ourselves that we are dealing with *external* influences on the equilibrium of the American economy. It is basically its internal workings, the domestic factors that influence and determine the behavior of consumers, producers, and governments that will move the economy out of

2. Higgs, Robert "Wartime Prosperity., A Reassessment of the U.S. Economy in the 1940s" *Journal of Economic History* 52, 1992.
3. Henderson, David R., "The Economics of War" San Francisco Chronicle, November 28, 2001. Also *The Joy of Freedom, An Economic Odyssey. Financial Times*, Prentice Hall, 2001

recession. This, as we saw in the chapter on economic cycles, has occurred many times. Robert Parry[4], President of the Federal Reserve Bank of San Francisco, says: "The Economy *will* recover and in the long run, its fundamentals are strong." Virtually all economists would argue that it is those fundamentals, not external shocks that will determine the economy's long–run growth path.

SUMMING UP

1. In spite of substantial long-term real income growth, the U.S. has experienced movements about its "target" of growth with stable prices. In this chapter, we looked at an aggregate demand-aggregate supply model of real income and prices. This model is quite different from the single product supply and demand model of price and quantity demanded in the chapter on supply and demand.

2. Aggregate price levels and levels of real income are established by the interaction of aggregate demand and aggregate supply. The equilibrium price level and the equilibrium level of income are established where aggregate quantity demanded equals aggregate quantity supplied. Equilibrium real income does not, however, necessarily correspond to desired real income.

3. Aggregate demand is a measure of the entire desired spending on final goods and services at each level of prices. The four factors that make up and determine aggregate demand are (a) consumption expenditures, (b) investment expenditures, (c) government expenditures, and, (d) net exports. Consumption expenditures depend on disposable incomes, cost and availability of credit, and expectations. Investment expenditures depend on interest rates, the expectations of producers, and government policy. Government expenditures are complex in determination but depend on such things as varying economic conditions, political philosophies, national emergencies, and efforts to secure re-election. Net exports (exports minus imports) can be either negative or positive and depend on exchange rate changes, trade policy, and politics. Thus, aggregate demand is equal to consumption expenditures (C) + investment expenditures (I) + government expenditures (G) + net exports (X_N).

4. Aggregate demand curves slope downward. The lower the price level, the greater the aggregate quantity demanded. The higher the price level, the lower the aggregate quantity demanded. The reason for the negative slope is not the same as with individual demand curves. Instead, the effects of interest rate changes, the effects of wealth changes, and the effects of relative price changes between domestic and foreign goods explain why AD slopes downward.

5. Aggregate supply is a measure of the entire desired output of final goods and services at each level of prices and real income. The factors which affect aggregate supply are (a) cost and availability of resources, (b) capacity and investment plans, (c) technology;, (d) productivity, and (e) government policy. Firms observe and act on increases in resource prices quickly, as their total costs and profitability are affected. Any economy's aggregate supply is constrained in the short run by its capacity stock of plants and equipment and other productive

---

4. Parry, Robert T. "The U.S. Economy After September 11". Federal Reserve Bank of San Francisco, Weekly Letter, December 7, 2001.

resources. In the long run, this capacity is increased by investment. Technological change increases the productivity of all resources and both results from and causes investment. Productivity, output per unit of input, depends on many things, including investment in human capital. Concerns have been raised about slower productivity growth in the United States than in other industrial nations. Expectations play a role in all decision making including supply plans, and changes in these expectations may importantly affect such plans. Government policy has many influences on supply plans. Tariffs, tax rates, and environmental decisions all affect costs and profitability and, thereby, supply.

6. Aggregate supply curves slope upward. As the price level rises, aggregate quantity supplied rises. As the price level falls, aggregate quantity supplied falls. The explanation for the positive slope appears to lie in the ultimately rising real cost of production from using resources of diminishing productivity as aggregate income rises. Thus, short-run aggregate supply curves slope upward on the assumption that productivity diminishes but factor prices in the short run are constant as aggregate prices rise. This assumption has to be modified to examine long-run aggregate-supply conditions.

7. Equilibrium (actual) levels of real income and prices may or may not be equal to potential (full employment) levels. At full employment, an economy operates at its natural rate of unemployment or that corresponding to frictional unemployment with inflation that neither tends to increase or decrease. Thus, equilibrium income and prices may create a GDP gap that is positive; i.e., an economy may operate with an unemployment rate greater than the natural rate. Alternatively, the economy may operate with an unemployment rate below the natural rate. Finally, equilibrium (actual) and potential (full employment) may be equal in which case the economy operates with its natural rate of unemployment, thought to be about 5 to 6 percent or less for the United States in 2005.

8. Equilibrium, real income, and price levels are subject to changes from demand shifts (changes in aggregate demand), as well as from supply shifts (changes in aggregate supply). Both aggregate demand and aggregate supply may increase or decrease. Either change will produce a change in the equilibrium level of income for the economy as well as a change in the level of prices.

9. An increase in aggregate demand will increase equilibrium real income and the price level, and will cause a movement along the aggregate supply curve. A decrease in aggregate demand will decrease equilibrium real income and the price level, and also cause a movement along the aggregate supply curve. Many factors, including changes in the money supply and changes in government expenditure and taxation, can cause such aggregate demand shocks.

10. An increase in aggregate supply will increase equilibrium real income and decrease the price level, and will cause a movement along the aggregate demand curve. A decrease in aggregate supply will decrease equilibrium income and increase the price level, and will also cause a movement along the aggregate demand curve. Many factors, including all factors that change input prices and the costs of production, can cause such aggregate supply shocks.

11. General economic conditions determine whether and how much production costs change as output (supply) changes. The three ranges or possibilities of aggregate supply response are (a) unemployment, the economy has large quanti-

ties of unemployed resources, (b) bottlenecks, the economy is approaching full employment, and (c) full employment, the economy is operating at capacity. In range (a), aggregate demand growth will cause rising real income at a stable level of prices. In range (b), aggregate demand growth will cause rising real income but with rising levels of price. In range (c), aggregate demand growth in the short run can only result in rising prices since an increase in real income is unattainable.

12. For decades, public economic policy has focused on adjusting aggregate demand to accomplish macroeconomic objectives of income, employment, and price stability. By the 1980s, "supply-side" advocates voiced the view that public policy should center more on adjusting aggregate supply through enhanced incentives to production. The debate between the two groups continues.

13. Measurements of aggregate levels of prices in an economy are called *price indexes*. They are necessary to reduce a vast heterogeneous mix of goods and services to a common denominator, their monetary values, and to permit comparisons of price changes from one year to another.

14. Index numbers, used to measure inflation, first require establishing a "market basket" of goods and services in a particular year whose prices can then be measured. The index for a year is calculated against the prices of that same basket of goods and services in a base or reference year.

15. Two of the most widely used indexes of the federal government are the consumer price index (CPI) and the GDP price index or GDP deflator.

16. By comparing the average of the weighted prices in the current year with those in the base year, we can see what has happened to average prices over that period. We can use this resulting index to deflate or inflate the changes in nominal or money GDP to obtain a measure of the growth or decline in real GDP.

17. There are various things affecting economic welfare that are not reflected in indexes and real GDP growth. Thus, the measure is an imperfect reflection of welfare change.

18. The consumer price index (CPI), unlike the GDP deflator, is a fixed-weight index. It assumes that the spending patterns of consumers do not change from year to year. It also ignores qualitative improvements in goods and services. For this reason, it probably overstates inflation and leads to increased inflationary pressures from cost-of-living adjustments and understatement of tax obligations where tax rates are tied to changes in real, rather than nominal income.

19. The macroeconomy may be subject to external aggregate demand shocks and external aggregate supply shocks. These are factors outside the domestic economy that alter it's income and price level. When production costs are raised sharply by an external supply shock such as oil price increases, there is a shift upward or to the left of aggregate supply. This occurred twice (1973-1974 and 1979-1980) (OPEC I and OPEC II) in the past 35 years.

20. According to economic principles, an upward shift in aggregate supply will cause a decline in the equilibrium level of real output as well as an increase in the price level. Where the aggregate supply effect is large, the effects on income and prices will also be large.

21. In the case of OPEC II, the 1979-1980 oil prices increases were very large. As a result, prices rose by 13.5 percent and unemployment rose from 5.8 percent to 7.1 percent. Real income declined. Although it is unlikely that the entire set of effects can be traced to the supply shock, it was clearly a major factor.

22. Supply shocks, since they are often unpredictable and difficult, if not impossible, to control, introduce an element of instability into national economic policy.

23. Supply shocks can be and tend to be minimized. In the case of OPEC II, efforts to minimize the effects led to increasing efficiency in energy use, a diminishing importance for oil as a primary energy source, increased output by non-OPEC suppliers, and, finally, decreasing stability of the oil carte and a reduced ability of Saudi Arabia to support oil prices.

24. By the mid-1980s, reductions in quantities of oil demanded and increases in quantities supplied made downward pressures on oil prices irresistible.

25. Average oil prices fell by 50 percent between late 1985 and April 1986. This helped set in motion a reverse or positive supply shock for the economy. The shift downward, or to the right, of AS helped to diminish price increases and to increase the equilibrium level of real income.

26. Supply shocks can have both negative and positive effects on the economy. They can help to solve economic problems as well as cause them. In 2001, the American economy was shocked by terrorist attacks; a "war on terrorism" has ensued

27. Some argue that the war on terrorism, like other wars, will tend to increase output and jobs. They argue that (1) war expenditures will increase aggregate demand and (2) falling energy prices will increase aggregate supply. The combined effect of the two influences will help to pull the American economy out of recession.

28. Others argue that the war on terrorism will tend to decrease aggregate supply as (1) the costs of security increase, and (2) decreased consumer confidence decreases aggregate demand. The two influences combined will make economic recovery more difficult.

29. Long term effects of the current shocks will depend in part on how long they last. Arguments about the effects of government war spending continue. Some argue that such expenditures do not contribute to consumer welfare and should be ignored from that standpoint. Most economists concede, though, that such expenditures create jobs.

30. Although external influences or shocks can have important effects, the internal workings of the American economy are most influential in its recovery from recession. If those fundamentals are strong, the economy will recover as it has done many times.

KEY TERMS

Aggregate demand
Aggregate demand shift
Aggregate supply
Aggregate supply shift
Consumer price index
Equilibrium level of prices and real income
GDP price index or deflator
Investment in human capital
Price indexes
Ranges of aggregate supply
External Aggregate demand shocks
External Aggregate supply shocks

QUESTIONS

1. How are individual market prices for commodities and services established? How is this different from the determination of aggregate prices and real income?

2. How do aggregate demand and aggregate supply interact to create an actual level of real income as well as a price level in an economy?

3. What is aggregate demand? What four components make up aggregate demand? What factors influence each component?

4. Which of the components of aggregate demand are largest and which are most volatile?

5. What are the three explanations for the negatively sloped aggregate demand curve? Is the reason for a negatively sloped aggregate demand curve the same as the reason for a negatively sloped demand curve for an individual good? If not, why not?

6. Upward sloping aggregate supply curves are based on what explanation? On what assumption about input prices is the short-run aggregate supply curve based? Would such an assumption be warranted in the long run?

7. How is aggregate supply defined? What influences determine aggregate supply?

8. What is the difference between the actual level of unemployment and the level of unemployment at full employment with a stable inflation rate called? Can this difference be zero? Why not?

9. Can the equilibrium level of income exceed the potential (full employment) level? If so, what is the relation between the natural and actual rates of unemployment?

10. If the equilibrium, (actual) national income and the potential (full employment) income are equal, with what rate of unemployment is the economy operating?

11. What is a demand shift? What is a supply shift? What affects will such shifts have on an economy's equilibrium income and price level?

12. What is meant by saying that "changes in aggregate demand cause movements along aggregate supply"? What may cause such changes in aggregate demand (demand shocks)?

13. What is meant by saying that "changes in aggregate supply cause movements along aggregate demand"? What may cause such changes in aggregate supply (supply shocks)?

14. "When aggregate demand changes, its effects on the price level depend on the range of aggregate supply in which the economy is operating." Explain.

15. What is the heart of the disagreement between "supply-siders" and "demand-siders" over achieving macroeconomic objectives?

16. Answer the questions below based on the information about aggregate demand (AD) and aggregate supply (AS) contained in the figure below.
    a. The equilibrium level of income is (Q_2), (Q_3), or (Q_1)?
    b. The equilibrium level of prices is (P_2), (P_3), or (P_1)?
    c. At what price level (P_3, P_1, or P_2) is there excess aggregate supply? Aggregate demand?

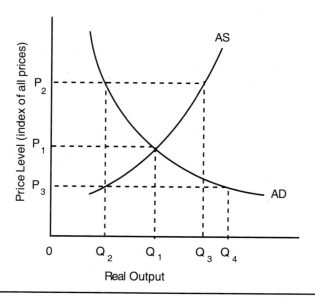

17. What is an "index number"? What is measured by the GDP index? The consumer price index?

18. What is the formula for calculating a price index in the year 1994?

19. What is meant in saying that the consumer price index is a "fixed weight" index? If the price of the CPI market basket in 1995 is $42 and the price of that basket in 1987 was $35, what is the CPI in 1995? What distortions in the economy are caused by using the CPI as a measure of inflation?

20. What are the major differences between the CPI and the GDP price index or deflator? Compute the GDP price index for 1995 based on (a) price of market basket in 1995 = $28, and (b) price of market basket in 1987 = $20.

21. What effect did the oil price increases of 1973-1974 (OPEC I) and 1979-1980 (OPEC II) have on aggregate supply?

22. According to economic principles, what macroeconomic effects will result from a decline in aggregate supply?

23. How important were the price, employment, and output effects of OPEC II?

24. Why is achieving national economic policy objectives more difficult in the face of supply shocks?

25. The price increases from OPEC II led to efforts to minimize their adverse effects. What things were done in these respects?

26. Oil prices fell dramatically in 1985-1986. From what did this seem to result? What happened to real income and employment as a result of "OPEC III"?

27. In macroeconomic terms, what should we expect to happen as a result of "positive" supply shocks such as the oil price decreases in late 2001?

28. What are external aggregate demand shocks? External aggregate supply shocks?

29. What are possible negative economic effects of a "war on terrorism"?

30. What are possible positive economic effects of a "war on terrorism"?

31. What does Robert Higgs argue about the effects of war expenditures on an economy?

Chapter 9: Aggregate Spending in the Macroeconomy
Classical and Keynesian Theories

Classical Theory
A body of economic theory that concludes that full employment is the norm for a market economy and that non-intervention by government is appropriate macroeconomic policy.

In the chapter on aggregate demand and aggregate supply, we obtained an overview of the macroeconomy through understanding the concepts of aggregate demand and aggregate supply. In this chapter and in the chapter on equilibrium in the macroeconomy, we will build on that foundation to show how spending and saving interact to create an equilibrium level of income and employment for a society. In doing so, we will strongly contrast two very different theories about the structure and operation of the macroeconomy. One is **classical theory**; in its extreme form it assumes that the aggregate supply curve is vertical, or that the economy operates at capacity and that full employment is the norm. The theory suggests that laissez faire or non-intervention in the market by government is appropriate government macroeconomic policy. The other is **Keynesian theory**; in its extreme form, it assumes that the aggregate supply curve is horizontal or that unemployment is often found in the macroeconomy. This theory suggests that significant government intervention is called for in order to move the macroeconomy toward full employment.

Keynesian Theory
A body of economic theory that concludes unemployment is possible for a market economy and that significant government intervention is appropriate macroeconomic policy.

As the chapter on economic fluctuations shows, a central problem of any economy is to control the destructive forces of unemployment and inflation. The classical and Keynesian views of the economy continue to fuel debates about economic policy in the U.S. While the Keynesian view has dominated those debates through much of the period since World War II, there remains much controversy, and a clear understanding of the two perspectives is important to following the policy controversies of the early twenty first century. After contrasting the two theories, we will develop the Keynesian model in stages.

In this chapter we will build the foundations of the Keynesian model. Building on these foundations, we will construct the full Keynesian model in the chapter on equilibrium in the macroeconomy. We want you to learn from these chapters the basic facts of the modern demand-based theory of income and employment. Though controversial, this theory continues to exercise great power over government policy and, thus, your money, your standard of living, and even the laws that govern you.

CLASSICAL ECONOMIC THEORY

Before Keynes wrote *The General Theory of Employment, Interest, and Money* in 1936, most economists belonged to the school called *classical economics.* Many aspects of classical economics are still accepted by most economists. Indeed, the theory has been refined as we shall see in the next chapter. However, in this chapter, we are analyzing only the classical theory of income and employment. We will also see that Keynes challenged some of the basic tenets of that theory.

Classical economists[1] said that a market-oriented economy had enough built-in self-corrective mechanisms that, if left to its own devices, its income would move to that level at which its labor force would be fully employed. They also claimed that if unemployment occurred (1) it would be due to temporary over-production and would be quickly corrected by market forces, or (2) it would be due either to interference by the government or to insufficient degrees of competition, or (3) it would be due to the unwillingness of workers to adjust their wage demands downward in response to market forces.

Three theories led classical economists to this conclusion that income would of its own accord move toward the level at which full employment exists:

1. Say's law
2. Savings, investment, and money markets
3. The theory of wage and price flexibility

Say's Law

Say's Law
In its simple form, the law states that supply creates its own demand.

Jean Baptiste Say (1767-1832) was a French historian writing around 1800. Economists know him mainly for **Say's law**. The simple version of that law is: *Supply creates its own demand.* We can best illustrate Say's law by the simple 2 sector circular-flow model (Figure 9-1). Recall its basic premise that households provide all the resources, labor, land, capital, and entrepreneurship, to firms, and firms pay households for these resources. Using these resources, firms produce goods for consumption by households. In turn, households pay for these goods and services with the income they get from selling their resources to firms.

In terms of the simple circular-flow model, "Supply creates its own demand" means that firms, while they are in the process of turning out all the goods and services that constitute supply, are at the same time acting as the sources of the income that households need to buy the firms' output. We saw in the chapter on economic fluctuations that gross domestic product creates an equivalent amount of gross domestic income. The level of that income is stabilized at the point of full employment. When firms employ all the labor available, households receive enough income to buy all the firms' output produced by that labor. Say's law is stunning in its simplicity. Unfortunately, it does not hold up in real life, at least not in its simple form.

---

1. Classical economists include David Ricardo and John Stuart Mill in the nineteenth century, and Alfred Marshall and Arthur Pigou (Neo *classical*) in the twentieth century.

Figure 9-1
Simple Two Sector Circular Flow Model

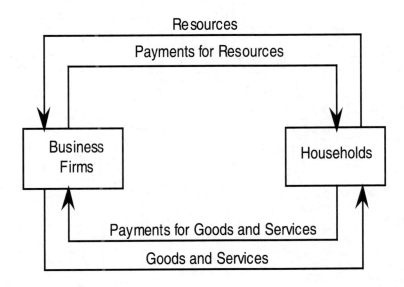

Savings, Investment, and Money Markets

Classical economists readily agreed that the simple circular-flow model illustrating Say's law was not adequate for an industrialized twentieth-century economy. However, they maintained that even a more complex circular-flow model (Figure 9-2) showed that income, left to itself, would move toward the level at which full employment would exist.

This is the classical reasoning. Households must use some of their money for savings and taxes, which means that savings and taxes siphon off some income that they would otherwise spend on consumption. Firms get most of their support, that is, demand for their output, from households. But firms *also* derive support from two other sources: government expenditures and investment. Economists of the classical school used to maintain that these four factors, taxes, savings, government expenditures, and investment, could be linked so as not to disturb the basic theory that income would adjust itself to the level at which full employment existed.

When people worried that these taxes and government expenditures would have a disturbing effect on this finely balanced model, the classicists had an answer: Just see to it that government expenditures and taxes are *equal*, and keep them both at the lowest possible levels. They'll balance each other off, and this will keep the effects of government fiscal activity to a minimum.

What about savings and investment? Would *they* balance each other off? Or would they create an imbalance and perhaps cause instability and nudge income to a level that would mean equilibrium at less than full employment?

Figure 9-2
A More Complex Circular-Flow Model

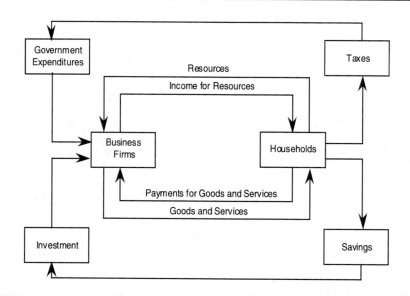

Abstinence Theory of Interest
An argument that people will save because interest payments induce them to abstain from current consumption.

Classical economists argued that savings and investment would be coordinated through interest rates established in money markets. They explained this link by using the **abstinence theory of interest**. People prefer to consume goods and services now, rather than later, because present consumption yields greater satisfaction than future consumption. If people are to be induced to save, that is, to abstain from consumption, they must be given a reward. This reward is called *interest*. Given interest, the consumer is willing to abstain from present consumption, in other words, save. Then in the future the consumer will be able to consume more because he or she will have more money (savings plus interest) with which to do so. The higher the interest rate (the reward for saving), the larger the quantity saved. Thus, the abstinence theory of interest provides the link between savings and investment.

The amount of money saved determines, in money markets, the *supply of loanable funds*. As Figure 9-3 shows, the curve for the supply of loanable funds slopes up to the right because the higher the interest rate, the larger the quantity saved. Therefore, the abstinence theory of interest explains why the supply of loanable funds slopes up to the right.

The decisions of businesses to expand their productive capacity by building new plants and equipment are what determine the demand for loanable funds. A person will make an investment when the return realized from that investment is at least equal to the cost of the interest on the money borrowed to make it. In other words, people make investments that have a rate of return equal to or greater than the interest rate. Classical economists said that the rate of return on an investment was determined by its productivity and thus, in the long run, by the state of the economy's technology. The demand curve for loanable funds in Figure 9-3 slopes downward to the right because falling interest rates make for greater profitability on investments. One could say that the interest rate is like rent paid on money. More investment is profitable at a 6 percent interest rate than at a 10 percent one, because the 6 percent rate also includes all investment that has a rate of return between 6 and 10 percent.

Figure 9-3
Supply of and Demand for Loanable Funds in Money Markets

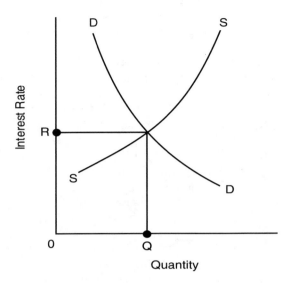

The supply of loanable funds (S) slopes up to the right because the higher the interest rate, the more people wish to save. The demand for loanable funds (D) slopes down to the right because the lower the interest rate, the more investment there is that yields a rate of return equal to or greater than the interest rate.

Thus, the interest rate links investment and savings. And the intersection between the supply of loanable funds (amount of money saved or withhold from the demand for consumption to become equal to the investment that businesses wish to add to the demand for consumption. The equality always becomes evident; demand always uses up the supply. The level of employment of resources still determines the level of income. The level of income still moves to full employment.

Wage-Price Flexibility

Classical economists recognized that there can be temporary overproduction in certain areas, because of either errors in estimating consumer demand or a failure of the interest rate to bring what people are willing to save into line with what businesses are willing to invest. Fluctuations in the market prices of labor and of products, however, quickly wipe out these temporary states of overproduction. As overproduction develops, workers lose their jobs and start to compete with workers who are still employed. This has the effect of reducing wages. As wages fall, lower costs and competition between firms forces prices down. Declining wages and declining prices together eliminate overproduction.

Elimination of overproduction is brought about by two effects of falling wages plus falling prices: (1) Total demand by workers is maintained, even though the money volume of spending declines, because prices of products fall in the same proportion as wages. Competition forces down wages, but also forces down prices. Classical economists assume that, because of competition, the decline in prices will be proportional to the decline in wages. The worker is no worse off, in effect, when wages fall 10 percent if prices also fall 10 percent. (2) The fall in prices causes those with savings to demand more goods, which eliminates excess supply. As prices fall, people with savings have greater wealth or purchasing power, their savings can buy more at the new lower prices.

Feeling richer, savers buy more, and save less. This increase in savers' consumption, as prices in general fall, is called the **Pigou effect**, after its classical originator, Arthur Pigou.

Pigou Effect
The argument that falling prices increase people's wealth or purchasing power and cause them to consume more.

To review: if the nation's budget is balanced (and balanced at a low level) so that government does not affect the market, and if there is enough competition in both the labor market and the product market, then the level of the nation's income automatically adjusts itself to the point at which there is full employment. In other words, classical economists concluded that there would not be long-term involuntary unemployment.

In the early 1930s the British government, in the throes of the Great Depression, sought answers from various classical economists. Surely these economists could work some magical cure that would revive the economy so that the level of income would rise to the point of full employment. Obviously the mechanism that ordinarily achieved this state of affairs did not seem to be working (or working quickly enough). Something was interfering with it.

Government fiscal activity was the culprit, said the classical economists. Let the government balance its budget and reduce its expenditures as much as possible, they recommended. So the British government in the early 1930s slashed expenditures and raised taxes. That will do for a start, said the classical economists, but in addition, because wage-price flexibility is not working, you must counter the influence of labor unions by forcing down wages; when the cost of wages falls, prices will fall, too, and demand will then increase.

Keynes, pondering the situation from his chair at Cambridge University, disagreed with these recommendations. He believed that they would worsen rather than lessen the depression. Keynes's ideas had been anticipated by his fellow economists, and many of them were being discussed by his contemporaries. However, it was Keynes who finally put these ideas together.

THE KEYNESIAN CRITIQUE

Keynes[2], who died in 1946, has been called the most influential economist of the twentieth century. His *general theory* disputed the classical income-determination theory, that held that the level of income would automatically move toward a position in which there was full employment. His argument largely replaced classical income theory for several decades and, as we noted earlier, dominated the theory and policies down to the 1980s. Today most, though not all, economists are Keynesians in some sense. At the least, they accept certain of his basic ideas and use his framework of analysis. Some economists today, however, regard the Keynesian system of analysis and its policy recommendations as outdated and appropriate only to depression-like conditions. But more about that after we have surveyed the Keynesian arguments.

What About Say's Law?

Keynes said that Say's law did not apply to a modern industrial society. In Say's eighteenth-century French world, production was small-scale and craft-oriented. People worked with simple machines. It did not take huge amounts of capital to repair them or replace them. Investment was therefore modest, and so was the

2. Keynes, J.M. *The General Theory of Employment, Interest and Money.* London/New York. McMillan, 1936.

need for savings. Households and firms (as viewed in the simple circular-flow model) were correspondingly small. Cottage industry abounded, and very often products were made to order. However, Say's law was an oversimplification even in his own day, because much of the French economy, and even more of the British, was taken over by larger-scale industries, as the Industrial Revolution accelerated during the latter part of the eighteenth century.

Classical economists replied that they recognized the oversimplification of Say's law and came up with the complex circular-flow model, which made adjustments for the more complex world.

The Abstinence Theory of Interest: Not True Said Keynes

A major feature of the classical theory of income was the *abstinence theory of interest*, which linked the desired level of savings (remember that savings always means decreased consumption) to the desired level of investment (which always means increased demand) through the interest rate. With government expenditures and taxes balanced, at the lowest possible levels, the classical view of the economic world seemed to be fairly valid.

But Keynes questioned the classical theory that desired or planned savings and desired or planned investment are always linked. He sought to invalidate the abstinence theory of interest, as follows:

1. *Savers and investors are different groups and are differently motivated.* Business groups make all the investment decisions and base them on comparative costs and on returns on investment. Profitability is the main reason for investment. Households are the main savers. They outsave businesses, even though large corporations do save great amounts in the form of undistributed profits. But in a wealthy society, households also save great amounts. Their motivation for saving, however, naturally differs from that of the business investors. But the simple fact of these differences in motivation is not important. The important point is: *Why should the interest rate link savings and investment?*

2. *The interest rate does not determine the level of savings.* People who save are going to save regardless of the level of the interest rate, and their motives vary. Some save because of custom or morality. Some save to provide security in old age; some to pay for a large purchase, such as a house or automobile. Some save to provide a fund for emergencies; some save to send their children to college. In sum, *people's motivations for savings are varied and are not merely influenced by the level of the interest rate.* Therefore, a certain rate of interest is not necessarily required to make people save. Many people would probably set aside money each month even if no interest rate existed.

3. Not only did Keynes seek to break the tie between planned investment and savings, by showing that the interest rate did not solely determine the amount of savings, but he also weakened the tie between investment and the interest rate. He said that businesses, in computing the probable returns on their investments, had to estimate future business conditions. Therefore, if you want to analyze why businesses invest, you must take into account their expectations of future conditions. This inclusion of expectations, a psychological factor that classical economists failed to give any weight to, weakened the relationship between planned investment and the level of interest rates.

So economists, according to Keynes, were left without the comforting mechanism of the interest rate that coordinated savings and investment at full employment. Without this, the economy could experience declining demand and unemployment, or increasing demand with resulting rises in employment, and possibly inflation. Let us see why.

Look at Figure 9-2 again. If planned savings are greater than planned investment, consumer demand for the firms' output of consumer goods shrinks, and investment demand does not take up all the slack. So total demand falls, and along with it, output, income, and employment fall.

Now suppose the reverse occurs. Suppose that savings are less than planned investment. This means that savings do not cause consumer demand for the output of firms to decrease as much as investment causes the firms' output to increase. As total demand increases, so does output, income, and employment. Eventually, when full employment exists, further increases in demand only generate increases in prices.

Lack of Wage-Price Flexibility

What did Keynes have to say about the classical economists' reliance on wage and price flexibility to correct any excess supply that might lead to unemployment? Remember that the classical economists said that a temporary oversupply of goods would cause unemployment, which would cause workers to compete harder for jobs, and that this would push wages down, which in turn would force prices down. Proportionate declines in wages and prices would leave real income unchanged, and thus real levels of demand for goods. People with savings would increase their level of consumption, and this would stimulate demand, and so on. Keynes said there were three factors that weakened this theory:

1. The flexibility of wages and prices is not great enough to generate these movements. Many corporations, possessing monopoly power in product markets, can keep prices from moving downward. Many labor unions also exercise monopoly power in factor markets in the same way; the unions are able to keep wages from moving downward. To Keynes's arguments, one can add that since 1936, governments have interfered more and more in the workings of the market, rendering it more inflexible. This has been true especially in areas such as minimum-wage laws and price-support systems for agriculture.

2. Even if wages and prices were both to decline, it is unlikely that real spending for goods and services would remain unchanged. After all, prices and wages never fall uniformly. Therefore, some groups would be hurt and some helped. And the two groups would never exactly offset each other. Furthermore, the burden of debt of workers would siphon away a large percentage of their incomes, thus cutting down on their spending. Finally, people are psychologically conditioned to plan their spending on the basis of money in hand rather than real income.

3. Even if one could overcome the obstacles generated by both factor 1 and factor 2, in order for the economy to expand very much as a result of increased real savings brought about by a decline in prices, there would have to be sharp drops in prices, and prices would have to stay low for a long time. There are easier ways to stimulate demand during periods of excess supply.

To summarize the Keynesian view: (1) Wage-price flexibility does not exist in sufficient amounts. (2) If it did, real spending would drop anyway. (3) Even leaving aside factor 1 and factor 2, there are easier ways to eliminate a generalized excess supply in the economy.

Aggregate Supply: The Keynesian Assumptions

The Keynesian theory we will set forth in this and the chapter on equilibrium in the macroeconomy focuses on aggregate demand and its role in determining the level of real income and employment. The model treats price levels as constants in order to center on income and employment effects of aggregate demand and changes in demand.

What kind of supply behavior would be consistent with this simple Keynesian model of demand-determined real income at stable prices? The answer can be seen in Figure 9-4. Notice that short-run aggregate supply is horizontal; planned or desired output responds to all changes in aggregate demand at a constant level of prices (up until we hit near full employment levels of output). The economic conditions that would explain this are those in the range of aggregate supply in which there is substantial unemployment or excess capacity. This supply-price relationship may be a reasonable assumption about firms offering to sell more at existing prices as long as they have idle or under utilized plant and equipment. In effect, firms have horizontal supply curves and the aggregate supply curve, as a result, is also horizontal at P*, the constant aggregate level of prices.

Note that in Figure 9-4, a change (shift) in aggregate demand, from AD_0 to AD_1, results in an increase in real income from Y_0 to Y_1. Both real incomes are consistent with the same level of prices, P*. The key point here is that:

Given the Keynesian assumption about short-run aggregate supply, aggregate demand determines real income, and that demand can be adjusted to any level required to accomplish income and employment goals with stable prices.

Figure 9-4

Determination of Real Income with a Keynesian Short-Run Aggregate Supply Function

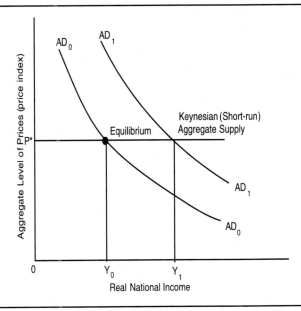

In a simple short-run Keynesian model, real income is determined by the location or amount of aggregate demand. Y_0 here is the equilibrium real income. A stable level of prices (P*) is consistent with a growing real income up to the point at which bottlenecks appear.

THE KEYNESIAN CONCLUSIONS

Classical economists, according to the Keynesian critique, were at least partially mistaken when they said that income would automatically move toward a level that would ensure full employment. Of course, the level of real national income may arrive at a position at which there is full employment and relatively stable prices, but there are no mechanisms that ensure that if this occurs, it will do so in an acceptable period of time. Therefore, it is more likely, say Keynesians, that the level of income will be either at a position at which there is unemployment or at which there is inflation. Both states are undesirable. So let's ask ourselves, what factors determine the level of income?

In the Keynesian view, as we noted earlier, it is the level of *aggregate demand*, the total demand for commodities and services, that determines an economy's level of real income. A business will produce only if it can expect profits. It can sell its goods only if there is demand for the product. In this case, what's true for one business is true for the entire economy: Output, and therefore income, will move in the same direction as aggregate demand. Increased income and employment will follow from increases in aggregate demand. Reduce demand and income and employment will suffer. But remember, according to Keynes, *there are no automatic market mechanisms that can force aggregate demand to the level at which there is full employment.*

This being so, the implication of Keynes' theory is that to achieve full employment, the government must manipulate aggregate demand. Not since the days of **mercantilism**, from the sixteenth through the eighteenth centuries, has economic theory made it the responsibility of the government to maintain economic welfare. That is why some economists have called Keyneianism modern-day mercantilism.

Incidentally, when we talk about the level of income here, we mean the *equilibrium income*. Recall from Figure 9-4 that equilibrium real income is established where aggregate quantity supplied is equal to aggregate quantity demanded. It is the central tendency of real income that equates the plans of consumers with those of producers. It is the income we have after all the forces in the model have worked themselves out. It is a stable level of income, so long as the various factors in the model *do not* change.

There are, as we saw in the chapter on aggregate supply and aggregate demand, four factors that determine the level of aggregate demand are:

1. Consumption expenditures
2. Investment expenditures
3. Government expenditures
4. Net exports

Three of these, consumption, investment, and government expenditures, make up *effective demand*. Increases in these items increase demand; decreases in any of them reduce demand. Savings and taxes siphon off the purchasing power of people and prevent them from using this money to satisfy their consumption demands.

Because these four factors determine demand, they also determine income and employment. So let's analyze the nature of the first three, consumption, savings, and investment, and show how they relate to changes in the level of income. Then, in another chapter, we will first take a simple nongovernment model and show how these factors determine an equilibrium

Mercantilism
A school of economic thought that held that government should take the responsibility for maintaining economic welfare.

level of income; finally, we will make the model more complex by adding in government expenditures and taxes.

Consumption, Savings, and Investment

You are already familiar with the idea of a function or curve. In the analysis of demand and supply, you saw that demand is not a relationship between a specific price and a specific quantity of a good or service, but between various quantities at various prices. When you draw a diagram of the demand schedule, it becomes a demand curve, which shows the functional relationships between prices and quantities demanded.

The same thing is true for the **consumption function**. It is not a specific quantity consumed by people at some given income level; it is a schedule, showing the relationships between levels of income and quantities consumed during a particular period of time. A diagram of this schedule, such as that in Figure 9-5, shows the functional relationship between income levels and quantities consumed.

Figure 9-5
The Consumption Function or the Relationship Between Income and Consumption

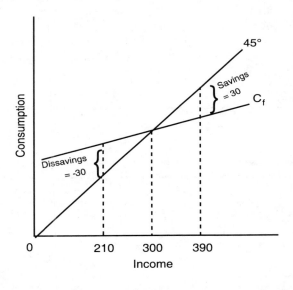

The distance from the income axis to the 45° line is the same as the distance from the 45° line to the consumption axis. Each point on the 45° line shows where income (the distance right on the axis) is equal to consumption (the distance up to the 45° line). Where the consumption function C_f, crosses the 45° line, (at income 300) consumption is equal to income. Where the consumption function lies above the 45° line (income level 210) the distance from the 45° line to C represents dissaving (30). Where the consumption function lies below the 45° line (income = 390), the distance from C_f to the 45° line represents savings (30).

Consumption Function

A schedule showing the relationships between levels of income and quantities consumed during a particular period of time.

Savings Function

A schedule showing the amounts people save at different levels of income in a particular period of time.

Investment Function

A schedule showing the amounts invested at different levels of income in a particular period of time.

The *consumption schedule*, or *function*, relates quantities consumed to levels of income. One must understand it in order to identify all the factors that influence the level of employment and income. Therefore, one must relate the various factors involved to income. So we shall deal not only with the consumption function, with how much people *consume* at different levels of income. We shall also deal with the **savings function**, the schedule showing amounts people *save* at different levels of income during a particular period of time, and with the **investment function**, the schedule showing amounts *invested* at different levels of income during a given period of time.

Let's build our income model in steps, just as we did our supply-and-demand model. First we show consumption schedules for individuals; then we add individual schedules to get an economy-wide consumption schedule. We diagram this and have a consumption function or curve for the whole economy. Again, as before, we assume that income is the only thing that changes. All other factors affecting the quantity of goods and services that people consume are fixed.

One could construct a consumption schedule for an individual in much the same way as one constructs a demand schedule for an individual. Ask each individual how much she or he would spend on consumption at each level of income and how much he or she would save. Table 9-1 shows consumption schedules for three individuals, A, B, and C. Note that each differs from the other. However, each shows that quantity consumed increases as income increases but *not as rapidly as income increases*. When one adds the consumption schedules and the income schedules of all the individuals, one obtains an economy-wide consumption schedule.

Table 9-1
Consumption Schedules for Individuals

A		B		C	
Income	Consumption	Income	Consumption	Income	Consumption
$2,000	$3,500	$2,000	$3,000	$2,000	$3,000
4,000	5,000	4,000	4,000	4,000	4,800
8,000	8,000	8,000	6,000	8,000	8,400
12,000	11,000	12,000	8,000	12,000	12,000
16,000	14,000	16,000	10,000	16,000	15,600
20,000	17,000	20,000	12,000	20,000	19,200
24,000	20,000	24,000	14,000	24,000	22,800
28,000	23,000	28,000	16,000	28,000	26,400

Table 9-2

Consumption and Savings Schedule

Income (billions of dollars)	Consumption (billions of dollars)	Savings (billions of dollars)
210	240	–30
240	260	–20
270	280	–10
300	300	0
330	320	10
360	340	20
390	360	30
420	380	40
450	400	50

Table 9-2 is an example of a consumption schedule for an entire economy. It shows that at low levels of income, people live beyond their means by consuming more than income (income levels 210, 240, and 270). At income level 300, consumption just equals income and savings are zero. Above income level 300, consumption is less than income, so the economy can save as well as consume. Figure 9-5 is a diagram of the data in Table 9-2.

To bring our analysis into focus, we have drawn, in Figure 9-5, a line from the origin upward, at an angle of 45 degrees. We shall call that line the 45 degree line. Note that consumption and income are equal to each other at any point on the 45° degree line.

There are different theories about the exact shape of the consumption function. However, for our purposes, we make the simplifying assumption that the consumption function, C_f, is a straight line, slopes up to the right, and crosses the 45 line. Where the consumption function crosses the 45 line (at 300), quantity consumed is equal to income. Whenever the economy drops below income level 300, consumption is greater than income. For example, note in Table 9-2 that at income level 210, consumption is 240, which leaves the economy 30 in the hole (negative savings). At that point, note in Figure 9-5 that the consumption function lies above the 45 line. When that happens, economists have a word for it: **dissavings**, the opposite of savings. Dissavings means that more is being consumed than is being produced within the economy.

On the other hand, if the income level is above 300 (e.g., at 390 in Figure 9-5), consumption for the economy is less than income, and the consumption function lies below the 45 line. The distance from the consumption function to the 45 line measures savings of (30).

To sum up, if the economy's C_f is *below* the 45 line (income levels over 300), positive savings take place. If the C_f lies *above* the 45 line (income less than 300), negative savings, or dissavings, take place.

Everyone knows how easy it is for private citizens to consume more than their income and wind up dissaving. They perhaps start out by drawing on their savings, until the savings are gone; then they borrow or perhaps apply for

Dissavings
The term used to describe negative savings by people in a society.

public assistance. In a fairly similar way, an entire economy can consume more than it produces, and experience overall dissavings. An economy can draw on its accumulated savings, its capital stock, by the mere fact that it does not produce enough capital to replace worn-out and obsolete capital; its net investment becomes negative, and it comes face to face with dissavings. The economy can borrow from other countries, which means that foreigners' money gets invested in one's own country. Or it can obtain foreign aid, in the form of gifts or international charity. The last two options, borrowing or accepting charity, mean that more is imported than is exported. In other words, the economy is consuming more than it is producing.

An example of dissaving occurred during the depression of the 1930s which was so severe that in the United States and several other countries net investment was negative and consumption exceeded income. Israel, several times during its brief existence, has been forced into dissavings by the necessity of maintaining a strong military stance and the need to absorb a constant flood of new immigrants. Israel has financed its excess of consumption over income in part by international borrowing, but primarily by gifts from the world's Jewish community, and especially by aid from friendly nations such as the United States.

Figure 9-6
The Savings Function

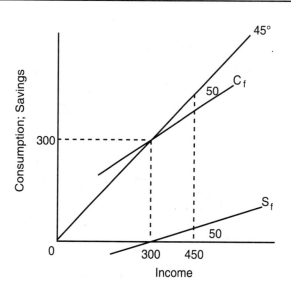

One can plot the savings function (S_f) from Table 9-2 or derive it from the consumption function (C_f). The distance from C_f to the 45° line measures savings. These distances should be marked off from the income axis to the savings function.

The Savings Function

Out of any given income, people either consume or save. So once you know the consumption schedule (see Table 9-2) or the consumption function (Figure 9-5), you can find the savings schedule and savings function, since savings is the act of *not* consuming. In brief:

$$income = consumption + savings.$$

In Table 9-2, the third column, the savings schedule, is the difference between income and consumption. Figure 9-6, expresses this savings function graphically. However, you could have used the consumption function in Figure 9-6to derive the savings function. The distance from the consumption function to the 45 line represents savings, either positive (incomes above 300) or negative (incomes below 300). If you measured off those distances on the income axis, with negative savings (dissavings) lying below the income axis, you would also have a savings function.

A Change in Consumption and Savings

When we talked about demand and supply, we stressed the distinction between a change in *quantity demanded* and a change in *demand*. The same distinction applies to other functions. A change in quantity consumed or quantity saved is a movement along a specific C_f (consumption function) or S_f (savings function) caused by a change in income. When a *non*income factor changes, it changes the entire schedule of consumption and savings and results in a shift of these functions. This constitutes a change in consumption and in savings. Let us look at the factors that can cause such shifts in consumption spending and savings.

Figure 9-7 shows a *change in quantity consumed* as a movement along C_1 from A to B because of a change in income. A *change in consumption* itself is a shift from C_1 to another consumption function, C_2, because of a change in one of the *non*income factors listed below:

Figure 9-7
Change in Consumption and Change in Quantity Consumed

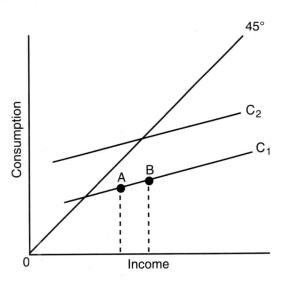

1. *Changes in social customs, mores, or attitudes toward savings.* Many of us have heard about the "Protestant ethic" hard work, thrift, and rational investment that lead to economic success. The stronger people's feelings about thrift, the higher the savings function. Today, people seem to be less concerned with personal savings, since institutional programs, such as pension funds and insurance programs, have apparently reduced the perceived need for individual saving.

2. *Changes in assets of consumers.* There are three ways of looking at people's asset positions: (a) What are their liquid assets? (b) What is their debt level? (c) What is their stock of goods (especially durable goods)?

Liquid Assets
Assets such as savings accounts or government bonds that may be quickly converted into money.

First, **liquid assets** are assets in the form of money or something that can be quickly converted into money, such as savings accounts and government bonds. People like to have some assets in liquid form for several reasons, mainly being prepared for an emergency. Once people have accumulated comfortable amounts of liquid assets, they can use their incomes for consumption. Second, paying off debt reduces income available for consumption over a period of time. When people accumulate debt quickly, this temporarily increases their consumption. However, when people are paying off debt, they consume less, out of necessity.

Since the level of debt affects consumption, the terms of consumer debts are important factors in determining consumption. What is the interest rate? How long a time will it take for repayment? These and other conditions of consumer loans encourage (or discourage) consumers from borrowing, and thus affect their level of consumption.

When you accumulate durable goods (cars, refrigerators, and so on), your consumption in the immediate future usually drops off sharply. If today you go on a spree and buy a washer, a dryer, and a plasma television set, you will probably not need new ones for several years, and this will surely lower your spending rate.

3. *Changes in expectations about future earnings.* If people expect that their earnings will increase in the future, and if they feel secure, they are inclined to consume more now than they would if they were pessimistic about future earnings. Young couples just starting a family borrow heavily to establish a home, expecting that their income will increase over the years. However, if there is a recession and they start to feel insecure about their jobs, or if inflation is cutting into their real income, people cut present consumption and increase their savings, to hedge against future wants.

4. *Changes in taxes.* When taxes go up, the amount people have to spend on daily consumable items naturally becomes smaller, no matter what their income is. Households pay part of their taxes out of income that they would otherwise spend for consumption, and part out of income that they would save. The effect of increased taxes is to decrease both consumption (increased taxes shift the C_f down) and savings (taxes shift the S_f down).

5. *Changes in the distribution of income; changes in demographic (population) factors.* Changes in the way income is distributed have a strong effect on the consumption function. Poor people have to consume a much larger proportion of their incomes than rich people do. Therefore, if something happens to redistribute the wealth so that the poor get a larger portion of it, the consumption function will shift upward and slope upward at the same time. Changes in the age distribution of the population also affect the position of the consumption function. The larger the percentage of people in age groups that are not income earning, the more people there are who are consuming without working to finance that consumption (for instance, children and the elderly). The baby boom that lasted from 1946 through 1964 was a strong element in keeping consumption high. But the large drop in the birthrate over the period from 1955 to 1975 reduced aggregate consumption in the succeeding period.

The five factors listed above can be divided into two broad categories: objective (or economic) factors and psychological factors. We consider changes in assets of consumers, changes in taxes, and changes in distribution of income and demographic factors to be objective or economic factors. We consider the psychological factors to be changes in social customs, mores, or attitudes toward savings, and changes in expectations about future earnings.

The Intended Investment Function

Autonomous Investment
Those investments not affected by changes in people's incomes and consumption.

Induced Investment
Those investments induced or generated by changes in income and consumption.

There are two kinds of investment: *autonomous* and *induced*. **Autonomous investment** is *not* affected by changes in people's incomes and consumption. It is affected by factors outside the model. In other words, the level of autonomous investment is independent of the factors within the model. **Induced investment**, on the other hand, is induced or generated by changes within the model, specifically by changes in income and consumption. For example, if the level of income increases, the quantity consumed also increases. This increases the need for plant and equipment (that is, for capacity) to produce the increased quantity of consumer goods demanded. This increased investment needed to expand capacity to take care of increased consumption is *induced* investment. For purposes of our model here, we shall assume that induced investment is zero and that we are dealing only with autonomous investment. Later, when we have completed our model, we shall add induced investment.

What Determines Autonomous Investment?

www.whitehouse.gov/fsbr/ esbr.html
For more information on investment visit this web site.

Businesses keep on investing, that is, creating capital, just as long as they expect that the returns from an investment are going to be at least equal to the cost of that investment. There are two factors that determine how much they invest. These factors are: (1) the cost of investing and (2) the expected rate of return.

1. *The interest rate*. When you invest your money in something, such as a machine or a building, and you put down some cash and borrow the rest. The cost of investing is not the price of the machine or building since you get this purchase price back by the device of *depreciation*, which is a legitimate cost of producing the product. Depreciation is built into the final price of any product. The *cost* of the investment is the interest that you must pay on the money you borrow to buy the thing *or* the interest you forego by using your funds instead of lending them out. In other words, if you had not bought that thing, you would have had an *opportunity* to lend your cash to somebody else and have interest payments flowing back to you.

Marginal Efficiency of Capital
The function that shows the quantity of investment made at each of several interest rates or the quantity that yields an expected return equal to or greater than each interest rate.

2. *Marginal efficiency of capital*. The marginal efficiency of capital is the expected rate of return on capital. In other words, it is the stream of income that businesses expect to receive over the life of the capital relative to its price. Two main items, plus a number of smaller factors, determine the marginal efficiency of capital:

   a. *Productivity of capital*. The more productive the capital, the greater the profit one can expect to receive back from an investment. The productivity of capital changes with the development of new machines that reduce the costs of labor or capital, or with the development of a new process, a new product, or new markets. So it can be said that any growth in productivity means greater potential profits to investors.

   b. *Expectations*. Since the marginal efficiency of capital deals with future returns, it is bound to be influenced by the future economic activity investors expect. This introduces a psychological and potentially irrational element. A President may have a heart attack, a war may occur in a part of the world that supplies petroleum, or meteorologists may predict a severe winter, and people in business may overreact. They may become more pessimistic, or more optimistic, than economic conditions warrant, and their attitudes may change almost overnight.

c. *Other factors*. Some of the other factors that affect the marginal efficiency of capital are the price of capital itself (for example, the sale price of a machine); the risks connected with the investment; taxation (especially in the case of taxes such as investment tax credits, that are directly tied to the investment); and, in the case of house construction, population growth and migration.

How Much Investment Will People Make?

Figure 9-8 shows how to go about figuring how much autonomous investment is likely to be made. The MEC (**marginal efficiency of capital**) curve shows the quantity of investment likely to yield an expected rate of return equal to, or greater than, the interest rate. The MEC curve slopes down to the right. This is so because as the interest rate falls, larger amounts of investment (capital instruments) will yield an expected return equal to or greater than the interest rate.

Figure 9-8
MEC curve

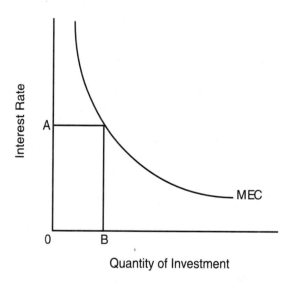

The marginal efficiency of capital (MEC) curve shows the quantity of investment at various interest rates. Investments must yield a rate of return equal to or greater than the interest rate. To find out how much investment is likely to take place, one must know the rate of interest that an investor is going to have to pay in order to borrow the money to make the investment.

Instability of Investment

In good times and bad, over the years consumption and savings have shown amazing stability. Gross private domestic investment, the other hand, has varied greatly as Figure 9-9 shows.

Figure 9-9

The Instability of Investment, Annual Changes in Real Gross Private Investment and GDP, 1958-2009

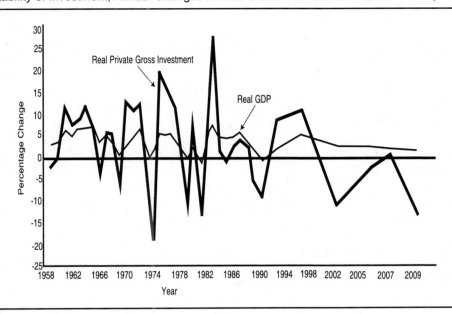

Source: Economic Report of the President, 2009.

Investment spending is highly volatile. In comparing changes in real investment and real GDP, we observe that the annual percentage changes in investment are greater than the percentage changes in GDP.

It has also, as Figure 9-9 shows, varied much more than real GDP. You can understand this pattern of investment if you just stop to think of the instability of the factors that determine the quantity invested. Interest rates fluctuate widely. The influences on people's expectations about the future are both rational and irrational. The flow of technological innovations is not even, so that industry improves its production techniques in fits and starts. Furthermore, the government itself may inject instability into the investment scene through changes in its economic policies and through loss of public confidence due to scandals.

However, since World War II, a number of changes have tended to increase the stability of investment. For one thing, the Employment Act of 1946 committed the government to economic stabilization. This has probably given business people greater confidence than they formerly had and reduced the likelihood of short-term variations in investment. Corporate retained earnings increased, so that corporations have not had to depend so heavily on the capital markets for investment funds. However, investment is still the most unstable component in the aggregate demand model of income.

Figure 9-10

Equilibrium Income: Relation Between Consumption (C_f), Savings (S_f), and Intended Investment (II)

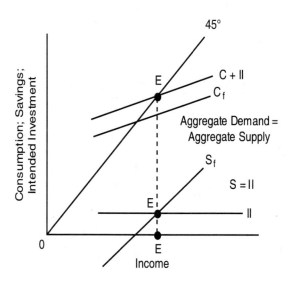

The bottom of the diagram shows intended investment in relation to savings. To find equilibrium income (E), one assumes that savings equals intended investment. Or one can add intended investment to the consumption function, so that aggregate demand equals aggregate supply. Both approaches give the same equilibrium income (E).

How Does Investment Fit Into Our Model?

We have made a number of assumptions: (1) We have assumed that the consumption function is a straight line that slopes upward to the right. This means that as people's incomes increase, they spend more on consumer goods, but they spend lower *percentages* of their incomes on these goods. (2) We are including in our category of intended investment only autonomous investment. (To review, *autonomous* investment is investment that is not affected by people's levels of income.)

Now look at Figure 9-10, which takes two different approaches to the matter of intended investment as it relates to the equilibrium level of income. (Note that II in Figure 9-10 stands for "intended investment," *not* roman numeral two!) Remember that the equilibrium level of income is the one that will not change unless one of the factors in the model changes.

One approach, called the **savings-equals-intended-investment approach**, is located on the bottom of the diagram. This shows the relation of savings (which *reduces* consumer demand) to investment (which *adds* to consumer demand). Note that the intended investment function that intersects the savings function is parallel to the income axis. Since the vertical distance from the income axis to the II function measures intended investment, and since it must be the same at all levels of income if it is to be consistent with the fact that investment is not affected by income, the two lines are parallel.

The second approach, called the **aggregate-demand-equals-aggregate-supply approach**, adds the intended investment function to the consumption function. Putting the II function here points up the relation of aggregate demand to aggregate supply. (Both these approaches will be discussed further in another chapter.) Note again that C + II is parallel to the consumption function (C_f). The vertical distance from C_f to C + II measures intended

Savings-Equals-Intended-Investment Approach
The determination of equilibrium income by equating savings and intended investment.

Aggregate-Demand-Equals-Aggregate-Supply Approach
The determination of equilibrium income by equating aggregate demand and aggregate supply.

investment. Intended investment must be the same at all levels of income to be consistent with the fact that autonomous investment is not affected by income. The two lines, thus, are parallel.

SUMMING UP

1. This chapter builds on the foundation discussed in the chapter on aggregate demand and aggregate supply to show how spending and saving interact to create an equilibrium level of national income. It focuses on two theories or approaches to this subject, the *classical theory* and the *Keynesian theory.*

2. *Classical economists* theorized that the aggregate supply curve is vertical or that in a market-oriented economy the level of income would automatically move to a position at which there would be full employment and capacity. Classical theory is based on: (a) Say's law, (b) the abstinence theory of interest, and (c) the theory of wage and price flexibility.

3. *Keynesian economists* theorize that the aggregate supply curve is horizontal or that there can be unemployment in the macroeconomy and government intervention may be necessary to move toward full employment.

4. *Say's Law* states in its simple form that supply creates its own demand. In terms of the simple circular-flow model, owners of resources receive incomes generated by producing supply and use those incomes to buy the total supply of goods and services that the economy produces.

5. In terms of the complex circular-flow model, the classical economists said that taxes and government expenditures need not have disturbing effects if both factors were kept equal and balanced at as low a level as possible. The way to get rid of the disturbing effects of savings and investment is through the rate of interest, as analyzed in the abstinence theory of interest.

6. The *abstinence theory of interest* states that people would rather consume now than save now and consume later. Therefore, people need a reward, interest on savings, to make them save. The higher the reward, the larger the quantity saved. Thus, the curve showing quantities of loanable funds saved slopes upward to the right when measured against the interest rate.

7. How much people invest depends on the rate of return, which in turn depends on the productivity of technology. Thus, the curve showing the quantities of loanable funds demanded at various interest rates slopes down to the right. More investment yields returns equal to (or greater than) the interest rate at a lower interest rate than at higher interest rates.

8. The equilibrium interest rate is the rate at which the *quantity supplied* of loanable funds is equal to the quantity *demanded* for the loanable funds. Therefore, the interest rate is the stabilizer that causes the amount of savings people wish to accrue (decreasing demand) to equal the amount of investment people wish to make (increasing demand).

9. If industry produces a temporary surplus, this surplus is quickly eliminated, because industry lays off workers, and the unemployed then compete for jobs, so wages fall. Also, as firms compete to sell off excess goods, prices fall. However, the worker's real income, and in general real demand, do not fall, since wages and prices fall proportionately. Because lower prices mean that the purchasing power of each dollar is greater, people with savings feel wealthier and thus increase the quantity of goods and services they demand (the *Pigou effect*).

10. John M. Keynes, in his 1936 book, *The General Theory of Employment, Interest, and Money*, rejected the classical conclusion that income always tends toward a position at which there is full employment.

11. Keynes said that Say's law was a gross oversimplification not only of the twentieth-century industrial world but also of Say's own eighteenth-century French world.

12. Keynes felt that the abstinence theory of interest was not valid because the interest rate does not correlate intended savings with intended investment, for these reasons: (a) The people who save are different from the people who invest and have different motivations. (b) The interest rate does not determine the level of savings, since the reasons why people save are largely unrelated to the level of the interest rate. (c) Business groups' expectations of the future are not strongly affected by the interest rate. Expectations are largely a psychological factor. Yet they have a strong influence on the rate of investment. These criticisms by Keynes weakened the traditional belief in the relationship between investment and the interest rate.

13. Since the interest rate, according to Keynesians, does not correlate savings and investment, desired savings can exceed desired investment. This reduces demand, and, eventually, income. On the other hand, desired savings can be *less* than desired investment. People can spend too freely. This increases demand and income.

14. Keynes attacked the remaining support of the classical income theory, wage and price flexibility, by making the following arguments: (a) Wages and prices are not flexible enough because there is not enough competition. (b) Even if wages and prices were to be flexible enough, real spending would drop anyway. (c) Leaving (a) and (b) out of the picture, there are easier and faster ways to get rid of a general excess supply of goods and services in the economy.

15. In the Keynesian model, it is aggregate demand that determines the level of income and employment. At least in the short run, price levels are considered constants since aggregate supply is in the range in which prices do not rise as aggregate demand increases.

16. The aggregate supply behavior that is consistent with the Keynesian assumption about constant price levels is one in which the aggregate supply curve is horizontal to the real income axis. Desired output responds to all changes in aggregate demand at a constant level of prices. Firms offer more for sale at existing prices, at least up to capacity rates of output.

17. Keynes concludes: (a) There is no market mechanism to make the actual level of income coincide with the preferred level of income at full employment. The actual level may exist at full employment, at less-than-full employment, or at full employment with inflation. (b) The level of income is determined by the level of *aggregate demand*, in other words, by the total spending in the economy.

18. Several factors determine the level of aggregate demand: intended consumption, intended investment, government expenditures (these three add to effective demand), intended savings, and taxes (these two detract from effective demand.)

19. The *consumption function* shows the functional relationship between quantities consumed and various levels of income. One assumes two things: (a) that all *non*income factors affecting the quantity consumed are fixed, and (b) that the consumption function is a straight line that crosses the 45° line (consumption is equal to income at that point) and slopes upward.

20. One can derive the *savings function* from the consumption function, since income is equal to consumption plus savings. Therefore, the difference between consumption and income is savings. The savings function is a straight line that crosses the horizontal axis and slopes upward. The distance from the savings function to the horizontal axis is equal to the distance from the consumption function to the 45° line.

21. A change in the quantity consumed or saved is due to a change in income, which causes a movement along the curve of the consumption or savings function. A change in both consumption and savings is due to a change in a *non*income factor, which causes the whole consumption and savings functions to shift.

22. Nonincome factors that may cause a change in consumption and savings are (a) changes in social customs, mores, or attitudes toward savings, (b) changes in assets of consumers (both quantity and composition), (c) changes in expectations about future earnings, (d) changes in taxes, and (e) changes in distribution of income and changes in demography (the distribution and density of population).

23. In this book we deal with two kinds of investment: autonomous and induced. *Autonomous investment* is influenced only by factors other than income and consumption. *Induced investment* is determined by changes in income and in quantity consumed. To keep our model simple, we assume here that induced investment is zero.

24. People make that amount of investment for which they can expect a rate of return equal to or greater than the cost of the investment. The cost of an investment is equal to the interest paid for the funds needed to finance it. The expected rate of return is the *marginal efficiency of capital*, and it is determined primarily by increases in productivity and by expectations of future economic activity.

25. Of the three components that increase effective demand, investment is the most unstable. The reason is that there are fluctuations in the three main factors determining the volume of investment: interest rates, expectations of the future, and the flow of technological improvements.

26. If one is making a diagram of the relation between consumption, savings, and intended investment, one can put the intended investment function above and parallel to the horizontal axis, and it will intersect the savings function. This emphasizes the relation of savings (which reduce the demand for consumption) to investment (which adds to it). This is called the *savings-equals-intended-investment approach*.

27. Alternatively, one can add the intended investment function to the consumption function; this is called aggregate demand. This function emphasizes the effect of total demand on income and is called the *aggregate-demand-equals-aggregate-supply approach*.

KEY TERMS

Abstinence theory of interest
Aggregate-demand-equals-aggregate supply approach
Autonomous investment
Classical theory
Consumption function
Dissavings
Induced investment
Investment function
Keynesian theory
Liquid assets
Marginal efficiency of capital
Mercantilism
Pigou effect
Savings function
Savings-equals-intended-investment approach
Say's law

QUESTIONS

1. Explain how a classical economist would defend the conclusion that the level of income always tends to move toward a point at which there is full employment. Include the role of Say's law, the abstinence theory of interest, and wage-price flexibility. What type of aggregate supply condition does the classical economist assume?

2. How did Keynes challenge the classical conclusion about income and employment, especially as it referred to the three foundations of classical theory: Say's law, the abstinence theory of interest, and wage-price flexibility?

3. What was Keynes' conclusion about the relationship between income and full employment? How is the level of income determined, according to Keynes?

4. What are the five factors that determine aggregate demand? How do changes in each of the five affect effective demand?

5. Which of the following factors change the quantity people consume or save, and in what direction? Why?

    a. An increase in the holding of consumer durables

    b. A decrease in taxes

    c. An increased desire for security in old age

    d. An increase in income

    e. A decrease in the amount of money that people hold

6. Answer the following questions based on the figure below:

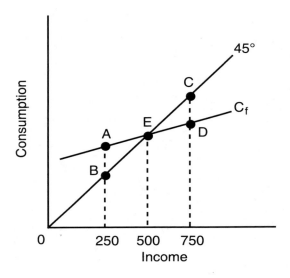

    a. The equilibrium level of income in the figure above is (1) 250, (2) 500, or (3) 750?

    b. Dissavings in the figure above is represented by the distance (1) CD, or (2) AB?

    c. Savings in the figure above is represented by the distance (1) CD, or (2) AB?

7. Distinguish between autonomous and induced investment.

8. Does autonomous investment increase or decrease when the following things happen? Why?

    a. The interest rate increases

    b. A new breakthrough in science opens up new areas of technological innovation for industry

    c. The stock market collapses and the general feeling is one of pessimism

9. What is the least stable element of aggregate demand as a part of GDP?

SECTION III:

Economic Policy in the Macroeconomy

SECTION III

Economic Policy in the Macroeconomy

In Section I, we laid the foundations for examining the macroeconomy. We did this through looking at the fundamental assumptions of economics and through discussing its basic methodology including its reliance on principles of supply and demand in understanding how a market economy functions. In Section II, we shifted focus from individual behavior and individual markets to examine the foundations of aggregate or macroeconomics. We looked at how aggregate income flows are measured as well as how we may understand the irregular variations or cycles in those flows. We then laid out the differences between classical and Keynesian economists about flexibility in the macroeconomy.

In Section III, we shall build further on this theoretical and empirical foundation by shifting from theory and measurement to economic policy. We will concentrate on two main areas of economic policy. Fiscal policy, variations in government expenditures and taxes are our first concern. We shall see what options governments have in financing their operations and what the different macroeconomic effects are of taxation and issuance of debt. After surveying the modern record of U.S. fiscal policy, we shall look at the widely perceived problems of federal budget deficits and the U.S. debt. Since the mid-1990s, the "supply-side" arguments about government policy and economic growth have reemerged and we will examine those arguments as well.

A second major focus of Section III is on monetary policy or variations in the supply of money. Since the mid-1990s, this has been the major tool of macroeconomic policy in the United States. We shall see not only how the money supply is created but also how monetary policy affects that creation

Chapter 10: Fiscal Policy, Deficit Financing, and the National Debt

The nature and extent of the federal government's role in influencing and guiding the economy toward growth, full employment, and price stability are subjects of continuing controversy. That controversy played a major role in the presidential election of 2008. In 1946, the Employment Act spelled out the federal government's macroeconomic responsibility as follows:

"It is the continuing policy and responsibility of the Federal Government to use all practical means consistent with its needs and obligations and other essential considerations of national policy to coordinate and utilize all its plans, functions, and resources for the purpose of creating and maintaining, in a manner calculated to foster and promote free competitive enterprise and the general welfare, conditions under which there will be afforded useful employment opportunities, including; self-employment for those able, willing, and seeking to work, and to promote maximum employment, production, and purchasing power."

Fiscal Policy
Variations in government expenditures and taxation.

Thirty two years later, the Full Employment and Balance Growth Act of 1978 (also known as the "Humphrey-Hawkins Full Employment Act") was passed as an Act to "...assert the responsibility of the Federal Government to use all practicable programs and policies to promote full employment, production, and real income,.." among others. For most of the period since World War II, **fiscal policy**, variations in government expenditures and taxation, has been a major tool in federal government efforts to guide the economy toward growth and acceptable levels of employment. From the previous chapter, we know that the Keynesian model suggests what that role should be. It also suggests how fiscal policy can be used to fill deficiencies in aggregate demand during recessions and restrain excessive aggregate demand during inflationary periods.

Against this backdrop, in this chapter we will look at the various ways tax changes and expenditure changes affect the macroeconomy. We will also examine the record of modern fiscal policy as well as the federal government's budgetary process to assess the widely perceived problems of large deficits and accumulation of national debt. Finally, we will look at "supply-side" arguments that were again gaining prominence as fiscal policy was reexamined in the mid-1990s. That reexamination required looking not only at effects on aggregate demand but also at effects on aggregate supply.

Discretionary Versus Automatic Fiscal Policy

Discretionary Fiscal Policy
Deliberate changes of government expenditures and/or taxes to achieve particular economic goals.

Most fiscal policy discussions focus on **discretionary fiscal policy** which deals with changes in expenditure and tax plans designed to achieve specific macro-economic goals of full employment and price stability. Such changes result from decisions by Congress and the federal executive, and frequently take the form of legislation. There are also **automatic stabilizers** or non- discretionary changes in the government tax receipts and expenditures that are connected with fluctuations in economic activity. For example, during recessions, people are automatically pushed into lower income tax brackets and are subject to lower marginal tax rates as incomes fall. Similarly, government transfer payments in the form of unemployment benefits automatically rise during recessions as more people lose their jobs and become qualified to receive such benefits (the opposite happens as the economy recovers and moves towards full employment). These built-in features on the revenue and spending sides of the fiscal balance help stabilize the economy by keeping disposable income from falling less than what would have otherwise been the case. They should not, however, be viewed as a substitute for discretionary fiscal policy which becomes necessary especially during periods of significant recession and inflation.

Automatic Stabilizers
Changes in expenditures and tax policies that reduce instability in income and employment.

Expansionary Versus Contractionary Fiscal Policy

Fiscal changes, whether discretionary or automatic, can be classified based on whether they are intended to stimulate the economy or slow it down. When the economy is in recession and suffers from high unemployment, fiscal policy should be expansionary (stimulative). On the other hand, if the economy is operating at the full-employment level of output and inflationary pressures are building up, then fiscal policy should be contractionary (restrictive). Therefore, the state of the economy determines the appropriate nature of fiscal policy to counter it. How are the variations in taxes and spending specifically used? What are their effects on the federal government fiscal balance (budget surplus or deficit)? To answer these questions consider the following definition of the government fiscal balance:

Expansionary fiscal policy
involves tax cuts, increase in government purchases, and/or higher government transfer payments.

$$\text{Fiscal balance} = \text{Revenues} - \text{Expenditures} = (T+NT) - (G+TR)$$

Contractionary fiscal policy
involves tax hikes, decrease in government purchases, and/or lower government transfer payments.

where, T is tax revenues, NT is nontax revenues, G is government purchases of newly produced goods and services, and TR is transfer payments. **Expansionary fiscal policy** involves *lower* T, *higher* G and/or *higher* TR than before (NT is not typically employed as a tool of fiscal policy). So the basic idea is to pump more spending into the circular flow. An increase in G directly shifts aggregate demand (AD) to the *right*, while tax cuts and increases in transfers do this indirectly (why?) **Contractionary fiscal policy**, on the other hand, involves *higher* T, *lower* G and/or lower TR. The idea here is to drain spending from the circular flow, directly or indirectly, and cause a shift in AD to the *left*.

Keynesian Arguments About Fiscal Policy

Compensatory Fiscal Policy (Functional Finance)

The argument that fiscal policy changes can vary aggregate demand and lead to output growth with stable prices.

Keynesians argue for **compensatory fiscal policy** (or functional finance) that uses fiscal policy tools to create changes in aggregate demand (AD). These changes, it is argued, acting through multiplier effects, will generate increased employment and growing output with stable prices. How does this work? Figure 10-1 illustrates this in a case when the economy is in recession and expansionary fiscal policy (tax cuts and/or spending increases) shifts AD to the right.

Figure 10-1

Using Compensatory Finance to Eliminate a Recession: Keynesian and Non-Keynesian (Classical) AS

a. Augmenting aggregate demand in the Keynesian (constant price level) range of the AS curve

b. Augmenting aggregate demand in the intermediate (rising price level) range of the AS curve

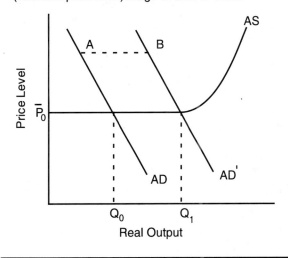 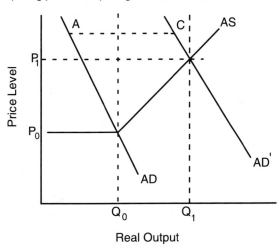

In Figure 10-1, the output level needed to eliminate a recession is Q_1 and the existing level of income is Q_0. A Keynesian fiscal policy is to increase aggregate demand from AD to AD'. In part (a), the increase in AD needed to increase output to Q_1 with stable prices is AB. In part (b), however, in the intermediate (upward sloping) range of AS, prices rise as AD increases and, because AS rises more slowly, a greater increase in aggregate demand (AC) is necessary to increase output from Q_0 to Q_1.

Suppose that the Keynesian assumption about aggregate supply (AS) is warranted. That is, AS is flat (the "Keynesian range") reflecting high unemployment and excess capacity and no price pressures due to a deep recession as in part (a). The economy, because of recession, is operating at real output level Q_0 with aggregate price level P_0. To achieve the full employment level of output Q_1, it is necessary to augment (shift) aggregate demand from AD to AD', or by the distance AB. Whether done through tax cuts or through government expenditure increases, Q_1 can be achieved with a stable price level, P_0.

Suppose, on the other hand, the economy is operating in the upward sloping portion of AS, as in part (b). Though compensatory finance may be still employed to increase AD and induce the necessary growth in real output to reach full employment, results differ from the Keynesian case in two ways: (1) inflation, the price level rises from P_0 to P_1, and (2) the amount of tax or expenditure stimulus required to achieve full employment is larger (AC versus AB) to compensate for the fact that rising price level reduces the increase in output associated with a given shift in AD. Stated differently, it matters *where* along AS the shift in AD occurs. The closer the economy is to its full-employment level of output that steeper is AS and the less expansionary is the effect of a given shift in AD.

Deficit Finance and the Public Debt

Budget Deficit
The amount by which government expenditures exceed government revenues.

Budget Surplus
The amount by which government revenues exceed government expenditures

Whether seen from the Keynesian viewpoint or from the classical perspective, an important dimension of functional finance is not represented at all in Figure 10-1. Use of government tax and expenditure policies to achieve employment goals may lead to expenditures that are not financed out of current revenues. Tax reductions and expenditure increases in periods of recession mean that the government runs a **budget deficit**, the amount by which current government expenditures exceed current government revenues. Of course, if government deficits during recessions were offset by comparable **budget surpluses** (revenues in excess of expenditures) in periods of economic expansion, the budget would be balanced over the course of business cycles. Keynes himself seems to have favored this "cyclically balanced budget" when he noted that "The boom, not the slump, is the right time for austerity..." This leads us to an important point: the timing of deficit reduction is important. Premature attempts to reduce budget deficits (often under political pressures) can prolong and/or increase the intensity of recession.

Federal Revenues and Expenditures

As noted previously, changes in revenues (mainly tax receipts) and expenditures are major quantitative tools of fiscal policy. Moreover, these changes reflect the effects of automatic stabilizers and/or deliberate tax and spending decisions. Figure 10-2 shows how total federal revenues and expenditures, expressed as a percent of GDP, have changed since 1960. Note that the dollar amount of revenues and expenditures are not strictly comparable over time due to inflation. Also, as the economy (GDP) gets larger so do revenues and expenditures. These problems make meaningful comparisons difficult which is why expenditures and revenues are divided by GDP first.

What can we learn from the figure? First, neither federal revenues nor expenditures, when put in perspective, has been growing "out of hand" contrary to common beliefs. In fact, there are several period during which the ratios fall implying that the revenues or expenditures (the numerator) did not grow as fast as the size if the economy (the denominator). Second, with the exception 1998-2001, the expenditures-to-GDP ratio exceeded the revenues-to-GDP ratio resulting in deficits. Third, the expenditures-to-GDP typically rises and the revenues-to-GDP ratio falls during recessions (denoted by shaded bars). The opposite happens after recessions (why?). This phenomenon is most pronounced during the Great Recession (2007-2009). Other factors, such as legislative actions to cut taxes, spending increases, and/or wars also affect the ratios.

Figure 10-2

Federal Government Total Revenues and Expenditures as a Percent of GDP

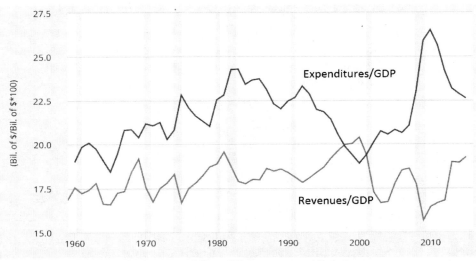

Source: Federal Reserve Bank of St. Louis, Office of Management and Budget

Deficits and the Gross Public Debt

Gross Public Debt
Value of all outstanding
debt of the federal
government.

What does the federal government typically do when its expenditures exceed its revenues? It fills the fiscal gap or deficits by borrowing money ("printing money" and raising taxes are less frequently used alternatives). This involves auctioning the Treasury Department issued bonds and other securities (I.O.U.'s) in the credit market. The buyers or investors are in essence lending money to the federal government in return for interest payments to them by the government until the bonds mature. The financing of deficits, therefore, adds to what the federal government, on behalf of the nation, owes to its lenders or bond holders. It is helpful to think of deficits as a river that flows into a lake that is **gross public debt** (also referred to as national or federal debt). If more water flows in the volume or stock of water accumulated in the lake increases. If there is an outflow (this happens when the federal government runs a surplus *and* uses it to retire some of its outstanding debt), then the stock of national debt falls. Figure 10-3 depicts this relationship between the federal deficits and national debt.

Figure 10-3

Federal Government Deficit and Public Debt as a Percent of Gross Domestic Product

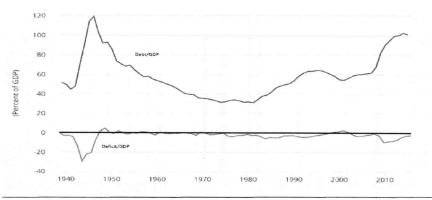

Source: Federal Reserve Bank of St. Louis

As can be seen, the debt-to-GDP ratio grew sharply during World War II as a result of deficit financing of much of the cost of the war. It rose from approximately 52 percent in 1940 to a peak of over 120 percent in 1946. While the dollar amount of the federal debt significantly increased in the next three decades, the debt-to-GDP ratio steadily fell from that peak reflecting the fact that GDP grew at a faster pace than the debt. This declining trend was sharply reversed in the early 1980s. Between 1980 and 2000, the absolute size of the debt increased by more than six times! Along with that, the debt-to-GDP ratio increased from a trough of over 34 percent in 1981 to over 55 percent in 2000. The size of the debt more than tripled in the first fifteen years of the new millennium and became roughly equal to 102 percent of the GDP (debt = $18.1 trillion and GDP=$17.8 trillion) in 2015.

Recall that the change in the debt-to-GDP ratio (the lake) mirrors the size of deficit (or surplus)-to-GDP. The large growth of the federal debt in the 1980s, for example, reflected the growth in federal deficits primarily due to a fall in tax revenues (as a percent of GDP) following the massive cut in individual income tax rates by the Reagan administration in 1981 which was not offset by spending reductions. The dollar amount of deficits almost tripled between 1980 and 1990 and increased from 2.5 percent to 3.7 percent of GDP. The Clinton tax hikes of 1993 coupled with strong economic growth during much of the 1990s translated into a budget surplus (for the first time since 1969) during 1998-2001. The surplus soon evaporated as a result of G.W. Bush tax cuts, increases in defense spending associated with two major wars in the post 9-11 period and continuous rise in spending on entitlement programs (Social Security, Medicare and Medicaid). During 2008 and 2009, the U.S. economy experienced the most severe recession since the Great Depression. Loss of tax revenues due to a weak economy accompanied by Obama administration's extraordinary economic "stimulus" package to counter the recession pushed the size of the deficit to extraordinary high levels by the post-World War II standards. Deficits exceeded $1.4 trillion in 2009 (nearly 10 percent of GDP). However, as the economy recovered, the deficit-to-GDP ratio began to fall steadily. In 2015, the absolute size of budget deficits was about $438 billion (2.5 percent of GDP).

The Distribution of the Public (National) Debt Ownership

To whom we owe the debt? Another way of asking this question is who owns what portion of total outstanding U.S. debt? As of September 2015, the size of total (gross) public (national) debt, or the cumulative value of all Treasury securities sold, was roughly 18.1 trillion dollars. According to Figure 10-4, about 28 percent of this total was held by various government agencies and trust funds. (In 2015, for example, Social Security held about 5 trillion dollar worth of the Treasury bonds, purchased using its surpluses over time, which represents the amount it lent to the federal government). Once we subtract from gross public debt the portion of the debt held by "Government Accounts," we arrive at **net public debt** (or "debt held by the public") which was about 72 percent of the total. The distinction between "gross" and "net" public debt is important, because the interest paid on the portion of the debt held by the federal government itself does not constitute a net financial burden on its budget. Moreover, net debt is a more accurate measure of the demands put on the private credit market by the government through its borrowings, for it excludes what one component of the government lends to another (the Treasury).

Net Public Debt
Debt held by the public.

Figure 10-4
Distribution of Total U.S. Public Debt Ownership (September 2015)

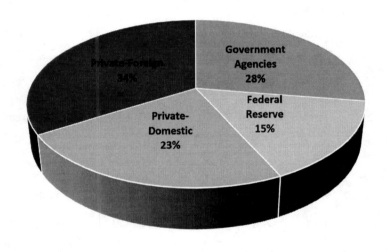

Source: The U.S. Department of Treasury

Note that the portion of the debt owned by the Federal Reserve (an independent quasi-public institution) is significant (about 15 percent) and is counted as part of net public debt; although the Federal Reserve returns the interest it receives back to the Treasury Department. (As we shall see in Chapter 13, the Federal Reserve uses the Treasury bonds it holds as a tool of monetary policy). A large number of private-domestic actors (including depository institutions, pension funds, insurance companies, mutual funds, state and local governments, and investors in U.S. Savings Bonds) collectively held over 23 percent of the debt. Finally, about one-third of the total debt was owed to foreign holders (governments, institutions, and individuals) of the U.S. bonds.

What are some of the implications of the debt ownership? First, a large number of people worldwide, directly or indirectly, buy the Treasury bonds in preference to private bonds as an investment vehicle. One major reason is that

Treasury bonds and other debt instruments are considered as one of the safest financial investments in the world, because the U.S. Government has never defaulted on its debt. So the bonds, while the *liability* of the U.S. federal government, are an important class of *asset* that individual and institutional investors desire to add to their portfolios for reducing their risk while enjoying competitive returns on a risk-adjusted basis. Second, the interest payments on the debt held domestically constitute a redistribution from taxpayers to bondholders (many but not all taxpayers are bondholders at the same time). This redistribution, however, is an *internal* one (among U.S. citizens). The bonds will be inherited by future generations who are also both taxpayers and bondholders (interest receivers). Third, interest payments to the fast growing portion of the debt owed to foreigners, on the other hand, is an external redistribution (from "us" to "them"). The large size of foreign-owned debt and the associated interest payments have been disconcerting to many and raised the specter of undue foreign influence ("China owns us.") To put this in perspective, net interest payments (that is, what the federal government pays minus what it receives) in 2015 it was equal to over $223 billion (1.3 percent of GDP and 6.1 percent of government spending) roughly a third of which were paid to foreign owners of the U.S. debt. The "half-full part of the glass" is that had it not been for the willingness of foreigners (including China) to invest their savings in Treasury bonds, the cost of borrowing would have been higher and interest rate sensitive spending lower in the U.S. than what actually observed.

What are the Major Concerns?

1. The *magnitude* of the deficits and the related debt have come to be a major concern. What is perhaps equally troublesome is that the deficits are actually *understated*. In all recent years, the Social Security Trust Fund (into which all social security tax receipts are paid) has accumulated large surpluses. The purpose of the fund is to pay for future retirement benefits of many "baby boomers" who are beginning to retire in the twenty-first century. To include these social security tax receipts as current revenues understates the "true" budget deficit. Many economists feel the fund should be "off budget." In the recent past, however, the impact of "off budget" surpluses was rather small (an average of under $40 billion between 2012 and 2015). A caution is, however, in order here. That the social security surplus is (and should be) invested in U.S. government securities enhances the security of the fund and does not mean it is used to fund "overspending" by the federal government.

2. A second major concern is connected to the rising percentage of the federal budget that consists of interest payments on the federal debt. Net interest payments by the federal government rose from an average of $126 billion over the period 1981-1990 to $191 billion during pre Great Recession period of 2001-2007 and to nearly $200 billion over the period 2008-2015. More appropriate comparisons, however, put these amounts in perspective: net interest as percentage of GDP for the three periods were 2.8, 1.6, and under 1.4 percent, respectively. This drop, in part, reflect our current low interest rate environment. Regardless of how we measure the interest cost of the debt, the magnitudes are large and the payments mandatory (default is not an option!) This suggests fiscal action associated with countering recessions results in a significant opportunity cost as there is less money left to spend on critical areas like infrastructure, health and education. What complicates the matter, however, is that inaction will cost the economy too (what are some of the costs of doing nothing?)

3. A third major concern is with the cyclical timing of the deficits. Throughout the history of the United States, federal deficits have usually occurred in periods of cyclical downturn as prescribed by Keynesians (for example, in the 1930s), or in periods of wars and urgent defense needs (for example, during World War II). Although recessions in the early 1980s and 1990s contributed to the size of deficits, clearly, large deficits would have existed even if the economy had operated at or near full employment! Large deficits in an economy operating at low rates of unemployment raise fears of demand-pull inflation.

Cyclical Deficit
A temporary or short-term deficit that results from revenue losses and increases in expenditures during a recession.

4. Another concern is about the composition of the budget deficit. Specifically, the total (or headline) deficit is the sum of the ***cyclical deficit*** and the ***structural deficit***. The cyclical deficit reflects the phase of the business cycle: it increases during recessions as tax revenues fall and certain government expenditures rise, due to automatic stabilizers and short-term stimulus measures, and shrinks as the economy enters the recovery phase. It is a *temporary* deficit and arguably a necessary deficit. The structural deficit, however, reflects a chronic mismatch between the federal revenues and expenditures and persists even if the economy is operating near or at the full-employment level of output and is growing at a normal rate. It is an ongoing deficit mainly resulting from large and popular Social Security, Medicaid, and Medicare programs. According to an estimate by the Congressional Budget Office (CBO), the total deficit in 2011 was equal to $1.3 trillion (the largest ever in absolute terms) out of which $367 billion was due to cyclical factors and $928 billion structural in nature. Admittedly, these two types of deficit are not entirely independent and separable. However, the distinction between them is important when it comes to addressing the "deficit problem."

Structural Deficit
An ongoing or long-term deficit reflecting a chronic mismatch between the government revenues and expenditures.

"Crowding-Out" Effect
The decline in investment spending that may occur as deficit financing raises interest rates.

5. There is real concern that large deficits will result in a **"crowding-out" effect**. The principle concern is that financing the deficits will increase the demand for financial savings and raise interest rates which, in turn, will reduce investment spending. As this happens, net investment falls leading to a smaller future productive capacity for the economy. Whether this will happen depends on whether it is private consumption or investment that is reduced at the higher interest rates and larger government expenditures. To the extent that investment is "crowded-out," future generations bear the burden because they will "inherit" an economy with less productive capacity. To the extent that present consumption is "crowded-out," the current generation bears the burden.

With the exception of the 1992 federal tax increase, financing of deficits in the 1980s and 1990s was accomplished through sales of government debt in money markets. It appears to us, therefore, that if crowding-out has occurred, most of it was against investment goods and, thus, that the burden lies primarily on future generations' reduced ability to produce and consume. There are, however, two qualifications to this presumed burden on future generations:

a. *The nature of government expenditures.* Just as private expenditures may be on present consumption or on investment, so may government expenditures. If the expenditures giving rise to the deficit are essentially for consumption (food stamps, increased benefits for public employees, and the like), then it is investment that will be "crowded-out" and future generations bear the burden. On the other hand, if the expenditures are for public investment (harbors, dams, flood control on the Mississippi, repairing levees on the Gulf Coast, and the like), then future productive capacity may actually grow though there will be relatively more public capital and relatively less private capital.

b. *The employment effects of government expenditures.* We assumed earlier that most (deficit creating) government expenditures in the 1980s and

1990s occurred when the economy was operating at or near full employment. Some economists have concluded that much of this deficit finance actually *moved* the economy towards full employment through a set of Keynesian multiplier effects. Thus, if substantial unemployment exists when the initial government outlays take place, a movement toward the (full employment) production-possibilities curve can occur without a burden on *either* current consumption or capital investment. This is demonstrated in Figure 10-5.

Figure 10-5

The "Crowding-Out" Effect and the Investment Demand Effect of Government Expenditures

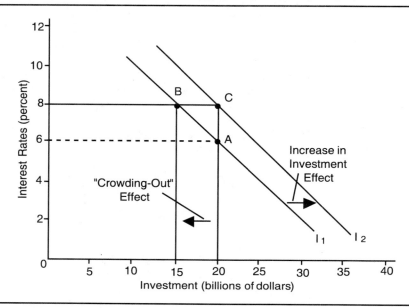

According to the "crowding-out" effect, an increase in interest rates caused by financing a federal deficit will reduce investment expenditures and the productive capacity of the economy inherited by future generations. In this illustration, I_1 is the original investment demand curve. Financing the deficit causes interest rates to increase from 6 percent to 8 percent and the quantity of investment to decline (point A to point B) from $20 billion to $15 billion with a $5 billion "crowding-out." However, the increased government expenditures stimulate the economy, improving business profit expectations and leading to an increase in investment demand from I_1 to I_2 (point B to point C). With interest rates at 8 percent and investment demand I_2, the amount of private investment is $20 billion, and the increase in the investment effect offsets the "crowding-out" effect.

In Figure 10-5, the economy represented is in recession, operating below its production-possibilities curve. The federal debt is increased through deficit financing and, as a result, interest rates rise from 6 percent to 8 percent. With investment demand I_1, the interest rate increase causes the quantity demanded of private investment to decline from $20 billion to $15 billion. The $5 billion decrease in investment represents the "crowding-out" effect of deficit financing and leads to a burden on future generations who will "inherit" a less productive economy. As government expenditures financed by the deficit grow, however, employment increases and business profit expectations improve. Expecting higher future profits, firms increase their demand for investment from I_1 to I_2. With the higher investment demand schedule, $20 billion is again the investment demanded even at the higher interest rate of 8 percent.

Crowding-in-Effect
Increases in private investment and consumption expenditures as deficit spending by the government stabilizes the economy and restores confidence.

The central point of this Keynesian argument is that if the "crowding-out" effect occurs it may be offset (as in Figure 10-5), more than offset, or partially offset by the stimulative effects on aggregate demand and investment demand when deficits occur in periods of recession. Research in the 1980s by economists Paul Evans and Robert Barro[1] supports the view that, in fact, government deficits do *not* lead to higher interest rates. Evans and Barro, thus, question the whole notion of "crowding-out." To summarize, the crowding out effect is subject to an important qualification: it is more likely when the economy is operating at or close to full-employment level of output (where the size of the economic pie cannot expand by much) and, therefore, an increase in public spending needs to come at the expense of private spending. However, when the economy is suffering from high unemployment and excess capacity and private investment and consumption expenditures are frozen as a result fear and uncertainty, then deficit spending by stabilizing the economy and improving confidence can actually have a **crowding-in effect** on private spending (as observed during the Great Recession).

Unfounded Concerns About the Debt and Deficit

There are two often expressed concerns about deficits and associated debt growth that are basically false and unfounded. The first is that the debt will ultimately grow so large that the government, unable to fund its activities, will become bankrupt. The second is that growing debt places an increasing burden on future generations. Let us look at each in turn.

Will Federal Deficits and Growing Debt Bankrupt the Nation?
Will the continued growth of debt ultimately mean the government will be unable to meet its obligations or "pay its bills" as can happen to private individuals and firms? Fundamentally, the answer is no. The reasons for this are three-fold:

1. *Raising revenues.* Under the Constitution, the federal government has the authority to impose and collect taxes. Since 1913, that authority has extended to income taxes, today the largest source of federal revenues. There is usually resistance to tax increases (one of which is the expected negative effects on investment and consumer spending), and there has been much debate in recent years about the federal tax system as well as its rates. The point, though, is that the authority to impose and increase taxes belongs to the government alone. Thus, individuals and firms may become bankrupt; the federal government *cannot.*

2. *Ability to refinance the debt.* The Treasury Department and the Federal Reserve refinance a part of the debt as it comes due each month. There is, thus, no practical reason why the debt *must* be reduced or eliminated. New government bonds can be sold to retire or repay maturing ones. Although expenditures could be cut or taxes increased to do the same thing, refinancing is a viable alternative. An important caveat, however, is that the debt must be sold to other countries (eg, China and Japan), these countries, faced with a declining exchange value for the U.S. dollar may resist greatly increasing the holding of U.S. federal debt.

1. Evans, Paul. "Interest Rates and Expected Future Budget Deficits in the United States." *Journal of Political Economy*, 95. February, 1987.
   Barro, Robert. "The Ricardian Approach to Budget Deficits." *Journal of Political Perspectives*, December 3, 1986.

3. *Control over the money supply.* At times, sovereign governments, faced with difficulty in meeting financial obligations, simply create (through the printing press or otherwise) enough money to pay their bills. This, too, is a power alone of governments. Of course, the amount of money created may greatly exceed the growth of goods and services, and inflation will result. There may be severe problems as a result of this but not, in any direct sense, the bankruptcy of the nation.

Will Federal Deficits and Growing Debt Burden Future Generations?

Could the debt be repaid? Yes. Would there be a major effect if it were repaid? Emphatically, yes! Repayment would require major increases in taxes and/or reductions in federal expenditures on non-debt service activities. Since the debt is not uniformly held by Americans repayment would result in a massive transfer and redistribution of income. The result would not, however, be a decline in total assets or wealth in the United States but a redistribution of those assets and that wealth. Most economists believe that the debt need not be (fully) repaid, anyway.

If the burden of the debt is not on future generations, where does it lie? The opportunity cost of the debt is borne by the generation in which it is created. Some of the debt increase since the 1980s has been due to rapid growth in programs that the federal government seemed unable or unwilling, for domestic political reasons, to restrain. Many of its expenditure programs (cost of living increases for social security recipients, growth of welfare benefits, growth of Medicare benefits, stimulus expenditures, and the like) fall into this category. A significant part of the debt increase was also to fund increased defense spending during the "cold war." Now that the "cold war" is over (we won) and the Soviet Union is gone, what was the burden of this failure to fund increased government expenditures (particularly defense goods) out of current (tax) revenues? The answer will take you back to the very definition of opportunity cost. The burden lies in the myriad of other goods and services that could have been consumed if the resources used to produce the actual defense and non-defense goods had been used to produce other goods. In addition, the production of defense goods shifted resources away from capital goods so the next generation will inherit an economy with less productive capacity. There is, thus, a type of inter generational burden.

In a 1995 study, Auerbach, Gokhale, and Kotlikoff[2] conclude that with present government policies, intergeneration balance would require raising income taxes *permanently* by 43 percent, and cutting federal transfers by 33 percent or government purchases by 32 percent in 1996! In other words, the conclusion is that present fiscal policies are significantly unbalanced in a generational sense. However, there is another aspect of intergeneration effect of debt that is worth noting. Sever economic contractions can deprive millions of their basic needs, dignity, and future. Left alone, they put the economy on a lower growth path. If deficits are incurred to counter the economic, social, and other costs of sever contractions and do so, to a large extent, by boosting public investments in human and physical capital and technology (as opposed to

---

2. Auerbach, Alan J., Jagdish Gokhale and Laurence J. Kotlikoff. "Restoring Generational Balance in U.S. Fiscal Policy What Will It take?" *Economic Review*, Federal Reserve Bank of Cleveland, Vol. 31, No. 1, 1995. Quarter 1.

defense or current expenditures), then future generations will benefit from an economy whose growth rate is higher than would have otherwise been the case. They will also enjoy the benefits of, for example, improved education, health care, and highway systems, faster and more environmentally friendly modes of transportation as well as cleaner and less expensive new sources of energy. So debt becomes a way of spreading the cost to the society of what matters (including economic stability itself) across many generations. As debt can be refinanced, there is little chance that it will be paid off by a particular generation (see also Application II).

Debts, Deficits, and the Balance of Trade

We have looked at both the real and the misplaced concerns about the effects on the domestic economy of accumulated federal deficits and debt. Were the United States a closed economy, the concerns could be left at that. Foreign trade (exports and imports) and its finance are not only part of the American economy, however, but an area of increasing importance. Many, though not all, economists believe that there are problems associated with federal budget deficits that make it more difficult to achieve a balance of trade (exports = imports). Paul McCracken[3], a former member of the Council of Economic Advisors, argues that the currency depreciation or a weakening dollar (more dollars necessary to buy foreign currencies) experienced in 1995 is, in other words, a vote of no confidence in an American fiscal policy that has failed to move toward a balanced budget. McCracken says that the deficit problem is not that the federal government is "going broke" and that the declining dollar is not a reflection of a weak macroeconomy or of poor monetary policy. He says it is also not the work of speculators. The increased deficits, says McCracken, have caused the Treasury to compete for and take more and more of the supply of domestic savings (which are relatively small anyway) to finance and refinance federal debt. In the 1970s, financing those deficits took about 10 percent of domestic savings; in the 1980s and 1990s, that percentage rose to 20 and 25 percent, respectively and since 2005, the figure has risen to about 25 percent. This has caused a decline in the growth of the domestic capital stock and, as a corollary, a decrease in real income growth. It is true, says McCracken, that net foreign inflows of capital covered some of the difference. The net inflow of foreign *investment*, foreign savings used to finance an increased stock of productive capital, however, has become *negative* (repayments exceeding new investments). McCracken is concerned that the declining exchange rates reflect an underlying decline in confidence that foreign investors have in the future growth of an economy burdened with a low rate of savings coupled with deficit financing that is diverting both domestic and foreign savings into assets (federal government bonds) that do not contribute to increases in future productive capacity. McCracken's argument is directed to the failure of the Balanced Budget Amendment in 1995. We will have more to say about efforts to change federal budgeting in the upcoming section.

---

3. McCracken, Paul W. "Falling Dollars? Blame the Deficit" *Wall Street Journal*. April 13, 1995.

Traditional Arguments About Budget Deficits and Trade Deficits

There are traditional arguments about the relationship between federal deficits and trade deficits that focus on monetary policy, interest rate changes, dollar appreciation, and trade deficits. Though these do not seem to entirely fit the circumstances of the American economy since the early 2000s, it is important to mention them. We see the traditional chain of causality between budget deficits and trade deficits in Figure 10-6. In the first link in the chain, financing a federal budget deficit increases the demand for domestic savings and raises U.S. interest rates relative to those in other nations. In the second link are two effects: (1) a "crowding-out" of domestic investment, and (2) an increased demand for (relatively high interest rate) U.S. securities. As U.S. securities are sold to foreigners, the foreign debt of the U.S. increases (the U.S. is now the world's biggest debtor nation). In the third link, foreigners buy more U.S. dollars to purchase U.S. securities, and this increased demand for U.S. dollars causes the fourth link, an appreciation of the dollar against other currencies (pound sterling, yen, German mark, etc.). Because the dollar is now more expensive, in the fifth link, there is a decrease in (more expensive) U.S. exports and an increase in (less expensive) U.S. imports. In the final link, as imports rise relative to exports, the U.S. balance of trade becomes negative (exports < imports).

Figure 10-6

The Traditional View of Federal Budget Deficits and Balance of Trade Deficits

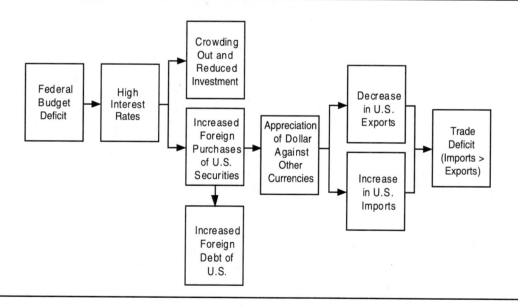

The view of many economists is that federal budget deficits lead, through a series of effects, to trade deficits. First, the deficit increases the demand for savings and leads to higher interest rates in money markets and monetary policy that is restrictive. Higher interest rates lead to "crowding-out" and less domestic investment. The higher interest rates lead to an increased foreign demand for U.S. securities and, thus, to greater foreign debt. Financing the increased purchases of U.S. securities raises the exchange rate of the dollar against other currencies. U.S. exports are now more expensive; U.S. imports are cheaper. The relative increase in imports leads to a deficit in the U.S. balance of trade.

It is worth noting that one conclusion of this traditional analysis is that fiscal policy of the sort suggested by the Keynesian model may not be as expansionary as its proponents claim. Deficits employed to fill demand gaps and to increase employment may be at least partially offset by a decline in exports as the dollar appreciates, and declining jobs in the export sector may offset some of the increased employment in the domestic economy.

An Alternative to the Traditional View

Ricardian Equivalence Theorem
The view that deficit finance has the same effects whether done through credit market borrowing or through current tax increases.

There are some economists, including several who are very prominent, who challenge the traditional view. They argue that even if the government goes into credit markets to finance a deficit, the increased demand for savings will not necessarily lead to higher interest rates and the set of linked effects shown in Figure 10-6. These contrarians base their argument on the **Ricardian Equivalence Theorem** which states that financing a deficit by credit market borrowing has the same economic effects as financing it through a current tax increase.

The argument is based on the reactions of individuals to current deficits that must be financed in the future. Aware that deficits today will require higher future taxes to finance the deficits, individual households cut current consumption because they anticipate a reduction in future after-tax incomes and, instead, save more to be able to pay the higher expected future taxes. If this argument is accepted, the first link in the chain of causal events in Figure 10-6 is broken. The increased supply of domestic savings by household entirely offsets the increased demand for domestic savings by the government and the rise in interest rates is avoided destroying the linkage, so the argument goes. Adherents of the traditional view, who probably constitute most economists, believe that the experience of the American economy since 1980 contradicts the Ricardian Equivalence Theorem. Both Budget and trade deficits have increased during much of this period. Moreover, there is little evidence that the private savings rate went up in response to larger budget deficits as predicted by the theorem.

Rethinking the American Fiscal System Since the 1990s

In spite of some misplaced concerns, huge deficits and rising federal debt have also ignited real and well-placed concerns not only among economists but also among millions of Americans. The Congressional elections of 1994 focused on some of those concerns. The Presidential election of 2008 again focused, at least partly, on these concerns. For at least a decade, proposals have been made, even some laws passed, to change the federal fiscal system. As we write this revision, major revisions of the system seem uncertain. The complexity of the system and its web of interrelated effects on incentives to risk taking and innovation, and saving and investment, together with its effects on income distribution, promise to make the efforts at revision contentious and difficult. Let's now look at some of the revisions already undertaken as well as some of the proposals for the future.

Efforts at Change Already Made

By the mid-1980s, it was clear to many that budget deficits and the federal debt were skyrocketing. Several Congressional efforts in succeeding years have been undertaken to impose fiscal discipline that would restrain deficits and debt growth.

Gramm-Rudman-Hollings Act (GRH), passed in late 1985, the legislation was intended to produce reductions each year in federal deficits with a goal of achieving a balanced budget by 1991. In 1987, the act was revised to provide for smaller deficit reductions and the goal of a balanced budget shifted forward where it remains.

The basic intent of GRH was to encourage Congress and the president to work together toward annual deficit reductions. Failure to do so would trigger automatic spending cuts. The recession of 1991, together with the huge federal expenditures associated with the Savings and Loan bailout, made GRH unfeasible. The automatic cuts were never made and, in effect, GRH was abandoned.

Budget Legislation Since the 1990s

Passed in late 1990, the Budget Reconciliation Act of 1990 was intended to trim $500 billion of budget deficits between 1991 and 1996. This was to be done through (1) an increase in the top marginal income tax rate, (2) lower deductions, (3) new "luxury" taxes, (4) higher excise tax rates, and (5) higher payroll taxes for Medicare. Decreases in federal spending in the same period of $260 billion were to contribute to deficit reduction. In addition, the Budget Enforcement Act of 1990 required that any increases in federal expenditures (other than emergency expenditures) must be accompanied by equal-sized cuts in existing expenditures or increases in taxes. Tax reductions also were to require equal and offsetting tax increases or expenditure cuts.

These measures, together with the Budget Reconciliation Act of 1993, which raised tax rates, increased taxes on social security benefits, and imposed higher excise taxes on tobacco and other goods, reduced budget deficits in the early twenty-first century. None, however, even has as a goal a balanced budget in the 1990s. (Indeed, deficits have grown again in the early years of the twenty first century.)

Proposals for Further Change

In the 104th Congress that took office in January 1995, a flurry of activity designed to further reform the American fiscal system took place. Some of the most important actions and proposals considered were:

1. A *balanced budget amendment* to the Constitution. The most restrictive action proposed has been to amend the Constitution to require an annual balance in the federal budget. Passed by the House of Representatives in March 1995, the proposal was narrowly defeated in the Senate. Proponents of the amendment argue that only a Constitutional restraint will have sufficient force to cause Congress and the president to take responsible steps to prevent large deficits and continued growth of the debt. Opponents say that such an amendment would tie the federal government's hands in periods of recession and deny it the ability to use compensatory fiscal policy as a counter-cyclical tool. Opponents also point out that in 1993, federal debt as a percent of the GDP fell as a result of the budget actions in the 1990s that we have already discussed. The proposal for a Constitutional amendment seems likely to continue as a way to deal with the country's perceived fiscal problems.

2. *Line-item veto.* Many public finance economists believe that the president should have the authority to veto specific items in appropriations bills while signing the other provisions of the bill into law. It has long been a practice to attach special interest expenditures favorable to groups in a particular congressional or senatorial district to an appropriations bill that contains many other expenditures beneficial to the country as a whole. Without a line-item veto, the president must sign or veto the entire bill. Many see the present system as one that is prone to fiscal "blackmail" and one that makes expenditure reductions

very difficult. In early 1995, line-item veto provisions were passed by both the House of Representatives and the Senate.

3. *Privatization*. Proposals continue to be made to make many government programs private. There are three ways in which this may be done: (1) contracting out government activities so that they are undertaken by private firms, (2) selling government assets (oil reserves, power plants, public lands) to private owners, and (3) providing consumers with vouchers which may be used to buy goods and services. Proposals to sell government assets such as the (quasi-public) U.S. Postal Service and Amtrak would yield revenue with which to reduce deficits. Contracting out would lower the cost of government. All such activities rely on the assumption that private firms, faced with an incentive to minimize cost, would be more efficient. Governments could establish standards for such activities but private sector incentives would reduce the amount of resources used to produce the goods and services. Vouchers would allow private individual consumers to make choices about purchases but, again, rely on private firms to produce those goods and services efficiently. Proponents say that government agencies, absent the profit motive, have less incentive to behave efficiently.

4. *Changes in budgetary procedures*. Many public finance economists believe that major changes are needed in federal budgetary procedures.

a. *Budgeting for entitlement programs*. Entitlement programs (social security, food stamps, Medicare, Medicaid, farm subsidies, and the like) pay benefits to any eligible American and have no cap on funding. Such programs, while estimated annually in cost, are not subject to expenditure limits. They are also the most rapidly growing of federal expenditures. As economist Michael Walden[4] says, "Any serious attempt to control federal spending must address the 'open-wallet system' employed with such programs." Proposals have been made to "means test" some; other proposals suggest limiting their growth to inflation and the growth of the eligible population. All such ideas promise to be difficult to enact since they are likely to be opposed by well-organized interest groups with strong preferences to preserve the "open-wallet" approach.

b. *Current account-capital account budgeting*. Current federal budgetary procedures treat all items as being on current account. We know from our earlier discussion that some federal expenditures (roads, bridges, water projects, and the like) involve capital or infrastructure building, projects whose benefits will exist for many years. Other federal expenditures (employee salaries, transfer payments and the like) are to pay for current services or current benefits. The federal government would do well, say many economists, to emulate the practices of private businesses and divide its budget into these two components. The current budget might well be constrained so that all expenditures must be paid out of current revenues. On the other hand, projects in the capital budget might be funded by borrowing just as private firms do. It would still be necessary, of course, to consider whether the resources needed to implement the capital budget would be more productive in the public or in the private sector.

---

4. Walden, Michael. "How Big is Government?" and "Who Pays the Tax Bill?" Chapter 5 in *Economic Issues, Rhetoric and Reality*. Prentice Hall, Englewood Cliffs, New Jersey, 1995.

What Should be Government's Share of the GDP Pie?

A fundamental way to deal with governmental fiscal problems is to ask: What should be its economic role and what part of the GDP must it claim to carry out that role? One could require by law or by constitutional amendment that government spending not exceed that percentage of the GDP. It would, though, be extremely difficult to decide and agree on government's role (something we have been arguing about throughout our national history) as well as its corresponding share of GDP. Even the policy statement of 1946 with which we began this chapter offers no guidance.

A Recap

Throughout our history as a nation, the role of government and its claims on resources to execute its role have been controversial. That controversy has never been more intense than in the period since the 1990s. From the 1960s to the 1980s, Keynesian fiscal policy was in ascendancy and compensatory fiscal policy was used at various times to move the economy toward lower rates of unemployment. In the 1980s, faced with (1) supply-side arguments to use tax cuts to spur economic growth, (2) rising defense expenditures to fight the "cold war," and (3) entitlement programs that were on "automatic pilot" or "open-wallet," federal expenditures grew more rapidly than federal revenues. The financing of the ensuing large deficits lead to a huge increase in the federal debt. Since 1985, various efforts have been made to restrain these deficits and the growth of the debt. While some of the efforts in the 1990s produced short-term deficit reductions, no long-term approach has yet been adopted. There were large deficits in 2009-2012 and these deficits have decreased dramatically since 2013 but, it may be likely that a combination of approaches, one that limits the rate of growth of federal expenditures, will be adopted. It is, however, by no means clear what that combination will be. In light of the large deficits of 2009-2011 and those that are projected through 2015, it may be likely that a combination of approaches, one that limits the rate of growth of federal expenditures, will be adopted. It is, however, by no means clear what that combination will be.

Application I: The "Share Economy," A Replacement for Keynesian Demand Management?

As we have seen in the immediately preceding chapters, the percentage of people unemployed (those who did not work last week and have been looking for work for at least four weeks) has been up and down in a near roller coaster fashion for the last 70 years. The "Keynesian revolution" ascribed this tendency of instability to a lack of wage and price flexibility in the economy. The Keynesian recipe for dealing with that perceived flaw in a modern market economy, was government management of aggregate demand, i.e.; expenditure and tax programs to push the economy toward full employment at stable prices.

From the mid-1980s to the present, there has seemed to be appreciably less enthusiasm for this type of macroeconomic policy. Faced with escalating federal debt and seemingly intractable budget deficits, Keynesian demand management would be difficult to pursue even if it enjoyed widespread political support. A number of economists have undertaken to identify ways to create a tendency toward full employment without major fiscal policy involvement by the federal government. A prominent such effort is that of Economist Martin Weitzman[5] of MIT. In a book entitled *The **Share Economy***, Weitzman argues that both inflation and unemployment problems can be solved by making wages

Share Economy
A proposal under which some of the wage earnings of labor would be tied to the profitability of firms.

more flexible and by tying the pay of workers at least partly to the profitability of the firms that employ them.

A Two Wage System

Under Weitzman's proposal, wages would be separated into two components: (1) a base pay that does not vary with firms' profits, and (2) a second component that would fall as profits diminish and rise as profits increase. The current wage system in the U.S. results in lay-off of workers in a recession as firms' cut back production. The result is an increase in unemployment. Under the "share economy" proposals, the (1) non-base component of wages would fall as firms revenues decline, (2) costs of production would decrease, (3) prices could be cut to increase sales, and (4) the work force would be maintained (a scenario of wage and price flexibility similar to the classical one that Keynes sought to disprove). Weitzman thus believes that full employment could be maintained even in the face of a recession.

Weitzman argues that even if only 15 to 25 percent of workers' wages were in the form of profit sharing, this stabilizing influence on unemployment would be effective. This would happen in a "share economy" without sacrificing the resource mobility essential to any capitalist system. Workers would not be laid off when there was a declining demand for a firm's products. If the decline continued though, the firm's profitability and the wages it would offer workers would fall relative to those in growing industries. When the wage gap grew large enough, labor would relocate to higher wage areas of the economy. Those would be the areas where consumers apparently prefer those labor resources to be used (in view of the higher prices they are willing to pay for the growing industry's output).

When, asked if this "share economy" proposal has been tried elsewhere, Weitzman points to Asia. "Japanese workers receive 25 percent of their pay as a bonus. In South Korea and Taiwan about 15 percent of pay comes as a bonus. Even government workers in Korea have their pay tied to profitability." The proposal would of course, cause workers to assume some of the risks of business; in other words, workers would become partly venture capitalists. Because of this, Weitzman expects the greatest opposition to his proposal to come from unions whose senior member's are least vulnerable to lay off and who through seniority, command the highest wage premiums. Such workers would be asked to accept more wage variability in order to assure a higher and more stable level of employment.

Critiques of the Share Economy

It might be reasonable to suppose that Keynesian economists would oppose Weitzman's proposal for it would seem to diminish the role of demand-management in macroeconomic policy. In fact, some of the most prominent "Keynesians," while expressing doubts about the proposal, have urged that it be seriously investigated. Lawrence Summers formerly of Harvard (and the U.S. departments of Labor and Treasury and economic advisor to the Obama administration) says: (1) in view of the widely held belief that a natural rate of unemployment precludes effective long-run trade-offs between inflation and unemployment, and (2) that the gains achievable by increasing the average level of employment make other macro-economic goals seem trivial.

---

5. Weitzman, Martin."The Share Economy-Can It solve Our Economic Ills?" *U.S. News and World Report*, August 26, 1985.

Nonetheless, Summers argues that there is no free lunch offered by the share economy. Negative effects could come about from two sources: (1) fellow worker problems, and (2) investment problems. The fellow worker problem derives from the incentives of workers faced with a declining revenue pie to resist hiring additional workers and an incentive to let the least productive workers go. Workers, concludes Summers, would be in competition with each other which would be exactly the opposite of the Japanese system. The investment problem comes from fixing the profit share of the revenue pie while allowing the wage component to vary. This, according to Summers, seems likely to reduce incentives to investment.

Another prominent macroeconomist, Alan Blinder[6] of Princeton University (and the Federal Reserve Board), says the Weitzman plan may be seen in two somewhat different ways. As a device for ending unemployment, it is a "bottle half full"; as an intrusion on the business cycle (with its elimination of less productive enterprises) it is a "bottle half empty." Blinder, who sees unemployment elimination as *very* important, believes the bottle "three quarters full." In addition, he says, by giving workers greater job security and a greater stake in the companies they work for, there might be higher productivity and less resistance to labor-saving technical change.

Blinder refuses to reject the Keynesian idea that "shorter and shallower" recessions are better, and continues to argue that the externalities of firms' actions (effects on consumers incomes) "justify government intervention to smooth business cycles."

What is the Status of the Share Economy?

Clearly, the wage-price system of the American economy continues to be different from the share economy. Indeed, as Blinder notes, even if the Weitzman plan is socially optimal, it will not be adopted unless it is also seen as privately optimal. To this end Weitzman has argued for a tax subsidy to firms that would cause them to adopt the plan. Blinder says that there are numerous other practical problems that would have to be solved as well. Many economists, Keynesians and non-Keynesians alike, feel that the proposal is worth serious study.

Application II: Fiscal Policy vs. Fiscal Politics

The 30th U.S. president Calvin Coolidge (1923-1929) once said that "There is no dignity quite so impressive, and no one independence quite so important, as living within your means." A champion of small government and deregulation, he cut taxes, federal government expenditures and the size of public debt. Today, many polls indicate that members of the public also associate reducing the federal deficit and debt with a fiscally responsible and prudent behavior. The "Roaring Twenties," ended with the deepest and most devastating economic contractions in the modern U.S. history, known as the "Great Depression," that soon spilled over to other countries. Ironically, like many other episodes of economic crisis before and after it, the Great Depression was, to large extent, caused by the bursting of speculative bubble in the stock and (residential) real estate markets fueled by high private debt. The unemployment rate reached nearly 25 percent in 1932 during President Hoover's term (1929-33) and was accompanied by mass poverty and homelessness and sharp increase in bank failures and decrease in industrial production and foreign trade. The Depression officially ended in 1933 when GDP began to rise, but the economy went through

6. Blinder, Alan S. "The Share Economy: A Bottle Half Full." *Challenge.* November-December, 1986.

another contraction during 1937-38 (a recession within the Depression) caused, in part, by a premature attempt to balance the federal budget. However, GDP did not reach its pre-Depression level until the early 1940s when the U.S. entered WWII.

The Depression era was an inflection point in the U.S. government fiscal and regulatory activism. Under President Franklin D. Roosevelt (1933-45), a large number of new public works projects, programs (including Social Security) and regulatory agencies were introduced to achieve the "3Rs" of "Relief, Recovery, and Reform." President Roosevelt instinctively understood the importance of restoring public confidence ("the only thing that we have to fear is fear itself") and deficit spending in boosting the level of aggregate demand consistent with the Keynesian prescription. The deficits in the 1930s, however, were relatively small as spending increases were in part supported by higher taxes on high income earners. The massive increase in military spending during WWII and resultant increase in employment finally pushed the level of GDP to new highs, but they also increased the public debt to GDP ratio to a record level of nearly 120 percent in 1946. The wars in Korea, Vietnam, introduction of Medicare and Medicare under President Johnson (1963-69) increased government expenditures in the 1950s, '60s, and '70s. The deficit to GDP ratio remained fairly stable and the debt to GDP ratio actually sharply fell during much of these three decades reflecting relatively higher GDP growth rates. The ratios, however, began to trend upward from the early 1980s on (with the exception of the 1990s) for reasons that were explained earlier (see the "Federal Revenues and Expenditures" section and Application II in Chapter 6).

The first decade of the new millennium witnessed a repeat of the Great Depression on a smaller scale (the Great Recession) mainly caused (again) by an abrupt end of the speculative boom in the housing and stock markets and accumulation of high private debt. It resulted in a near collapse of the financial system and exacted huge economic as well as human tolls. Massive interventions by the federal government were deemed necessary to prevent the Recession from turning into another Depression (see Application I in Chapter 1). Figure 10-7 shows legislative and non-legislative fiscal changes that affected the path of fiscal deficit over the period 2001-2011. It suggests as a consequence of these changes, the fiscal balance went from a projected cumulative surplus of $5.9 trillion to an actual cumulative deficit of $6 trillion. This is almost a 200 percent reversal! The figure also suggests that the deficit incurred in relation to countering the Great Recession (the "Recovery Act") was relatively small.

Against the backdrop of this brief historical review of fiscal policy changes that increased the cyclical and structural budget deficits and public debt, we attempt to address some of the misperceptions and issues that shape public opinion and drive "fiscal politics." As noted in the first paragraph, members of the public expect the (federal) government to live within its means. *After all, if individuals and businesses "balance their checkbooks" why shouldn't the government?* Aside from the fact that many individuals may not practice what they preach (the private debt to GDP ratio, depending on how it is measured, has been quite high and even higher than the public debt ratio), this way of looking at the issue ignores the fact that the scope of responsibilities of the federal government is vastly larger than those of individuals and businesses. An individual is responsible for his/her family welfare and a company for its shareholders and employees. The federal government, however, has to be concerned about the nation's *collective* welfare. In the realm of macroeconomics, this translates into mitigating the economic and social impacts of severe downturns by stabilizing the economy and lowering the unemployment rate. (As noted before, the federal government is *required* by

Acts of Congress to respond to "economic disasters" which often inflict more damages than the most devastating natural disasters). Stated differently, managing the macroeconomy is not the same as managing household or corporate finances. While a corporation, for example, can downsize and layoff its workers in the face of economic adversity and/or relocate to another state or country in search of greener pastures (lower taxes and wages and fewer labor and environmental regulations, for example) the government cannot do that.

Figure 10-7

Changes in deficit projections since January 2001

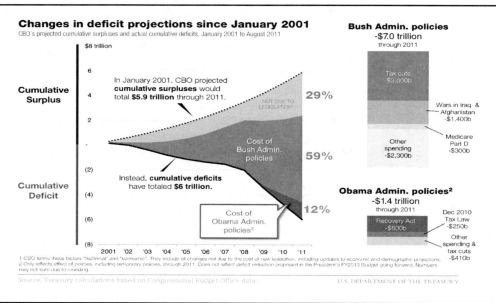

But doesn't deficit spending basically involve the government spending of private money? That is true when the government borrows from the private investors to support deficit spending. However, the point worth emphasizing is that, especially during severe economic contractions, private consumption and investment expenditures are depressed as a result of loss of income, uncertainties, fears, and limited profitable business opportunities. Under these conditions, deficits inject spending into the economy which might not have otherwise materialized in a timely fashion to stop the downward spiral in economic activity. As argued by Jerry Bernstein and Richard Kogan[7], deficits act like shock absorbers for the entire economy as they reduce the volatility in expenditures and taxes, and economic growth over economic busts and booms (and across generations). They contend that, far from being a fiscal evil, deficits are downright good when *properly managed.*

So are concerns about deficits and accumulating debt unfounded? To be sure there are some legitimate concerns, but obsession with the fiscal deficit is unhealthy. As the noted economist (and the former Secretary of Treasury and Harvard University President) Lawrence Summers pointed out, we have many deficits (in areas such as health, education, and infrastructure) and the fiscal deficit is not the most important one. He argues that it is economically unwise not to borrow at historically low interest rates prevailing in the (post) Great

7. Jared Bernstein and Richard Kogan. "Bumpy deficits, smoother ride: The historical evolution of budget deficits and growth rate" Vox, August 18, 2015.

Recession years in order to invest, for example, in our decaying infrastructure (such as roads, bridges, and airports). These investments yield higher rates of return than the cost of borrowing money and benefit the economy through stimulating aggregate demand, creating jobs, and boosting future economic growth through expanding productive capacity. As such, they benefit both current and future generations. This leads to another important point in deficit spending: *what the government does with borrowed money is important.* While there are compelling moral and ethical reasons for helping the needy and vulnerable members of the society to maintain a basic standard of living through transfer payments (especially during tough economic times), priority should be given to public investments.

When is then the "right time" for cutting deficits and lowering the public debt? As discussed before, the cyclical component of the total deficit tends to go up during economic downturns and shrink when the economy recovers, but the structural component may persist even during periods of economic boom. The "right time" for cutting deficits of any kind, however, is when the economy is well into its recovery phase and not when it is in a slump. Premature deficit reductions, under political pressures, may make the contraction deeper and longer and, ironically, raise the deficit (debt) to GDP ratio! (What may happen to GDP, the denominator?) This explains why an annually balanced budget requirement is likely to make a bad situation worse, or is pro-cyclical (why?)

What can be done to reduce deficits (debt) the timing issue aside? Many members of the public and politicians focus on the need to deal with "waste, fraud, and abuse" associated with "big government." As important and sizable as these may be, eliminating them is likely to have a modest impact. As many credible studies have suggested, it takes a *combination* of spending cuts and tax hikes to bring the fiscal deficit and debt to a sustainable lower level. However, while the arithmetic of deficit reduction is very simple its politics is complicated and often toxic. "Conservatives" want to significantly cut most taxes and non-defense expenditures that they perceive as wasteful even more. In contrast, "liberals" want to maintain and even increase non-defense expenditures and pay for them by more tax revenues generated through eliminating tax loopholes and "corporate welfare," and imposing higher tax rates on the "rich." Finally, most importantly, there are many members of the public (and the interest groups representing them) who, as many polls have shown, are in favor of lower deficits, debt, and smaller government in abstract, but seem to be unwilling to do what it takes to achieve these goals in practice. They want higher taxes, but as long as they are not the ones who pay them. (Don't tax me. Don't tax him. Tax that fellow behind the tree!) They are also for cuts in government spending so long as their favorite government benefits and programs remain intact. (What is mine is mine and what's yours is negotiable!) The implications are disconcerting but familiar: through lobbying efforts and political pressures, the necessary tax rate increases and tax codes reforms are blocked and popular entitlement programs (Social Security, Medicaid, and Medicare) and defense spending, whose huge costs are behind the rise in the structural component of the total deficit, are shielded from reasonable modifications. The essence of this dilemma and a major contributing factor to our fiscal imbalances seems to be that people want more government then they are willing to pay for. The rhetoric about our fiscal issues and government masks an important question that begs an answer: how much each of us is willing to give up to achieve a balanced budget and low debt?

SUMMING UP

1. The economic role of government has always been controversial. However, both the Employment Act of 1946 and the Humphrey-Hawkins Full Employment Act of 1978 assigned the federal government a broad responsibility (but not a commitment) to create and maintain full (high) employment.

2. *Fiscal policy*, variations in government expenditures and taxation, was a major counter-cyclical tool of the federal government from the 1960s to the 1980s.

3. *Discretionary fiscal policy* consists of changes in expenditures and taxes that are made to achieve specific macroeconomic goals. There are also *automatic stabilizers*, changes in taxes and expenditures that are triggered by fluctuations in economic activity that result in changes in income and employment.

4. Keynesians argue for *compensatory fiscal policy*, the use of fiscal policy (tax, expenditure) tools that will shift aggregate demand and result, during recession, in increased employment and income at stable prices. This argument is based on the Keynesian assumption that changes in aggregate quantity supplied can equal changes in aggregate demand without increased prices (the horizontal range of aggregate supply). If, on the other hand, a more classical aggregate supply (upward sloping range of aggregate supply) conditions hold, expansionary fiscal policy will lead to aggregate price rises and a larger fiscal stimulus will be required to achieve the same fiscal goal.

5. Use of fiscal policy tools in either range of aggregate supply may result in government *budget deficits* (expenditures > revenues) unless funded out of current revenues. *Budget surpluses* may result if revenues exceed expenditures.

6. A major concern about the deficits is their very large magnitudes. Also troubling is that, by including Social Security Trust Fund revenues as current general revenues, the deficit is actually understated. Another concern is that interest payments on the debt which constitute a rising percentage of the federal budget, reduce discretionary expenditures, those which may be subject to reduction.

7. The timing of the deficits is a further concern. Though deficits, historically, have occurred during recessions and wartime, most recent deficits have occurred when the economy was operating with low rates of unemployment. This development leads to fears about Demand-pull inflation.

8. An often expressed concern about deficits is that financing them in credit markets will lead to "crowding-out," a decline in net investment spending as federal demand for funds causes interest rates to rise. Future generations, thus, inherit a less productive economy. If consumption is "crowded-out," the current generation bears this burden.

9. The authors conclude that if "crowding-out" has occurred, it has been at the expense of investment with future generations bearing the burden. Two qualifications, however, are (1) government expenditures that are deficit financed may be for investments in which case, future generations will benefit from a more productive economy, and (2) government expenditures in times of significant unemployment may, through Keynesian effects, move the economy toward full employment with little or no burden on current consumption or investment.

10. An unwarranted concern about the deficits and the national debt is that the government will ultimately be unable to fund its activities and will go bankrupt. This is false because governments can (1) refinance their debts and, (2) unlike individuals can raise revenues through taxation and "printing" money.

11. Seventy seven percent of the federal debt consists of assets (bonds) owned by Americans. It is, thus, a debt of the government but mainly an offsetting credit to American citizens. While it could be repaid, doing so would result in a massive redistribution of income and wealth since the assets funding it are not uniformly held by Americans. The real opportunity cost of the; debt is on the generation in which the debt is created for that generation foregoes the goods and services that are not produced.

12. Some economists, including Paul McCracken, believe that the continuing deficits undermine the confidence of foreign investors. As the Treasury competes for a larger percentage of a (limited) supply of domestic savings, foreign investors foresee a decline in the capital stock of the U.S. and the net inflow of foreign capital becomes negative. As foreign capital leaves the country, exchange rates of the dollar against foreign currencies decline.

13. In the traditional view, federal deficits are related to trade deficits through monetary policy, interest rate changes, and dollar *appreciation*. A budget deficit leads to tight money and higher interest rates, which leads to crowding out and reduced investment, rising foreign purchases of U.S. securities, and increased foreign debt of the U.S., which causes the dollar to appreciate, which causes decreased U.S. exports and increased U.S. imports, which, in turn, leads to a trade deficit.

14. "Keynesian" expansionary fiscal policies may lead to decreased exports and trade deficits. This reduction in aggregate demand means that such policies may be less expansionary than Keynesians have argued.

15. A contrary view of the effects of budget deficit finance is seen in the *Ricardian Equivalence Theorem*. This theorem holds that financing deficits through credit market sales of bonds has the same effects as financing them through tax increases. If bonds are sold, individuals, aware that future tax increases will be required to finance the deficits, will cut consumption and save more to pay the expected higher taxes. This increased saving causes deficit financing not to lead to higher interest rates and, breaks the tie between deficit financing and trade deficits.

16. A major push to rethink and reshape the American fiscal system has occurred since the early 1990s. The system is very complex and has major effects on incentives to risk taking, innovation, saving and investment, and the distribution of income. Its revision will be difficult.

17. Changes in the fiscal system that have already occurred include (1) the Gramm-Rudman-Hollings Act of 1985 that could have lead to automatic spending cuts but has, instead, been abandoned, and (2) the Budget Reconciliation and Budget Enforcement Acts in 1990 and 1993, which require offsetting expenditure cuts or tax increases when new expenditures are authorized.

18. Proposals for future changes include (1) a Balanced Budget Amendment to the Constitution that would require an annual balance in the federal budget, (2) the Line-Item Veto which would allow the president to veto particular appropriations that serve narrow interest groups, and (3) privatization that could take the form of contracting out government activities, selling government assets, and providing consumers with vouchers to buy goods and services.

19. Many economists suggest that needed changes in federal budgetary procedures include (1) entitlement programs should be subject to expenditure caps rather than the "open-wallet" system, and (2) the federal government should adopt a current budget/capital budget format which would permit federal borrowing for capital projects but restrict payments for current services to current revenues.

20. A most fundamental fiscal reform would be to restrict the Federal government's share of the GDP to that which is necessary to carry out an agreed on role. That share is now 23 percent including retirement programs. Defining the role, however, would be very difficult.

21. The Keynesian arguments for government intervention to manage aggregate demand and reduce the severity of business cycles have been less well received since the 1980s. One of the proposals to replace this demand management is contained in the idea of a "share economy" advanced by Martin Weitzman.

22. Under the share economy proposal, there would be two components of the wage payment to workers. Most of the payment would be in the present contract form which guarantees a wage but not permanent employment. The second component would be tied to the profitability of firms, with that share rising as profits increase and falling as profits diminish.

23. Under the share economy proposal, wages would fall in a recession. This would result from falling demand and reduced profits of firms. Thus, firms will not lay off workers but will cut prices to restore sales.

KEY TERMS

Automatic stabilizers
Budget deficit
Budget surplus
Compensatory fiscal policy
"Crowding-out" effect
Discretionary fiscal policy
Fiscal policy
Ricardian Equivalence Theorem
Share economy

QUESTIONS

1. What is the basic macroeconomic role assigned to the federal government by the Employment Act of 1946?

2. Explain what is meant by *fiscal policy* and what its role in economic stability was from the 1960s to the 1980s.

3. Explain the differences between *discretionary fiscal policy* and *automatic stabilizers*. What are examples of each?

4. What is the Keynesian assumption about aggregate supply during periods in which *compensatory fiscal policy* is employed? What is the classical assumption? Which of the two assumptions increases the amount of compensatory fiscal policy stimulus required to achieve employment goals?

5. What is meant by budget deficit? Budget surplus? Which has been characteristic of federal budgets since 1960?

6. In what year did the federal debt as a percentage of GDP reach its maximum? What caused this maximum?
     a. What happened to the federal debt as a percentage of GDP from 1960 to 2015? What were the major causes of the changes during this period?
     b. What causes budget deficits? What is the relationship between federal budget deficits and the federal debt?

7. What are the four major current concerns about federal debt?

     a. In what sense is the magnitude of the federal deficits understated?
     b. Interest on the federal debt has risen as a percentage of the federal budget. Why is this viewed by many as a problem?
     c. Deficits in recent years have frequently occurred when the economy was operating with low levels of unemployment. Why is this timing a matter of concern?

8. What is the "crowding-out" effect? How is this effect related to the burden of deficits and debt on present and future generations?

9. How do the nature of government expenditures and the employment effects of government expenditure qualify any conclusion about the burden of deficits and federal debt?

10. How, according to Keynesians, may the "crowding-out" effects of deficits during periods of recession be at least partially offset by their stimulative effects?

11. Explain why concerns about federal bankruptcy and federal debt burdens on future generations are basically unwarranted?

12. What would be the major effect of a repayment of the federal debt?

13. What was the major burden of large increases in the federal debt during the post-1980 period?

14. Explain, step by step, how a federal budget deficit may, in the traditional view, lead to a budget deficit. Why does this view support the idea that fiscal policy stimulus to the economy may be less than expected by Keynesians?

15. What is the Ricardian Equivalence Theorem? How does it break the chain of events in the traditional view of the relationship between budget deficits and trade deficits?

16. Why will it be complex and difficult in the 1990s to reshape the American fiscal system?

17. What were the provisions of (1) the Gramm-Rudman-Hollings Act (1985), (2) the Budget Reconciliation Act of 1990, (3) the Budget Enforcement Act of 1990, and (4) the Budget Reconciliation Act of 1993?

18. How would a Balanced Budget Amendment change the American fiscal system? How does Line-Item Veto change the system? Privatization of federal programs?

19. What is meant by the "open-wallet" system of budgeting for entitlement programs? What proposals have been made to change this system?

20. How would adoption of a current-account and capital-account in the federal budget change the American fiscal system? What is the rationale for adoption of this type of budgeting procedure?

21. Why would it be very difficult to limit federal government spending by limiting its share of GDP?

22. What is the Keynesian solution to the problem of the business cycle?

23. What would be the system of wage payment in a "share economy?" How does this differ from the present wage-price system?

24. If the "share economy" system were adopted, what would be the effect on wage-price flexibility?

25. Would there be labor immobility in a share economy? Explain.

26. What nations have wage systems similar to that in the "share economy"?

27. Who would you expect to strongly oppose a share economy? Why?

28. Why has the acceptance of a natural rate of unemployment heightened interest in the "share economy"?

29. What does Summers mean by fellow worker problems and investment problems associated with a share economy?

30. What might the share economy do to worker job security, labor productivity, and implementation of labor-saving technological changes?

31. Identify some of the problems in getting agreement to create a "share economy."

Chapter 11: Money in the Modern Economy

In this and upcoming chapters, we will examine the basic roles of money in a modern market economy. Policy debates concerning the supply of money took on even greater importance beginning in the 1990s. These have grown stronger in 2009-2011 because of the efforts of the central (Federal) reserve bank to use monetary policy to deminish the effects of a severe recession. But before we can talk about monetary policy, it is necessary to understand what money is and what essential functions it performs.

First, let's note that, although money is an important part of an economy, the factors of production, the resources essential to producing things (land, labor, capital, entrepreneurship) do not contain money. Money does not directly produce anything although resources are required to produce money. In view of this, how does money contribute to turning out automobiles or computers, or any of the myriad of goods and services we consume each year?

Before we can trace a clear relationship between the supply of money and the production of goods and services, there are some questions we must answer in this chapter and in the next about money itself: What is money? What are its functions? How is it increased or decreased, and how is this process controlled? How does the system of banks and non-bank financial institutions work? How does money affect the level of economic activity and prices? Most important, how can monetary policy changes influence the supply of money in order to bring about a higher level of income and employment, with stable prices?

Barter: An Early System of Exchange;

Barter
A system in which goods are exchanged for other goods.

People can produce goods and services without the existence of money; where there is no money, goods must be exchanged for other goods. When this happens, the system of exchange is called **barter**.

For example, Farmer Nielson needs a hundred bushels of wheat and a pair of shoes, size eleven. He looks around his farm to see what he can barter and decides that his 250-pound pig is surely worth a hundred bushels of wheat and a pair of size-eleven shoes. He takes his pig to his nearest neighbor, Farmer Gomez, a wheat farmer, and offers to barter the pig for the wheat and the shoes. Farmer Gomez agrees that it's a fair exchange, but although he has the wheat, he doesn't have the size-eleven shoes. So Farmer Nielson goes down the road to Farmer Camilla McGrath. Her father died recently and left a closet full of size-eleven shoes, but she has no wheat. Her brother on the next farm also has some of their late father's size-eleven shoes, and he has plenty of wheat, but he doesn't want the pig. Farmer Nielson will probably make his trade eventually, but it may cost him a lot of time and effort.

Double Coincidence of Demand
A situation in which there is a mutuality of needs and in which one individual is willing to exchange goods with another.

The central requirement of the barter system is what is called a **double coincidence of demand**, or of wants. Not only must Farmer Nielson want what the other person has, but also the other person in the exchange must want what Nielson has. Establishing mutuality of needs is usually time consuming and therefore inefficient. How much easier it would be for Nielson to take the pig to the butcher in town, sell it for money, buy the wheat from the miller, and then drop by the shoe store and pick up a pair of size-eleven shoes.

Money: A More Modern System of Exchange

Modern economies are much more complex than early ones, and this creates pressure to replace barter with a more efficient system of *money exchange*. As a society specializes its labor and other resources, it must also specialize the means by which exchanges are made.

Your instructor is not only a teacher, not only a college teacher, but, even more specialized than that, an economics instructor, producing a service called education. How should he or she be paid? In a society without money, would one student barter potatoes, another mow the instructor's lawn, or another clean the classroom? Although barter was used earlier in this and other countries, it is too cumbersome today (though governments occasionally engage in barter trade with each other). The existence of money makes possible, an efficient flow of goods and resources, and a more highly developed economy.

But what is money? What is the essential ingredient that makes a thing money?

Money
Anything that people accept in exchange for goods and services.

A thing becomes **money** when people accept that thing in exchange for goods and services in general. *Money is money because people say it is money* and accept it in exchange for almost anything else. Governments may decree that something be accepted as payment for all debts, public or private. Although this *encourages* acceptance of that thing as a medium of exchange, it does not guarantee it. In the past, money consisted of gold and silver or paper backed by gold and silver. You could exchange a paper five-dollar bill for a five-dollar gold piece. This increased its acceptability as money. Today if you take a five-dollar bill to a bank, you will get in return only a new five-dollar bill. And yet you can still exchange it for goods and services.

In the long run, it is just the *acceptance* of the thing called money in exchange for goods and services that makes it money.

The Functions of Money

There are four basic functions that money performs:

1. Money acts as a *medium of exchange*. The central ingredient of money is its acceptability by others. When money is exchanged for goods and services, it is functioning as a medium of exchange and relieves a society of the need to use barter.

2. The second function is a corollary of the first. Money is a *standard of value or unit of account*. Money serves as a measure by which a value can be set on goods and services. In a barter economy, if Farmer Nielson wanted to know the value of his pig, he compared it with the value of other goods. The pig might be worth a hundred bushels of oats and the extraction of an aching tooth, and so on.

     In a money economy, the pig's value is set in terms of the monetary unit of the country. The monetary unit of the United States is the dollar, so here the pig is valued in dollars. Although other nations have differing standard units (Euros, pounds, francs, and so on), in each country money functions as a standard of value or unit of account and makes it possible for people to place a value on goods and services. It is, thus, a common denominator of all goods and services.

3. Money is the most liquid of assets and acts as a *store of value*. In a barter economy, how can Farmer Nielson *save*? He can do so only by storing goods. He can stash away wheat or preserve the products of the pig (bacon, ham, sausages), or he can accumulate larger numbers of things. But it costs a lot to store these things, and such products can deteriorate over a period of time. It would be simpler if Nielson could sell his output and save the accumulated *money*. (Money occupies little space; it doesn't rot or breed weevils. It just sits there and frequently earns interest.)

     But money *does* fluctuate in value, because of increases or decreases in prices. Inflation reduces the purchasing power of money and therefore reduces its value. Deflation causes the reverse to happen. This factor reduces the efficiency of money as a store of value.

4. Money is a *means of deferred payment*. Money facilitates lending and the repayment of loans. In a barter economy, borrowing is a most cumbersome affair. Suppose that Nielson's land is next to the river, and one year the river floods and destroys his wheat crop. He goes to Farmer Gomez, who lives in the unaffected uplands, and borrows wheat so he can plant a new crop. But because of the flood, wheat is now relatively scarce, that is, in short supply, with a high relative exchange value. The following year the weather is fine, and there is a bumper crop. Nielson, with plenty of wheat today, pays Gomez back for the wheat he borrowed last year. But with this year's abundance of wheat, the scarcity value of wheat has declined markedly, compared with last year, and wheat has a low relative exchange value.

     It is more efficient to base credit on a general medium of exchange: money. One expects money and its scarcity value (in simple language, its purchasing power) to be less subject than barter items to variations outside people's control.

     However, the value of money, its purchasing power, does vary as prices vary, and this, as we said earlier, reduces the usefulness of money. There have been times in history when the supply of money increased so rapidly that it led to monetary disaster. During the American Revolution, for example, the Continental Congress issued so much currency with no backing that the people lost confidence in it. The purchasing power of that money dropped so low that the currency was not accepted in exchange for goods and services and the expression "not worth a Continental" became a part of our language.

Characteristics of a "Good" Money

Many things have performed the function of money. During the American Revolution, in Massachusetts wheat served as money, and in Virginia tobacco was legally defined as money. American Indians used strings of colored beads called wampum as money; some African tribes have used cattle and cowry shells, and some groups in the South Sea Islands have used large stones. Apart from paper currency, gold, silver, and copper are the materials that most commonly serve as money.

What characteristics should one look for in a good money? (1) It should be portable, or easy to carry; (2) it should be easy to recognize, but hard to counterfeit or duplicate illegally; (3) it should be easily subdivided, to allow for small as well as large purchases; (4) the cost of storing it, that is, physically storing it in a safe place, or storing it in an accounting sense, should be low; (5) it should be durable, and not wear out or rot quickly; and (6) the relative supply should not vary so greatly that large variations in relative scarcity value occur, since purchasing power changes as prices vary.

The Supply of Money: How to Define and Measure It

Defining and identifying the supply of money in the United States has become more difficult in recent decades. Ideally, we would like the definition to include all financial instruments that may readily be used in the short-term exchange of goods and services. Because of institutional and legal changes in our monetary system since the early 1970s, the exact identification and measurement of those instruments has become more complex for reasons we will look at in this and the succeeding chapter. As a first approximation, however, let's define money in the following way:

Money consists of all liabilities in commercial banks and other financial institutions that are subject to demand plus currency and coin in circulation.

Demand Deposits
Accounts that are subject to withdrawal by means of a check.

Demand deposits are what you know as *checking accounts*. They are called demand deposits because you can withdraw these deposits "on demand," by presenting a check.

A *check* is merely an order to a financial institution from the holder of a demand deposit to transfer some money from the deposit and pay it to someone else. The deposit is the money, not the check. If there is no deposit, the check is worthless.

About 40 percent of our money supply, as defined, is in the form of demand deposits. This is so, because it is both more convenient and safer to make large transactions this way. Another 33 percent is in other checkable accounts. However, the economic importance of "checkbook money" is even greater than that, since about 90 percent (by value) of all economic transactions are accomplished by means of checks drawn against demand deposits.

Depository Institutions
Those institutions that hold demand deposits.

The keepers of demand deposits are called **depository institutions**. Commercial banks are the largest part of the institutions that hold our demand deposits. Since demand deposits comprise the bulk of the U.S. money supply, commercial banks hold most of the supply of money in the United States. (As we shall see later, however, many other institutions in the United States now hold and create money.) The second largest component of our narrowly defined money supply is *currency in circulation*, which means currency that is in use rather than in the vaults of banks or of the Federal Reserve. Currency; is the paper money in the U.S. economy and consists of Federal Reserve Notes that are issued by the Federal Reserve Banks.

Coins are another part of the supply of money. Though relatively small, they are a vital part of that supply. These metal tokens are minted by the Treasury, but also issued through the Federal Reserve Banks. Today both currency and coin are called **fiat money**. Their value as monetary instruments is greater than their value as commodities. The five-dollar bill as a monetary instrument is worth five dollars in goods and services.

Cartoon Feature Syndicate

"I'm holding onto my cash, I think money is going to come back."

As a *commodity* (waste paper or perhaps a wall decoration) it is worth very little. The twenty-five-cent coin, if it were melted down and sold as metal, would be worth far less than twenty-five cents. Currency and coin are also defined as **legal tender**, which is any money the law says must be accepted as payment for all debt, public (owed to or owed by the government), or private (owed by one individual to another). The smallest part of our money supply is travelers checks which make up less than one percent of the total.

Coins and Gresham's Law

Coins are a clear example of fiat money. Governments long ago discovered that they could "profit" from issuing coins that contain less precious metal (gold, silver) than their face value. Though the United States did issue non-debased coins (such as the famous gold double eagles) earlier in our history, all coins in the U.S. money supply today are debased, that is, they contain mostly base (less valuable) metal. The fact is that all of the non-debased coins today are collectors items and, depending on condition, sell for more than their face value. When sold, they end up in museums, private collections, or being melted down. This is a clear illustration of **Gresham's Law**, which asserts that debased money always tends to drive non-debased money out of circulation. In other words, coins con-

Fiat Money
Monetary instruments that have less value as commodities than as money.

Legal Tender
All forms of money that, by law, must be accepted in payment of private or public debt.

Gresham's Law
The assertion that debased money will drive non-debased money out of circulation.

taining mainly base metal will circulate while the dear (precious metal) coins will be driven out of circulation.

Each of the three different kinds of money, demand deposits, currency, and coin, has its own advantages and disadvantages. The convenience of paying for things, especially expensive items, through the medium of checks that transfer demand deposits is fairly obvious. One does not have to carry large sums in currency. Most people use demand deposits most of the time to pay for larger bills or expenses.

However, checks have two disadvantages: (1) Not everyone is willing to accept a check in economic exchange. The fear of fraud or of inadequate funds in the check payer's demand deposits, plus the trouble of collecting on bad checks, reduces the acceptability of checks as money. (2) For small purchases, a check ordering a transfer of a demand deposit is a very inefficient form of money. Imagine a child in a candy store pulling out a checkbook to pay for a fifty-cent purchase. Coins and currency are more efficient in such cases.

Money Is Debt

www.federalreserve.gov/ fomc/

www.federalreserve.gov
For more information on the money supply visit the Federal Reserve web site listed above.

Demand deposits are liabilities of institutions that create them. Currency is a liability of the Federal Reserve banks. Both are non-interest-bearing debt. In effect, the supply of money is the monetization of certain forms of debt. The commercial bank or other institution that holds your demand deposit promises to pay you in money the amount of your account when you demand it. If you go into the bank and demand the deposit, the bank will give you currency. But what is currency? A ten-dollar bill says on its face that it is a Federal Reserve Note. The Federal Reserve promises to pay you ten dollars for it. Like the demand deposit, the ten-dollar bill is a promise to pay. But if you go to the Federal Reserve Bank and demand payment, you will receive only a new bill or change for the old one.

Since government will not exchange anything tangible for currency, like gold or silver, what is currency good for? What are demand deposits good for? Their worth lies in the fact that people are willing to exchange goods and services for them. Thus, by definition, currency is money. The value of money is not the gold or silver that backs it up (there is today no gold or silver backing the U.S. supply of money), but the goods and services that the money can buy. That value depends on the *prices* of the goods and services to be bought in relationship to the supply of money. The lower the prices, the more a given amount of money can buy, and thus the higher the value of money.

Measures of the Money Supply

M_1

The money supply we have talked about above, demand deposits, coin, currency and travelers checks, is a measure of money that focuses on those things that serve as a medium of exchange. That measure is referred to as M_1 money.

M_1 = Currency, Coin, Travelers Checks and all Checkable Deposits

M_1
A measure of money supply that includes currency, coin and travelers checks plus all deposits that are subject to checks.

Remember though, that money also serves as a standard of value, a store of value, and a means of deferred payment. To focus on these functions of money and to correlate the money supply more closely with changes in GDP, we shall define the money supply two other ways.

M_2

M_2
A measure of the money supply that includes all M_1 money plus small time deposits and money market mutual funds.

Near Monies
Assets with all of the characteristics of money except that they do not circulate as a medium of exchange.

M_3
A measure of the money supply that includes all M_1 + M_2 money + large value certificates of deposits (CDs).

M_2

M_2 includes all of the components of M_1 plus savings deposits, small time deposits and money market mutual funds. These last three elements are called **near monies**, assets that have all the characteristics of money (particularly as a store of value) except that they do not circulate as a medium of exchange. To get some idea of the relative importance of M_1 and M_2 in 2001, M_1 amounted to 1.34 trillion dollars while M_2 was equal to 6.2 trillion dollars.

$$M_2 = M_1 + \text{Savings Deposits} + \text{Small Time Deposits} + \text{Money Market Mutual Funds}$$

M_3

A third, and still broader, definition of the money supply is also possible. **M_3** consists of all the components of M_2 plus negotiable certificates of deposit (CDs). This is the broadest of the three money supply measures. In 2001, its value was 4.28 trillion dollars.

$$M_3 = M_2 + \text{Large Value Certificates of Deposit}$$

Summing Up the Money Supply

For many purposes, the money supply can no longer be defined simply as currency, coins and checkable deposits (M_1). There are so many new (and ever changing) near monies in America's financial markets that we must take account of these if we are to have an adequate measure not only of the things that serve as a medium of exchange but also serve to store value, serve as a standard of value and as a means for deferred payments. The near monies we will look at are:

1. *Savings Deposits*, those that earn interest but do not mature at a specific date. These deposits are found not only in commercial banks but also in savings and loan associations, mutual savings banks and credit unions. They are not subject to routine checking demands and thus, are not included in M_1.

2. *Time Deposits*, those that have a specific maturity date that typically is as short as thirty days and range up to several years. Some financial institutions offer similar non-negotiable certificates of deposit with fixed interest rates. They are not included in M_1 because they cannot be resold and must (subject to large penalties) be held to maturity.

3. *Money Market Fund Accounts*. First introduced by Merrill Lynch in 1971, they exist in large amounts but are not included in M_1 because of restrictions on checking against them and also because minimums are established for these checks. They are, in other words, not sufficiently flexible to be included as a medium of exchange.

4. *Negotiable Certificates of Deposit* Certificates that have some of the characteristics of money but are usually denominated in large sums ($100,000+) and are not subject to checking. For these reasons, they are included neither in M_1 nor M_2.

Near Monies, Liquidity, and Credit Cards

When an economy has a large amount of near money (that is, is in a highly liquid state), the average and marginal propensities to consume tend to increase. If the economy is already in an inflationary gap, high liquidity may worsen the inflation. However, if the economy is in a recession, with a deflationary gap, high liquidity may soften or cushion the contraction.

Credit Cards

Credit Cards: Where do they fit? Are they substitutes for money? The credit card is only a quick and convenient way to *borrow* money. At the end of the month, the borrower gets a statement of purchases made with the credit card during the month and must pay in *money* for what was charged. All a credit card does is reduce the inconvenience and risk of carrying around a large amount of money. It is not a substitute for money. But credit cards do enable people to increase their purchasing power temporarily. This can affect total demand, and thus the level of income, employment, and prices. Furthermore, the public's ability to vary purchasing power temporarily by using credit cards can make it harder for the government to carry out a stabilization policy.

The Origins of Commercial Banking: Goldsmith Banking

To understand how M_1 is created, we must understand the original depository institutions and their role in creating demand. The origins of today's commercial bank lie with the goldsmiths of seventeenth-century England.

In the early 1600s in England, the safest places to store valuables were the vaults and safes of the goldsmiths of London, who made useful items out of gold. Wealthy people put their gold and silver in these vaults for safekeeping; the goldsmiths charged a fee for this watchdog service. At first, the goldsmiths had to return the same gold and silver that people had entrusted to their care. However, after a while, people said the goldsmith did not have to return the piece of gold that was deposited, just an amount of gold of equivalent value. This relaxing of the rules began a series of developments that eventually led to the modern commercial bank.

The depositor, the person who left gold with the goldsmith, received a document stating the value of the gold deposited. (This document was equivalent to your bankbook, which shows how much you have deposited.) When Lady Upton-Chase found that she needed money or wanted to buy something, she could take this document and transfer ownership of all (or any part) of the gold to a third party. She would write, "I order you, the goldsmith, to pay to the third party so-and-so much of the gold on deposit."

Thus, the modern check was born. Since the goldsmiths were internationally known, these endorsements of deposits to another person were widely accepted as a means of payment. Thus, they functioned as money. Deposits of gold at goldsmiths eventually became today's demand deposits. But the story does not end there.

The goldsmith became known as a person with money to lend, and people who needed money began borrowing from the goldsmith. At first goldsmiths lent their own gold. In time, they realized that people who stored gold with them would not want that gold back for a while. There was always a certain amount of stored gold in their vaults, so they began to lend some of it. After a while the borrowers, instead of taking the gold, accepted documents stating that they had gold on deposit with the goldsmith. The borrowers would *endorse* these documents of deposit (write checks) over to those people they wished to make payments to.

The goldsmiths were soon creating documents of deposits in amounts much larger than the amounts of gold they actually had in their vaults. Since these documents attesting to deposits were accepted as payment, they functioned as money. Thus the goldsmiths, by making loans and creating deposits (attested to by documents), were creating and increasing the supply of money.

The goldsmiths, however, had to be prepared to give gold back when people presented these documents transferring deposits (checks). Fortunately, not all of these documents were presented at the same time. Thus, the goldsmiths were able to keep a prudent supply of gold, enough to meet these demands, on hand at all times. This was the origin of the **fractional reserve principle**, that is, the need to have on hand an amount of reserves (in this case gold) smaller than the total amount of deposits, to meet possible demands for withdrawal of deposits in gold.

Fractional Reserve Principle
The need to maintain on hand a reserve less than the amount of total deposits.

So one sees in seventeenth-century English banking the *origins* of our modern commercial banking system: (1) deposits that can be withdrawn on demand; (2) the check as a means of transferring these deposits and the functioning of these deposits as money; (3) the practice of lending money by creating a deposit and increasing the supply of money; and (4) the need to keep reserves of gold in amounts that are fractions of total deposits, which make possible the lending and creation of new deposits, and thus a larger supply of money.

In another chapter you will see how commercial banks and other depository institutions today are like the goldsmiths of long ago: By their lending activities, these institutions increase and decrease the amount of demand deposits and, thus, the M_1 money supply.

The Future of Money, or Can the Computer Replace Currency and Coin?

Today, as we have seen, there are many forms of money and near money. It is possible to create a scenario in which M_1 money or at least coin and currency may lose most if not all of its importance as a medium of exchange.

Imagine an economy without currency and coin, and also without checks as you know them. Imagine a great central computer. In its memory banks are entered all expenditures and all receipts of money. All receipts of income are fed directly into the computer and added to each individual's account. No more depositing of paychecks, no more lugging around dirty, germ-covered currency and coin.

Everyone has an account. Everyone has her or his own card, perhaps keyed to the thumbprint. Every place that sells things, every place at which people make payments has terminals connected to the computer. When you buy something, you take your debit card, slip it into the terminal, and it types out the deduction to be made from your account at the computer.

No more bad checks. If you overdraw your account, lights will instantly flash, and a recorded voice from the computer terminal will say, "You're overdrawn." No more hours spent figuring your bank balance. You can obtain it on request from the computer. No more hiding income from the Internal Revenue Service. The computer knows all. Big Daddy will indeed have become a machine.

Have we not begun to see this process in the 2000s? Want to buy gasoline or groceries? No need for cash, your automatic teller machine card is used instead and the amount automatically deducted from your bank balance. A recent study by John Caskey and Gordon Sellon, Jr.[1], suggests that debit card use will grow rapidly, though there are cost barriers that limit that expansion.

The Economy and the Supply of Money

How do changes in the supply of money affect the level of economic activity? Two major factors are (1) the absolute size of the supply of money and (2) the rapidity with which the supply of money changes hands in a given period of time.

Consider a simple economy with only three people: Farmer Martinez, Mo Courington the shoemaker, and Vee Jackson the baker. The supply of money in the economy is $20. Vee Jackson buys $20 worth of sausages from Farmer Martinez. Therefore, Farmer Martinez exchanges $20 worth of output for $20 in money. Farmer Martinez buys $20 worth of shoes from Mo Courington, and again exchanges $20 in output for $20 in money. Finally, Mo Courington, buys $20 worth of bread from Vee Jackson, and there is a further exchange of $20 in output for the same $20 in money. Although the supply of money is only $20, this $20 has changed hands three times, and the total output supported through this process is $60. Figure 11-1 shows this process through a circular-flow diagram.

The Equation of Exchange

Equation of Exchange (MV = PQ). The supply of money times its velocity equals the price level times the amount of net goods and services.

One can express the circular-flow process in Figure 11-1 in the form of an equation, called the **equation of exchange**:

$$MV = PQ.$$

M stands for the supply of money and V is the *velocity of exchange*, or the number of times the supply of money changes hands in a given period. One might call MV the *effective supply of money*. Also, if P is the average price level of the goods sold, and Q is transactions in physical terms and can be restricted to include only the output of net final goods and services, then PQ (the money value of that output) is *net national product.*

$$MV = PQ = NNP.$$

Let's make an equation from our example: M, the supply of money, is $20; V, the velocity of exchange, is three (since the money changed hands three times); and Q, physical output, consists of the sausages, shoes, and bread. It can be seen that MV equals PQ, since 20 x 3 = 20 x 3.

So the equation of exchange works perfectly in this extremely simple model. Although the gigantic economy of the United States, with its 300 million people and its multitude of transactions and output, is vastly more complex, it operates the same way. (We have considered PQ as being NNP and velocity, V, as being essentially the velocity of income. Now we can define Q as including *all* economic transactions. We can say that Q includes the buying and selling of intermediary products, financial instruments, and even used items. When one defines transactions, Q, that way, velocity, V, is much higher. One can call it the velocity of transactions. Here, in order to keep our analysis simple, we shall consider only the velocity of income.)

---

1. Caskey, John P. and Gordon H. Sellon, Jr. "Is the Debit Card Revolution Finally Here?" *Economic Review*, Federal Reserve Bank of Kansas City, Vol. 79, Number 4, Fourth Quarter, 1994.

Figure 11-1
The Circular Flow of Money and Output

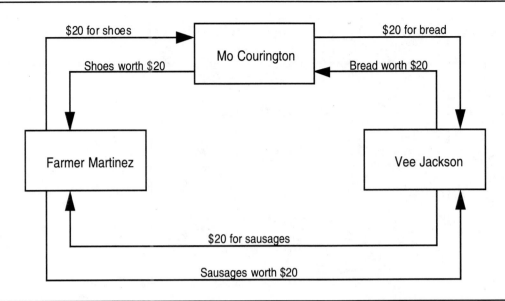

Source: Economic Report of the President, 2004, G.P.O. Washington D.C.

The Velocity of Exchange (V)

www.federalreserve.gov
For more information on
the velocity of money visit
this web site.

You now see that the dollar value of output PQ is determined by changes in the supply of money, and also by changes in the velocity of exchange (the number of times the money supply M changes hands). The supply of money is controlled by the monetary authority responsible for doing so. (In the United States, it is the Federal Reserve.) The velocity of exchange, on the other hand, cannot be controlled. It depends on the structure of the financial system and on the actions of the public. One can easily measure velocity by dividing the net national product by the supply of money. Table 11-1 shows that measure of the velocity of exchange for recent years between 1986 and 2003.

The data in Table 11-1 show that the velocity of exchange (V) since the mid-1980s was rather constant though declining in recession years (1991–1992). It is true that V rose earlier between 1960 (3.3) and 1985 (5.7). The reasons for the increase between 1995 and 2009 seem to have been because the public was able to use the supply of money more and more efficiently for three reasons: (1) Financial institutions and financial markets have grown both more complex and more available to the public. The increased use of savings accounts, money market accounts, stocks and bonds, government securities, and various forms of private short-term commercial credit have moved money more rapidly from one use to another. (2) The public has greatly increased its use of credit cards, which has cut down its need to hold money. (3) The public has increased its use of institutions such as banks and other financial intermediaries, reducing its need to hold money for longer periods of time. We should also note that there may be a problem with M_1 as the money supply here. Other assets may be so liquid that some other measure of the money supply may correlate better with NNP than M_1. This is a complex subject of great controversy among monetary economists.

Table 11-1
The Velocity of Exchange

	M$_1$ (billions of dollars)	NNP (billions of dollars)	V NNP$\div$M$_1$
1986	724.5	3,799.2	5.24
1990	826.4	4,965.1	6.01
1991	897.7	5,114.3	5.70
1992	1,024.8	5,367.3	5.24
1994	1,149.9	6,264.7	5.4
1998	1,094.8	7,738.2	7.1
2003	1,287.1	9,835.7	7.6
2005	1,368.9	10,786.2	7.9
2009	1,684	14,399.6	8.6

Output, Prices, and *M* (for Money): A Simple First Look

To examine the way changes in the supply of money affect output of goods and services and their prices, we must make a simplifying assumption: We will assume that V (the velocity of exchange) is constant (an assumption that seems warranted for recent years).

Given the equation of exchange, MV = PQ, when M (some measure of the supply of money) increases and V (the velocity of exchange) is constant, then PQ (the value of output) must increase. The important question is: Will P (prices) increase, or will Q (output) increase? There we pointed out that during a recession, when there is high unemployment and excess capacity in factories, output can increase without much increase in prices. This is because an increase in aggregate supply can occur without increases in prices from private producers. Therefore, if the United States has a recession, and the supply of money (M) increases, prices (P) will remain relatively stable and output (Q) will increase. We also said in another chapter that as an economy approaches full employment, some resources will be in shorter supply than others, and prices will begin to increase. This is because aggregate supply under these conditions is upward sloping. An increase in aggregate quantity supplied in response to an increase in the money supply occurs only with rising costs and prices. Therefore, as money (M) increases and the economy approaches full employment, prices (P) begin to rise, along with output (Q). Obviously, when the economy is at *full* employment, any increase in the supply of money (M) will only result in an increase in prices (P). Output (Q) cannot increase any further, because all resources are fully employed.

If economic policy is geared toward increasing output and employment, the appropriate monetary policy is to increase the supply of money. On the other hand, if the policy seeks to decrease inflation, the appropriate monetary policy is to decrease the supply of money.

But remember, we are assuming that the velocity of exchange (V) is constant. When V changes, it may either reinforce or counteract the effects of changes in the supply of money.

The Demand for Money: An Alternative

There is another way of looking at the way the supply of money affects output and prices. For many reasons, people need to hold part of their assets in the form of money (as opposed to real estate and other assets). People do not receive income at the same time that they have to pay for the goods and services they buy. For example, professors are paid once a month. Although they pay the usual recurring bills on the first of the month, they must keep some money on hand to buy food, gasoline, haircuts, and so forth, for the rest of the month. This is called holding money for *transaction purposes*. People also need to hold money for emergencies: The car breaks down, the water heater springs a leak, or someone gets sick. This is called holding money for *precautionary purposes*. In addition, people hold money to take advantage of economic opportunities. Stock prices may be low, or there may be a sale on coats. One needs money on hand to take advantage of these opportunities. This is called holding money for *speculative purposes*.

Whatever the reason, people want to hold certain amounts of money. How much they hold depends on their incomes, the amounts and kinds of assets they have accumulated (durable goods, liquid assets, and so on), and their personal lifestyles. If the supply of money increases, people find themselves holding more cash than they wish, and they may invest all or part of it, or they may spend all or part of it on more consumer goods and services. Therefore, when money increases, both investment and consumption demand increase.

Suppose the supply of money decreases. Then people have less cash on hand than they want, so they have to either decrease their consumption (an uncomfortable solution) or convert other assets into cash. That is why investment and consumption demand both fluctuate with the supply of money.

Because people want to hold a certain amount of their assets in the form of money, they react when their actual holdings do not correspond to their desired holdings. If they have more assets in the form of money than they want when the supply of money increases, they increase their investments. They also buy more consumer goods. This expands the economy. Income increases, which has the effect of increasing the amount of money that people wish to hold. This process continues until what people wish to hold becomes equal to the increased supply of money. When the supply of money decreases, the reverse occurs.

Thus the two monetary approaches (the equation of exchange and the demand for money) lead to the same conclusions. An increase in the supply of money increases aggregate demand and expands the economy. A decrease in the supply of money decreases aggregate demand and contracts the economy. We shall have more to say about this in the upcoming chapter.

SUMMING UP

1. This chapter examines the basic roles of money in a modern market economy.

2. When people use the *barter* system, they exchange goods for goods and do not use money. The most serious flaw in the barter system is the need for *double coincidence of demand.* That is, the person you wish to trade with must have what you want, and also want what you have.

3. When people use a *money exchange* system, they exchange goods for money and then money for goods. This is a much more efficient way to carry out the four functions money performs: (a) It is a *medium of exchange.* (b) It is a *standard of value or unit of account.* (c) It is a *store of value.* (d) It is a *means of deferred payment.*

4. The characteristics of a good money are the following: (a) It is portable, or easily carried. (b) It is easily recognized, but hard to counterfeit or duplicate. (c) It is easily subdivided. (d) It costs little to store. (e) It is durable. (f) The supply of it is relatively stable.

5. The *supply of money* in the United States has become more difficult to define and measure. One definition is that it consists of all *demand deposits* and all currency and coin in circulation. About 75 percent of the supply of money, thus defined, is in the form of demand and other checkable deposits *(checking accounts). Depository institutions* are those financial firms that hold demand deposits and honor checks written against them. *Currency* is issued by the Federal Reserve, while *coins* are minted and issued by the Treasury. *Fiat money* is any money that has greater value as a monetary instrument than as a commodity. *Legal tender* is any money that the government says is to be accepted for all debts, public and private.

6. Coins are an example of fiat money. Almost all coins today are debased (contain less valuable metal). Those that are not debased (contain valuable metal) have been driven from circulation by the debased coins. This illustrates Gresham's Law that debased money will drive non-debased money out of circulation.

7. Money is debt. *Demand deposits* are debts (liabilities) of commercial banks. *Currency* is a debt (liability) of the Federal Reserve.

8. Measuring the money supply as demand deposits, currency and coin is known as M_1, a measure of the highly liquid financial instruments that are quickly used as a medium of exchange.

$$M_1 = \text{Currency, Coin, Travelers' Checks and Checking Deposits}$$

9. Since money also serves as a standard and store of value as well as a means of deferred payment, we can broaden the money supply measurement to include those financial instruments that serve these additional purposes. This measure is known as M_2 and adds near monies, things that have all the characteristics of money except that they do not readily serve as a medium of exchange. Included in M_2 are the components of M_1 plus savings deposits, small time deposits and money market mutual funds.

$$M_2 = M_1 + \text{Savings Deposits} + \text{Small Time Deposits} + \text{Money Market Mutual Funds}$$

10. The broadest conventional measure of the Money supply, M_3 adds long-term negotiable financial instruments, especially large denomination certificates of deposit.

$$M_3 = M_2 + \text{Large Value Certificates of Deposit}$$

11. Credit cards are not money. They are simply instruments that permit individuals to borrow against future income. As such, they may affect short-term variations in demand but serve none of the four functions of money; neither are they near money.

12. Goldsmith banking in seventeenth-century England established the basic structures of modern commercial banking including the *fractional reserve principle*.

13. One can use the *equation of exchange,* $MV = PQ$, to describe how changes in the supply of money affect economic activity. In this equation, M is the supply of money, V is the velocity of exchange, P is the price level, and Q is actual output.

14. The *velocity of exchange* (V) is calculated by dividing NNP by M_1. Though it grew between 1960 and 1985, it has been rather constant since.

15. Assuming *velocity of exchange* (V) to be constant, when the supply of money (M) increases, PQ increases. If there is unemployment and unused plant capacity as M increases, output (Q) increases and price (P) is relatively stable. As the economy approaches full employment, price (P) begins to increase while M is still increasing, and when the economy reaches full employment, only prices increase.

16. An alternate approach to how changes in the money supply affect economic activity examines why people hold money. They hold it for purposes of *transactions, precaution,* and *speculation.* The amounts they want to hold depend on their incomes, the quantities and kinds of assets they have, and their lifestyles.

17. When the supply of money increases, people have more money on hand than they want, and they try to convert it to other assets (invest it) or they spend it on more consumption. If the supply of money decreases, people have less money on hand than they want, and they try to increase their cash on hand by cutting back on their consumption or by reducing their investments (or both).

KEY TERMS

Barter
Demand deposits
Depository institutions
Double coincidence of demand
Equation of exchange
Fiat money
Fractional reserve principle
Gresham's Law
Legal tender
M_1 money
M_2 money
M_3 money
Medium of exchange, standard of value, store of value, means of deferred payment
Money
Near monies

QUESTIONS

1. What are the four basic functions of money? How does rapid inflation affect the performance of these functions?

2. "Money is the root of all evil." Why don't we do away with it?

3. Suppose that our government suddenly printed up enough money to give everyone a new fifty-dollar bill. What would happen to output and prices? State clearly the assumptions you are making about employment and velocity of exchange.

4. Why are near monies not included in M_1?

5. How does M_3 differ from M_2?

6. In what ways did goldsmith banking create the foundations for present day banking?

7. What are the characteristics of a good money? Pick three commodities, and analyze their favorable and unfavorable characteristics as a good money.

8. "Money is money because people say it's money." Do you agree? Why?

9. Why do non-debased coins not circulate as part of the money supply?

10. What effects do credit cards have on the supply of money?

Chapter 12: Commercial Banking and the Creation of M_1 Money

In the previous chapter, we discussed the functions, the characteristics, and a little of the history of money. We mentioned that the bulk of the M_1 money supply is in the form of demand and other checkable deposits, which are held primarily by commercial banks but also by other financial institutions. So in analyzing how the supply of money is increased or decreased, and how it is controlled, we must look again at commercial banking.

The Simple Economy: Four Assumptions About a Simple Model

The U.S. financial system is complex and the best way to approach it is to abstract from that complex reality and set up a simple model. We will call it the Simple Economy and make four assumptions about its financial system to enable us to analyze the process of increasing and decreasing the supply of money in basic terms. Then we will drop these assumptions, one by one, so that the analysis will gradually become more complex and realistic. Finally, we will examine, the U.S. financial system.

Here are the four simplifying assumptions:

1. The only financial institution in the Simple Economy is a single bank. That bank, the First National Bank, is a monopoly bank, or in other words, it is the Simple Economy's banking system.

2. The government has no control over the First National Bank, so there are no regulations that restrict its banking activities.

3. There is no paper currency or coin. The Simple Economy's entire money supply consists of the demand deposits (checking accounts) in the First National Bank.

Table 12-1

The First National Bank's Balance Sheet

Assets		Liabilities and Net Worth	
Loans	$1,000,000	Demand deposits	$1,000,000
Buildings and equipment	500,000	Net worth	500,000

4. The Simple Economy is closed, that is, there is no international trade. This last assumption is the only one we will not drop later in the discussion. If we were to take international trade into account, we would make our discussion of banking transactions unnecessarily complex at this stage. We will introduce open economy banking and monetary policy in the next chapter.

First we will analyze the process of increasing and decreasing the supply of money in the simplest model. Then we will drop assumption 3 and show what effects currency and coin have on the money supply. Then we will drop assumption 2 and show what happens when the government regulates the supply of money. Finally we will drop the assumption that there is only one bank and analyze the functioning of the multibank system with many separately incorporated banks. At that point we will analyze the U.S. banking system in relation to the supply of money.

Now let's consider the First National Bank, an established and ongoing commercial bank (Table 12-1 shows its balance sheet), with *liabilities* of $1 million, all in demand deposits. In other words, the First National owes its depositors $1 million. It also has $500,000 in *net worth*, which represents the equity or ownership of the stockholders in the bank. Last, it has $1.5 million in assets, $1 million in the form of loans. The First National has loaned that $1 million to the citizens of the Simple Economy. The other $500,000 in assets is in the form of the bank's buildings and equipment. Remember that for the First National's books to balance, the bank's assets and liabilities plus net worth have to be equal, just as they must in any company's accounting balance sheet.

The following short tables will show only *changes* in the balance sheet. This will help us focus on the effects of banking transactions on the supply of money. Note that there is only $1 million in money in the Simple Economy, and remember that all of the Simple Economy's money is in the form of demand deposits (no currency and no coin).

Table 12-2

The Effect of a Loan on the First National Bank's Balance Sheet

Assets		Liabilities	
Loans	+$10,000	Demand deposits	+$10,000

Money Creation in the Simple Model

Joe Bloggs, one of Simple Economy's more ambitious citizens, has made a discovery which he hopes will make him rich. He has invented mottled-gray bubble gum that will blend into sidewalks. He goes to see Elvira Snodgrass, president of the First National Bank, to tell her of his discovery. "Wonderful!" says Snodgrass. "No more of those unsightly pink blobs on our sidewalks. You'll make a pile out of this invention, son!"

When Bloggs asks to borrow $10,000 to set up a bubble-gum factory, Snodgrass approves the loan. Table 12-2 shows what happens then.

First, Bloggs signs a promissory note, stating that he will pay the bank $10,000 in six months' time. To the bank, this promissory note is an asset, since Joe Bloggs now owes the First National Bank $10,000. The category "Loans" increases by $10,000. But now the First National must pay Bloggs that money he has borrowed. It does this by increasing his demand deposits at the bank by $10,000; by this act, it increases the supply of money in the Simple Economy by $10,000.

"But," you may say, "where did the First National Bank get the $10,000 to give Joe Bloggs?" The answer is simple. The bank created that demand deposit by simply writing on Bloggs' account, "plus $10,000." *The bank creates demand deposits to pay for the loans that it makes*. It cannot just take the demand deposit from somebody else's account, because what would *that* person do if he or she wanted to use that demand deposit? Nor can the bank take it from accounts in its own name, because that would mean that the bank owed money to itself, which is an absurdity. The point we are trying to make is that commercial banks create demand deposits when they make loans.

With that $10,000 demand deposit, Bloggs first hires a contractor to build his factory and pays the contractor $2,500. He makes this payment by writing a check on his account. So Bloggs' account goes down by $2,500 and the account of the contractor goes up by $2,500. There is no change in the Simple Economy's supply of money, for accounts are only transferred. Bloggs then buys machinery for $2,500, and writes another check to pay for it. Again his account shrinks by $2,500, while the machinery seller's demand deposits increase by $2,500. Again, there is no change in the supply of money, only transfers of demand deposits. When Bloggs buys raw materials for $2,500, the same thing happens. And it happens again when he hires workers and starts producing bubble gum.

In effect then, as Bloggs spends his demand deposit, his account is slowly transferred to those to whom he makes payments by writing checks. The supply of money changes hands as the demand deposit at the bank is transferred. (Isn't this like your own experience with commercial banks?)

Table 12-3
Decrease in the Supply of Money

Assets		Liabilities	
Loans	-$10,000	Demand deposits	-$10,000

Now Bloggs starts selling bubble gum to retail stores, which the store owners pay for by writing checks drawn on their own demand deposits. Bloggs deposits those checks, so his account increases while the accounts of the store owners decrease. Still no change in the *supply* of money. Joe makes profits, and eventually his demand deposits increase to $10,000.

Now Bloggs can pay off his promissory note to the bank. He goes to the office of President Snodgrass and writes a check for $10,000. Snodgrass writes "Paid" on the promissory note and deducts the amount from Bloggs's account. (In effect, Bloggs has received and paid off an interest-free loan. To keep our analysis simple, we have avoided the subject of interest on loans.)

Table 12-3 shows the transactions on the books of the First National Bank. Note that the account called "Loans" decreases by $10,000 as Bloggs pays off the note. The First National Bank's demand deposits are also decreased by $10,000 as the bank deducts the check from Bloggs' demand deposits. The Simple Economy's supply of money actually decreases by $10,000, for Bloggs's check to the bank decreases only his own demand deposit and is not transferred to any other account.

What has this analysis shown us? (1) When a commercial bank (First National Bank) makes a loan, and creates a demand deposit in order to make the loan, the supply of money is increased. (2) When a loan is paid off by means of a check that decreases demand deposits, the supply of money is decreased.

Enter Currency and Coin

We are about to drop assumption 3 because there are two basic weaknesses in this simple model: (1) For small purchases, it is very inefficient to write checks transferring demand deposits; one needs paper currency and coin. (2) The existence of currency and coin provides an automatic check on the ability of the First National Bank to expand the supply of money.

The first weakness (no currency or coin) is apparent. When a supply of money consists only of demand deposits, all transactions, no matter how small, have to be made by checks and transferring demand deposits. When you buy a newspaper, you would have to write a check for fifty cents. The cost of handling checks for these small amounts would be greater than the value of the transactions. Therefore, one important function of currency and coin is to provide a more efficient form of money for small-value transactions.

Table 12-4

The Effect of the Government's $1 Million Deposit of Currency and Coin on the Balance Sheet of the First National Bank

Assets		Liabilities	
Cash in vault	+$1,000,000	Demand deposits	+$1,000,000

The second weakness is that in this simple model without currency or coin, the bank (by lending) can expand the supply of money without limit. When we introduce currency and coin, you will see that they provide an automatic check on the ability of the bank to expand loans and thus to expand the supply of money.

We said that people in the United States find it most comfortable to hold about 25 percent of the M_1 supply of money in the form of currency and coin. (This percentage varies somewhat from place to place and from one month to another.) We will assume that the Simple Economy people are like Americans. They also want to hold 25 percent of the supply of money to be used for exchange purposes in the form of currency and coin. And we will also assume that this percentage does not vary.

Let's introduce currency and coin into the economy. The Simple Economy's government wants to spend $1 million more than it receives in taxes. To cover this deficit, it issues $1 million in currency and coin. What happens when the government deposits the currency in the First National Bank? Table 12-4 shows the effect on the First National's balance sheet.

The bank now has an asset of $1 million called "Cash in vault," and also a liability of $1 million, which is the demand deposit held by the government that represents the deposit of currency. The Simple Economy's supply of money has increased by $1 million, the demand deposit owned by the government. Remember that the actual cash in the First National Bank's vault is not yet part of the supply of money, because it is not yet in circulation.

The government spends the $1 million for various goods and services, like roads, bombers, and education. This spending transfers the demand deposit from the government to the individuals who sell these goods to the government. Remember, though, that people want 25 percent of their supply of money in the form of currency and coin. Therefore, they withdraw from their demand deposits $250,000 in cash.

Table 12-5 shows the results. Only $750,000 remains in the vault in cash, and demand deposits are only $750,000. The supply of money, however, is still $1 million consisting of $750,000 in demand deposits and $250,000 in currency and coin in circulation, in people's pockets.

Now the First National Bank has assets in a form that does not earn it any income (the $750,000 cash in its vault). The bank's officers want to put those assets to work earning income. So they lend out $1 million, which, as you already know, creates demand deposits of $1 million.

Table 12-5

The Effect on the First National Bank of a Withdrawal by Depositors of $250,000 in Cash from Their Demand Deposits

Assets		Liabilities	
Cash in vault	$750,000	Demand deposits	$750,000

Table 12-6

The Effect on the First National Bank's Balance Sheet of a Second Withdrawal of $250,000 by Depositors

Assets		Liabilities	
Cash in vault	$500,000	Demand deposits	$1,500,000
Loans	1,000,000		

Remember that the bank can lend more money than the amount of cash it holds in its vault because the depositors want to keep only 25 percent of the supply of money in the form of currency and coin.

Now the demand deposits are $1 million fatter. What happens? Well, the people still want to keep 25 percent of the country's money in the form of, currency and coin, so they withdraw *another* $250,000 in cash. Table 12-6 shows the net results. "Cash in vault" is down to $500,000 and the total of demand deposits is $1.5 million. The supply of money is now $2 million, $1.5 million in demand deposits and $500,000 in currency and coin in circulation.

The First National Bank still has assets in a form that does not earn them any income (the $500,000 "Cash in vault"). The bank's officers want to put the assets to work, so they extend *more* loans. Let's say they loan $2 million, and thereby create demand deposits of an additional $2 million. The citizens of the Simple Economy still wish to keep 25 percent of their M_1 money in the form of currency and coin. To do this they withdraw $500,000 in cash, reducing demand deposits by a like amount.

Table 12-7 shows the net results. The First National Bank's vault no longer has any cash at all. Loans and discounts are $3 million and demand deposits are $3 million. The country's supply of money is now $4 million; that is, $3 million in demand deposits and $1 million in currency and coin in circulation. If the bank extends still more loans, and thereby creates still more demand deposits, the depositors, to get the 25 percent of the total money supply in currency and coin that they want, will demand more currency than the bank has.

Table 12-7

The First National Bank's Balance Sheet When It Increases Loans to $3 Million

Assets		Liabilities	
Cash in vault	0	Demand deposits	$3,000,000
Loans	3,000,000		

In effect, *the amount of currency and coin in the vaults of the bank places a limit on the amount that the bank can lend.* Since the people want to hold 25 percent of the money supply in the form of currency and coin, the country's total supply of money is limited to four times the amount of currency and coin available, or one dollar in cash for every three dollars in demand deposits. In order to increase its lending, and thus the supply of money (demand deposits), the First National Bank would have to get more currency and coin from the government.

To summarize, currency and coin perform two functions: (1) For purchases that have small value, they are a more efficient form of money than demand deposits. (2) They provide an automatic check on the ability of the bank to make loans, create demand deposits, and increase the supply of money.

Enter the Government

Let us now drop our second assumption, that there is no government regulation. The Simple Economy's government creates a Central Bank for the purpose of controlling lending by the First National Bank. The government requires that the First National Bank keep assets in the form of reserves equal to a specific percentage of its demand deposits, and gives the Central Bank the power to increase or decrease these reserves. (Bear in mind that Central Banks, such as the Federal Reserve, are only bankers' banks. They do not engage in banking activities involving the public.)

www.federalreserve.gov
For more information on banking regulation visit this web site.

Reserve Requirements

Remember that a bank's reserves are not demand deposits, but some form of assets that the banking authority defines as reserves. The U.S. government defines *reserves* as all deposits by *depository institutions* in the Federal Reserve, plus currency and coin held in the vaults of these institutions.

Enter the Federal Reserve (Courtesy Federal Reserve System)

Table 12-8
Reserves Versus Demand Deposits for the First National Bank

Assets		Liabilities	
Required reserves	$200,000	Demand deposits	$1,000,000
Excess reserves	800,000		
Total reserves	$1,000,000		

Let's say that the Simple Economy's Central Bank defines reserves as the U.S. Federal Reserve does. This means that the First National Bank may count as reserves all First National Bank deposits at the Central Bank, plus all currency and coin the First National Bank holds. The law says that the First National Bank must keep a minimum quantity of reserves equal to a certain percentage of its demand deposits. This percentage is called the **required reserve ratio**. For example, suppose that the required reserve ratio is 20 percent and that the First National Bank has $1 million in demand deposits. According to law, the First National Bank must have $200,000 in reserves (20 percent of $1 million) or $200,000 in deposits at the Federal Reserve Bank, and/or in currency and coin.

Table 12-8 shows that the First National Bank has $1 million in reserves and also $1 million in demand deposits. Since there is only a 20 percent required reserve ratio, to comply with the law, the First National Bank is required to hold only $200,000 of those reserves. The other $800,000 of its

Required Reserve Ratio
The minimum ratio of reserves to deposits that depository institutions are required to maintain.

reserves are not required, and are called **excess reserves**. A bank's required reserves plus its excess reserves equal its *total reserves*.

Excess Reserves
Reserves of depository institutions that are above the required reserve ratio.

Now consider the excess reserves of the First National Bank, assets it is not required to have and that are not earning income for it. What can the First National Bank do to remedy this? Table 12-9 shows the First National Bank's accounts after it lends out $1 million, which in turn creates (or increases demand deposits by) $1 million (the payment of the loan). The First National Bank's total reserves are still $1 million, because there has been no change in deposits at the Central Bank and no change in currency and coin. All that the First National Bank has done is to create a loan, and therefore to create a demand deposit. However, demand deposits are now $2 million, and the amount of reserves that are required (which must be 20 percent of demand deposits) increases to $400,000. Excess reserves decrease, to $600,000, since some of those excess reserves now become part of required reserves.

Table 12-9

The First National Bank's Accounts After It Lends an Additional $1 Million (thus increasing demand deposits by $1 million)

Assets		Liabilities	
Required reserves	$400,000	Demand deposits	$1,000,000
Excess reserves	600,000		
Total reserves	$1,000,000		
Loans	$1,000,000		

Table 12-10

The First National Bank's Accounts After It Lends an Additional $3 Million More and Reduces Its Excess Reserves to Zero

Assets		Liabilities	
Required reserves	$1,000,000	Demand deposits	$5,000,000
Excess reserves	0		
Total reserves	$1,000,000		
Loans	$4,000,000		

The First National Bank still has $600,000 worth of non-income-earning assets (the remaining excess reserves of $600,000). Table 12-10 shows that the bank's officers finally increase their loans by $3 million, which increases demand deposits by the same amount, to $5 million. Nothing has happened to the First National Bank's total reserves because there has been no change in either its deposits at the Central BankCC or its holdings of currency and coin. However, required reserves (20 percent of demand deposits) now equal total reserves, and there are no excess reserves left in the bank. So the First National Bank cannot lend another penny to anyone.

Each time a bank extends loans and creates demand deposits, its required reserves must increase by 20 percent of the increase in demand deposits. Since the act of lending and creating demand deposits does not affect total reserves, this increase in required reserves must come out of excess reserves. Now the First National Bank has reached the position (see Table 12-10) of zero excess reserves. It cannot lend any more money, because, if it tried to, the law would require it to hold more reserves than it has, and it would be violating the banking laws. The bank must have excess reserves before it can lend more and increase its demand deposits further. These excess reserves can then quickly become required reserves to comply with the law that specifies 20 percent required reserves.

In comparing Tables 12-8, 12-9, and 12-10, one can see that $800,000 in excess reserves enables the bank to create five times that amount in demand deposits. Because the required reserve ratio is 20 percent, the First National Bank can expand the supply of money by five times its excess reserves. This means that it needs only one dollar of reserves for every five dollars of demand deposits. This is the bank's **fractional reserve requirement**. If the required reserve ratio were to be increased to 50 percent, the bank would need one dollar of reserves to create two dollars of demand deposits. If the required reserves were to be increased still further, to 100 percent, the bank would have to hold one dollar for every dollar it loaned. In other words, required reserves and demand deposits would have to be equal.

Fractional Reserve Requirement
The minimum percentage of reserves against deposits that depository institutions must legally maintain.

Enter Many Other Banks

Now remember the first assumption that the First National Bank is the only commercial bank in Simple Economy. It is a *monopoly* bank; it is, in fact, the entire commercial banking system. A monopoly bank can lend money and create demand deposits (money) that are a multiple of its excess reserves. The First National Bank can do this because depositors cannot write checks and deposit them in other banks. There *are* no other banks.

The behavior of an individual commercial bank in a multibank system differs from that of a monopoly bank with respect to its excess reserves, lending, and creation of demand deposits.

Now we will drop the assumption that there is only one bank, a monopoly bank, in the economy. Let's assume that there are more than 15,000 separately incorporated, privately owned, commercial banks, and that the economy being discussed is that of the U.S. Now we can begin to analyze the U.S. banking system.

The Federal Reserve and Clearing Checks

The United States has had a Central Bank since 1913. It is called the Federal Reserve System or "Fed" for short. The nation is divided into *twelve* reserve districts, each with a Federal Reserve Bank. Federal Reserve Banks perform an important function not previously discussed, they serve as a national clearinghouse for checks. Now what does that mean?

In our system, with its many commercial banks, you can write a check on your account in one bank and have it deposited in an account in another bank. How do banks collect or receive payment for such checks from other banks? They do it through the Federal Reserve (Fed) collection process.

Table 12-11 shows what changes take place in this collection process. You write a check for $1,000 on a demand deposit in the Bank of America in California, and this check is deposited in the First National Bank of Boston. The

Table 12-11

The Effect of One Check on the Federal Reserve and Two of Its Member Banks

Bank of America		Federal Reserve	First National Bank of Boston	
Assets	Liabilities	Deposits	Assets	Liabilities
Reserves	Demand deposits	First National Bank of Boston	Reserves	Demand deposits
−$1,000	−$1,000	+$1,000	+$1,000	+$1,000
		Bank of America		
		−$1,000		

demand deposits in the First National Bank of Boston are increased by $1,000. To collect its money, the First National Bank sends the check to the Federal Reserve, which increases the First National Bank's deposits with the Fed. In other words, the reserves of the First National Bank increase by $1,000. Meanwhile, back at the Bank of America, the situation is the opposite. The Federal Reserve reduces the Bank of America's deposits with the Fed by $1,000. In other words, the reserves of the Bank of America decrease by $1,000. The Federal Reserve then sends the canceled check to the Bank of America, which reduces *your* demand deposits by $1,000.

In brief, at a multibank system, when a check is drawn on an account in Alpha Bank and deposited in Bravo Bank, there is a transfer of both demand deposits and reserves (deposits at the Federal Reserve). The Federal Reserve acts as the third party, the go-between.

Lending by Individual Banks: A Little Goes a Long Way

Now we are going to deal with a number of independent banks in the Federal Reserve System. Let's call our four representative banks Alpha, Bravo, Charlie, and Delta. An individual bank in a multibank system can lose both demand deposits and reserves overnight to other banks, through a flow of checks. Therefore, Alpha Bank, an individual bank in a multibank system, cannot lend money and create demand deposits that are a multiple of its excess reserves. Alpha Bank, following a conservative rule, lends an amount *equal only to its own excess reserves*. If it lends more, it runs the risk of losing (through a flow of checks) so much of its reserves that it cannot meet the law's reserve requirements.

Table 12-12 shows the changes in the relevant accounts for Alpha Bank as it applies this rule. Part (a) shows that Alpha Bank, before it lends $800,000, has $1 million of established demand deposits. On the basis of its past experience, Alpha Bank estimates that these deposits will remain with the bank. Alpha Bank also has $1 million in reserves, of which $200,000 are required and $800,000 are excess, since the required reserve ratio is 20 percent.

Part (b) of Table 12-12 shows Alpha Bank lending only an amount equal to its excess reserves. Suppose, however, that the worst occurs (part c) and that all these new demand deposits flow out as checks to other banks, for example, to Bravo Bank.

Table 12-12
Changes in the Relevant Accounts for Alpha Bank

(a) Alpha Bank Before it Lends $800,000		(b) Alpha Bank After it Lends $800,000	
Assets	**Liabilities**	**Assets**	**Liabilities**
Required reserves $200,000	Demand deposits $1,000,000	Reserves $1,000,000	Demand deposits $1,800,000
Excess reserves $800,000		Loans $800,000	
Total reserves $1,000,000			
(c) Alpha Bank After Checks Have Cleared		**(d) Bravo Bank After Receiving Checks**	
Assets	Liabilities	Assets	Liabilities
Reserves $200,000	Demand deposits $1,000,000	Reserves $800,000	Demand deposits $800,000
Loans $800,000			

Bravo Bank now has an increase in demand deposits of $800,000 (part d). It sends these checks to the Federal Reserve, which promptly increases Bravo's deposits there by $800,000 and at the same time reduces Alpha's deposits there by $800,000. The Federal Reserve then sends the canceled checks to Alpha Bank, which duly notes the fact that its demand deposits have shrunk by $800,000.

Part (c) shows us, however, that even though Alpha Bank has lost $800,000 in reserves and demand deposits, it can still meet its obligations. It still has its required reserves ($200,000 in reserves is adequate because the bank has $1 million in demand deposits and the required reserve ratio is 20 percent).

In Table 12-13, part (a) shows that Bravo Bank now has excess reserves of $640,000. Part (b) shows Bravo lending up to its limit of $640,000, thereby creating demand deposits of $640,000.

Now suppose the worst happens (part c). All the checks drawn on Bravo Bank's newly created demand deposits flow to Charlie Bank. Charlie Bank now has an increase in its demand deposit of $640,000.

Charlie Bank sends these checks to the Federal Reserve, which increases Charlie Bank's deposits with the Federal Reserve (and its own reserves) by $640,000 (part d). At the same time, the Fed deducts $640,000 from Bravo Bank's deposits at the Fed (and lowers Bravo's reserves by that amount). When Bravo gets these canceled checks back, it records the information that it has $640,000 less in demand deposits.

Bravo Bank has followed the rule and lent only as much as it held in excess reserves. Even though it has lost the newly created demand deposits and equivalent reserves, it can still satisfy the legal reserve requirement.

Table 12-13

Changes in the Relevant Accounts for Bravo Bank

<table>
<tr><th colspan="2">(a) Bravo Bank Before it Lends $640,000</th><th colspan="2">(b) Bravo Bank After it Lends $640,000</th></tr>
<tr><th>Assets</th><th>Liabilities</th><th>Assets</th><th>Liabilities</th></tr>
<tr><td>Required reserves $160,000</td><td>Demand deposits $800,000</td><td>Reserves $800,000</td><td>Demand deposits $1,440,000</td></tr>
<tr><td>Excess reserves $640,000</td><td></td><td>Loans $640,000</td><td></td></tr>
<tr><td>Total reserves $800,000</td><td></td><td></td><td></td></tr>
<tr><th colspan="2">(c) Bravo Bank After Checks Have Cleared</th><th colspan="2">(d) Charlie Bank After Receiving Checks</th></tr>
<tr><th>Assets</th><th>Liabilities</th><th>Assets</th><th>Liabilities</th></tr>
<tr><td>Reserves $160,000</td><td>Demand deposits $800,000</td><td>Reserves $640,000</td><td>Demand deposits $640,000</td></tr>
<tr><td>Loans $640,000</td><td></td><td></td><td></td></tr>
</table>

We could continue to analyze this process at great length. At each round of lending, the excess reserves diminish (as excess reserves are reclassified as required reserves), so that excess reserves decrease only to the limit of its excess reserves, creating demand deposits (money) to pay for the loans. However, as excess reserves filter through all the banks, the whole banking system makes loans and creates demand deposits that are a multiple of the original excess reserves in Alpha Bank.

Table 12-14

Demand Deposits Created

Bank	Amount
Alpha Bank	$800,000
Bravo Bank	640,000
Charlie Bank	512,000
Delta Bank	409,600
Rest of the banks	1,638,400
	$4,000,000

Table 12-14 shows what happens. Alpha Bank created $800,000 in demand deposits. This money, by means of checks, was transferred to Bravo Bank. Bravo Bank took this $800,000 and created $640,000 in demand deposits. If we had continued our analysis, you would have seen that Charlie Bank then created $512,000 in demand deposits. And when that money got over to Delta Bank, Delta Bank created $409,600. As the money went further and further, the other banks in the system created $1,638,400. Because the required reserve ratio is 20 percent, the whole banking system could create $4 million in new demand deposits, even though each bank made loans and generated new demand deposits only up to the amount of its excess reserves. If each bank lends an amount equal to its excess reserves and uses only demand deposits to pay out money for the loans, the formula for the multiple that demand deposits may be of the required reserve ratio, the **deposit multiplier** (DM) is:

$$DM = 1/R,$$

where R is the required reserve ratio. In our example, R is 20 percent. The deposit multiplier equals:

$$DM = 1/.20 \text{ or } 5$$

But What About Leakages That Restrain Demand Deposit Creation?

We have seen that it is technically possible, with a 20 percent required reserve ratio, for banks to have a maximum potential of creating new demand deposits five times the original excess reserves. However, the full multiple creation of demand deposits rarely takes place. There are what are called **leakages**, factors in the creation of demand deposits in the process, which reduce the ability of the depository institutions to expand demand deposits.

1. *Currency and Coin (C).* Suppose that people who borrow from the bank withdraw currency and coin from their demand deposits. This has the effect of withdrawing reserves from the banking system, thus reducing the amount of demand deposits that can be created. For example, suppose that when Alpha Bank lends out the original $800,000, one of the borrowers demands $100,000 in currency as payment, instead of a demand deposit. So, instead of $800,000 in checks being transferred from Alpha Bank to Bravo Bank, only $700,000 in checks is transferred. Reserves (deposits at the Federal Reserve) shifted from Alpha to Bravo are $700,000 (not $800,000). Bravo's excess reserves are thus $560,000, not $640,000. Bravo Bank cannot make as many new loans or create as large demand deposits, and this effect is passed on through the rest of the system. The $100,000 taken as currency in payment of loans at Alpha Bank reduces the original excess reserves in the banking system, and thus the total of new loans and demand deposits.

2. *Excess Reserves (E).* We have assumed so far that each independent bank lends up to the limit of its excess reserves, that it lends every penny it can, provided it can maintain enough reserves to meet the legal minimum. In practice, bankers are often much more conservative and want to keep a cushion or extra reserve in case checks are drawn against them in amounts greater than the amounts of the new demand deposits. What if some depositors write checks against Alpha Bank's original deposits and this money flows into other banks? If Alpha has not kept some of its excess reserves on hand, it will not be able to meet these unexpected transfers of demand deposits and reserves. However, if

Deposit Multiplier
The formula for determining the multiple that demand deposits may be of required reserves.
DM = 1/R

Leakages
Factors in the creation of demand deposits which reduce the ability of depository institutions to expand demand deposits.

banks do lend out amounts less than their excess reserves, then the amount of the demand deposits created in the system is much less.

3. *Demand for Loans*. The fact that the banking system has excess reserves (the ability to make loans) does not mean that there are always good opportunities to lend. During a business slump, bankers may fear that some potential borrowers will not be able to repay loans. So when times are bad, bankers may not lend up to the maximum. Also, at times there may not be much demand for loans even when interest rates are low.

When we take these leakages into consideration, the formula for the deposit multiplier becomes more complex:

$$DM = \frac{1}{R + E + C}$$

where R is the required reserve ratio, E is excess reserves, those *not* used by the banking system to create loans, and C is the currency withdrawn by those receiving loans. We cannot factor loan demand conditions into the formula because it focuses only on the ability to supply loans.

The Role of Excess Reserves

In our analysis of the way money is created under government regulation, we have pointed out the crucial role of excess reserves. Without excess reserves, banks cannot extend loans and create demand deposits. Therefore, control over the amounts of reserves in the banking system means control over the amount of lending that is done, and, by extension, control over the supply of M_1 money itself. As the supply of the many near monies we looked at earlier has grown, the Fed's ability to control all forms of money has been somewhat diminished. As we saw with the sharply restrictive monetary policy of the Fed in 1981-1982, however, its power to control money and economic activity remains very great and its authority over reserve requirements was extended in the 1980s to all depository institutions, not simply commercial banks. Only the Federal Reserve has the power to increase or decrease the required amount of excess reserves in the system. If it wishes to increase economic activity it can lower deposits creating reserve requirements. On the other hand, if it wishes to restrict the growth of economic activity, it can raise reserve requirements. How it may do this is a subject we will look at in the next chapter.

A Final Word About Excess Reserves

Federal Funds Market
The market in which banks, through inter-bank transfers, lend their excess reserves to other banks.

Excess reserves can be used to create earnings for financial institutions. Though cautious, bankers naturally tend therefore, to minimize the amount of excess reserves they hold. One important way they do this is to turn them into very-short-term earning assets by lending them to other banks that are short of required or desired reserves. A market has been created in which such transfers occur. That market, the **federal funds market**, handles billions of dollars of such inter-bank transfers through brokers. If Alpha Bank is short of reserves, it contacts a broker who arranges a short-term (often overnight) transfer of excess reserves from Bravo Bank. The interest rate at which such reserve loans is made is known as the *Federal Funds Rate*. A key point, in other words, is that excess reserves do not just sit around idly in the American financial system.

Application I: First Steps in Banking

The following selection from *Punch*, the late British humor magazine, requires no introduction.

Q.What are banks for?
A.To make money.

Q.For the customers?
A.For the banks.

Q.Why doesn't bank advertising mention this?
A.It would not be in good taste. But it is mentioned by implication in references to Reserves of £249,000,000 or thereabouts. That is the money they have made.

Q.Out of the customers?
A.I suppose so.

Q.They also mention Assets of £500,000,000 or thereabouts. Have they made that too?
A.Not exactly. That is the money they use to make money.

Q.I see. And they keep it in a safe somewhere?
A.Not at all. They lend it to customers.

Q.Then they haven't got it?
A.No.

Q.Then how is it Assets?
A.They maintain that it would be if they got it back.

Q.But they must have some money in a safe somewhere?
A.Yes, usually £500,000,000 or thereabouts. This is called Liabilities.

Q.But if they've got it, how can they be liable for it?
A.Because it isn't theirs.

Q.Then why do they have it?
A.It has been lent to them by customers.

Q.You mean customers lend banks money?
A.In effect. They put money into their accounts, so it is really lent to the banks.

Q.And what do the banks do with it?
A.Lend it to other customers.

Q.But you said that money they lent to other people was Assets?
A.Yes.

Q.Then Assets and Liabilities must be the same thing?
A.You can't really say that.

Q.But you've just said it. If I put £100 into my account the bank is liable to have to pay it back, so it's Liabilities. But they go and lend it to someone else, and he is liable to have to pay it back, so it's Assets. It's the same £100, isn't it?

A. Yes, but ....

Q.Then it cancels out. It means, doesn't it, that banks haven't really any money at all?

A.Theoretically....

Q.Never mind theoretically. And if they haven't any money where do they get their Reserves of £249,000,000 or thereabouts?

A.I told you. That is the money they have made.

Q.How?

A.Well, when they lend your £100 to someone they charge him interest.

Q.How much?

A.It depends on the Bank Rate. Say five and a half per cent. That's their profit.

Q.Why isn't it my profit? Isn't it my money?

A.It's the theory of banking practice that....

Q.When I lend them my £100 why don't I charge them interest?

A.You do.

Q.You don't say. How much?

A.It depends on the Bank Rate. Say half a percent.

Q.Grasping of me, rather?

A.But that's only if you're not going to draw the money out again.

Q.But of course, I'm going to draw it out again. If I hadn't wanted to draw it out again I could have buried it in the garden, couldn't I?

A.They wouldn't like you to draw it out again.

Q.Why not? If I keep it there you say it's a Liability. Wouldn't they be glad if I reduced their Liabilities by removing it?

A.No. Because if you remove it they can't lend it to anyone else.

Q.But if I wanted to remove it they'd have to let me?

A. Certainly.

Q.But suppose they've already lent it to another customer?

A.Then they'll let you have someone else's money.

Q.But suppose he wants his too...and they've let me have it?

A.You're being purposely obtuse.

Q.I think I'm being acute. What if everyone wanted their money at once?

A. It's the theory of banking practice that they never would.

Q. So what banks bank on is not having to meet their commitments?

A. I wouldn't say that.

Q. Naturally. Well, if there's nothing else you think you can tell me…?

A. Quite so. Now you can go off and open a banking account.

Q. Just one last question.

A. Of course.

Q. Wouldn't I do better to go off and open a bank?

SUMMING UP

1. Our analysis of the banking system of the imaginary Simple Economy is based on four assumptions: (a) There is only one bank in the system, the First National Bank. (b) There are no government regulations. (c) There is no currency or coin. The economy's supply of money is limited to the amount of demand deposits in the First National Bank. (d) There is no international trade.

2. The First National Bank increases the supply of M_1 money by extending loans, which are paid to the borrower by creating new demand deposits. The borrowers pay off the loans by checks drawn on their demand deposits. This decreases the supply o M_1 money in the economy.

3. The Simple Economy banking system, limited by our four assumptions, has the following weaknesses: (a) For purchases of small value, demand deposits are a very inefficient form of money. (b) The First National Bank's ability to expand the supply of M_1 money through lending is unlimited. But we can eliminate these weaknesses by dropping our third assumption and introducing currency and coin.

4. People like to hold a certain percentage of a nation's money in the form of currency and coin. The amount of currency and coin held provides an automatic check on the bank's ability to extend loans and increase demand deposits. As the bank lends out money, it creates more demand deposits, and demand deposits are money. Then people withdraw more currency and coin from the bank in order to maintain that desired percentage of the money supply in the form of currency and coin. When the bank no longer has any currency and coin left in its vaults, it can no longer lend, and create new demand deposits.

5. Varying the quantity of currency and coin is not an efficient way to regulate the total money supply. A more efficient system is to (a) establish a central bank, such as the Federal Reserve System, (b) require commercial banks to keep assets in the form of reserves equal to a certain percentage of demand deposits, and (c) empower the central bank (the Federal Reserve in the case of the United States) to vary the amount of reserves. In the U.S. financial system, *reserves* are defined as deposits of depository institutions at the Federal Reserve plus cash in the vaults of those institutions.

6. In a one-bank (monopoly) system, loaning money creates demand deposits, but does not affect total reserves. However, in a system that has a government-imposed *required reserve ratio,* an increase in demand deposits raises the figure for required reserves. Banks must then count their *excess reserves* as part of their required reserves. When all its reserves come under the heading of "required," a commercial bank cannot extend loans, because it has no more excess reserves that it can reclassify as required reserves when demand deposits increase.

7. Because the required-reserve ratio is less than 100 percent, that is, it is *fractional*, depository institutions can create demand deposits that are a multiple of their reserves.

8. In our simple model of the banking system in the Simple Economy, the monopoly bank need not be concerned about a flow of checks and reserves to other banks because there is only one bank in the system. Therefore, a monopoly bank can expand the supply of money (create demand deposits) by lending out money equal to a multiple of its reserves. The size of the multiplier depends on the size of the required reserve ratio.

9. When we drop the assumption that there is only one bank and assume that there are 12,000 banks, with the Federal Reserve controlling all of them, we are approximating a model of the U.S. banking system. The Federal Reserve acts as a national clearinghouse for checks. When Alpha Bank receives a check from Bravo Bank, Alpha sends it to the Federal Reserve. The Federal Reserve increases Alpha's deposits (reserves) with the Federal Reserve and reduces Bravo's deposits (reserves) with the Fed. When Bravo Bank receives the check, it reduces the demand-deposit account on which it is drawn.

10. When checks flow from one bank to another, both reserves and demand deposits are transferred. To avoid letting its reserves fall below the required level, an individual bank in a multibank system makes loans (and thus creates demand deposits) only up to the level of its excess reserves. But as these excess reserves gradually filter through the banking system, the banking system creates demand deposits (money) that are a multiple of the original excess reserves.

11. In the real world, the banking system does not increase the supply of M_1 money by the full multiple of its excess reserves because of the following *leakage* effects: (a) Some borrowers want *currency and coins* instead of demand deposits in payment for their loans, which has the effect of withdrawing reserves from the banking system, thus reducing the amount of demand deposits that can be created. (b) Some banks, as a matter of prudence, will wish to keep *excess reserves* because they fear that an unexpected flow of checks to another bank might drain off reserves not only from their new demand deposits, but also from old demand deposits. (c) If there is a business slump, some banks will not lend money up to the limit of their excess reserves, because they fear that some loans will not be repaid. Sometimes, too, there is not much demand for loans, even when interest rates are low.

12. Banks, nonetheless, minimize the holding of excess reserves. Banks that have excess reserves lend them, for very short periods, to other banks that need reserves. This is done through the Federal Funds Market at a rate of interest known as the Federal Funds Rate.

KEY TERMS

Deposit multiplier
Excess reserves
Federal funds market
Fractional reserve requirement
Leakages
Required reserve ratio

QUESTIONS

1. What effects do the following transactions have on the demand deposits and reserves of Alpha Bank? On the whole commercial banking system? Why? (The required reserve ratio is 20 percent.)

    a. Ernie Jones withdraws $100 from his demand deposit account in Alpha Bank.

    b. Susan Smith borrows $500 from Alpha Bank, but puts the proceeds into Bravo Bank.

    c. Betty Cohen deposits $200 in her account at Alpha Bank by a check drawn on someone else's account at Alpha Bank.

    d. Susan Smith pays off her loan at Alpha Bank by a check drawn on her account at Alpha Bank.

2. What effects do these four transactions have on the supply of money? Why?

3. Why must a commercial bank maintain a certain level of reserves under the U.S. banking system? What are excess reserves, and what is their significance?

4. In a commercial banking system, how is the supply of money increased and decreased?

5. In a multibank system, an individual bank makes loans only up to the level of its excess reserves, while the whole commercial banking system can lend out money that is a multiple of the original bank's excess reserves. Why is there this difference?

6. What leakages can prevent a commercial banking system from lending at the full multiple of its original excess reserves?

7. What is the Federal Funds Market? What is the Federal Funds Rate?

Chapter 13: Monetary Policy
Central Banking in Financial Markets That are Deregulated and International

Money, as we have seen, plays a vital role in the economic life of people. The money supply and changes in the money supply affect the decisions of every consumer and producer, as well as the activities of the government. Because of the important link between money and the levels of income, employment, and prices, all modern governments exercise some degree of control over their system of financial institutions. In the United States, these controls began taking their modern form with the creation of the Federal Reserve System (the "Fed") in 1913.

Control by the Fed generally increased from its inception to the 1980s. This was especially true with the banking reforms of the 1930s. By the 1970s, it became clear to many that regulation of monetary institutions had, in some respects, gone too far. As a result, and, in response to rapidly evolving financial markets, substantial deregulation occurred in the 1980s and 1990s and continued to occur into the early 2000s. At the same time, in recognition of the macroeconomic importance of controlling the money supply, some regulatory powers of the Fed have been broadened.

How to control as well as measure the money supply remains an area filled with controversy. After we have examined the workings of the Fed, America's central bank, we will in the application in this chapter, assay some of the controversies between Keynesians and Monetarists, as well as arguments about how effective, if at all, are discretionary macroeconomic policy changes.

Figure 13-1
Boundaries of Federal Reserve Districts and Their Branch Territories

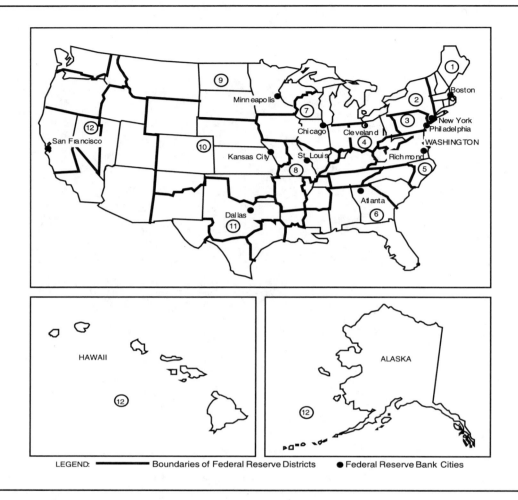

LEGEND: ▬▬▬▬ Boundaries of Federal Reserve Districts ● Federal Reserve Bank Cities

Source: Federal Reserve Bulletin. Reproduced by permission of the Board of Governors of the Federal Reserve System.

THE STRUCTURE OF THE FEDERAL RESERVE

Central Bank
A financial institution
established by government
to oversee a nation's
monetary system.

Where do *banks* go when they want to go to the bank? They go to a Federal Reserve Bank, which is a banker's bank or a **Central Bank**, one that is established by the government to oversee the country's financial system.

When Congress passed the Federal Reserve Act of 1914, it did not create just one bank. It divided the country into 12 Federal Reserve Districts, with a Federal Reserve Bank in each. Figure 13-1 shows the 12 districts and the location of the 12 Federal Reserve Banks. For example, the first Federal Reserve District takes in all of New England. Its Federal Reserve Bank is in Boston. The twelfth district consists of seven western states plus Alaska and Hawaii. Its bank is in San Francisco.

National Banks
Commercial banks
chartered by the federal
government.

State Banks
Banks chartered by state
governments.

www.federalreserve.gov
For more information on
the structure of the Federal
Reserve visit this web site.

All **national banks** (commercial banks chartered by the federal government) are required to be members of the Federal Reserve System. **State banks** (commercial banks chartered by the various state governments) can join it if they wish. Not all commercial banks are members of the Federal Reserve System. Those that are, however, comprise the larger commercial banks in the United States, and control more than 70 percent of U.S. banking assets. It is important to note that the Depository Institutions Deregulation and Monetary Control Reform Act of 1980, while permitting all depository institutions to offer checkable deposits, imposed uniform reserve requirements on all depository institutions, bank and non-bank alike. The distinction between members and non-members has, thus, become much less important.

Each Federal Reserve Bank is technically owned by the commercial member banks in its district. On becoming a member, each commercial bank must buy stock in its District Federal Reserve Bank, the amount depending on the size of its capital surplus. It receives a fixed annual dividend on these shares.

The main policy-making body of the Federal Reserve is the board of governors, in Washington, D.C. There are seven governors including the chairman, who are appointed for terms of 14 years by the President, with the advice and consent of the Senate. Though not a separate branch of government, the Board of Governors of the Federal Reserve is substantially independent of the executive branch of government. Only rarely has a President had the chance to appoint a majority of the board of governors, since a President ordinarily appoints a new member only once every two years. Therefore, a President who wanted to try to play God with the nation's money supply would not be able to do so unless all seven members of the Board of Governors of the Federal Reserve died or resigned at the same time. Some regard this as a built-in safety valve.

There are two main committees that help the board of governors formulate policy:

1. *The Federal Open Market Committee (FOMC)* controls decision making about the most important weapon the Fed has in controlling excess reserves, lending, and the supply of money: open market operations, which we will say more about later. This committee is made up of the members of the Board together with five of the Presidents of the District Reserve Banks.

2. *The Federal Advisory Council* consists of 12 prominent bankers, one from each of the 12 boards of directors of the Federal Reserve Banks. They meet periodically with the Board and advise the governors about problems in the various districts of the system. The Council, however, has no policy-making authority.

Each of the 12 Federal Reserve Banks has a nine-member board of directors. Three are appointed by the board of governors in Washington, to represent the national interest. Three are elected by the member commercial banks, one from the large banks, one from the medium-size banks, and one from the small banks; they represent banking interests in the particular district. These six appoint the remaining three, who represent the general economic community.

So we see a mixture of both quasi-public and pure public elements in the Federal Reserve System. The national board of governors, with its two main support committees and its three appointed members on each board of directors of the 12 Federal Reserve Banks, is the public element. The ownership of the 12 district Federal Reserve Banks by the commercial banks in that district, plus the fact that the commercial banks appoint three members to the board of directors of their district Federal Reserve Bank, is the quasi-public element. Unquestionably, however, the pure public element is the dominant influence in monetary decision making, and it is important to remember that the Fed is not a profit-making institution. Early in our history, the Congress created two "almost" Central Banks that were both public and private in their functions. The Fed was an effort to create a true Central Bank or "bankers' bank."

General Powers of the Federal Reserve

In the previous chapter we pointed out that commercial banks must have excess reserves in order to make loans and create demand deposits, and that as a bank increases its demand deposits, it must transfer or reclassify excess reserves as required reserves. Also, in a multibank system, the individual commercial bank needs a prudent margin of excess reserves in case its customers decide to write an unexpectedly large number of checks, thereby transferring demand deposits and reserves to other banks. Its ability to participate in the Federal funds market helps it to maintain this margin.

General Power
The authority of the central bank (Fed) to increase or decrease the required reserve ratio.

The device we used earlier to explain the Central Bank was a hypothetical economy, the simple economy, with one Central Bank that had the power to vary the amount of excess reserves held by commercial banks. This power is called the **general power** because it enables a central bank to increase or decrease the excess reserves that a commercial bank must have in order to make any kind of loan.

The U.S. Federal Reserve has three means at its disposal to influence excess reserves: through open-market operations, through the discount rate, and through the required reserve ratio.

Open-Market Operations
What is for sale in the open market? There are many instruments, including debt instruments that are short term (maturing in 90 days to one year), highly liquid (easily sold for a cash return), and relatively free of risk. Examples are *prime commercial paper* (promissory notes of large secure corporations), *banker's acceptances* (short-term debt of banks), and *Treasury bills* (short-term debt of the federal government).

In the open market, the Federal Reserve (FOMC) is an important customer. It buys and sells already issued federal government debt (primarily Treasury bills), which has the effect of increasing or decreasing excess reserves in the commercial banking system. This effect makes open-market operations the most important of the Fed's three weapons. The added advantage of this weapon is that it can be applied selectively. Remember that in open-market operations, the bonds are not bought directly from the Treasury.

1. *Increasing reserves.* To increase a depository institution's excess reserves, the Federal Reserve buys government-debt securities on the open market, as shown in Figure 13-2.

Figure 13-2

Changes in Assets and Liabilities of both the Federal Reserve Bank and the Commercial Bank When the Commercial Bank Sells Government Securities to the Federal Reserve

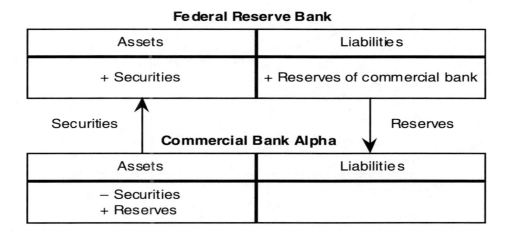

Let's say that a certain commercial bank, Alpha Bank, has customers begging for loans, but Alpha does not have enough excess reserves to lend any more money or to create any more demand deposits. Instead of going to the Federal Funds Market, let's suppose that the Fed comes along and buys some assets, government securities, from Alpha Bank. To pay for these assets, the Fed increases Alpha Bank's deposits with the Federal Reserve. This means that the Fed is taking on a liability. Alpha Bank is exchanging its government securities for a deposit at the Federal Reserve Bank. So Alpha's total reserves increase, and thus its excess reserves also increase.

But what happens when the Federal Reserve buys government securities from private individuals? (See Figure 13-3). Along comes an ordinary citizen, Joe Reed. The Fed buys a government security from him and gives him a check in return. Reed deposits the check in his account at his commercial bank, Alpha Bank. Alpha sends the check to the Federal Reserve, which increases Alpha's deposit with the Fed. That is, it increases Alpha Bank's reserves. The Federal Reserve; has an increase in its assets (the government security it bought from Joe Reed) and an equal increase in its liabilities (the deposits of the commercial bank at the Fed). Joe Reed's total assets are unchanged. The decrease in his holdings of government securities is exactly equal to the increase in his demand deposits. The effect of all this on Alpha Bank is an increase in assets (its reserves increase because its deposits with the Federal Reserve increase), and an increase in liabilities (Reed's demand deposit account). Thus Alpha Bank's total reserves have increased and, therefore, so have its excess reserves.

Figure 13-3

Changes in Assets and Liabilities of the Federal Reserve Bank, Plain Citizen Joe Reed, and Commercial Bank Alpha When the Federal Reserve Bank Buys Government Securities from a Private Citizen

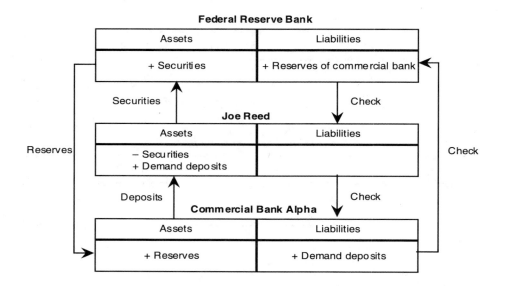

2. *Decreasing reserves.* To decrease depository institutions' excess reserves, and also to decrease their total reserves, the Federal Reserve sells government securities. Figure 13-4 shows how this works.

First, lets say that the Federal Reserve sells the government security to a commercial bank (Bravo Bank). When Bravo Bank buys a government security from the Fed, it pays for it by accepting a reduction in its deposits with the Federal Reserve. The Fed's assets decrease (by the amount of the securities sold to Bravo Bank). Its liabilities also decrease, because Bravo Bank's deposits with the Fed decrease. This means that Bravo Bank's total reserves decline. Therefore, Bravo Bank's excess reserves decline.

Figure 13-4

What Happens to Assets and Liabilities of the Federal Reserve Bank and Commercial Bank Bravo When the Fed Sells Government Securities to Commercial Bank Bravo

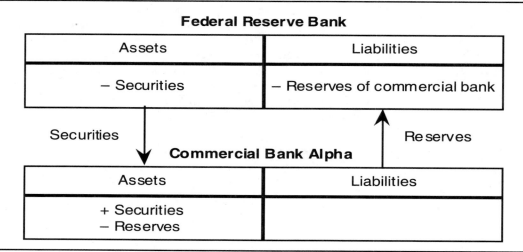

How does it affect excess reserves and the supply of money when the Federal Reserve sells government securities to *non*-commercial banking institutions, or to private individuals? Figure 13-5 shows what happens.

Figure 13-5

What Happens to Assets and Liabilities of the Federal Reserve Bank, Maria Deluca, and Commercial Bank Charlie When the Fed Sells Government Securities to a Private Citizen

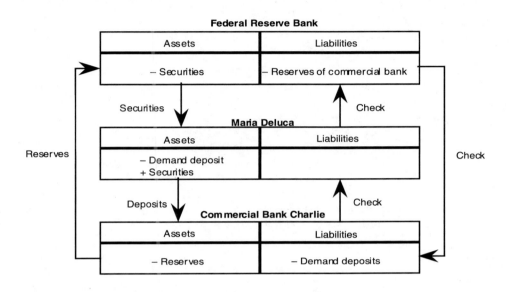

Here is Maria Deluca, citizen, who buys a government security from the Fed and gives a check in return. The Fed collects on the check by reducing the deposits with the Fed of Charlie Bank, the commercial bank that holds Deluca's demand deposits. The Fed sends Deluca's check to Charlie Bank, which reduces the amount of demand deposits in her account. The Fed's assets decrease by the amount of the securities sold to Deluca. There is an offsetting decrease in the Fed's liabilities (Charlie Bank's deposits with the Federal Reserve). The total assets of Maria Deluca are unchanged. Her holdings of government securities increase and her demand deposits decrease by equal amounts. Charlie Bank's assets decrease (its reserves, that is, its deposits at the Federal Reserve, are less) and there is an equal decrease in its liabilities (the demand deposits of Maria Deluca).

Therefore, when the Federal Reserve sells government securities, the effect is to reduce total reserves, and thus to reduce excess reserves of the whole commercial banking system. Because of this decrease in the excess reserves of commercial banks, their lending ability decreases, and so does their power to increase demand deposits (the supply of money).

The Discount Rate

The Federal Reserve Bank, as we have said, is a banker's bank to depository institutions: It holds deposits for them and helps collect or clear checks between institutions. The Fed also makes loans to member commercial banks and other thrift institutions by buying either their promissory notes or by buying from the banks IOUs of nonbanking corporations or individuals defined as acceptable by the Fed. When the Fed buys such promissory notes, it deposits the proceeds in the depository institution's Federal Reserve account, increasing the bank's total reserves, and thus increasing its excess reserves.

Depository institutions do not get all these services free. The Federal Reserve Bank charges interest for making these loans. It is called a *discount* rather than interest, because the Fed collects the interest charge when it makes the loan.

For example, a commercial bank, Delta Bank, sells the Fed a $1,000 promissory note that matures in three months. The **discount rate** (interest rate) is eight percent per year, a two percent discount for the three-month period. Delta Bank actually receives from the Fed only $980, or $1,000 less two percent. Delta's deposits at the Federal Reserve increase by $980. In other words, Delta pays the Fed $20 for the privilege of using $1,000 for three months.

If the Federal Reserve wants to encourage depository institutions to increase their reserves this way (that is, to increase their deposits with the Fed), it can reduce the cost of borrowing by *lowering the discount rate.* If the Fed wants to discourage institutions from increasing reserves this way, it can increase the cost of borrowing by *increasing* the discount rate.

Note: The Federal Reserve cannot reduce the reserves of depository institutions by this device. It can only use the discount rate to *encourage* or *discourage* the increasing of reserves. In addition, the Federal Reserve in recent years has restricted its lending through discounting to situations in which depository institutions are in temporary need of reserves. Remember, though, institutions can borrow each other's excess reserves through the   Federal Funds Market.

Note: There is a difference between discount-rate policy and discount policy. *Discount-rate policy* has to do with variations in the discount rate and their effects. The *discount policy* has to do with the availability of discounts. As a means of power over excess reserves, the Fed's ability to manipulate the discount rate is not as important as its operations in the open market.

However, through the responses of the depository institutions, the Federal Reserve discount rate controls interest rates on loans of all sorts: mortgage loans, car loans, and so forth. When the Fed raises its discount rate, this is a sequence of repercussions in the economy: (1) Everybody knows the higher rate is a signal that the Fed is tightening credit. (2) The higher rate discourages institutions from increasing their reserves, and thus keeps them from making as many loans. (3) The higher discount rate pushes up all other interest rates.

The Required Reserve Ratio

When a depository institution makes a loan, as you know, the essential ingredient is excess reserves. The institution cannot loan more money and create more demand deposits once it reaches the bottom of its excess-reserve barrel, because it might risk dropping below its required reserves. The final and most powerful tool which the Fed can employ to affect the banking system is that it can change the **required reserve ratio**, the percentage of reserves against deposits that financial institutions are required to maintain.

Varying the required reserve ratio does not change the total reserves of a depository institution, just the proportion of total reserves that the bank must have on hand, that are *required.* Therefore, it changes the proportion that is counted as excess.

For example, a commercial bank has $100,000 in demand deposits and $25,000 in total reserves. If the required reserve ratio is 20 percent, its required reserves would be 20 percent of $100,000 (the amount of demand deposits) or $20,000. Its excess reserves would be $5,000 ($25,000 minus $20,000). If the Fed were to reduce the required reserve ratio to 10 percent, the commercial

Discount Rate
The rate of interest charged by the Fed when it makes loans to member banks and other depository institutions.

Required Reserve Ratio
The percentage of reserves against deposits that financial institutions must maintain.

bank's required reserves would be $10,000 (10 percent of $100,000) and its excess reserves would be $15,000 ($25,000 minus $10,000). In other words, if the Fed lowers the required reserve ratio, the commercial bank's excess reserves increase.

If the Fed were to increase the required reserve ratio from 20 percent to 25 percent, the commercial bank's required reserves would increase to $25,000 (25 percent of $100,000) and its excess reserves would decrease to zero ($25,000 total reserves minus $25,000 required reserves). In other words, if the Fed increases the required reserve ratio, the commercial bank's excess reserves decrease.

Clearly, the Fed's ability to vary the required reserve ratio is a very powerful tool, since it means that the Fed can readily change the excess reserves of the whole commercial banking system. The problem is that it is *too* powerful to be used often. Small percentage changes in the reserve ratio can have enormous effects on the reserve position of financial institutions. That is why the Fed varies its activity on the open market on an ongoing basis, giving the economy the ongoing changes in M_1 money that are needed to carry out its monetary policy. Only rarely and cautiously does it tamper with the reserve ratio. Changes in the reserve ratio usually signify major shifts in Federal Reserve policy.

A Review: How the Fed Nudges the Banking System

If the Federal Reserve wishes to *increase* the excess reserves of commercial banks to enable them to increase loans and create more demand deposits (the supply of money), it can do the following: (1) *buy* government securities on the open market, (2) *lower* the discount rate, or (3) *lower* the required reserve ratio.

If the Federal Reserve wishes to *decrease* banks' excess reserves, to reduce commercial banks' ability to make loans and create more demand deposits, it can do the following: (1) *sell* government securities on the open market, (2) *raise* the discount rate, or (3) *raise* the required reserve ratio.

A Word About Paying Interest on Reserves

The Fed has historically controlled the money supply through open market operations, changing the discount rate, and changing reserve requirements. In 2008 another tool became available to the Fed to help control the money supply. This new tool is the ability for the Fed to pay interest on reserves. That is, when a bank holds reserves on deposit at the Fed, the Fed now pays the bank interest on those deposits. This change gives the Fed another tool with which to influence the economy. The higher the interest rate on reserves, the more reserves banks will choose to hold. Thus, an increase in interest rate on reserves will tend to increase the reserve ratio, lower the money multiplier, and lower the money supply. Because the Fed has paid interest on reserves for a relatively short time, it is not yet clear how important this new instrument will be in the conduct of monetary policy.

Specific Powers of the Federal Reserve

No sooner had Congress passed the Federal Reserve Act of 1914, which brought the Federal Reserve Bank into existence, than people came forth with ideas to strengthen its authority. So, over the years Congress has passed amendments giving the Federal Reserve additional powers, especially in the areas of lending and credit. Powers added to the Fed over specific areas of lending are called **specific powers**.

Margin Requirements on Stocks

The **margin requirement** is the percentage of cash required as a down payment on the purchase of a share of stock. The Bank Act of 1933 gave the Federal Reserve power to set the *margin* that buyers of stock in the various stock exchanges must pay when they buy corporate stock. The purpose of the margin requirement is to control speculation on the stock market.

If the Federal Reserve wants to reduce speculation on the stock exchange, it can increase the margin requirement. Let's say that the Federal Reserve increases the margin from 50 percent to 75 percent. This means that a person buying stock must pay cash equal to 75 percent of the value of the stock and can borrow only 25 percent of its purchase price. It works in reverse too. For example, in 1974 the stock market fell drastically from the high 900s to below 600. (These figures are from the Dow Jones Industrial Index, which measures changes in the prices of stock on the New York Stock Exchange) To stimulate demand for securities, the Federal Reserve dropped margin requirements from 65 percent to 50 percent. It did not do so in October, 1987, however, because the market recovered rather quickly and steadily.

The Federal Reserve's responsibility for watchdogging speculation in the stock market does not clash with its responsibilities for controlling excess reserves. Variations in stock-market margin requirements do not affect the total or excess reserves of commercial banks.

Regulations X and W

Beginning in World War II, Congress gave the Federal Reserve the power to regulate consumer and real estate loans. **Regulation X** concerned loans on consumer goods, while **Regulation W** involved real estate loans. These regulations made the Federal Reserve responsible for determining the minimum down payment on a loan and the maximum length of time in which a loan could be repaid.

Regulation Q

Regulation Q empowered the Federal Reserve to set the maximum interest rates that commercial banks could pay on savings accounts (time deposits) and on demand deposits. While this authority existed, the Fed would not allow banks to pay interest on demand deposits and, also, set the maximum interest rates payable on savings accounts.

Deregulation and Financial Markets: The 1980s

A movement to reverse some of the regulatory controls established or expanded in the 1930s took hold in the United States in the late 1970s. Although deregulation began with the airline industry, financial markets, including commercial banking, were not far behind. Regulation Q had placed controls over banks regarding interest rates, the kinds of assets they could invest in, and the kinds of financial instruments they could issue. By the late 1970s, this regulation seemed to many, including many in the banking industry, to be anachronistic. Banks, by

---

Specific Powers
Additional authority of the Fed beyond the general power to control lending and credit.

Margin Requirement
The percentage of cash required as a down payment on stock purchases.

Regulation X
Empowered the Fed to control loans on consumer goods.

Regulation W
Empowered the Fed to control real estate loans.

Regulation Q
Empowered the Fed to set maximum interest rates commercial banks could pay on savings accounts.

then, were only an (important) part of a much larger financial industry comprised also of savings and loan associations, mutual savings banks, brokerage houses and other thrift institutions. It seemed inequitable and inefficient to many that banks should be subject to regulations that did not apply to the other institutions. Perhaps more importantly, it seemed that the American economy and its people would benefit from allowing all the players in these markets to compete on an equal footing in an increasingly competitive industry.

The "Deregulatory Act" of 1980

The Depository Institutions Deregulation and Monetary Control Reform Act of 1980, which repealed Regulation Q, was seen by many as a move toward a more competitive set of financial institutions. The law provided that:

1. Controls over interest rates on deposits were to be phased out over five years.
2. All deposit-taking institutions could issue checking accounts.

3. Thrift institutions could now make a wider range of loans.

4. Reserve requirements were extended uniformly to all depository institutions.

5. All depository institutions would be able to avail themselves of the services of the Fed (clearinghouse, borrowing, etc.).

All in all, the 1980 Act went a long way toward creating a competitive, though not, as we shall see, a necessarily stable environment in American financial markets.

How well has deregulation worked?

The push for financial market deregulation ran up against a severe set of failures in such markets in 2008-2009. We examined some of those problems and government reaction to them in Application I (The Financial Crisis of 2008-2009: background, Causes and Effects) and recommend that you read that application again.

Regulation in the Banking System

The banking crisis of 2007- 009 demonstrated that financial regulation is a continuing process - that regulations will and should change over time to keep up with the changing world. In the aftermath of the crisis, an overhaul of financial regulation was clearly needed. In 2010 U.S. Congress enacted a bill that represented an effort to respond to the events of the preceding years. Like most legislation, the Wall Street Reform and the Consumer Protection Act often referred to as the 2010 Dodd-Frank Bill. This bill contains four main elements: consumer protection, derivatives regulation, regulation and shadow banks, and resolution authority over non-bank financial institutions that face bankruptcy. After many years of deregulation the Dodd-Frank Bill was an important step in the regulation of our financial system.

How Sound Are America's Financial Institutions?

In many respects, the 1980s were more turbulent for American financial institutions than any period since the 1930s. Major U.S. banks (including Continental Illinois) failed or were "bailed out." Others saw much of their loan portfolios (to underdeveloped nations, to farmers, etc.) on the verge of becoming non-performing or written off as bad debts. The Savings and Loan Associations had an even more rocky period with 17 percent of them disappearing in the first two years of the 1980s and continued failures with a massive "bail-out" of these institutions agreed to in the late 1980s. Partly in response to the perceived instability in the industry (more a threat to shareholders than to depositors who are insured), the Garn-St. Germain Act was passed in 1982. The legislation was designed primarily to increase the borrowing authority of savings and loan associations and thereby to avoid a wave of bankruptcies in that industry. At the same time the Act authorized all depository institutions to sell money market mutual funds, adding further to the competitiveness of financial markets.

In spite of the Garn-St. Germain Act, the years since 1982 have been turbulent ones for America's financial institutions, both its commercial banks and its thrift institutions (savings and loan firms, credit unions, and the like). Between 1982 and 1991, more than two thousand failed. Many more have failed in the financial crisis of 2008-2009. More than half of the failed thrift institutions were savings and loan associations, with the recession of 1990-1991 putting further pressure on marginal financial institutions. If the financial services sector was just another (big) industry in the American economy, this "shaking out" of weak firms might be seen as the ordinary working of an increasingly competitive marketplace. There are two basic reasons, however, for viewing the failure of so many financial institutions differently.

1. We have seen that banks and other depository institutions are key to the operation of our monetary system. They not only hold the money deposits of businesses and individual households, but as we have seen, create most of America's money supply through making loans. Some of the institutions that failed were large; only quick intervention prevented a serious threat to regional economies, perhaps even the larger national economy.

2. The intervention, though substantially successful, has been at a huge cost to taxpayers. Recall that we earlier said that beginning in the 1930s, the Federal Government provided its full backing to protect checking and savings deposits in banks and thrifts. The Federal Deposit Insurance Corporation (FDIC); and the Federal Savings and Loan Insurance Corporation (FSLIC); were pledged to pay for most of the losses in the more than 2,000 insured financial institutions. By 1995, the estimate of this cost to taxpayers has risen to over $500 billion including interest payments.

Are the Nation's Financial Institutions Still in Trouble?

At first, it appeared that many of the Nation's commercial banks were in peril and more than 1,300 did fail between 1982 and 1991. Even a few large banks failed with one (the Bank of New England) becoming insolvent in the recession of 1990-1991. However, the Federal Deposit Insurance Corporation (FDIC) was authorized in 1991 to borrow from the Federal Government, many banks were reorganized or acquired by sounder ones, and the improved economy in 1993 and 1994 brought renewed financial health to most banks. Since 2000, many mergers and acquisitions further strengthened remaining banks. The wave of failures in 2008-2011 has re-exposed the unacceptably of firms to engage in highly risky additions of poor quality loans to their portfolios.

Savings and loan associations (S&Ls), however, have not fared as well. More than one-third of all S&Ls in business since 1987 have gone out of business or merged with commercial banks (a process that continues on 2008-2011). There are three main reasons why failure in this area of our financial services industry continues to be a serious concern.

1. Deregulation. Deregulation, as we have noted, has substantially increased competition among financial institutions. The Savings and loan association (S&Ls) had, since the 1930s, enjoyed a virtual monopoly on home mortgage loans. These relatively long-term, well-secured assets helped to create a stable, low-risk industry. With deregulation, other financial institutions could compete for home mortgage loans and could also attract savings deposits with higher interest rates since deregulation had removed interest rate caps. S&Ls, stuck with low interest rate mortgages and the need to attract savings deposits with higher interest rates, shifted their loans toward high risk loans of all types.

2. Problems of Insuring Against Risk. In 1980, the Federal Deposit Insurance Corporation (FDIC) insurance was raised to $100,000 per account with no limit on the number of individual accounts. In 2009 this insurance was raised to $200,000. Though FDIC's original purpose in the 1930s was to stabilize financial markets through averting panics, the ironic result of deposit insurance in the 1980s and 1990s was able to reduce stability. This seems to be at least partially the result of the **problem of moral hazard**, the problem that insuring individuals (depositors) against risk reduces the individual's incentive to prevent the occurrence of losses. The strategy of the S&Ls to offer extraordinarily high interest rates to attract deposits worked in part because depositors took no risks in putting their funds in shaky financial institutions. Insurance also permitted S&Ls to make higher risk loans than they would otherwise have done. After all, if the loans were successful, S&L shareholders would benefit; if the borrowers defaulted and the S&Ls became bankrupt, the FDIC, not the shareholders, would cover the losses of depositors.

3. Fraud and Loan Defaults. There were many defaults and S&L failures in oil-producing states (especially Texas). Defaults on many loans escalated as oil prices fell sharply in the 1990s. At the same time, less restrictive oversight by bank regulators led to widespread fraud by some S&L officers. One estimate in the 1990s is that there were fraudulent practices in about 40 percent of the failed S&Ls.

Further Reform of Financial Services

The 1990s saw further substantial reforms. In 1989, the Financial Institutions Reform, Recovery, and Enforcement Act (FIRREA) established the **Resolution Trust Corporation (RTC)** to preside over the dissolution of insolvent S&Ls. We mentioned earlier that by one estimate, the cost to taxpayers of the RTC's activities was estimated to be $500 billion. FIRREA's other changes included: (1) putting all deposit insurance under FDIC control, (2) increasing insurance premiums for banks and thrifts, (3) raising capital requirements for S&Ls, (4) permitting S&Ls to receive deposits from businesses, and (5) directing the Fed to allow bank holding companies to acquire financially sound S&Ls. Since the mid-1990s, further reforms have occurred including allowing banks to enter the insurance business.

Problem of Moral Hazard
The problem that insuring individuals against risk reduces their incentive to prevent losses.

Resolution Trust Corporation (RTC)
A federal agency created in 1989 to preside over the dissolution of insolvent S&Ls

A Further Movement Toward Competition? Interstate Banking

Throughout American history, the number of banks has been large relative to that of other industrial nations such as Canada and Great Britain. The reason for the disparity has lain in the tradition and often legal insistence on branch banking. Some states have even insisted on unit banking, the requirement that a bank have one location and no branches even within the same state. Interstate branches are forbidden by Federal law, though permitting the practice would probably increase the competitiveness of the industry. Resistance to changing the restrictions on interstate banking led to the formation of **bank holding companies**, corporations that may own several banks, even banks in different states. Nearly all big banks in the United States today are owned by holding companies who not only offer diversified banking services but also such collateral activities as leasing and credit cards. In 1995, the Congress passed legislation that removed restrictions in interstate banking.

Bank Holding Companies
Corporations that may own several banks, even in different states.

Financial Institutions: A Summing Up

We witnessed a number of fundamental changes in American financial institutions in the 1980s and 1990s. It became easier to enter financial markets, and as a result they have become more broadly defined. At the same time, it became easier to fail. Many questions remain to be resolved. Should deposit insurance continue to encourage depository institutions to take excessive risks? Are regulatory functions adequate to protect society's interests? How do we measure the money supply so that, once defined, a supply exists that can be closely correlated with changes in income and unemployment. As Keynes wrote, "We can draw the line between "money" and "debt" at whatever point is most convenient for handling a particular problem."

The Powerful Fed: A Summary of Its Functions

We have seen that the Fed is a powerful agency and that its authority over the financial institutions of America in many respects, grew in the 1980s. Although we have mentioned some of its powers before, let's summarize them.

The Fed Regulates the Supply of Money

Through its control over the excess reserves of depository institutions, the Federal Reserve regulates the supply of M_1 money. By means of its operations in the open market, and its variations in the discount rate and in the required reserve ratio, the Federal Reserve may increase or decrease excess reserves. Depository institutions must have excess reserves in order to make loans and create new demand deposits, which are the main form of money.

A great economist, Joseph Schumpeter, once said that whoever controls credit or access to financial capital is akin to the judges (ephors) of ancient Egypt who had power of life or death over all that nation's citizens except for the Pharaoh. To Schumpeter, bankers who controlled access to credit exercised this power in a modern capitalist society. If Schumpeter is right, is the Fed their Pharaoh? After all it controls the ephors (bankers and lenders at all depository institutions) in the United States.

The Fed Acts as a National Clearinghouse for Checks

When a depository institution receives a check written against an account in another financial institution, it gets paid by sending the check to the Federal

Reserve Bank. The Federal Reserve Bank, when it receives the check, increases the deposits with the Federal Reserve of the institution sending the check and reduces the deposits of the bank on which the check is drawn. The Federal Reserve institution then sends the check to the depository institution on which it is drawn. *That* institution reduces the amount of demand deposits in the account of the person who wrote the check.

The Fed Issues Paper Currency

The Federal Reserve issues all the paper money in circulation. The Federal Reserve does not use the issuance of currency as a device to control the overall supply of money, but it must make certain that there is enough currency around to meet the economy's needs. For instance, the need for currency varies from season to season.

Before Christmas, people want to hold cash to buy Christmas presents so demand for paper currency increases. As people withdraw currency from their demand-deposit accounts, depository institutions run low on cash in their vaults. They therefore order more currency from the Federal Reserve, which fills their currency order and reduces their deposits with the Fed by an equal amount. In this way the Fed increases the supply of currency in the economy each Christmas season.

After Christmas, business falls off and people become uneasy about holding more currency than they actually need, so they deposit the excess in their demand-deposit accounts. The depository institutions now have more cash in their vaults than they want, so they send the excess back to the Federal Reserve, which stashes away the cash and increases the banks' deposits with the Fed. In this way the Fed withdraws currency from circulation. This high elasticity in the supply of currency helps take care of seasonal changes in the volume of business.

The Fed Regulates and Examines Member Banks

Congress has given the Federal Reserve the power to regulate many of the activities of depository institutions. To check whether these institutions are obeying the rules, the Fed periodically examines their books. Some believe that this regulatory function needs further strengthening.

The Fed Acts as a Banker's Bank

When depository institutions want to go to the bank, they go to the Federal Reserve, which loans them money by accepting, at a discount, to be sure, their short-term debt instruments. The Federal Reserve also holds deposits of depository institutions, deposits that form part of their total reserves.

The Fed Is a Fiscal Agent and Bank for the U.S. Treasury

The U.S. Treasury itself keeps deposits at the Federal Reserve and writes checks on them. Furthermore, the Federal Reserve handles the national debt for the government. When the Treasury issues the federal debt, the Federal Reserve sells the debt instruments and collects the proceeds for the Treasury. When this debt *matures* (is due for payment), the Federal Reserve pays what is owed out of the Treasury's account.

The Fed Is a Fiscal Agent for Foreign Central Banks and Treasuries

A number of foreign central banks and treasuries use the Federal Reserve as their bank in the United States. The Federal Reserve treats them as impartially as it does its own member banks or the U.S. Treasury. It loans money, buys and sells debt instruments, and in general acts as their fiscal agent.

Monetary Policy

Monetary Policy
Decisions of the Fed regarding changes in the money supply and interest rates.

Monetary policy consists of the decisions of the Fed regarding changes in the money supply and interest rates to achieve economic goals. The most important goal is to reach acceptable levels of growth, employment and price stability. Therefore, in order to understand monetary policy, one needs to know how changes in the money supply affect interest rates and influence income, employment, and prices.

Varying the Supply of Money

Earlier we looked at the effects of changes in the money supply on employment and prices. We saw that increases in the supply of money expand effective demand, while contractions reduce it. Therefore, to counter unemployment, a nation's monetary policy should be to expand the money supply. On the other hand, to counter inflation, a nation's monetary policy should be to cut back the money supply.

Table 13-1
The Federal Reserve's Monetary Policy

What should the Fed do about unemployment?	What should the Fed do about inflation?
Increase excess reserves	*Decrease excess reserves*
Buy government securities	Sell government securities
Lower the discount rate	Raise the discount rate
Lower the required reserve ratio	Raise the required reserve ratio

Varying Interest Rates

What happens to an economy when interest rates vary? When interest rates go up, people do not want to borrow as much to buy consumer goods, because the cost of borrowing money has risen. Businesses do not want to buy as much new plant and equipment, for the same reason. So investment decreases. (Remember that investments need to have an expected rate of return equal to or greater than the interest rate.) Also, when interest rates go up, government expenditures at the state and local levels that are financed by borrowing tend to go down. State and local governments must be concerned about their taxpayers moving to other locales, with lower tax rates. So state an local governments are more sensitive than the federal government about raising taxes to pay increased interest costs on borrowed money. (You knew, didn't you, that state and local governments have to borrow heavily in order to see themselves through the fiscal year?)

All in all, raising interest rates decreases aggregate demand by decreasing consumption based on consumer borrowing as well as investment, and debt-financed expenditures by state and local governments.

What happens when interest rates go down? Just the reverse of what happens when they go up. People more readily borrow money to buy consumer goods because credit is cheaper. Businesses increase their investment spending because there are more investments that yield a return equal to or greater than the cost of the interest. And state and local governments increase their deficit-financed expenditures, too, because the price of money is low.

Some Recommendations on Monetary Policy

During a recession, when there is a lot of unemployment, monetary policy should aim at expanding total spending by increasing the supply of money and decreasing the interest rate. During an inflation, monetary policy should aim at decreasing total spending and discouraging price increases by reducing the supply of money and increasing the interest rate. Table 13-1 outlines the methods the Federal Reserve can use to combat unemployment or inflation.

What to Do When Recession Hits
Suppose there is a recession. Aggregate demand is low, unemployment is high and nobody is buying much. What can be done? The monetary policies that increase the supply of money also lower interest rates and combat unemployment.

During a period of high unemployment, the Federal Reserve should follow policies that increase excess reserves. In the discussion of the Fed, you learned how this can be done. The Federal Reserve should do one or more of the following:

1. *Buy government securities on the open market.* The proceeds are used to increase the deposits of commercial banks with the Federal Reserve; that is, the commercial banks' total and excess reserves rise, so that they can lend out more money.

2. *Lower the discount rate.* This encourages commercial banks to discount acceptable short-term debt and increase their total and excess reserves.

3. *Lower the required reserve ratio.* This does not change commercial banks' total reserves, but it does lower the percentage of reserves that are required, and thus it creates mor excess reserves.

Figure 13-6
Credit Market Equilibrium

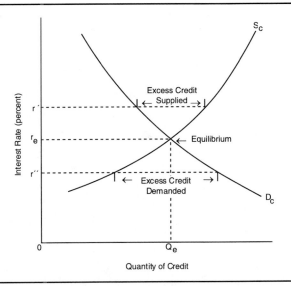

The Supply of Credit (S_c) is upward sloping, and the demand for credit is downward sloping as functions of interest rates. Equilibrium is established at interest rate r_e, where quantity demanded = quantity supplied. Other interest rates (such as r′ and r′′ are disequilibrium rates associated with excess supply or excess demand.

The Monetary Transmission Mechanism: Credit Markets in a Recession

Let's suppose the monetary policy task is to increase real income and reduce unemployment while minimizing inflationary pressures on prices. Whichever of the three "tools" or combination of them it employs, the effects of Federal Reserve action will be felt in credit markets. Let's trace through how those effects occur.

In Figure 13-6, we see the workings of a credit market. Remember that most of our money is in the form of credit (interest bearing loans), created by depository institutions. There are, thus, many credit markets. For convenience, however, let's aggregate them into a hypothetical credit market as in Figure 13-6. The supply of credit (S_c) slopes upward (holding everything else but interest rates constant); as interest rates rise more credit is offered because savings move from non-interest bearing form (e.g., stocks) into interest bearing deposits at banks, savings and loan associations and the like. The demand for credit (D_c) is downward sloping (holding everything else but interest rates constant). The quantity demanded rises because firms, consumers, and even governments borrow more at lower interest rates. Equilibrium is established where the quantity demanded equals the quantity supplied of credit at interest rate r_e. Any other interest rate than r_e would lead to either excess quantity supplied (at r′) or excess quantity demanded (at r′′).

Figure 13-7
Credit Market Response to an Increased Supply of Credit

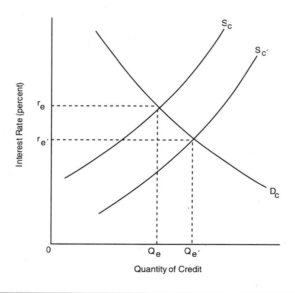

The Fed follows an "easier" monetary policy and the supply of credit (S_c) increases to (S_c′). The equilibrium interest rate falls and the quantity of credit demanded (borrowing) rises from Q_e to Q_e′

A Recession: Enter the Fed

Let's suppose that credit markets are in equilibrium with market clearing interest rates but that the economy is in recession. The Fed (Federal Open Market Committee, Board of Governors) decides to fight the recession with an "easier" monetary policy. Through whatever means (discount rate, reserve requirements, open market purchases of government securities, etc.), the Fed, acting through depository institutions, creates an increase in the supply of credit as in the shift of supply from S_c to $S_c{}'$ in Figure 13-7. As a result interest rates fall from r_e to $r_e{}'$.

Short-run Effects

As the above happens, we see in Figure 13-8 that short-run equilibrium real income is affected. As depository institutions expanded credit in Figure 13-7, interest rates fell. In 13-8 that leads to investment increases that shift aggregate demand in the short run from AD to AD.$'$ Real income grows from Q_e to $Q_e{}'$ and prices rise modestly from P_e to $P_e{}'$.

Note: There would have been no upward pressure on prices if aggregate supply had been horizontal at price level P_e. That aggregate supply assumption, however, is the Keynesian assumption. Monetarists do not necessarily agree with the idea that resource idleness is so widespread that increases in aggregate demand that cause real income growth always occur with no short-run upward pressure on prices.

Figure 13-8
Short-Run Aggregate Demand Increase from the Increased Investment Effect of Monetary Policy Easing

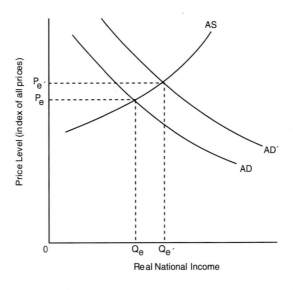

As interest rates fall with an easing of monetary policy, investment increases cause a growth of aggregate demand (AD to AD$'$). Real income rises from Q_e to $Q_e{}'$ and prices rise modestly from P_e to $P_e{}'$.

Long-run Effects

What about the long-run effects of easing monetary policy? We see these in Figure 13-9. What we have seen so far is a monetary policy transmission mechanism that looks like this when put in Keynesian terms.

Easing of Monetary Policy $\rightarrow$ Increase in Supply of Credit $\rightarrow$ Decrease in Interest Rates $\rightarrow$ Increase in Investment $\rightarrow$ Increase in Aggregate Demand in Short Run $\rightarrow$ Increase in Real Income and Prices.

Now we must factor in the long-run supply effects of the investment increases resulting from lower interest rates. In Figure 13-9, we see that in the long run, further shifts that occur in aggregate supply from AS to AS′ resulting in a growth in real income from $Q_e′$ to $Q_e″$. Note that the supply increase results in lowering prices from $P_e′$ back to P_e. Note also that it is not necessarily a monetarist assumption that money supply growth is price neutral in the long run. Rather, the important point is that increasing aggregate supply in the long run will reduce the upward pressures on prices from increased spending or increased aggregate demand. Completing the transmission mechanism (in Keynesian terms), it becomes:

Easing of Monetary Policy → Increase in Supply of Credit → Decrease in Interest Rates → Increase in Investment → Increase in Aggregate Demand in Short Run → Short-run Increase in Real Income and Prices → Long-run Increase in Aggregate Supply → Further Growth in Real Income and Reduced Pressure on Prices.

Figure 13-9
Long-Run Aggregate Demand and Aggregate Supply Effects of Monetary Policy Easing

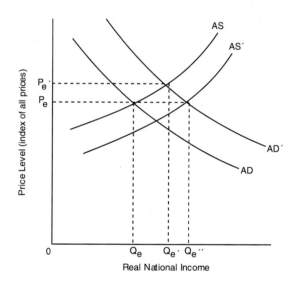

The short-run increase in real income (Q_e to $Q_e′$) and increase in prices (P_e to $P_e′$ from Figure 13-8) leads to the long-term increase in aggregate supply (AS to AS′) that restores price equilibrium at P_e and further increases real income ($Q_e′$ to $Q_e″$).

What to Do When Inflation Hits

Suppose there is an inflation. Aggregate demand is high, and prices are rising fast. What can be done? During a period of rising prices, the Federal Reserve should follow policies that decrease the supply of money and increase interest rates. From the discussion of the Fed, you know how this can be done. The Federal Reserve should do one or more of the following:

1. *Sell government securities on the open market.* This has the effect of reducing the financial institutions' deposits at the Federal Reserve, which means that their excess reserves go down by a like amount, and they have fewer loanable funds.

2. *Raise the discount rate.* This makes it more expensive for financial institutions to borrow from the Federal Reserve, and, therefore, discourages them from increasing their reserves by means of short-term debt.

3. *Raise the required reserve ratio.* This leaves financial institutions' total reserves untouched, but makes them hold a higher percentage of their total reserves as required reserves, which leaves a smaller percentage of excess reserves.

Remember that each of these general powers has different effects. Open-market operations can increase excess reserves or decrease them, and they are also more selective than the other powers. For ordinary monetary policy operations, the Federal Reserve uses mainly open-market operations. Varying the discount rate cannot decrease excess reserves, but it does have a strong immediate impact on interest rates. It causes the interest rates for various kinds of debt instruments (mortgages, personal loans) to fluctuate readily. Varying the required reserve ratio, as we noted before, is too strong and unselective a weapon for the Federal Reserve to use often. The use of this weapon generally signals a major change in Federal Reserve policy.

The Monetary Transmission Mechanism: Credit markets in Inflation

Let us suppose now the economy we are looking at has a serious (demand-pull) inflationary problem. Imagine that it is like the American economy in 1979-1980 with "double-digit" inflation. The job of the Fed, using any of the above "tools" is to "cool-off" the economy with a restrictive monetary policy. Go back to Figure 13-6 and imagine that equilibrium interest rates are too low, that is they are creating inflationary levels of aggregate demand. How can the Fed get interest rates up? Look again at Figure 13-7, but let's have the Fed decrease the supply of credit (S_c' to S_c in 13-7), which reduces the quantity demanded of credit (Q_e' to Q_e) and cause interest rates to increase from r_e' to r_e. Put again in Keynesian terms, the transmission mechanism in the short run is:

A "Tightening" of Monetary Policy; $\rightarrow$ Decrease in Supply of Credit $\rightarrow$ Increase in Interest Rates $\rightarrow$ Decrease in Investment $\rightarrow$ Decrease in Aggregate Demand $\rightarrow$ Lower Level of Prices.

The effects of the decrease in investment can be seen in a reduction of aggregate demand such as from AD' to AD in Figure 13-8. As AD falls, price levels diminish as from P_e' to P_e, and real income will fall. Of course, if the inflation is pure demand pull, aggregate supply may have a vertical (capacity range) look as in Figure 13-10. Here the economy has reached its maximum (capacity) real income at Q_e and is operating with its natural rate of unemployment. Increasing aggregate demand cannot cause a growth in real income so, instead, with "too many dollars chasing an unchanged quantity supplied of goods" prices are pushed up from P_e to P_e'. The Fed decreases the supply of credit by the proper amount, interest rates rise and aggregate demand decreases from AD' to AD. The economy in the short run then enjoys both full employment and price stability (established as a target level of prices).

Figure 13-10

The Effects of Restrictive Monetary Policy on Aggregate Demand, Real Income, and the Price Level When the Economy is Operating at Capacity

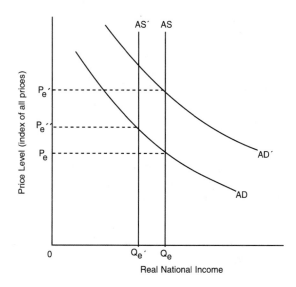

The inflationary economy is operating at capacity with an aggregate supply that is vertical at real income Q_e. Increasing AD is causing demand-pull price pressures that raise prices from P_e to P_e'. The Fed reduces the supply of credit, interest rates rise and aggregate demand decreases from AD' to AD. Prices are stabilized at P_e and real income maintained at capacity, Q_e.

What happens in the long run? The higher interest rates would be expected to lead to a short-run decrease in investment and a long-run decrease in aggregate supply (as from AS to AS' in Figure 13-10). The consequence of the supply effects of restrictive monetary policy might be less than full employment with lower real income (Q_e to Q_e') and higher prices (P_e to P_e''). A falling level of real income and rising prices would probably be seen as a slowing of productivity growth and a call, as we witnessed in the 1980s, for stimulating the supply side of markets. To do that, of course, the Fed would have to reverse course, ease up in credit markets, and let interest rates drift downward.

The Main Point

The main point of the preceding discussion is to emphasize the complexity of the cause-and-effect relationships in monetary policy. These depend on: (a) credit markets, (b) interest rates as signals to borrowers and lenders, (c) investment effects of changing interest rates, (d) demand effects of investment decisions and, in the long run, (e) the supply effects of investment decisions.

There are some who say that in view of all these complexities, discretionary monetary policy is a job for a "philosopher king," not a Federal Reserve chairman. In this regard, some would argue for a simple monetary rule (increase the supply of credit by X percent per year) as opposed to discretionary changes from week to week. It is no easy job being Chairman of the Fed. If you are right about direction and magnitude of choice, you may get some credit (Paul Volcker in the 1980s). If you are wrong about direction and amount, you may be blamed for a recession or depression (ironically, the same Paul Volcker for the 1981-1982 recession).

Weaknesses of Monetary Policy

Monetary policy cannot be expected to provide solutions to all economic problems. Here are six reasons why:

1. *Inadequate demand for credit.* During a serious recession or a depression, monetary policy may be quite ineffective in stimulating the economy. Depository institutions may already have all the excess reserves they need. (a) As business goes into a slump, people may shy away from borrowing to such an extent that more loans are paid off than are made. So excess reserves increase without the help of the Federal Reserve. (b) With the economic outlook so gloomy, lending institutions are often unwilling to run the risk of lending. So no matter what the Fed does to increase excess reserves, lending institutions refuse to increase loans and the supply of money. (This is what the commercial banks did during the Great Depression of the 1930s.) (c) The depository institutions may have money they are willing to lend, but people are just not borrowing. During a mild recession, however, monetary policy aimed at increasing excess reserves may work well, as it did in the recession of 1954. That recession was caused by the decline of defense expenditures at the end of the Korean War. At that time, people's confidence in the economy was strong. There was a tax cut; and an easy-money policy increased excess reserves, thus stimulating bank lending, increasing the supply of money, and reducing interest rates.

2. *Non-demand-pull inflation.* Monetary policy may curb inflation, provided that it is a demand-pull inflation of the type in Figure 13-10. The Federal Reserve can dry up excess reserves so much that depository institutions cannot make loans. Then people cannot get money to buy things with. However, if the inflation is caused by factors *not* susceptible to control by the lowering of aggregate demand (cost-push and administered-price inflation), monetary policy may not be the cure. For example, the inflation of 1973-1974 was caused in part by the raising of oil prices by OPEC (Organization of Petroleum Exporting Countries) and the rise in agricultural prices. The Federal Reserve tried to use monetary policy to decrease prices. But its tight-money policy, that is charging very high interest rates on the money it lent, only led to commercial banks raising *their* interest rates to 12 percent. A liquidity crisis (that is, a shortage of assets that could be easily converted into money) in the banking system was predicted. The Fed was forced to back off from its tight-money policy before the double-digit inflation could be contained.(*Double-digit* meaning at any rate of 10 percent or more per year.)

3. *Recognition and Implementation Lag.* Only a philosopher king has perfect foresight. A Fed chairman (and board) rely on data that is always lagged and that may or may not be an accurate measure of current economic activity. Monetary policy changes, thus, may be a reaction to an incorrect perception of problems, akin to giving someone a dose of medicine for an ailment that the patient no longer has!

Even a philosopher-king cannot have orders carried out instantly. While some Fed policies can be changed quickly (open-market operations) others take 30 months or more to fully implement. Lower interest rates may find a few firms with investment plans on the shelf waiting for the right present value; many other firms will only *begin* planning new investments as interest rates fall. Implementation lags can seriously slow the workings even of correct monetary policy.

4. *Distributive effects.* During inflation, a tight-money policy of raising interest rates does not affect the economy *evenly.* It hits some groups harder than others. For instance, in the construction industry, high interest rates cause the demand for new houses to plummet. Each time there has been a period of tight-money policy and high interest rates, the construction industry has experienced serious cutbacks, with consequent layoffs of workers.

Depository institutions, as their excess reserves dwindle, do not lend their reduced supply of money evenly. Safe customers get loans, but risky ones do not. The more risky firms (generally smaller-scale, new firms) not only face higher interest rates, but also have difficulty getting loans. Larger corporations do not have this problem. They are isolated from the tight-money situation because, when *they* want money, they can dip into their own retained earnings and depreciation funds.

Figure 13-11

Expectations Effects on the Demand for Credit Result in perverse effects of Monetary Policy

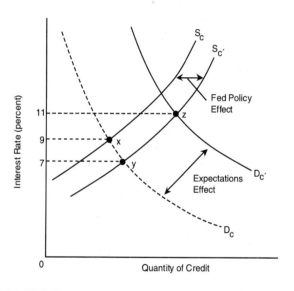

The Fed seeks to lower interest rates from their initial equilibrium at X (D$_c$ intersects S$_c$) and nine percent. The target interest rate is seven percent, which can be attained by increasing the supply of credit from S$_c$ to S$_c$' (S$_c$' intersects D$_c$) at point Y. The public, expecting higher inflation to result, attempts to lock in the lower interest rate and increases its demand for credit from D$_c$ to D$_c$'. At the new equilibrium, point Z, (D$_c$' intersects S$_c$') interest rates rise to 11 percent.

5. *Changes in Velocity.* As the Federal Reserve increases the money supply during a recession and decreases it during an inflation, changes in the velocity of exchange may partially counteract these trends. During a recession the velocity of exchange may decrease, which reduces the impact of an increased supply of money. Pessimistic consumers and businesses try to hold on to their money. During an inflation, the velocity of exchange, V, may increase, which reduces the impact of a decreased supply of money. Optimistic consumers and businesses, expecting that prices will go up still higher, continue to buy at an ever greater rate. Although monetary velocity, as we saw earlier, has been relatively constant in recent years, it can change as it did in the 1970s.

6. *Changes in Inflationary Expectations.* To execute its monetary policies through credit markets, the Fed must set up equilibrium interest rate targets. Suppose, for example, that the Fed wants to expand the economy and decides to

try to get interest rates down from an average of nine percent to seven percent. To do this, it uses some set of the previously discussed policy tools to increase the supply of credit as in Figure 13-11 from S_c to $S_c{}'$. With demand D_c, the Fed's target would be achieved. The public, however, expecting this increase in the quantity demanded of credit to cause a higher rate of inflation, tries to lock in the seven percent rate and increases its demand for credit from D_c to $D_c{}'$. In the new credit market equilibrium, the interest rate effect of the Fed's action is not to lower interest rates to seven percent but to raise them to 11 percent!

Monetarism

Monetarism
An approach to macroeconomic policy in which the supply of money is the dominant factor.

Monetarism is an approach to macroeconomic policy in which the supply of money plays the dominant role. Nobel Laureate Milton Friedman, the economist who founded the monetarist school, maintains that both fiscal policy and monetary policy based on Keynesian analysis are wrong. He and other monetarists charge that the Keynesians underestimate the effects of the supply of money on the economy. Friedman, as well as newer monetary theorists, says that people have a stable and predictable demand for money, a demand related to the size of the economy. Therefore, the supply of money and its relationship to national income should be the key to government policy, both fiscal and monetary. To control unemployment and inflation, the monetarists say, the government should follow a policy of increasing the supply of money at a proper and constant rate.

In the mid-1990s, some economists suggested that discretionary monetary policy was becoming less and less effective. One important reason cited was that international capital markets had become so large and so efficient that a single central bank, even one as powerful as the Fed could have little overall influence on credit supplies and interest rates. These issues plus the monetarist attack on Keynesian fiscal and monetary policy deserves full treatment. So, in the following application we will explore these controversies.

Application I: How Much Does Money Matter? Monetarists Versus Keynesians

The most serious challenge to Keynesian theories of economics, especially to the monetary and fiscal policies, has come from Milton Friedman and the monetarist school of economics. These economists say that monetary policy is more important than fiscal policy, and that in order to stabilize an economy, a steady rate of growth in the supply of money must be ensured. The monetarists do not simply say that money matters, as would Keynesians, they go further, and say that money supply policy matters more than any other economic policy.

The Monetarists' Position
The basic tenet of the monetarists is that the biggest single factor in determining money income, real income, and the level of prices is the *rate of growth of the money supply.* They contend that people want to keep a fixed percentage of their assets in the form of money, a percentage that depends on their real incomes, their standards of consumption, and the composition of their other assets. As you know, if the supply of money increases too quickly, people find themselves holding more money than they wish. They try to re-establish the old equilibrium, by demanding more nonconsumption assets, such as land, machinery, stocks, and bonds; and/or more consumer goods, either of which causes the economy to expand. If the supply of money shrinks, the reverse happens, and the economy contracts.

This variation in the supply of money also affects prices. Monetarists do not accept the Keynesian view that an economy with growing expenditures can expand indefinately with stable prices. Beyond some point, as the economy expands, demand-pull inflation sets in. Conversely, as the supply of money and the economy contract, excess capacity and excess inventory drive prices down.

Some but not all monetarists are critical of discretionary policy. They recommend that the Federal Reserve concentrate on monetary rules maintaining a steady increase in the money supply, at about two to four percent per year. This, they say, would force the economy into a stable growth with low inflation.

The 4 percent growth in the money supply would provide enough expansion to accommodate the three percent increase in productivity that some economists feel is historically what can be sustained. It would also provide enough flexibility to reinforce sectors of the economy that have less capacity than others, so that inflation would be mild.

Monetarists challenge the assumption that by means of continuous adjustments in fiscal policy and monetary policy, one can cause the economy to grow with relative stability. He says that changes in fiscal policy are ineffective and that the monetary policy of changing the interest rate also accomplishes little, since it is the *percentage rate of change in the supply of money* that is most closely correlated with changes in levels of income and employment. Furthermore, because nobody can accurately predict future business trends, it is dangerous to use changes in the rate of growth of the money supply for fine-tuning purposes.

Thus, monetarists who support decision by rule make simple and direct recommendations for government economic policy: Let the monetary authority (the Federal Reserve) increase the supply of money at a fixed rate of two to four percent per year and the economy will adjust itself. Although this will not eliminate all economic instability, it will avoid extreme variations. As Friedman notes: "We do not know enough to avoid minor fluctuations. The attempt to do more than we can will itself be a disturbance that may increase rather than reduce instability."

Discretionary monetary policy has at times seemed to complicate stabilization rather than solve the problems of economic fluctuations. After World War II the Federal Reserve used its open-market operations to peg the price of government securities, and neglected the postwar inflation. In 1957 the Fed enforced such a tight policy, in an attempt to fight inflation, that it contributed to the 1958 recession. Often just before or during an inflation, the Fed has increased the supply of money by greater amounts than the four percent recommended by Friedman. This has fed the inflation; 1973 is a good example.

It is somewhat ironic that the sharply restrictive monetary policy practiced by the Fed in 1981-1982 has been both hailed as a triumph of correctly timed monetary restraint and pointed to as an example of overreaction by some monetarists. While the decrease in money supply growth did, as we have already seen, lead to a reduction in inflation, it also caused a fall in real GDP and a sharp increase in unemployment.

The Keynesian Defense

While Keynesians do not deny the importance of the money supply, they regard it as a complementary tool to fiscal policy. Commenting on the rapid growth in income and jobs in the mid-1980s, a leading Keynesian and Nobel Laureate James Tobin[1] remarked that "the patent success of fiscal stimulus in promoting recovery in the United States in 1983-1984 reinforces the Keynesian side of this old debate."

A flaw in the monetarists' theory is the implied assumption that velocity of exchange remains constant. (The monetarists say that V is constant in the short run, but not in the long run.) As you saw earlier, V can change in the long run. These variations indicate the economy's responses to changes in many factors, including fiscal policy (taxes and government expenditures). Variation in the supply of money, say the Keynesians, is not the main stimulus that brings about changes in money income and real income. It is only one of a number of factors, including variations in fiscal policy and interest rates, that cause such changes. Critics of monetarism claim that the rigid link that the monetarists would forge between money and economic activity just does not exist.

A leading economist and former chairman of the Council of Economic Advisers, Martin Feldstein[2], says, however, that perfectly stable or predictable trends in velocity are not necessary, merely that "controlling monetary aggregates is better than the alternative bases for guiding monetary policy."

The monetarists' demand for a rigid monetary rule opens up several areas of debate. What money are they talking about? Is it to be just demand deposits plus all currency and coin in circulation (M_1)? Or does it also include various forms of near money (M_2)? If near money is excluded, don't variations in these highly liquid assets affect the situation?

Debates about whether to include M_2 elements of near monies and which to include explain some theoretical differences. This explains also some of the conflict in policy recommendations.

Also, how much time elapses between an increase in the supply of money (however one defines it) and the effect of that increase in the form of improved economic activity? The data that Friedman presents show great variability in time lags.

If, as is questionable, there is any validity to the Phillips Curve and if there is some trade-off between inflation and unemployment, what clue does one get from the monetarists that can be used to decide at what level the trade-off should be with this fixed growth in the money supply? If the Federal Reserve should increase the money supply at a certain fixed annual rate, this would force into the open certain changes in the economy. There might be fluctuations in interest rates that might be too large for comfort.

A Conclusion

Milton Friedman and the monetarist school have affected the thinking of many economists and public policy makers. People have begun to pay a lot more attention to the role of the money supply and monetary policy. These factors have assumed greater importance in government economic policy, even if making monetary policy effective is more difficult in a world of huge and efficient international capital markets. Nearly everyone agrees that money does matter. However, many economists are unwilling to concede that money is the only, or even the only major, thing that matters. Nor are they willing to completely abandon discretionary fiscal policy as a tool to affect the economy, although, its use is much more restricted today than in earlier decades. Many continue to espouse correcting for ups and downs in economic activity by making periodic adjustments in fiscal and monetary policy, a little of this and a dash of that, and prefer

1. Tobin, James. "Monetarism, An Ebbing Tide?" *The Economist*, April 27, 1985.
2. Feldstein, Martin. "Monetarism: Open-Eyed Pragmatism?" *The Economist*, May 3, 1985.

this on-the-spot approach to the measured-recipe method of following the rigid monetary rule and adding four percent to the money supply each year.

Keynesian and Monetarist Views: A Summary of Differences

The Keynesian-Monetarist debate is far from over. Both see the growth of the 1980s as providing supporting evidence for their views. Table 13-2 gives a summary of their contrasting views.

Monetary practitioners (e.g., Paul Volcker at the Fed in the 1980s) see discretionary monetary policy as a powerful and effective force. Milton Friedman sees the problem with discretionary policy as being people inadequate to a task. (Friedman: "Clearly the problem is not the person who happens to be chairman, but the system.") Thus, the crux of the debate *among* monetarists.

Keynesians see both views as too narrow, believing that discretionary fiscal and monetary policies can be linked together to achieve macroeconomic targets of growing real income and stable price levels. James Tobin regards the pure monetarist view as an "ebbing tide: which enjoyed its heyday in the 1960s and 1970s". The debate, in other words, is far from over.

Table 13-2
Keynesian Versus Monetarist Views

Item	Keynesian View	Monetarist View
Demand for Money	Determined by people's incomes, (opportunity) cost of holding money, interest rates.	Determined by inflationary expectations, people's incomes, the level of prices, rates of returns on various forms of wealth and institutional factors.
How Money Affects the Economy	Increases in money supply lower interest rates, increase investment, and raise aggregate demand.	Increases in money supply cause increases in consumer spending as well as investment, which raise real income.
Discretionary Fiscal Policy	Very important as a tool to raise aggregate demand, lower unemployment, and raise real income.	Ineffective if not counterproductive in reaching real income targets because deficits lead to crowding out and politicians are short sighted.
Discretionary Monetary Policy	Useful, but not as potent a tool as discretionary fiscal policy.	Seen as very powerful and important by many monetarists while other prefer a fixed monetary rule.

Monetary Policy and International Markets Monetary Policy

Whatever the eventual outcome of the Keynesian-Monetarist debate, its importance has diminished from a policy standpoint. As we have seen, aggregate demand management, however effective or ineffective it might be, is severely constrained by the reality of the large federal debt together with the acceptance of the view that a natural rate of unemployment makes demand management ineffective or even counterproductive in the long run. That same debt and the necessity to finance it, together with the extreme ease with which capital funds move internationally, seems also to be making discretionary monetary policy more difficult to administer.

Much of the federal debt is held by foreigners. The Japanese are the largest holders of this debt. In order to attract foreign capital in these amounts, U.S. long-term interest rates have to be competitive with those in other major capital markets, such as Germany and Japan. When those rates rise, U.S. rates have to be kept high also even if domestic concern for a recession might otherwise cause the Fed to move toward monetary ease.

.   An article in *The Wall Street Journal* in March, 1990 relates a case in which the Fed acted in December 1989 to increase the money supply (buying treasury bills) to act against a possible recession: Although long-term interest rates fell briefly, they quickly moved upward and were soon *above* the rate existing before the easing of the money supply.

Then-Fed Chairman Alan Greenspan, asked whether the powerful Central Bank could still do its job of managing the money supply in a contracyclical manner, responded to a congressional committee: "To what extent have we lost control over our economic destiny? The Fed can still do its job but it's more difficult." Former New York Fed Chairman Anthony Solomon compares the difficulty with trying to juggle three balls at the same time: (1) economic growth, (2) inflationary pressures, and (3) foreign holdings of U.S. debt together with the need to attract long-term capital from abroad. At this point, few doubt that the Fed *can* do so, but it certainly is a more difficult task in the early twenty first century.

Application II: The Federal Reserve's Unorthodox Policies

As noted in Application I of Chapter 1, financial deregulations contributed to accumulation of risk in the U.S. financial system and its near collapse in the 2008-2009 period. One aspect of the financial crisis was a sharp drop in lending by banks to other banks and to consumers and businesses known as a "credit freeze." This reflected the banks' fear that the loans would not be paid back. As the "lender of last resort" and in order to thaw the credit freeze the Federal Reserve began injecting liquidity into the financial system through several new lending programs or "facilities." These programs went beyond the traditional way of granting member banks loans through the Fed's "discount window." They basically involved making short-term collateralized loans (with eligible collaterals specified by the Fed) to banks and other financial actors as a result of which they were able to swap their less liquid financial assets for the Treasury securities or cash. For the first time, eligible borrowers included "primary dealers" (the bond dealers through whom the Fed conducts its open market operations) who received direct loans from the Fed. While the Fed defended these measures as part of its efforts to mitigate the effects of the financial crisis and restore financial stability, it was criticized for "bailing out" banks. The latter was especially controversial, for it is generally perceived that banks were not required by the Fed to aggressively lend to consumers and businesses in return. There is some support for this perception as commercial and industrial loans by commercial banks reached its peak in October 2010 and have not returned to that level since then. Bank loans to consumers, however, reached its peak in February 2009, declined for more than a year after that, surpassed its peak in April 2010, and continued to rise since then.

Another unorthodox policy adopted by the Fed had to do with its role as the conductor of monetary policy. As the federal funds rate (the short-term rate on interbank loans) approached near zero ("zero lower bound") due to the Fed's expansionary monetary policy, the Fed had to resort to other measures to maintain the easy stance of monetary policy. The Fed initiated a series of "large-scale asset purchases" (LSAPs) from commercial banks and other private institutions in late 2008. These financial assets included mortgage-backed securities (MBS) and longer-term Treasury securities. They were purchased with the stated objectives of supporting mortgage lending and housing markets and improving conditions in private credit markets. In effect, LSAPs made more liquid assets available to the sellers (more reserves with the Fed in the case of banks), reduced the risk of holding financial assets with longer maturity periods, and brought down *long-term* interest rates such as mortgage rates. Since LSAPs increase the quantity of money they are more generally known as "Quantitative Easing" or QE. The magnitudes of QEs were indeed large. Based on the change in the value of assets on the Federal Reserve's balance sheet they totaled well over $2.0 trillion. This has raised the specter of higher future inflation among some critics. The Fed emphasizes that part of its interventions involved merely swapping assets with short-term maturity with assets with long-term maturity. Moreover, the Fed points out that it has an "exit strategy" which involves reversing its purchases and raising interest rates when signs of inflationary pressures begin to emerge. Several recent studies support the downward effects of QEs on long-term interest rates. As for their effects on inflation, while no material increase in inflation expectations and actual inflation rate has been observed to date, the jury is still out.

SUMMING UP

1. The Federal Reserve System (the Fed) is organized as follows: (a) There are 12 Federal Reserve Banks in 12 districts. (b) All national commercial banks must be members of the system, while state banks may join if they wish. (c) Each member bank must buy some stock in its particular district Federal Reserve Bank. (d) A seven-member board of governors in Washington controls the system. Its members are appointed by the President, with the advice and consent of the Senate, for terms of 14 years. (e) The Federal Open Market Committee (FOMC) and the Federal Advisory Council are the two main committees under the board of governors. (f) Each Federal Reserve Bank has nine people on its board of directors: three appointed by the board of governors, three elected by the member banks, and three from the local community.

2. The so-called "general powers" of the Federal Reserve, including those granted in the Deregulatory Act of 1980, entitle it to control the excess reserves of all depository institutions, bank and non-bank alike by the following devices: (a) *Open-market operations.* To increase all institutions' excess reserves, the Fed buys government securities in the open market; it buys them from the commercial banks and pays for them by increasing deposits with the Federal Reserve. To reduce excess reserves, the Fed sells government securities on the open market to the depository institutions and deducts the amount of the sale from their deposits (reserves). (b) *Varying the discount rate.* When the Fed wants to encourage an increase in excess reserves, it lowers the *discount rate,* so that money becomes cheaper for the depository institutions to borrow. The institutions therefore borrow more, which increases their deposits with the Fed and increases their excess reserves. When the Fed wants to discourage the discounting, it increases the discount rate. (c) *Varying the required reserve ratio.* The Fed can lower or raise the percentage of a depository institution's total reserves that are considered "required," which in turn raises or lowers the reserves that are counted as "excess."

3. The Federal Reserve has or has had *specific powers* over certain aspects of lending. (a) The Fed sets the *margin requirement* for stock purchases. The *margin* is the percentage of cash required as a down payment on a purchase of corporate stock. The balance may be borrowed. (b) Regulation Q, the authority of the Fed to set maximum interest rates, was repealed in 1980. The act made all depository institutions subject to uniform reserve requirements and gave all such institutions access to the Fed's services. In general, it created a much more competitive American financial industry.

4. Financial markets were substantially deregulated in the 1980s. Controls over interest rates were removed, all depository institutions were permitted to create checkable deposits, loans by thrifts were expanded, and the Fed became available as a lending agency to all depository institutions.

5. The 1980s and early 1990s were turbulent for American financial institutions. Many banks and S&Ls failed. Two important concerns are (a) such institutions are primarily responsible for making loans and, thereby, creating most of America's money supply, and (b) taxpayers have absorbed a huge cost through the FDIC and Federal Savings and Loan Insurance Corporation (FSLIC) of guaranteeing depositors in the failed institutions.

6. The banking industry recovered in the 1990s because of reorganization and improved lending conditions. The S&L industry remains a problem. This seems to be because (a) deregulation has increased competition for savings and loan associations, which caused them to pay higher interest rates to attract depositors, and (b) insuring depositors against risk results in the *moral hazard problem* in that it reduces incentives by depositors to prevent losses.

7. Financial reform legislation; in 1989 created the *Resolution Trust Corporation (RTC)* to preside over the dissolution of failed S&Ls. The legislation also broadened FDIC authority over deposit insurance and allowed bank holding companies to acquire sound S&Ls while raising capital requirements for S&Ls to the same levels as that of banks.

8. The functions of the Federal Reserve are the following: (a) It regulates the supply of money. (b) It acts as a national clearinghouse for checks. (c) It issues all paper currency. (d) It regulates and examines member banks. (e) It acts as a banker's bank. (f) It acts as a fiscal agent and bank for the U.S. Treasury. (g) It acts as a fiscal agent for certain foreign central banks and treasuries.

9. Monetary policy works through credit markets that are controlled by interest rates. Using any one or a combination of its powers, the Fed can increase or decrease the supply of credit in these markets and, thereby, cause interest rates to rise or fall. As they rise, the quantity demanded of credit falls. As they fall, the quantity demanded of credit rises.

10. A lowering of interest rates, seen in Keynesian terms, leads to an increase in investment. As investment increases, aggregate demand grows, leading to an increase in real income and prices in the short run. In the long run, there is also an increase in aggregate supply that will cause further growth in real income and may partially or entirely offset the short-run price increase.

11. Increasing interest rates leads to a reduction in investment. Seen in Keynesian terms, as investment decreases, aggregate demand falls, leading to a decline in the short run real income and prices. In the long run, the decline in investment may lead to a decline in aggregate supply and a reduction in real income.

12. Discretionary monetary policy is based on complex relationships involving credit markets and interest rate targets. Some argue that it is so easy to be wrong about direction and magnitude of policy change that it would be better to have a monetary rule or fixed rate of increase in the supply of money and credit.

13. *Monetary policy* involves manipulating the supply of credit and interest rates so as to achieve low unemployment and only slight price increases. The Board of Governors of the Federal Reserve is the group responsible for administering monetary policy.

14. To overcome unemployment, one should increase the supply of credit and decrease interest rates in order to increase investment, aggregate demand, and income. In the long run, this should increase aggregate supply and further increase real income. To increase excess reserves, and thereby increase the money supply, the Fed should: (a) buy government securities on the open market, (b) lower the discount rate, or (c) lower the required reserve ratio.

15. To overcome inflation, one should decrease the supply of credit and increase interest rates; this should decrease aggregate demand and reduce prices. To decrease excess reserves, and thereby decrease the money supply, the Fed should: (a) sell government securities on the open market, (b) raise the discount rate and (c) raise the required reserve ratio.

16. The weaknesses of monetary policy are: (a) Inadequate demand for credit. During a severe recession, the policy may not work. People are afraid to invest, so they pay off loans and shy away from further borrowing. As a result, excess reserves increase without Fed interference. (b) Non-demand-pull inflation. During an inflation, monetary policy may be ineffective in dealing with kinds of inflation that are not susceptible to the lowering of aggregate demand (cost-push and administered-price inflation). (c) Monetary policy becomes ineffectual when inflation accompanies high unemployment. (d) Lags of recognition and implementation. (e) Changes in inflationary expectations may offset the plans of the Fed about interest rate changes.

17. Milton Friedman and some other economists of the monetarist school of thought reject discretionary fiscal and monetary policy aimed at stabilizing aggregate demand. They believe that a constant and proper level of increase in the supply of money is the key to containing both inflation and unemployment.

18. The monetarists claim that the rate of growth of the money supply is the primary factor that influences the level of economic activity (employment and prices). Some argue that deliberate (discretionary) monetary policy that changes the money supply may have a perverse effect on economic activity. This, plus the fact that no one can accurately predict future business affairs, makes discretionary, monetary, and fiscal policy ineffective and dangerous. Some monetarists therefore advocate a simple monetary rule: Let the government increase the supply of money by a fixed rate of two to four percent per year. Other monetarists regard discretionary monetary policy as effective and important in achieving economic growth and stability objectives.

19. The Keynesians point to the following weaknesses in the monetarist position: (a) The velocity of exchange is not constant, either in the short or long run. Therefore, there is no rigid link between the economy and the supply of money. (b) The monetarists leave a number of questions unanswered: What do they define as being money? What about variations in time between changes in the supply of money and changes in the economy?

20. Keynesians believe that discretionary monetary and fiscal policies can be devised to achieve real income and price-level goals.

21. The debate between Keynesian and monetarist views continues. All economists, nonetheless, regard the supply of money as an important macroeconomic variable.

KEY TERMS

Bank holding companies
Central bank
Discount rate
General power
Margin requirement
Monetarism
Monetary policy
Moral hazard problem
National banks
Regulation Q
Regulation W
Regulation X
Required reserve ratio
Resolution Trust Corporation
Specific powers
State banks

QUESTIONS

1. What is a central bank? How does it differ from private banks?

2. Which is more important, the pure public element or the quasi-public element of the structure of the Federal Reserve?

3. Given that the required reserve ratio is 20 percent, describe the way the following transactions would affect the following accounts: Required Reserves, Excess Reserves, Total Reserves, and Supply of Money.

> a. A commercial bank *buys* $10,000 in government securities from the Federal Reserve Bank.
> b. A commercial bank *sells* $10,000 in government securities to the Federal Reserve Bank.
> c. A commercial bank discounts a $1,000 note at 8 percent for 90 days at the Federal Reserve.
> d. The Federal Reserve raises the required reserve ratio to 25 percent.
> e. The Federal Reserve lowers the required reserve ratio to 15 percent.

4. What are the general powers of the Federal Reserve? How do they work? Why are they called general powers?

5. How do federal reserve policies affect credit markets?

6. What would you advise the board of governors of the Fed to do in case of an inflation? of a recession? What would you have advised them to do in the 1981-1982 inflationary situation?

7. When the Federal Reserve practices a policy of tight money in order to combat inflation, who pays the cost? Give reasons why these groups bear the cost.

8. How does non-demand-pull inflation complicate monetary policy?

9. You have just been appointed to the Board of Governors of the Federal Reserve System. The chairman has asked you to review monetary policy and present your recommendations on:
      a. Federal Reserve policy to counter inflation or unemployment.
      b. the groups in the economy that obtain advantages or disadvantages from your recommendations.
      c. the economic justification for your recommendations.
      d. how you would deal with significant amounts of inflation and unemployment at the same time.

10. How may changes in inflationary expectations complicate reaching Fed policy objectives?

11. What were the major changes since the 1980s in American financial institutions? What is the present role of the Fed vis-a-vis these institutions?

12. What seems to have caused widespread failures of banks and S&Ls in the 1980s and early 1990s?

13. What was the original purpose of deposit insurance? What is the problem of moral hazard and how was it related to financial failures in the 1980s and 1990s?

14. What was the purpose of the Resolution Trust Corporation?

15. What are the basic elements of the monetarists' position? Do they seem justified? Why?

Chapter 14: Economic Policy Controversies
Supply-Side Economics, Rational Expectations, New Views by Keynesians;, Classical Economists, and the Post-Keynesians

As America entered the 1980s, its economy seemed to face some unprecedented challenges. Having survived the supply shocks of the early to mid-1970s, (OPEC I) and the late 1970s (OPEC II), it found itself in 1981 with an inflation rate of almost nine percent (briefly over 10 percent), an unemployment rate rising to almost 10 percent (in 1982), and a growth in real GDP declining sharply through much of the early 1980s. As often happens in periods of economic difficulty, the nation looked for new ideas or old ideas re-expressed to fit the times.

Supply-Side Economics
Arguments about efforts and incentives to stimulate growth in aggregate supply.

In electing Ronald Reagan as President, the country, at least in part responded to his promise of new policies to reinvigorate the American economy. Prominent among Reagan's arguments and those of his advisers was that of using **supply-side economics**, arguments about efforts and incentives to stimulate growth in aggregate supply. These efforts were designed to ensure real income growth at stable prices. Growth was to occur rapidly enough to create jobs at a rate that would bring down unemployment. In this chapter we are going to look at some of these supply-side arguments, arguments that are again being advanced in the early twenty first century, and the evidence regarding policies undertaken in their support. We will also look at some of the reservations expressed by those who argue that such discretionary government policies can have little or no macroeconomic effect. Finally, we will look at new views about macroeconomic theory, including those of rational expectations, new Keynesians, new classical economists, and the post-Keynesians.

Figure 14-1
Changes in Aggregate Demand, Aggregate Supply and Prices

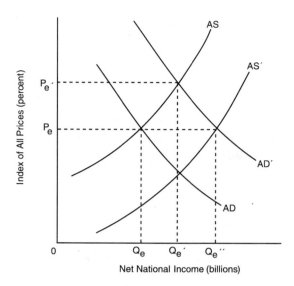

The initial equilibrium real income is Q_e with price level P_e (AD = AS). If aggregate demand is increased through fiscal or monetary policy, the short-run effect is to shift AD to AD′. The new equilibrium real income (AD′ = AS) is Q_e′ with price level P_e′. In the long run, if aggregate supply grows, AS shifts to AS′ and prices reequilibrate at P_e with real income Q_e′′.

Short Run Aggregate Supply and Aggregate Demand: A Review

Recall from a previous chapter that equilibrium real income and the equilibrium price level are established where aggregate quantity demanded equals aggregate quantity supplied (the level of output and prices at which the plans of those making expenditure decisions are made equal to the plans of those making production decisions). The initial equilibrium in Figure 14-1 is at real income Qe and price level Pe, where aggregate quantity demanded equals aggregate quantity supplied. Now suppose that aggregate demand grows to AD′ as the result of stimulative fiscal (tax cuts, etc.) or monetary policy. With aggregate supply unchanged, real income grows to Qe′ but prices rise to Pe′. In the interest of price stability, an increase in aggregate supply is called for such as from AS to AS′. It would then be possible to establish a new higher level of real income at e′′, where a new aggregate quantity demanded equals a new aggregate quantity supplied. Prices, then, stabilize at the old level Pe.

How Do We Stimulate Aggregate Supply?

The shift of aggregate supply in Figure 14-1 could be a reaction to long-run investments that occur because of the larger aggregate demand. That simple Keynesian view of aggregate supply changes as responses to changes in aggregate demand is disputed, however, by "supply-side" economists. These economists assign aggregate supply a much more important and autonomous role in achieving the macroeconomic objectives of real income growth and price stability. Let's look, then, at the foundations of supply-side economics.

Fundamentals of Supply-Side Views

F. Thomas Juster[1] has argued that supply-side economics is based on four elements or hypotheses:

1. Entitlement programs (unemployment compensation, social security payments, etc.) have lowered work incentives; reducing such programs will, therefore, restore incentives and cut the tax burden on tax payers and investors.

2. America's system of taxes is biased against effort, saving, and investment. Lowering taxes, thus, will increase labor supplies and savings and investment.

3. Public regulation designed to protect consumers and employees raises costs and reduces investment. Many such activities offer few benefits relative to their costs. The view of supply-side proponents is that this applies both to (1) industrial regulation of particular industries that often creates monopolies or cartels with less efficiency and higher costs, and (2) social regulation such as pollution control health and safety regulation that raises costs and prices without being subjected to a cost/benefit calculation.

4. The long use of monetary and fiscal programs to stimulate aggregate demand has created a climate of inflationary expectations. Changing those expectations (through, for example, a commitment to balanced budgets) will help, therefore, to reduce inflationary pressures.

While Juster expresses sympathy for some of these four propositions, he expresses serious doubt about the linkage between tax reductions, labor supplies and the volume of savings. One should not forget, though, that supply-side policies are founded not only in economic theory but also in political philosophy. As President Reagan said in his *Economic Report* of 1987: "Government should play a limited role in the economy, It should encourage a stable economy in which people can make informed decisions. It should not make those decisions for them or arbitrarily distort economic choices...."

Tax Policy, Keynesian Expenditure Reductions or Supply-Side "Wedges?"

Tax Wedge
The supply-side view that taxes are a wedge between resource prices and the prices of final goods and services.

To Keynesians, tax increases are seen as a reduction of the ability of consumers and firms to purchase goods and services. Tax increases, thus, reduce aggregate demand and are contractionary. Supply-siders, on the other hand, believe that most tax increases ultimately are incorporated as higher costs by producers and finally are shifted forward to consumers by way of higher prices. Tax increases, therefore, create a cost-push effect on aggregate supply. In the decades of the 1970s and 1980s, for example, federal payroll taxes (primarily social security taxes), as well as state and local government excise and sales taxes were boosted substantially. Supply-siders see such tax increases as a "**tax wedge**" between the prices of resources and the prices of final goods and services. In other words, as government taxes have increased, costs of production and prices have risen and aggregate supply has been reduced (shifted to the left). To supply-siders, rever-

---

1. Juster, F. Thomas. "The Economics and Politics of the Supply-Side View." *Economics Outlook USA*, Autumn, 1981.

sal of this trend of rising taxes would lower production costs and prices and lead to an increase in aggregate supply (a shift to the right).

The Tax Cuts of 1981: How Well Did They Work?

We witnessed numerous changes in Federal taxation in the 1980s. The 1981 changes reduced the highest marginal income tax rate from 70 percent to 50 percent (by 1984). Income taxes were indexed to prevent "bracket creep," rising marginal tax rates associated with growth in nominal but not real income. In line with article (2) of the supply-side propositions, this was expected to increase savings and investment, as well as to encourage a larger supply of labor. It might also be added that it was expected to encourage legal transactions as opposed to the **underground economy**, those transactions that give rise to taxable income but are not reported for tax purposes. In 1985, Reagan proposed a further reduction in the highest marginal tax rate to 31 percent; a proposal that went into effect in 1987 (although, in 1993, it was raised to 33 percent).

Underground Economy
Economic transactions that give rise to taxable income but are not reported for tax purposes.

It is still difficult to assess the long-term relative aggregate supply and aggregate demand effects of the 1981 tax cuts. It is, of course, still too early to forecast the long-run effects of the 1987 tax law. President Reagan, in his 1987 *Economic Report*, regarded the 1981 cuts as a clear success, reporting that "businesses fixed investment set records as a share of real gross domestic product in 1984 and 1985 and remains high by historical standards." Some economists have criticized the correlation saying that increased investment rates were merely a reaction to the extraordinarily low investment rates during the severe recession of 1981-1982 rather than a long-term improvement in savings and investment. Benjamin Friedman[2], a Harvard economist, says that attacking the deficits will be necessary before such a long-term change in savings and investment rates can occur. That argument was joined forcefully in the intense debates in the mid-1990s over reducing federal deficits and is being renewed in the wake of the deficits of 2002 to the present.

Supply-Side Economics: Why So Controversial?

That there was a significant recovery of the American economy between 1982 and 1990 is unquestionable. That it constitutes the second longest sustained recovery in the economy's peacetime history is also correct, as is the statement that relatively stable prices (inflation rates of two to four percent) and declining unemployment (5.2 percent in early 1990) accompanied the expansion. In many respects, this would seem to validate the idea that proper coordination between changes in aggregate demand and changes in aggregate supply can produce sustained real income growth *and* relative price stability. Why, then, the controversy over supply-side economics? In substantial measure, the controversy (at least at the macroeconomic level) derives from the large budget deficits of the 1980s that we examined in another chapter. Many supply-siders argued that real income growth could occur with no need to incur such deficits because federal revenues would grow in spite of tax cuts as the economy expanded.

---

2. Friedman, Benjamin M. "Did Regan's 1981 Tax Incentives Work? The Vaunted Investment Boom Is a Bust." *New York Times*, July 7, 1985.

The Laffer Curve: Too Much Taxation Reduces Revenue

Laffer Curve
A theoretical association between various tax rates and the tax revenues collected at each rate.

An early precept upon which supply-side economic arguments were founded was a proposition named for economist Arthur Laffer and called the **Laffer curve**. This is a theoretical association between various tax rates and the tax revenues collected at each rate. We see a hypothetical Laffer curve in Figure 14-2. Note that as tax rates rise from point 0 to point B, tax revenues rise and reach a maximum of $1,000 billion ($1 trillion) at point B. As rates rise above 40 percent, revenues decline. Cutting tax rates from 75 percent to 40 percent could, thus, increase revenues (from $500 billion to $1 trillion). It follows from the curve that there is more than one rate that will generate a specific amount of revenue. Notice that points A and C correspond to the same revenue ($500 billion) but to very different tax rates (25 percent and 75 percent). The reasoning underlying the Laffer curve is that of point (B) in our supply-side elements: taxes are biased against effort, saving and investment. Beyond some point, as they rise, they lead to reduced effort (or diversion of resources to the underground economy) as well as reduced saving and investment. As they are cut, the supply of effort increases as does savings, investment, income, and the tax base.

Figure 14-2
A Hypothetical Laffer Curve for an Economy

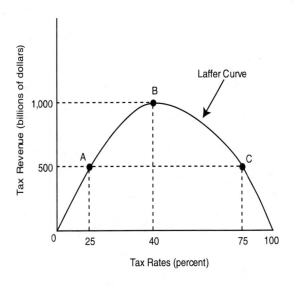

As tax rates rise, tax revenues rise. At (A), a tax rate of 25 percent yields revenues of 500 billion dollars. That same revenue would be yielded however at Point C with a tax rate of 75 percent. Tax revenues are at a maximum ($1,000 billion) at Point B.

A major problem with the Laffer curve is in making it operationally testable. How can we know where point B lies in reality? If we want to produce a certain amount of tax revenue, how can we structure taxes in advance and in the proper way to avoid the disincentives of proceeding past point B? President Reagan and others were apparently persuaded of the validity of the Laffer argument in the case of the 1981 tax cuts. Although there may be some who say investment lags simply postponed the revenue inflow, many others point to the deficits and question the Laffer curve concept itself. A second problem with the Laffer curve is the sensitivity of incentives to work and save and invest when tax rates are reduced. Some empirical studies by critics suggest that these incentive effects will be smaller than supply-siders believe. Thus, tax cuts in a growing economy may primarily expand aggregate demand and may result in budget deficits and inflation. What effects will the tax cuts of 2003 have on aggregate demand and aggregate supply?

Can Discretionary Policy Changes Alter Growth Anyway? Rational Versus Adaptive Expectations

Economists of whatever view agree that expectations play an important role in private economic decision making. Consumers must form expectations about the future including such things as incomes, prices, taxes, interest rates, and inflation rates. Firms must form expectations about future events including many of the same things. Neither group can make informed present decisions without some perspective on the future.

Adaptive Expectations Hypothesis
The argument that decision makers form their view of the future on the basis of actual events that have occurred in the recent past.

Differences exist among economists as to how expectations are formed. A traditional idea is that called the **adaptive expectations hypothesis**, which holds that decision makers form their view of the future on the basis of actual events that have occurred in the recent past. Consider the question of inflation rates. As we noted earlier, annual inflation rates since 1983 have generally ranged from two to four percent. Adaptive expectationists would argue that this range is probably the prevailing view that we have of the immediate future. Suppose now that the monetary authority increases the supply of credit and inflation rises to 10 percent. Wage demands of labor (and other costs) will not likely rise immediately to offset the difference between expected and actual inflation rates. As a result, firms' (real) costs fall, profits rise and investments are likely to increase. In the long run, of course, resource suppliers will adapt to the new inflation rate and adjust their resource price demands upward to offset the change in inflationary expectation. In the short-run, though, monetary (or fiscal) policies could work to stimulate the economy.

Rational Expectations Hypothesis
The argument that decision makers form their view of the future partly on the basis of events in the recent past but also on the basis of present events.

A more recent view associated in particular with Robert Lucas, Jr. and Thomas Sargent of the University of Minnesota, is called the **rational expectations hypothesis**[3]. This hypothesis is that private decision makers form their inflationary expectations partly on the basis of events in the recent past but also on the basis of present events. People not only learn from what *has* happened but from what *is* happening. Combining the two sources of information, they anticipate future events including inflation rates and changes in inflation rates. Suppose that this view is accepted. If the monetary authority increases the supply of credit, private decision makers quickly build this information into their view of the future. If they now expect (without the lag of adaptive expectations) that inflation rates will rise, they adjust their wage and other price demands upward, raising costs, reducing the profitability of investment, and offsetting the investment effects of the macroeconomic efforts to stimulate the economy.

Rational expectationists would argue, thus, that discretionary macroeconomic policy, especially monetary policy, is not only ineffective but even destabilizing. Only if the macroeconomic policy change was greater than expected by firms and consumers would it work. If one accepts this idea, it would seem almost impossible to fool all private decision makers in some systematic way. Discretionary macroeconomic policy would seem to be ruled out, and macroeconomic policy by rule would be called for.

---

3. In McCallum, Bennett. "The Significance of Rational Expectations Theory." *Challenge,* November-December, 1980.

How Influential is Rational Expectations Theory?

There is no doubt that rational expectations theory is some what influential. It has caused some economists to rethink and even question some of their beliefs about the degree of effectiveness of various macroeconomic policy tools (money supply changes, tax cuts, etc.). Many economists, nonetheless, are not prepared to abandon their view that the macroeconomy can successfully be nudged toward more rapid growth or price stability through selectively applied policy changes. As recently as 1981-1982, a powerful dose of monetary restraint did moderate inflation as well as impel the economy into recession. In 1992-1993, a powerful series of monetary growth stimuli does seem to have helped foster an economic recovery. Policy changes, in other words, may work; they just may not work as well as adaptive expectations conclude, but not as poorly as rational expectationists conclude.

Beyond Traditional Keynesian and Classical Policy Arguments

Let's sum up some of the policy controversies that continued throughout the 1970s and 1980s, and continue today between the Keynesians and the classical schools of economic thought. These policy differences focus on three aspects of the modern macroeconomy.

1. *How well do markets work?* Are they competitive, and, if so, competitive enough so that flexibility of resource and product prices will tend to create a tendency toward full employment? Classical economists believe that the answer to both questions is yes. Keynesians, on the other hand, doubt that there is enough flexibility in market prices to eliminate the necessity for discretionary government fiscal and monetary policies designed to increase the economy's move toward full employment.

2. *Will markets eliminate excess supply and excess demand?* Even if there are flexible prices, will markets work efficiently, that is move resources with sufficient mobility to achieve macroeconomic equilibrium quickly? Classical economists, while realizing that there is not perfect mobility (there are barriers such as monopoly, discrimination, and lack of information), argue that there is sufficient mobility to move toward market clearing uses of resources in socially acceptable periods of time. Keynesian economists, by contrast, believe that the barriers to mobility are sufficiently great that excess supply and excess demand can exist in markets for significant periods of time. In their view, this justifies use of government fiscal and monetary policies to eliminate these "bottlenecks" in the macroeconomy.

3. *Expectations, rational or adaptive?* Many classical economists accept the view that consumers and producers in the modern macroeconomy are so knowledgeable about the effects on the aggregate price level of government demand management that such Keynesian policies can have no systematic affects on aggregate demand/ aggregate supply equilibrium. There is, after all, much effort to forecast such effects and react to them. Keynesians, however, argue that such forecasts are imperfect and that there are major variations from the forecasted results. There is room, therefore, say Keynesians, for government policies to affect the macroeconomic equilibrium in a systematic way.

The Post-Keynesians, Today's Contrarians

Post-Keynesians
A school of economists who argue the need for widespread government intervention in the economy because of private market failures.

Incomes Policy
An argument of post-Keynesians that government intervention should include wage and price controls as well as extensive economic planning.

Keynesians and classical economists continue to argue about the scope and effectiveness of discretionary macroeconomic government policies. Neither group, however, argues that the private macroeconomy is so clogged with monopoly and market imperfections that it simply cannot work. Rather, the two groups argue about how serious the imperfections are and whether particular kinds of market intervention by government are warranted and effective. A third small, but vocal group of economists do, however, argue that the modern private macroeconomy is subject to so many such large-scale *structural* problems that recurrent crises characterize its operations. This group called **Post-Keynesians** argue, thus, for permanent government intervention to offset the private market failures they believe to be widespread. They cite price rigidities, monopolization of product and resource markets, and concentrated financial markets as evidence that the economy is "sick" and that their concerns are warranted. Rather than deal with the symptoms, as they believe Keynesians would do, post-Keynesians, in a position akin to that of Marxians, argue for systematic government intervention in the economy. This intervention would take the form of direct regulation of industries and use of tax and expenditure policies to alter the system of incentives about resource usage. Many post-Keynesians argue for an **incomes policy** that would move government's role to one of (1) wage, price and profit controls, and (2) substantial economic planning. Post-Keynesians differ from Marxians in that the former support a private market system that is extensively "managed" by government, while the latter group support direct government ownership of the means of production. Prominent post-Keynesians include the late English economist Joan Robinson and the prominent American economist, the late John Kenneth Galbraith.

SUMMING UP

1 As America entered the 1980s, it had high inflation, rising unemployment and a declining rate of growth in real GDP.

2. Macroeconomic policy under the Reagan administration was partly based on supply-side economics, policies designed to stimulate growth in aggregate supply at stable price levels.

3. The equilibrium level of real income and prices is established where aggregate quantity demanded equals aggregate quantity supplied. In the face of growing aggregate demand, price stability requires incentives to increase aggregate supply through savings and investment.

4. "Supply-siders" have argued that macroeconomic growth and stabilization policy, which had long focused on aggregate demand changes, should shift emphasis to treat changing aggregate supply as an autonomous variable.

5. Supply-side views seem to be founded in four ideas: (a) entitlement programs reduce incentives; their reduction will raise incentives and cut tax burdens, (b) taxes are biased against saving and investment: lower taxes will mean more effort as well as savings and investments, (c) much public regulation to protect consumers and employees, both directly of industries and also social regulation such as pollution controls, has high costs and relatively few benefits,

(d) stimulating aggregate demand through monetary and fiscal policies has created high inflationary expectations and there is a need to lower these expectations.

6. The tax cuts of 1981 were intended to stimulate saving and investment and to redirect resources away from the underground economy of non-taxed transactions Marginal tax rates were cut in 1981 and again in 1987. The tax cuts of 2001, 2002 and 2003 are similar in structure.

7. There was an increase in investment rates after 1982; it is unclear how much of that increase is attributable to the tax cuts.

8. The main controversy over supply-side economic policies is not in the post-1981 sustained growth or relative price stability but rather in the large federal deficits that have resulted.

9. According to the Laffer curve, tax rates can be so high that disincentives to work, save and invest set in and actually reduce tax revenues as rates rise beyond some level. The Laffer curve apparently had some influence in the 1981 tax cuts.

10. A major problem with the Laffer curve is implementing it. We do not know whether the cuts in 1981 raised tax revenues through incentive effects or through aggregate demand effects. What we have observed is that revenues did not rise as rapidly as expenditures and large deficits resulted. Another problem is with the sensitivity of work and savings incentives to tax cuts. Supply-siders believe the incentives to be very sensitive, critics disagree.

11. Expectations play an important role in private decisions by consumers and by firms. The adaptive expectations hypothesis holds that expectations are formed by people on the basis of recent events. Macroeconomic policy changes, thus, can be influential in affecting savings and investment in the short-run because resource prices are based on current expectations and are not immediately adjusted upward in the face of rising rates of inflation.

12. Expectations, say some economists, are formed according to the rational expectations hypothesis, that is, on the basis not only of recent events but also current events. Combining both sets of information, private decision makers anticipate the consequences of current macroeconomic policy changes such as the higher inflation that may result from a growing money supply. Thus, resource prices adjust quickly and negate any stimulative effect from the policy change. Discretionary policy does not work; policy by rule is called for.

13. Rational expectations theory has been influential. It still appears to many economists, however, that discretionary policy changes such as the 1981 curtailment of the money supply and the monetary policy changes of the early 1990s worked, at least in the short run.

14. Keynesians and classical economists argue about the scope and effectiveness of government macroeconomic policies. Post-Keynesians, however, argue that widespread failures in the private economy make necessary permanent and extensive government intervention in a modern macroeconomy. This intervention, they argue, should take the form of direct and detailed regulation of industries as well as an incomes policy which would involve wage, price and profit controls. Post-Keynesians differ from Marxists in that they do not argue for public ownership of the means of production.

KEY TERMS

Adaptive expectations hypothesis
Incomes policy
Laffer curve
Post-Keynesians
Rational expectations hypothesis
Supply-side economics
Tax wedge
Underground economy

QUESTIONS

1. What were the general macroeconomic conditions of the American economy in the early 1980s?

2. What is meant by the term "supply-side economics?" What kinds of macroeconomic policies do supply-siders argue for?

3. In the face of growing aggregate demand, what is necessary to ensure price stability?

4. On what four propositions are supply-side economic views founded?

5. What were the intended effects of the 1981 tax cuts? What are the intended effects of the tax cuts of 2002, and 2003?

6. Were the 1981 tax cuts successful? If so, in what sense?

7. What is the source of the major controversies surrounding the supply-side policies of the 1980s?

8. In the figure below a hypothetical Laffer curve is drawn. Answer the following questions about the curve.

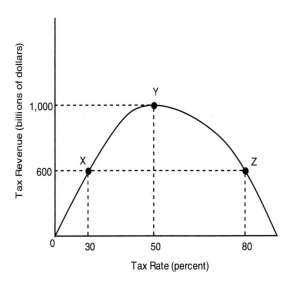

a. What is the Laffer curve argument about the association between tax rates and tax revenues?
b. At what tax rate do revenues reach a maximum?
c. Why are there two tax rates (30 percent, 80 percent) that yield the same revenue?
d. What causes tax revenues to decline beyond point Y?
e. What are the principal problems with using the Laffer curve as a basis for tax policy?

9. Explain the difference between the rational expectations hypothesis and the adaptive expectations hypothesis? Under which of the two may short-run charges in discretionary macroeconomic policy be successful?

10. What is the view of Keynesians and classical economists about the role of government in direct management of the economy?

SECTION IV:

International Trade

Chapter 15: Patterns of International Trade

Closed Economy
An economy that engages only in domestic economic activities.

Open Economy
An economy that engages in both domestic and international activities

Throughout this book, we have looked at the many facets of a single market economy. For the most part, we treated that economy as *closed* or as one that engages in domestic economic activities only. The purpose of this was part of the larger approach of the text; to begin with simple principles and then gradually to make them more general and more complex until they could shed light on a wide range of economic problems

Now, let us look at the American economy as *open* or as one that engages in both domestic and international economic activities. This means that America not only trades with other nations, but also must finance that trade. In the early years of the twenty–first century, international trade by the United States is not only growing, but also becoming a more important part of its economy. Arguments have flared again, as they have any times in our history, over the conditions under which this country should trade with others. One thing is clear, however: with combined exports and imports, in the year 2000, of more than two and one third *trillion* dollars, the U.S. is the world's largest trading nation and a nation for which trade has again become a key sector of its economy.

What Makes Up Trade?

Exports
Commodities and services sold to other nations.

Imports
Commodities and services bought from other nations.

Trade consists of **exports**, commodities and services sold to other nations, and **imports**, commodities and services bought from other nations. Suppose that a dealer in San Francisco imports a Toyota. The price the importer pays (plus any shipping charges paid to foreign shippers) is added to the total of U.S. imports. Similarly, when a Japanese grain dealer imports American wheat, the payments that U.S. wheat sellers receive (plus any payments to our own shippers) are added to the total of our exports.[1]

---

1. Although the 2008-2009 financial downturn temporarily slowed this growth.

Visible Items
Those physical commodities that are exported or imported by a nation.

Invisible Items
The services including financial services associated with exports and imports by a nation

International trade, thus, is made up of both **visible items** and **invisible items**. The visible items are the commodities (cars, wheat, television sets, petroleum, machinery, and so on) that are exported and imported. Invisible items are the services, including financial services (services of exporters and importers, ship rentals, cost of financing, and so on) which are exported and imported.

How Important is Trade to America?

Only a few decades ago many might have said: "Look, the U.S. is a big nation; it produces a great variety of goods and services and has vast natural resources. Surely trade with other nations isn't all that important to us. Why devote a whole chapter to it?" Now, hardly a day passes without reference in the media to the importance of foreign trade to our economy and to the jobs of its people. Deficits in trade (imports > exports) are front page news to which stock markets react. Negotiations between the U.S. and China over further opening of Chinese markets to American exports are both economically and politically sensitive. Arguments about "free trade" versus "fair trade" are not merely academic issues. International trade and the financing of that trade have, by the early 21st century, become vital issues and seem likely to increase in importance as the nation continues to progress into the remaining part of the century.

America's Balance of Trade and Net Foreign Trade

It is worthwhile to repeat that both commodities and services are traded internationally. Commodity exports (X) (wheat, computers, and the like) and commodity imports (M) (autos, textiles, and the like) determine the **commodity balance of trade** so that when only commodities are considered:

Commodity Balance of Trade (X-M)
The value of commodity exports less the value of commodity imports.

$$X - M = \text{Commodity Balance of Trade}$$

When the commodity balance of trade is positive (X > M), a nation is selling more of its goods and services abroad than it is purchasing from other nations. This positive balance is commonly referred to as a "favorable" balance of trade. When the commodity balance is negative (X < M), the nation is purchasing more goods and services from abroad than it is selling to other economies; the negative balance is commonly referred to as an "unfavorable" balance of trade. While one should be cautious about reading too much into the terms "favorable" and "unfavorable," it is well to remember that differences between exports and imports (sales and purchases) must be financed each year by every nation.

Net Foreign Trade (NFT)
A measure of the trade balance that includes services. It is measured by taking the commodity balance and adding in net services (service exports – service imports).

When services (transportation, insurance, financial services, and the like) are included in the balance, however, we arrive at a measure of **net foreign trade**, or one which subtracts imports from exports (X – M), but adds in net services (S_N) (service exports – service imports). Thus net foreign trade is:

$$(X - M) + S_N = \text{Net Foreign Trade (NFT)}$$

NFT, thus, is a measure of the balance on both goods and services. Clearly, one way in which a deficit in the commodity balance (X < M) may be financed is through a positive net services (service exports > service imports) balance.

Table 15-1

U.S. Exports, Imports, Net Services, and Net Foreign Trade, 1960-2008 (billions of dollars)

Year	Merchandise Exports (X)	Merchandise Imports (M)	Net Services (S_N)	Net Foreign Trade* $(X - M) + S_N$
1960	19.7	14.8	-1.4	3.5
1965	26.5	21.5	-.3	4.7
1970	42.5	40.0	-.3	2.2
1975	107.1	98.2	3.5	12.4
1980	224.3	249.8	6.1	-19.4
1985	215.9	338.1	0	-122.1
1990	389.3	498.3	31.0	-78.8
1995	575.8	749.5	73.9	-99.8
1996	612.0	802.6	82.8	-107.8
1997	678.4	876.5	63.2	-107.8
1998	670.4	917.1	68.1	-178.6
1999	684.6	1,030.0	73.9	- 261.8
2001	718.7	1,164.1	62.5	- 382.9
2008	1,276,994	2,117,245	142	-698.2

Source: *Economic Report of the President*, 2010.

*Merchandise plus Services (may not add because of rounding)

www.oecd.org
For more information on foreign trade visit this web site.

What has been the record of the American economy in recent decades regarding the commodity balance and net foreign trade? From Table 15-1, several trends may be seen in both the commodity balance and in net foreign trade. From 1960 to 1975, America had a "favorable" commodity balance (X > M), even though there were typically small deficits in net services (service exports < service imports). Overall, net foreign trade, though typically small, was positive, reaching $12.4 billion in 1975. After 1975, America had consistently "unfavorable" commodity trade balances (X < M) reaching nearly 700 billion in in 2008. At the same time, after 1985, it began experiencing large positive net service balances (service exports > service imports), which partially offset the commodity deficits. In 2002, however, the NFT deficit grew to $406.9 billion and by 2004 had reached $665.4 billion. Exports, however, grew after 2004 as the declining value of the dollar stimulated exports. The dramatic growth of the average NFT deficit (after 1980) seems to have come about because of: *Changes in exchange rates.* Between 1980 and mid 1985, U.S. dollar/foreign currency exchange rates soared. Against the currencies of America's major trading partners, the dollar increased in value almost 70 percent. Goods imported into the U.S. became relatively cheaper while American exports became relatively more expensive. Our rising quantity demanded of imports and the declining quantity demanded of our exports pushed X − M to ever larger negative figures. After mid 1985, the dollar declined against the currencies of our major trading partners, a trend that has continued into 2009. Because of this, export growth was strong, more than doubling between 1985 and 1993. From 2003 into 2009, the dollar again declined but export growth has been weak because of low economic growth among many US trading partners.

Table 15-2

Export of Goods and Services as a Percentage of GDP, Selected Countries, 2008

Country	Exports as Percentage of GDP 2008
Netherlands	61
Canada	41
Germany	37
New Zealand	33
Spain	31
Italy	30
France	29
United Kingdom	27
Japan	14
United States	12.8

Source: IMF, International Financial Statistics, 2009.

Real Income Growth. In the face of the tax changes and other stimulative actions from 1982 on, the American economy and the real incomes of its citizens grew (except for the recession years of the early 1990s, the early 2000s and the recession years of 2008 and 2009). Since Colonial days, Americans have had a strong (income-related) taste for imported goods. A growing demand for imports, even in the face of rising prices, added fuel to the large deficits, which were only partially offset by positive net service balances.

But is Trade as Important to us as to others?

Perhaps you are saying, "All right, granted that foreign trade *can* have an effect on the U.S. economy, and will continue to do so in the twenty-first century; is the effect really important compared to the other factors that influence jobs and the welfare of Americans?" One way to answer the question is to look at how large a part exports or sales abroad are of the GDP or final value of all goods and services produced in America. Table 15-2 shows that for the U.S., exports make up a smaller percentage of GDP than they do for many of the other nations. Trade today constitutes only about 12.8 percent of U.S. total output, but for the other nations, which account for a large part of the world's trade, the figure ranges up to 61 percent (Netherlands).

Do these figures mean that trade is relatively unimportant to the U.S.? The answer, emphatically, is *no*, for the following reasons:

Growth in importance. The percentage of total output made up of exports has almost doubled since 1970. The 12.8 percent represents an important part of the demand for U.S. output and thus the derived demand for labor (jobs) and other resources. If this foreign market for U.S. goods were to disappear, it would mean not just an 12.8 percent reduction in GDP, but a much larger reduction.

Greater firm efficiency. The additional demand created by trade enables American firms to operate more efficiently and to achieve economies of scale that might not otherwise be possible. Because of this international trade, manufacturers are able to lower their costs. This means not only potentially lower prices to consumers (both for exported goods and for goods produced in the U.S. from exported inputs), but also more profitable investment opportunities and demand for labor (jobs).

Reversal of historical decline. The growth of export importance is interesting historically. Early in U.S. history, trade was very important to the economy of the U.S. Then as the U.S. came of age the importance of foreign trade declined. Now there is a clear resurgence of international trade as a mainstay of the U.S. economy.

Importance of raw material imports. One big reason for the increased importance of trade is the growing dependence of the U.S. on imports of raw materials. The U.S. now imports more than 50 percent of the petroleum it uses (as late as the 1950s it was an exporter of oil). And although the U.S. has huge mineral resources, it must import 100 percent of the chromium and tin it uses, as well as between 90 and 100 percent of such minerals as cobalt, manganese, platinum, and nickel. In other words, the U.S. *needs* foreign trade for the sake of our industrial economy.

Of course the U.S. must, as we noted earlier, pay the countries from which it imports in their own currencies. Japanese business firms want yen, not dollars, so that they can pay their workers and other costs. In turn, to earn these foreign currencies, the U.S. must export its own goods and services as well as import capital.

The Gains from Trade

Earlier in our history there were those who argued for isolationism, both politically and economically. Today, we are seeing a resurgence of such arguments. Today there might be some who would say: "Apart from those needed minerals (and we can probably find substitutes even for many of them in the long run), I fail to see that we are necessarily better off because of trading. After all, we can use macroeconomic policy to achieve full employment, even without trade. Surely if we made the effort, we could produce just about everything we want. Let's keep the jobs at home in the U.S. Where is the advantage to be had from trade?"

The answer to the above question is not obvious. The U.S. is among a few fortunate nations that probably could, from a technical point of view, achieve **autarky**, economic self-sufficiency. Most food can be grown in the U.S., even tropical fruits. The nation could achieve self-sufficiency in energy too, if it chose to do so. But is complete self-sufficiency necessarily desirable for

Autarky
Economic self-sufficiency.

the U.S. or for any nation? Virtually all economists say no, for reasons we shall now examine.

Trade and Comparative Advantage

In discussing the reasons for trade among nations, one immediately encounters two terms: the **absolute advantage** and the **comparative advantage** that each nation has in producing things. We can best define these terms by example.

Absolute Advantage
The ability of a given nation to produce all commodities more cheaply (that is, using up few resources per unit of output) than any other nation with which it might trade.

Let's say that you are a graduate engineer, and you set up a personal small business of your own. You have an assistant named Pat Bloggs, who does the filing and other routine jobs in your office. You pay Bloggs $30 a day to perform these tasks, while you, as a professional engineer, earn $100 a day. After a particularly hellish week, in which drawings have gone to the wrong firm, you review the operation of the office. You realize that you can do these routine chores much more efficiently than Bloggs. Thus you have an *absolute advantage* over Bloggs. Should you fire Bloggs and do the job yourself? Comparative advantage says no. The $100 a day you earn as an engineer reflects your marginal revenue productivity (MRP); the $30 reflects Bloggs' *MRP*. Therefore, you should stick to your specialty of engineering, because in this you have a *comparative advantage*. In other words, you are relatively more productive as an engineer than as an office assistant. There is a lesson to be learned here. Even a person with an absolute advantage in doing *every* task should specialize in that field in which her or his comparative advantage lies.

Comparative Advantage
A situation in which a nation is relatively more efficient at producing some goods than at producing others, compared with the production capabilities of other nations with which it trades.

We demonstrated how this principle works when we were discussing the market system of a single country: for efficiency's sake, resources should move to their most productive alternative uses. A city could hire engineers to sweep the streets, and they would probably do a great job. But it would be foolish for a society to employ its engineers in this way, since their comparative efficiency is greater when they are building roads, bridges, and offshore drilling rigs.

Now let's apply this idea of comparative advantage to trade between nations. In the real word, international trade involves many nations and thousands of commodities and services. To keep things simple in this illustration, though, we shall deal with only two nations, the U.S. and Honduras. We will examine the trade in only 2 commodities that each country can produce, tractors and bananas.

Discussing additional goods and countries would not change the basic principles; it would just make the relationships more complex.

Table 15-3 shows the production-possibilities (PP) schedules for the U.S. and Honduras. Each country is capable of producing both bananas and tractors. However, note that the rate at which tractors can be traded off for bananas (that is, the rate at which the output of tractors decreases as the output of bananas increases) is very different for the two countries. The reason is that there are different resource endowments in the two countries including climate and human capital.

Figure 15-1 illustrates the PP for the two countries. Unlike the PP curves we saw earlier, these "curves" are straight lines. That is, they reflect a constant rate of exchange of tractors for bananas (we are assuming that the cost of producing each item is constant). Later in this chapter we will discuss PP curves that are concave to the origin and reflect increasing real cost.

Table 15-3

Production-Possibilities Schedules, United States and Honduras (hypothetical)

United States		Honduras	
Units of Tractors	Units of Bananas	Units of Tractors	Units of Bananas
50	0	0	100
40	5	5	80
30	10	10	60
20	15	15	40
10	20	20	20
0	25	25	0

Figure 15-1

Production Possibilities for the United States and Honduras

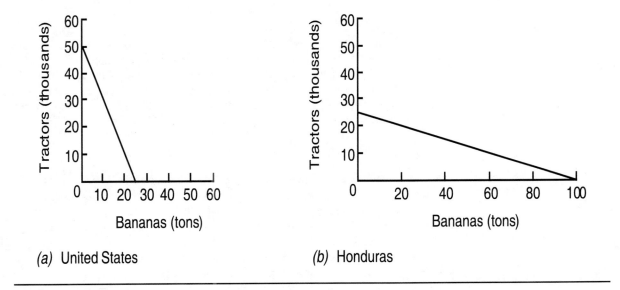

(a) United States (b) Honduras

The Terms of Trade

From the tables above it can be seen that the U.S. should, for the sake of trade gains, specialize in producing tractors, and Honduras should specialize in bananas. Now the real **terms of trade** (the relation for a nation at which its exports exchange for imports) must be decided. That is, a ratio must be determined at which Honduran bananas will be exchanged for U.S. tractors. There must be an advantage for each country. The Americans must get more than 1/2 unit of bananas for each unit of their tractors, and the Hondurans more than 1 unit of tractors for 4 units of their bananas.[2]

Each country must get more for its products in the world market than it would if it had sold them domestically. If both countries are to benefit, the actual exchange rate must lie between 1T = 1/2 B (preferred by Honduras) and 1T = 4B (preferred by the U.S.).

Terms of Trade
The rate at which a nation's exports and imports exchange. In real terms, the number of its exports necessary to obtain its imports. In financial terms, the ratio of export prices to import prices x 100.

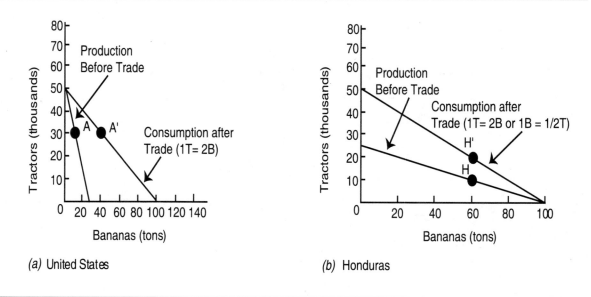

(a) United States

(b) Honduras

The exact terms of trade will depend on the market demand for both products. Market demand depends on the degree to which one can substitute other products for either commodity, and on the relationship of demand to supply. If there are no good substitutes for tractors, and if demand for them is large relative to supply, the exchange rate (terms of trade) will be in favor of the U.S. If conditions are reversed, the terms of trade will be favorable to Honduras.

Gains from Trade

Suppose that the exchange rate moves to 1T = 2B. Figure 15-2 shows what happens to production and consumption in both countries. Look at the replotted PP curves of both countries. The dark lines (called consumption-possibilities curves), indicating consumption after trade, show what each country can consume if it specializes in the good in which it has a comparative advantage and exports part of its output. We can see first how this process of mutually beneficial exchange occurs through an arithmetic example. Table 15-4 shows what happens when one tractor can be exchanged for two tons of bananas (1T=2B). That exchange rate is the same as one ton of bananas for one half a tractor (1B=1/2T). Each country benefits by taking some of the output of the good in which it has a comparative advantage (tractors for the U.S., bananas for Honduras) and exchanging with the other country for the good in which it does not have a comparative advantage (bananas for the U.S., tractors for Honduras).

To illustrate the trade benefits, let us assume that the before-trade production and consumption bundles for U.S. and Honduras are A (T=30 and B=10) and H (T=10 and B=60), respectively. Let us further assume that each country wishes to maintain the before-trade level of consumption of the good in which it has a comparative advantage (T= 30 for U.S. and B=60 for Honduras),

---

2. We are working here with the real terms of trade. In reality, of course, it is the prices of exports and imports that determine a nation's (financial) terms of trade.

but increase the consumption of the other good through trade. With complete specialization, U.S. produces 50 units of tractor, keeps 30 units for domestic consumption, and exports the extra 20 units to Honduras in exchange for 40 units of banana. Similarly, Honduras produces 100 units of banana, keeps 60 units for domestic consumption, and exports the extra 40 units to U.S. in exchange for 20 units of tractor. The after-trade bundles for U.S. and Honduras are A? (T=30 and B=40) and H? (T=20 and B=60), respectively. These bundles, as can be seen from Figure 15-2, lie outside the pre-trade production possibilities lines. This means that trade made a previously unattainable bundle attainable.

Table 15-4

(Hypothetical) Consumption Possibilities Schedules after trade, United States and Honduras

United States		Honduras	
Units of Tractors	Units of Bananas with trade	Units of Tractors with trade	Units of Bananas
50	0	0	100
40	20	10	80
30	40	20	60
20	60	30	40
10	80	40	20
0	100	50	0

The important result that Table 15-3 together with Table 15-4 and Figure 15-2 enables us to see is:

As long as a nation has a comparative advantage in producing some things, it should specialize in producing those things. It should then export part of the goods for which it has a comparative advantage and import goods in which it has a comparative disadvantage. By so doing, it will increase the total utility of both nations.

This is true even if the nation has an absolute advantage in producing everything it consumes.

What Determines Comparative Advantage?

Since we have shown that comparative advantage is a mutually advantageous basis for trade, we need to identify the factors that determine a nation's comparative advantage. Also we want to ask the question: Are nations locked into a particular comparative-advantage position, or do their positions change?

First, *nations have differing comparative advantages,* for the following reasons:

Different endowments. Different nations have different endowments of natural resources, both in quantity and quality. For example, nations such as the U.S.,

Canada, Russia, and the People's Republic of China have large quantities (although different proportions) of relatively high-grade resources (petroleum, mineral deposits, topsoil, and so on).

Different physical features. Different nations have different physical features (mild or extreme climate, many or few natural harbors).

Different stages of development. Different nations are at different stages of development of markets. For example, the U.S., Japan, and the countries in Western Europe have well-developed capital markets, reflecting large supplies of savings that can be transformed through investment into capital, including human capital (skills and abilities resulting from investment in education). In other countries, markets may be either rudimentary or nonexistent.

Different supplies of productive factors. Different nations have different supplies of factors of production, including labor. For example, China and many other less-developed countries have large supplies of labor relative to capital. A country tends to specialize in products (or services) that intensively use those resources in which it is relatively rich.

Second, the *comparative advantages of nations change.* Nations are not locked into a position with respect to comparative advantage. For example, the U.S. began as a nation rich in land and short of capital and labor. Today, it is relatively rich in capital and land, and relatively short of labor. (This has nothing to do with our unemployment rate. It means that as the U.S. presently produces things, even at full employment, capital and land are abundant relative to labor.) Up until the Civil War, the U.S. specialized in land-intensive agricultural exports (cotton, tobacco, rice, and so on). Today, it specializes in exports that are capital-intensive and land-intensive. For example, in 2000 more than 45 percent of U.S. exports were comprised of capital (non-automotive) goods. Another 10 percent were grains and cereals, which are land-intensive. Thus, almost half of U.S. exports were derived from processes that were capital- and land-intensive. On the other hand, the U.S. imports many things (coffee, cocoa, inexpensive textiles, handicrafts) that are relatively labor-intensive. (Although automobiles, steel, and other such goods are exceptions.)

Demand Considerations

As we have seen, domestic economic trade is based on the benefits of voluntary exchange. International trade, whether between nations or, as is most often the case, between individuals, is also based on the expected benefits of voluntary exchange. We saw in Figure 15-2 that supply (cost-based) considerations make it possible for nations, through exchange, to consume more with trade. There are also important benefits to trade that derive from demand considerations. The structure of demand differs greatly from one country to another as well as from one part of the world to another. The primary reason for these differences lies in the diversity of tastes and preferences that exists among individuals within countries as well as between different nations. Consider tastes in food and clothing. Americans (both North Americans and Latin Americans) prefer coffee; the English and many Asians prefer tea. The Japanese prefer fish; Americans have a much stronger taste for beef, pork and chicken. Out of these differences arises a willingness to pay prices for goods and services that differs substantially from one area to another and thus gains to be had in exporting.

There are many arguments about changing the comparative advantages of countries, especially about whether comparative-advantage trade tends to help the poor-trading nations to develop. In the application in this chapter, we will examine some of these arguments.

Increasing Costs and Other Cautions

In the case involving the U.S. and Honduras, we concluded that each would produce only its most advantageous good, tractors or bananas. We showed that bilateral exchange between the two nations would make both better off in terms of the quantities of the 2 goods available for consumption. There are some qualifications to the argument, however.

Increasing costs. As each country reallocates its resources from the disadvantageous good to the advantageous one, it will run into *increasing costs*. For example, as the U.S. produces more tractors, the cost (in bananas not produced) may rise, until it reaches a point at which it would be better off if it produced some bananas of its own rather than always exchanging tractors for Honduran bananas. Honduras, whose costs of producing bananas also rise, may be better off producing some of its own tractors. The point is that increasing costs cause international specialization to be less than complete.

Employment effects. When two countries specialize in making things in which they have a comparative advantage and then trade with each other, achieving the greatest possible production, we assume that there is full employment in the trading nations. However, at times this trade means reallocating resources and, when this results in unemployment, the countries' output may fall below the PP curve. So there are some possible undesirable effects for a country from trade. But there are various macroeconomic (fiscal and monetary) tools that a nation can use to achieve its employment goals, and there are microeconomic tools that can be used to reallocate resources in efficient resource markets (job retraining, for example). Thus, many economists feel that the risk of creating temporary unemployment is not a compelling reason to forego trade.

Assumption of competitive trade. The principle of comparative advantage depends heavily on *competition* in international trade. If the tractors are produced by a monopolistic firm but the bananas are exported by competitive firms, Honduras may not fully reap the benefits of trade. If monopolistic export boards (perhaps government ones) negotiate the terms of trade (American wheat for Russian oil, for example), one cannot tell what the outcome will be. This is also true of bilateral monopoly. The end result depends on the relative skills and bargaining strengths of the participants.

Externalities. If there are *externalities*, the terms of trade may not reflect the real costs of production. The countries may produce and exchange either too little or too much. (Suppose that the tractor factories pollute the water and air and that their costs do not reflect the added social costs of cleaning up the environment.)

Prices may not reflect relative scarcity. The principle of comparative advantage depends on the fact that relative prices (the American price of tractors and the Honduran price of bananas) reflect relative scarcities of resources in each nation. If the prices do not reflect these scarcities, an international (as well as domestic) misallocation of resources occurs. Suppose that the U.S. subsidizes the tractor industry. Then international prices of tractors (the terms of trade) would not reflect underlying relative scarcity and companies would produce more tractors than is efficient (and trade them). (Americans would, in effect, be producing tractors when they should be producing bananas.)

Figure 15-3
How a Protective Tariff Works

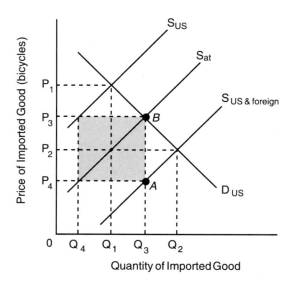

Figure 15-3 illustrates the effects of a protective tariff. The domestic supply of the good is S_{US} and the domestic demand is D_{US}. Without trade equilibrium price is P_1 and Q_1 of the good is sold. If free trade in the good occurs, imports increase the domestic supply to $S_{US \& foreign}$. As a result of trade, price declines to P_2 and Q_2 of the good is sold. Both the decline in price and the increased consumption of the good ($Q_2 - Q_1$) are benefits to consumers attributable to trade. If a protective tariff of AB is imposed, supply declines to S_{at}, with the tariff, price rises to P_3 and quantity sold declines to Q_3. Both the increase in price (P_2 to P_3) and the decrease in consumption of the good ($Q_2 - Q_3$) are costs to consumers attributable to protectionism.

Protectionism
Efforts by governments to protect domestic firms and industries from the competition of imported goods

Protectionism. The biggest obstacle to trade being conducted according to comparative advantage is **protectionism**, the efforts of governments to protect domestic firms or industries from the competition of imported goods. Consequently, there has been little completely free trade in modern times (or indeed at any time). Let us now look at how nations may protect trade and the arguments surrounding these practices.

The Means of Protection

There are two principal means by which countries usually intervene to protect their own industries from overseas competition: tariffs and quotas.

Tariffs
Taxes levied on imported goods

Tariffs
The most common means of protection are **tariffs**, which are taxes levied on imported goods. Figure 15-3 shows how a protective tariff works and also shows its effects on trade and prices. Before trade begins, the U.S. demand for bicycles is D_{US} and the supply is S_{US}. Equilibrium price is P_1 ($Q_1 D_{US} = Q_1 S_{US}$). At this price, Q_1 of bicycles are sold. (Presumably, bicycles are goods in which this country has a comparative *dis*advantage.) Now trade opens up. The U.S. begins to import foreign bicycles (from Japan, Italy, and France). The supply of bicycles increases to $S_{US \& foreign}$. Equilibrium; price falls to P_2, and Q_2 bicycles are sold. The supply increases until the price of bicycles in the U.S. is equal to the price of bicycles abroad (not including transportation costs). As long as the American price is higher, foreign producers will continue to export

bicycles in order to sell in the more profitable American market. Now suppose that the bicycle manufacturers complain to Congress, as the Bicycle Manufacturers' Association did in the 1970s. They argued as follows:

> *A deluge of imported bicycles into the U.S. has increased imports from 19.8 percent of our market in 1964 to 37.1 percent in 1972. We don't feel our business should go down the drain. Standards must be established that would automatically impose restrictions on imports competing with American products.... This is not protectionism.*

Let's say that the bicycle lobby convinces Congress that this argument is valid, so that Congress and the President levy a tax, a tariff, on imported bicycles. The tax which is equal to AB in Figure 15-3 increases the cost of importing bicycles and reduces the supply to S_{at} (supply after tariff). The new equilibrium price is P_3, which is higher than the pre-tariff price (by $P_3 - P_2$). The number of bicycles sold goes down (by $Q_2 - Q_3$) to Q_3. Note that part of the gain to consumers from all the foreign bicycles coming into the country is eliminated. If the tariff had been higher, imports might have ceased altogether, and supply might have fallen back to S_{US}. Then price would have gone back up to P_1 (with only Q_1 sold).

So the tariff hurts consumers, because now they must buy bicycles at a price higher than the free market international price, and they are getting fewer bicycles. The tariff also hurts foreign bicycle manufacturers, because the net price they receive (after paying the tariff) is P_4. In addition, the tariff hurts U.S. firms that may use the product as an input (messenger services and the like). The total revenue to the U.S. government from the tariff is shown by the shaded area. This is the unit tariff per bicycles ($P_3 - P_4$) times the number of bicycles imported ($Q_3 - Q_4$). (At price P_3, American manufacturers supply Q_4.)

Cartoon Feature Syndicate

"He wasn't even warm, was he, Mom?"

Figure 15-4
The Burden of a Tariff with Inelastic Demand

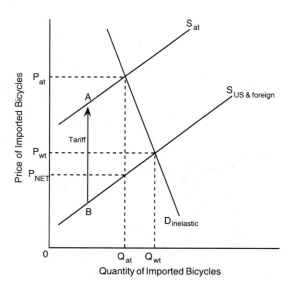

The burden of a tariff is related to the elasticity of demand for the imported good. Figure 15-4 illustrates the relationship for the case in which demand is price *in*elastic. Without a tariff, supply is S US & foreign, price without tariff is P_{wt}, and quantity sold before the tariff is Q_{wt}. A tariff of AB on the imported good decreases supply after tariff to S_{at}. As a result, price rises to P_{at} and quantity sold declines to Q_{at}. There is a large increase in price (P_{wt} to P_{at}) relative to the decline in sales ($Q_{wt} - Q_{at}$). Most of the burden of the tariff is borne by consumers in the form of higher prices, though foreign producers also are burdened by the lower net price (P_{NET} as opposed to P_{wt}).

Figure 15-5
The Burden of a Tariff with Elastic Demand

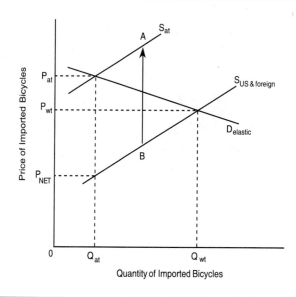

Elasticity and the Burden of the Tariff

You may recognize that the burden of the tariff (either the higher price to consumers or the lower net price to sellers) is distributed on the basis of the price elasticity of demand for the imported good. We see in Figure 15-4 and Figure 15-5 how the distributive burden of the tariff is related to elasticity. There may be both a *consumer burden*, the portion of a tariff paid by consumers in higher prices, and a *producer burden,* the portion of a tariff paid by importers in a lower net price and reduced sales of the imported good.

In Figure 15-4 the demand for the imported good is price inelastic, implying that poor substitutes exist for the good or that consumers spend relatively little of their incomes on it. With unrestricted trade, the bicycle market clears at Q_{wt} (quantity without tariff) and at price, P_{wt} (price without tariff). After tariff AB is levied, supply is reduced from $S_{US\ \&\ foreign}$ to S_{at} (supply after tariff). Now the market is cleared at Q_{at} and P_{at} (quantity and price after tariff). Most of the market burden ($P_{at} - P_{wt}$) is borne by consumers in the form of higher prices but part, $Q_{wt} - Q_{at}$ is borne by producers in the form of reduced sales and a lower net price (P_{NET}). Consumers absorb most of the burden. We see in Figure 15-5 how the burden of a tariff is distributed when the demand for the imported good is price elastic. Before the tariff, with elastic demand $D_{elastic}$ and supply $S_{U.S.\ \&\ foreign}$, price is P_{wt} and the quantity sold of the good is Q_{wt}. When the same amount of tariff AB is now imposed, costs of importing the good rise, and supply declines to S_{at} resulting in a higher price (P_{wt} to P_{at}) and a decrease in the quantity of the good sold (Q_{wt} to Q_{at}) and a lower net price (P_{NET}) to foreign producers. There is a large decrease in quantity sold relative to the increase in price and most of the burden of the tariff falls on firms importing the good. The demand for the imported good is price elastic; implying that relatively good substitutes for the imported good exist or that consumers spend a significant part of their income on it. With unrestricted trade, the market clears at Q_{wt} and P_{wt}. After tariff AB is imposed, supply falls from $S_{US\ \&\ foreign}$ to S_{at} and the market clears at Q_{at} and price P_{at}. The consumer burden ($P_{at} - P_{wt}$) is relatively small while the producer burden ($Q_{wt} - Q_{at}$) and the lower net price ($P_{wt} - P_{NET}$) is relatively large. Clearly, when demand is elastic, most of the burden falls on producers in the form of reduced sales and lower net prices.

Is anyone better off as a result of the tariff? Yes, the American bicycle manufacturers are. They do not have to pay the tariff, so they keep the full price (P_{at}) of their product. This is higher than P_{NET}, which is the price foreign makers have after they pay the tariff. The federal government is better off by the amount of revenue. The tariff, in other words, represents a loss in income by consumers, which is transferred to the government and to protected domestic firms.

Beyond the burden, two points about tariffs should be emphasized: (1) When the government imposes a tariff, it makes a *net addition to domestic monopoly power.* In our example, bicycle manufacturers had been getting a competitively set international price for their product. Now they are getting a more monopolistically established price instead. (Though in this case the government, rather than private business, is the agent that creates the monopoly influence.) Thus, tariffs defeat our objective of having a competitive market system. (2) When the government imposes a general tariff (or other trade restriction), it *reduces the number of good substitutes that consumers have for domestically produced goods.* This, in turn, may make the demand *more price inelastic* and (because it increases monopoly power) may cause prices in the long run to rise by an even greater amount than the amount of the tariff itself.

Import Quotas

Import Quotas
Restrictions imposed by governments on the quantity of a good that may be imported.

The second major means governments use to protect their industries against competition from abroad is **import quotas**, that is, restrictions on the quantity of goods that may be imported. In one way, the effects of quotas are much like those of tariffs. Look again at Figure 15-3. Suppose that Congress, instead of enacting a tariff, had said that only $Q_3 - Q_4$ bicycles could come into the U.S. Supply would still have dropped to S_{at} (or we could call this S_{aq} to stand for supply after quota). Total supply (Q_3) would have been domestic supply (Q_4) plus foreign supply ($Q_3 - Q_4$). Consumers would be affected just as adversely and U.S. bicycle makers would still get the higher price, P_3. The difference is that *a quota is not a revenue-producing device* (the shaded area would not exist), so the government would not get any extra tax revenue. Foreign bicycle makers would get the same price as domestic makers, P_3 (less transportation costs, of course), and domestic consumers would carry the burden of the quota.

Import Embargo
A prohibition, imposed by government, against importing certain goods.

The most extreme form of a quota is an **import embargo**, which is an absolute prohibition against importing a good. If Congress had imposed an embargo on foreign bicycles, supply would have reverted to S_{US}. Price would have risen to P_1 (domestic producers would have been restored to whatever monopoly power they originally had).

Embargoes are relatively rare in American history. In 1808, during the Napoleonic wars, President Jefferson imposed one. After 1962, the U.S. government embargoed trade with Cuba (no Cuban cigars, sugar, or rum). Until the 1970s, there was a U.S. embargo on trade with the People's Republic of China. It is worth noting that when embargoes are lifted, they are usually lifted in the interest of political expediency (détente, for example) rather than in the interests of free trade. Embargoes are usually short-term political penalties against antagonistic nations. In 1996, the decades long embargo against Cuba was intensified after tensions rose between the two governments.

Export Quotas: Rational Ignorance by Consumers?

As we have seen, quotas have effects similar to tariffs except that they do not generate revenues for governments. In protecting domestic producers, governments sometimes assign shares of their domestic markets to foreign exporters. Examples of this in the U.S. include imports of textiles, apparel, and sugar. The American government assigns quotas to foreign governments (Dominican Republic, Taiwan, etc.), and those governments, recall, assign the quotas to their own producers. In all cases, of course, American consumers pay prices above the world price (for example, more than twice the world price of sugar). Clearly, American sugar producers have benefited as well as foreign producers who are able to obtain quota shares. By one estimate, the value of these monopoly rights (rents) to foreign producers in 1993 was over $11 billion.

Why, you may ask, do such clear and obvious impediments to free trade exist when millions of consumers are harmed and a few thousand (domestic and foreign) producers reap the benefits. Why should consumers ignore these added costs rather than inform themselves fully and attempt to resist efforts by government to impose such costs? Many economists believe that the explanation lies in the concept of **rational ignorance**, the rationality of consumers in ignoring many proposals of government in view of the large costs of informing themselves about such proposals and the small individual benefits of doing so. It is worth reminding ourselves of this idea. Take the case of sugar quotas which were renewed in 1996. Would you, for example, as a consumer of sugar, bother to inform yourself about monopoly sugar prices in the U.S. and lead a campaign to overturn the public decision to impose a quota system? Even if you were successful in eliminating quotas (a very unlikely result for one

Rational Ignorance
The argument that when the benefits of a public choice are highly concentrated and its costs highly diffused, it is rational for those who bear its costs to ignore them.

voter), the benefit/cost ratio of this activity to you would be unfavorable. Notice, though, that the same calculus would not apply to most private consumption decisions. Would you inform yourself about the private choice between a Chevrolet Corvette and a Nissan 350-Z? In the latter instance, the benefits and costs would be quite different and most likely would make it irrational to ignore the information needed to be fully informed.

Many economists would argue that quotas are clearly less preferred to tariffs where governments intend to restrict international trade. Notice that tariffs create tax revenues whereas quotas generate benefits only to private producers. At least with tariffs, the revenues *could* be used to reduce other taxes as well as to fund public expenditure programs. It is for this reason that some economists, faced with the political difficulties of eliminating quotas, have proposed auctioning the rights to export quotas. Presumably, the rights would bring something close to the $11 billion referred to earlier.

Arguments in Favor of Protection

As already noted, the U.S. has rarely if ever practiced completely free trade. (Neither have most other countries.) Americans frequently say they believe in competition. But many, including many of their elected representatives, seem to argue against it when it is to their financial advantage. Economists in general, most U.S. economists, that is, sing the praises of free trade. But apparently, the economists who make public policy cannot completely convince the government. In the mid 1990s, we again saw efforts to impose new restrictions on trade between the U.S. and other nations. Similar arguments for protectionism have arisen during the sharp economic downturn of 2008-2010. In view of these continuing efforts to push for protectionism, let's examine the arguments most commonly advanced in favor of restricting trade.

The Infant-Industry Argument

The infant-industry argument is as follows: Industries that are just starting cannot meet the pressures of competition by similar, already established industries located in other, more industrially mature countries. Such infant industries deserve the protection of a tariff or other protective device, and they should be sheltered until they have become big enough to take advantage of economies of scale.

This argument may seem reasonable. However, there are opposing arguments: (1) Tariffs and other forms of protection, once enacted, are extremely hard to abolish. For example, the bicycle industry still enjoys tariff protection. So do the automobile and steel industries and many other U.S. industries that are hardly infants. (2) If an industry needs to be protected before it is mature, direct government subsidies are preferable, since they make the costs of such protection explicit. (3) The logic of the infant-industry argument is difficult to apply, since it is hard to know (in either a developed or underdeveloped nation) *which* infant industries will (and should) survive. Short of pursuing a goal of autarky, a nation must choose, without any clear guidelines, *which* infant industries to put into its protective and expensive incubator. The protecting nation runs the risk not only of distorting its uses of resources but even of ending up with an industry that fails anyway, especially if the protection is finally withdrawn.

The National-Security Argument

The national-security argument is as follows: The U.S. can never really be certain of the supply of a good produced in a foreign country. The nation cannot even depend on its present friends to help in a tight spot. This means that, when it comes to defense goods, U.S. security must take precedence over U.S. economic efficiency.

This argument is difficult for economists to judge, since there are no objective criteria by which to evaluate the trade-off between increased national security and decreased industrial efficiency. Economists can only identify the costs involved in (1) levying tariffs, or (2) directly subsidizing firms that make defense goods. Most economists would say that direct subsidies are preferable, because they more clearly identify the costs involved.

Figure 15-6
History of American Tariffs, 1820-1980

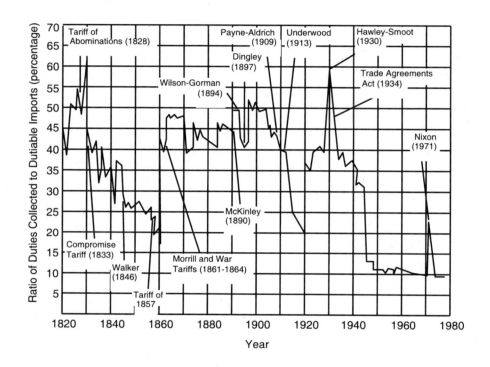

Source: U.S. Department of Commerce, Historical Statistics of the U.S. and Statistical Abstract of the U.S., 1982.

Figure 15-6 shows the wide variations in American tariffs between 1820 and 1980. Since 1980, tariffs have declined with the free trade agreements such as those with Canada, Mexico and other nations increasing the volume of goods not subject to import duties.

The Cheap-Foreign-Labor Argument

The cheap-foreign-labor argument can best be summed up in two examples. The American textile industry, say proponents of protection, must be protected from imported textiles from nations such as Malaysia, Thailand, and the Peoples Republic of China. Wages in Thailand and other such nations are so low that American firms cannot price their textiles low enough to compete. Florida farmers must be protected from the winter produce of Mexican farms where much agricultural labor is paid $3 per day. How, say some Florida farmers and their elected representative, can they possibly compete with Mexican farmers whose labor costs are only 3 to 5 percent of their own? Although this argument is persuasive to many people, it is irrelevant to economists because (1) the higher wages of Americans presumably reflect higher marginal productivity; (2) it is socially inefficient to have an American firm that cannot compete with labor-intensive imports try to do so; and (3) it is less costly to retrain labor and reallocate resources to more efficient uses than it is to protect an inefficient industry (however, remember the exception: the national-security argument.); and (4) wage costs are only part of the costs of production. Costs per unit of product produced depend not only on prices paid for labor but on labor's productivity. Much of the seeming advantage of low wage countries seemed to disappear in the 1990s. Much of this advantage has been in "blue collar" labor cost, which is declining and will continue to decline as a portion of total cost in the twenty-first century. Already, as Peter Drucker[3] has observed, this no longer provides a competitive edge to low wage countries. As a result, in spite of the continued movement of some industries to low wage countries and the continuing controversy over "outsourcing" of U.S. jobs, we are witnessing a net return of industries to the U.S. to take advantage of lower transport costs.

The Macroeconomic-Employment Argument

The macroeconomic-employment argument is that during hard times the U.S. can "export" some of its unemployment. (This is sometimes called a *beggar-thy-neighbor* argument.) Large segments of the business community (except big importers) and of labor often support this idea. The principle is to create more jobs at home by excluding, or sharply restricting, imports. Such an increase in domestic demand for formerly imported goods causes the U.S. to move toward full employment. Has the U.S. followed the beggar-thy-neighbor principle? Figure 15-6 shows what has happened to tariffs during our "hard-times" periods. You can see that tariffs have been high during most recession and depression periods, such as the mid-1870s, 1890s, early-1900s (though they were falling then), and 1921. They were especially high in the early years of the Great Depression (the Hawley-Smoot tariffs, in 1930, were the highest in modern American history). The purpose of the so-called Tariff of Abominations (1828) was to protect U.S. infant industries such as textiles and iron. Tariffs have from time to time protected American makers of every sort of commodity. Cheese, watches, cameras, musical instruments, and machinery are some that come to mind.

Economists usually feel that a beggar-thy-neighbor action is not likely to succeed. Even if it does work initially, the cost is great because such actions invite retaliation in the long run by other countries. (If the U.S. raises its tariff on bananas, Honduras will raise *its* tariff on tractors.) A trade war is likely to result and every nation will be hurt.

The reason why nations will be hurt is that as tariff walls go up, governments try to stimulate domestic demand, through tax cuts, increased government spending, and lowered interest rates. Assuming that previous international trade has reflected a comparative advantage, the U.S. will increase its domestic output, substituting homemade products for imported ones, at the expense of efficiency. Without trade, even if the U.S. reaches full employment, there will be relative inefficiency in the industries producing these products. Thus, the level of U.S. production of goods and services will be lower than if the tariff had not been introduced.

---

3. Drucker, Peter J. "Low Wages No Longer Give Competitive Edge." *The Wall Street Journal*, March 16, 1988.

Retaliation for "Unfair" Trade Practices

Proposals to restrict trade are often based on the view that they are necessary to punish unfair trading practices by other nations. Such proposals frequently include the following reasoning: "Since free trade does not, and perhaps cannot exist, trade restrictions can be used as leverage against unfair traders to create a system of fair trade." This rationale is found in the provisions of the Trade Agreement Act of 1979. Among the provisions of the act is one prohibiting foreign firms from dumping or selling products in the U.S. at prices lower than those in their own domestic markets. The act provides that, on a finding of dumping by the International Trade Commission, the President may impose penalties against foreign producers.

Economists are divided on the question of penalizing dumping. Some say that dumping is merely a subsidization of domestic consumers by foreign producers. Why turn down a gift? Others say that dumping may be predatory, an attempt to suppress competition or prevent its development through entry into an industry. The problem with this rationale for trade restrictions is that it supposes that dumping may create monopoly. Many economists would say that if it does, the monopoly profits will serve as a stimulus to entry anyway, and tend to eliminate the benefits of dumping. We will see more about retaliation in the Applications section of this chapter.

The Rustbelt: Protecting Declining Industries

Many of the arguments for trade restriction in recent decades have came from elected officials of areas with declining industries or industries containing antiquated plants and equipment. An argument advanced was the reverse of the infant-industry argument. Such industries, it is said, need temporary protection while they phase out or cut back production and during the period in which jobs are found for workers in other industries. While plausible, the argument suffers from many of the same problems as the infant-industry argument. Which industries should be protected? How much cost is reasonable? An illustration will suffice. About 75 percent of all shoes sold in the U.S. are imported (mainly from Brazil, Taiwan, China and The Republic of Korea). In an effort to protect this declining industry, Congress, in 1985, studied imposing import restrictions that would have saved more than 30,000 jobs in the industry. The cost *per job*, however, in terms of higher prices and other costs, would have been about $68,000! Publicity about the costs led to the demise of the proposal.

An equally serious problem is in choosing the industries that are declining and face ultimate elimination. Only a few years ago, the American steel industry seemed a candidate with the closing of much of its older plants and equipment and the consequent loss of jobs in the Mid-west. With the exchange rate changes of 1987–1988, however, the steel industry again became more competitive and operating at high levels of capacity. The "rustbelt" prospered in the 1990's and had low unemployment rates. In the early 2000s, exchange rates moved against the dollar and the American steel industry sought and received temporary protection. Was this protection either necessary or economically wise?

International Trade Policy Since World War II

General Agreement on Tariffs and Trade (GATT) An international organization created in 1947. Its objectives included fostering freer trade throughout the world.

As we have seen, tariff levels have fluctuated greatly throughout American history. After World War II, the U.S. was instrumental in creating the **General Agreement on Tariffs and Trade (GATT)** in 1947. From 23 original members, it has grown to more than 117 nations in 1995 and now includes much of Eastern Europe and even such nations as the People's Republic of China and Russia. Dedicating itself to fostering trade and lowering tariffs, GATT has held a series of meetings, or "rounds." Three of the more recent rounds, the Kennedy Round (1967), the Tokyo Round (1979), and the Uruguay Round (1994), resulted in major tariff reductions. The Uruguay round alone reduced tariffs world-wide by 40 percent. Further GTO meetings have, however, been less successful.

World Trade Organization (WTO) A successor organization to GATT whose primary purpose is to further liberalize world trade.

The Uruguay round also resulted in the creation of a new international organization, the **World Trade Organization (WTO)**. The WTO is the successor to GATT and has the same basic objective, that of further liberalizing trade. All member states have rights and obligations within this organization. A difference between the WTO and GATT, however, is that developing nations, like the industrial nations, have an obligation to liberalize trade. Indeed, in2002, preferential trade policy treatment for the developing nations was eliminated. A new legal system now exists within the WTO to resolve trade disputes among the member nations.

Regional Trade Agreements

While GATT and WTO grew after 1947 as organizations that are global in scope, a parallel pattern emerged in which nations have joined to form regional agreements also designed to liberalize trade among their members. These agreements have taken three different forms:

1. Common markets

2. Customs unions

3. Free trade agreements

Common Markets Agreements for free trade, common tariffs and free movement of capital and labor.

The most comprehensive of the three are **common markets**, which provide for (1) free trade among the members, (2) common tariffs for trade with non-member states, and (3) free movement of capital and labor among the members. A **customs union**, on the other hand, is less comprehensive and provides for free trade among members and common tariffs for trade with non-members. Finally, a **free trade agreement** is least comprehensive providing only for free trade among member states.

Customs Unions Agreements for free trade and common tariffs.

Free Trade Agreements Agreements for free trade among members.

Current Regional Trade Arrangements

The most successful free trade agreement since World War II is the European Union (EU). Many nations that did not wish to join the EU formed the European Free Trade Association (EFTA) in 1960, and have since negotiated free trade agreements with the EU. The combination of EU-EFTA nations forms a free trade area which encompasses a population of over 300 million and constitutes the largest free trade market today.

Western hemisphere nations are moving to create a free trade market that may be even larger than that in Europe. In 1988, the U.S. and Canada signed a free trade agreement that eliminated tariffs on all goods and virtually all services by 1999. The *bilateral* free trade flows are the largest in the world. In 1993, the agreement was expanded with the inclusion of Mexico and an agreement to phase out all tariffs in this trilateral trade over a period of 15 years. The **North American Free Trade Association (NAFTA)** included a provision to ultimately include all western hemisphere nations. This goal has proved difficult to achieve, however, in view of the continuing controversies surrounding NAFTA and the narrow margin of its congressional approval in 1993.

The Trans-Pacific Partnership (TPP)

As this book goes to print, the U.S. and 11 other countries are in the final stages of a trade agreement — the Trans-Pacific Partnership (TPP) — that would, if completed, be the biggest trade agreement in recent history. It would cover countries accounting for over 40% of the world trade and economic output. It will have far-reaching implications for public health, environmental conservation protection in the United States and around the world. If it is to truly reflect a "21st-century trade agreement" as President Obama has outlined, it will need to include meaningful, and enforceable environmental provisions and not include back door mechanisms that undercut bedrock protections for people's health and the planet.

Multilateral Free Trade: Its Future

The period since 1947 has seen impressive gains in free trade through much of the world. World trade today is probably freer (though not yet fully free) than it has ever been. Does this mean that the culmination of the trade liberalization of the past half century will be truly global free trade? While most economists would wish the answer to be yes, the answer is not that clear. There are at least two alternatives to free trade that will contend for dominance over the next 10 to 20 years.

Regional trading blocs. Growth of regional trading blocs that erect barriers to external trade while furthering free trade among members (for example, a European bloc contending with a western hemisphere bloc.)

State-directed trade. Growth of state-directed trade: in spite of the seeming demise of central planning (the old Soviet Union, the "old" People's Republic of China, etc.), forces may already be seen urging at least a partial return to state economic direction. That urge seems strongest in parts of Latin America.

Economists are sure only of this: Although both of the above arrangements may produce some short term gains for some states, both will produce greater real losses in contrast with global free trade. If this conflict of trade policy philosophies or ideas is compared to a prize fight, world trading history since 1947 seems to have free trade ahead on points, but no knock-out is in sight!

Free Trade: A Reprise

Before 1947, the U.S. and other trading nations were free to impose or raise tariffs. Tariff increases frequently lead to retaliation and, at times, "trade wars" with major reductions in the volume of trade. The 1930s, as we have seen, were especially characterized by these conditions. Many economic historians conclude that protectionism contributed significantly to the lengthening of the great depression.

Lowering of tariff and other trade barriers since World War II have doubtless increased stability and reduced the effects of trade wars such as that of the 1930's.

Application I: Does Trade Create Development?

From 1960 through the early 2000s, it became apparent that nations such as Mexico, Brazil, Korea, Taiwan, Singapore, Malaysia, India and China were developing major manufacturing sectors and that international trade was playing a key role in this process. Indeed, these nations came to be known as the newly industrializing countries (NICs), in contrast with the less-developed countries (LDCs). The emergence of the NICs seemed to reignite a long-standing debate among economists and others, not only about the future course of economic development, but also about the role of international trade in fostering such development.

In the 1980s, the "debt crisis" of some of the NICs and many of the LDCs further complicated efforts to assay the relationship between trade and development. In the early twenty first century, pressures to move away from free trade have arisen again, especially, as pointed out above, in Latin America. Opponents have even rioted during meetings designed to promote free trade. That these issues will continue to be important to all nations, rich, poor and in between, seems nearly certain. Development cannot begin or continue without capital and other imports, and importing cannot occur unless nations have export earnings with which to finance imports. Likewise, debt cannot be serviced, much less repaid except out of export-derived revenues. In an increasingly interdependent international economy, few issues take on more importance than the relationship between trade and development. Few also are likely to be more contentious.

The Relation Between Trade and Development

To establish this relationship, we must find a relation between exporting-importing and the increase in productivity that is the key to development. Opinions are divided about whether trade, especially trade based on comparative advantage, enhances economic development. In this application we will examine some of the controversies surrounding this subject.

The Classical View

Early economists, including Adam Smith and David Ricardo, believed that trade was essential to economic development, or to what Smith called "The Wealth of Nations." Writing about the country's efforts to produce things that it could import more cheaply, Smith said, "The value of its annual produce is certainly more or less diminished, when it is thus turned away from producing commodities evidently of more value than the commodity which it is directed to produce."

This idea of maximizing the wealth of a nation through trade, however, is based on a static situation (*static* meaning timeless). Much of the argument over its validity arises from the distinction between the static economic position of a country at a point in time, and the improvement (or deterioration) in the country's position that occurs over time. Let's illustrate the difference between these two perspectives.

At its beginning, the U.S. started out with a certain endowment of land, labor, capital, and entrepreneurship. For simplicity, assume that all its resources were integrated into the market system. Now ask yourself the following questions: (1) In any given year, for instance, 1940, would the per capita national income be higher if the U.S. followed a policy of free trade? Or would it be higher if it imposed restrictions on trade? (2) Which policy, restricted trade or unrestricted trade, would cause income to grow faster from one date to another (for instance, from 1940 to 2000)?

Figure 15-7 will help you visualize the answer. It shows that in 1940 the U.S. could have two levels of per capita income: $1,300 or $1,350. The $1,300 figure corresponds to the level if the government enforced protective practices (such as tariffs or quotas). It represents many possible levels of income resulting from different combinations of trade restrictions. Each of the combinations causes resources to be used in ways that are *less* productive than would be the case if there were free trade, or if there were comparative-advantage trade. The $1,350 represents the *free*-trade (comparative advantage) case.

Therefore, the answer to question 1 is that at any point, its process of development, a nation will have a higher income if it engages in free trade and utilizes all its resources on the basis of comparative advantage.

Figure 15-7
Hypothetical Growth Paths of the United States: Free Trade and Protectionism, 1940 to 2000

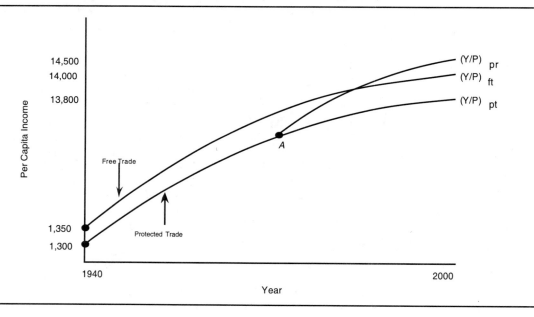

Now what about *growth* as it relates to international trade? Which policy, comparative-advantage (free) trade or some sort of protective tariffs or quotas, would yield the U.S. the greater growth in income during the period from 1940 to 2000? Adherents of the classical economic view say that comparative-advantage trade would give the greatest growth, because a nation that trades according to the principle of comparative advantage allocates its resources to their most productive uses. Thus, the nation is maximizing its productivity. With free trade, as income grows over time, along $(Y/P)_{pt}$ in Figure 15-7, the size of the nation's market grows. There is specialization and division of labor. Capital increases and productivity increases as well.

The growth path with protected trade $(Y/P)_{ft}$, begins at a lower level ($1,300) in 1940 and in 2000 results in a lower level of per capita income ($14,500) as well. This is because even with full employment of its resources, allocation is less efficient and productive with protection than with (comparative advantage) free trade. This is the traditional view of the relationship between trade and development and the reason why many economists espouse free trade as the desired policy objective of developing nations.

Reservations About the Traditional View

There are objections to the above scenario. Some economists feel that a policy of comparative-advantage trade is not, in the long run, the best policy for developing nations. They feel that one cannot prove an explicit relationship between growth and free international trade. Economist Hollis Chenery[4] has been one of the doubters. Chenery, a long time official of the U.S. Agency for International Development (USAID), has argued that there are five reservations that point to the wisdom of modifying comparative advantage as a policy to enhance economic development for NICs and LDCs:

1. *Factor costs.* The benefits of comparative advantage trade depend on factor markets producing equilibrium prices of resources. This means that the prices reflect "true" relative costs of production. Consider the imperfections in labor or capital markets that one sees in developing countries (for example, the U.S. in the 19th century or in virtually all LDCs today). As development takes place, markets perform more efficiently. There are often dramatic changes in factor costs, and thus in comparative advantage.

2. *Export markets.* Comparative-advantage trade gives rise to specialization. NICs and LDCs frequently come to specialize in producing, and exporting, just one, or a very few, raw materials. Then they must import food and raw materials that they do not produce along with manufactured (and semi-manufactured) products. The result is an unstable economy, which is tied to the fluctuating prices of raw materials. (For example, the world price of copper plunged 65 percent in the early 1970s. Chile, which produces one-eighth of the world's copper, suffered acutely.) You can see that following a policy of comparative-advantage trade makes it hard for an underdeveloped nation to keep its economy stable. In addition, price and income elasticities of demand for these countries' raw materials are low, though data are conflicting. (When the price of copper falls on the world market, and a country's chief export is copper, it cannot make up in export earnings for the drop in price by selling a greater quantity to its industrialized neighbors.) So the terms of trade, the ratio of export prices to import prices, may turn against the exporter of the raw material. The reason is that the developing nation, for example, Chile, must continue to import manufactured goods, whose prices (compared to the price of the exported copper) are now relatively much higher.

Many economists fail to see factors 1 and 2 as being necessarily valid arguments against a developing country's specializing in its comparative advantage raw-material exports. In their view, a developing nation's rate of return on investment in its raw material is greater than the rate of return it *would* receive if it tried to build up other internal projects, such as factories, even after correcting for factor costs and fluctuating world prices.

---

4. Chenery, Hollis B. "Comparative Advantage and Development Policy." *American Economic Review,* 51:1 March, 1961.

3. *Productivity changes.* Manufacturing, by its very nature, may enhance the skills of labor and management more than agriculture does. So some economic advisers urge a developing nation to stress manufacturing, even at the expense of·comparative-advantage exports. Some of the NICs appear to have done so. Others disagree, asking whether such an advantage exists. Perhaps, they say, the developing nation could make as much headway by concentrating on agriculture as by concentrating on manufacturing. Some of the LDCs are attempting to reemphasize agriculture. All agree, however, that the nation must make allowances for productivity changes in allocating its resources, even if it does not, in the long run, opt for manufacturing as the area of concentration.

4. *Dynamic external economies.* As an industry grows, its costs fall. Or demand for its output increases. As a result, the costs of other industries may also fall. There may, in fact, be a whole group of investments that are profitable *only if they are undertaken together.* Comparative advantage, manifested in market signals such as equilibrium prices, does not under these conditions indicate to a nation how it should allocate its resources. Suppose, for example, that the underdeveloped nation increases its investment in industry and realizes certain of these external economies. This will reduce the costs of more than one industry. But, some economists say, perhaps it would have realized even more external economies if it had allocated its capital to comparative-advantage agriculture. For example, it could have built fabricating plants, including expanding the production of the raw material.

5. *Uncertainty and flexibility.* Some economists feel that changes in markets can happen so quickly, and are so hard for policy makers to foresee, that a diversified economy, one that can quickly adjust to changes in supply and demand, is better (and certainly more flexible) than one that relies on a single product, or only a few products. Economists Peter Lindert and C. P. Kindleberger[5] have argued that the terms of trade now discriminate against the raw-material-exporting nations and favor the industrialized nations, because the raw-material-exporting nations lack flexibility. So it seems that a developing nation might be well advised to sacrifice some short-term efficiency in the interests of longer-term flexibility, and a capacity to adjust more rapidly to changes in world supply and demand.

A serious problem with this, though, is that inefficiency often involves creating monopoly privileges and rents that are very difficult to eliminate in the long run. Many examples of this problem can be found in some of the NICs and LDCs. A report in the Wall Street Journal in November 1986 indicated that in Indonesia, a country possessed of many exportable natural resources including oil, export revenues have done little to finance broadly based economic development programs. Principal among the reasons for this has been the substitution of bureaucratic import controls and corruption for free trade. A small oligarchy, including the then President's family, received monopoly rights over imports and control over access to import quotas along with (monopoly) distribution rights to products within the country. Such monopoly pricing might ordinarily attract investors into these industries but investment licensing has prevented that. Higher monopoly prices made Indonesian exports less competitive and reduced export earnings, thereby reducing the ability to finance

---

5. Lindert, Peter H. and Charles P. Kindleberger, *International Economics.* Homewood, Illinois, Richard D. Irwin. 1998.

developmental imports. In the 1990's, a proposal was made in Indonesia to develop an expanded automobile industry. A member of the President's family was given monopoly rights and partly as a result, an efficient competitive automobile industry did not materialize. It is not surprising that bureaucratization and corruption have made the export position of many LDCs less competitive. Indeed, their share of world exports has been falling since the 1950s.

Those With Reservations: Modify Free Trade

Those who have reservations about comparative-advantage trade and its ability to insure or accelerate growth argue for modifications in trade policy. Such modifications may involve significant departures from free trade. Some of the measures adopted include (1) rationing of trade (foreign exchange) earnings either direct controls or through multiple pricing (exchange rate) controls, (2) providing direct subsidies or tax incentives to firms that produce import substitute products, and (3) creating import-export monopoly agencies to obtain lower prices for imports and capture revenue from domestic producers for governmentally determined development uses. To the extent that these noncompetitive market interventions are effective, proponents say that the growth path with protection, $(Y/P)_{Pr}$ in Figure 15-7, can accelerate at some point (point A in Figure 15-7), utilizing dynamic externalities and other advantages to propel the nation onto a new path that will generate higher real income at the end of the period ($14,500 versus $13,000) than would be the case with free trade.

Debt Problems of the LDCs and NICs

With the dramatic exception of the "Asian Tigers" (South Korea, Taiwan, Hong Kong, Singapore, Malaysia, Thailand and in recent years China and India), the trade positions of the LDCs and NICs deteriorated in the 1970s and 1980s. Most of the LDCs exports continue in the early twenty first century to consist of primary commodities. For many of them (Indonesia and Venezuela excepted), agricultural primary commodities dominate their exports. Such products have declined in value from more than one-third in 1955 to less than 14 percent in 1986. While those that export fuels benefited (until the mid-1980s) from rising prices, this added, ironically, to the financial problems of others. The dramatic increase in manufactured engineering products has benefited some NICs (especially the "Asian Tigers") while it has had little effect on many LDCs whose manufactured products are not competitive in world markets.

Faced with rising import prices (especially fuels) and softening primary commodity export prices, many NICs and LDCs turned to international capital markets and borrowed heavily in the 1970s. In some instances, the long-term investment credits were wisely invested and resulted in dramatic productivity growth and growth in exports (e.g., South Korea). In other instances, the long-term credits appear to have been less wisely employed, often in the bureaucratic controls and corruption to which we referred earlier. Some countries, especially in Latin America (Brazil, Argentina, Peru) have, at times, appeared to be on the verge of inability to even service the interest payments on their debts (often 50 percent or more of their GDPs). Liberalization of economic policy in the 1980s and 1990s, especially in Argentina and Chile, eased some of these concerns in the 1990's, but serious problems reappeared in 2002, especially in Argentina.

Implications for Trade Policies

For many years, representatives of the LDCs and, to a lesser extent, the NICs, argued for creating a special system of trading and financial preferences for the "developing nations." At times, especially at the United Nations Conference on Trade and Development (UNCTAD), they lobbied for a system under which there would be guaranteed export prices for primary commodities, easier access to markets in industrial nations and long-term capital flows to LDCs and NICs at preferential interest rates. Those pressures, however, seemed to abate until the debt crisis of the 1980s.

In the 1980s and 1990s, we heard again arguments for trade preferences. One NIC (Brazil) temporarily suspended interest payment on its debt. An LDC (Peru) announced it would pay no more than 15 percent of its GDP in interest payments on its external debt. Two American Secretaries of the Treasury argued for more public and private capital flows to LDCs and NICs at below market interest rates. Arguments in support of these policies have reemerged in the early twenty first century. Which shall it be in the future, free trade in commodities services and capital or a "new (non-free trade) order" of trading relationships? As we indicated in the preceding chapter, free trade has gained, but there are real concerns about the future. Economists are not of one mind about which trade policies are consistent with sustained growth and development. Many would agree with Arnold Harberger[6] that free trade, and a minimum of government involvement in domestic and international economic affairs, is preferable. Other economists would agree with Hollis Chenery that free (comparative-advantage-based) trade may be stacked against the LDCs and NICs. For them, government action is called for to encourage the real and financial trading relationships that will permit more and more LDCs to become NICs and for the NICs to become major industrial countries.

Application II: Steel Tariffs

The United States is generally perceived as having a free market economy. Within this structure, competitive markets, self sufficiency, and individualism are highly valued. This is why former President Bush's imposition of tariffs on imported steel-products came as a surprise to many Americans.

On March 5, 2002, the President announced that the U.S. would impose tariffs of up to 30 percent on 15 imported steel products, starting March 20 and lasting 3 years. These import tariffs were placed on the selected products in an effort to protect the U.S. steel industry from lower cost foreign producers.

Some of the President's liberal political opponents criticized the plan for not going far enough. They believed the U.S. steel producers were being treated unfairly by other nations' illegal "dumping" of steel in the U.S., below the cost of production in their home countries. Conservative allies of the President and many economists said this was a step away from the commitment to freer trade that had characterized foreign economic policy of both democratic and republican administrations since World War II.

It appears politics played an important part in President Bush's' decision to impose steel tariffs. The tariffs were good news for several Rust Belt swing states such as Pennsylvania and West Virginia.

These economic sanctions ignited an enormous international controversy. The European Union announced that it planned to immediately impose retaliatory tariffs on the U.S. to be started on June 18, 2002. Many people feared this would inevitably be the start of a major trade war. The retaliatory tariffs never materialized but in the fall of 2003, the World Trade

---

6. *World Economic Growth: Cases of Developed and Developing Nations.* San Francisco: Institute for Contemporary Studies, 1984.

Organization (WTO) stated that dumping was not a significant problem and that these American tariffs represented an illegal barrier to trade.

In late 2003, with trade wars still looming, President Bush decided to lift the tariffs which, by this time, had been drawing criticism at home from several industries, including automobile manufactures and other large steel users. This early withdrawal of the tariffs drew criticism from many steel producers, but was applauded by steel importers and free trade proponents.

The steel tariffs of 2002-2003 demonstrate again not only the tug and pull of our economic relations with other nations but also the clear nexus between economic policy and domestic politics.

SUMMING UP

1. In this chapter, we looked at a market economy as one that is open, or that trades (exports, imports) with the rest of the world. For the U.S., international trade has grown in its importance to its economy.

2. Trade consists of *exports*, commodities and services sold to other nations, and *imports*, commodities and services purchased from other nations. Exports and imports consist of both *visible items* (commodities) and *invisible items* (services).

3. The *commodity balance of trade* measures the difference between commodity exports and commodity imports (X - M).

4. *Net foreign trade (NFT)* is the commodity balance (X – M) difference between exports (X) and imports (M), plus net services (service exports – service imports):

$$NFT = (X - M) + S$$

Foreign trade is important, even to a diversified economy such as that of the U.S.

5. NFT can exert a significant macroeconomic influence on the level of income and employment, the demand for goods, services and the creation of jobs. This is so even in the U.S., in which exports (and NFT) form a smaller percentage of output than they do in many other major trading nations. (However, in dollar volume, the U.S. is by far the largest international trader and the percentage of its output made up of exports has nearly doubled since 1980.)

6. Between 1960 and 1980, the U.S. usually ran a small trade surplus or trade deficit (X < M). Since1983, the U.S. has run up increasingly large trade deficits that seem to be due to exchange rate changes and the income taste of Americans for imported goods.

7. Trade is important to the U.S. for several reasons: (a) Trade constitutes an important part of demand for U.S. output, and hence demand for labor (that means more jobs) and other resources. (b) Demand that results from trade enables many U.S. industries to operate more efficiently and on a larger scale. (c) The percentage of U.S. GDP represented by trade has grown in recent years. This reflects a greater interdependence with other nations. (d) The U.S. needs

imports of raw materials, such as certain key minerals, in order to operate many industries.

8. *Autarky* (economic self-sufficiency), although it may be technologically possible for the U.S., is economically unwise, because the U.S., by specializing in items in which it has a comparative advantage, can realize gains from trade.

9. *Absolute advantage* refers to a nation's ability to produce all of a good it consumes more efficiently than any other nation. (Some nations may have an absolute advantage in all goods.) *Comparative advantage* refers to a nation's being more efficient in producing some good or goods than in producing others (even though the nation may also be absolutely more efficient than its neighbors in producing everything).

10. At any given time, nations have certain production possibilities. These are reflected in their PP curves (assuming full employment and a given technology level). So long as any two nations have different internal rates of exchange (trade-offs) between producing the same 2 goods, it is mutually beneficial for each to specialize in producing the good in which it has a comparative advantage.

11. By specializing in producing those things in which it has a comparative advantage, and by trading what it does not consume to other nations for goods in which *they* have a comparative advantage, a trading nation can have more goods to consume (the consumption-possibilities curves will be above the domestic PP curve). Differences in tastes and preferences of consumers in different countries also create utility gains from trade.

12. Comparative advantage derives from (a) different endowments of natural resources, (b) different physical features (climate, harbors, and so on), (c) different states of development of markets (for example, some nations have well-developed capital markets), and (d) different supplies of labor.

13. Comparative advantages change, sometimes dramatically. The U.S. began with a comparative advantage in land-intensive commodities, which it exported. Today it has a comparative advantage in capital-intensive as well as land-intensive goods.

14. If nations run into a certain level of increasing costs as they specialize, the specialization may not be complete. That is they will produce a wider variety of goods. (For example, Honduras will produce some of its own tractors, the U.S. will produce some of its own bananas.)

15. Some people disapprove of foreign trade because of the unemployment that occurs when resources (especially labor) must be reallocated as a result of that trade. To economists, this is not a compelling argument against an open economy. They point to the macroeconomic tools that can be used to increase employment, and the microeconomic tools that can be used to reallocate resources (for example, job retraining).

16. Comparative advantage depends on competition. When competition does not exist, or when nations with equal advantage do not trade competitively with each other, some of the benefits of comparative-advantage trade are lost.

17. Trading nations that are burdened by *externalities* may produce and trade too much or too little for comparative advantage to work. Prices for goods exported should accurately reflect relative scarcity of resources.

18. The theory of comparative advantage depends on relative prices reflecting relative scarcities of resources in each nation. If prices do not reflect these scarcities, an international misallocation of resources occurs.

19. The major obstacle to free trade is *protectionism,* the effort to protect farmers and industries from the competition from lower-priced goods imported from foreign countries when there is free international trade.

20. The two major means of protectionism are (a) *tariffs,* which are taxes levied on imported goods, and (b) *quotas,* which are limitations on the quantity of imports.

21. Tariffs and other trade restrictions reduce the supply of goods and raise the prices charged consumers. They may also add to the monopoly power of domestic producers, and they may reduce the number of good substitutes available to consumers, making domestic demand for a good more inelastic. One thing in their favor is that they produce revenue for the importing governments.

22. The burden of a tariff consists of a *consumer burden,* that part of the tariff paid by consumers in a higher price, and the *producer burden*, that part paid by sellers in a lower net price and reduced sales. The more inelastic is the demand for the imported good, the greater is the consumer burden. The more elastic is the demand for the imported good, the greater is the producer burden.

23. Quotas do not produce revenue for governments. Otherwise the effects of quotas are similar to those of tariffs. They reduce supply, raise prices to consumers, and enhance the monopolistic position of domestic producers. The most extreme form of quota is an *embargo,* an absolute prohibition against importing a certain good or trading with a certain country. Export quotas are sometimes assigned not only to protect domestic firms but to favor foreign countries and firms. Voters (consumers) may not resist the higher prices of these quotas because of rational ignorance.

24. Some arguments in favor of protectionism are as follows: (a) the *infant-industry argument* (firms that are new and small need to be protected until they are large enough to compete with more established firms in foreign industries); (b) the *national-security argument* (uncertainty of foreign supply, plus need for a reliable source of military hardware, means that domestic producers must be protected, even if they are inefficient); (c) the *cheap-foreign-labor argument* (domestic firms that must pay high wages should be protected against imports from countries in which wages are low); (d) the *macroeconomic-employment argument* (recessions and depressions can be "exported" if a nation puts up barriers to trade that reduce imports without reducing exports); (e) retaliation for "unfair" trading practices (make them trade fairly) and; (f) protection of declining industries (help such industries temporarily) during phasing out.

25. Economists generally reject these arguments that favor protectionism, with the exception of the national-security argument, for which there is little objective basis for evaluation. However, even in the case of protection given to industries producing goods needed for national security, economists feel that there

should be direct subsidies instead of tariffs, so that the costs of protection are clearly identified.

26. Beggar-thy-neighbor tariffs are likely to be ineffective, even counterproductive. When one nation sets up high tariffs, other nations retaliate. As a result, without specialized trade, nations have fewer goods and services to consume, even when they have full employment.

27. In 1947, the world's major trading nations created GATT, the *General Agreement on Tariffs and Trade*. By 1995, it had grown to over 117 nations dedicated to liberalizing trade.

28. The Uruguay round of GATT talks (1994) created a new trade organization, the *World Trade Organization (WTO)* which seeks to further increase trade liberalization in both developing countries and industrial nations.

29. Regional trade agreements have grown since World War II. They have taken the form of (a) common markets, (b) custom unions, and (c) free trade agreements.

30. *Common markets* provide for free trade, common tariffs, and free movement of capital and labor. *Customs unions* provide for common tariffs and free trade. *Free trade agreements* provide only for free trade.

31. The future of free trade is being clouded by (a) the growth of regional trade agreements and (b) the re-emergence of state-directed trade.

32. Major free trade arrangements include the European Union-European Free Trade Association (EU-EFTA) Agreement and NAFTA (North American Free Trade Association).

33. Policy makers today must face a major question: Can international trade provide the primary basis for the economic development of poor nations? Evidence since the 1960s of growth of the newly industrialized countries (NICs) seemed to suggest yes.

34. Views differ as to the relation between trade and development. Classical economists (Adam Smith, David Ricardo) felt that comparative-advantage trade was essential to increasing output and maximizing the wealth of a nation.

35. Much of the debate over the relation between trade and development involves the distinction between the static principles of comparative-advantage and the dynamic principles of growth.

36. One can show that, in a static sense (that is, at a point in time), a nation can maximize its output if it allocates all its resources to their most productive uses. However, there is no certainty that if a nation does this, the growth of its output over a period of time will be greater than it would have been if it had departed, selectively, from comparative-advantage trade.

37. Those who argue for restricting comparative advantage, as the basis for trade, argue on the basis of: (a) *Factor costs*. Imperfections in the factor markets of underdeveloped nations cause their factor costs not to reflect their real relative cost. (b) *Export markets*. Comparative-advantage specialization on the part

of the poor nations may result in unstable economies. Low income and price elasticities of demand for raw-material exports may turn the terms of trade against the nation that specializes. (c) *Productivity changes.* In an economy based on manufacturing, the skills of labor and management increase and diversify more rapidly than they do in an economy based on agriculture. (d) *Dynamic external economies.* Several investments, a whole package of them, may have to be made simultaneously in order to make them succeed, or pay off. This is more likely to happen in an industry-based economy than in an agriculture-based economy. (e) *Uncertainty and flexibility.* A diversified economy is more flexible, and can adjust more readily to changes in supply and demand, than an economy that specializes in a few raw-material exports. Thus, it can better resist the effects of worsening terms of trade.

38. Economists generally discount points (a) and (b), from the above paragraph as reasons to abandon comparative-advantage trade. However, they should take into account factors (c), (d), and (e) when they are working out trade policy.
39. Deviations from free trade seem often to give rise to bureaucratic red tape in LDCs and to monopoly grants and corruption. These impediments to productivity growth raise prices and make LDC exports less competitive in world markets

40. Faced with rising import (especially fuel) prices in the 1970s and falling primary commodity prices, LDCs and some NICs borrowed heavily in world capital markets. Where the capital was not wisely invested, a "debt crisis" arose in which threats to default or limit payments created serious problems in financial markets.

41. For years LDCs and NICs have argued for a "new international economic order" with restrictions on free trade involving guaranteed export prices, easier access to markets, and below market interest rates for capital.

42. Economists generally espouse free trade. Many, probably most American economists, argue that free trade is preferable to trade restrictions as a means to create productivity growth and minimize the distortions of bureaucracy and corruption. Some, however, argue that free trade is stacked against LDCs and NICs and that trade preferences should be considered.

KEY TERMS

Absolute advantage, comparative advantage
Autarky
"Beggar-thy-neighbor" argument
Burden of a tariff (consumer burden, producer burden)
Cheap foreign labor argument
Commodity balance of trade
Common markets
Customs unions
Exports, imports
Free trade agreements
General Agreement on Tariffs and Trade (GATT)
Infant-industry argument
National security argument
Net foreign trade

Open economy, closed economy
Protectionism
Rational ignorance
Tariffs, quotas, embargoes
Terms of trade
Visible items, invisible items of trade
World Trade Organization (WTO)

QUESTIONS

1. What is meant by the term "open economy?" "Closed economy?"

2. What imported goods do you often buy? How would you be affected if the U.S. restricted international trade or stopped trading with other nations entirely?

3. Why are most production-possibilities curves *not* straight lines? What happens to international specialization when such curves are truly curves?

4. Consider the following hypothetical production-possibilities schedules for the U.S. and Honduras:

United States		Honduras	
Units of Tractors	Units of Bananas	Units of Tractors	Units of Bananas
50	0	0	100
40	5	5	80
30	10	10	60
20	15	15	40
10	20	20	20
0	25	25	0

  a. Plot the production-possibilities curves.
  b. Is there a basis for mutually beneficial trade between the two countries?
  c. What will determine the terms of trade that are established between the two countries?

5. Based on the arguments advanced in this chapter, why, in your opinion, did the beggar-thy-neighbor tariff (Smoot-Hawley tariff) of 1930 perhaps slow the American recovery between 1930 and 1934?

6. What happens to the trade from either developed or underdeveloped nations when monopoly export and import agencies are set up? Why?

7. Evaluate the following statements:
  a. "Free trade forces domestic producers to pay attention to consumer tastes and preferences."
  b. "Free trade would be desirable, but we can't afford to rely on the Russians, or the French, or even the British, for our military hardware."
  c. "High tariffs to create more jobs will work for the U.S. because other, less powerful nations wouldn't dare retaliate."
  d. "In several recent years, the U.S. has run a large commodity trade deficit. What we should do to counteract this is to buy less from abroad."
  e. "In several recent years, the U.S. has run a large commodity trade deficit. We don't need to worry, though, because exchange rate changes will eliminate the deficit."

8. In the following graph, we see the demand for and supply of an imported good. D_d is the domestic demand, S_d is the domestic supply. S_{ft} is the supply with free trade of both domestic producers and imports, and S_{at} is the supply after a tariff is imposed.

a. What is the price and quantity of the good without trade? With free trade? After a tariff is imposed?
b. Who bears most of the burden of the tariff, consumers or importing firms? What is the burden of each?
c. Who benefits from the tariff? What is the price benefit?

9. What are the differences between common markets, customs unions and free trade agreements? Which of these is the most comprehensive form of trade agreement.

10. What was the basic role of GATT? What is the basic objective of the WTO?

11. What are the major threats to further world trade liberalization?

12. What are the differences between the static view of comparative advantage and the dynamic view of growth?

13. If you were recommending economic policy to a developing low-income country, at what point would you recommend that it follow a policy of comparative-advantage trade, and at what point would you recommend that it sacrifice a certain amount of efficiency in the use of its resources in order to achieve more growth?

14. Consider an underdeveloped country (for example, Chile), and suppose that it primarily exports one raw material (for example, copper). How can low price and income elasticities of demand for copper affect Chile's export earnings, its ability to import other necessary goods, and its terms of trade?

Glossary

Ability-to-pay principle A principle of taxation under which those who have a larger income are deemed capable of paying not only a larger tax but a larger percentage of their income in taxes.

Absolute advantage The ability of a given nation to produce all commodities more cheaply (that is, using up few resources per unit of output) than any other nation with which it might trade.

Abstinence theory of interest A theory that people prefer to consume goods and services now, rather than later; therefore, people will save (postpone consuming) only if they are given a reward. That reward is called interest.

Accelerator principle The general rule that changes in the rate of change of consumer demand cause much larger changes in induced investment. The accelerator is positive if a change in the increase in consumer demand causes induced investment to increase. It is negative if the change in induced investment decreases.

Accounting profit The difference between total revenue and total explicit cost.

Adaptive expectations hypothesis The view that decision makers form their inflationary expectations on the basis of events of the recent past.

Adjustable-peg system A system of exchange in which currencies are pegged, or are not allowed to change in value by more than a specific percentage. The pegs themselves, however, may be changed from time to time.

Administered-price inflation A kind of inflation that occurs when firms with some control over price use that power to raise prices more rapidly than cost increases.

Administered pricing A term used by some economists to refer to prices that are set by the administrators of firms rather than established by independent influences of supply and demand.

Age-earnings profile A profile that shows the relationship between annual incomes and age for groups with various levels of education.

Aggregate-demand-equals-aggregate-supply approach (Keynesian) An approach to the problem of finding equilibrium income in a simple economic model without government and foreign trade. According to this approach, the equilibrium is at that level at which *aggregate supply*, consumption plus savings (C + S), is equal to *aggregate demand*, consumption plus intended investment (C + I).

Aggregate-demand-equals-aggregate-supply approach (General) An approach that holds that equilibrium real income is established where aggregate quantity demanded equals aggregate quantity supplied.

Aggregate demand shock A term used to describe a shift in aggregate demand.

Aggregate production function The relationship in physical (nonmonetary) terms between output and employment for a given economy (at a specific time). A "recipe" for output.

Aggregate supply shock A term used to describe a shift in aggregate supply.

Allocative inefficiency The tendency for monopoly firms to set prices above marginal costs and to allocate fewer resources to producing their products than consumers prefer.

Antithesis In Marxist theory, the force arising from a social contradiction that compels a change in the existing thesis (or set of social arrangements).

Arbitrage The practice of buying international currencies at low prices and quickly selling them at high prices.

At factor prices Method of computing national income using the prices paid in the factor markets. This measuring practice excludes indirect business taxes.

At market prices Method of computing national economic accounts using the prices paid in the markets for goods and services. This measuring practice must utilize all market costs incurred in production.

Autarky Economic self-sufficiency.

Automatic stabilizers Structures built into the U.S. economy that have a moderating influence on recessions and inflations. They are automatic in that they operate without being invoked by government policy makers. They are not considered strong enough to prevent, by themselves, the occurrence of business fluctuations. The progressive personal income tax is an example.

Autonomous investment Investment that is not affected by changes in the nation's overall level of income and consumption.

Average propensity to consume The percentage of their incomes that people at a given level of income tend to consume:

$$APC = C/Y$$

Average propensity to save The percentage of their incomes that people at a given level of income tend to save:

$$APS = S/Y$$

Average revenue Total revenue divided by output.

Average total cost Average fixed cost plus average variable cost.

Backward-bending labor supply curve A graphic illustration of a situation in which the quantity of labor supplied decreases as the wage increases beyond a certain level.

Balance-of-payments statement The annual accounting statement disclosing the status of a nation's foreign trade, including its capital transactions. The statement reveals what was bought and sold, and how any difference between the two was financed. (The balance-of-payments account must balance.)

Balance of trade The monetary value of exports minus imports:

$$X - M.$$

Balance to be financed In the balance-of-payments statement, the combination of the basic balance plus the short-term capital account.

Balanced-budget multiplier The multiplier that makes itself felt when a balanced-budget change in government expenditures and taxes (that is, government expenditures and taxes moving in the same direction and by the same amount) causes the level of national income to change in the same direction and by the same amount as the expenditure-tax change. *See also* Multiplier effect.

Bank holding companies Corporations that own one or more banks.

Barriers to entry Factors that prevent other firms from entering a market.

Barter A system of exchange that does not involve money; the trading of goods directly for other goods.

Basic balance In the balance-of-payments statement, the balance in the current account plus the balance in the long-term capital account.

Benefits-received principle of taxation The theory of taxation according to which people pay taxes that are commensurate with, or in line with, the benefits they receive from government services.

Bilateral monopoly A market situation in which a single seller bargains with a single buyer.

Bonds Instruments of debt, guaranteeing payment of the investment (face value) plus interest by a certain date. Interest on bonds is a cost of production to a business firm that raises capital by selling bonds.

Break-even point or price Occurs when a firm just covers its opportunity costs. A price that equals average cost and marginal cost is a break-even price.

Bretton Woods Conference International monetary conference held in 1944, which established the International Monetary Fund (IMF) and the International Bank for Reconstruction and Development (IBRD).

Budget restraint The limits on purchases of goods imposed by a consumer's income and by the prices of the goods bought.

Business cycles Variations in a nation's general economic activity; fluctuations in output, income, employment, and prices.

Capital account The account, in a nation's balance-of-payments statement, that is made up of long-term and short-term capital flows.

Capital broadening (constant capital-to-labor ratio) The situation in which capital instruments grow at the same rate as the amount of labor employed.

Capital consumption allowance *See* Depreciation.

Capital deepening The situation in which a nation's employers use more capital relative to the amount of labor used, thus raising the capital-to-labor ratio for the economy.

Capital gains tax A tax placed on the increase in the value of an asset, which is realized on the sale of the asset. It is considered a tax loophole because the tax rate on such gains tends to be lower than on other forms of income.

Capital-intensive process A production process that uses relatively more capital than labor or land.

Capitalism An economic system with two essential ingredients: (1) the private ownership of the means of production, and (2) the expression of economic decisions through a system of interrelated markets.

Capture hypothesis The view that regulatory agencies are often captured by the industries they regulate and serve industry interests rather than those of the public.

Cartel A group of producers who join forces and behave like a monopoly with respect to price and output.

Ceteris paribus In economic analysis, the practice of holding certain variables constant and permitting other *key* variables to change.

Change in demand A shift in a demand curve (by which more or less of a good is bought at all prices) that results from a change in (1) income, (2) tastes, (3) prices of other goods, (4) number of consumers, or (5) consumers' expectations of future prices.

Change in quantity demanded A movement along a demand curve that results from a change in the price of that good.

Change in quantity supplied A movement along a supply curve that reflects a change in the amount of a good offered for sale as only the price of that good changes.

Change in supply A shift in a supply curve that reflects that more or less of a good is offered for sale by a firm at all prices.

Check An order to a bank from the holder of a demand deposit to transfer money from that demand-deposit account and pay it to someone else.

Checking accounts *See* Demand deposits.

Closed market economy A market economy consisting of interrelated product and factor markets that does not trade products, services, or resources with other economies.

Closed shop An employment situation in which workers *must* join a union in order to get or hold a job.

Coins Metal tokens minted by the Treasury and issued through the Federal Reserve Banks.

Command economy An economy in which the problems generated by scarcity are solved by a system of central government planning.

Commercial bank Any bank that holds demand deposits.

Common property resources Those that are open to use by everyone. They have, thus, no individual owners (also called common access resources).

Common rent *See* Quasi-rent

Common stock Instruments of ownership of a corporation. People who own shares of common stock can vote on all matters requiring stockholders' consent, and there are no limitations on the amount of dividends they can receive. However, they receive dividends only after all prior claims against the company (interest on bonds, and so on) have been paid.

Comparable worth A proposal under which wages would be based on the intellectual and physical demands of various jobs. Points would be created for each job and jobs with the same numbers of points would receive equal wages.

Comparative advantage A situation in which a nation is relatively more efficient at producing some goods than at producing others, compared with the production capabilities of other nations with which it trades.

Compensatory fiscal policy *See* Functional finance.

Competing interest laws Those in which special interest groups on both sides of a legislative issue vie for favor in order to obtain concentrated benefits.

Competition The market form in which no individual buyer or seller has influence over the price at which she or he buys or sells. *See also* Pure competition.

Complementary investment An investment that increases the productivity of other investments.

Complements Products used in conjunction with each other.

Concentration ratios A measure of the combined market shares of an industry's largest firms.

Conscious parallelism A practice in which a dominant firm sets its prices and other firms set theirs in a way that parallels those of the price leader.

Constant capital-to-labor ratio *See* Capital broadening.

Constant-cost industry An industry in which the cost curves of individual firms remain the same as the output of the industry varies.

Constant GNP *See* Real GNP.

Constant returns to scale The condition for a firm when all inputs are increased at the same proportion and output increases by this same proportion.

Consumer choice A theory of demand that rests on four assumptions about consumers: (1) Consumers buy competitively. (2) Consumers have limited money incomes and full information. (3) Consumers are rational. (4) Consumers maximize their utility or satisfaction.

Consumer price index An index that measures price changes for a certain market basket of goods likely to be purchased by a family of four living in an urban area. Compiled and published monthly by the Bureau of Labor Statistics.

Consumers' surplus The difference between what consumers would be willing to pay for a good and what they actually pay for it.

Consumption function Schedule of the quantities that people are willing and able to consume at different levels of income during a given time period.

Contestable market One in which there are no significant losses from entry or exit due to sunk costs.

Contraction phase That part of the business cycle in which the level of economic activity falls.

Control through the ruble Control that the Soviet Union exercises over business firms through the medium of the Gosbank (central bank). A business firm's account at the Gosbank is credited with the value of its assigned production goal. As the firm uses resources, it pays for them by checks on its account. If the firm uses up its account before it achieves its assigned goal, it fails in its assignment.

Corporate profits The return to entrepreneurship in firms that are incorporated. Corporate profits equal dividends plus retained earnings (undistributed corporate profits) plus corporate taxes.

Corporation A legal entity or form of business enterprise, created by the process of incorporation, which functions separately from its owners.

Cost-plus pricing A form of administered pricing in which a firm first computes its variable cost, then its overhead or fixed cost, and finally adds its expected profit per unit. The result is the price it charges to consumers.

Cost-push inflation The kind of inflation that occurs when suppliers of resources increase their prices faster than productivity of manufacturers increases. Costs of production then go up, which forces prices up.

Countervailing power The idea that monopoly power often exists on both sides of a market. The monopsony power of buyers is counterbalanced by the monopoly power of sellers.

Coupon economics The system by which a government rations the output of the economy by issuing ration coupons to consumers, which consumers must redeem in order to buy rationed products.

Covert collusion A situation in which representatives of various firms in the same industry meet and decide on prices, shares of the market, and other conditions of the market.

Creeping inflation A kind of inflation in which there is a moderate rise in prices that continues for an extended period of time.

Criticism and self-criticism program A program in the Soviet Union that requires individual citizens to identify and report deviations from the government's economic plan.

Cross price elasticity of demand The percentage change in the demand for one good divided by the percentage change in the price of another good.

Crowding theory A theory that explains the effects of discrimination by tracing the impact that discrimination has in forcing women, blacks, or other minorities into certain kinds of employment and out of others.

Cultural Revolution A mass social movement that took place in the People's Republic of China in 1966-1969, supported by the Chinese government and aimed at rooting out bourgeois and antirevolutionary thought and action.

Currency in circulation Currency (both paper money and coins) that is actually in use, not in the vaults of banks or in the Treasury.

Current account An account in the balance-of-payments statement that is like the income and expense statement of a nation. It includes all current transactions, but excludes short-term and long-term movements of capital.

Current account balance The balance in the interpayments accounts obtained by adding exports of goods and services minus imports of goods and services plus net unilateral transfers.

Customer discrimination Job and wage discrimination resulting from tastes of buyers (for example, diners in restaurants preferring to be served by men or whites).

Cyclical deficits component That part of the federal deficit which arises from automatic stabilizers.

Deadweight loss of monopoly A welfare loss to society of consumers' and producers' surplus that results from monopoly. It is a loss not captured by someone else.

Decreasing-cost industry An industry in which external economies cause costs of all individual firms in the industry to fall as the output of the industry as a whole increases.

Deflating current GNP The act of decreasing current GNP to take into account a rise in prices; expressing GNP in terms of dollars of constant purchasing power.

Deflation A general lowering of prices in an economy.

Deflationary gap The increase in aggregate demand necessary to make aggregate demand equal to aggregate supply at full employment.

Demand A set of relationships representing the quantities of a good that consumers are willing to buy over a given range of prices in a given period of time.

Demand curve A graphic plotting of the demand schedule, or a set of relationships between various prices of a good and the quantities of it that the public will buy at each of those prices in a given period of time.

Demand deposits Deposits in commercial banks that can be withdrawn "on demand" by one who presents a check.

Demand-pull inflation A rise in prices that occurs when demand for goods exceeds the ability of the economy to supply these goods at existing prices. The result is that the market rations this short supply through the medium of increased prices.

Demand schedule Indicates the quantity demanded at each price level.

Democratic socialists Those who believe in using democratic procedures to gain political power and curtail capitalism.

Dependent variable The factor in a two-variable system that changes as a result of changes in the independent factor.

Deposit multiplier That formula for determining the multiple that demand deposits may be of the required reserve ratio.

Depreciation An account allowance for the capital that "wears out" (either through use or obsolescence) while being used to produce the final goods and services of an economy in a given period of time.

Derived demand A demand for one thing that depends on the demand for something else. (For example, the demand for labor depends on the demand for the goods produced by labor.)

Dialectical materialism A philosophy in which material things are viewed as the subject of all change, and technology and the natural environment as the main forces that cause society to change continually.

Diminishing marginal utility of income The theory that people get less and less satisfaction from each increase in their incomes.

Diminishing rate of transformation The idea that the rate at which one good may be traded off, or transformed, into another decreases.

Direct The relationship between the independent variable and the dependent variable is direct if the dependent variable changes in the same direction as the independent variable.

Direct democracy A governmental system in which citizens directly choose the rules under which they will be governed.

Dirty float A system of managed exchange rates in which exchange rates are "pegged" or allowed by central banks to move with certain limits.

Discommunication The problems that a large organization encounters in trying to communicate in order to achieve effective decision making; due in part to large size.

Discount rate The rate of interest that the Federal Reserve charges depository institutions when it discounts acceptable short-term debt at the Federal Reserve, to enable the institutions to obtain reserves.

Discretionary fiscal policy Day-to-day fiscal policies established by government officials, designed to cope with changing economic conditions.

Diseconomies of scale The disadvantage a firm may encounter when it increases the size of its plant and increases its output, only to find that the cost of each unit produced is greater than before.

Dissavings Consuming more than is produced, or consuming more than one's income.

Double coincidence of demand In a system of barter exchange the requirement for a mutuality of needs; each party to a transaction must want what the other has.

Double taxation A situation that arises when a corporation pays taxes on its gross receipts. Then it distributes its dividends from these receipts to its stockholders, who must then pay income tax on the previously taxed money.

Duopoly An industry dominated by two interdependent major sellers, although there may be a number of fringe firms as well.

Durable goods Commodities (such as automobiles) that are used up at a very slow rate; that is, it takes a long time (years) to use them up.

Dynamic efficiency Over a period of time, using resources in ways that maximize the long-term benefits from their employment.

Dynamic framework A concept or set of relationships by which one can explain the way certain things change through time.

Economic capacity The level of long-run production that is achieved with the lowest per-unit cost at the optimal plant size.

Economic determinism Assuming that all actions are reactions to changing economic reality.

Economic development The long-term process by which the material well-being of a society's people is significantly increased.

Economic dualism The coexistence within a society of two or more different economies (frequently, one with markets and cash incomes and the other with barter).

Economic imperialism A Marxist concept according to which capitalists ward off a fall in profits and lessen the severity of economic crises by exploiting the underdeveloped countries. Supposedly, capitalists do so by using the underdeveloped countries as a source of demand for their output and supply of cheap raw material and as places to invest capital.

Economic integration The degree to which an economy's resources are employed in their most productive uses.

Economic institutions Social institutions through which economic decisions are made (for example, the Federal Reserve System).

Economic loss The excess of total costs over total revenues.

Economic loss with production A situation in which a firm's short-run total revenue is less than its total costs, but greater than its total variable costs. The firm minimizes its loss by continuing to produce.

Economic loss with shut down A situation in which a firm's short-run total revenue is less than its total costs, but greater than its total variable costs. The firm minimizes its loss by continuing to produce.

Economic loss without production A situation in which a firm's short-run total revenue is not only less than its total costs, but also less than its total variable costs. The firm loses less by closing down altogether.

Economic profit Profit that is above normal profit. When there is economic profit, total revenue is greater than total cost (including the opportunity cost of entrepreneurs).

Economic rent The payment made to a resource whose supply is perfectly inelastic.

Economics The social science that deals with the analysis of material problems, how societies allocate scarce resources to satisfy human wants.

Economies of scale Achieved by a firm when the cost of each unit produced falls as output increases with larger plant size.

Effective demand The total aggregate demand for commodities and services in an economy.

Elasticity of (product) supply A measure of the rate of change in quantity supplied divided by the rate of change in price.

Elasticity of resource demand The rate at which the quantity of a resource demanded changes as its price changes:

$$\%\Delta Qd / \%\Delta P$$

where Q = quantity of the resource demanded, P = price of the resource, and (Greek delta) = "change in."

Elasticity of resource supply The rate of change in the quantity of an input supplied as its price changes:

$$\%\Delta Qs / \%\Delta P$$

where L = amount of labor, W = wage rate, and (Greek delta) = "change in."

Elasticity of supply of labor The rate of change in the quantity of labor supplied divided by the rate of change in the wage or:

$$Qs Qs / W W,$$

where W equals the wage rate.

Embargo An absolute prohibition against importing certain goods.

Employment The situation in which a unit of resource (labor, land, capital, entrepreneurship) is used in some economic activity.

Entrepreneurship The function of organizing labor, land, and capital into a firm capable of producing and marketing a commodity or service.

Entry limit pricing The practice by monopoly and oligopoly firms of setting prices below profit maximizing levels in order to deter entry of new firms.

Equation of exchange $MV = PQ$, where M = supply of money, V = velocity of exchange (number of times M changes hands), P = price level, and Q = number of transactions.

Equilibrium exchange rate The rate of exchange between two currencies that clears the market or eliminates excess supply and demand.

Equilibrium income The level of income that results from the central tendency of a model. This level will be maintained as long as the factors in the model (savings and investment) remain the same.

Equilibrium price The market-clearing price, or the price at which quantity demanded equals quantity supplied.

Equity stock *See* Common stock.

Ex-ante investment The amount of investment firms plan to make.

Ex-post investment The investment that firms actually undertake (not simply plan to undertake).

Excess demand The excess of quantity demanded over quantity supplied at a price lower than the equilibrium price.

Excess reserves Assets that depository institutions hold in the form of reserves, but which are over and above that required by Federal Reserve regulations.

Excess supply The excess of quantity supplied over quantity demanded at a price higher than the equilibrium price.

Exchange controls Devices governments use to ration foreign currencies or eliminate excess demand for those currencies.

Exclusive unions Bargaining agents that agree to restrict union size and maximize the wage gains of their members.

Expansion The process by which a society's output grows as it uses more and more resources.

Expansion phase That part of the business cycle in which economic activity rises.

Expenditure approach A method of computing national income accounts that is concerned with the kinds of goods people buy, with what kinds of expenditures they make.

Explicit costs Those costs of a firm that result from contracting for resources in the markets.

Exploitation In neoclassical economic theory, a payment to a resource that is less than its value of the marginal product.

Exports Commodities and services sold to other nations.

External diseconomies of scale An increase in a firm's costs caused by changes in the output of the industry as a whole.

External diseconomy A cost increase originating outside of the individual firm.

External economies of scale A decrease in a firm's costs caused by increases in the output of the industry as a whole.

External economy A cost decrease originating outside of the individual firm.

Externalities The differences between privately expressed (market) costs and benefits and publicly expressed (nonmarket) costs and benefits. *See also* Spillovers.

Factor markets Those in which the prices of resources like land, labor, capital, and entrepreneurship are established and in which these resources are allocated.

Fascism An economic system combining private property rights with centralized choices about what to produce.

Featherbedding A practice in which unions require a certain number of jobs for the production of goods or services, and there is no need for that number of jobs.

Federal funds market The market in which banks lend their excess reserves to each other over night at the federal funds rate.

Fiat money Money that has greater value as a monetary instrument than as a commodity. It is money because the government issued it and says that it is money, and because people accept it as such.

Final goods and services Goods and services sold to the ultimate user.

Final-value method Method of computing GNP that sums up the prices to final buyers of all goods and services produced by the economy. Avoids double counting by eliminating intermediate production, and leads to the same statistical result as the value-added method of computing GNP.

Financial capital Capital in the form of money; savings that are available for investment in physical capital.

Fine tuning Discretionary changes in fiscal and monetary policy leading to counterchanges in the state of the economy.

Fiscal policy Manipulation of the expenditures and taxes of the federal government to achieve certain economic goals.

Fixed costs Costs that do not vary with output.

Fixed exchange rates A system of international exchange in which the currency of each nation has a certain fixed relationship to the currencies of other nations that is established by government decision. Rates are not allowed to vary with changing market conditions.

Foreign-trade multiplier effect (FTM) The change in GNP resulting from a change in net foreign trade:

$$FTM = GNPX{-}M'$$

where X = exports, M = imports, and (Greek delta) = "change in."

Fractional reserve requirement The percentage of deposits that depository institutions must hold as reserves. As a result, such institutions can lend out amounts that are a multiple of their reserves.

Free good A good with a price of zero. Supply is greater than demand at any price above zero.

Free rider problem Refers to the fact that once public goods are produced, they are available for consumption by individuals who may have contributed nothing to the cost of producing them.

Freely-floating exchange rate A competitive system of international exchange in which the currencies of the various nations are valued according to supply and demand in the international money market. The exchange rate is free to move up or down to eliminate excess supply or excess demand.

Frictional unemployment Short-term unemployment resulting from workers moving from one job to another.

Full capacity A situation in which a firm or industry is at the low point on its long-run average-cost curve.

Full economic integration When all resources of a society are employed and used in their most productive uses.

Full employment A situation in which everyone in the labor force is employed except those who are frictionally unemployed.

Full-employment budget The budget that balances government expenditures against the level of receipts (taxes) that the government would receive if the economy were at full employment.

Functional distribution of income An approach to the distribution of income that emphasizes the *sources* of income: wages, interest, rent, and profit.

Functional finance A policy that aims at compensating for changes in aggregate demand in the private sector by varying the public sector's expenditures and taxes.

General powers of the Federal Reserve System Powers that enable the Federal Reserve to increase or decrease the amounts of excess reserves that commercial banks need in order to make loans.

General price index Index construction by the Commerce Department to convert current GNP to constant GNP.

Giffen goods Those inferior goods with an income effect that moves in the same direction as price and for which the income effect is larger than the substitution effect.

GNP gap The difference between potential GNP and actual GNP achieved.

GNP implicit price deflator *See* General price index.

Gold-flow point The disequilibrium exchange rate at which it is cheaper to buy and ship gold in payment for trade than to buy currencies.

Gold standard The system of international exchange used up until the 1930s, according to which currencies were valued in terms of gold and were convertible into gold, and each nation was obligated to exchange its currency for gold.

Gold tranche position The amount of gold a member nation can borrow from the International Monetary Fund (IMF).

Gosbank The state bank in the Soviet Union, used to control and audit individual firms' activities. All firms have accounts with Gosbank, and all their purchases and sales go through the bank.

Gosplan An agency in the Soviet Union that translates overall goals into a comprehensive plan for the economy. Gosplan is the central planning committee of the Soviet Union.

Government expenditures In the national economic accounts, the measure of all government purchases of goods and services.

Great Leap Forward Second 5-year plan of the people's Republic of China (1958-1962). Execution of the plan was such a disaster that it was abandoned in 1960.

Gross national income (GNI) Total income at market prices generated in the production of all final goods and services during a specific time period. GNI = wages and salaries + rent + interest + proprietors' income + corporate profits + depreciation + indirect business taxes.

Gross national product (GNP) Total dollar value of all final goods and services produced in a given time period. GNP = consumption + gross investment + government expenditures + net foreign investment (export - imports).

Gross private domestic investment Investment including depreciation or capital consumption allowance. *Private* means counting only nongovernment investment; *domestic* means counting only investment made in the U.S. Investment is the act of creating capital, manufactured producer goods that aid in producing consumer goods and other capital goods.

Growth The intensive process by which the productivity (output per hour of labor employed or income per capita) increases.

Hedonism A philosophical school that argues that self-satisfaction is the primary goal of individuals.

Hedonist One who argues that people act to achieve self-satisfaction.

Herfindahl index A measure of market concentration obtained by summing the squared percentage market shares of firms in an industry.

Historical materialism The view that society throughout history has undergone a continual process of change and development from one form to another. The guiding factors in this process are the natural environment and changing technology.

Historical period A period of time in which technology changes.

Homo communista Communist or communal man.

Homo economicus A term meaning "economic person."

Homogeneous product A product so standardized that buyers do not differentiate between the output of different firms.

Horizontal mergers Are mergers between firms in the same industry.

Human capital The improvement in labor skills (marginal physical product) attributable to education or other training, innate ability and acquired skills.

Implicit costs Those costs associated with using self-owned resources.

Import duties *See* Tariffs.

Imports Commodities and services bought from other nations.

Inclusive unions Bargaining agents that seek to expand the number of jobs offered, and thus, the size of the union.

Income approach Computation of the national income accounts based on measuring the kinds of income generated in producing the output of the economy.

Income effect In demand analysis, the change in the quantity of a good that consumers demand as a result of a change in its price and thereby the consumers' purchasing power, or real income.

Income elasticity of demand An estimate of the rate at which the demand for a good varies as consumer incomes vary:

$$\%\Delta Q / \%\Delta Y$$

where Q = output and Y = income

Income-inferior goods Those goods that consumers tend to buy less of as their incomes increase, and more of as their incomes fall.

Incomes policy A policy that frequently involves wage and price controls by the government. In general, a cooperative effort of labor, management, and government to find mutually agreeable goals for the economy and the means to achieve these goals.

Increasing-cost industry An industry in which individual firms experience increasing costs caused by increases in output by the industry as a whole.

Increasing marginal utility of income The assumption that people get more and more satisfaction from each additional increase in their incomes. (This is not generally accepted as true).

Increasing opportunity cost The assumption that as a nation chooses to produce more of one good, it must (ultimately) give up increasing amounts of the other good.

Incremental capital-output ratio The additional capital needed to produce additional output.

Independent variable In a set of relationships, the variable that changes first.

Indicative planning The kind of planning one finds in France, where the government draws up targets for the economy and brings together employers and unions to discuss and modify the proposals. Firms and workers, with government support, move to implement these plans.

Indirect business taxes Taxes on goods and services passed on to consumers in the form of higher prices (for example, excise and sales taxes).

Induced investment Investment generated by changes in income and in quantity consumed. An increase in income leads to greater quantities consumed. Then there is an increase in investment to expand capacity in order to satisfy the new demand.

Inferior goods Goods that you cut back consumption of as your income increases.

Inflating current GNP Increasing current GNP to take into account a fall in prices; expressing GNP in terms of dollars of constant purchasing power.

Inflationary gap The excess demand at full employment that causes prices, rather than output, to increase.

Innovation Introduction of new products or processes.

Input-output relationships The complex set of interrelated requirements for inputs needed by the economy to produce various combinations of output (arranged by industries).

Instantaneous multiplier A multiplier effect that takes place without an intervening period of time. *See also* Multiplier effect.

Interdependency A situation in which economic actions depend on each other (for example, when firms in an industry act on the assumption that their price and output policies are dependent on the actions of other firms in that industry).

Interest The return to the owners of capital. Only interest paid by businesses is included in gross national income. (Interest on the national debt or interest on consumer loans is not included.)

Interlocking directorates A practice in which individuals serve on the boards of directors of more than one firm in the same industry.

Internal economies of scale Decreasing costs from a firm's increased output in the long term. These decreasing costs are due to changes made within the firm.

Internalizing costs and benefits The process through which the prevention of spillovers or externalities is accomplished by having all costs, private and public included in the price of a good.

Internal rate of exchange The rate at which a nation gives up one good in order to produce another.

International monetary fund (IMF) An organization set up at the Bretton Woods Conference in 1944 to facilitate international trade, especially to assure the financing of such trade and to administer the adjustable peg system of post-World War II exchange rates.

International reserves Assets available to central banks and other agencies that are accepted in payment of international debts.

Inverse The relation between independent and dependent variables is inverse if the dependent variable changes in the opposite direction from the independent variable.

Investment function A schedule of the quantities that people are willing and able to invest at various levels of income during a given period of time.

Invisible hand argument The idea attributable to Adam Smith that self-interest based voluntary exchanges can make all those involved in the exchanges better off.

Invisible items The services, including financial services (as opposed to physical commodities), that are exported or imported by a nation. Items not normally reflected in merchandise exports and imports.

Involuntary additions to inventory *See* Unplanned additions to inventory.

Involuntary reductions to inventory *See* Unplanned reductions in inventory.

Jawboning The use of persuasion on the part of the government to get business and industry to comply with government guidelines.

Job discrimination A situation in which workers are employed on the basis of some consideration other than their productivity, such as race or sex.

Kibbutz A community that operates on the principle of complete income equality. In Israel in 1973, there were 240 kibbutzim, with more than 85,000 members.

Kinked-demand curve A demand curve that is based on the assumption that firms in an oligopoly follow suit when competitors' prices decrease, but ignore other firms' price increases.

Labor-intensive process A production process that uses relatively more labor than capital or land.

Laffer curve A theoretical association between various tax rates and the tax revenues collected at each rate.

Law of demand The general rule that consumers buy more at lower prices than they do at higher prices; that price and quantity demanded are inversely related.

Law of diminishing marginal utility The general rule that as more of a particular good is consumed in a given time period, the additional utility of each additional unit of the good will ultimately decrease.

Law of diminishing returns *See* Law of variable proportions.

Law of supply The general rule that the quantity supplied rises as price rises, and falls as price falls; that price and quantity supplied are directly related.

Law of variable proportions (diminishing returns) The general short-run rule that as a firm uses successive equal units of a variable input in conjunction with a fixed input, additions to output (marginal output) derived from the variable input begin to diminish beyond some point.

Leading indicators Certain kinds of economic activity that lead the business cycle by increasing or decreasing before the rest do. Measurements of these indicators are "weather vanes" for the economy.

Leakages Factors in the multiple creation of demand deposits that reduce the ability of depository institutions to expand the supply of money or demand deposits.

Legal tender Anything that the law requires be accepted in payment of a debt.

Limited liability A legal term that means that those who own the corporation (stockholders) are not responsible for its debts. Stockholders' liability (or the amount stockholders are liable for if the firm goes bankrupt) is limited to the purchase price of their stock.

Liquid assets Assets, such as savings accounts or government bonds, that can be quickly converted into money with little risk of loss.

Liquidate To sell a firm or to convert its plant capacity to producing other goods.

Logrolling The practice of trading votes or trading support for one issue in order to obtain support for another.

Long-run period A planning period of a firm or industry, in which all inputs are variable. During this period, the firm can choose any plant size permitted by present technology and by its financial limitations.

Lorenz curve A curve that shows the degree of inequality in the distribution of income for a specific year. The percentage of people in different groups is shown on the horizontal axis, and the percentage of income going to each group is shown on the vertical axis.

Loss minimization *See* Profit maximization.

M1 money A measure of the money supply that consists of currency, coin and checking deposits and travelers checks.

M2 money A measure of the money supply that consists of all components in M1 plus savings deposits, small time deposits and money market mutual funds.

M3 money A measure of the money supply that consists of all the components of M2 plus large value certificates of deposit.

Macroeconomics The study of the forces that determine the level of income and employment in a society.

Malthusian specter The nineteenth-century view, advanced by Thomas R. Malthus, that the supply of people (increasing at a geometric rate) would outrun the supply of food (increasing at an arithmetic rate), and that widespread starvation would result.

Margin requirements Regulation by the Federal Reserve of the percentage of the selling price of stock that a purchaser must put down in cash in order to buy a stock. The purchaser may borrow the rest from a bank or a stockbroker.

Marginal cost The cost of producing an additional unit of output.

Marginal efficiency of capital The expected rate of return on capital; the stream of income a business expects to obtain over the life of a piece of capital in relation to the price of that capital.

Marginal physical product The additional amount of product that a firm can produce as a result of hiring an additional unit of input (labor, capital, and so on).

Marginal private cost or benefit Cost or benefit that individuals derive from producing or consuming an additional unit of a good.

Marginal propensity to consume The percentage of any change in income that people tend to spend:

$$MPC = \Delta C / \Delta Y$$

where C = consumption, Y = income and (Greek delta) = "change in."

Marginal propensity to save The percentage of any change in income that people tend to save:

$$MPS = \Delta S / \Delta Y$$

where S = savings, Y = income and (Greek delta) = "change in."

Marginal resource cost The amount it costs a firm to hire one more unit of a resource or factor.

Marginal revenue The change in total revenue due to a small or one-unit change in output.

Marginal revenue product The addition to total revenue attributable to using an additional unit of a resource. One finds it by multiplying the marginal physical product of the resource times the marginal revenue from selling the additional units of product it produces.

Marginal social cost or benefit Cost or benefit to society caused by producing and consuming an additional unit of a good.

Marginal tax rates The rates on additional taxable income.

Marginal utility The additional satisfaction derived from the consumption of the last unit (or additional unit) of a good purchased.

Marginal utility of income The change in satisfaction derived from a change in income.

Marginal utility of leisure The change in satisfaction derived from change in leisure time.

Market period The period of time in which a firm has already produced its output. All costs are fixed costs.

Market system The set of means by which exchanges between buyer and seller are made.

Marxist socialism A system of philosophy of government and economics that grew out of the writings of Karl Marx in the nineteenth century.

Materials-balance approach An explanation of environmental problems based on the amount of input used in production and the disposal of waste products created in the consumption of that output.

Means of deferred payment The function of money that is concerned with facilitating lending and the repayment of loans.

Medium of exchange The function of money that deals with exchanging goods for money and money for goods.

Mercantilism A system of economic thought, at its peak from the sixteenth to nineteenth centuries, according to which governments were responsible for the welfare of the economy.

Microeconomics The study of disaggregated economic activities or how a market economy allocates resources through prices.

Midpoint formula A device used in calculating the price elasticity of demand by dividing the average rate of change in quantity demanded by the average rate of change in price.

Mixed economies Economic systems that combine elements of private and public property rights and centralized as well as decentralized choices about resource usage.

Model A device economists use to create a systematic analogy to actual economic behavior.

Monetarism An approach to economic policy that emphasizes the dominant role of the supply of money. It calls for a fixed and appropriate increase in the money supply each year as the basic policy for economic stabilization.

Monetary policy A government's manipulation of the money supply to achieve economic goals.

Money Anything that performs the functions of a medium of exchange, standard of values, store of value, and standard of deferred payment.

Money (current) GNP Output of a given year valued at the prices of that year. Data on GNP before being adjusted for price changes.

Money income The number of dollars received in income; does not reflect purchasing power.

Monopolistic competition A market situation with three main characteristics: (1) many firms, (2) differentiated products, and (3) relative ease of entry into and exit from the market.

Monopoly power A firm's ability to influence the price of its product.

Monopsony A market situation in which there is only one buyer.

Monopsony profit *See* Technical factor exploitation.

Moral suasion The use of persuasion by the Federal Reserve to get depository institutions to do what it wants.

Multinational corporations (MNCs) International firms that buy raw materials, sell finished products, and have production facilities in many countries.

Multiplier effect The multiple change in income due to a given initial change in aggregate demand. *See also* Balanced-budget multiplier.

Multiplier formula

$$M = 1/ \text{MPS or } 1/1\text{- MPC}$$

where MPC = marginal propensity to consume and MPS = marginal propensity to save.

National banks Commercial banks chartered by the federal government.

National income (NI) Net income of a country using factor prices generated in the production of all goods and services in a given period of time. NI = wages and salaries + rent + interest + proprietors' income + corporate profits.

National income at factor prices Net income of a country obtained by using only market prices of factors rather than market prices of finished commodities or sales on the commodity markets.

Natural monopoly A market situation for an industry in which there are economies of scale up to the output rate that fills the market. A single firm is more efficient than any larger number of firms.

Natural rate of unemployment The difference between what economists consider full employment and a zero level of unemployment. Basically it is frictional unemployment.

Near money Assets that have all the characteristics of money except that they are not used as a medium of exchange.

Negatively sloped A curve sloping downward, to the right, on a diagram.

Negative net investment A situation in which gross investment is less than depreciation. In such a case, the capital stock of the economy is contracting.

Negative savings *See* Dissavings.

Negative sum game When losses exceed the winnings in a game.

Neoclassical economics School of economic thought developed during the late nineteenth century. Many aspects of this thought are considered valid today, and others have been changed and expanded. For example, Keynesian economics (named after John Maynard Keynes) evolved from a basic change in one aspect of neoclassical economics.

Net foreign trade (NFT) The difference between exports and imports:

$$NFT = X - M,$$

where X = exports and M = imports.

Net national income (NNI) A nation's net income at market prices generated in the production of all final goods and services during a given period of time (excluding depreciation) NNI = wages and salaries + rent + interest + proprietors' income + corporate profits + indirect business taxes.

Net national product (NNP) The net value of all final goods and services a nation produces during a given time period (excluding depreciation), NNP = consumption + net investment + government expenditures ± net exports.

Nomenklatura The term used to describe the Soviet elite whose special entitlements increase their real incomes.

Nondurable goods Commodities, such as food, that are used up fairly quickly.

Nonprice competition Forms of competition between businesses that do not involve price. May include competition in styling, services, advertising, and quality.

Normal goods Those that consumers buy more of as their real incomes rise and less of as their real incomes fall.

Normal profit A profit just large enough to keep the firm producing in the long run. Normal profit equals the entrepreneur's opportunity cost (what entrepreneurship could earn in other uses). A normal profit is included in total cost.

Normative economics Economic discussions that make judgments about the way things should be.

Official reserve transactions account An account of those sources such as borrowing from other official agencies that finance the basic balance.

Official reserve transactions balance In a nation's balance of payments, the account showing how a payment deficit is financed.

Oligopoly An industry characterized by (1) the existence of a few firms that dominate an industry, each of which can affect the actions of others in the industry; (2) either homogeneous or differentiated products; and (3) significant barriers to entry.

Oligopsony A situation in which there are few buyers in the market.

OPEC An acronym for the Organization of Petroleum Exporting Countries, an international oil export cartel that sets the price of (most) exported oil.

Open market economy A market economy that does exchange products, services, or resources with other economies or nations.

Open-market operations The buying and selling, by the Federal Reserve, of highly liquid, short-term, low-risk government debt.

Opportunity cost The best alternative good one gives up when one chooses to produce a certain thing.

PACs or political action committees Organizations that channel funds from special interest groups to the election campaigns of politicians.

Paradox of thrift An ironic situation in which, during a recession, if people all try to increase their savings, the equilibrium level of income of the nation and the actual quantity saved decrease.

Paradox of value That some goods have great total utility in use (e.g.; water) but little in exchange while other goods have relatively little value in use (e.g.; diamonds) but great value in exchange. The price we are willing to pay for a good is based on its value in exchange.

Pareto optimal A situation that makes at least one person better off while making no one else worse off.

Parity A level for farm-product prices, maintained by governmental support and intended to give farmers the same purchasing power for each product sold as they had in some designated base period.

Partnership A business arrangement in which two or more individuals combine to operate an unincorporated business enterprise.

Per capital real GNP The figure obtained by dividing real GNP by the size of the population.

Per se rule A rule in law that certain acts are illegal in and of themselves, no matter what their intent.

Perfect economic integration The situation in which units of a resource are paid the same amount in all uses of that resource.

Perfect elasticity The situation in which price elasticity of demand approaches infinity. This means that as the quantity demanded changes, there is no change in price. The demand curve is horizontal.

Perfect inelasticity The situation in which price elasticity of demand equals zero. This means that as price changes, there is no change in quantity demanded. The demand curve is vertical.

Perfect integration The situation in which units of a resource are paid the same amount in all uses of that resource.

Perfect price discrimination The situation in which a firm charges the same consumer a different price for each unit sold. The price is the maximum that the consumer will pay for each unit.

Perfectly contestable market One in which there are no losses from entry or exit due to sunk costs.

Periodic multiplier A multiplier effect that takes place over time. *See also* Multiplier effect.

Personal disposable income The portion of personal income that people may either spend or save. PDI = personal income - personal taxes.

Personal income All income received by people, whether from production or from transfer payments. PI = national income + undistributed corporate profits + corporate taxes ± net transfer payments.

Phillips curve A curve that shows the trade-off between unemployment and price changes. If employment increases, prices will increase; if unemployment increases, price increases will go down.

Physical capital Capital in the form of tools and instruments of production.

Pigou effect An economic reaction whereby, as prices fall, people with savings have greater purchasing power; therefore, savers increase their demand for goods and services.

Positive economics Economic discussions that consist of pointing out what *is*, positive economics contains no value judgments.

Positive net investment A situation in which gross investment exceeds depreciation; this means that the capital stock of the economy is expanding.

Positive sum game When winnings exceed losses in a game.

Positively sloped Sloping upward, to the right on a diagram.

Precautionary purposes One reason why people want to hold money; they want cash in hand in case of emergencies.

Preferred stocks Stocks that have preference status when it comes to receiving dividends and assets of a given corporation, in case the corporation should have to liquidate. Preferred stocks usually do not carry voting privileges, and the amount of dividends is usually limited.

Present discriminatory activity Basing jobs and wages on goods other than productivity.

Price discrimination The charging of different prices for a good to different consumers. A situation in which the price of a unit of some good, divided by the marginal cost of that unit, is not the same for all customers. The seller of the good discriminates against some customers.

Price elastic A term describing a market situation in which the quantity of a good demanded changes at a faster rate than the price of the good:

$$\%\Delta Q/\%\Delta P > 1$$

where Q = quantity, P = price, (Greek delta) = "change in, "and > = "greater than."

Price elasticity of demand (E_d) An estimate of the rate at which the quantity demanded of a good varies in response to its price:

$$E_d = \%\Delta Q/\%\Delta P$$

where Q = quantity demanded, P = price, (Greek delta) = "change in."

Price elasticity of supply An estimate of the rate at which the quantity of a good supplied changes as the price of the product changes:

$$E_s = \%\Delta Qs/\%\Delta P$$

where Q = quantity supplied, P = price, (Greek delta) = "change in."

Price floor A target price, usually established by government, below which the market price is not allowed to move.

Price index A measure of changes in a price level.

Price inelastic demand A term describing a market situation in which the quantity of a good demanded changes at a slower rate than the price of the good:

$$\%\Delta Q/\%\Delta P < 1 \text{ where Q = quantity demanded, P = price,}$$
(Greek delta="change in," and < = "less than.")

Price leadership In an oligopoly, a form of implicit collusion in which a leader firm sets prices that are observed and followed by others in the industry.

Price rivalry The contest in which sellers watch what prices others charge and then react to those prices.

Price seeker A firm that must set the price of its product(s) as well as determine its most profitable output rate.

Price taker A firm which acts on a price that is beyond its control. This generally occurs in perfect competition.

Primary demand Demand for a commodity (such as cars or refrigerators) by those who have not owned that commodity before: first-time owners.

Private equilibrium The *market* equilibrium between the buyer's privately and noncollusively determined benefits from the sale of a commodity and the seller's privately determined costs (including the profit necessary for entrepreneurship).

Private rates of return Rates of return on investment that do not take into account indirect social costs and benefits (called external costs and benefits).

Producers' surplus The difference between the actual selling price of a good and the marginal cost of producing it.

Product differentiation An attempt to make your product different, or appear to be different, from your competitors product.

Production-possibilities curve A graphic representation of the production-possibilities function. *See also* Production-possibilities function.

Production-possibilities function A relationship expressing those combinations of goods that the full-employment use of a society's resources can produce during a particular period of time (using the best available technology).

Profit A return or payment to the entrepreneur.

Profit maximization To produce an output level where profits are maximized. Profit is said to be maximized or loss minimized when production is at the level at which marginal cost is equal to marginal revenue.

Profit-push inflation *See* Administered-price inflation.

Profits of unincorporated businesses. *See* Proprietors' income.

Progressive tax A tax with a rate that increases as the tax base increases.

Proletariat Workers in the factories of the industrial societies developed since the eighteenth century.

Property rights Rights of ownership to use, to transfer, and to benefit from the employment of factors of production.

Proportional tax A tax with a rate that remains the same as the tax base changes.

Proprietors' income The return to entrepreneurship in firms that are not incorporated.

Protectionism The government's effort to protect domestic firms or industries from free (competitive) international trade by imposing tariffs or quotas on imported commodities.

Public goods Goods that can be used by a person without reducing the amount available for other people to use.

Pure competition A market form that has the following characteristics: (1) No single firm can influence price. (2) There is no collusion. (3) Products are homogeneous. (4) There are no barriers to entry or exit. (5) Prices are flexible. (6) Buyers and sellers have full information.

Pure economic determinism The assumption that the actions of people and institutions are reactions to changing economic reality.

Pure economic rent The payment to a resource whose supply is perfectly inelastic.

Pure monopoly A market form in which (1) there is just one firm, and (2) the firm's product has no close substitutes.

Pure monopsony A labor market situation in which there is one employer that sets wage rates.

Pure number A number that is independent of the units of measure of the factors involved in compiling it.

Quantity adjuster A firm that has no control over the price at which it sells its product. It decides only how much to produce.

Quasi-rent or common rent The difference between the actual payment to a resource in relatively inelastic supply and its opportunity cost.

Quotas Restrictions on the quantities of goods that may be imported into, or exported from, a country.

Random variations Variations that cannot be accounted or planned for, since they do not follow any regular pattern.

Rational expectations hypothesis The view that decision makers form their inflationary expectations on the basis of current and recent past events and thus anticipate future events.

Rate of exchange The price at which one nation's currency is exchanged for that of another.

Rate of transformation The rate at which one good is traded off for another.

Rational ignorance The argument that when the benefits of a public choice are highly concentrated and its costs highly diffused, it is rational for those who bear its costs to ignore them.

Real GNP The output of a nation for a given year, adjusted for price changes between that year and given base year.

Real income The value of what one can buy with one's money income.

Regressive tax A tax with a rate that declines as the tax base increases.

Regulated monopoly A market situation in which one firm usually has a franchise from government, but a government regulatory commission sets prices and other conditions that the firm must follow.

Regulation Q A government regulation that empowered the Federal Reserve to set the maximum interest rates that commercial banks can pay on savings accounts and demand deposit (checking) accounts. This regulation was abolished in the early 1980s.

Regulations X and W Government regulations that empowered the Federal Reserve to set minimum down payments and maximum length of loans for consumer lending and real estate lending; expired in the 1960s.

Relative rent Differences in rent payments to a resource in different uses.

Rent (national income measures) In the calculation of gross national income, the payments to owners of land. Includes an estimated rent on homes occupied by their owners.

Rent (resource market payments) A payment to resource owners above that which would just induce them to employ resources in a particular use.

Rent seeking activities Those activities undertaken by special interest groups to obtain privileges from governments that will raise their return above opportunity cost.

Replacement demand *See* Secondary demand.

Representative democracies Systems of government in which voters choose elected representatives to make public choices.

Required reserve ratio The percentage of depository institutions' demand deposits that the Federal Reserve requires these banks (financial institutions) to keep in the form of assets called reserves.

Reserve army of the unemployed A Marxist term denoting the number of people who are unemployed in capitalistic societies because of the increased use of capital and improved technology (that is, machines replacing labor).

Reserves Eligible assets (their eligibility determined by the Federal Reserve) that must be held by depository institutions.

Resource externalities Changes in the costs of resources that are not attributable to the actions of a single firm but are due to changes in the industry, or in the natural or political environment.

Resources The inputs (land, labor, capital, entrepreneurship) used to make consumer and producer goods.

Results of historical discrimination The effects on present patterns of jobs and wages attributable to previous economic discrimination.

Retained earnings Undistributed corporate profits.

Rule of reason A rule under which there is a broad judicial determination of the reasons for a firm's conduct and the effects of that conduct on restraint of trade.

Sales maximization hypothesis The argument that firms seek to maximize sales or the size of the firm rather than the firm's profit.

Satisficing A decision to seek an acceptable or satisfactory level of profit as opposed to a maximum level of profit.

Savings-equals-intended-investment approach An approach to the problem of finding equilibrium income, in a model without government and foreign trade, according to which the intended investment curve is placed above the x axis (measured income) in relation to the savings function ($S = II$).

Savings function Schedule of the quantities that people are willing and able to save at different levels of income during a given period of time.

Say's law Supply creates its own demand

Scarcity The relation between limited resources and unlimited wants which results in the inability to satisfy all human wants for goods and services.

Seasonal variations Fluctuations in employment, money supply, and cash flows that occur regularly at certain periods each year.

Second degree price discrimination The practice of charging different prices to different groups of buyers.

Secondary demand Demand by consumers for commodities to replace consumer goods.

Secular trend The expansion or contraction of an economy over very long periods of time. The long-term trend in any time series.

Services Those products of an economy (haircuts, medical attention, and so on) that are not commodities. The value of services is included when GNP is computed.

Short-run period The period of actual production, in which some resources used by a firm are variable and at least one resource is fixed.

Shut down point or price The rate of output that corresponds to a price equaling average variable cost. Total revenue equals total variable cost and the firm's loss is no greater with than without production.

Signaling The idea that employers pay higher wages to more educated workers because the education is a signal of other aspects of productivity increasing behavior.

Single-tax movement A school of thought in the late nineteenth century, led by Henry George, which proposed taxing away all land rents and using the revenues to fund governments. Henry George believed this would be the only tax needed to finance an economy.

Social costs Private costs plus spillovers (externalities). *See also* Externalities; Spillovers.

Socialism A social system in which there is collective or governmental ownership of the means of production and distribution of goods. There are many brands of socialism, encompassing many gradations of political and economic thought. Common to all of them is the idea that control of the means of production should be in public, not private, hands.

Sole proprietorship A form of business enterprise in which one person is the owner, and is solely responsible for that enterprise.

Special drawing rights (SDRs) A system of international reserve assets, the so-called "paper gold"; a market basket of currencies established by the International Monetary Fund (IMF). Nations that are members of the IMF may borrow these SDRs to ease currency crises.

Special interest laws Those that confer concentrated benefits but impose diffused costs on voters.

Specific powers of the Federal Reserve Powers of the Federal Reserve to regulate particular areas of lending, such as margin requirements on stock purchases; Regulation Q, W, and X were part of these powers.

Speculative purposes One reason why people wish to hold some of their assets in the form of money: they want to be able to take advantage of unforeseen opportunities to invest, to buy bargains, and so forth.

Spillovers Differences between *private* costs and benefits and *public* costs and benefits. *See also* Externalities.

Standard of value The function of money that enables people to place values on goods and services.

State banks Commercial banks chartered by the various state governments.

Static efficiency At a point in time, using resources in ways that produce the most desired mix of output.

Stationary state A condition in which a given society has reached the upper limit to its growth in per capita income.

Store of value The function of money that enables holders of money to save by a process of transferring value from the present to the future.

Structural deficits component That part of the federal deficit that arises from discretionary fiscal policy.

Structural unemployment A kind of unemployment caused by changes in the structure of the economy, either in the composition of demand or in technology. Either one of these types of changes may cause changes in the composition of the demand for labor.

Substitutes Products that may be consumed in place of each other.

Substitution effect An effect that appears when there is a change in the quantity of a good demanded resulting from a change in its price relative to other goods' prices. This effect comes to light during analysis of demand in a given market. A relatively cheaper good is substituted for relatively more expensive goods.

Sunk costs Outlays on resources that have already been made. Also called fixed costs.

Superior goods Those whose consumption varies in the same direction as but at a greater rate than real income. The elasticity of income is greater than 1.

Supply A set of relationships representing the quantities of a product that a firm (or all firms in an industry) will offer for sale at each possible price in a given period of time.

Supply curve A graphic plotting of the supply schedule, or a set of relationships between various prices of a good and the quantities of it that a firm supplies.

Supply of M_1 money All demand deposits in commercial banks, plus all currency and coin in circulation.

Supply of resources The quantities of a resource offered for sale at various prices in a given period of time.

Supply side economics Efforts and incentives to stimulate growth in aggregate supply.

Surplus value Marxist term for the differences between the wages paid to workers and the market value of what workers produce. Surplus value, to Marxists, measures the degree of exploitation of the proletariat (working class).

Synthesis In Marxist theory, the system that evolves after the antithesis has forced social changes.

Tariffs Taxes on imported goods.

Tax avoidance The process by which tax obligations are minimized by lawful use of the provision of tax laws.

Tax evasion The illegal process by which tax obligations are either not reported or incorrectly reported in order to evade tax payment.

Tax rate With respect to income, the percentage of income a citizen must pay annually in taxes. With respect to property, the percentage of the value of property the owner must pay to the government annually in taxes.

Technical factor exploitation In factor markets, the failure of a monopsonistic employers to pay resources their value of marginal product or marginal revenue product (also called monopsony profit).

Technocrats Term used by John Kenneth Galbraith to describe those who hold power in large corporations (also used to apply to those who would "manage" the economy).

Technological change Growth in knowledge or advances in techniques that result in more productive capital goods and more efficient organization.

Technostructure Term used by John Kenneth Galbraith to describe the many interlocking committees of people with technical expertise in large corporations, who make the essential corporate decisions.

Terms of trade Relationship between a nation's export prices and its import prices:
$$T = P_X P_I \text{ where } P_X = \text{prices of exports and } P_I = \text{prices of imports.}$$

Thesis In Marxist theory, the set of social arrangements existing at a given time.

Tight money policy A policy of a nation's central banking authority that aims at reducing aggregate demand by decreasing the supply of money in an economy.

Time deposits Savings accounts for which depository institutions can require prior notice before the account holder can withdraw the funds.

Total cost Total fixed cost plus total variable cost.

Total utility The entire satisfaction from consuming a good.

Transactions purposes One reason for holding some assets in the form of money. People do not receive their income at exactly the same time that they need to pay out money. Thus, they want to hold money to be able to meet these day-to-day payments.

Trust An organization that controls the voting shares of an industry and thus can set output rates and prices like a multi-plant monopoly.

Turnover tax A tax on goods as they pass through the various stages of production. The Soviet Union uses turnover taxes to increase prices so that the quantities of goods available (quantity supplied) will be equal to the quantities demanded. It is also employed in some Western European countries.

UNCTAD United Nations Conference on Trade and Development.

Underemployment An employment situation in which units of resources are not employed in their most productive uses.

Unemployment A situation in which a unit of a resource is unable to find use as an input.

Underground economy Transactions that occur and give rise to taxable income but are not reported for tax purposes.

Union shop A labor market in which individuals who are employed by a firm must then join the union.

Unions Organizations formed by employees for purposes of collective bargaining with employers.

Unit elastic demand A term describing a market situation in which quantity demanded of a good changes at the same rate as its price:

$$\%\Delta Q / \%\Delta P = 1$$

where Q = quantity demanded, P = price, and (Greek delta) = "change in."

Unit of account *See* Standard of value.

Unlimited liability A situation in which there is no differentiation between the assets of the business and the personal wealth of its proprietor. If the business suffers reverses, the owner is personally liable for all its debts.

Unlimited life A situation in which a corporation can continue to exist no matter who owns its stock.

Unplanned additions to inventory A situation in which a business firm produces more of its product than the public is willing or able to buy, which must then be added to inventory. The result is that the business acts to reduce supplies and reduce amounts produced; income moves toward equilibrium.

Unplanned reduction in inventory A situation in which a business firm does not produce as much of its product as the public is willing and able to buy. The result is that the business acts to increase its orders and increase the amounts produced; income moves toward equilibrium.

Utility theory A theory of demand that assumes that consumers buy things on the basis of their evaluation of the satisfaction to be derived from various combinations of goods, and of their effort to maximize that satisfaction.

Value-added method A method of computing GNP in which one adds all additions to the value of a product made at each stage of production; the total of these additions for a given product equals the final value of that product.

Value of marginal product The value to consumers of the output produced by using an additional unit of a resources. One computes this value by multiplying the marginal physical product of the resource times the price of the good produced by the resource.

Variable costs Costs of factors of production (such as labor, raw materials, and so forth) that vary according to variations in the firm's output.

Veblen good A good whose appeal is greater at higher prices than at lower prices.

Velocity of exchange The number of times the supply of money changes hands in a given period of time.

Vertical mergers A merger of firms producing inputs to be used in the production of a final product.

Visible items Those commodities (such as cars, food, and machinery) that are exported or imported by a nation.

Wage and price controls Mandatory limits on wages and prices established by a regulatory authority and enforced by law.

Wage and price guidelines Suggested rules for levels of wages and prices. The government suggests these rules, but compliance with them is voluntary.

Wage discrimination A form of price discrimination in which employers use, as criteria to determine the wages they pay to their employees, certain characteristics that have nothing to do with the productivity of the employees, such as race or sex. They may pay lower wages to blacks than to whites, to women than to men, and so forth.

Wages and salaries The money income, including social security taxes, that is the return to labor; figured into the computation of gross national income.

Waste of monopolistic competition The failure of monopolistically competitive firms to produce at minimum long-run average cost or, in other words, the tendency to product with excess capacity.

Wholesale price index An index that measures change in wholesale prices.

Zero economic growth (ZEG) The idea or belief that an economy's GNP should not increase. ZEG is usually based on a concern for preserving or improving the physical and cultural environment.

Zero population growth (ZPG) The slogan advanced by people who feel that the birth rate should equal the death rate so that population will not increase.

Zero sum game When winnings are equal to losses in a game.

Index

Study Guide

Table of Contents

Chapter 1: Breaking the Ice

PART 1

First, read the section entitled "Summing Up" at the end of Chapter 1. The summary offers a thorough review of the chapter.

Things to Watch For

Economics—originally called "political economy"—has existed as a separate area of study for about two centuries. Early economists (called classical economists), beginning with Adam Smith, were generally pessimistic about the future of people's material well-being. Twentieth-century economists are much more optimistic about the ability of society to manage or even, in the long run, to solve economic problems. By economic problems, they mean the ability of a society to provide for the material well-being of its people.

Chapter 1 deals with the role of self interest: What motivations underlie people's economic behavior? It traces the efforts of economists, ever since the eighteenth century's Adam Smith, to answer this question. Smith said that self-interest is the dominant motivation of people. He maintained that the role of government should be to make sure that the self-interested efforts of private citizens contribute as much as possible to the public interest. Benthamites (nineteenth-century followers of Jeremy Bentham) believed that humans are walking calculators of pain and pleasure, and that all they want is to maximize pleasure (a view known as hedonism).

Later economists, such as Alfred Marshall, rejected the notion of precise maximization of pleasure, but continued to believe that the pursuit of monetary gain, as well as the satisfaction to be derived from consuming the goods bought with money, is people's most powerful economic motivation. John Maynard Keynes, writing in the 1930s, observed that the economic problem—scarcity and the limits it imposes on satisfying human wants—might be solved. However, he felt that until scarcity could be eliminated, nations would have to continue to rely on human self-interest to create savings, investment, and growth. Most modern economists agree that self-interest, although not the *only* economic motivation, is the most powerful one. They feel that business firms *almost* maximize profits and consumers *almost* maximize satisfaction.

Radical economists maintain that **homo communista** (communist man) will replace the old idea of the self-interested **homo economicus** (economic man). The communist citizen, they say, will be concerned with the interests of the group and the community as a whole, not with the interests of self. In the early twenty-first century, as more and more societies seek to create self-interest incentives to economic growth, homo communista seems endangered.

Chapter 1 defines economics, describes the methods used by economists, and discusses why a knowledge of those methods is important. The definition of economics emphasizes these basic facts: (1) Economics is a social (rather than a physical) science. (2) It is analytical rather than simply descriptive. (3) It is concerned with the material well-being of people.

Chapter 1 explains that economists seek to analyze world problems by a method that ordinarily encompasses three stages: (1) A *descriptive* stage, in which economists gather the facts that bear on the causes of the problem. (2) A *theorizing* stage, in which economists formulate a **model**, or a simplified set of relationships that form an analogy to reality. In this stage they may also formulate a hypothesis—that is, assume a certain relationship between variables contained in the model—and then test the model to see to what extent a change in the "problem" variable can be explained by changes in the other variables stated in the hypothesis. (3) A *policy-making* stage, when economists know the results of the testing and are prepared to make recommendations on an *economic policy*. Bear in mind that economic policies are a part of overall social policies; economists themselves rarely make those policies.

As you study economics, always be aware that the principles you learn won't lead you to *unique* conclusions about solutions to economic problems. Not even experienced professional economists have *unique* solutions to the world's problems.

Throughout the text you will find sections called applications. These applications are short articles about economic problems. Each is designed to illuminate the economic theory you have learned in the preceding chapter. You will find that you are already familiar with most of these problems; the only new thing will be the approach, or the *way* the problem is treated, using economic principles. Each time you finish an application, consider how those principles may be applied to other problems you are aware of. You will be surprised at how universally applicable the tools of the economist are. In the first chapter of your textbook are several short applications. These six applications deal with important issues currently being addressed in the United States. They deal with Social Security reform, saving in the nation, problems of public education, affordable housing, and the cost and availability of health care. As you read these applications, notice the extent to which these are economic as well as social and political issues. Note also the "economic way" of thinking about these issues leads not to unique solutions but to the identification of alternative solutions. A useful approach to maximizing your understanding of economic principles is to read these applications now for general familiarity with the subjects addressed. As you complete the course, come back to chapter 1 and reread them in light of what you have learned. See if your understanding or perhaps even your viewpoints have changed.

When you get to the end of a chapter, carefully read the summary of it, entitled "Summing Up," which gives a point-by-point list of the main things to remember.

As you work your way through the book, don't be anxious about how much mathematics you are expected to know. A major feature of this book is its mathematical simplicity. We believe that a student can learn basic principles of economics and how to apply them, without having calculus or any of the other mathematical tools that are useful in advanced economics courses. We do, however, make extensive use of graphs as visual illustrations of economic relationships. The combination of verbal explanations and graphical illustrations will reinforce your understanding of both principles and problems.

Part 2

Define the following terms and concepts.

1. Hedonism
2. Model
3. Hypothesis
4. Homo economicus
5. Homo communista
6. Economics
7. Experimental economics
8. Positive economics
9. Normative economics
10. Macroeconomics
11. Microeconomics
12. Independent variable
13. Dependent variable
14. Inverse relationshi
15. Direct relationship

Part 3

Answer the following questions and problems.

1. How has the view of people's economic motivation changed over the last hundred years?

2. Why did nineteenth-century philosophers call economics "the dismal science"? What has happened to make it less dismal in the twentieth and twenty first centuries?

3. What are the three basic stages in economic analysis? What is the role of the economist in the third stage?

4. Using Figure 1-1, do the following things:

    a. Label the axes on which one measures changes in the dependent variable and the independent variable.

    b. Draw "curves," showing (1) an inverse relationship between the two variables; (2) a direct relationship between them; (3) a curve that is positively sloped; (4) a curve that is negatively sloped; (5) a curve in which all change is in the dependent variable; and (6) a curve in which all change is in the independent variable. Label the curves 1, 2, 3, and so on.

Figure 1-1
Graph for Problem 4

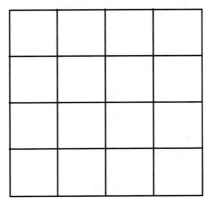

5. Why are more and more societies relying on self-interest as the basis for incentives to economic activity?

6. What is the difference between macroeconomics and microeconomics?

7. What is the difference between an independent variable and a dependent variable?

8. Why does economics use so many graphs & equations?

Part 4 Self-test

Section A True/false questions

T F 1. Unless businesses exactly maximize profits and consumers exactly maximize satisfaction, self-interest is ruled out as an economic motivation.

T F 2. If a curve is negatively sloped, there is a *direct* relationship between the dependent and independent variables.

T F 3. A model exactly describes reality.

T F 4. A hypothesis is a statement of relationships that are known to be true.

T F 5. Economists can generally create controlled laboratory conditions that permit them to repeat laboratory experiments dealing with economic behavior.

T F 6. Economists assume that material problems are the only important problems.

T F 7. In order to make economic policy, a person must be an economist.

T F 8. Economists are generally more optimistic today about the *ability* of people to solve problems of material well-being than they were 150 years ago.

T F 9. Economists assume that business firms maximize profits to the greatest degree possible because firms precisely behave this way.

T F 10. Most economists accept the old assumption of *homo economicus* as an appropriate way to explain the behavior of consumers and producers.

T F 11. Applying economic problems to the analysis of social problems leads to unique solutions.

T F 12. Alfred Marshall, considered to be the founder of modern economics, argued that self-interest and acquisitiveness were the primary economic motivations of people.

T F 13. Economics is the social science that deals with the analysis of material problems.

T F 14. There are four basic stages in Economic Analysis.

T F 15. Positive economics consists of determining what is.

Section B Multiple-choice questions

1. Which one of the following do most economists *not* assume to be true of economic behavior?
    a. Consumers and producers have clear objectives.
    b. Consumers seek to obtain as much satisfaction as possible.
    c. Producers seek to obtain as much profit as possible.
    d. Consumers and producers are more concerned with the interests of others than with their own interests.

2. Which of the following statements is *positive*?
    a. We should break up all large corporations.
    b. Consumers ought to be represented in the Cabinet.
    c. Unions are bad.
    d. The deficit in the federal budget last year was about $400 billion.

3. Which of the following statements is *normative*?
    a. American Telephone and Telegraph (AT&T) earned 9.6 percent on its investment last year.
    b. There are more telephones in the United States than in any other nation.
    c. New telephones put into service last year numbered 200,000.
    d. The breakup of AT&T into several companies was a good decision.

4. Adam Smith believed that the public interest is best served by
    a. government planning.
    b. monopolistic firms.
    c. wage-price controls.
    d. self-interest harnessed to the public good.

5. Alfred Marshall argued that the economic motive of people is to achieve
    a. a contemplative life.
    b. power over others.
    c. monetary gain.
    d. subjective social welfare.

6. In the early twenty-first century, self-interest as a motivation to economic activity and growth
    a. is largely disappearing as governments rely more and more on the incentives of homo communista.
    b. has reappeared in Western Europe and North America.
    c. is reappearing in formerly socialist states of Eastern Europe and Asia.
    d. is disappearing as more and more nations rely on central planning.

7. Marxists seek to discredit *homo economicus* because they believe that, in a capitalist society,
   a. concentration of power in the hands of business firms leads to alienation of workers and consumers.
   b. business people are concerned with social welfare.
   c. government prevents maximization of profit and satisfaction.
   d. people don't have enough information to act rationally.

8. A positively sloped curve is one that
   a. slopes up or to the right.
   b. slopes down or to the left.
   c. involves an inverse relationship between two variables.
   d. expresses no clear relationship between variables.

9. Which of the following is *not* a characteristic of economics?
   a. It is analytical.
   b. It is a social science.
   c. It deals with material relationships.
   d. It deals mostly with things that cannot be quantified.

10. The economist's method is based on all but which one of the following?
    a. Gathering of facts
    b. Model building
    c. Transcendental meditation
    d. Hypothesizing

11. Vernon Smith's research on economic behavior concludes that
    a. Experimentation to test economic arguments is impossible
    b. Experimentation is too new to test arguments about economic behavior
    c. Experimentation is an appropriate way to test arguments about economic behavior
    d. Experimentation has lead to no conclusions about the validity of economic principles

Section C Matching questions

Match the phrases in column B to the terms in column A.

Column A	Column B
1. Model	(a) Assumed relationship(s)
2. Positive statement	(b) Analogy to reality
3. Inverse relation	(c) Self-satisfaction
4. Hypothesis	(d) What *should* be
5. *Homo communista*	(e) What *is*
6. Direct relationship	(f) Mankind interested in self
7. Hedonism	(g) Mankind interested in the community
8. Economic problem	(h) Limits imposed by scarcity
9. Normative statement	(i) Independent and dependent variables move in opposite directions
10. *Homo economicus*	(j) Independent and dependent variables move in the same direction
11. Alfred Marshall	(k) Mankind seeking monetary gain

ANSWERS

Part 4

Section A 1, F; 2, F; 3, F; 4, F; 5, F; 6, F; 7, F; 8, T; 9, F; 10,T; 11, F; 12, F; 13, T; 14, F; 15, T
Section B 1, d; 2, d; 3, d; 4, d; 5, c; 6, c; 7, a; 8, a; 9, d; 10, c, 11, c
Section C 1, b; 2, e; 3, i; 4, a; 5, g; 6, j; 7, c; 8, h; 9, d; 10, f; 11, k

Chapter 2: Scarcity and Economic Development

Part 1

First, read the section entitled "Summing Up" at the end of Chapter 2. This summary offers a thorough review of the chapter.

Things to Watch For

Chapter 2 starts off with a discussion of markets. A market system is a set of means by which buyer-seller exchanges are made. The invisible hand argument proposed by Adam Smith indicates that the self-interest decisions of buyers-sellers can maximize the public good through the actions of markets (the invisible hand argument).

The rest of the chapter deals with scarcity and its relationship to economic development and to the making of economic decisions. Scarcity is the relationship between limited resources and unlimited human wants. Because of scarcity, societies cannot satisfy all wants for goods and services. They must devise means by which to choose which goods to produce and who is to get them.

In a capitalist society, one in which ownership of the means of production is primarily private, economic questions relating to scarcity are answered through a system of markets, the medium through which buyer-seller exchanges are made. These questions, then, are common to all societies: (1) What goods shall be produced? (2) How shall they be produced? (3) For whom shall they be produced? If it were not for scarcity, all goods and services would be available to everyone at no opportunity cost. Furthermore, they would be free; that is, they would have no price, the means through which output is rationed. Scarcity, though, exists in all societies at all times. Thus people must find solutions to these three interdependent questions.

Answering questions involves making choices. One way for a society to view its economic choices is through the device of the production-possibilities function, a relationship showing the combinations of goods and services that a society, at full employment and using all its resources according to the best available technology, can produce during a given period of time. When one graphs these choices, the resulting curve is called a production-possibilities curve (PP curve). The PP curve represents a frontier or outer limit to a society's productive capacity.

However, neither the production-possibilities function nor the PP curve can tell us what combinations of goods and services a society will actually choose to produce. Each nation must establish its own means for making these choices. The means a society uses may range from letting markets alone dictate the choices to turning the responsibility over to a group of government bureaucrats. Most societies use some combination of these two means.

A production-possibilities curve is a useful device for understanding various aspects of employment. Employment is the condition in which a unit of resource (land, labor, capital, or entrepreneurship) is used in an economic activity. Full employment, exists when all units find uses. Unemployment exists when there are units of resources that cannot find uses within an economic system. Underemployment exists when resources find some employment, but in activities that are less than their most productive uses.

Full employment, in terms of the production-possibilities curve, means that a nation is on that curve, its production frontier. Underemployment or unemployment means that a nation is below the curve. (In the United States, it is conventional to define full employment as no more than 4 percent unemployment; this allows for people who are between jobs.)

In a developing society, the production-possibilities curve naturally shifts from time to time. The choices a society makes now will influence its PP curve in the future. If it chooses to produce more capital (heavy machinery, factories, and so on) now, it will experience more growth or shift in productivity in the future than if it chooses more consumer goods now and gives up a certain amount of growth in productivity in the future.

A major factor in a nation's economic development is economic integration. A nation's resources are in perfect integration when all of them are being used in the most efficient way possible, and each is paid the same in all its uses. However, there are many barriers (political and social, as well as economic) to such integration. Because integration is difficult to achieve, all societies usually have some degree of economic dualism, whereby a modern, efficient exchange economy coexists with an economy that is traditional and non-exchange-oriented.

Production-possibilities curves are usually drawn as bowed or concave to the origin of a graph. This reflects an assumption of increasing opportunity cost. Opportunity cost is the alternative goods you give up when you choose to produce a certain thing. (For example, a society may forgo the opportunity to produce a certain number of tractors in order to put up some needed low-cost housing.) Economists usually assume that opportunity cost ultimately increases in any society; that is, there is a diminishing marginal rate of transformation in moving resources from the production of one good to another. In other words, a society will gradually give up more and more of one thing in order to produce more and more of another. Gradually, it will opt for specialization of its resources. Now land, labor, and capital are more productive when used to produce some things than when used to produce others. This means that a society that expands its output of one good will finally begin to use resources that would have been more productive if used in some other way. So the society ultimately experiences increasing opportunity cost as one good is substituted for another.

Economic institutions-the social arrangements through which economic decisions are made-have a lot to do with which choices a society makes about using its resources, and also with how well the decisions are carried out.

Chapter 2 also deals with economic development, the process by which the material well-being of a society's people is significantly increased. Economists generally are in favor of economic development-not because it necessarily makes people happier, but because it increases the choices available to people. Remember these points:

1. Economic development is an evolutionary process, a set of interdependent actions.

2. Economic development has multiple origins, both economic and noneconomic.

3. Economic development has multiple results, economic and noneconomic.

The last two points mean that economic problems aren't just economic and that solving them will affect far more than just economic relationships. One cannot, then, view economic problems from the standpoint of pure economic determinism. In other words, it is not realistic to think that people and their institutions react only to changes in economic alternatives or economic facts. Social, political, cultural, and religious influences are interdependent with economic influences.

The reason economic development is so hard to measure is that it has so many sources and so many effects-effects on income, on distribution of income, on life expectancy, and on a multitude of other things. Most economists, though, feel that the growth in real per capita product gives the best approximation to a correct measurement (even if it must be qualified in particular cases). Real per capita product can be calculated in two steps.

Total national product - price increases = real national product
Real national product ÷ population = real per capita national product

The shortened formula for this second equation is Y/P where Y = real national product and P = population.

Looking at data for Y/P in recent years shows us that (1) the income gap between rich and poor countries is growing; (2) many countries with small populations and low incomes find it difficult to create modern economies (mainly because of the size of capital investment needed in modern industries); and (3) huge income gaps exist throughout the world.

It's hard to determine what is a significant increase in Y/P, because significance differs from one country to another. This is so mainly because various nations' resistances to development differ. (1) There are social and cultural resistances. Does a given society accord high esteem to its entrepreneurs, or not? Does the society encourage birth control, or discourage it? Resistances such as these often affect, whether a society has a surplus (in other words, whether it does not consume now everything it produces). If it does have a surplus, it will have the savings it needs to invest in capital and in the education of its own people. If it doesn't, it won't. (2) There are also technological and technical resistances. The poor country with its less well-developed means of allocating resources runs into a diminishing rate of transformation much sooner than the rich nation.

It is often very hard for poor nations to import and use the advanced technology developed by the rich industrial nations. The low-income nation may have a low incremental capital-output ratio. That is, it may require relatively little capital to produce a given increase in output. Nonetheless, it may well lack even that amount of capital. It usually also lacks the labor skills and managerial and technical knowledge that would enable it to use industrial technology as effectively as the industrial nations do. In addition, advanced technology draws on socially complementary things (good transportation, health facilities, schools, and educated labor pool) that are uncommon in many poor nations. Finally, modern technology is frequently indivisible. It must be adopted as a whole, and the sizes of the markets in low-income countries do not permit this.

Endowments of natural resources are one advantage some low-income countries do have. This is a major reason why such countries as Saudi Arabia are no longer among the ranks of low-income nations. Perhaps it is also one reason why China, with its massive oil reserves, may in the future leave the ranks of the low-income countries. However, structural reforms and reliance on market incentives seem to be an even more important factor in the case of China. For many underdeveloped areas, though, natural riches are only potential resources, not resources that are available for economic use with present technology.

Data for the years since 1960 show that the income gap between rich and poor nations has grown, though some new countries have joined the ranks of the rich. Will the gap ever decrease? Much will depend on population pressures. The poor nations continue to have the highest rate of population growth. Recent projections of population growth indicate that world population will approach a maximum later in the twenty-first century.

Part 2

Define the following terms and concepts.

1. Basic economic questions
2. Capital intensive process
3. Complementary investment
4. Diminishing marginal rate of transformation
5. Economic development
6. Economic dualism
7. Economic institutions
8. Economic integration
9. Employment, unemployment, underemployment
10. Entrepreneurship
11. Free goods
12. Human capital
13. Increasing opportunity cost
14. Incremental capital/output rates
15. Interdependency
16. Invisible hand argument
17. Labor intensive process
18. Marginal rate of transformation
19. Market system
20. Opportunity cost
21. Outsourcing
22. Production-possibilities function
23. Property rights
24. Pure economic determinism
25. Real Per Capita National Product
26. Resources
27. Scarcity

Part 3

Answer the following questions and problems.

1. What is meant by the "Invisible Hand"? How can it make people better off?

2. What kind of economy would exist for you and for other people in a world without scarcity? Would you want or have a job in such a world?

3. Can scarcity and affluence exist at the same time for the same people?

4. Why must all economies devise a means for answering the basic economic questions of what to produce, how to produce, and who is to get the output?

5. What seem to be the basic problems that low-income countries face in "closing the gap"?

6. Three things are common to both rich and poor countries: economic dualism, imperfect economic integration, and increasing opportunity cost. What are the differences in growth potential of rich countries and poor countries?

7. Consider the hypothetical production-possibilities schedule in Table 2-1.

   a. Use Figure 2-1 to plot the production-possibilities curve of India from the data in Table 2-1.

   b. What is the rate of transformation from points B to C?

   c. What happens to the rate of transformation as movement along the curve occurs? Why?

   d. What would the rate of transformation look like if all resources used in producing wheat and trucks were equally productive in either use?

Table 2-1
Production Possibilities for Wheat and Trucks, India

Product	Production Rates				
	A	B	C	D	E
Wheat (thousands of tons)	0	20	40	60	80
Trucks (thousands)	60	53	38	20	0

8. What factors could shift the production-possibilities curve in Figure 2-1?

Figure 2-1
Production Possibilities

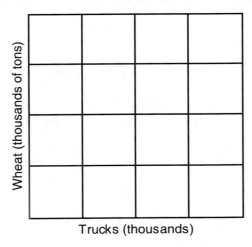

Trucks (thousands)

9. Draw points in Figure 2-1 that correspond to positions of

   a. full employment.

   b. underemployment.

10. How important is the rate of growth?

11. Why does the Production-Possibilities Curve bow out, what if it was straight?

12. What is the invisible hand?

Part 4 Self-test

Section A True/false questions

T F 1. The "Invisible Hand" is the watchful eye of a benevolent government.

T F 2. Economic dualism exists only in low-income countries.

T F 3. If jobs can be found for everybody in the labor force, underemployment will be eliminated.

T F 4. Perfect economic integration means that a resource is paid the same in all its uses.

T F 5. A nation is usually on its production-possibilities curve.

T F 6. The income gap between rich and poor nations has widened since 1960.

T F 7. If resources are not specialized at all, a production-possibilities "curve" will be a straight line.

T F 8. Opportunity cost is likely, ultimately, to increase for any nation.

T F 9. The reason why nations experience a diminishing rate of transformation is that societies don't make wise choices about how to use resources.

T F 10. Labor productivity tends to increase with increased specialization.

T F 11. The production-possibilities curve of the United States shifted greatly in the twentieth century.

T F 12. Free goods are in such abundant supply that the have a zero price.

T F 13. Economic development is the long-term process by which the material well being of a society's people is significantly increased.

T F 14. The production possibilities curve bows out because resources are equally productive in all uses.

T F 15. According to the text, unemployment is lacking a gainful occupation.

T F 16. Underemployment is the condition in which a resource is unable to find a use to produce goods.

T F 17. Opportunity cost is always the dollar amount given up in order to produce more of one particular good.

Section B Multiple-choice questions

1. Which one of the following best fits the idea of Adam Smith's "Invisible Hand"?
   a. Actions of God favor market economies
   b. Actions of a benevolent government make the right choices for the people
   c. Actions of buyers and sellers in a market environment maximize the benefit from markets
   d. Central planning in the former Soviet Union

2. Which one of the following is not a reason why we need a means of allocating resources?
   a. Scarcity
   b. Limited resources
   c. Unlimited wants
   d. Low incomes

3. Which one of the following is not a basic question confronting all economic societies?
   a. What shall be produced?
   b. How should markets be made competitive?
   c. For whom shall goods be produced?
   d. How is output to be produced?

4. Which of the following is not necessarily one of the benefits of economic development?
   a. Higher per capita incomes
   b. More happiness
   c. More freedom of choice
   d. More leisure

5. Which of the following is not characteristic of economic development?
   a. It is an evolutionary process.
   b. It is simple and does not change relationships.
   c. It has multiple origins.
   d. Its effects are broad.

6. Which of the following is not a social or cultural barrier to economic development?
   a. A caste system
   b. Religious belief that resources should be used only in certain ways
   c. Cultural belief that restricts mobility in the choice of occupations
   d. Cultural belief that lays great stress on savings

7. According to W. Arthur Lewis, the development of a nation would not depend on which one of the following?
   a. Knowledge
   b. Favorable climate
   c. Will to economize
   d. Capital

8. A major technological advantage, which some people argue that low-income countries have, is
   a. a well-developed educational system.
   b. large complementary investments in entrepreneurial skills.
   c. low incremental capital-output ratios.
   d. large quantities of labor skills.

9. Which one of the following statements about natural resources is correct?
   a. Virtually all low-income countries are well endowed with natural resources.
   b. None of the low-income countries has significant natural resources.
   c. Rich countries have become rich mainly because of their natural resources.
   d. Natural resources, in order to be usable, require complementary investments in human capital and transportation.

10. The income gap is growing in every area of the world except
    a. the Near East.
    b. Latin America.
    c. Asia.
    d. Africa.

11. Which one of the following is not one of the fundamental factors necessary for shifting a nation's production-possibilities curve?
    a. Economic integration
    b. Technological change
    c. Decreasing opportunity cost
    d. Basic structural or institutional change

Section C Matching questions

Match the phrases in column B to the terms in column A.

Column A	Column B
1. Economic integration	(a) Resource paid same price in all uses
2. Basic economic questions	(b) Buyer-seller exchanges
3. Economic development	(c) Limited resources, unlimited wants
4. Entrepreneurship	(d) Zero price
5. Market system	(e) Growing real per capita product
6. Production-possibilities curve	(f) What we give up to produce something
7. Opportunity cost	(g) Organization of diverse resources
8. Scarcity	(h) Land, labor, capital, and entrepreneurship
9. Resources	(i) What, how, for whom
10. Free goods	(j) Output frontier or limit
11. Outsourcing	(k) Substitution of less expensive factors of production

ANSWERS

Part 4

Section A 1, F; 2, F; 3, F; 4, T; 5, F; 6, T; 7, T; 8, T; 9, F; 10, T; 11, T; 12, T; 13, T; 14, F; 15, F; 16, F; 17, F

Section B 1, c; 2, d; 3, b; 4, b; 5, b; 6, d; 7, b; 8, c; 9, d; 10, a; 11, c

Section C 1, a; 2, i; 3, e; 4, g; 5, b; 6, j; 7, f; 8, c; 9, h; 10, d; 11, k

Chapter 3: Supply and Demand-Price Determination in Competitive Markets

Part 1

First, read the section entitled "Summing Up" at the end of Chapter 3. It constitutes a thorough review of the chapter.

Things to Watch For

This chapter deals with how prices are set in a competitive (that is, a free, private-enterprise) capitalist economy. Competition is the market form in which individual buyers and sellers have no influence over the price at which they buy and sell. In such markets there is no price rivalry. Prices in such markets are determined by the independent influences of supply and demand.

Demand is a set of relationships showing the quantities of a good that consumers will buy at each of several prices within a specific period of time. The factor that determines quantity demanded for a good is price, while the factors that determine demand are (1) incomes of buyers, (2) tastes and preferences of buyers, (3) prices of other products (both complements, which are goods used in conjunction with another product, and substitutes, which are used in place of another product), and (4) consumers' expectations about future prices and market conditions. These four factors determine an individual's demand. Total demand for a good (or for all goods) is influenced by a fifth factor as well: the number of consumers, or the population.

One may establish a hypothetical demand curve for a good by holding constant all variables influencing the demand for that good except its price. (This is the ceteris paribus, or certain other-things-being-equal, assumption.) The resulting demand schedule or curve (when plotted) reflects the facts that (1) people buy more of a good at low prices than at high prices (the law of demand), (2) there is a price above which consumers drop out of the market, and (3) the strength of a person's taste for a good probably declines as the person gets more of it.

A demand curve ordinarily slopes down to the right. This happens for two reasons. (1) As the price of a good falls, consumers buy more of it and substitute the good for other, relatively more expensive ones (substitution effect). (2) As the price of a good falls, consumers' purchasing power increases, so they buy more of that good (income effect).

Exceptions to the downward-sloping demand curve are rare. They include (1) goods that are so very income-inferior that people buy less of them as their price falls and use their increased purchasing power to buy other, more desired goods (for example, beans in a poor country), and (2) Veblen goods, goods that have greater appeal to consumers at higher prices than at lower prices (perhaps super yachts).

Learn the difference between a change in demand and a change in quantity demanded. A change in demand involves a shift of the demand curve. It arises from a change in income, tastes, prices of other goods, people's expectations, or number of consumers. A change in the quantity demanded involves a movement along a demand curve. It may be caused only by a change in the price of the good itself. (A change in the quantity of eggs demanded can be caused only by a change in the price of eggs.)

To arrive at a curve for market demand, one sums up the demand curves of individuals. Generally, economists assume that there are no interdependencies between the demand curves of individuals. Thus the adding up is simple. (Occasionally, though, people jump on a bandwagon. They rush out to buy a Frisbee, or some such thing, because someone else has one. In such a case, the process of adding up can become complicated.) At any rate, the curves depicting market demand, like the curves depicting individual demand, usually slope downward to the right.

The other side of the market is supply. Supply is a set of relationships showing the quantities of output that a firm will offer for sale at each possible price within a specific period of time. While quantity supplied is determined by price, supply is determined by 1) the technology used to produce it, (2) prices of inputs or resources, (3) prices of other goods, and (4) the firm's expectations about future prices.

Learn the difference between a change in supply and a change in quantity supplied. A change in supply involves a shift of the supply curve. It may be caused by (1) a change in technology, (2) a change in prices of inputs, (3) a change in the price of other goods, or (4) a change in the firm's expectations about future prices. A change in the quantity supplied involves a movement along the supply curve and may be caused only by a change in the price of the good itself. (When the price of cars goes up, the quantity of cars supplied goes up as a result.)

A supply schedule, when plotted, is called a supply curve. According to the law of supply, supply curves slope up to the right. When prices are high, firms offer to sell larger quantities than they do when prices are low.

To arrive at a schedule for market supply, one sums up the supply curves of individual firms. As in the case of demand, the adding up assumes that there are no interdependencies (that is, no collusion) between firms. For competitive suppliers this assumption works well, since no single firm has any influence over price or any reason to observe what another firm is doing.

Prices are established by the forces of supply and demand, which operate jointly but-under competition-independently of each other. An equilibrium price is a price at which quantity supplied equals quantity demanded.

A disequilibrium price may be either higher or lower than the equilibrium price. If a price is higher, there is excess supply. Firms offer to sell more than consumers want to buy. If a price is lower than equilibrium, there is excess demand. Consumers want to buy more than firms want to sell. Therefore, an equilibrium price is a market-clearing price. It is a price that eliminates excess supply or demand.

Now for a summary of the conditions necessary for competitive pricing: (1) flexible prices, with no floors or ceilings, (2) full information on the part of buyers and sellers, (3) expectations that prices will hold constant in the future, (4) free entry into and exit from the industry (mobility of resources), (5) maximizing of profit by firms and maximizing of satisfaction by consumers, and (6) absence of conspiracies or collusion.

Finally, we discuss the effects of government established prices in general and, more specifically, government imposed rent controls. Rent controls or ceiling prices create a disequilibrium and, in this case, an excess demand. With a price fixed below the equilibrium, quantity demanded increases and quantity supplied may decrease. The quality of housing will also probably decline.

The chapter discusses who gains and who loses with rent control and why. Finally, it discusses justifications for controls and, given that most U.S. economists oppose such controls, what may be the reason for their enactment and their continuation.

The best case with rent control exists where supply is perfectly inelastic (a vertical line). Excess demand occurs because of the increase in quantity demanded under the lower controlled rent. The worse case exists where supply slopes up and excess demand occurs because of both increases in quantity demanded and decrease in quantity supplied with a lower than equilibrium (controlled) rent. If rent control also reduces supply or shifts the supply curve to the left, excess demand is even greater.

Part 2

Define the following terms and concepts.

1. Competition
2. Demand schedule, demand curve
3. Change in demand
4. Change in quantity demanded
5. Ceteris paribus assumption
6. Income-inferior goods
7. Veblen goods
8. Income effect
9. Substitution effect
10. Supply
11. Change in supply
12. Change in quantity supplied
13. Law of demand
14. Law of supply
15. Aggregation
16. Equilibrium price
17. Excess demand
18. Excess supply
19. Complements, substitutes

Part 3

Answer the following questions and problems.

1. What conditions must exist in order for a market to function competitively? Is it easy to create these conditions? Why?

2. In an economy that grows rapidly for a long period of time, what is the most important factor affecting demand? Why is this so?

3. In an economy that grows rapidly, what factor has the strongest influence on supply? Why?

4. Evaluate the following statement: The only thing that can't cause a change in the demand for gasoline is a change in the price of gasoline.

5. Under what conditions does the law (hypothesis) of demand not hold true?

6. Consider Figure 3-1 and do the following things:

   a. Label both axes properly.

   b. Label the demand curve and the supply curve.

   c. Label the equilibrium price.

   d. What does one call the distance CD? Label it.

   e. What does one call the distance AB? Label it.

   f. Why is the equilibrium price the price that tends to be created?

Figure 3-1
Equilibrium Pricing

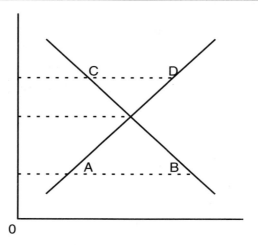

7. Your local newspaper reports the following: The owners of the New Orleans Sandwich Shop in Seattle, Washington, found that when they priced their hot dogs (reportedly the Rolls-Royce of the tube steaks) at $3.00 each, "sales were awful." When they raised the price to $3.45, sales doubled. When they raised the price to $3.75, sales doubled again!

   a. Draw a diagram to show what the demand curve for these hot dogs apparently looked like.

   b. Can you think of a reason why sales rose as price increased?

   c. What term do economists use for a good such as this one?

   d. The New Orleans Sandwich Shop slipped into oblivion when the Frankfurter opened down the street and sold hot dogs for $1.50. Why?

8. For most goods, would the income effect or the substitution effect of a price change have a greater influence on the change in quantity demanded? Why?

9. Draw the diagram of a housing market that has a perfectly inelastic supply with a downward sloping demand curve. Indicate excess demand under rent control. Do the same for a case in which the supply of housing is upward sloping and the demand

downward sloping; indicate the increase in excess demand. What happens to excess demand when the supply of housing decreases?

10. What is the difference between a demand schedule and a demand?

11. In the rent control example, how can the supply curve for housing be vertical?

Part 4 Self-test

Section A True/false questions

T F   1. In the case of most goods, rising incomes cause the quantity demanded to increase.

T F   2. Veblen goods probably appeal to the snobbishness of people.

T F   3. If the price of a good goes up, the demand for it decreases.

T F   4. If the price of butter goes up, the demand for margarine is likely to increase, since margarine is a substitute for butter.

T F   5. It probably won't take much of an increase in the price of gasoline to decrease the demand for gasoline.

T F   6. One person's demand curve is likely to be very much like another person's.

T F   7. If the price of video tapes goes up, the quantity of them that is supplied will increase.

T F   8. The law of supply tells us that the price of a good and quantity supplied are inversely related.

T F   9. Market solutions to economic problems involve using price to ration output.

T F   10. Rent controls tend to create an excess demand.

T F   11. In a purely competitive market, the producer can set the price

T F   12. Excess supply is the quantity of a good firms can not sell at a price above equilibrium.

T F   13. If prices are below equilibrium price, there is a shortage.

T F   14. Prices are set by demand only.

T F   15. The only thing that can cause movement along the demand curve for a product is a change in price of that product.

T F   16. Consumers' tastes and preferences can change demand.

Section B Multiple-choice questions

1. In a competitive market, all but which one of the following conditions exist?
   a. Full knowledge on the part of buyers and sellers
   b. Price flexibility
   c. Absence of collusion
   d. Barriers to free entry and exit

2. Demand depends on all but which one of the following?
   a. Tastes and preferences of buyers
   b. Prices of complements and substitutes
   c. Incomes of buyers
   d. The existence of competitive market conditions

3. Supply depends on all but which one of the following?
   a. Income
   b. Prices of other goods
   c. Technology of production
   d. Prices of inputs

4. Complementarity is illustrated by which one of the following?
   a. Demand for bread increases as price of margarine falls.
   b. Demand for pizzas rises as price of hamburgers increases.
   c. Demand for used cars decreases as price of new cars falls.
   d. Demand for mass transit increases as price of gasoline rises.

5. Substitutability is illustrated by which one of the following?
   a. Demand for recreational facilities rises as income increases.
   b. Quantity of housing demanded falls as price of housing rises.
   c. Demand for beer increases as the price of whiskey increases.
   d. Demand for paint increases as the price of housing decreases.

6. Which one of the following is not a characteristic of equilibrium price?
   a. Quantity supplied equals quantity demanded.
   b. Excess supply equals zero.
   c. Price never changes.
   d. Excess demand equals zero.

7. Demand curves normally slope down to the right because of all but one of the following factors. Which?
   a. Law of demand
   b. Veblen-goods effect
   c. Substitution effect
   d. Income effect

8. Which one of the following is least likely to be an income-inferior good?
   a. Beans
   b. Rice
   c. Education
   d. Corn

9. Which of the following is not true about rent controls?
   a. Quantity demanded increases
   b. Quantity supplied may decrease
   c. Quality may decrease
   d. Excess supply appears

10. Which of the following is true about rent controls?
    a. Most economists favor rent controls
    b. Governments use it because it subsidizes landlords
    c. Those who live in rent controlled housing are strong political supporters of such legislation
    d. All those who wish to rent are benefited by rent control

11. Which of the following will generate the most excess demand in rent controlled situations?
    a. A vertical supply
    b. Upward sloping supply
    c. Unchanged demand
    d. Reduced supply and downward sloping demand

Section C Matching questions

Match the phrases in column B to the terms in column A.

Column A	Column B
1. Equilibrium price	(a) No influence over price
2. Inferior good	(b) Quantity demanded falls as price falls
3. Change in demand	(c) Other things being equal
4. Monopolistic pricing	(d) People buy more of one good as price of other goods fall
5. Expectations	(e) People buy more as price increases
6. Competition	(f) Market clearing
7. Veblen good	(g) Shift of demand curve
8. Ceteris paribus	(h) Cartel
9. Upward-sloping curve	(i) Future prices
10. Complementarity	(j) Price and quantity directly relate
11. Rent controls	(k) Excess demand
12. Change in quantity demanded	(l) Movement along a demand curve

ANSWERS

Part 4

Section A 1, F; 2, T; 3, F; 4, T; 5, F; 6, F; 7, T; 8, F; 9, T; 10, T; 11, F; 12, T; 13,T; 14, F; 15, T; 16, T

Section B 1, d; 2, d; 3, a; 4, a; 5, c; 6, c; 7, b; 8, c; 9, d; 10, c; 11, d

Section C 1, f; 2, b; 3, g; 4, h; 5, i; 6, a; 7, e; 8, c; 9, j; 10, d; 11, k; 12, l

Chapter 4: Components of an Economic Society

Part 1

First, read the section entitled "Summing Up" at the end of Chapter 4 for thorough summary of the material presented in the chapter.

Things to Watch For

Chapter 4 is divided into five main sections. The first four deal with a closed macroeconomy, one that does not trade with other economies. In the first one, there is a discussion about circular flow models of how our economy functions. (These aren't the first models we've presented. Remember the production-possibilities curve in the discussion of scarcity in Chapter 2.) The circular-flow model brings out the interrelationships between the components of the economy and the economic activities of each in factor and product markets. You could compare the interconnecting or circular nature of economic activity to the case of the chicken and the egg. There is no beginning or end to economic activity.

The remainder of Chapter 4 points out some important aspects of the three main components of the economy: households (or the people), business firms, and governments, and introduces the question about social responsibility of business.

The chapter's second section, on households, deals with the way income is distributed to households and what the households spend that income on. In this part, be sure you can distinguish between functional distribution of income and personal (or size) distribution of income. Remember that a Lorenz curve measures the degree of equality or inequality in the personal distribution of income.

The third section, on businesses, talks about the three forms of business organizations (sole proprietorships, partnerships, and corporations) and identifies the major strengths and weaknesses of each. It's important that you keep in mind the distinctions introduced in this part. Part 3 closes with a discussion of some of the concerns created by large corporations.

The fourth section concerns governments: federal, state, and local. First this section gives some figures to show what governments spend money on. Then it discusses taxation, or where governments get their money. It is important that you understand the two principles of taxation-benefits received and ability to pay-and the three kinds of tax structures-progressive, regressive, and proportional. Equally important is the question of who pays the taxes (the incidence of taxation). When it comes to the question of how progressive our tax structure is, it's difficult to arrive at any hard-and-fast answers. In this section, we look at the distribution of income and how it is affected by taxes, transfer payments and payments in kind. This section concludes by looking at some of the many implications of the distribution of income and changes in that distribution.

Next, the chapter notes how governments also affect the economy by making laws that set the rules of the game, and by the activities of various regulatory bodies.

Finally, the chapter briefly deals with an open economy, or one that exports to and imports from other economies.

The most important conclusion on the question of social responsibility of business seems to be that it's very hard to define what the social responsibility of business really is. This suggests that even if business is socially responsible to the people, this cannot really solve the fundamental social problems of our economy. One may well ask, "Should social responsibility on the part of businesses even be expected to solve our problems?" The section deals with the responsibility of businesses to their shareholders and with the relationship between competition and socially responsible behavior by firms. A key question asked is: "When will markets punish or reward socially responsible behavior by firms?"

Part 2

Define the following terms and concepts.

1. Open economy
2. Closed economy
3. Factor markets, product markets
4. Functional distribution of income
5. Lorenz curve
6. Sole proprietorship
7. Partnership
8. Corporation
9. Unlimited liability
10. Limited liability
11. Unlimited life

12. Bonds
13. Preferred stock
14. Common stock
15. Double taxation
16. Multinational corporations
17. Benefits-received principle of taxation
18. Ability-to-pay principle of taxation
19. Progressive tax
20. Regressive tax
21. Proportional tax
22. Tax rates

Part 3

Answer the following questions and problems.

1. In Figure 4-1, label the boxes and the connecting lines with their appropriate titles. Use arrows to show the correct flows of economic activity for the complex circular-flow model.

2. Using the circular-flow diagram (Figure 4-1), start at any point and explain how the circular flow of economic activity works.

3. Using Figure 4-1 again, explain how the flow of economic activity can be decreased; how it can be increased.

Figure 4-1
Complex Circular-Flow Model

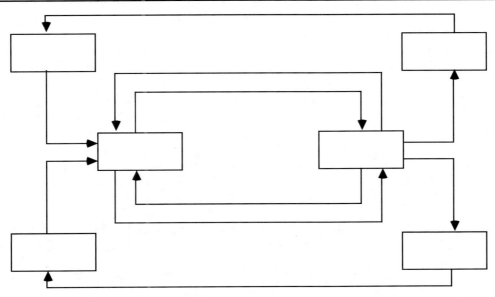

4. List, in order of increasing magnitude, incomes classified according to the functional distribution of income. Review factors that have affected this distribution.

5. Review the various factors that have affected the personal distribution of income since 1935.

6. Using Figure 4-2 and Table 4-1, draw a Lorenz curve for column A and also one for column B. Which distribution is more nearly equal?

Figure 4-2
Lorenz Curves for Distributions A and B

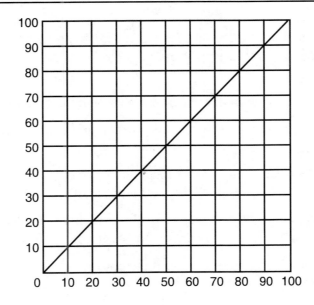

Table 4-1
Distribution of Personal Income

	A	B
Percentage of People	**Percentage of Total**	**Percentage of Total**
Lowest one-fifth	6	4
Second one-fifth	12	8
Third one-fifth	18	16
Fourth one-fifth	24	28
Highest one-fifth	40	44

7. Review the advantages and disadvantages of sole proprietorships, partnerships, and corporations.

8. Why are some economists concerned about the concentration of economic power in large corporations?

9. What economic and political problems and benefits are created by multinational corporations?

10. What are the principal kinds of expenditures made by the federal government? by state governments? by local governments?

11. Explain and criticize the benefits-received principle of taxation; the ability-to-pay principle.

12. What is the most important source of tax revenue for the federal government? for state governments? for local governments?

13. Taking taxes as a whole, including taxes collected by all levels of government combined, is our tax structure progressive, regressive, or proportional? Explain your answer.

14. What are the problems with deciding what is a "fair" distribution of income?

15. List and briefly describe the function of five regulatory commissions of the federal government.

16. Who should exhibit corporate social responsibility: governments, or the managers or the stockholders of corporations? Explain your answer; be complete.

17. What are the arguments of critics that profit maximizing behavior by firms is consistent with private interests but conflicts with public interests?

18. What factors have caused an increase in the competitiveness of the American economy in recent decades?

19. When will markets reward socially responsible behavior by firms? When will they punish such behavior?

20. What is the Lorenz curve trying to show us?

Part 4 Self-test

Section A True/false questions

T F 1. Increases in savings and taxes expand the circular flow of economic activity; increases in investment and government expenditures contract it.

T F 2. Data on the functional distribution of income indicate that since 1935 there has been a relative shift from wages and salaries to corporate profits.

T F 3. Between 1935 and the mid-1950s, the personal distribution of cash income became more nearly equal; from then to the early 1990s it has not changed.

T F 4. Looked at from a demand point of view, saving contracts an economy because it decreases the demand for consumer goods.

T F 5. The form of business enterprise that is easiest to establish is the sole proprietorship.

T F 6. An advantage of partnership over sole proprietorships is that partnerships have unlimited life.

T F 7. Corporations may have limited liability.

T F 8. Common stock differs from preferred stock in that it offers greater voting rights but is limited in the amount of dividends its owners can receive.

T F 9. To say that taxes from all levels of American government are at most only mildly progressive is a correct generalization.

T F 10. The benefits-received principle of taxation supports the conclusion that taxes are best when based on the size of a person's income.

T F 11. The advantage of the benefits-received principle of taxation is that there is little difficulty in computing who receives the benefits from the goods and services provided by government.

T F 12. The best example of a proportional tax is the sales tax, because the same tax rate is applied no matter how large the purchase.

T F 13. Since corporate executives are professional managers of their enterprises, they have expertise in deciding what is socially desirable for our society.

T F 14. According to the chapter, socially responsible behavior by firms will never be rewarded by markets.

T F 15. According to William Shepherd, non-competitive forces have grown in the American economy in recent decades.

T F 16. For an individual firm, lack of information or perspective may make socially responsible behavior difficult to undertake.

T F   17. All government expenditures are productive.

T F   18. The distribution of cash income in the US is equal.

T F   19. The three main forms of business organizations are the sole proprietorship, the partnership, and the government.

Section B Multiple-choice questions

1. For a corporation, limited liability means that
   a. the corporation is limited in its obligation to pay its debts, up to a certain percentage of its net worth.
   b. the managers are limited in how much debt they can cause the corporation to incur.
   c. the corporation is limited in paying dividends to stockholders to periods in which it has made profits.
   d. the stockholder has no further financial obligation to the corporation beyond the money paid for the stock.

2. In comparison with taxes collected by the federal government,
   a. state and local taxes are both more progressive.
   b. state and local taxes are both more regressive.
   c. state taxes are more progressive, while local taxes are regressive.
   d. local taxes are more progressive, while state taxes are regressive.

3. The ability-to-pay principle of taxation is best illustrated by a
   a. property tax.
   b. sales tax.
   c. personal income tax.
   d. corporate income tax.

4. Through which of the following do governments affect economic activity?
   a. Expenditures and taxation
   b. Enactment of laws
   c. Use of regulatory agencies
   d. All of the above

5. Of the three forms of business enterprise discussed in the text, which can most effectively raise financial capital?
   a. Sole proprietorships
   b. Partnerships
   c. Corporations
   d. All are equally effective

6. In what aspect does the corporation not represent the dominant form of business enterprise?
   a. Share of wages paid
   b. Share of capital invested
   c. Share of number of firms
   d. Share of output

7. Which one of the following combinations of taxes and expenditures represents the major source of income and major type of expenditure for local governments?
   a. Property tax; education
   b. Sales tax; welfare
   c. Sales tax; education
   d. Personal income tax; highways

8. Which of the following statements is not true?
   a. Householders supply the resources and demand the consumption output.
   b. Firms supply both resources and output.
   c. Savings and taxes reduce households' demand for the output of firms.
   d. Investment and government expenditures increase the demand for the output of firms.

9. Which of the following combinations of expenditures and taxes represents the most important form of expenditures and taxes for the federal government?
   a. Defense expenditures; corporate income taxes
   b. Income security; personal income taxes
   c. Education; sales and excise taxes
   d. Defense expenditures; personal income taxes

10. Multinational firms are difficult for any one country to control because
    a. they are chartered and regulated by the United Nations.
    b. unions cooperate with them on an international scale.
    c. they can shift purchases and production from one country to another.
    d. they are incorporated in more than one country.

11. A weakness of the argument in favor of social responsibility on the part of corporations is represented by which of the following?
    a. Although corporate managers are trained to make profits, they have no expertise in determining what actions are socially responsible.
    b. There is no objective way to define social responsibility.
    c. Corporate executives are insulated from reality by their positions and have difficulty understanding what constitutes a socially responsible position.
    d. During a business contraction, profits contract, and firms may cut back socially responsible activities just when they are most needed.
    e. All of the above.

12. According to William Shepherd, the competitiveness of the American economy
    a. increased from 1960 to 1980 but has declined since.
    b. has declined significantly in the past three decades.
    c. has increased substantially in the past three decades.
    d. has not changed in recent decades.

13. According to Adam Smith, greedy behavior by firms is effectively limited by
    a. firms' desires to promote the public's welfare.
    b. public regulation of firms.
    c. the invisible hand of competition.
    d. the organization of consumers.

14. Critics of profit maximizing behavior by firms argue that governments should do which of the following?
    a. Ban socially undesirable products.
    b. Establish minimum standards for products.
    c. Regulate the marketing of products.
    d. All of the above.

Section C Matching questions

I. Match the terms in column B with related terms in column A.

Column A	Column B
1. Labor	(a) Rent
2. Capital	(b) Wages
3. Land	(c) Profits
4. Entrepreneurship	(d) Interest

II. For each of the terms in column A, write (if applicable) an S for sole proprietorship, a P for partnership, and a C for corporation in column B.

Column A	Column B
1. Existence as a legal entity	_____
2. Unlimited liability	_____
3. High level of incentive	_____
4. Ease of formation	_____
5. Unlimited life	_____
6. Access to capital by use of special financial instruments	_____
7. Limited life	_____
8. Specialized management functions	_____
9. Separation of management and ownership	_____
10. Tendency to suffer from management inefficiency	_____
11. Higher cost of formation	_____
12. Possibility of being subject to special laws	_____

III. Match the terms in column A with related terms in column B.

Column A	Column B
1. Progressive	(a) Property tax
2. Regressive	(b) Federal income tax
3. Proportional	(c) Sales tax

ANSWERS

Part 4

Section A 1, F; 2, F; 3, F; 4, T; 5, T; 6, F; 7, T; 8, F; 9, F; 10, F; 11, F; 12, F;
13, F; 14, F; 15, F; 16, T; 17, F; T; 18, F; 19, F
Section B 1, d; 2, b; 3, c; 4, d; 5, c; 6, c; 7, a; 8, b; 9, b; 10, c; 11, e; 12, c; 13, c;
14, a
Section C I.1, b; 2, d; 3, a; 4, c
II.1, C; 2, S and P; 3, S; 4, S; 5, C; 6, C; 7, S and P; 8, P and C; 9, C;
10, S; 11, P and C; 12, C
III.1, b; 2, c; 3, a

Chapter 5: Measuring Domestic Income and Product

Part 1

First, read the section entitled "Summing Up" at the end of Chapter 5 for a thorough summary of the material presented in the chapter.

Things to Watch For

Chapter 5 explains the concepts you need in order to understand the ways governments compute the level of aggregate activity in the economy. All of us hear these measures of national output and income continually bandied about. Not only economists and politicians but also the news media constantly refer to measures of national income and product, especially when they are discussing the state of the nation or the health of the economy. The subject is also important because these concepts will be used in building more sophisticated concepts and theories further along in the text.

The chapter is divided into three parts. The first part defines the five major measures of economic performance and shows how each is computed. To be able to understand discussions of the nation's economy, you need to remember the distinctions among these five measures beginning with Gross Domestic Product (GDP). The text leads you through them one by one, from the first measure, GDP/GDI, through NNP/NNI, NI, PI, and DPI, showing what is excluded and what is added in each case. The chapter explains the difference between gross domestic product and gross national product. The chapter, as well, details the components of GDP, namely, personal consumption expenditures (C), gross private domestic investment (I), government (G), and net exports (X_N).

Note that we use the terms output or product and income interchangeably. Since the expenditure and income approaches lead to the same numerical result, output and income are equal. It is important that you remember the reasoning behind that result.

The second part of Chapter 5 presents several topics that add depth to our understanding of the five national economic accounts. First, the distinction between gross domestic and gross national product is not only shown but the rationale for adopting GDP measures is explained. Statisticians use two approaches-the final-value method and the value-added method-to add the data to obtain these measures of output and income. You should know the distinction between money (or current) GDP and real (or constant) GDP. You should also be able to convert money GDP to real GDP by the use of a price index. The last section discusses the various forms of output and of economic transactions that are not included in GDP.

To complete the approaches to macroeconomics measurement, the components of gross domestic income (GDI) are explained. Those components are wages and salaries (W), rent (R), interest (INT), profit (P), capital consumption allowance (D), and indirect business taxes. In adding to the total GDI, we see that it is (must be) equal to GDP.

Lastly, there is a discussion on GDP as a measure of human well-being that concludes the inadequacies in the measurement of GDP are significant enough to make one question the validity of its use as a measure of human welfare. These inadequacies are: (1) GDP does not include most nonmarket forms of output; (2) GDP does not take into account external costs and benefits of production and consumption (especially pollution of various kinds); (3) GDP does include output that many people feel does not contribute to human welfare (output such as excessive advertising and defense expenditures); and (4) GDP cannot take into account the economic effects on future generations of the depletion of nonreproducible resources by present production. Note: Be sure you understand Arthur Okun's positions on the subject.

Part 2

Define the following terms and concepts.

1. Expenditure approach to national economic accounting
2. Income approach to national economic accounting
3. Gross domestic product
4. Gross domestic income
5. Final goods and services
6. Private consumption expenditures
7. Durable goods
8. Nondurable goods
9. Net exports
10. Gross private domestic investment
11. Government expenditures
12. Income at market prices
13. Income at factor prices
14. Factors of production
15. Wages and salaries
16. Rent
17. Interest
18. Proprietors' income
19. Corporate profits
20. Capital consumption allowance (depreciation)
21. Indirect business taxes
22. Net national product
23. Net national income
24. Positive net investment
25. Negative net investment
26. National income
27. Personal income
28. Disposable Personal income
29. Final-value method of income estimation
30. Value-added method of income estimation
31. Money (current) GDP
32. Real (constant) GDP
33. Consumer price index
34. Wholesale price index
35. General price index
36. Per capita real GDP
37. Inflating current GDP
38. Deflating current GDP

Part 3

Answer the following questions and problems.

1. What do we mean when we say that the national economic accounts are definitional concepts?

2. Why are the statistical results of the expenditure and income approaches of estimating national income accounts always equal?

3. Define and give a formula for computing the following national economic accounts:

    (a) gross domestic product, (b) gross domestic income, (c) net national product,

    (d) net national income, (e) personal income, and (f) disposable personal income.

4. Show how the value-added method of computing GDP equals the final-value method in terms of final results.

5. What is the difference between money GDP and real GDP? How do you convert money GDP to real GDP?

6. List the kinds of output that are not included in GDP for the United States. Why are they not included?

7. List the kinds of economic transactions that are not seperately included in GDP. Why are they not included?

8. From the data in Table 5-1, compute the five major accounts: GDP, NNP, NI, PI, and DPI. (This one is easy.) The answers are given after Part 4.

Table 5-1
Data for Problem 8 (billions of dollars)

Consumption	300
Gross private domestic investment	75
Government expenditures	100
Net exports	-5
Depreciation	25
Indirect business taxes	10
Corporate taxes	15
Retained earnings	10
Net transfer payments	15
Personal taxes	25

9. Using all the formulas available plus the data in Table 5-2, compute the five major national economic accounts: GDP, NNP, NI, PI, and DPI. (This one is more difficult.) Answers and hints are given after Part 4.

Table 5-2
Data for Problem 9 (billions of dollars)

Consumption	350
Rent	15
Gross private domestic investment	100
Personal taxes	75
Corporate taxes	15
Wages and salaries	400
Personal savings	30
Indirect business taxes	20
Net private domestic investment	75
Domestic business interest	20
Dividends	5
Proprietors' income	25
Retained earnings	10
Interest on consumer loans	10

10. In Table 5-3, fill in the column for real GDP. (The answers are given after Part 4.)

Table 5-3
Hypothetical Data for Problem 10

Year	Nominal GDP	Price Index	Real GDP
1950	55.6	50.6	
1960	284.8	80.2	
1970	684.9	110.9	
1980	974.1	135.3	

11. In Table 5-4, first compute the price index using 1962 as the base year for the hypothetical prices; then compute the price index using 1972 as the base year. (The answers are given after Part 4.)

Table 5-4
Hypothetical Data for Problem 11

Year	Price	Price Index (1962 = 100)	Price Index (1972 = 100)
1957	12		
1962	14		
1967	18		
1972	27		
1982	32		

12. GDP statistics fail to take into account costs that are outside the marketplace. What are these costs? Do you agree that they reduce the effectiveness of GDP as a measure of well-being?

13. Some people argue that large amounts of output included in GDP do not really contribute to material well-being. What kinds of output may fall into this category? Do you agree that they do not contribute to our well-being?

14. What was Okun's advice to those computing the accounts? Why?

15. Explain the distinction between gross domestic and gross national product.

16. Why do we need both real GDP and current GDP?

17, Why is some output excluded from GDP?

Part 4 Self-test

Section A True/false questions

T F 1. If the price level rose between one year and another, you must inflate the GDP figure for the latter year in order to compute real GDP change.

T F 2. When you convert money GDP to real GDP, you must divide real GDP by the price index.

T F 3. If gross investment is greater than depreciation, the economy has negative net investment, and as a result the economy contracts.

T F 4. The wages of used-car salesmen are included in gross domestic income.

T F 5. The market value of a car built and sold in 1987 and resold in 1989 is not included in 1989's GDP.

T F 6. Net investment is included in GDP, while gross investment is included in NNP.

T F   7. The value of total transactions in an economy exceeds the value of GDP.

T F   8. Capital gains from the resale of personal property are not included in GDP.

T F   9. Profits are part of national income, but all profits are excluded from personal income.

T F   10. When one is computing GDP, one excludes interest on the national debt from government expenditures; when one is computing GDI, one includes interest on the national debt as part of interest.

T F   11. No doubt exists that real GDP is not a good measure of material well-being because GDP does not include all output.

T F   12. Since one does not include external costs of production and consumption in the market calculation of price, such costs do not affect real GDP as a measure of material well-being.

T F   13. Because some people consider that certain types of output do not contribute to material well-being, they argue that real GDP, which includes these, cannot be considered a useful measure of material well-being.

T F   14. The opponents to economic growth argue that in the long run a high level of GDP decreases future well-being because it depletes the world supply of nonreproducible resources.

T F   15. Arthur Okun argued that real GDP was not designed to be a measure of material well-being and therefore should not be computed.

T F   16. Gross domestic product excludes imports and exports while gross national product includes them.

T F   17. The work of children doing household chores is counted a part of GDP.

T F   18. A car is a durable good.

T F   19. GDP measures the value of all intermediate goods and final services in a given period of time.

T F   20. Illegal goods and services are included in the GDP.

T F   21. The transactions involved in buying and selling of used items are included in the GDP.

T F   22. National income includes only wages and salaries.

Section B Multiple-choice questions

1. In the calculation of GDP, which of the following is not considered investment?

   a. Construction of a factory to produce widgets

   b. Construction of a house to be lived in by the owner

   c. An increase in inventory on the shelves of a supermarket

   d. Increased purchases of shares of stock in AT&T

2. Suppose that a CD player is produced in 1993 but not sold until 1994; it affects GDP

   a. as a consumption good only in 1993.

   b. as a net addition to inventory in 1994 only.

   c. as a net addition to inventory in 1994 and a consumption good in 1993.

   d. as a net addition to inventory in 1993 and a consumption good in 1994, with a net decrease in inventory in 1994.

3. Which of the following is not subtracted from national income to arrive at personal income?

   a. Personal taxes

   b. Retained earnings

   c. Corporate taxes

   d. Social security taxes

4. Suppose that the money GDP was $800 billion in 1988 and $900 billion in 1989. We may

   a. conclude that more was produced in 1988.

   b. not compare the real output of the economy in 1988 and 1989 without knowing changes in prices.

   c. conclude that prices were higher in 1989.

   d. conclude that real output was larger in 1989 than in 1988.

5. The difference between net national income and national income is

   a. proprietors' income.

   b. depreciation.

   c. social security taxes.

   d. indirect business taxes.

6. Interest on consumer loans is included in which one of the following?

   a. Gross domestic income

   b. National income

   c. Net national product

   d. Personal disposable personal income

7. To compare real GDP of one year with real GDP of another, we must

   a. correct for changes in the price level.

   b. divide by total population.

   c. correct for changes in the size and composition of the labor force.

   d. correct for changes in firms' accounting procedures.

8. Which of the following items is not calculated in national income?

   a. The rent a homeowner would have to pay if he or she did not own the home

   b. Social security payments to people over 65

   c. Tips received by a waiter

   d. Pay received by an army private

9. One of the following is included in GDP. Which?

   a. The work of housewives

   b. Illegal production

   c. The production of services

   d. Labor on do-it-yourself projects

10. Value added is computed by

   a. subtracting the figure for GDP for one year from the figure for GDP for the following year.

   b. adding up the values added at each stage.

   c. subtracting the amount allowed for depreciation of machinery from the amount of total production of the machinery.

   d. subtracting the amount of transfer payments received from the government from the amount of transfer payments paid to the government.

11. Some people say that real GDP fails to include all output and all cost, and that therefore it is not a measure of material well-being. Which of the following items does not support their argument?

    a. The contributions of housewives

    b. Air pollution

    c. Current production for military defense

    d. Water pollution

12. Some people say that real GDP contains output that fails to contribute to material well-being. Which of the following items does not support their argument?

    a. Intermediate products, such as steel that goes into an automobile

    b. Many forms of advertising

    c. Output of a chemical plant that contributes to pollution

    d. Unnecessary levels of defense expenditures

13. A main point in the argument that present economic growth reduces future material well-being is that

    a. full employment increases inflationary tendencies.

    b. increases in productivity lead to greater unemployment, since employers do not need to hire as many workers.

    c. economic growth reduces the supply of nonreproducible resources available for the future.

    d. GDP does not take into account an increase in leisure time.

14. Which of the following best states Arthur Okun's plea to the calculators of the national economic accounts?

    a. Real GDP is not an accurate measure of material well-being, and thus we should abandon it as an indicator.

    b. Real GDP is not an accurate measure of material well-being, and those who calculate it should do whatever is necessary to correct that deficiency.

    c. Real GDP is an accurate measure of material well-being, and we should ignore its critics.

    d. Real GDP is not an accurate measure of material well-being, nor is it meant to be. People who calculate real GDP should not try to meet the criticisms.

15. The difference between GDP and GNP is:

    a. depreciation is subtracted from GDP.

    b. all international trade is subtracted from GNP.

    c. personal taxes are subtracted from GNP.

    d. GDP is a measure of the value of output that is occurring in this country regardless of who owns the domestic resources that produces the output.

Section C Matching questions

Match phrases in column B to the terms in column A.

Column A	Column B
1. Final goods and services	(a) Gross investment exceeds depreciation
2. Factor prices	(b) Uses a price index
3. Positive net investment	(c) Does not take into account changes in prices
4. Money (current) GDP	(d) The price index is below 100
5. Real (constant) GDP	(e) Do not include intermediary products as separate items
6. Inflating current GDP	(f) Is equal to income approach
7. Corporate profits	(g) Includes only domestic business interests
8. Rent	(h) Excludes indirect business taxes
9. Expenditure approach	(i) Includes rent on owner-occupied homes
10. Interest	(j) Equals dividends + corporate taxes + retained earnings
11. Measured economic welfare	(k) NDP + leisure and non-market services - regrettable necessities and disamenities

ANSWERS

Part 3

8. See Chapter 5 for definitions.

$$GDP = C + Ig + G + Xn = 300 + 75 + 100 + (-5) = \$470$$

$$NDP = GDP - D \text{ (depreciation)} = 470\text{-}25 = \$445$$

$$NI = GDP\text{-}D\text{-}IBTX \text{ (indirect business taxes)} = NDP\text{-}IBTX = 445\text{-}10 = \$435$$

PI = NI + (incomes received but not earned)-(incomes earned but not received) = 435 + (net transfer payments)- (corporate taxes + retained earnings)= 435 + (15)-(15+10) = \$425

DPI= PI- (personal income taxes) = 425-25 = \$400

Additional questions:

Did the country overconsumed or underconsume its GDP? By how much?

Answer: It overconsumed its GDP by $5 which is equal to its net import from abroad (Xn = -5).

Was the country (i) a net lender to and/or buyer of assets from the rest of the world or (ii) a net borrower from and/or seller of assets to the rest of the world?

Answer: (ii) because the country had to pay for its overconsumption.

Did the country's capital stock expand, contract, or stayed the same?

Answer: The change in capital stock is equal to net investment, or In=Ig-D=75-25=50. Since the net addition to capital stock was positive, it expanded during the data period.

9. We don't have the data for G and Xn to compute GDP based on the expenditure approach as in the previous problem. So we start from the bottom and build up!

Compute DPI = consumption + personal savings + interest on consumer loans = 350 + 30 + 10 = $390

Compute PI= DPI + personal taxes = 390 + 75 = $465

Compute NI= wages and salaries + rent + proprietors' income + business interest payment + corporate gross profits = wages and salaries + rent + proprietors' income + business interest payment + (retained earnings + dividends + corporate taxes) = 400+15+25+20+ (10+5+15) = $490

Compute NDP (same as NNP assuming zero net factor incomes from abroad) = NI + IBTX = 490 + 20 =$510

Compute GDP = NDP + D (not directly given) = NDP + (Ig-In) = 510 + (100-75) = $535

Frustrated? Remember that these are highly simplified versions of reality!

10. 109.9, 355.1, 617.6, 720.0

Solve problem 10 by dividing nominal GDP by the price index and multiplying by 100 for each year.

11. 1962: 85.7, 100, 128.6, 192.9, 228.6 1972: 44.4, 51.9, 66.6, 100, 118.6

Solve problem 11 by dividing the price of each year by the prices of the base years and multiplying by 100.

Part 4

Section A 1, F; 2, F; 3, F; 4, T; 5, T; 6, F; 7, T; 8, T; 9, F; 10, F; 11, F; 12, F; 13, T;
         14, T; 15, F; 16, F; 17, F; 18, T; 19, F; 20, F; 21, F; 22, F
Section B 1, d; 2, d; 3, a; 4, b; 5, d; 6, d; 7, a; 8, b; 9, c; 10, b; 11, c; 12, a; 13,c; 14, d; 15, d
Section C 1, e; 2, h; 3, a; 4, c; 5, b; 6, d; 7, j; 8, i; 9, f; 10, g; 11, k

Chapter 6: Economic Fluctuations

Part 1

First, read the sections entitled "Summing Up" at the end of Chapter 6 for a detailed and thorough summary of the material in the chapter.

Things to Watch For

Chapter 6 is not a difficult chapter. It consists primarily of descriptions and definitions. However, it is an important chapter, for it gives you a background for the study of a big problem in our economy: fluctuations in the level of business activity.

Chapter 6 is divided into four parts. The first part discusses business fluctuations in a general sense. It defines what fluctuations are and describes the various phases of the business cycle. The most important point made here is that each cycle differs in length and intensity, or in other words, use of the word cycles, does not imply regularity in occurrence or length. In fact, both the cycle as a whole and its various stages differ in length and intensity. Within a given cycle, all economic activity does not vary in the same direction at the same time. However, there is enough uniformity for economists to be able to identify certain leading indicators. These indicators are very useful to economists when they are trying to predict the course of a business cycle.

The second part is concerned with unemployment. It defines full employment as well as the various kinds of unemployment (frictional unemployment, cyclical unemployment, and structural unemployment) and discusses some implications of each. These definitions are very important. You'll run into them again later on, in the analysis of government economic policy. The concept of a GDP gap, the difference between full employment and actual GDP is developed. The part ends with a discussion of the costs of unemployment-economic, social, and psychological.

The third part analyzes inflation and the economic effects of variations in prices. It first defines the two kinds of inflation (demand-pull inflation and cost-push inflation) and discusses some economic problems of each. These definitions, too, are very important. In our analysis of government economic policy they'll be used frequently. There is next a discussion of the effects of price variations (decreases as well as increases) both on the distribution of real income and real wealth, and on output.

The fourth part deals with the interaction between employment and prices. This section stresses two main points: (1) Full employment and stable prices may be difficult to maintain at the same time. The closer an economy gets to full employment, the higher the rate of increase in prices becomes. (2) The Phillips curve indicates that there is a set of relationships between various degrees of unemployment and the rate of inflation. The fourth part winds up with an analysis of what happens when the Phillips curve shifts up to the right. At the same level of unemployment, a higher level of inflation exists. It is important that you keep these changing unemployment-inflation relationships in mind, because they are a key factor in the effectiveness of government economic policy.

The application within Chapter 6 surveys the problems of trying to establish an acceptable unemployment goal for the American Economy. Attention today is focused on identifying the economy's natural rate of unemployment, one at which the rate of inflation is not only acceptable but also neither accelerating or decelerating. The natural rate argument leads to the conclusions that (a) the actual unemployment rate may be impossible to push below the natural rate in the long run, and (b) efforts to push unemployment below the natural rate lead to higher inflation rather than less unemployment. The application surveys some of the evidence about what has happened to the natural rate for the U.S. (it seems to have risen) as well as some of the ways through which the natural rate might be reduced.

Part 2

Define the following terms and concepts.

1. Secular trend	12. GDP gap
2. Business cycle	13. Inflation
3. Seasonal variations	14. Cost-push inflation
4. Random variations	15. Demand-pull inflation
5. Contraction phase	16. Deflation
6. Expansion phase	17. Real interest rate
7. Leading indicators	18. Stagflation
8. Full employment	19. Inflationary expectations
9. Frictional unemployment	20. Okun's Law
10. Structural unemployment	21. Natural rate of unemployment
11. Cyclical unemployment	

Part 3

Answer the following questions and problems.

1. Distinguish among secular trends, business cycles, seasonal variations, and random variations.

2. Name the four phases of the business cycle and note what happens to prices, output, and employment in each.

3. Why do some economists prefer the term business fluctuations to the term business cycles?

4. Over a business cycle, why do the prices and outputs of durable-goods industries behave differently from those of nondurable-goods industries?

5. What do economists mean by leading indicators? What function do these leading indicators perform?

6. Distinguish among the three kinds of unemployment and give an example of each. How would you go about reducing each of these kinds of unemployment?

7. Describe each of the types of inflation.

8. If we assume that total output is unchanged, how do price increases redistribute real income? What groups benefit? Who suffers? Apply the same questions to price decreases.

9. During an inflation, who benefits: debtors, creditors, or savers? Why? What happens during a deflation?

10. How may a high rate of inflation lead to recession and unemployment?

11. Why may a moderate rate of inflation be beneficial to output?

12. How do the authors justify viewing creeping inflation as a threat to economic stability?

13. Whereas a moderate deflation may be beneficial to economic expansion, a rapid decline in prices tends to reduce output. Why?

14. Why may the goals of full employment and stable prices be contradictory? Draw a Phillips curve as part of your explanation.

15. What does the line labeled Potential GDP in Figure 6-1 represent? What does the line labeled Actual GDP represent? From 1994 to 1998 line Actual GDP was on or below potential GDP. What does that Potential GDP mean? From 1986 to 1990 Actual GDP was on or above Potential GDP. What does that mean?

Figure 6-1
The GDP Gap

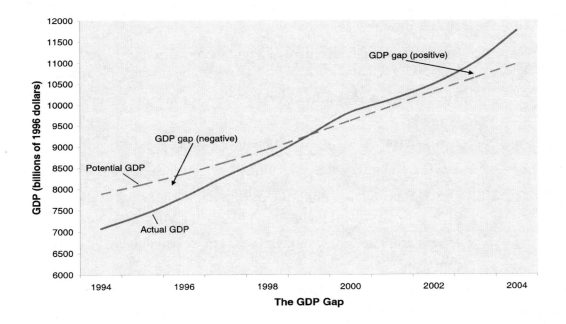

16. What is meant by the natural rate of unemployment?

17. Why is it difficult in the long run to push an economy's actual unemployment rate below its natural rate?

18. What seems to have happened to the natural rate of unemployment of the American economy? How might the natural rate be lowered?

19. How are unemployment and inflation related?

20. Why is understanding leading indicators important?

Part 4 Self-test

Section A True/false questions

T F 1. The nondurable-goods sector of the economy experiences wider fluctuations in price and smaller fluctuations in output than the durable-goods sector, because it is characterized by such high degrees of competition that no one firm has much control over the price.

T F 2. Before 1969, inflation and unemployment moved together during the business cycle; high unemployment was associated with high rates of inflation.

T F 3. When prices increase, savers benefit, while debtors do not.

T F 4. Business cycles are recurrent and nonperiodic variations in the level of economic activity.

T F 5. In a market-oriented economy, some level of frictional unemployment will always exist.

T F 6. If there is enough information about job opportunities and an adequate level of total demand, there will be no frictional unemployment.

T F 7. The Phillips curve shifts outward whenever the rate of unemploy-ment increases.

T F 8. A cost-push inflation occurs whenever wages are rising during an inflation.

T F 9. Stagflation hinders the government's efforts at economic stabilization.

T F 10. Some argue that the Phillips curve has shifted upward to the right because of the greater role of competition in causing inflation.

T F 11. The natural rate of unemployment is one at which there is a zero rate of inflation.

T F 12. A major problem with identifying the natural rate of unemployment is due to shifting inflationary expectations.

T F 13. The natural rate of unemployment for the U.S. has fallen in recent years.

T F 14. The changing composition of the American labor force has had a major effect on the nation's natural rate of unemployment.

T F 15. The natural rate of unemployment cannot be lowered.

T F 16. Okun's Law states that GDP will decline 2 1/2% for each 1% of employment above the natural rate.

T F 17. Leading economic indicators reflect how an economy has already changed.

T F 18. Inflation causes a decrease in the purchasing power of the dollar.

T F 19. Business cycles are regular in length and average between 2 to 4 years.

T F 20. During a recession phase inflation tends to move downward.

T F 21. In the long run, an economy cannot be pushed below its natural rate of unemployment.

Section B Multiple-choice questions

1. Which one of the following may be interpreted as demand-pull inflation?

   a. At full employment, demand exceeds the ability of the economy to produce at existing prices.

   b. Prices increase slowly over a long period of time.

   c. Costs of resources rise more rapidly than productivity rises.

   d. Prices increase very rapidly due to a rapid increase in the supply of money.

2. If OPEC quadruples the price of crude oil in 2005, the resulting inflation will be called

   a. creeping inflation.

   b. hyper-inflation.

   c. cost-push inflation.

   d. demand-pull inflation.

3. Which of the following is true?

   a. Business cycles tend to be recurrent and periodic.

   b. All phases of the business cycle tend to take an approximately equal length of time.

   c. All phases of the business cycle tend to be about equal in intensity.

   d. All the above are false.

4. In which industry do the most substantial variations in output and employment occur during a business cycle?

   a. Medical services

   b. Automobiles

   c. Food

   d. Furniture

5. If we assume that real output is unchanged, which generalization is not true about the effects of inflation?

   a. Debtors benefit.

   b. Savers benefit.

   c. Lenders are hurt.

   d. Both lenders and debtors are hurt.

6. Over a business cycle, prices in nondurable-goods industries tend to fluctuate widely while output tends to be relatively stable, because

   a. these industries are concentrated industries in which certain firms have the power to control output.

   b. consumers are limited in their ability to postpone new purchases from these industries because of the nature of the product.

   c. firms in these industries are small and therefore cannot get enough resources to keep output stable.

7. The shift outward of the Phillips curve can be attributed to

   a. increased amounts of structural unemployment.

   b. increased importance of cost-push inflation.

   c. increased impact of international inflationary forces beyond the control of domestic stabilization policies.

   d. all of the above.

8. The Phillips curve measures the tradeoff between

   a. unemployment rate and price level changes.

   b. wages and profits.

   c. quantity demanded and quantity supplied.

   d. employment rates and rates of inflation.

9. Which of the following generalizations about the relationship between price changes and output is usually true?

   a. A strong inflation can lead to a recession.

   b. A mild inflation tends to encourage economic expansion.

   c. A strong deflation tends to lead to economic contraction.

   d. All of the above are usually true.

10. Government economic policy may not achieve full employment and stable prices at the same time because

   a. full employment is impossible, since some workers are always unemployed as people move from one job to another.

   b. business groups within the country will not allow the achievement of this objective because it cuts down on their profits.

   c. some kinds of resources are in shorter supply than others.

   d. all of the above explain why both goals cannot be achieved.

11. Which of the following best describes the natural rate of unemployment concept?

   a. The unemployment rate associated with no unemployment.

   b. The unemployment rate associated with no change in the rate of inflation.

   c. The unemployment rate associated with creeping inflation.

   d. The unemployment rate associated with mild deflation.

12. Which of the following is not a way to lower the natural rate of unemployment?

   a. Creating a better match between job locations and available workers.

   b. Enhancing barriers to resource mobility.

   c. Creating a better match between skills of available workers and job openings.

   d. Reducing barriers to labor mobility such as economic discrimination and union membership requirements.

13. An attempt to reduce the actual rate of unemployment below the natural rate will likely result in which of the following?

   a. A short-run rise in the rate of unemployment.

   b. A short-run increase in the rate of inflation.

   c. A long-run decrease in the rate of unemployment.

   d. A short-run decrease in the rate of inflation.

Section C Matching questions

Match the phrases in column B to the terms in column A.

Column A
1. Secular trend
2. Leading indicators
3. Frictional unemployment
4. Structural unemployment
5. GDP gap
6. Demand-pull inflation
7. Cost-push inflation
8. Price increases
9. Real income
10. Phillips curve
11. Natural rate of unemployment

Column B
(a) A situation in which actual output is less than potential output
(b) Depends on degree of mobility of labor
(c) Savers suffer
(d) A situation in which demand exceeds supply
(e) Fall before economy falls, rise before economy rises
(f) Expresses what money income can buy
(g) Depicts the tradeoff between price changes and unemployment
(h) A situation in which prices of resources increase more than productivity
(i) Long-term movements in the economy
(j) Depends on changes in technology and composition of demand for output
(k) Has risen in the U.S. in recent decades

ANSWERS

Part 4

Section A 1, T; 2, F; 3, F; 4, T; 5, T; 6, F; 7, F; 8, F; 9, T; 10, F; 11, F; 12, T; 13, F; 14, T; 15, F; 16, T; 17, F; 18, T; 19, F; 20, T; 21, T
Section B 1, a; 2, c; 3, d; 4, b; 5, b; 6, b; 7, d; 8, a; 9, d; 10, c; 11, b; 12, b; 13, b
Section C 1, i; 2, e; 3, b; 4, j; 5, a; 6, d; 7, h; 8, c; 9, f; 10, g; 11, k

Chapter 7: Economic Growth

Part 1

First, read the sections entitled "Summing Up" at the end of Chapter 15. They offer a thorough review of the material.

Things to Watch For

Prior to this chapter, the book has dealt primarily with static principles, those dealing with economic relationships at a point in time. Dealing with growth and the problems relating to growth requires a dynamic framework-one that explains how economic relationships change as time goes by.

Chapter 15 begins by making a distinction between extensive growth and intensive growth. Extensive growth is the extensive process by which the total output of an economy grows as the economy has more and more resources. Intensive growth is the intensive process by which productivity, which is output per hour of labor (or income per capita), increases.

Since extensive growth comes about when the economy uses more resources, a nation's total supply of resources is the key to its expansion. Land represents natural resources. As we've seen before (in Chapter 2), resources are not fixed. They change, particularly as new technology makes it possible to use things previously not recognized as resources, or viewed only as potential resources. Labor is another resource. It represents the human skills and abilities of a society, without which there is no economic activity. Expansion via growth in the supply of labor can come about from an increase in population or from increased participation of people in the labor force (people working longer hours, more women entering the labor force, and so on). Capital, another resource, represents the results of investment. It may take the form of either an investment flow (financial capital) or a stock of plant and equipment (physical capital). Remember that capital basically affects the productivity of people. As workers have available more capital, and more sophisticated forms of capital, their productivity rises.

What determines the amount of capital people have to work with? One of the most important factors is market size. As a market grows, consumer purchasing power increases to the point at which aggregate demand warrants investment in plants, tools, and other forms of physical capital. Thus, areas or countries with low incomes and scanty populations employ less capital and have a less productive labor force than high-income areas or countries that have large populations.

Growth, the intensive process, is primarily the result of increasing efficiency. Relatively little of our increased output in the twentieth century has resulted from just increased use of resources. Most of it has resulted from increased output per unit of input (that is, increased productivity). Two developments account for this increase in productivity: (1) Specialization. As a market grows, it becomes possible to specialize in uses of resources within that market. (2) Technological change. Growth in technological knowledge results in greater productivity of capital goods and greater efficiency of organization.

Studies suggest that technological change has been the biggest cause of intensive economic growth. This is because it is the influence of technology that helps overcome the barriers to growth. There are at least two important barriers to growth: (1) The effect of diminishing returns (the law of variable proportions). There is a gradual decrease in efficiency associated with using more of certain inputs with a fixed amount of certain others. Many classical economists saw land as the fixed input. The effect of overcrowding-of more people on the same amount of land-is decreased efficiency. (2) Population pressures. If population increases more rapidly than the earth's capacity to sustain people (which mainly involves its capacity to produce food), the ceiling to growth will be very low. This pessimistic theory concerning barriers and population pressures is called the Malthusian specter, after T. R. Malthus.

Thus we say that technological change is a shift factor. It shifts the whole growth path of a society upward and prevents the above-mentioned barriers from producing stagnation, or a stationary state. Technological improvement has been the most important shift factor in the growth of the U.S. economy. One study concludes that between 1929 and 1957, 20 percent of economic growth in the United States resulted from improved technology and another 27 percent from improved education and training (in other words, greater investment in human capital).

Population growth retards the growth of low-income countries. However, it has been a significant factor in increasing demand and market sizes in the United States since 1900. The increase in U.S. population from 90,000,000 to more than 290,000,000 in the early twenty-first century has also increased the labor force and made possible the extension of mass production. Nowadays-especially because children in an urban industrial society are consumers, not producers, and because people prefer other goods to more children-we appear to be moving toward zero population growth.

In recent years U.S. economists have been interested less in a rapidly growing labor force than in expansion of capital. Production techniques have become more capital-intensive (increased capital/labor ratio) rather than more labor-intensive (increased labor/capital ratio). A situation of increased capital/labor ratio is referred to as capital deepening, in contrast to capital broadening, which is what happens when you have growth with a constant capital/labor ratio.

In a final section of the chapter, evidence regarding a slowing of productivity growth in the U.S. is discussed. According to Edward Denison, the rate of growth between 1973 and 1983 fell. Denison cites the reasons for this decline as (1) changing composition of the labor force, (2) changing composition of output, (3) growth in government regulation, (4) rising resources prices, and (5) declining rate of capital formation. A changing composition of output toward (labor intensive) services may be the most important of the causes.

William Baumol, on the other hand, argues that the American economy has not lost its productivity edge. Baumol cites the facts that, (1) productivity growth has simply returned to its historic rate, (2) productivity growth has declined in all industrial nations, and (3) productivity (output per unit of labor employed) of American labor remains the highest in the world.

The first application deals with the question of whether or not the growth of the United States depends on military spending. Some economists, such as Douglas Dowd, believe that since World War II the relative economic stability of the United States has indeed depended on defense-related purchases. Other economists, such as Arthur Okun, point out that military spending is like any other kind of federal spending in terms of its effect on

GDP (that is, on aggregate demand). This is an extension of the point established by John Maynard Keynes in 1936.

Examining the record on military spending leads to the following conclusions: (1) If there had been no defense spending in this country since World War II, and if it had not been replaced by other spending, unemployment would have been much higher. (2) Defense spending has been a fairly stable part of government spending. (3) Changes in defense spending in the 1960s had much less impact on the growth of U.S. potential than did changes in monetary and fiscal policy.

As to the effect of military spending on technological change and industrial capacity, some feel that military spending does little to increase capacity and that we could better use our resources in ways that do increase capacity. Others feel that defense spending has helped bring about advances in technology (new processes, new techniques) and that this has enhanced our productivity. It is impossible to say which view is correct. If both are correct, we should try to find out what the tradeoff is between the technology we gain by military spending and the capacity we lose by it. One thing is clear. Defense spending in the 1970s, 1980s, and 1990s did not fill the gaps in either employment or capacity. The application concludes with a note that declining defense spending in the 1990s did not necessarily have undesirable effects on economic growth. Rising defense spending after 2001 may or may not have such effects.

Optimism about continued growth and improvement in material welfare has been tempered by recognition of the need to establish tradeoffs between more growth and protection of the environment. These tradeoffs are the subject of the second application. Economists generally don't believe that decay of the environment is due to growth, per se. They do, however, believe that economic causes are at the root of environmental problems; these causes are connected with the pattern of growth.

Economists have differed with some ecologists on the following points: (1) Given certain unfavorable externalities, ecologists dispute the amount of real growth that has occurred in the industrialized nations. (2) Ecologists see absolute limits to growth, whereas economists see tradeoffs and generally feel that growth must continue. (3) Ecologists usually see government action as the primary means of solving environmental problems, whereas many economists believe that the market system can provide solutions as well.

Economists feel that the market system can be made to incorporate the externalities (the costs of cleaning up air and water to acceptable levels of purity). Two ways to do this are (1) setting standards for industrial effluents, and (2) taxing industrial effluents. One would circumvent the market; the other would use market signals.

Ecologists feel that the limits of growth are established by nature. Economists such as Kenneth Boulding agree that we must take natural limits into account as we move from an open-frontier (unlimited-growth) society to a "spaceship-earth" society, where nature imposes limits. Some ecologists feel that growth itself is the source of the problem and must be stopped. Pressures for zero population growth (ZPG) and zero economic growth (ZEG) are continuing.

Economists rebut these ideas by arguing that (1) resources will continue to grow (not remain static, as assumed in "doomsday" models), (2) not using resources today will deny future generations the new capital that would result from their use, and (3) advocates of ZPG and ZEG underestimate the flexibility and usefulness of the market system in finding solutions to environmental problems.

The application concludes with a notation that improvement in environmental quality is an increasing concern. Economists and most ecologists have increasingly agreed that: (1) environment repair need not require elimination of economic growth, and (2) two market forces can be useful in accomplishing environmental goals that do not require sacrificing economic growth.

Part 2

Define the following terms and concepts.

1. Dynamic framework
2. Static framework
3. Extensive growth
4. Intensive growth
5. Disembodied technological change
6. Human capital
7. Technological change
8. Stationary state
9. Malthusian specter
10. Capital-intensive production
11. Labor-intensive production
12. Capital broadening
13. Capital deepening
14. Zero economic growth
15. Zero population growth

Part 3

Answer the following questions and problems.

1. In what ways has military spending played an important economic role in the United States since World War II? In what ways has this kind of spending been no more important than-or even less important economically than-other kinds of government expenditures?

2. What are the major differences between economists and ecologists when it comes to suggesting solutions to environmental problems? Is there a growing concensus between economists and ecologists about growth and environmental repair? Explain.

3. What is the "Malthusian Specter"? Why has it not occurred in industrial nations? What will be necessary to avoid it in less-developed nations?

4. Consider Figure 7-1, and do the following things.

   a. Draw a growth path that illustrates the classical view of an eventual "stationary state."

   b. Explain why the growth path is shaped the way you have drawn it.

   c. Explain what factors can shift this growth path upward (raise productivity and real per capita income).

Figure 7-1
Growth Path of an Economy

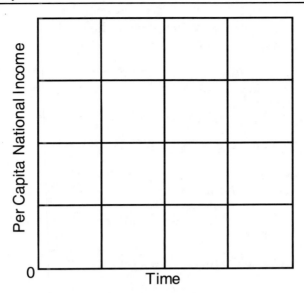

5. What role has population increase played in the economic growth of the United States? What role has immigration played in this growth?

6. What, according to Edward Denison, are the reasons for the declining growth of productivity in the United States since 1973? Which of these factors has/have been most important in decline?

7. William Baumol concludes that U.S. labor has not lost its productivity edge. What factors does he cite in reaching that conclusion?

8. What problems are associated with diverting investment to environmental-cleanup uses? What are solutions to these problems? Which solution do you favor? Why?

9. How important is the rate of growth?

10. How has the composition of the labor force changed?

Part 4 Self-test

Section A True/false questions

T F 1. Economists and ecologists seem to be coming to an agreement on the role of markets in finding solutions to environmental problems.

T F 2. Technological change has been the most important source of American growth since 1929.

T F 3. Growth and expansion are basically the same thing.

T F 4. Changes in military spending have done much to reduce unemployment since 1960.

T F 5. Economists generally believe that the market system can be used to force firms to incorporate externalities in their costs.

T F 6. When an economy is at a stationary state, this always means that it is at a level of near-starvation.

T F 7. Population increase always retards economic growth.

T F 8. Only dynamic theory is useful in economics.

T F 9. Economists believe that the pattern of growth, not growth itself, causes environmental pollution.

T F 10. According to Edward Denison, productivity growth has been faster than average since 1973.

T F 11. Technological change results in growth through increased efficiency.

T F 12. Human Capital consists of investment in the education of the workforce.

T F 13. Methus argued that food production grows geometrically.

T F 14. Military spending (federal expenditure) adds to aggregate demand.

T F 15. A growing economy's growth is always accompanied by full employment.

Section B Multiple-choice questions

1. According to Walter Heller, economists and ecologists disagree on all but which one of the following?

   a. Whether real growth has occurred

   b. Whether there are absolute limits to growth

   c. Whether growth can be stopped

   d. Whether markets can provide solutions to environmental problems

2. Ecologists believe in all but which one of the following?

   a. Zero population growth

   b. Zero economic growth

   c. Need for stimulants to private investment

   d. Government antipollution standards

3. Which one of the following courses of action open to government does not stimulate spending?

   a. Reducing federal expenditures

   b. Increasing federal expenditures

   c. Decreasing taxes

   d. Increasing government spending more than taxes

4. Which of the following represents capital?

   a. Offshore oil

   b. The building in which Congress meets

   c. A steel plant

   d. Your private automobile

5. Which of the following is the most important source of recent growth in the United States?

   a. Additional labor

   b. Additional land

   c. Better technology

   d. Wage and price controls

6. Which of the following does not help to explain the slowing of productivity growth in the United States since 1973?

   a. Decline government regulation

   b. Rising resource prices

   c. Decreases in the rate of capital formation

   d. A changing composition of output in favor of services.

7. William Baumol argues that U.S. labor has the highest productivity in the world and that it has not lost its productivity edge. What factors does he cite in support of this conclusion?

   a. Productivity growth has slowed in all industrial nations.

   b. Service sector employment in the U.S. has grown less rapidly than in almost all other industrial nations.

   c. Productivity growth in the U.S. has returned to its historic average.

   d. All of the above are cited by Baumol.

Section C Matching questions

Match the phrases in column A to the terms in column B.

Column A	**Column B**
1. Extensive process	(a) Stationary state
2. Fixed input(s)	(b) Dynamic
3. Classical economics	(c) Static
4. Capital/labor ratio rises	(d) Growth
5. Characterized by changes over time	(e) Expansion
6. Relation of employment to output	(f) Malthus
7. Specter of starvation	(g) Diminishing returns
8. Capital/labor ratio is constant	(h) Capital broadening
9. Existing at a point in time	(i) Capital deepening
10. Intensive process	(j) Aggregate production function

ANSWERS

Part 4

Section A 1, T; 2, T; 3, T; 4, F; 5, F; 6, T; 7, F; 8, F; 9, F; 10, T; 11, T; 12, T; 13, F; 14, T; 15, F

Section B 1, c; 2, c; 3, a; 4, c; 5, c; 6, a; 7, d

Section C 1, e; 2, g; 3, a; 4, i; 5, b; 6, j; 7, f; 8, h; 9, c; 10, d

Chapter 8: Aggregate Demand and Aggregate Supply

Part 1

First, read the sections entitled "Summing Up" at the end of Chapter 7. They offer a thorough review of the chapter.

Things to Watch For

Chapter 7 introduces a very important series of chapters; those discussing how the level of income, output, employment, and prices are determined. This chapter shows how the equilibrium level of real income and prices is determined through the interaction of aggregate demand and aggregate supply.

First, the chapter introduces and defines the concept of aggregate demand and explains the factors that determine it. Then the downward-sloping nature of the aggregate demand curve is explored. Second, the concept of aggregate supply is introduced, defined and its determinants are detailed. The upward-sloping nature of aggregate supply is then examined. Finally, the two curves are put into the same diagram with prices on the vertical axis and real income/output on the horizontal axis. Equilibrium, where aggregate quantity demanded equals aggregate quantity supplied, will establish the level of prices and real income in the economy. You should remember that although the analysis seems much like the supply-and-demand model presented in Chapter 3, it has important differences. Know these differences. Furthermore, the student is cautioned that equilibrium and full employment are not necessarily the same.

Rounding out the discussion, the chapter analyzes the effects of changes in aggregate demand and aggregate supply under conditions in which there are demand shocks and supply shocks. It is also important to remember the three ranges of aggregate supply in its relationship between prices and employment.

Before the application, the chapter concludes with two further subjects. First, is a brief comment on supply-side economics-the main point here is that policy advocates of it concentrate on policy that would increase the ability of the economy to produce. More on supply-side policies will be included in a later chapter. Second, is a discussion of price indexes including the Consumer Price Index and computing the GDP price deflator.

The application reviews the economic effects of the (oil-price determined) supply shocks of 1973 and 1979 in terms of the aggregate demand-aggregate supply model introduced in Chapter 7. The application continues with an examination of the reverse shocks of falling oil prices in the 1980s and 1990s. In conclusion, the application looks at the economic effects of terrorist attacks on the United States in 2001 and how those attacks may influence the recovery from recession of an economy mobilizing to fight terrorism.

Part 2

Define the following terms and concepts.

1. Equilibrium level of prices and real income
2. Aggregate demand
3. Aggregate supply
4. Aggregate demand shock
5. Aggregate supply shock
6. Supply-side economics
7. OPEC I, II, III
8. Investment in human capital
9. Ranges of aggregate supply
10. Price indexes
11. GDP price index or deflator
12. Consumer price index
13. External aggregate demand shocks
14. External aggregate supply shocks

Part 3

Answer the following questions and problems.

1. Draw a diagram representing aggregate demand and aggregate supply.

    a. Label all curves and axes.

    b. Show equilibrium and indicate and explain an excess supply or excess demand.

    c. Explain how equilibrium is achieved.

    d. Show the results of a demand shock.

    e. Show the results of a supply shock.

2. Explain why the aggregate demand curve slopes downward. Why does aggregate supply slope upward?

3. State each of the determinants of aggregate demand, and explain what happens when they shift.

4. State each of the determinants of aggregate supply, and explain what happens when they shift.

5. Explain how equilibrium employment and full employment may differ.

6. What is an aggregate demand shock? Show by use of a diagram how it affects prices and real income.

7. What is an aggregate supply shock? Show by use of a diagram how it affects prices and real income.

8. Using a diagram, show the three ranges of aggregate supply. What causes these different ranges to exist?

9. What are external demand and supply shocks?

10. What were the external oil supply shocks of the 1970s and 1980s and how did they affect the economy?

11. What is supply-side economics? What government policies do you think would be consistent with it's arguments?

12. Make up a numerical problem that illustrates how a 2000 GDP price index would be computed using a market basket price in 2000 and a market basket price in 1987.

13. Why is the CPI considered such an important index? How may it overstate aggregate price changes?

14. Summarize the possible aggregate demand and aggregate supply effects of the "war on terrorism." What caveats apply to those effects?

15. If the economy is not in equilibrium, how does it get back?

16. What is the largest component of aggregate demand (AD)?

Part 4 Self-test

Section A True/false questions

T F   1. As with the supply-and-demand model of a particular market, the equilibrium price level and equilibrium real income are determined by the intersection of aggregate demand and aggregate supply.

T F   2. The aggregate demand curve slopes downward for the same reason as does the demand curve for a particular commodity.

T F   3. Among other factors, aggregate demand is determined by consumption, investment, and government expenditures.

T F   4. Expectations about future economic events become more optimistic as the aggregate demand curve shifts down to the left.

T F   5. Aggregate supply curves slope upwards so that real income increases as prices increase.

T F   6. Among other things, the aggregate supply curve is determined by cost of resources, technology, and productivity.

T F   7. If our expectations about future economic activity become more optimistic, the aggregate supply curve shifts to the right.

T F   8. Equilibrium between aggregate supply and aggregate demand is always at full employment.

T F   9. When there is an aggregate demand shock due to increased demand, the aggregate demand curve shifts to the right with both real income and the price level increasing.

T F 10. The aggregate supply curve has three ranges:

>1. No increases in prices as real income increases.
>
>2. Increases in the price level as real income increases.
>
>3. Increases in the price level with no increases in real income.

T F 11. OPEC I (1973-74) increased prices as the reduced supply of oil decreased real income.

T F 12. The increase in oil supply known as OPEC III (early 1980s) caused a reduction in the price level and an increase in real income.

T F 13. Supply-side economics is concerned with how the ability of the economy to produce can be increased.

T F 14. The consumer price index is used as the GDP price deflator.

T F 15. A war on terrorism is likely to reduce aggregate demand.

T F 16. The aggregate supply curve has a positive slope.

T F 17. Aggregate demand is a measure of the entire planned spending on final goods and services at each level of prices and real incomes.

T F 18. The CPI consumer price index is one of the most widely used indexes of the federal government.

T F 19. Supply shocks have only positive effects on the economy.

Section B Multiple-choice questions

1. When diagramming aggregate demand and aggregate supply

   a. real national income is placed on the vertical axis and the price level on the horizontal axis.

   b. the price level is placed on the vertical axis and real income on the horizontal axis.

   c. employment is placed on the vertical axis and the price level on the horizontal axis.

   d. government expenditures are placed on the horizontal axis and employment on the vertical axis.

2. Which one of the following is not a determinant of aggregate demand?

   a. Consumption expenditures

   b. Investment expenditures

   c. Technology

   d. Net exports

3. Which one of the following is not a determinant of aggregate supply?

    a. Cost and availability of resources

    b. Capacity and investment plans

    c. Productivity

    d. Disposable personal income

4. Which one of the following does not cause the aggregate demand curve to slope downward?

    a. Changes in real output

    b. Interest rate changes

    c. Wealth effects

    d. Changes in relative prices between foreign and domestic goods

5. Which of the following relationships is correct?

    a. Equilibrium employment and full employment may not be the same.

    b. Equilibrium employment and full employment are always the same.

    c. Equilibrium employment and full employment are never the same.

    d. Equilibrium employment and full employment are unrelated.

6. Which of the following is not correct?

    a. Real income will increase without increases in prices when there is substantial unemployment.

    b. Both real income and prices will increase when there are bottlenecks in the supply of some resources.

    c. When full employment is reached, only prices can increase.

    d. When full employment is reached, only increases in real income can occur.

7. With aggregate demand shocks

    a. the aggregate demand curve moves up the aggregate supply curve and increases prices and real income.

    b. the aggregate supply curve moves up the aggregate demand curve and increases price but reduces real income.

    c. the aggregate supply curve moves down the aggregate demand curve and reduces prices and increases real income.

    d. the aggregate demand curve moves down the aggregate supply curve and increases both prices and real income.

8. An improvement in technology will

    a. increase aggregate demand.

    b. decrease aggregate demand.

    c. increase aggregate supply.

    d. decrease aggregate supply.

9. Which of the following was not a factor limiting the severity of the effects of the oil supply shock of 1979-80?

    a. More efficient use of energy.

    b. Increase in use of alternative sources of energy.

    c. Increased suppliers of non-OPEC oil.

    d. More rapid worldwide economic growth.

10. The oil shock in 1979-80 was an example of

    a. an external demand shock increasing prices and real income.

    b. an external supply shock increasing prices and decreasing real income.

    c. an external supply shock decreasing prices and increasing real income.

    d. an external demand shock decreasing prices and real income.

11. Oil price changes in 1985 and 1986 are an example of

    a. an external supply shock decreasing prices and raising real income.

    b. an external demand shock increasing prices and reducing real income.

    c. an external supply shock increasing prices and reducing real income.

    d. an external supply shock increasing prices and reducing real income.

12. The negative effects of a war on terrorism are likely to be

    a. a decrease in aggregate supply and an increase in aggregate demand.

    b. an increase in aggregate supply and an increase in aggregate demand.

    c. an increase in aggregate supply and a decrease in aggregate demand.

    d. a decrease in aggregate supply and a decrease in aggregate demand.

13. The positive effects of a war on terrorism are likely to be

    a. an increase in aggregate supply and a decrease in aggregate demand.

    b. a decrease in aggregate supply and a decrease in aggregate demand.

    c. an increase in aggregate supply and an increase in aggregate demand.

    d. an increase in aggregate demand and a decrease in aggregate supply.

Section C   Matching Questions

Match the phrases in Column B to the terms in Column A

Column A	Column B
1. Aggregate demand	(a) Reduced aggregate demand
2. Aggregate supply	(b) Downward sloping curve
3. Increased cost of credit	(c) Increased aggregate demand
4. Increased disposable personal income	(d) GNP gap is zero
5. Equilibrium real income	(e) OPEC oil price increases of the 1970s
6. Equilibrium income = potential income	(f) Less real income demanded at each price level
7. Aggregate supply shocks	(g) Aggregate quantity supplied = Aggregate quantity demanded
8. Aggregate demand shock	(h) Upward sloping curve
9. Full-employment aggregate supply	(i) No increase in real income
10. External aggregated demand and supply shocks.	(j) Influences outside the domestic economy
11. Colas	(k) Determined by the consumer price index

ANSWERS

Part 4

Section A 1, T; 2, F; 3, T; 4, F; 5, T; 6, T; 7, T; 8, F; 9, T; 10, T; 11, T; 12, T; 13, T; 14, F; 15, F; 16, T; 17, T; 18, T; 19, F

Section B 1, b; 2, c; 3, d; 4, a; 5, a; 6, d; 7, a; 8, c; 9, d; 10, b; 11, a; 12, d; 13, c

Section C 1, b; 2, h; 3, a; 4, c; 5, g; 6, d; 7, e; 8, f; 9, i; 10, j

Chapter 9: Aggregate Spending in the Macroeconomy

Part 1

First, read the section entitled "Summing Up" at the end of Chapter 8. It offers a thorough review of the chapter.

Things to Watch For

You may find Chapter 8 rough going, but if you are willing to work your way through it step by step, you will be rewarded. Chapter 8 is the first of three chapters that will lead you through the Keynesian model of income determination. This model is named after the economist John Maynard Keynes (whose name rhymes with gains). This chapter will give you a theoretical foundation for our later discussion of economic policies that governments use to stabilize a nation's economy and for some of the controversies surrounding those policies..

The chapter is divided into three sections. The first explores the macroeconomic theory most widely accepted before Keynes formulated his model. This earlier theory is called classical income-determination theory. Classical theory held that a market economy, if left alone, would achieve a level of income and output that would bring about full employment. What was necessary, such economists believed, was a low and balanced government budget plus competitive markets. The three concepts that underlie their thinking are Say's law, the abstinence theory of interest, and wage and price flexibility.

The second section of Chapter 8 explains Keynes's ideas about income determination by analyzing his criticisms of the classical model. Keynes attacked the abstinence theory of interest by breaking the relationship between the interest rate and savings, and reducing the strength of the relationship between the interest rate and investment. He also challenged the effectiveness of wage and price flexibility as a device for eliminating a temporary oversupply of firms' inventories. If you want to understand the relationships discussed in the next chapters, it is important that you understand this reasoning. It is important to remember Keynes' assumption about aggregate supply, i.e., that supply is horizontal and increases in response to increased demand without increases in prices (the unemployment range of aggregate supply).

The third section of this chapter sets up the basic elements of the Keynesian model. Keynes said that the level of income may be such that the economy may be at full employment, above full employment (inflation), or below full employment (unemployment). The thing that determines the level of income in the Keynesian model is the level of effective demand or aggregate demand. The five factors that determine effective demand are consumption, savings, investment, government expenditures, and taxes. The latter part of the chapter explores the relationship between the first three factors and the level of income, and brings together in diagrammatic form the elements contained in the Keynesian model. It is essential that you thoroughly understand this section, because the next chapters build on it. The Keynesian theory of income determination is a key concept, and this chapter sets forth the crux of this theory.

Part 2

Define the following terms and concepts.

1. Classical theory
2. Say's law
3. Abstinence theory of interest
4. Wage-price flexibility
5. Pigou effect
6. Effective demand
7. Consumption function
8. Savings function
9. Investment function
10. Dissavings
11. Liquid assets
12. Autonomous investment, induced investment
13. Marginal efficiency of capital
14. Aggregate-demand-equals-aggregate-supply approach
15. Savings-equals-intended-investment approach
16. Keynesian theory
17. Mercantilism

Part 3

Answer the following questions and problems.

1. What do classical economists conclude about full employment in a market-oriented economy? Under what two conditions do they feel that unemployment can exist? What three concepts underlie their conclusions?

2. What is Say's law? Illustrate it with a simple circular-flow diagram.

3. When a complex circular-flow diagram rather than a simple one is used, what additional problems confront the classical economist with respect to income determination? How does the abstinence theory of interest solve those problems?

4. Explain the abstinence theory of interest. Explain how the interest rate links savings to investment.

5. Explain how, according to classical economists, wage and price flexibility does away with unemployment and a temporary oversupply of firms' goods. What role does the Pigou effect play in this process?

6. What arguments did Keynes use to refute Say's law? To refute the abstinence theory of interest? Explain how Keynes challenged the relationship between planned savings and the interest rate, and cast doubt on the relationship between planned investment and the interest rate.

7. Keynes denied the assumption that wages and prices are flexible enough to move the economy toward full employment. Explain the points he used to support his conclusion.

8. After he had refuted classical conclusions about the level of income, what did Keynes conclude about it? What did he say determines the level of income?

9. Draw the aggregate supply curve that is consistent with the Keynesian assumptions. What level of employment must be assumed? Why?

10. Name five factors that determine the level of effective demand. Which of these factors increase demand as they increase, and which decrease demand as they increase?

11. Draw a diagram showing the 45? line, the consumption function, and the savings function. What is the significance of the 45? line? Given the consumption function you have drawn, what are you assuming about the relationship between the percentage of income that people consume and the various levels of income? Between the percentage of income that people save and the various levels of income?

12. What does it mean when we say that individuals sometimes dissave?

13. Distinguish between a change in the quantity consumed and saved on the one hand and, on the other, a change in consumption and savings.

14. What are five factors that can cause a change in consumption or savings?

15. The level of autonomous investment is determined by the cost of investing and the expected rate of return. What determines the cost of investing? What determines the expected rate of return, or the marginal efficiency of capital?

16. Use a diagram to show how the quantity of autonomous investment is determined. (Be sure to label the diagram properly.)

17. Why is the quantity of investment so unstable? What factors have tended to reduce this instability?

18. Add intended investment to your diagram of the consumption and savings functions, using the following two approaches. What set of relationships does each approach emphasize?

   a. The savings-equals-intended-investment approach.

   b. The aggregate-demand-equals-aggregate-supply approach.

19. What is the difference between Classical and Keynesian economics?

20. Why is investment so volatile over time?

Part 4 Self-test

Section A True/false questions

T F   1. According to Say's law, supply creates its own demand, so that unemployment cannot long exist.

T F   2. Classical theory maintains that the economy can only temporarily deviate from full employment.

T F   3. Classical economists, knowing that saving reduces consumer demand, believe that demand will be equal to supply only if people do not save.

T F   4. Classical theorists considered unemployment a temporary problem because of considerable monopoly in both the product and the labor markets.

T F   5. Although Keynes agreed that the level of saving is determined by the interest rate, he felt that the level of investment is not deter-mined by it, because of business expectations.

T F   6. Keynes concluded that an economy's level of income may be such that the economy may be at full employment, or at inflation, or below full employment.

T F   7. The aggregate supply curve that is consistent with the Keynesian model slopes upward showing that increases in demand will increase both real income and prices.

T F   8. The position of the consumption function depends on the level of income, but the quantity of goods and services consumed depends on many other factors.

T F   9. If the interest rate decreases, the amount of investment also decreases because the profits investors expect to make decrease.

T F   10. An individual can dissave by decreasing his or her accumulated savings, but the economy as a whole cannot dissave.

T F   11. The marginal-efficiency-of-capital curve slopes down to the right because, as the interest rate falls, larger amounts of investment yield a return equal to or greater than the interest rate.

T F   12. Induced investment is the result of increased buying.

T F   13. Classical theory believes that the supply curve is vertical.

T F   14. Say's Law says that demand creates supply.

T F   15. Keynesian economists theorize that government intervention is not necessary to move to full employment.

Section B Multiple-choice questions

1. The classical conclusion that a market economy has built-in mechanisms that will keep income at the full-employment level is supported by which of the following assumptions?
   a. Wage and price flexibility
   b. Say's law
   c. The abstinence theory of interest
   d. All of the above

2. The abstinence theory of interest does not maintain that
   a. people would rather consume now than later.
   b. total demand equals total supply only when savings are zero.
   c. the higher the interest rate, the larger the quantity saved.
   d. the lower the interest rate, the smaller the quantity saved.

3. Wage and price flexibility will eliminate a temporary oversupply of goods and also unemployment by
   a. decreasing wages and prices and thus increasing quantity demanded.
   b. increasing the purchasing power of workers as wages fall more slowly than prices.
   c. increasing the purchasing power of entrepreneurs as wages fall faster than prices.
   d. decreasing wages and prices and thus decreasing quantity demanded.

4. Which of the following did Keynes present as an argument for maintaining that the interest rate does not equate desired savings and desired investment, and that the abstinence theory of interest is wrong?
   a. Those who save are not the same as those who invest.
   b. Motivations for saving are not entirely related to the rate of interest.
   c. Expectations about future economic activity weaken the relationship between investments and the interest rate.
   d. All of the above.

5. Which of the following arguments did Keynes use in challenging the idea that wage and price flexibility is sufficient to bring about a situation of full employment and no surpluses?
   a. Monopoly power is rare in the U.S. market economy.
   b. Wages always fall more rapidly than prices.
   c. Workers are more concerned with real income than with money income.
   d. None of the above.

6. After analyzing the classical conclusions about the level of income and employ-ment, Keynes concluded that
   a. the level of income will always be such that there is full employment.
   b. the level of income will always be such that there is less than full employment.
   c. the level of income may be such that there is full employment, or unemploy-ment, or inflation.
   d. the level of income is unrelated to the level of employment.

7. Which of the following is not correct about the aggregate supply curve consistent with the Keynesian assumptions?
   a. Prices do not increase with increases in output.
   b. Unemployment exists.
   c. Both prices and real income increases with increases in demand.
   d. The aggregate supply curve is horizontal.

8. Effective demand will increase if
   a. consumption, investment, and government expenditures increase.
   b. taxes and savings increase.
   c. consumption decreases and savings increase.
   d. government expenditures decrease.

9. The quantity consumed may change if there are changes in
   a. institutions or customs.
   b. the level of income.
   c. liquid assets or taxes.
   d. tax laws.

10. Which of the following is most correct? The quantity of autonomous investment changes when there are changes in
    a. interest rates.
    b. expectations about future economic activity.
    c. productivity of investment.
    d. interest rates, expectations, and productivity of investment.

11. Of all the factors that influence effective demand, the most unstable over time is
    a. consumption.
    b. savings.
    c. investment.
    d. government expenditures.

Section C Matching questions

Match the phrases in column B to the terms in column A.

Column A	Column B
1. Classical economics	(a) Investment in relation to savings
2. Say's law	(b) Income increases, quantity consumed increases
3. Abstinence theory of interest	(c) Income always tends toward a level at which there is full employment
4. Wage and price flexibility	(d) Consume now rather than save and consume later
5. Pigou effect	(e) Consumption exceeds income
6. Consumption function	(f) Supply creates its own demand
7. Autonomous investment	(g) Eliminates temporary oversupply
8. Dissavings	(h) Not affected by income
9. Marginal efficiency of capital	(i) Expected rate of return
10. S=II	(j) Savers feel wealthier as prices fall, and they demand more consumption

ANSWERS

Part 4

Section A 1, T; 2, T; 3, F; 4, F; 5, F; 6, T; 7, F; 8, F; 9, F; 10, F; 11, T; 12, T; 13, T; 14, F; 15, F

Section B 1, d; 2, b; 3, a; 4, d; 5, d; 6, c; 7, c; 8, a; 9, b; 10, d; 11, c

Section C 1, c; 2, f; 3, d; 4, g; 5, j; 6, b; 7, h; 8, e; 9, i; 10, a

Chapter 10: Fiscal Policy, Deficit Financing, and the National Debt

Part 1

First, read the section entitled "Summing Up" at the end of Chapter 10. It provides a thorough review of the material in the chapter.

Things to Watch For

The first part of Chapter 10 deals with the fiscal policy implications of the Keynesian model. Fiscal policy consists of variations in government expenditures and taxation. The policy based on that model is called compensatory fiscal policy or functional finance. First, be clear on the distinction between discretionary policy and automatic stabilizers. Second, be able to explain how functional finance would work in theory. The result of this policy is that a budget deficit would tend to result in its use during a recession and a surplus during inflation.

The second part is concerned with budget deficits and the rapidly increasing federal debt. First presented, are relevant statistics on the relationship between federal debt, GDP, interest on debt, total and per capita debt. Understand which of these are most relevant to an understanding of the seriousness of the debt. Next, there is a discussion of the major concerns that economists have about the size and growth of the federal debt. Be sure you can distinguish between relevant and unfounded concerns about the debt. In this discussion the crowding-out effect is most important and should be given close attention.

The question of the burden of the federal debt is also very important. Be sure to understand the income redistribution effects and the possible opportunity cost effects of the debt. Another area where budget deficits may affect the economy is through its affect on the balance of trade and payments. Be sure to understand both the traditional arguments and alternatives to the traditional view.

Beginning in the 1970s, efforts have been made through legislation and legislative proposals to reduce the growth in the federal debt and to reduce the budgetary deficits. The Gramm-Rudman bill of 1985 is one early example. Be familiar with these efforts. Finally, include the balanced budget amendment controversy, the line item veto controversy, privatization of federal programs, and changes in budgetary procedures.

The chapter ends with Martin Weitzman's proposal for a share economy to reduce the reliance on Keynesian demand management. Understand the workings of the two-wage system. Also, understand the various critiques of the system, both pro and con. The chapter concludes an application on the national debt and where we are headed

Part 2

Define the following terms and concepts.

1. Fiscal policy
2. Discretionary fiscal policy
3. Automatic stabilizers
4. Compensatory fiscal policy
5. Budget deficit

6. Budget surplus
7. Crowding-out effect
8. Ricardo Equivalence Theorem
9. Share economy

Part 3

Answer the following questions.

1. Explain the difference between discretionary policy and automatic stabilizers.

2. Explain how functional finance or compensatory fiscal policy would work according to the Keynesian model.

3. What are the concerns about the growing federal debt discussed in the text? Explain why they should be of concern to you.

4. Explain the "crowding-out" effect. What factors would tend to offset the crowding-out effect?

5. Discuss the fallacies of the concern over the federal government going bankrupt.

6. In what various ways are the burdens of the debt increased? For the present generation? For future generations?

7. What is the traditional view about the relationship between budget deficits and the balance of trade? What alternative view is presented in the text?

8. Name and discuss four pieces of legislation, passed or proposed, aimed at resolving the large federal budget deficit.

9. Discuss the pros and cons of the share economy proposal of Martin Weitzman.

10. What are the potential problems if a rapidly growing national debt?

11. What does discretionary mean?

Part 4 Self-test

Section A True/false questions

T F 1. Automatic stabilizers are structures in our economy that were designed specially to moderate inflations and recessions.

T F 2. Discretionary fiscal policy involves varying the supply of money and the interest rate.

T F 3. During a recession, functional finance would increase government expenditures and or decrease taxes.

T F 4. A more valid measure of the significance of the national debt, thus the absolute total of debt, is the amount of interest as a percentage of per capita income.

T F 5. There is little difference between the economic impact of private debt and the economic impact of federal debt.

T F 6. Since the economic cost of a war is financed by government debt, it is passed on to the generation that has to pay off the debt.

T F 7. When it comes to the problem of redistribution of income, it makes little difference who owns the national debt.

T F 8. The traditional view of the relationship between federal budget deficits and the balance of trade is that deficits increase interest rates that appreciate the dollar, reducing exports and increasing imports.

T F 9. The Gramm-Rudman bill was a last ditch effort of legislation to increase the power of discretionary fiscal policy.

T F 10. The share economy is based on a two-tier wage system with one tier based on the firms profits.

T F 11. Automatic stabilizers are discretionary factors that reduce the likelihood of recession.

T F 12. Crowding out is when government receives funds that would otherwise go to private users.

T F 13. Taxing and spending are both part of fiscal policy.

T F 14. Budget Deficits are defined as the amount by which government expenditures exceed government revenues.

Section B Multiple-choice questions

1. Compensatory fiscal policy, or functional finance, during a recession would

   a. compensate for low levels of aggregate demand by increasing government expenditures and or reduce taxes.

   b. compensate for high levels of aggregate demand by decreasing government expenditures and or increase taxes.

   c. increase the interest rate and reduce the supply of money.

   d. decrease the interest rate and increase the supply of money.

2. Who pays the economic cost of a war financed by federal debt?

    a. the generation that pays taxes to pay off the debt resulting from the war

    b. the generation that fights the war, since resources are siphoned away from consumption and investment to the production of military goods

    c. no one, in that there are no economic costs to wars, since they stimulate the economy

    d. all of the above

3. Under a share economy wages would be

    a. entirely tied to the profitability of employing firms.

    b. entirely separated from the profitability of employing firms.

    c. unrelated to the profitability of employing firms.

    d. partially tied to the profitability of employing firms and partly determined by fixed wage contracts.

4. Which of the following is true about compensatory fiscal policy?

    a. It operates automatically and is one of the automatic stabilizers.

    b. During a recession, it would decrease the deficit in the federal budget.

    c. It would use fiscal policy to counteract inadequate levels of demand to achieve full employment and stabilize prices.

    d. It would compensate for improper changes in the interest rate.

5. Which of the following is not a major concern of economists about the federal debt?

    a. The federal government would go bankrupt if it had to pay off the debt.

    b. The interest on the debt is so high that it reduces the ability to move towards a balanced budget.

    c. The crowding-out effect reduces investment.

    d. Large deficits during low levels of unemployment increases the fear of inflation.

6. Which of the following does not tend to counter the argument about the crowding-out effect?

    a. Increased demand for output due to deficits stimulates demand for investment.

    b. Government debt, due to deficits does not have a direct affect on the interest rate.

    c. Part of government expenditures are for investment purposes, such as roads and schools.

7. It is generally assumed that deficits in the federal budget would

   a. have no affect on the balance of trade.

   b. tend to increase exports and decrease imports.

   c. tend to increase imports and decrease exports.

   d. tend to increase both exports and imports.

8. Which one of the following is not a proposal to impose some fiscal discipline that would restrain debt growth?

   a. The Employment Act of 1946

   b. Gramm-Rudman-Hollings Act of 1985

   c. Balanced budget amendment to the constitution

   d. Line-item veto

Section C Matching questions

I. Match the phrases in column B to the terms in column A.

Column A	Column B
1. Fiscal policy	(a) Expenditures exceed taxes
2. Discretionary fiscal policy	(b) A two-tier wage system
3. Automatic stabilizers	(c) Varying taxes and government expenditures
4. Compensatory fiscal policy	(d) The same results occur from debt increase or tax increase
5. Budget deficit	(e) Work without policy action
6. Budget surplus	(f) Interest increases and investment decreases
7. Crowding-out effect	(g) Need policy action
8. Ricardo Equivalence Theorem	(h) Compensates for improper levels of aggregate demand
9. Share economy	(i) Taxes exceed expenditures

ANSWERS

Part 4

Section A 1, F; 2, F; 3, T; 4, T; 5, F; 6, F; 7, F; 8, T; 9, F; 10, T; 11, F; 12, T; 13, T; 14, T
Section B 1, a; 2, b; 3, d; 4, c; 5, a; 6, b; 7, c; 8, a
Section C 1, a; 2, g; 3, e; 4, h; 5, a; 6, i; 7, f; 8, d; 9, b

Chapter 11: Money in the Modern Economy

Part 1

First, read the section entitled "Summing Up" at the end of Chapter 11 for a thorough review of the chapter.

Things to Watch For

Chapter 11 is an introduction to money and its importance to an economy. (Chapter 12 will discuss the banking system and Chapter 13 monetary policy.)

This chapter first tackles the question of what money is. It analyzes a barter economy (in which there is no money) and then a money economy. It states the four functions of money and gives the characteristics of a good money along with emphasizing the fact that money is debt. Next the chapter discusses the supply of money and analyzes the three kinds of money that make up this supply: demand deposits, currency in circulation, and coins in circulation. It contains a number of definitions (Part 2 gives a complete list of new concepts) so that you can distinguish between money and near money (for example, the money in savings accounts and government debt) and also credit cards. Finally, the chapter distinguishes between, M1, M2, and M3 money as alternative measures of the money supply.

Keep in mind that money is money because people accept it as money. Money becomes money because people accept it in exchange for goods and services. It is a social convention to reduce the real costs of exchanging goods and services.

To give you a glimpse of the banking system and its role in the supply of money, Chapter 11 offers a brief look at goldsmith banking in seventeenth-century England. The goldsmith system had most of the elements of the modern commercial bank: demand deposits, checks, fractional reserves, loans, and the creation of demand deposits. The next chapter will lead you again (but this time very slowly) through the workings of the commercial bank system as it affects lending and the supply of money.

The last question Chapter 11 deals with is: How do changes in the supply of money affect output and prices? The chapter gives two approaches: (1) the equation of exchange (MV = PQ), the velocity of exchange and (2) the demand for money. Both lead to the same conclusions. If you increase the supply of money, the economy expands. If there is full employment, this expansion is shown only in increases in prices. If you decrease the supply of money, the level of demand declines. It is important that you understand this last section, because the chapter on monetary policy will bring you back to the equation of exchange and the problem of the effect on the economy of changes in the supply of money.

Part 2

Define the following terms and concepts.

1. Barter system of exchange
2. Double coincidence of demand
3. Money
4. Medium of exchange
5. Standard of value or unit of account
6. Store of value
7. Means of deferred payment
8. Checking accounts or demand deposits
9. Depository institution
10. Fiat money, legal tender
11. Near money
12. Fractional reserve principle
13. Equation of exchange
14. M1 money
15. M2 money
16. M3 money
17. Legal tender
18. Gresham's Law

Part 3

Answer the following questions and problems.

1. Contrast a barter system of exchange with a money system. Which is more efficient? Why?

2. What makes something money? What are the functions of money in an economy?

3. Pick something that you think would serve as a good form of money and list characteristics that would favor its use as a money. Also list any characteristics that might make it unfavorable.

4. What are the advantages and disadvantages of the three forms of M1 money in the U.S. economy?

5. Define M1, M2, and M3 money. What do you think are the advantages and/or disadvantages of each as measures of the money supply?

6. The text maintains that money in our economy is debt. What does the text mean by that?

7. Why aren't credit cards considered money? Why are traveler's checks considered money?

8. The text describes seventeenth-century goldsmith banking as the origin of today's commercial banking system. How did goldsmiths in those days affect the supply of money?

9. State the equation of exchange and explain what each letter symbol in the equation stands for.

10. Use the equation of exchange to show what would happen during a recession if the supply of money increased. What if there were full employment?

11. What is a double coincidence of wants?

12, If fiat money is not backed by gold, why does fiat money have value?

Part 4 Self-test

Section A True/false questions

T F 1. Money is anything that people accept as an asset.

T F 2. Savings deposits are near money but are not regarded as M1 money.

T F 3. Checking-account deposits are not money, because not everyone will accept a check.

T F 4. Money is not wealth, since it is almost costless to produce.

T F 5. The purchase of goods with a credit card is an illustration of money serving as a medium of exchange.

T F 6. Because prices can vary, money is sometimes not a good store of value.

T F 7. During an inflationary period, increases in the velocity of exchange tend to hold down increases in prices.

T F 8. According to the quantity theory of money, a ten-dollar bill that circulates five times has the same effect as fifty dollars circulating once.

T F 9. If we assume that Q increases and MV is constant, we can safely conclude that prices will decrease.

T F 10. The major weakness of the barter system of exchange is that it requires double coincidence of demand.

T F 11. M2 money is smaller in quantity then M1 because it does not include M1 money.

T F 12. M3 money is the narrowest of the alternative measures of the money supply.

T F 13. Batter is a system in which goods and services are exchanged for other goods and services.

T F 14. Demand deposits are also known as savings accounts.

T F 15. Gresham's Law states that gold and silver will be taken out of circulation and fiat money will circulate.

T F 16. Money is only acceptable in the form of paper or metal.

T F 17. Credit cards are not money.

T F 18. Travelers checks are considered part of the money supply.

Section B Multiple-choice questions

1. The chief difference between near money and money is

   a. near money is fiat money, whereas money is not.

   b. near money consists of all deposits in commercial and savings banks, whereas money does not include deposits.

   c. near money is not directly spendable, whereas money is directly spendable.

   d. None of the above.

2. If people hold money because they need to spend money before their next paycheck, this is an example of

   a. the transactions demand of money.

   b. the quantity theory of money.

   c. the velocity of exchange.

   d. None of the above.

3. Which one of the following generalizations can be derived from the equation of exchange?

   a. In deflationary periods, creditors gain at the expense of debtors.

   b. At full employment, any increase in the money supply tends to increase prices.

   c. In inflationary periods, producers increase prices to counter rising costs.

   d. All of the above can be derived from the equation.

4. Fiat money is

   a. money backed by gold.

   b. something more valuable as a monetary instrument than as a commodity.

   c. anything that the government says is money.

   d. All of the above.

5. The largest single component (in terms of total value) in the M1 money supply is

   a. coins.

   b. currency.

   c. demand deposits.

   d. savings deposits.

6. When we are talking about money in an economy, it is incorrect to say that

    a. money is anything that is accepted as a medium of exchange, as a standard of value, as a store of value, or as a means of deferred payments, even if there is no gold to back it up.

    b. the stock of money does not include government bonds.

    c. demand deposits are by far the largest part of the supply of money in the United States.

    d. an economy's supply of money is a good measure of its wealth.

7. People hold money

    a. to have money for purchases in between receipts of income.

    b. to have money in case of unforeseen emergencies.

    c. to have money to take advantage of economic opportunities as they arise.

    d. for all of the above purposes.

8. If income and GDP rise and the supply of money remains constant, economic theory would predict

    a. a rise in the velocity of exchange if prices are constant.

    b. a fall in prices if the velocity of exchange remains constant.

    c. a rise in the demand for cash balances and reductions in demand for consumer goods.

    d. All of the above.

9. Which of the following combinations does not go together?

    a. Medium of exchange and means of deferred payments

    b. Barter system of exchange and double coincidence of demand

    c. Demand deposits and near money

    d. All are valid combinations.

10. In which of the following situations would money function as a store of value?

    a. The husband checks the prices at the local supermarket.

    b. The wife checks the balance in the family savings account.

    c. You take out a loan at the local bank.

    d. In all of the above, money functions as a store of value.

11. M2 money is:

  a. All demand deposits plus all currency and coin in circulation.

  b. M1 money plus near money.

  c. M3 money plus near money.

  d. M3 money plus all currency and coin in circulation.

12. Which of the following is not included in the M3 money supply?

  a. Currency and coins.

  b. Check deposits and time deposits.

  c. Large value certificates of deposit.

  d. All of the above are included in M3 money.

Section C Matching questions

Match the phrases in column B to the terms in column A.

Column A	Column B
1. Fiat money	(a) The rate of turnover of the money supply
2. Near money	(b) Any bank that holds demand deposits
3. Store of value	(c) The function of money as a unit of account
4. Equation of exchange	
5. Demand deposits	(d) He wants what I have and I want what he has
6. Velocity of exchange	(e) Money deposited in checking accounts
7. Standard of value	(f) Holds money in case of emergencies
8. Depository institution	(g) Expresses the quantity theory of money
9. Double coincidence of demand	(h) The function of money as a means of saving
10. Precautionary purposes	(i) More valuable as a monetary instrument than as a commodity
11. M3 money	(j) Savings accounts
	(k) Large value Certificates of Deposit

ANSWERS

Part 4

Section A 1, F; 2, T; 3, F; 4, F; 5, F; 6, T; 7, F; 8, T; 9, T; 10, T; 11, F; 12, F; 13, T; 14, F; 15, T; 16, F; 17, T; 18, T
Section B 1, c; 2, a; 3, b; 4, b; 5, c; 6, d; 7, d; 8, d; 9, c; 10, b; 11, b; 12, d
Section C 1, i; 2, j; 3, h; 4, g; 5, e; 6, a; 7, c; 8, b; 9, d; 10, f; 11, k

Chapter 12: Commercial Banking and the Creation of M1 Money

Part 1

First, read the section entitled "Summing Up" at the end of Chapter 12. It offers a thorough excellent review of the chapter.

Things to Watch For

Chapter 12 leads you step by step through the workings of the depository banking system, especially as they relate to the process of increasing and decreasing the supply of M1 money.

    The chapter begins with the simplest of models, which assumes the following: (1) There is only one bank. (2) There is no government control. (3) There is no currency and no coin. (4) There is no international trade. In this simple model, you learn that the supply of money (demand deposits) is increased when the commercial bank extends a loan and creates a demand deposit in payment. The supply of money is decreased when the loan is paid off and there is a necessary reduction of demand deposits.

    Then the text introduces currency and coin into the model. You learn that currency and coin perform two main functions: (1) they provide a more efficient form of money for small-value purchases, and (2) they provide a check on the ability of the commercial bank to expand loans and the supply of money.

    Next government regulation is introduced. In its regulations, the government has an efficient method of controlling the bank's lending activities and the effects of these activities on the supply of money. The regulations require the bank to keep reserves equal to a certain percentage of its demand deposits. (This is called the required reserve ratio.) In order to make loans and thus increase demand deposits (money), the bank must have more than the required amount of reserves (excess reserves). If the required reserve ratio is less than 100 percent (if a fractional reserve requirement is in effect), the commercial bank can lend more than a dollar for each dollar of total reserves, thus increasing demand deposits. If the bank is a monopoly bank, it can lend a multiple of its total reserves, because it is the banking system and checks cannot flow to other banks.

    We all know, though, that other banks do exist. When we drop the assumption of there being only one commercial bank in the banking system, our model approaches that of the U.S. banking system, with its more than 15,000 commercial banks. The Federal Reserve must now function as a national clearinghouse for checks. When someone deposits a check in a bank other than the one the account is in, the check goes to the clearinghouse (the Federal Reserve) and demand deposits and reserves (the commercial bank's deposits at the Federal Reserve) are transferred. Because of this, the individual commercial bank within this multibank system does not lend a multiple of its excess reserves. Instead it lends only up to the amount of its excess reserves, thereby increasing demand deposits by that amount. As these excess reserves work through the commercial banking system, the whole system creates loans and demand deposits that are a multiple (reciprocal of the required reserve ratio) of its excess reserves. This multiple is known as the deposit multiplier. The multiplier effect is reduced, however, by the effects of leakages and the desire of lending institutions to maintain excess reserves. Those excess reserves can be loaned to other banks at an interest rate called federal funds market rate.

Bear in mind that although the Federal Reserve controls this process, it is commercial banks (and other financial institutions) that are the primary instrument through which the supply of money is changed. Commercial banks vary the money supply by making loans and having loans paid off, transactions that increase and decrease demand deposits.

The application, "First Steps in Banking," is a reprint from the British humor magazine Punch. In a lighthearted vein the application discusses many of the basic characteristics of commercial banking, and the process of increasing and decreasing the supply of money.

Part 2

Define the following terms and concepts.

1. Required reserve ratio	4. Deposit multiplier
2. Excess reserves	5. Leakages in money creation
3. Fractional reserve requirement	6. Federal funds market

Part 3

Answer the following questions and problems.

1. Using the simple model of Chapter 12 (assuming that there is only one bank, no government regulation, no currency and coins, and no international trade), explain how the supply of money is increased and how it is decreased.

2. Now add currency and coin to the simple model (but keep the other assumptions). What two functions do currency and coin perform? Explain how they are carried out.

3. Now add government regulation to the simple model (but keep the assumption that there is only one bank). Show how the rule that a bank must keep reserves equal to a percentage of demand deposits restricts the monopoly bank's ability to expand loans and demand deposits (the supply of money).

4. In a banking system with only one bank (a monopoly bank), why is that bank able to expand the supply of money by an amount that is a multiple of its excess reserves?

5. Explain what occurs in a multibank system in which the Federal Reserve acts as the collection process, when checks written on accounts in one bank are deposited in another bank. Make up a numerical example.

6. Why would an individual bank in a multibank system use the conservative rule of making loans and creating demand deposits only up to the amount of its excess reserves? Make up a numerical example to illustrate your answer.

7. What is the deposit multiplier? How can a multibank system increase the supply of money by a multiple of its original excess reserves? Again use a numerical example to illustrate.

8. Although technically a multibank system can expand the supply of money by a multiple of the original excess reserves, it is rare that the system does so. There are leakages in this process of expansion of the money supply. Explain what these leakages are, and indicate how they reduce the ability of the banking system to expand the supply of money.

9. Suppose that the changes detailed below take place in the following accounts: demand deposits, loans, total reserves, excess reserves, and required reserves. Show what happens to these accounts. Use Table 12-1 and Table 12-2 to record your answers. Work the transactions separately; they are not cumulative. Indicate whether the accounts affected increase or decrease, and by how much. Do this for Bank A in Table 12-1 and also for the whole banking system in Table 12-2, which includes Bank A. The required reserve ratio is 20 percent. (The answers are given after Part 4.)

   a. Bank A is established with a capital of $100,000. For its stock, the bank receives $25,000 in currency and $75,000 in checks drawn on other banks. All checks are cleared. (Remember that total reserves consist of all deposits at the Federal Reserve, plus all currency and coin in the vaults of the bank.)

   b. Mr. Lopez deposits a check for $1,000 to his account at Bank A. That check is drawn on a deposit at another bank. All checks are cleared.

   c. Ms. Clark borrows $10,000 from Bank A and deposits the proceeds in Bank A.

   d. Ms. Jones withdraws $500 in currency from her account in Bank A.

   e. Mr. Lopez writes a check for $500 on his account in Bank A and deposits it in another account in Bank A.

   f. Ms. Clark pays off her $10,000 loan at Bank A with a check from another bank. All checks are cleared.

Table 12-1
Bank A

	Required Reserves (RR)	Excess Reserves (ER)	Total Reserves (TR)	Loans	Demand Deposits
a.					
b.					
c.					
d.					
e.					
f.					

Table 12-2
The Whole Banking System

	Required Reserves (RR)	Excess Reserves (ER)	Total Reserves (TR)	Loans	Demand Deposits
a.					
b.					
c.					
d.					
e.					
f.					

10. Table 12-3 lists three balance sheets for Bank A, a commercial bank. The required reserve ratio is 20 percent for balance sheet A, 25 percent for balance sheet B, and 50 percent for balance sheet C. Use the table to do the following problems. (The answers are given after Part 4.)

   a. For Bank A, compute the required reserves for each of the three balance sheets.

   b. Compute the excess reserves for each of the three balance sheets.

   c. How much could Bank A safely extend in new loans if it were one bank in a multibank system?

   d. How much could Bank A safely extend in new loans if it were the only bank in the commercial banking system?

Table 12-3
Balance Sheets for Bank A (thousands of dollars)

	A	B	C
	RRR 20%	**RRR 25%**	**RRR 50%**
Assets			
Reserves	80	100	150
Loans	200	150	200
Government bonds	70	60	50
Liabilities			
Demand deposits	300	240	300
Net Worth			
Capital	50	50	100
a. Required reserves			
b. Excess reserves			
c. New loans, multibank system			
d. New loans, monopoly bank system			

11. In the application, identify the questions and answers that apply to loans, demand deposits, and reserves.

12. What is the reserve requirement?

Part 4 Self-test

Section A True/false questions

T F 1. When a commercial bank extends a loan and increases demand deposits in payment, it increases the supply of money. Once created, this money cannot be decreased.

T F 2. The two functions of currency and coin are (a) to provide an effi-cient form of money for small-value purchases, and (b) to provide a check on the ability of a bank to extend loans and expand the supply of money.

T F 3. When borrowers from a commercial bank accept currency rather than a demand deposit, the potential for money expansion increases in the whole banking system.

T F 4. A commercial bank in a fractional reserve system is required to hold reserves equal to its demand-deposit liabilities, in case people withdraw currency.

T F   5. A single bank in a multibank system can make loans and create demand deposits only up to an amount equal to its excess reserves. However, the commercial banking system as a whole can make loans and expand demand deposits by a multiple of its excess reserves. If there are no leakages, the size of the multiple depends on the size of the required reserve ratio.

T F   6. When a check written on an account in Bank A is deposited in Bank B and cleared through the Federal Reserve, demand deposits flow from Bank A to Bank B, while reserves flow from Bank B to Bank A.

T F   7. The banking system may not expand loans and demand deposits by their greatest multiple because banks may fear larger-than-usual withdrawals.

T F   8. Total reserves equal all deposits made at the Federal Reserve by member banks, plus currency and coin in the vaults of banks; total reserves also equal excess reserves plus required reserves.

T F   9. Although the Federal Reserve controls the process, privately owned, profit-motivated corporations called commercial banks are the primary instruments through which the supply of money is increased or decreased.

T F   10. The most important reason for the legal reserve requirement is to prevent harm to depositors and stockholders if the bank should fail.

T F   11. Banks can create M1 money by making loans from their required reserves.

T F   12. Leakages limit the creation of money by the banking system.

T F   13. The deposits multiplier is 1/excess reserves.

T F   14. The Required Reserve Ratio is the minimum ratio of reserves to deposits that depository institutions are required to maintain.

T F   15. Banks that have excess reserves lend them to other banks that need reserves.

Section B Multiple-choice questions

1. Commercial banks increase the supply of money

    a. whenever they accept currency and coins in circulation in exchange for a demand deposit.

    b. whenever they extend loans and create demand deposits.

    c. every time they pay out currency or coin from the vaults when a depositor presents a check for payment.

    d. under all of the above circumstances.

2. The reserve requirements that the law imposes on commercial banks

    a. are primarily for protection of depositors in case customers make excessive withdrawals.

    b. are primarily to protect the stockholders against business losses by management.

    c. are primarily to set limits on the supply of money.

    d. serve all of the above purposes.

3. Suppose that Bank A, the only commercial bank in the economy, has no excess reserves and that the required reserve ratio is 20 percent. Sylvia Bloggs empties many years' spare change out of her cookie jar and deposits $500 in currency into the bank. Now Bank A can expand the supply of money by

    a. $2,000.

    b. $400.

    c. $500.

    d. $2,500.

4. Now suppose that Bank A of question 3 is only one bank of many in a multibank system. The right answer would now be

    a. $2,000.

    b. $400.

    c. $500.

    d. $2,500.

5. If the $500 deposit in question 3 had been a check drawn on another account in Bank A of a multibank system, the answer would now be

   a. $0.

   b. $2,000.

   c. $400.

   d. $500.

6. Which one of the following transactions leads to a change in the supply of money?

   a. Harry Smith deposits his paycheck in his checking account at his bank.

   b. Bertha Jones obtains a loan from her commercial bank and receives a demand deposit in return.

   c. Sally Robinson pays cash for a tool set at the local hardware store. The manager of the store deposits the cash in the store's checking account.

   d. All of the above affect the money supply.

7. Suppose that the required reserve ratio is 20 percent and that a given bank's total reserves are $1,000, with $200 in excess reserves. The total amount of demand deposits is

   a. $4,000.

   b. $5,000.

   c. $800.

   d. None of the above amounts.

8. Suppose that the amount of excess reserves in a commercial bank increases. One can conclude

   a. that the bank is making more profits from the loans made.

   b. that the amount of loans-and thus of demand deposits-will increase.

   c. that the potential for expanding loans and the money supply has increased.

   d. None of the above.

9. A commercial banking system does not expand loans and the supply of money by its full multiple effect because of which of the following leakages?

   a. Some borrowers may choose to get currency rather than a demand deposit in payment for a loan.

   b. Some banks may hold excess reserves because they fear that deposits and reserves may be lost by a greater-than-normal flow of checks to other banks.

   c. Economic conditions may be so uncertain that commercial banks may not lend out as much as they could.

   d. All of the above act as leakages.

10. The ability of an individual commercial bank in a multibank system to lend and create demand deposits is limited by

    a. possible withdrawals of currency by its depositors.

    b. possible flow of checks to other banks, which would transfer demand deposits and reserves to those banks.

    c. the need to maintain the amount of reserves required by law.

    d. All of the above.

11. The federal funds market is a financial market in which

    a. the federal government sells its new bond issues.

    b. depository institutions borrow from the fed.

    c. banks lend each other their excess reserves for long periods of time.

    d. banks lend each other their excess reserves for short periods of time.

Section C Matching questions

Match the phrases in column B to the terms in column A.

Column A
1. Federal Reserve
2. Excess reserves
3. Monopoly bank
4. Individual bank
5. Currency and coin
6. Extending loans
7. Required reserve ratio
8. Total reserves
9. Deposit multiplier
10. Federal funds market

Column B
(a) Can extend loans and create demand deposits only equal to its excess reserves
(b) Percentage of demand deposits required to be kept in reserve
(c) Creates demand deposits
(d) Functions as a national clearinghouse for checks
(e) A better form of money for small-value purchases
(f) Excess reserves plus required reserves
(g) Amount of reserves above that required
(h) Can expand credit and supply of money by a multiple of excess reserves
(i) Short-term loans from one bank to another
(j) Another potential growth in money supply from excess reserves

ANSWERS

Part 3

9. (a) The first transaction depicts the creation of a bank through the sale of capital stock. For Bank A, no deposits or withdrawals are made, and there are no loans. Bank A's total reserves increase by $100,000: $25,000 because of the increase in currency in Bank A's vault, and $75,000 because of the checks drawn on other banks, which are sent to the Fed for collection. This increases Bank A's deposits at the Fed. Required reserves are not affected, because demand deposits are not affected. Excess reserves, therefore, increase by the increase in total reserves ($100,000).

For the banking system as a whole, demand deposits decrease by $75,000, because $75,000 worth of checks are written to buy Bank A's stock and are not transferred to a demand deposit in Bank A. Loans are not affected. Total reserves increase by only $25,000, the currency taken out of circulation and now in the vault of Bank A. The $75,000 in checks simply transfers deposits at the Fed from the banks they were written on to Bank A, canceling the effect on the whole banking system. Required reserves decrease by 20 percent of the decrease in demand deposits, or $15,000. Excess reserves increase by $40,000 (TR = ER + RR).

(b) In transaction b, Bank A's demand deposits increase by $1,000 as the deposit is made. Loans are not affected. Bank A's total reserves increase by $1,000 when the check is sent to the Fed for collection, and Bank A's deposits at the Fed are increased. Its required reserves increase by $200, or 20 percent of the increase in demand deposits. Excess reserves increase by $800: TR (1,000) = ER (800) + RR(200).

There is no change for the banking system as a whole, since the increase in Bank A is offset by the decline in the bank the check was written on.

(c) In transaction c, Bank A's demand deposits increase by $10,000, because the proceeds of the loan are deposited in Bank A. Loans increase by $10,000 because a loan is made. Total reserves are unaffected, because neither cash in the vault nor deposits at the Fed are affected. Required reserves increase by $2,000 (20 percent of the increase in demand deposits); this must come from excess reserves, which decrease by $2,000.

Changes in the banking system as a whole as a result of transaction c are the same as the changes for Bank A. This transaction involves only Bank A, and thus there are no offsetting entries for other banks.

(d) In transaction d for Bank A, demand deposits decrease by $500 as the currency is withdrawn. Loans are not affected, since no loan is made or paid off. Total reserves decrease by $500, because now there is $500 less in Bank A's cash in vault. Required reserves decrease by $100 (20 percent of the decrease in demand deposits), and excess reserves decrease by $400: TR(-500) = RR (-100) + ER (-400).

For the banking system as a whole, transaction d brings the same changes as it does for Bank A, since only Bank A was involved in this transaction and there were no offsetting entries by another bank.

(e) Transaction e involves no change in any of the accounts for Bank A or for the banking system as a whole. It is merely a transfer of deposits from one account to another in the same bank.

(f) In transaction f for Bank A, no deposit or withdrawal is made, so demand deposits are unaffected. A loan is paid off, so Bank A's loans decrease by $10,000. Its total reserves increase by $10,000, since Bank A's deposits at the Fed increase due to the clearance of the check. Its required reserves are unaffected, since demand deposits are unaffected. Its excess reserves increase by $10,000, which is the same as its increase in total reserves.

For the banking system as a whole, demand deposits in the bank the check was drawn on decrease by $10,000. That check is used to pay off a loan and thus is not deposited in Bank A. Loans decrease by $10,000, the amount of the loan paid off at Bank A. Total reserves are unaffected, since, as the check is cleared, reserves (deposits at the Fed) are merely transferred from the account of the bank the check was written on to the account of Bank A. Required reserves decrease by $2,000 (20 percent of the decrease in demand deposits). Excess reserves increase by $2,000: TR (0) = RR (-2,000) + ER (2,000).

10. (a) Required reserves: A, 60; B, 60; C, 150.

(b) Excess reserves: A, 20; B, 40; C, 0.

(c) New loans, multibank system: A, 20; B, 40; C, 0.

(d) New loans, monopoly system: A, 100; B, 160; C, 0.

Part 4

Section A 1, F; 2, T; 3, F; 4, F; 5, T; 6, F; 7, T; 8, T; 9, T; 10, F; 11, F; 12, T; 13, F; 14, T; 15, T

Section B 1, b; 2, c; 3, a; 4, b; 5, a; 6, b; 7, a; 8, c; 9, d; 10, d; 11, d

Section C 1, d; 2, g; 3, h; 4, a; 5, e; 6, c; 7, b; 8, f; 9, j; 10, i

Chapter 13: Monetary Policy

Part 1

First, read the sections entitled "Summing Up" at the end of Chapter 13. It offers a thorough review of the material presented in the chapter.

Things to Watch For

Chapter 13 discusses the workings of the Federal Reserve System and examines the government's policy toward money.

The first part of the chapter sketches the structure of the Federal Reserve System. Note: The Fed is a combination of public and private structures. It is not simply an instrument to be used by those in power in the government.

The chapter analyzes the general powers of the Federal Reserve System. The Fed has the power to increase or decrease its member commercial banks' excess reserves. (Remember that excess reserves are the main ingredient necessary for loans and for the creation of demand deposits.) You should understand the workings of the Fed's general powers, because it is these powers (control over excess reserves and thus over the supply of money) that are the foundation of the government's monetary policy. A major component of these powers is the discount rate, or the rate charged, by the Fed in making loans to member banks. A second component is the required reserve rate, which determines the amount of reserves lending institutions must maintain.

In addition to its general powers, the Fed has specific powers-powers, for example, over specific areas of lending, including the power to set the margin requirement-the percentage of a cash down payment that a person must pay in order to buy stock. This means that the Fed can control to some extent speculation on the stock market. There was also Regulation Q, which gave the Fed control over interest rates on demand and savings deposits in commercial banks, and thus some control over the volume of funds available for mortgages. Remember the Deregulation Act of 1980; it repealed Regulation Q and, amongst other things, reduced regulation of banks. The now-lapsed Regulations X and W gave the Fed influence over consumption and real estate lending.

The discussion of the workings of the Federal Reserve closes with a section on the functions of the Fed. We have talked about most of these functions before: the fact that the Fed acts as a clearinghouse for checks, the fact that it regulates the supply of money, and so on. Here we introduce the facts that the Fed issues currency and that it functions as fiscal agent and bank for the U.S. Treasury, as well as for some foreign central banks and treasuries.

The next part deals with the Deregulatory Act of 1980. First, it lists the main features of the act and then discusses some of the consequences. Especially important, is the material dealing with the savings and loan crises of the 1980s and the problems of moral hazard exposed by these crises.

The sections of Chapter 13 dealing with monetary policy are very important. Like fiscal policy, monetary policy is a main tool by which the federal government can fight unemployment and inflation. Thus it is vital that you understand this area of economics thoroughly. In brief: To fight unemployment during a recession, the monetary policy of the government is to increase the supply of money and lower the interest rate. To achieve this, the Fed uses its general powers to increase the amount of excess reserves in commercial banks. To counter inflation, the government needs to decrease the supply of money and raise the interest rate. To achieve this, the Fed uses its general powers to decrease banks' excess reserves.

The effects of monetary policy are felt in credit markets. Chapter 13 illustrates how these markets react both in cases of unemployment and inflation to changes by the fed in the amount of excess reserves held by depository institutions. It is important that you understand the short-run as well as the long-run effects in both economic situations. Doing so will give you an appreciation of the complexity of implementing monetary policy in ways consistent with the government's macroeconomic objectives.

Monetary policy, in spite of its advantages, does have its weaknesses and limitations. One perplexing is the weakness it shares with fiscal policy: How should it function when significant inflation and unemployment exist at the same time? In addition, as Chapter 13 illustrates, changing inflationary expectations can affect monetary policy, even neutralize it, and, in some instances, even create perverse results for that policy. In addition, monetary policy can not assure adequate demand for credit.

The application considers the controversy between the monetarists and the Keynesians, especially as to the relative importance of monetary and fiscal policy. The monetarists maintain that money is the primary influence on a nation's output, income, and prices. These believers in monetarism feel that the supply of money should increase at a fixed and appropriate rate. They further maintain that fine tuning the economy through continual adjustments of fiscal and monetary policy is ineffective and maybe even dangerous.

Defenders of Keynesian policy say that there are a number of flaws in the monetarists' theory. (1) Monetarists' assumption that the velocity of exchange is constant is not valid. (2) Monetarists do not make it clear what they mean by "money supply," nor what time lag they consider to exist between a variation in the supply of money and the effect of that variation on the economy. (3) If inflationary forces other than demand-pull forces exist, monetarism is too indirect to work.

Part 2

Define the following terms and concepts.

1. National banks
2. State banks
3. General powers
4. Central bank
5. The discount rate
6. Specific powers
7. Margin requirements
8. Resolution Trust Corporation
9. Regulations X and W
10. Regulation Q
11. Required reserve ratio
12. Monetary policy
13. Monetarism
14. Bank holding companies
15. Moral hazard problem
16. Monetary policy

Part 3

Answer the following questions and problems.

1. The structure of the Federal Reserve System is a combination of public and private elements. Identify and briefly describe both the public and the private elements.

2. Explain how the Fed would use open-market operations to

   a. increase the amount of excess reserves of its member banks.

   b. decrease the amount of excess reserves of its member banks.

3. How does the Fed use the discount rate to affect the excess reserves of its member banks? Among the Fed's devices for controlling the money supply, why is the discount rate not as important as open-market operations?

4. How does a lowering of the required reserve ratio affect banks' excess reserves? What about an increase in the required reserve ratio? Make up a numerical example of how a lowering of the required reserve ratio affects banks' excess reserves.

5. Why does the Fed, in controlling excess reserves, rarely use its power to vary the required reserve ratio?

6. In four areas of lending, the Federal Reserve has (or has had) specific regulatory powers, called the specific powers of the Federal Reserve. List these specific powers and explain how they have functioned.

7. Why do you think there were so many failures of savings and loan banks in the 1980s?

8. What are the major provisions of the Deregulation Act of 1980?

9. The text lists seven functions of the Federal Reserve. Name and explain them.

10. During a recession, what monetary policy would you recommend with respect to the supply of money? with respect to the interest rate? Why? During an inflation, what monetary policy would you recommend with respect to the supply of money? with respect to the interest rate? Why? What should the Fed do to implement these recommendations?

11. Trace the monetary transmission mechanism for a recession. For an inflation.

12. The text lists weaknesses of monetary policy. Name and explain them.

13. Briefly describe what is meant by the monetarist school of economic policy.

14. Assuming that the required reserve ratio equals 20 percent, consider the following transactions. What changes occur in the accounts of commercial bank Alpha (given in Table 13-1) with respect to demand deposits, government securities, total reserves, excess reserves, and required reserves? Assume that each transaction is separate and not cumulative, and that all checks are cleared. (The answers are given after Part 4.)

Which of these transactions involve changes in the supply of money? By how much does the money supply change?

a. Alpha Bank buys $10,000 in government securities from the U.S. Treasury and deposits the proceeds in Alpha Bank.

b. Alpha Bank buys $10,000 in government securities from the Federal Reserve.

c. Mary Bloggs sells $10,000 in government securities to the Fed and deposits the proceeds in Alpha Bank.

d. Alpha Bank discounts $20,000 of prime commercial paper at the Fed.

Table 13-1
Accounts of Commercial Bank Alpha

	Required Reserves	Excess Reserves	Total Reserves	Government Securities	Demand Deposits
a.					
b.					
c.					
d.					

15. What role do inflationary expectations play in monetary policy? How may they interfere in monetary policy?

16. Assume that you belong to the monetarist school of thought. Defend your recommendation that the constant growth of the supply of money at an appropriate fixed rate should be a main component of government stabilization policy.

17. Why do the monetarists oppose fine tuning of the economy?

18. Discuss the various arguments the Keynesians present in opposition to Milton Friedman's monetarist position.

19. How can a bank create money?

20. Where do the bonds come from that the federal Reserve buys and sells to adjust interest rates?

Part 4 Self-test

Section A True/false questions

T F 1. The government owns and controls the Federal Reserve.

T F 2. The board of governors of the Federal Reserve is not under the direct control of the executive branch of the government.

T F   3. The Fed uses its general powers to control the amount of the basic ingredient needed for the extension of credit and the creation of demand deposits: excess reserves.

T F   4. An important general power of the Federal Reserve is its power to vary the discount rate, because by using this power the Fed can either increase or decrease total reserves.

T F   5. During a recession the Federal Reserve should buy securities in the open market, increase the discount rate, and increase the required reserve ratio.

T F   6. As one method of controlling the supply of money, the Fed varies the amount of currency in circulation.

T F   7. M2 money consists of all demand deposits, currency, and coin in circulation plus near money.

T F   8. A basic function of the Fed is to act as a national clearinghouse for checks, shifting reserves from one bank to another as checks flow between banks.

T F   9. Monetary policy was not effective in helping to cure the depression of the 1930s. The reason was that banks accumulated excess reserves without the help of the Fed, because the depression caused banks to lend less and borrowers to borrow less.

T F   10. During an inflation, when there is a tight money policy, certain groups suffer more from that policy than others. They include small and new firms, the construction industry, and borrowers for consumer purchases.

T F   11. The monetary policy transmission mechanism for a recession would be easing of monetary policy   increase in supply of credit   decrease in interest rates   increase in investment   increase in demand   increase in real incomes and prices.

T F   12. Although the monetarists call for a fixed and appropriate rate of growth of the supply of money, they agree that there should also be fine tuning in other areas of fiscal and monetary policy.

T F   13. The increasing ease with which capital moves internationally has made monetary policy easier to implement.

T F   14. The increased holdings of federal debt by non-residences increased the case of implementing monetary policy.

T F   15. During the 1980s the Savings and Loan Association prospered because of the Deregulatory Act of 1980.

T F   16. Regulation X deals with loans on consumer goods.

T F   17. Regulation Q was used to set the minimum interest rate banks could pay on savings accounts.

T F   18. The fed can control the supply of money.

T F 19. All national banks are required to be members of the Federal Reserve System.

T F 20. To overcome unemployment, one should decrease the supply of credit and increase interest rates.

Section B Multiple-choice questions

1. Which of the following statements about the Federal Reserve System is true?

    a. All commercial banks are members of the Federal Reserve System, since the law says that they must join it.

    b. All commercial banks have an option to join the Federal Reserve System if they wish.

    c. National banks must be members of the Federal Reserve System, but state banks may join or not, as they wish.

    d. Any commercial or savings bank may join the Federal Reserve System.

2. Which of the following is not one of the Fed's general powers over excess reserves?

    a. Carrying out open-market operations

    b. Varying the discount rate

    c. Varying the margin requirements on stock trading

    d. Varying the required reserve ratio

3. When the Fed buys government securities on the open market, the effect is to

    a. decrease demand deposits in depository institutions.

    b. reduce depository institutions' deposits at the Fed, that is, reduce total and excess reserves.

    c. decrease the price of government securities.

    d. increase depository institutions' deposits at the Fed, that is, increase total and excess reserves.

4. A decrease in the required reserve ratio

    a. increases excess reserves but does not affect total reserves.

    b. decreases both total and excess reserves.

    c. decreases excess reserves only.

    d. increases both total and excess reserves.

5. Which of the following is not a function of the Federal Reserve?

   a. To issue all currency

   b. To act as a national clearinghouse for checks

   c. To be a banker's bank: that is, to hold deposits of member banks and to extend loans to member banks

   d. To manage the debt of the federal government

6. During a recession, the monetary policy of the Federal Reserve should be to

   a. increase the supply of money and reduce the interest rate.

   b. decrease the supply of money and increase the interest rate.

   c. increase both the supply of money and the interest rate.

   d. decrease both the supply of money and the interest rate.

7. During an inflation, the monetary policy of the Federal Reserve should be to

   a. increase excess reserves by selling securities on the open market, lowering the discount rate, and decreasing the required reserve ratio.

   b. increase excess reserves by buying securities on the open market, raising the discount rate, and increasing the required reserve ratio.

   c. decrease excess reserves by buying securities on the open market, lowering the discount rate, and decreasing the required reserve ratio.

   d. decrease excess reserves by selling securities on the open market, raising the discount rate, and raising the required reserve ratio.

8. One of the following statements does not describe a weakness of monetary policy. Which?

   a. During a serious depression, monetary policy will not work because banks' excess reserves may increase without the help of the Fed.

   b. Monetary policy may not be effective against an inflation that is due to causes other than demand pull.

   c. Monetary policy cannot readily deal with a situation in which high inflation and high unemployment occur at the same time.

   d. Variations in the supply of money do not affect prices during an inflation.

9. Which of the following is not a weakness of monetary policy?

   a. During inflation, a tight money policy does not affect all groups in the economy equally; some suffer more than others.

   b. During an inflation, the policies needed to reduce the supply of money are just the opposite of those needed to increase the interest rate.

   c. The velocity of exchange can vary; when it does, this may counteract monetary policy to some extent.

   d. Monetary policy cannot readily counter inflation and unemployment at the same time.

10. Which of the following statements is true of monetarism?

   a. Monetarism is another term for monetary policy.

   b. Monetarism is a viewpoint that fiscal policy is more important than monetary policy because monetary policy is weak.

   c. Monetarism is a viewpoint that the supply of money is extremely important and should be increased at a constant and appropriate rate.

   d. Monetarism is a viewpoint that the monetary policy and fiscal policy are equally important and effective.

11. The basic recommendation of the Friedman monetarists is

   a. a constant and appropriate rate of increase in the supply of money and fine tuning of the economy in other areas of fiscal and monetary policy.

   b. a constant and appropriate rate of increase in the supply of money and no fine tuning of the economy in other areas of fiscal and monetary policy.

   c. a vigorous use of both fiscal and monetary policy to control inflation.

   d. A vigorous use of discretionary monetary policy.

12. Which one of the following statements would not be used by Keynesians to refute the beliefs of the monetarists?

   a. Velocity of exchange can vary. Such variations can counteract the effects of a constant increase in the supply of money.

   b. The stabilizing mechanisms of a free-market economy are not as "automatic" as the monetarists assume.

   c. Money itself-or the amount of it in circulation-does not have any effect on the economy.

   d. The monetarists are unclear on which supply of money is important to control.

13. According to James Tobin, the experience of the American economy in 1983-1984 leads to the conclusion that

    a. monetary policy is the most effective tool in stimulating an economy to recovery from recession.

    b. fiscal policy was poorly timed and ineffective in stimulating the economic recovery.

    c. fiscal policy was very successful in promoting economic recovery.

    d. combined monetary and fiscal policy was successfully timed to promote economic recovery.

14. Which of the following is not a reason why the Keynesian-Monetarist debate may become less important in the 1990s?

    a. The federal debt and budget deficits make Keynesian demand management less attractive as policy devices.

    b. U.S. interest rates have to be keyed to and competitive with those in other international capital markets.

    c. International capital movements are much larger and easier than in previous decades.

    d. The Keynesians and monetarists have agreed on the respective importance of the two policy approaches.

15. Changes in inflationary expectations may have which of the following effects on the effectiveness of monetary policy?

    a. They make monetary policy easier to implement.

    b. They may offset or even more than offset the policy effect of changes in the money supply.

    c. They always work to reinforce the desirable policy effects of changes in the money supply.

    d. They are unrelated to the policy effects of changes in the money supply.

16. During the 1980s which of the following was not true?

    a. Substantial numbers of banks and savings and loans experienced sever financial difficulties.

    b. All banks could have demand deposits at their bank.

    c. Banks could establish branches anywhere in the U.S.

    d. All banks had access to the Fed clearinghouse.

Section C Matching questions

I. Match the phrases in column B with the terms in column A.

Column A
1. National banks
2. State banks
3. General powers
4. Open-market operations
5. The discount rate
6. Required reserve ratio
7. Regulations X and W
8. Regulation Q
9. Margin requirements on stocks
10. Deregulation Act of 1980
11. Monetary policy
12. Monetarists
13. Board of governors
14. Currency

Column B
(a) Buying and selling of government securities
(b) Variations in it do not change total reserves, but the combination of required and excess reserves does change
(c) Issued to meet the needs of the general public
(d) Chartered by state governments
(e) Critical of Keynesian monetary and fiscal policy
(f) Controlled the interest member banks could pay on savings accounts and demand deposits
(g) Varies the supply of money and the interest rate
(h) Control over excess reserves
(i) Semi-independent of the President
(j) All banks can hold demand deposits
(k) Chartered by the federal government
(l) Control speculation in the stock market
(m) Controlled lending in consumer and real estate markets
(n) The rate at which the Federal Reserve lends to its member banks

II. Column A lists things the Federal Reserve can do to counteract recession and inflation. Put an R in column B if the action listed would help to fight a recession, or I if the action listed would help to fight an inflation.

Column A
1. Buy securities in the open market
2. Sell securities in the open market
3. Raise the discount rate
4. Lower the discount rate
5. Raise the required reserve ratio
6. Lower the required reserve ratio

Column B
_____
_____
_____
_____
_____
_____

ANSWERS

Part 3

12. (a) When the government deposits the proceeds in Alpha Bank, Alpha Bank's demand deposits increase by $10,000. Due to the purchase by Alpha Bank, government securities increase by $10,000. The bank's total reserves do not change, because neither its deposits at the Fed nor its cash in vault is affected. Its required reserves must increase by 20 percent of the increase in demand deposits ($2,000). This increase comes from excess reserves, which in turn decrease by $2,000.

      Notice that the bank's purchase of a government security from the Treasury has the same effect as the bank's loan to an individual.

(b) Alpha Bank buys $10,000 in government securities from the Fed. The Fed does not want money; it wants to reduce total and excess reserves. So there is no change in demand deposits. Government securities increase by $10,000. Since the Fed decreases Alpha Bank's deposits at the Fed, total reserves decrease by $10,000. Required reserves are not affected. All the decrease in total reserves comes from excess reserves, which decrease by $10,000.

(c) Mary Bloggs deposits in Alpha Bank the proceeds of her sale to the Fed of $10,000 in government securities. Alpha Bank's demand deposits increase by $10,000. The government securities in Alpha Bank are unaffected. Total reserves increase by $10,000 as Blogg's check is cleared and the Fed increases Alpha Bank's deposits at the Fed. Alpha Bank's required reserves must increase by $2,000 (20 percent of the increase in demand deposits). Excess reserves increase by $8,000 (since there is a $10,000 increase in total reserves and $2,000 is transferred to required reserves).

(d) Neither demand deposits nor government securities are affected. The Fed adds the proceeds of the discount to the deposits of Alpha Bank at the Fed, and total reserves increase by $20,000. Alpha Bank's required reserves are unaffected, but its excess reserves increase by $20,000.

Part 4

Section A 1, F; 2, T; 3, T; 4, F; 5, F; 6, F; 7, T; 8, T; 9, T; 10, T; 11, T; 12, T; 13, F;
        14, F; 15, F; 16, T; 17, F; 18, T; 19, T; 20, F
Section B 1, c; 2, c; 3, d; 4, a; 5, d; 6, a; 7, d; 8, d; 9, b; 10, c; 11, b; 12, c; 13, c; 14, d; 15, b;
        16, c
Section C I. 1, k; 2, d; 3, h; 4, a; 5, n; 6, b; 7, m; 8, f; 9, l; 10, j; 11, g; 12, e; 13, i; 14, c;
        II.1, R; 2, I; 3, I; 4, R; 5, I; 6, R

Chapter 14: Economic Policy Controversies

Part 1

First, read the section titled "Summing Up" at the end of Chapter 14. It offers a thorough review of the material presented in the chapter.

Things to Watch For

Chapter 14 reviews the policy recommendations of supply-side economics. Referring back to the aggregate supply-aggregate demand model of Chapter 7, it is theoretically possible to increase real income at stable prices by increasing aggregate supply. This is the premise of supply-side economics, and it is important that you understand it.

Next the chapter presents the fundamental supply-side views. While learning these fundamentals, remember that they are both political philosophy and economic theory. Also you should understand the intent and reality of the 1981 tax cut. To understand the 1981 tax cut, you should understand the Laffer Curve, which relates tax rates to various levels of total tax revenue. One of the tenets of tax cuts was that lowering tax rates would reduce the number of transactions in the underground economy. You should also understand why the concept is controversial as a basis for economy policy.

Chapter 14 also raises the question of whether discretionary policy changes can achieve the objectives predicted for them. Here serious consideration must be given to the concepts as well as to their effectiveness in view of expectations that are formed rational or adaptive. Those expectations may be either. Finally, the chapter deals with the views of the Post-Keynesians who argue for greater government intervention to affect market failures through an incomes policy.

Part 2

Define the following terms and concepts.

1. Supply-Side Economics
2. Laffer Curve
3. Adaptive Expectations Hypothesis
4. Rational Expectations Hypothesis
5. Tax Wedge
6. Post-Keynesians
7. Incomes Policy

Part 3

Answer the following questions and problems.

1. Review the aggregate supply and aggregate demand model presented in Chapter 7. What happens when aggregate supply increases?

2. Draw the Laffer Curve. What are its policy implications?

3. What is the fundamental premise of supply-side economics?

4. What, according to F. Thomas Juster, are the basic elements of supply-side economics?

5. What is the Laffer Curve? What are its implications for tax policy? Why is it difficult to draw tax policy conclusions from the Laffer Curve?

6. From your perception of the material presented in Chapter 14, assess the effectiveness of supply-side economics. What are its most controversial aspects?

7. Discuss the Post-Keynesian policy problems from both a supply-side and Keynesian perspective.

Part 4 Self-test

Section A True/false questions

T F 1. When aggregate supply increases, both real income and prices increase.

T F 2. When aggregate supply decreases, real income falls and prices increase.

T F 3. Acceptance of the rational expectations hypothesis leads to te conclusion that discretionary monetary policy is ineffective in stimulating the economy.

T F 4. The Keynesian view is that increased demand will cause supply to increase in the long run, while the supply siders feel that aggregate supply is independent of aggregate demand and has an autonomous effect on real income and prices.

T F 5. The Laffer Curve relates tax rates to various levels of total tax revenues.

T F 6. Adaptive expectations are formed on the basis of what people have done both in the past and in the present.

T F 7. Rational expectations depend on both past experience and present events.

T F 8. Acceptance of the adaptive expectations hypothesis leads to the conclusion that monetary policy can only be effective in the long run.

T F 9. Keynesians maintain that obstacles in the market will prevent macroeconomic equilibrium.

T F 10. Classical economists believe that rational expectations would neutralize government discretionary policy.

T F 11. Supply-side economics was reflected in the economic views of the Reagan administration.

T F 12. Supply-side economics argues for stimulating demand by creating incentives to entrepreneurship.

T F 13. The Laffer Curve shows that as taxes increase, government revenue always grow.

T F 14. Underground economy involves those transactions that give rise to taxable income but are not reported for tax purposes.

Section B Multiple-choice questions

1. Which of the following happens when aggregate supply increases?

   a. Real income increases while prices decline.

   b. Real income increases while prices increase.

   c. Real income declines while prices also decline.

   d. There are no changes in income and prices.

2. Which of the following is not a fundamental element of supply-side economics?

   a. Entitlement programs lower work incentives.

   b. Taxes in the U.S. are biased against effort, savings and investment.

   c. Tax cuts to the poor will raise demand and thus supply.

   d. Regulations raise costs and reduce investment.

3. The Laffer Curve suggests that

   a. lowering of tax rates may increase tax revenues by increasing work incentives.

   b. increasing tax rates will always increase tax revenues.

   c. increasing tax rates always decrease tax revenues.

   d. lowering tax rates would always decrease tax revenue.

4. Adaptive expectations

   a. only take into account expected future events.

   b. only take into account expected present events.

   c. only take into account past events.

   d. take into account past and expected present events.

5. Which of the following is/are fundamental presumptions of supply-side economics?

   a. Public regulation raises costs, reduces investment, and has a low benefit/cost ratio.

   b. Programs designed to stimulate aggregate demand have created a climate of inflationary expectations.

   c. Entitlement programs lower work incentives and taxes are biased against saving and investment.

   d. All of the above are fundamental to supply-side economics.

6. Which of the following changes in federal taxation were contained in the tax legislation in the 1980s?

   a. Marginal tax rates were reduced from a high of 70 percent to 50 percent by 1984.

   b. Tax rates were lowered to discourage the growth of the underground economy

   c. Marginal tax rates by 1987 were lowered from a high of 50 percent to 35 percent.

   d. All of the above were contained in tax legislation in the 1980s.

7. According to the Laffer Curve argument, the relationship between tax rates and tax revenues is

   a. tax revenues always increase with increasing tax rates.

   b. tax revenues increase initially with increasing tax rates, then fall as tax rates continue to increase.

   c. tax revenues rise with rising tax rates, reach a maximum, then fall as tax rates continue to increase.

   d. Both (b) and (c) are correct.

8. The reasons for the shape of the Laffer Curve are

   a. rising taxes are biased against effort.

   b. rising taxes are biased against saving and investment.

   c. rising taxes ultimately create incentives to use resources in the underground economy.

   d. All of the above reasons explain the shape of the Laffer Curve.

9. The relationship between effective macroeconomic (monetary, fiscal) policy and the expectations of economic decision makers is that

   a. macroeconomic policy can only be effective if expectations are rational.

   b. macroeconomic policy can only be effective if, in the short run, expectations are adaptive.

   c. macroeconomic policy can be effective if expectations are either adaptive or rational.

   d. macroeconomic policy can never be effective in the short run if expectations are adaptive.

10. Much of the controversy surrounding supply-side economic policies in the 1980s is due to

a. the decline in net national income between 1983 and 1989.

b. the high rate of inflation between 1983 and 1989.

c. the rising marginal federal tax rates in the 1980s.

d. the large budget deficits that seemed to contradict supply-side predictions.

Section C Matching Questions

Match the phrases in Column B to the terms in Column A

Column A	Column B
1. Supply-side economics	(a) Reduce work incentives
2. Income-price level equilibrium	(b) Permanent government policy
3. Post-Keynesian	(c) Past and present events
4. Laffer curve	(d) Stimulating growth in aggregate supply
5. Entitlement programs	(e) Tax rates-tax revenues
6. Reduced regulation	(f) Aggregate quantity supplied = aggregate quantity demanded
7. Rational expectations	(g) Lower costs and raises incentives
8. Adaptive expectations	(h) Actual events in recent past

ANSWERS

Part 4

Section A 1, F; 2, T; 3, T; 4, T; 5, T; 6, F; 7, T; 8, F; 9,T; 10,T; 11, T; 12, T; 13, F; 14, T
Section B 1, a; 2, c; 3, a; 4, c; 5, d; 6, d; 7, d; 8, d; 9, b; 10, d
Section C 1, d; 2, f; 3, b; 4, e; 5, a; 6, g; 7, c; 8, h

Chapter 15: Patterns of International Trade

Part 1

First, read the section entitled "Summing Up" at the end of Chapter 16. It provides an excellent review of the chapter.

Things to Watch For

In chapter 16 we relax the assumption that the economy examined is closed. Now we examine the impact of trade with other economies and how that trade is financed. Chapter 14 deals with exports (X, those things a nation sells to others) and imports (M, those things it buys from others). This trade is made up of visible items (the commodities) and invisible items (services, including financial services). The commodity balance of trade is the difference between exports and imports (X - M).

Net foreign trade (exports - imports + net services balance (SN)) can exert a powerful macroeconomic influence on a nation.

Trade is important for any nation except a nation that decides to pursue a course of autarky, or economic self-sufficiency. Autarky is economically disadvantageous, even for the United States, not in terms of absolute advantage (which exists when a given nation can produce all things more efficiently than any other nation can), but in terms of comparative advantage (which exists when a given nation can produce some things relatively more efficiently than others).

A production-possibilities schedule and a production-possibilities curve show that the internal rate at which a nation gives up one good to produce another ultimately increases. When one looks at these schedules and curves, the advantage to a nation of foreign trade becomes clear. By trading with one another, two nations that operate under comparative advantage can both have more of all goods and services than would be possible without trade.

The reason trade is beneficial is that the internal rate of exchange of one country (the slope of its production-possibilities schedule) is different from that of another country. Trade creates a new exchange rate, different from the internal rates of either nation. The actual exchange rate that is established is called the terms of trade. It is the rate at which one nation's goods are exchanged for the goods of another nation. (Later on in the chapter, we see that the terms of trade is also the ratio of the prices of exports to the prices of imports.)

Note these facts about comparative advantage: (1) Nations have differing comparative advantages based on varying endowments of resources, differing physical features, differing degrees of development of capital markets, and differing ratios of capital to labor. (2) As a nation develops, its comparative advantage changes. The main reason why specialization of trade on the basis of comparative advantage occurs is that a nation that does not practice such specialization encounters increasing costs. That is, a nation that wishes to produce both good A and good B finds that the necessary internal tradeoffs force it to give up larger and larger amounts of one of the two goods. Finally, it gets to the point at which it is cheaper to import some of the goods it would otherwise produce. Trade specialization is not, however, complete. This is so for a number of reasons: (1) International trade affects the internal level of employment. (2) There is a lack of competition in internal trade. (3) International trade carries certain externalities. (4) Relative prices between one country and another may not reflect scarcities. (5) There is protectionism, which means legal or government-established barriers to free trade.

The main devices governments use to practice protectionism are as follows: (1) Tariffs, or taxes on imports. Tariffs reduce the supply of the good that is being so taxed, raise the price of it, increase domestic monopoly power, and raise revenue for the government. (2) Quotas, or restrictions on the amounts of certain goods that may be imported. The effects of quotas are the same as those of tariffs, except that quotas do not raise revenue for the government. (3) Embargoes, or laws that prohibit the import of certain goods altogether. The effect of embargoes is to reduce the supply of the good to domestic sources, raise the price of the good, and enhance domestic monopoly power. Lack of effective opposition by consumers to import quotas may be attributable to rational ignorance.

The arguments in favor of trade protectionism are (1) the infant-industry argument, which holds that a newly begun, developing industry needs to be protected from mature foreign competitors; (2) the national-security argument, which holds that a nation should preserve its defense industries against competition from foreign defense materials, because it can never be sure of having a ready supply of any good that must be imported; (3) the cheap-foreign-labor argument; and (4) the macroeconomic-employment argument, which holds that protectionism restricts imports, stimulates exports, and as a result lowers unemployment.

Economists generally reject all these arguments as being fallacious and self-defeating, except for the national-security argument. Even in that case they feel that direct subsidies to defense industries are preferable to tariffs and quotas and embargoes, because subsidies give a clear picture of the costs involved. The United States has never allowed trade to be entirely free, but it also has only rarely set up extremely high tariffs or embargoes or other very restrictive trade rules. Those that it did enact were set up during wars, depressions, and other national emergencies.

GATT, the General Agreement on Tarrifs and Trade, was set up in 1947 to foster trade and lower various forms of obstacles to free trade.

In 1994, the Uruguay round of GATT created the World Trade Organization (WTO) to replace GATT. The WTO's purpose is to seek further trade liberalization. Various trade agreements have occurred since World War II. Their forms include common markets, custom unions, and free trade agreements. Be sure you understand the differences among them. Two present major free trade arrangements are the European Union-European Free Trade Association or EU-EFTA and the North American Free Trade Association or NAFTA.

The application deals with an issue very much in the forefront today. Does international trade help nations (especially the poor nations) to develop economically? The classical economists thought that it does. In fact, they felt that international trade is essential to a nation's economic development. The answer has been made more complicated by the appearance of a number of countries now called newly industrialized countries (NICs) and also the creation in the 70s and 80s and 90s of a very serious debt problem for many NICs and less developed countries (LDCs). The application shows that, if one takes a static approach (that is, if one ignores the changes that take place over time), this argument is compelling. Nations that trade will allocate their resources to their most productive uses, and thus will have a greater productivity and higher per capita income than nations that don't trade.

At least five points of doubt have been raised about whether international trade will have the same positive results over time. (1) Imperfections in the factor market. As these imperfections disappear, relative costs and comparative advantage change. (2) Unreliability of export markets. Some highly specialized raw-material economies are very unstable. They can't grow rapidly because of low price and income elasticities of demand for their products. The terms of trade are more unfavorable to them than to the developed industrialized nations. (3) Changes in productivity. Manufacturing, even when it is not dictated by comparative advantage, builds up supplies of resources and a pool of labor with sophisticated skills to a much greater degree than agriculture does. (4) Dynamic external economies. Equilibrium market prices do not indicate which investments must be taken together to be profitable. Thus, the market signals that emerge when nations trade under the comparative-advantage system may dictate the wrong investments. (5) Uncertainty and flexibility. An economy that is diversified in its trade relationships-one that does not base its trade strictly on comparative advantage-can respond more quickly and flexibly to changes in supply and demand (world prices) than an economy that is dependent on one or a few products.

Economists generally disregard the first two of these arguments. But they concede that the others may sometimes support an argument for a shift of economic policy away from comparative advantage. Recently, pressures have developed to create a "new economic order," one in which poor nations are given special trading arrangements and concessions. If such concessions are granted, they will probably involve a further move away from comparative advantage. Intense debate continues about whether free trade benefits the NICs and LDCs or whether special treatment should be afforded them to encourage growth. That the free trade argument seems to be winning is reflected in the rules of the new WTO that require both industrial nations and LDCs to follow the same free trade policies.

Part 2

Define the following terms and concepts.

1. Absolute advantage, comparative advantage
2. Autarky
3. "Beggar-thy-neighbor" argument
4. Burden of a tariff (consumer burden, producer burden)
5. Cheap foreign labor argument
6. Commodity balance of trade
7. Common markets
8. Customs unions
9. Exports, imports
10. Free trade agreements
11. General Agreement on Tariffs and Trade (GATT)
12. Infant-industry argument
13. National security argument
14. Commodity balance of trade
15. Net foreign trade
16. Open economy, closed economy
17. Protectionism
18. Rational ignorance
19. Tariffs, quotas, embargoes
20. Terms of trade
21. Visible items, invisible items of trade
22. World Trade Organization (WTO)
23. NAFTA
24. European Union-European Free Trade Association

Part 3

Answer the following questions and problems.

1. What problems would nations experience in trying to achieve autarky?

2. Consider the hypothetical production-possibilities schedule for the United States and Zaire shown in Table 15-1.

    a. What happens to the rate of exchange of trucks for copper in the United States? of copper for trucks in Zaire?

    b. What is the United States' initial rate of exchange of copper for trucks? Zaire's initial rate of exchange of trucks for copper?

    c. What causes the internal rate of exchange to change in each of the two countries?

    d. For trade to take place in this case (Zairian copper to the United States, American trucks to Zaire), what is the range within which the terms of trade must fall?

Table 15-1
Production-Possibilities Schedules: United States and Zaire

United States		Zaire	
Units of Trucks	Units of Copper	Units of Trucks	Units of Copper
100	0	0	100
80	10	5	80
60	20	10	60
40	30	15	40
20	40	20	20
0	50	25	0

3. In Figure 15-1, plot the production-possibilities schedules for (a) the United States and (b) Zaire from the data in Table 15-1. Then consider the following additions to this economic situation.

    a. What would the production-possibilities curves look like if resources were specialized in their uses?

    b. In Figure 15-1 plot the consumption possibilities after trade for both countries.

    c. What causes the internal rate of exchange to change in each of the two countries?

    d. For trade to take place in this case (Zairian copper to the United States, American trucks to Zaire), what is the range within which the terms of trade must fall?

    e. Would the United States benefit from trade with Zaire even if it had an absolute advantage in producing both trucks and copper? Why?

4. What are the major arguments for protectionism? Why do economists regard all but one as fallacious?

Figure 15-1
Production-Possibilities Curves

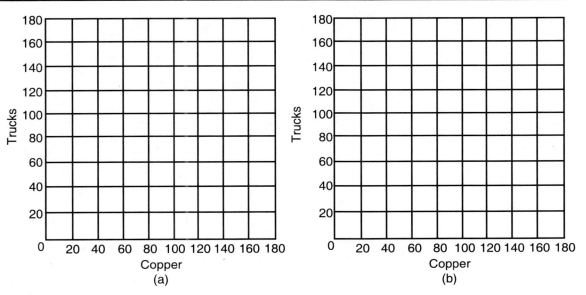

5. Consider Figure 15-2and then answer the following questions.

a. What is the equilibrium price of the imported good (including foreign imports)?

b. Draw a new supply curve reflecting a tariff on this good that partially reduces foreign supply. What happens to price? Who bears the burden of the tariff? Who benefits from the tariff?

c. What will the price of this good be if an embargo is placed on imports of it from abroad? Who benefits from-and who "pays" for-the embargo?

Figure 15-2
Effects of a Tariff

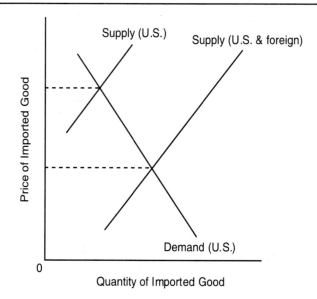

6. Why did the classical economists regard comparative-advantage trade as essential to the economic development of nations?

7. There are several arguments in favor of moving away from comparative advantage as the basis for a developing nation's trade policy. Which ones are regarded by some economists as valid?

8. What do you think is likely to happen in the future to free trade between rich and poor nations? What may the debt problems of NICs and LDCs have to do with this?

9. What is the difference between tariffs and Quotas?

10. What is absolute advantage?

Part 4 Self-test

Section A True/false questions

T F 1. The balance of trade measures the difference between exports, and imports, and services.

T F 2. Foreign trade is not important to the United States.

T F 3. The commodity balance of trade equals exports minus imports.

T F 4. Net foreign trade is equal to exports plus imports.

T F 5. The balance of trade affects the economy through its effects on GNP.

T F 6. A nation that has an absolute advantage in producing all its goods should not trade with other nations.

T F 7. In a real-world situation, production-possibilities curves are not likely to be straight lines.

T F 8. If internal rates of exchange are the same in two different nations, there is no advantage to be had from trade between them.

T F 9. The terms of trade express the prices at which the goods of one nation can be exchanged for the goods of another nation.

T F 10. The comparative advantage of the United States has changed little over the last century.

T F 11. Externalities may cause specialization of trade among nations to be incomplete.

T F 12. Tariffs decrease domestic monopoly power.

T F 13. The United States has never imposed an embargo in modern times.

T F 14. Economists accept all the arguments in favor of protectionism except the macroeconomic-employment argument.

T F 15. The classical economists saw little need for nations to trade with one another.

T F 16. At any given time, the nation that allocates its resources on the basis of comparative advantage is likely to have a greater output than the one that does not.

T F 17. One reason why nations should follow the principle of comparative advantage is the notion of dynamic external economies, which means that certain investments should be undertaken together.

T F 18. Price and income elasticities of demand may, according to some economists, weigh against raw-material-producing nations' use of trade as a basis for their economic development.

T F 19. A nation exporting one or just a few commodities is more likely to be able to adjust to changes in international supply and demand than a nation that exports many.

T F 20. The WTO was set up by the U.S. to protect U.S. industry from foreign competition.

T F 21. NAFTA is an agreement between the U.S., Canada, and Mexico to promote free trade.

T F 22. The World Trade Organization is the successor to GATT.

T F 23. The U.S. currently exports more than it imports.

T F 24. Imports are commodities and services bought from other nations.

T F   25. Tariffs and quotas are the two principle means by which countries usually intervene to protect their own industries from overseas competion.

Section B Multiple-choice questions

1. Which of the following is not a visible item of trade?

    a. Automobile exports

    b. Steel imports

    c. Petroleum imports

    d. Payments to foreign shippers

2. The commodity balance of trade is which one of the following?

    a. Exports minus imports

    b. Visible minus invisible items of trade

    c. Exports divided by imports

    d. The balance in the federal budget

3. Net foreign trade consists of

    a. exports plus imports.

    b. exports minus imports.

    c. exports minus imports plus net services.

    d. the value of services sold to other nations.

4. When imports increase which of the following occurs?

    a. the balance of trade increases

    b. the balance of trade decreases

    c. The balance of trade is unaffected

    d. GNP increases

5. The terms of trade express the relationship between

    a. exports and imports.

    b. total paid for exports and total paid for imports.

    c. prices paid for exports in relation to prices paid for imports.

    d. visible and invisible items of trade.

6. A nation's consumption-possibilities curve is probably affected by international trade in which one of the following ways?

   a. It is greater after trade.

   b. It is less after trade.

   c. It is unaffected by trade.

   d. The effect is indeterminate.

7. One of the following does not cause trade specialization to be incomplete. Which?

   a. Increasing costs

   b. Noncompetitive trading conditions

   c. Externalities

   d. Complete factor substitutability

8. Economists do not reject which one of the following arguments in favor of protectionism?

   a. Cheap foreign labor

   b. Infant industry

   c. Macroeconomic employment

   d. National security

9. A tariff is likely to do all but which one of the following?

   a. Reduce domestic prices

   b. Increase domestic supply

   c. Increase government revenues

   d. Increase domestic monopoly power

10. Economists generally accept all but which one of the following reservations about comparative-advantage trade among nations?

    a. Changes in factor cost

    b. Uncertainty and flexibility

    c. Dynamic external economies

    d. Changes in productivity

11. Which of the following changes seems least likely at this time to occur in international trade?

    a. Special trading privileges for poor countries

    b. Special borrowing privileges at the IMF for poor countries

    c. Movement in the direction of free trade

    d. Lower tariffs in rich nations for goods imported from poor nations

12. The World Trade Organization is

    a. a world customs union.

    b. a world common market.

    c. a free trade agreement between the United States and Europe.

    d. an organization to promote free trade.

Section C Matching questions

Match the phrases in column B to the terms in column A.

Column A	Column B
1. Autarky	(a) Exports minus imports + net services
2. Absolute advantage	(b) Excludes exports and imports
3. Internal rate of exchange	(c) Economic self-sufficiency
4. Terms of trade	(d) Producing all things more efficiently than others can
5. Net foreign trade	(e) Producing some things more efficiently than others can
6. Tariff	(f) Domestic tradeoff between goods for a nation
7. Embargo	(g) Price of exports ÷ prices of imports
8. Invisible items of trade	(h) Tax on imported goods
9. Dynamic external economies	(i) Prohibition against importing a certain good
10. Comparative advantage	(j) Return greater when a group of investments is taken together
11. Commodity balance of trade	(k) Exports minus imports

ANSWERS

Part 4

Section A 1, T; 2, F; 3, T; 4, F; 5, T; 6, F; 7, T; 8, T; 9, T; 10, T; 11, T; 12, F; 13, F;
14, F; 15, F; 16, T; 17, F; 18, T; 19, F; 20, F; 21, T; 22, T; 23, T; 24, T; 25, T
Section B 1, d; 2, a; 3, c; 4, b; 5, c; 6, a; 7, d; 8, d; 9, a; 10, a; 11, a; 12, d
Section C 1, c; 2, d; 3, f; 4, g; 5, a; 6, h; 7, i; 8, b; 9, j; 10, e; 11, k